International Financial Reporting and Analysis

International Financial Reporting and Analysis

Second Edition

David Alexander
Anne Britton
Ann Jorissen

THOMSON

Australia • Canada • Mexico • Singapore • Spain • United Kingdom • United States

International Financial Reporting and Analysis, second edition

David Alexander, Anne Britton, Ann Jorissen

Publishing Director
John Yates

Publisher
Patrick Bond

Editorial Assistant
Thomas Rennie

Production Editor
Helen Oakes

Manufacturing Manager
Helen Mason

Marketing Manager
Katie Thorn

Typesetter
Gray Publishing

Production Controller
Maeve Healy

Cover Design
Jackie Wrout

Printer
Zrinski d.d. Croatia

ISBN-10: 1-84480-201-9
ISBN-13: 978-1-84480-201-2

This edition published 2005
by Thomson Learning.

British Library Cataloguing-in-Publication Data
A catalogue record for this book is available from the British Library

Contents

Foreword *not written by author*

This book is overdue. With the decision taken by the European Union (EU) to require all listed EU companies to prepare their consolidated accounts in accordance with International Accounting Standards (IAS) from 2005 onwards, there is a pressing need to train people in the financial reporting language of the future. New is not so much that new standards are replacing old standards. New is that as a result of the political decision to use IAS in the future, accounting is no longer a national matter, which differs from country to country. The financial reporting language of the future is an international language. This requires an international approach in the teaching of that language.

The authors have opted for such an approach. They are right. Financial reporting is dealt with in this book as a subject in its own right without too much reliance on standards of one or more particular countries. The authors also put the emphasis on the whys and wherefores. More than ever, accountants and students of accountancy need to be trained to think about accounting. Although knowledge of the standards is important, those who favour IAS, favour a principles-based approach to standard setting. This requires those who apply the standards to carefully consider what the standard is trying to achieve rather than how a particular event or transaction can be brought into the scope of the standard so as to obtain the desired result.

Financial reporting is the only matter concerning listed EU companies which is now uniform throughout the EU. This is quite a radical change from the past. That change affects all Member States, although some more than others. For continental Europe, IAS is very much an Anglo-Saxon inspired reporting model. Applying and understanding IAS in these countries, requires a considerable effort in getting to know the new concepts and the approach of the standard setters with the trilogy of recognition, measurement and disclosure. But, as the authors of the book point out, there is virtually no UK listed company yet that already applies IAS. There is too often an inclination in the UK to believe that with the knowledge of UK GAAP, one is perfectly ready for the IAS revolution. This is clearly untrue.

Although the requirement to apply IAS does not extend to small and medium sized companies (at least not as an EU requirement), many Member States of the EU will, as a result of the modernisation of the Accounting Directives, amend their national accounting legislation in a manner which brings it closer to IAS. There can therefore be no doubt that it is difficult to conceive an accounting training in any Member State of the EU which does not enter into a detailed examination of IAS and the conceptual framework that underpins IAS. Equally, given the adoption of IAS also in Australia and a number of other countries in the world and the rapidly increasing influence of International Accounting Standards worldwide, the book should meet an important need in regions outside Europe.

I hope that this book will find a good reception and I congratulate the authors with their initiative.

Karel VAN HULLE
Head of Unit, Insurance and Pensions, Financial Institutions
European Commission
(formerly Head of Financial Reporting and Company Law, European Commission)

Preface

Why this book?

Financial reporting is changing. Accounting has always been a reactive service, changing and developing to meet the practical needs created by the environment in which it operates. This process of change can be illustrated by both time considerations and place considerations. In particular, in the days when most business operations were largely organized within national boundaries, accounting thought, practices and regulation grew up in significantly different ways in different countries, consistent with national environments and characteristics, a process discussed in more detail in Chapter 2.

Now, however, big business is international, and the process and its implications are moving at a very fast rate. Big business is global in its operations; the demand for finance is global and the supply of finance is global. The provision of information, the oil which lubricates any working market, is global in its reach and instantaneous in its transmission. Financial reporting must of necessity become global too. From slow beginnings, the International Accounting Standards Board is now poised to become the generally accepted regulator at this international level. From 2005, every listed EU company (and also in Australia) is *required* to produce its group financial statements in full accordance with International Accounting Standards and International Financial Reporting Standards. Other countries, as diverse as the USA and China, are seeking close convergence, at minimum, with IASB requirements.

The effects on accounting and reporting for business entities operating at a national or local level, many of them of the small-medium enterprise (SME) size, are unclear, and are likely to differ in different places. Two points are very clear to us, however. First, national needs, characteristics and ways of thinking will remain significant at the SME level. Second, the application of agreed International Accounting Standards, a subjective process of necessity, will continue to be influenced by the context and environment in which the application takes place.

This new book is written to reflect this new situation and its implications. A knowledge of the requirements of the International Accounting Standards is now essential to anyone studying financial accounting and reporting, whether the aim is the preparer focus implied by a desire to enter the accounting professions or the user focus implied by finance, business or MBA-type programmes aimed at management or the educated public.

But of course, knowledge is not enough. A critical understanding of issues and alternatives, of the whys and wherefores, is also required. The author team has been carefully constructed to contain significant academic, pedagogic and writing experience and to reflect the diversity of European and international thought and experience. Our approach is to expose the reader to the issues by a carefully developed sequence of exposition, student-centred activity and constructive feedback. This process provides a framework with which the reader can assimilate, understand and appraise the exposition of international requirement that follows. Only with such an overall understanding, enhancing both depth and breadth, will the reader be able to follow, and hopefully to take an active part in, the future development of financial accounting and reporting as the process of international change continues.

It is important to be clear that our emphasis is on the IASB requirements, and on a full understanding thereof. How those requirements will actually be applied in detailed practice in the many different countries and cultures involved has to be largely outside our scope. As already indicated, we certainly believe that there will continue to be material differences in the practical interpretation and application of international standards. We give a full justification and explanation of that belief, and provide a framework for analysing its implications. Nevertheless, it has to be up to the individual reader and/or teacher, situated in a 'local' context, to explore what the implications of that local context may be.

Structure and pedagogy

The broad structure of the book is as follows: Part One provides the essential conceptual and contextual background. Parts Two and Three explore the detailed issues and problems of financial reporting both in general and through the specific regulatory requirements of the International Accounting Standards Board – for individual company issues in Part Two and for group and multinational issues in Part Three. Part Four provides a summation by an in-depth consideration of financial statement analysis within a dynamic international context.

Each chapter follows a similar pattern in terms of pedagogic structure. Learning objectives set out what the student should be aiming to achieve, with an introduction to put the chapter in context. There are frequent activities throughout the chapter, with immediate feedback so that students can work through practical examples and reflect on the points being made. The chapter closes with a summary and exercises. Answers to some of the exercises can be found at the end of the book.

Supplementary materials

Companion website

A companion website to the book can be found at *www.thomsonlearning.co.uk/abj2e*. The site has an open access student and lecturer area and a password-protected lecturer area, as follows:

Student and lecturer area (OPEN ACCESS)
■ Information about the book
■ Useful weblinks
■ Handy introductions to accounting and finance techniques, disciplines and concepts taken from *The IEBM Pocket Encyclopedia of Business and Management*
■ Optional chapter covering industry-specific standards (e.g. IAS 30 and 41, and IFRS 6).

Lecturer area (PASSWORD PROTECTED)
■ Downloadable lecturer's guide, consisting of PowerPoint slides and answers to the exercises.

Target audience

This is not a book for those with no prior exposure to accounting. A one-year introductory course in accounting and a basic understanding of the principles of double-entry, or some practical business exposure, are assumed. However, we recognize that such earlier work may have taken any of a wide variety of different forms, have approached the subject from any of several different directions, and indeed may well not have been studied in the English language. The book will be particularly suitable for the middle and advanced years of undergraduate 3- or 4-year degree programmes, for post-graduate programmes requiring an internationalization of prior studies of a national system and for MBA-type programmes where a true understanding of the issues and the implication of accounting subjectivity and diversity is required. Readers requiring a training manual of 'how to do it', whether 'it' is preparation or unintelligent interpretation and analysis, may perhaps do better elsewhere.

Acknowledgements

We are grateful for constructive help and support from several quarters. First of all the authors are indebted to Christoph Müller (DHL) for the assistance given and the insight into the airline industry derived from discussion with him. Further, the authors want to thank Leo van der Tas (Erasmus University Rotterdam and Ernst & Young) for his comments on Chapter 2. We are especially grateful to Karel van Hulle for not only writing the Foreword, but also providing helpful comments to us. Jennifer, Pat, Paula, and many others have given every encouragement from Thomson Learning. Cynthia has helped immeasurably with the preparation of successive drafts of the manuscript. Three spouses and ten offspring have coped with the conflicting demands on our time and thoughts. Now, perhaps, it is your turn to help us, or to help us to help you. Suggestions for further development and improvement would be gratefully received by authors or publisher.

Finally, to come back to where we started, we hope that you, the reader, will be interested and stimulated. The internationalization of accounting is an unstoppable force, which will create new and demanding challenges. We believe that participation in this process will be a fascinating and rewarding experience. We hope that you will agree when you have finished studying this book.

David Alexander, University of Birmingham
Anne Britton, Leeds Metropolitan University
Ann Jorissen, University of Antwerp

Part One

Framework, Theory and Regulation

*In this first part we look at what financial reporting is all about –
what it is trying to achieve and how the accountant sets about
achieving it. We explore the international context, reasons for
national differences in accounting practice and tradition and the
developing international regulatory system designed to achieve
greater harmonization.*

Part One

Basics of financial reporting

After studying this chapter you should be able to:
- [ ] explain and discuss the scope of accounting in general and of financial reporting in particular
- [ ] describe the major types of user of published financial information and discuss the implications of their different needs
- [ ] list and discuss the characteristics of accounting information that are likely to maximize its usefulness
- [ ] describe and apply the traditional conventions applied in financial reporting
- [ ] discuss and illustrate the internal coherence or inconsistency of these conventions.

Introduction

At its simplest level, accounting is about the provision of figures to people about their resources. It is to tell them such things as:

1. what they have got
2. what they used to have
3. the change in what they have got
4. what they may get in the future.

You may have done quite a lot of 'accounting' already. In many cases, this will have consisted largely of technical manipulation – writing up ledger accounts, preparing profit and loss accounts and balance sheets and so on. Much of the emphasis is likely to have been on 'doing things with numbers'. Given a figure to start with, you can probably record it in a proper double-entry manner and see its effect through onto a balance sheet that actually balances.

But this is only part of the story. Suppose you are not 'given a figure'. Suppose you are given, or have available, a whole variety of figures all related to a particular item or transaction. Which figure or figures should you actually put into the double-entry system? More fundamentally, *how* are you going to decide which ones to put in? In very general terms, we can answer this question by going back to our original simple definition of accounting. Namely, that it concerns the provision of figures to people about their resources. Presumably, therefore, the figures that we as accountants should provide to people are the figures that they need to know for their own particular purpose.

So the key question is: What do people want to know about their resources? What use do they wish to make of the figures we as accountants provide? Once we have answered this question, we can go on to say that the figure we should put into our double-entry system is the one likely to be *most useful to the user of our accounting reports*.

Accounting therefore needs:

- an effective and efficient data handling and recording system
- the ability to use that system to provide something *useful* to somebody.

This book is essentially concerned with the second of these needs. We have to consider three fundamental issues:

1 *Who* are the users of accounting statements?
2 *What* is the purpose for which each particular type of user requires the information?
3 *How* can we provide the user with the information best suited to their needs?

However, we have also to remember that the accountant and the user have themselves to operate within, and under the control of, the community at large. There is, therefore, an element of *regulation* that has to be taken into account.

Users of financial reports

As readers will be aware, accounting can be divided into management accounting and financial accounting. Very broadly, management accounting is designed for the management user, i.e. for internal decision making, and financial accounting is designed for all other users. The theoretical distinction is that management, by definition, can obtain whatever information it needs from within the organization. External users, however, have to rely on negotiation or regulation in order to obtain information. Financial reporting is only concerned with external users and so is this book.

Activity 1.1

Nine user groups can be suggested for financial reporting, as follows:

1 The equity investor group, including existing and potential shareholders and holders of convertible securities, options or warrants.
2 The loan creditor group including existing and potential holders of debentures and loan stock and providers of short-term secured and unsecured loans and finance.
3 The employee group including existing, potential and past employees.
4 The analyst–adviser group, including financial analysts and journalists, economists, statisticians, researchers, trade unions, stockbrokers and other providers of advisory services, such as credit-rating agencies.
5 Suppliers and trade creditors, past, present and potential.
6 Customers, also past, present and potential.
7 Competitors and business rivals.
8 The government, including tax authorities, departments and agencies concerned with the supervision of commerce and industry and local authorities.

9 The public, including taxpayers, consumers and other community and special interest groups, such as political parties, consumer and environmental protection societies and regional pressure groups.

Taking each of these groups one at a time, consider first the sort of decisions that they are likely to wish to make using accounting information and, second, the implications from this as to what information they might need.

Activity feedback

The equity investor group

Essentially, this group consists of existing and potential shareholders. This group is considering whether or not to invest in a business: to buy shares or to buy more shares; or, alternatively, whether or not to disinvest, to sell shares in the business. Equity investors look for one or a combination of two things: income, a money return by way of dividend, or capital gain, a money return by way of selling shares at more than their purchase price. It should be apparent that these two are closely related. Indeed, the only difference is the timescale. However, the simple theory is made immensely more complex in practice by the effects on share prices of other equity investors' expectations.

For example, share prices for a company may rise because higher dividends are expected to be announced by the company. Alternatively they may rise because other people *believe* dividends will increase. A buys some shares in expectation of 'good news'. This causes prices to rise. B then buys some shares in expectation of the price rise continuing. This causes the price to rise again – a self-fulfilling prophecy – which brings in C as a buyer too. The original hope of 'good news' is soon forgotten. If, however, at a later date the news arrives and turns to be bad, everyone involved, A, B and C, may want to sell and the price will come crashing down.

The motivational and psychological arguments involved here are well beyond the scope of this book. It is the information requirements that concern us. If the investor is taking a short-term view then current dividends may be a major factor. As the time horizon of our investor lengthens then future dividends become more important and future dividends are affected crucially by present and future *earnings*. The focus then is on profits, which both determine future dividends and influence the share price.

One obvious point is that investors, both existing and potential, need information about *future* profits. The emphasis in published accounting information is almost wholly on past or more or less present profits. These may or may not be a good guide to the future. The need to make the past results useful for estimating (guessing?) the future is an important influence on some of the detailed disclosure requirements we shall explore later. The general trend is to make reported accounting statements as suitable as possible for the investor to make their own estimations. We should note an alternative possibility, however. This is that the company itself – through either the management or possibly through the auditors – should make a forecast. After all, the management and the auditor have a much greater insight into possibilities and risks than the external shareholder.

The loan creditor group

This group consists of long-, medium- or short-term lenders of money. The crucial question an existing or potential loan creditor wishes to consider is obvious: Will he or she get their money back? A short-term loan creditor will primarily be interested, therefore, in the amount of cash a business has got or will very soon get. As a safeguard, they will also be interested in the net realizable value (NRV) of all the assets and the priority of the various claims, other than their own, on the available resources. Longer term lenders will clearly need a correspondingly longer term view of the firm's future cash position. Their needs are thus similar to the needs of the equity investor group – they need to estimate the overall strength and position of the business some way into the future.

The employee group

Employees or their representatives need financial information about the business for two main reasons:

1 fair and open collective bargaining (i.e. wage negotiations)
2 assessment of present and future job security.

In these respects they too need to be able to assess the economic stability and vulnerability of the business into the future.

The employees, actual or potential, will have additional requirements as well, however:

1 They will often need detailed information at 'local' level, i.e. about one particular part of the business or one particular factory.
2 They will need information in a clear and simple non-technical way.
3 They will need other information that is inherently non-financial. They will want to know, for instance, about management attitudes to staff involvement in decision making, about 'conditions of service' generally, promotion prospects and so on. It can thus be seen that the employee group may require particular statements for its own use and that it may require information not traditionally regarded as 'financial' at all.

The analyst–adviser group

In one sense this is not a separate group. It is a collection of experts who advise other groups. Stockbrokers and investment analysts will advise shareholders, trade union advisers will advise employees, government statisticians will advise the government and so on. The needs of the analyst–adviser group are obviously essentially the needs of the particular group they are advising. However, being advisers and presumably experts they will need more detail and more sophistication in the information presented to them.

Suppliers and trade creditors need similar information to that required by short-term loan creditors. But they will also need to form a longer term impression of the business's future. Regular suppliers are often dependent on the continuation of the relationship. They may wish to consider increasing capacity specifically for one particular purchaser. They will therefore need to appraise the future of their potential customers both in terms of financial viability and in terms of sales volume and market share.

Customers will wish to assess the reliability of the business both in the short-term sense (will I get my goods on time and in good condition?) and in the long-term sense (can I be sure of after-sales service and an effective guarantee?) Where long-term contracts are involved, the customer will need to be particularly on his or her guard to ensure that the business appears able to complete the contract successfully.

Competitors and business rivals will wish to increase their own effectiveness and efficiency by finding out as much as possible about the financial, technical and marketing structure of the business. The business itself will naturally not be keen for this information to become generally available within the industry and it is generally recognized that businesses have a reasonable right to keep the causes of their own competitive advantage secret. Competitors may also wish to consider a merger or an amalgamation or a straight takeover bid. For this purpose they need all this information, plus the information required by the equity investor group. They also need information about what they – the bidders – could do with the business. In other words, they need to be able to form an opinion on both:

- what the existing management is likely to achieve
- and what new management could achieve with different policies.

The government

Everybody is aware that governments require financial information for purposes of taxation. This may be the most obviously apparent use by governments, but it is not necessarily the most important. Governments also need information for decision-making purposes. Governments today take many decisions affecting particular firms or particular industries, both in a control sense and in government's capacity as purchaser or creditor. Also, governments need information on which to base their economic decisions as regards the economy as a whole. This information is likely to need to be very detailed and to go well beyond the normal historic information included in the usual published accounting reports. Again, there is an obvious need for future-oriented information.

The public

Economic entities, i.e. businesses in the broadest and most general sense, do not exist in isolation. They are part of society at large and they react and interact with society at every level. At the local level, there will be concern at such things as employment, pollution and health and safety. At the wider level, there may be interest in, for example, energy usage, effective use of subsidies, dealings with foreign governments and contributions to charities in money or kind. Much of this information is non-financial. Indeed, some of it cannot be effectively measured at all. Whether it is accounting information is an open question. But it is certainly useful information about businesses.

Summary of user needs

Several general points emerge from the preceding discussion:

1 Many, although not all, of the information requirements are essentially forward looking.
2 Different users, with different purposes, may require *different* information about the *same* items.

3 Different users will require (and be able to understand) different degrees of complexity and depth.

4 Not all the information required is likely to be included in financial accounts.

Characteristics of useful information

Activity 1.2

Make a list of the desirable attributes or characteristics (such as relevance, for example) that financial information should have if it is likely to be useful.

Activity feedback

Seven general ideas occur to us, as follows.

Relevance

This sounds obvious, but on reflection is difficult to define and therefore to achieve. A report must give the user what he or she wants. As already indicated this presupposes that we, the accountants preparing the report, know:

1 who the user is
2 what their purpose is
3 what information he or she requires for this purpose.
   Clearly these requirements may change as time goes by.

Understandability

Different users will obviously have different levels of ability as regards understanding accounting information. Understandability does not necessarily mean simplicity. It means that the reports must be geared to the abilities and knowledge of the users concerned. Complex economic activities being reported to an expert user may well require extremely complicated reports. Simple aspects being reported to users with little or no background knowledge will need to be very simple. The problems really arise when we have the task of reporting on complex activities but to the non-expert user.

Reliability

The user should be able to have a high degree of confidence in the information presented to him or her. This does not necessarily mean that the information has to be factually correct, but it should be as credible, as believable, as possible. Preferably, it should be independently verified, e.g. by an independent, qualified auditor. However, unverified – or unverifiable – information may be better than no information at all.

Completeness

The user should be given a total picture of the reporting business as far as possible. This is a tall order. It implies large and complex collections of information. It may also imply problems of understandability.

Objectivity

The information presented should be objective or unbiased in that it should meet all proper user needs and neutral in that the perception of the measurer should not be biased towards the interest of any one user group. Objectivity is a confused notion, with several different possible meanings. We shall consider the problems in more detail later. The present proposition is that reports should not be biased by the personal perception, the personal opinion, of the preparer of those reports. The stated need is not for reports with *no* personal opinion, but for reports with *unbiased* personal opinion.

Timeliness

Essentially, this means that information should be provided to the user in time for use to be made of it. Information presented should be as up to date as possible. Approximate information, made available in time to assist with some decision or action, is likely to be more useful than precise and accurate information presented after the decision has already been made.

Comparability

Information about any one business for any one period should be presented so that:

1 it can be easily compared with information about the same business for a different period
2 it can be easily compared with information about a different business for the same, or even a different, period.

Clearly consistency of treatment is very important here – the application of generally accepted standards (and generally accepted regulatory standards).

Need for communication

So we have some idea of the various characteristics of useful information. But, more fundamentally, what is information? Remember our earlier suggestion that 'accounting is about the provision of useful figures to people about their resources'. The accountant has to provide figures to the user. But 'provide' does not just mean 'send'. It is not enough to send, to deliver, sheets of paper with words and figures on. There has to be *communication*, there has to be *understanding* by the user. The point about communication, the point about information, is that the receiver is genuinely informed. He or she must become mentally and personally aware.

If effective communication is to take place the language used must be such that the signs employed evoke in others the same response as if those others were to see the object represented instead of the signs. This is, of course, an idealistic position. A television news film can never really put the viewer in the same position in every respect as if they were physically present at the actual event filmed. Even less successful is a verbal description by 'someone who was present'. In accounting, the means of communication is essentially a few numbers, usually prepared by someone who was not actually involved in the financial events supposedly being portrayed anyway. But it is a useful idea to bear in mind, however impossible to achieve.

Another problem is the likely ignorance of the intended receiver of the information. Accounting 'signs' are highly 'coded'. The accountant knows what he or she means, but does anybody else? And how is the user requiring the information to specify exactly what is wanted from the accountant if they cannot 'speak the language'? Clearly, when we think about it, the accountant has to communicate the main features of the reports in *non-accounting terms*.

Financial accounting conventions

We have looked at some of the possible things that financial accountants *could* do in order to provide useful figures to people about their resources. We have looked at who the users are and what sort of information they might want. In this and the following chapters we look at what accountants usually *do* do. Many different words are used in textbooks, articles and statements to describe these ideas – concepts, conventions, assumptions, postulates for example. Some of them are described as being more 'fundamental' than the others. In this chapter we shall simply refer to all of them as 'conventions'. Later we shall look at how international bodies define and divide them, but here we concentrate on the ideas themselves.

We shall consider 12 separate conventions, as follows: business entity, duality, monetary measurement, cost, accounting period, continuity (going concern), conservatism (prudence), consistency, materiality, objectivity, realization of revenue and matching.

Business entity

This states that the business has an identity and existence distinct from its owners. To the accountant, whatever the legal position, the business and the owner(s) are considered completely separately. Thus the accountant can always speak of the business owing the owner money, borrowing money from the owner, owing profits to the owner and so on. Think of the basic business balance sheet:

Fixed assets	Capital
Current assets	Liabilities
Total	Total

As we know, a properly prepared balance sheet can always be relied on to balance. Why is this? The simple answer is because capital is the balancing figure. Capital is the amount of wealth invested in the business by the owner, the amount of money borrowed by the business from the owner or the amount the business owes the owner. None of these three statements could be made unless the accountant is treating the business as separate from, and distinct from, the owner. The accountant usually prepares the accounts of, i.e. the balance sheet of, the business. Transactions of the business are recorded as they affect the business, not as they affect the owner. In principle, another balance sheet always exists, namely for the owner as an individual. This will contain the owner's investment in the business, shown as one of his or her assets.

Duality

This may be regarded as a formalization of the basis of double-entry. It states that in relation to any one economic event, two aspects are recorded in the accounts, namely:

1 the source of wealth
2 the form it takes (i.e. its application).

Substance over form

In the simplest of terms, 1 is 'where it comes from' and 2 is 'what we have done with it'. The source it came from will have a claim back on it. Thus, again in balance sheet terms, we can say that the balance sheet shows the array of resources at a point in time (assets) and the claims on those resources (liabilities); it shows the application of what was available (assets) and the source of what is available (liabilities or claims).

Monetary measurement *(Stable unit of measurement)*

Accountants regard their job as dealing with *financial* information. This convention states that the accountant only records those facts that are expressed in money terms. Any facts, however relevant they may be to the user of the information, are ignored by the accountant if they cannot conveniently be expressed in money terms. It is often said that the greatest asset an effective and efficient business possesses is its workforce. So why does the workforce never appear on a business balance sheet? The short answer is that it would be extremely difficult to 'put a figure on' the workforce, i.e. to express this asset, this resource, in money terms. So the accountant does not even bother to try. Facts and outcomes that cannot be expressed in money terms are ignored. This convention and its limitations are sometimes queried.

Cost

This convention states simply that resources acquired by the business are recorded at their original purchase price. It follows on from the previous convention in that it tells us *how* that item is actually to be measured. This is the well-known historical cost (HC) convention. It does not always now receive the near universal support of earlier years.

Accounting period

This very simple convention recognizes that profit occurs over time and we cannot usefully speak of the profit 'for a period' until we define the length of the period. The maximum length of period normally used is one year. This is supported by legislation normally requiring the preparation of full audited accounts annually. This does not, of course, preclude the preparation of accounts for shorter periods as well. But the formal 'published accounts' period is nearly always one year.

Continuity (going concern)

This important convention states that in the absence of evidence to the contrary it is assumed that the business will continue into the indefinite future. This convention has a major influence on the assumptions made when evaluating particular items in the balance sheet. For example, the convention allows us to assume that inventory will eventually be sold in the normal course of business, i.e. at normal selling prices. Perhaps even more obviously it allows for the principle of depreciation. If we depreciate an item of plant over ten years, then we are assuming that the plant will have a useful life to the business (not necessarily a useful total *physical* life) of ten years. This assumption can only be made if we are first assuming that the business will continue – or keep going – for at least ten years. Notice, incidentally, that the going concern assumption does not say that the business is going to keep being profitable into the indefinite future. It merely assumes that the business will manage not to collapse altogether.

Conservatism (prudence)

This convention refers to the accounting practice of recognizing all possible losses, but not anticipating possible gains. This will tend to lead to an understatement of profits – to an understatement of asset values with no corresponding understatement of liability.

The accounts are in essence trying to give an indication of the current position (the balance sheet) and of the degree of success achieved through the accounting period (the profit and loss (P&L) account). This convention requires the accountant to attempt to ensure that the position or the degree of success is not overstated. Recognizing that absolute accuracy is not possible, the accountants, according to this convention, should ensure the avoidance of overstatement by deliberately setting out to achieve a degree of understatement. This requires that similar items, some of which are positive and some of which are negative, should not be treated identically or symmetrically.

Activity 1.3

Give some examples of regular non-symmetrical treatment of positive and negative aspects of otherwise similar items.

Activity feedback

There are many examples to choose from. Two examples are:

1 the treatment of inventory, which is usually shown at cost or NRV if lower (but not at NRV if higher) – see Chapter 15
2 the whole approach to contingent items – see Chapter 18.

Consistency

This is the practice of applying the same accounting rules, methods or procedures in each similar case. This convention should:

1 avoid short-term manipulation of reported results
2 facilitate comparisons within the firm over different accounting periods (intra-firm comparisons)
3 facilitate comparison between different entities (inter-firm comparisons).

Consistency can, of course, never overrule the requirements of proper and useful reporting. But the convention does certainly support the argument that where several alternative treatments or approaches are acceptable, the business should make a decision and then stick to it year by year for all similar items.

Materiality [mə,tiəri'æliti]

This is a statistical concept that, in its application to accounting, implies that insignificant items should not be given the same emphasis as significant items. The insignificant items are, by definition, unlikely to influence decisions or provide useful information to decision makers, but they may well cause complication and confusion to the user of accounts. Their detailed treatment may also involve a great deal of time and effort – and therefore of money! – for no useful purpose. Many firms, for example, treat smallish items that fulfil all the theoretical requirements of the definition of fixed assets, but cost below a defined minimum amount, as simple current expenses. This is not done because it is correct. It is done because it is easier and because it is 'good enough' for practical purposes and for users' informational needs.

Objectivity

This convention refers to an attribute or characteristic of accounting information generally regarded as desirable. This is that accounting measurements and information should permit qualified individuals working independently to develop similar measures or conclusions from the same evidence. In a nutshell, accounting information should be verifiable. Two schools of thought seem to have arisen in recent years over the full implications of this. One argues that the desire for objectivity implies as much factual content as possible. Facts, e.g. the actual cost figure specified in a contract, are easily verifiable. This idea surely corresponds with the everyday meaning of objectivity, i.e. the avoidance of subjectivity, the avoidance of personal opinion.

The second school of thought seems to argue that the degree of objectivity can be indicated not by the amount of formal (factual) verifiability, but by the degree of consensus achieved by several independent opinions. The question of whether a young woman is pretty or a young man is handsome clearly depends on the person giving the opinion ('beauty is in the eye of the beholder'). But this second school of thought would presumably argue that if, say, six people all say that they agree with such a statement, it becomes objective, becomes a fact ('the majority is always right'). You, the reader, must make your own mind up. But what is clear in any event is the convention that verifiability is a desirable element in accounting.

Realization of revenue

We have just established the convention that an asset acquired by the business is usually recorded at the original purchase price. It is thus based on a market transaction. It is obvious that, at the latest, when the asset is disposed of by the business, we must record the actual disposal price. So if we buy inventory for €30, €30 has to be recorded as having gone and inventory (of €30, cost convention) has to be recorded as being present. If we then sell the inventory for €50, we must record €50 as being present and inventory has to be removed from the accounts. Thus an asset of €30 has been replaced by an asset of €50, giving a profit of €20. Once the €50 is physically in, there is no other possibility than to record an asset of €50. But is there no possibility of recognizing an asset of €50 before, i.e. earlier than, the physical arrival of the money? Suppose we sell the inventory on 1 December and receive the money on 10 December. When did assets of €30 turn into assets of €50? Was it 10 December when we received the money? Or was it 1 December, when we acquired the expectation – indeed the right – to receive the money?

More importantly perhaps what *criteria* are we going to use to answer this question? On what *grounds* should we decide when the total asset figure increased, i.e. when the profit was made? This is a very complicated matter. We can first of all state the usual conventional answer: revenue is recognized as soon as, and is allocated to the period in which:

1 it is capable of objective measurement and
2 the asset value receivable in exchange is reasonably certain.

But this is really rather simplistic and we need to explore the area in more detail. (See Chapter 17.)

Before we do that, we should complete our overview by seeing how the revenue recognition question leads on to the calculation of profit. Since profit is revenue less expenses, we must explore the idea of matching expenses and revenues together.

Matching

Looking back over the conventions we have discussed so far, we have:

1 decided on the basic characteristics of the recording system (*business entity* and *duality*)
2 decided on how we are going to record items entering the business's control (*monetary measurement* and *cost*)
3 decided on how to record the proceeds from the disposal of such items (*revenue recognition*).

The essential item missing is clearly the mechanism for recording the actual loss of the item – its removal from the financial statements about the business. The earlier question was: When did assets of €30 turn into assets of €50? It is intuitively clear that whenever this did happen (and the revenue recognition convention tells us when), a profit of €20 was made. Thus, if the revenue, the benefit, is €50, then the expense, the amount used or lost, is €30. The matching convention covers this final stage in the process of profit calculation. It states that:

> Income (or profit) determination is a process of matching against revenue the expenses incurred in earning that revenue.

When an asset gets used, it becomes an expense. The question in effect is: At precisely what point does the accountant regard an asset as being 'used'? The answer is: At the point when the related revenue is recognized, so the process of profit calculation can be summarized as follows. First, we determine the point at which the revenue is to be recognized, the time when the proceeds are 'made'. Second, we *match* the *expense* against the revenue, i.e. we regard the expense as occurring at the same time as the revenue. So if the revenue from selling an item of inventory is recognized on 28 December as €50 then the expense of €30 is also recognized on 28 December. Accounts prepared in 31 December will include profit of €20 and an asset of €50 (debtors or cash). But if the revenue from selling an item of inventory is recognized on 2 January, then the expense will also be recognized on 2 January. Accounts prepared on 31 December will include an asset of €30 (inventory), no revenue and no expense, and therefore no profit or loss from this transaction.

The **matching convention** is often referred to as the **accruals convention**, although some writers distinguish between them. The accruals convention should be contrasted with the ideas of cash flow accounting (Chapter 22). The essence of the accruals convention is that the time when an item of benefit should be recognized and recorded by the accountant is determined by the reasonably ascertainable *generation* of the benefit – not by the date of the actual (cash) *receipt* of the benefit. Similarly, the time when an item of expense should be recognized and recorded as such by the accountant is determined by the *usage* of the item, not by the date of the acquisition of the item or of the *payment* for the item. The accruals convention is therefore another way of saying that the process of profit calculation consists of relating (matching) together the revenues with the expenses. It is not directly concerned with cash receipts and cash payments.

Coherent framework

Thus far we have considered, separately, 12 conventions. How do they relate together? The idea of an all-embracing framework is discussed more fully in Chapter 8. What we can usefully do at this stage is to look at the 12 conventions to consider whether they are 'coherent' or consistent with each other.

One of the most problematic conventions is that of prudence or conservatism. At its most basic this derives from the obviously sensible belief that it is important not to encourage the users of accounts to spend money or to consume resources they do not have. Consideration of this convention, together with several of the other conventions, gives rise to certain difficulties.

Activity 1.4

Suggest pairs of conventions that we have already discussed, which are, or may be, contradictory or in opposition to each other, and illustrate the possible problems between them.

Activity feedback

Here are some possibilities we thought of:

1 **Prudence** and **going concern**. The going concern convention argues that the firm will 'keep going', e.g. that it will not be forced out of business by competition or bankruptcy. This may be a likely and rational assumption, but it is not necessarily prudent – in certain circumstances it could be decidedly risky.

2 **Prudence** and **matching**. The matching convention, building on the going concern convention, allows us to carry forward assets into future periods on the grounds

that they will be used profitably later. This obviously makes major assumptions about the future that may not be at all prudent. The contradiction between these two conventions is one of the major problems of accounting practice. Should we, when in doubt, emphasize prudence or matching? Should we ensure that we never overstate the position or should we do our professional best to 'tell it like it is'? Should we report the worst possible position (prudence) or the most likely position (matching)?

3 **Prudence** and **objectivity**. Objectivity implies certainty and precision. It implies freedom from personal opinion, freedom from bias. Prudence, quite explicitly, implies that we *should* bias the information we choose to report in a certain direction. If accounting information could be genuinely objective, then prudence would be irrelevant by definition, because any bias would be impossible. In practice, of course, since accounting always has to make assumptions about future events, objectivity can never be completely achieved.

4 **Prudence** and the **cost concept**. This is a particularly interesting pairing of ideas. The cost concept is supported by objectivity (not on the grounds that it is objective, but on the grounds that it usually has a greater objective element than alternative valuation concepts) and is often regarded as being supported by prudence and, in some respects, it is.

Prudence suggests that in areas of valid choice, lower asset figures should be incorporated in accounts. In times of rising prices, use of replacement costs (RCs) could therefore be seen as imprudent, as compared with use of HC. But consider the effect on reported profits of using a RC basis rather than historical costs (HCs) (Chapter 5). This splits up the HC profit into operating profit and holding gain, enabling the 'genuine', and therefore safely distributable, operating profit to be distinguished. Nothing could be more imprudent than to distribute resources needed to maintain the business and HC accounting can easily permit this to happen.

Now try the following activity.

Activity 1.5

On 20 December 20X7 your client paid €10 000 for an advertising campaign. The advertisements will be heard on local radio stations between 1 January and 31 January 20X8. Your client believes that, as a result, sales will increase by 60% in 20X8 (over 20X7 levels) and by 40% in 20X9 (over 20X7 levels). There will be no further benefits.

Required

Write a memorandum to your client explaining your views on how this item should be treated in the accounts for the three years 20X7 to 20X9. Your answer should include explicit reference to at least *three* relevant traditional accounting conventions and to the requirements of *two* classes of user of published financial accounts.

Activity feedback

To: Client
From: Accountant

Treatment of advertising costs

There are a number of possible treatments:

- Write off the whole amount in 20X7. This could be justified on the grounds of *prudence* – any return being highly speculative.
- Write off the amount in strict proportion to the expected benefits. This would be supported by the *matching* convention, i.e. to allocate the expenses over the period of benefit in proportion to that benefit. This would imply expenses of €0 in 20X7 (as benefit does not commence in 20X7), €6000 in 20X8 and €4000 in 20X9.
- The conflict between prudence and matching is usually resolved through compromise, although in areas of real doubt and difficulty prudence should prevail and be given greater emphasis. A reasonable compromise in this case might well be to charge all the €10 000 as an expense in 20X8 – any returns in 20X9 being much more speculative than those expected in 20X8.
- The validity of this suggestion would depend on the particular circumstances, advice of advertising and industry experts, your earlier treatment of similar items (*consistency* is an important accounting convention) and also on the *materiality* of the amounts concerned. If the amounts concerned are small in relation to your results as a whole, then it is pointless to spend my time (and your money!) in a lengthy and detailed investigation.
- We should perhaps also consider the users of your accounting reports. For example, a *trade creditor* will be particularly interested in your assets and liability position. From this point of view, an asset that exists because of the speculative expectation of higher sales next year is not exactly a safe 'near-cash' security. Contrariwise, a *shareholder* will be concerned with the future trend of profits, and application of the matching convention is arguably an essential requirement for showing a fair indication of present profit and current and future trends.

The general conclusion from Activity 1.5 should be clear. A great deal of choice and subjectivity is involved in trying to produce useful financial information.

International dimension

This introductory chapter has discussed basic and general ideas. We have not been at all concerned with what is likely to happen in any particular country or any particular jurisdiction. Historically, accounting and reporting grew up largely independently, and often very differently, in different countries. Practice, regulation and, indeed, the mode and volume of regulation, differed, often very greatly.

With the global economy, instant communication and a global finance market, this situation has changed sharply and this process of change is continuing. The historical developments, and the reasons for them, are discussed in Chapter 2. The institutional and regulatory developments in the ongoing process of increasing harmonization, involving the European Union (EU) and the International Accounting Standards Board (IASB) in particular are discussed in Chapter 3. To put the practical effects of current developments in perspective, in 2005 some 7000 enterprises listed in European stock exchanges will be *required* to produce full consolidated financial statements under

International Accounting Standards (IAS), together with consistent comparative figures for 2004. To give but one example, the number of UK companies already doing this in 2004 was nil! A process of rapid change is under way. It is this process of change that necessitates the international approach taken by this book.

Terminology and the English language

Many readers of this book will be trying not only to master a subject new to them but also doing so in a language that is not their first. One added difficulty is that there are several forms of the English language, particularly for accounting terms. UK terms and US terms are extensively different. Some examples are shown in the first two columns of Table 1.1. At this stage, you are not expected to understand all these terms; they will be introduced later, as they are needed.

The International Accounting Standards Board (IASB) operates and publishes its standards in English, although there are approved translations in several languages. The IASB uses a mixture of UK and US terms, as shown in the third column of Table 1.1. On the whole, this book uses IASB terms, but UK terms tend to be used in the Fourth EU Directive. Familiarity with both is essential.

Table 1.1 Some examples of UK, US and IASB terms

UK	US	IASB
Stock	Inventory	Inventory
Shares	Stock	Shares
Own shares	Treasury stock	Treasury shares
Debtors	Receivables	Receivables
Creditors	Payables	Payables
Finance lease	Capital lease	Finance lease
Turnover	Sales (or revenue)	Sales (or revenue)
Acquisition	Purchase	Acquisition
Merger	Pooling of interests	Uniting of interests
Fixed assets	Non-current assets	Non-current assets
Profit and loss account	Income statement	Income statement

Summary

Financial reporting is concerned with the provision of information about business organizations to people outside the management function. We have thought about the various users of financial reporting, and the type and characteristics of information they might need. Finally we have explored the accountant's traditional approach to meeting these needs, i.e. the traditional underlying conventions of accounting. It can be demonstrated that they are often not mutually consistent. As we shall see in Chapter 2, different national traditions have sharply differing views on which conventions should be given priority.

1 Look up as many definitions of accounting as you can find, noting the source, country, original language and date of publication. Note, and try to explain, their differences.

✔ **2** Consider the relative benefits to users of financial statements of:
- information about the past
- information about the present
- information about the future.

✔ **3** Do you think that a single set of financial statements can be prepared that will be reasonably adequate for all major external users and their needs?

4 Which of the suggested conventions do you regard as most important? Why?

5 Which of the suggested conventions do you regard as most useful? Why?

6 Explain the differences, if any, between your answers to questions 4 and 5.

✔ **7** How objective is the traditional HC balance sheet?

8 Completeness is not compatible with the monetary measurement convention. Discuss.

9 A firm spends €10 000 developing a new product and €5000 on an advertising campaign for it. Which conventions will help you in deciding on the appropriate accounting treatment and what do they imply?

10 Which conventions underlie the usual accounting treatment of inventory and work in progress?

11 HC accounts are neither objective nor useful. Discuss.

12 The normal accounting practice of revenue recognition proves that accountants are prudent. Discuss.

13 How do accountants decide when to recognize revenue?

14 When do accountants usually recognize revenue?

15 Do your answers to questions 13 and 14 satisfy the objectivity convention?

16 Explain the relationship between revenue recognition and asset valuation.

17 A local group collects subscriptions from its members, and also has to pay 60% of them to central funds. In the year to 31 December 20X8 the group receives:

for 20X7	€20
for 20X8	€60
for 20X9	€10

It pays to central funds in that year:

for 20X7	€12
for 20X8	€30
for 20X9	nil

Required:

(a) Produce a summary of the subscription position for the group for the year 20X8, on
   (i) a receipts and payments basis,
   (ii) a revenue and expenses basis.

(b) Outline the advantages and disadvantages of each basis with reference to appropriate accounting conventions. Give the group leader your recommended method, with reasons. Discuss also any difficult decisions you have to make in deciding your answer to (a) above.

(ACCA – adapted)

2

International accounting differences

After studying this chapter you should be able to:
- [ ] describe and explain how the following elements influenced the development of financial reporting and the existing accounting systems in a country:
  - provision of finance
  - the legal system
  - the system of taxation
  - cultural values
- [ ] explain and appraise the influence of cultural values on accounting values
- [ ] explain how different systems of accounting regulation could develop
- [ ] describe the purpose of country classification exercises
- [ ] appraise whether these country classification exercises are still relevant today.

Introduction

Chapter 1 introduced you to the subject of accounting and why accounting matters. It also touched on the importance of international harmonization with respect to financial reporting. In this chapter we will focus on why accounting and financial reporting systems developed differently in different countries. At the end of this chapter we will pay attention to recent research approaches in studying differences in financial reporting between individual countries.

In Activity 2.1 we take another look at the main issues of Chapter 1.

Activity 2.1

Try to formulate in your own words the subject of accounting and especially financial reporting. Why does international harmonization matter?

Activity feedback

A company draws up its financial statements to reflect the effects of transactions and events within and outside the company on its assets and liabilities, financial position and income. Whether and in what way, events and transactions are reflected in the financial report depends on the accounting policies chosen by the company's management. For every kind of transaction and event management must decide, either explicitly or implicitly, whether and how to reflect it in the financial statements. The methods of recognition and measurement, consolidation, and presentation must be chosen and decisions made as to what data to disclose in what degree of detail. Within limits, these choices are at management's discretion.

The limits just mentioned are set by standard setters in different countries or international standard setters such as the IASB, which promulgate the methods of recognition and measurement, consolidation, and presentation that the company must comply with. Some standard setters allow many options with regard to those issues. Other standard setters are strict and prescribe, for example, one specific measurement method for a specific asset. Companies located in countries where standard setters allow many choices with regard to recognition and measurement issues etc. have much more accounting flexibility in the presentation and valuation of their assets, liabilities, results and financial position. As a result, users of financial statements of companies located in countries with accounting flexibility will face more problems comparing the performance of different companies with one another than users of annual accounts of companies located in countries with very little accounting flexibility. A discussion of the influence of accounting flexibility on financial analysis can be found in Chapter 26.

These differences in accounting systems are an obstacle towards the comparability of financial information published by companies using different sets of accounting standards. Companies operating in different countries and raising capital on different capital markets insist on more harmonization of accounting standards in the first place. Harmonization would increase the comparability of financial information and would create more transparency for the users of financial information. As a result, the information asymmetry between stakeholders and the companies would decrease. This will lead to a lower cost of capital for companies (see, for example, Leuz and Verrechia, 2000).

Activity 2.2

Remember the contents of Chapter 1 and list again a number of users of financial information and for what purpose they will use the information.

Activity feedback

From Chapter 1 we know that different external stakeholders of financial statements exist and that they use the information of the annual accounts in their own decision-making process.

Shareholders: They use information from the financial statements in order to determine whether or not they are going to invest or disinvest in a company.

Creditors: On the basis of the financial statements creditors will assess the capability of a company to repay its debt in the long term. Based on the results of that analysis credit will be granted or denied and the conditions will be negotiated.

Suppliers: They will assess the capability of the firm to repay their invoices in the short term before they decide to grant short-term credit.

Workforce: Employees will use financial statements data to get an idea about the financial health of their company.

Government: Governments use financial statements for several purposes, including for determining taxable income or making decisions about government grants to certain industries.

All over the world stakeholders use the information provided by financial statements in their decision-making process for the purposes enumerated earlier. Although the use of the information is more or less the same worldwide, the communication of that information can differ according to the location of the company (type of accounting standards used) or other influencing factors (e.g. legal system, development of the capital market, culture and so on).

Information from the annual accounts becomes useful for decision making if it can be compared to a certain benchmark. Very often data taken from the financial statements of other companies are used as a benchmark. As already mentioned in the feedback discussion of Activity 2.1 comparability will be hindered if the level of accounting flexibility differs among the companies. Accounting flexibility means that because of the freedom of choice the same kind of transactions and events can be reflected differently by different companies. This accounting flexibility is not only a problem related to comparability in those countries where accounting standards allow large freedom of decision. It was, and still is to a certain extent, also a major problem when shareholders and other external stakeholders compare the financial statement information provided by companies located in different countries with each other.

The performance of another company is only a yardstick for evaluation if comparability is not jeopardized by accounting flexibility or other factors (see Chapter 26). Comparing two financial reports that are based on different accounting policies is like comparing two lengths without knowing that one is in centimetres and the other in inches.

So if readers want to compare financial reports, which are the reflections of transactions and events as recorded under a particular accounting policy, it is important that the accounting policies do not differ to such an extent that the comparison of financial reports is meaningless. The accounting policies or accounting decisions of a company were, and still are to a large extent, influenced by the national environment and national accounting standards and practices.

As these national standards and practices differ from each other we will focus in this chapter on the differences between national accounting practices and standards and national accounting environments. In a period where international harmonization or even standardization seems to be almost realized, national differences still play a role. Empirical evidence exists (as we will see later in this chapter) that even the reporting behaviour of multinational companies listed on several international stock markets is still influenced by national accounting characteristics. That is the reason why we still pay attention to these national differences in the current volume.

Origin of national differences

Financial reporting in general can be viewed as part of a communication process. The report is a medium through which information is transferred by a sender to a receiver.

The nature and functions of reporting with respect to organizations differ depending on the nature of the sender and the receiver as well as on the nature of the information transferred. The sender and the receiver form an integral part of their environment, which at the time that financial reporting developed in the past centuries was merely a national environment.

Financial reporting was, to start with, mainly internal reporting. Early financial reports can hardly be called external, they were a means by which the owners could get an insight into their income and capital. The company was a part of and managed by its owners. One could hardly distinguish between internal and external financial reports. From the early 1800s on the increasing scale of companies resulted in finance problems and the need for a disconnection of management and capital supply. Private capital alone was insufficient to finance business activities, so capital was gathered from people outside the company.

This separation of ownership and management makes it possible to have the company managed by people specializing in management. The owners delegate control and the evaluation of the management to the board of directors. The board of directors has also the power to hire and fire top management and to approve any strategic decisions. The directors, by way of contrast, are accountable towards the owners for their deeds, decisions and policy. The external financial report provides a means of rendering account of this authority. Besides the functions of profit and capital determination, already mentioned, the financial report now also serves a stewardship role. An example of early external financial reporting are the accounts 'published' by the East India Company in the 18th century.

Financial reporting evolved from internal to external reporting, but for a long time external reporting meant providing information within the borders of a specific country. Because national environments have different characteristics, standard setters and accounting bodies have chosen different alternatives for recognition, measurement and presentation of assets, liabilities, equity, revenue and expenses. They have chosen those recognition, measurement, consolidation and presentation policies that best fitted their national environments. In each country annual accounts provide information on the financial position of a company and its result. Although the general mission is similar in most countries many differences between countries occur. In each country there was and still is a different mix of influences on financial reporting. These differences result from different environmental, institutional and cultural influences in the individual countries. We will now focus on the most important environmental, institutional and cultural differences that shaped financial reporting in the individual countries.

The causes discussed thus far have been identified by several researchers who focused on this topic especially in the last 25 years of the 20th century when the need for accounting harmonization started, as a result of increasing globalization of the business world. Among the most important causes referred to in the literature are: provision of finance; the existing legal system; the link between accounting and taxation; and cultural differences between societies.

Provision of finance

According to Nobes and Parker (2003, p. 21): 'This difference in providers of finance (creditors/insiders) versus (equity/outsiders) is the key cause of international differences in financial reporting.' We saw earlier in this chapter that through the increasing scale of companies two centuries ago, firms had to find extra capital to finance growth. Companies in different countries responded differently to this increased need for funds. In countries such as Germany, France, Italy, Belgium, banks became the major supplier of extra funds. Companies in these countries relied more on debt to finance their activities than on equity. In contrast, in the UK and the USA the extra funds tend to be provided by shareholders, often by many shareholders for small amounts. Companies in those countries rely more on equity for the financing of their activities. In those countries an active stock exchange was and still is present.

Table 2.1 presents some examples of countries in which companies are more shareholder oriented and countries in which companies are more credit/family/state oriented.

Table 2.1 Shareholder-oriented versus credit-oriented countries

Shareholder oriented	Credit/family/state oriented
United States	Germany
United Kingdom	France
The Netherlands	Belgium
Sweden	Italy
Australia	Spain
Canada	Portugal

Source: Adapted from Alexander and Nobes (2004), Nobes and Parker (2003) and Ordelheide and KPMG (2001)

Activity 2.3

Could you argue why especially this difference between credit/insiders versus equity/outsiders has an impact on financial reporting?

Activity feedback

Insiders or parties that have a power relation towards a company are in a position to ask for internal data about the financial position of the firm towards which they exercise power. The power relation of outsiders is much weaker: they are not in a position to ask for extra information and have to rely on public information. Especially in countries where widespread shareholdership exists, the power of the individual shareholder to get financial information is limited. Although the power of the individual shareholder is weak, in those countries where companies rely on the capital market for extra funding there is a strong incentive towards high-quality external financial reporting. Through financial reports companies communicate their financial situation to existing and potential shareholders.

So in countries where companies are largely financed through equity, financial statements will have an investor or shareholder orientation. This means that financial statements must provide the kind of information that will enable a potential shareholder to make the best investment decision. Financial information that enables investors to make those investment decisions is called 'high-quality' accounting information. In the last decade empirical research on the measurement of 'accounting quality' and 'quality of accounting earnings' has indicated that in these countries with a strong capital market influence, the quality of accounting earnings is higher than in countries with a creditor orientation. In countries where companies rely more on debt financing, the financial statements have a creditor orientation. In those countries information provided through the annual accounts must be useful to judge whether a company is able to repay its debt. Creditor protection becomes important in this respect.

These differences in financing are worth bearing in mind when companies from different countries are compared with each other for financial analysis purposes. (See further Chapters 26 and 27.)

Activity 2.4

If you were to compare the financial risk between companies on the basis of the debt/equity ratio calculated from the published annual accounts, in which countries would you come across firms with the highest ratio?

Activity feedback

If we exclude the impact of other influencing factors on the debt/equity ratio (e.g. type of industry, profit distribution versus reservation) and take into account only these national differences, then you would find, for example in Germany and France, companies with higher debt/equity ratios than in companies in the USA or in the UK. This difference is then due solely to national differences with regard to the way in which companies are financed.

Existing legal system

Over the years in the western world two types of legal system have developed: the so-called common law system and the code law system. Both legal systems have been exported in the 20th century to different parts of the world. The common law system originated in England and is developed from case law. The legal system in most commonwealth countries is the common law system. Common law is characterized as a legal system that is developed case by case and does not prescribe general rules that could be applied to several cases. In a common law situation accounting rules are not a part of the law. In common law countries accounting regulation is in the hands of professional organizations of the private sector. Company law in these countries is kept to a minimum. Detailed accounting regulation is produced by the private standard setter, as we will discuss later when we look at accounting regulation.

The code law system originated in Roman law and has developed in continental Europe. It is characterized by a wide set of rules that try to give guidance in all situations. In code law countries the company law is very detailed and accounting standards are often embodied in the company law. Accounting regulation in code law countries is in the hands of the government and financial reporting is in those circumstances often reduced to complying with a set of very detailed legal rules.

Table 2.2 gives some examples of code law and common law countries. (See also La Porta, Lopez-de-Silanes, Schleifer and Vishny, 1997 and 1998.)

Link between accounting and taxation

In some countries the fiscal authorities use information provided in the financial statements in order to determine taxable income. In countries like Belgium expenses are only tax deductible if they are also recognized in the profit and loss account. As a result financial reporting becomes tax influenced or even tax biased. In this respect Germany is well known for its *Massgeblichkeitsprinzip*, which stands for the fact that the tax accounts (*Steuerbilanz*) should be identical to the accounts published for external stakeholders (*Handelsbilanz*). This link between financial reporting and taxation is often found in those countries that do not have an explicit investor approach in their financial reporting orientation.

In countries like the USA, the UK and the Netherlands the link between taxable income and accounting income is much weaker. Separate accounts are filed for tax purposes. The measurement and recognition rules and estimates used in the tax accounts can differ from the valuation rules used in the preparation of the financial statements published for all external stakeholders.

Table 2.3 shows the general relationship between accounting and taxation using some examples based on the situation in the 1990s.

Table 2.2 Common law versus code law countries

Common law countries	Code law countries
England and Wales	Scotland
United States	France
Australia	Germany
Canada	Belgium
Ireland	The Netherlands
New Zealand	Portugal
Singapore	Spain
	Japan

Source: Adapted from Alexander and Nobes (2004), Nobes and Parker (2003) and Ordelheide and KPMG (2001)

Table 2.3 General relationship between accounting and taxation

Independence	Dependence
Denmark	Germany
Ireland	France
The United Kingdom	Belgium
The Netherlands	Italy
Czech Republic	Sweden
Poland	Norway

Source: Adapted from Alexander and Nobes (2004), Nobes and Parker (2003) and Ordelheide and KPMG (2001)

This relationship between accounting income and tax income can vary over time. For example, Spain was for a long time in the column of dependence; with the reform of 1989, however, the link between taxable income and accounting income became less strong and they are now moving towards independence.

Cultural differences

Research indicates that another cause of variation between national accounting systems is cultural differences. Cultural differences between nations are identified as an important influencing factor on reporting and disclosure behaviour with regard to financial statements. One of the prominent researchers on cultural differences is Hofstede (1984). He used four constructs to classify countries according to the cultural differences he observed in his empirical research. The constructs resulted from empirical survey-based research in one multinational (IBM; survey population 100 000 employees in 39 countries, 1984). Hofstede labelled his constructs as follows: individualism, power distance, uncertainty avoidance and masculinity. According to Hofstede these labels describe the following characteristics of a society.

Individualism versus collectivism
Individualism stands for the preference for a loosely knit social framework in society wherein individuals are supposed to take care of themselves and their immediate families only. Collectivism describes the preference for a tightly knit social framework in which individuals expect their relatives, clan or other in-group to look after them in exchange for unquestioning loyalty. The fundamental issue addressed by this dimension is the degree of interdependence a society maintains among individuals. This difference relates to the people's self-concept: 'I' or 'we'.

Large versus small power distance
Power distance is the extent to which the members of a society accept that power in institutions and organizations is distributed unequally. People in larger power distance societies accept a hierarchical order in which everybody has a place that needs no further justification. The fundamental issue addressed by this dimension is how a society handles inequalities among people when they occur.

Strong versus weak uncertainty avoidance
Uncertainty avoidance is the degree to which the members of a society feel uncomfortable with uncertainty and ambiguity. This feeling leads them to beliefs promising certainty and to maintain institutions protecting conformity. Strong uncertainty avoidance societies maintain rigid codes of belief and behaviour and are intolerant of deviant people and ideas. Weak uncertainty avoidance societies maintain a more relaxed atmosphere in which practice counts more than principles and deviance is more easily tolerated.

Masculinity versus femininity
Masculinity stands for the preference in society for achievement, heroism, assertiveness and material success. Its opposite, femininity, stands for the preference for relation- ships, modesty, caring for the weak and the quality of life.

Based on Hofstede's classification scheme Gray (1988) defined 'accounting values' that can be linked to the different cultural values as follows:

- professionalism versus statutory control
- uniformity versus flexibility
- conservatism versus optimism
- secrecy versus transparency.

Activity 2.5

Consider again the cultural values described by Hofstede. How do they link with the accounting value dimensions defined by Gray?

Activity feedback

Between some variables there is a direct relationship, between other characteristics and values the relationship is rather indirect.

Professionalism versus statutory control

The accounting value professionalism links to individualism. Professionalism is consistent with a society where the emphasis is on 'I' rather than 'we'. Professionalism also goes together with a society with small power distance. Statutory control is observed in the opposite situation, namely in societies with large power distance. In relation to the accounting profession, professionalism implies self-regulation by the accounting profession itself. Statutory control implies control by the government. Statutory control could also be linked to strong uncertainty avoidance.

Uniformity versus flexibility

First of all, uniformity can be linked to strong uncertainty avoidance. Uniformity leads to detailed regulations embedded in the law and adherence to consistency. Uniformity is therefore also associated with large power distance societies and societies in which the emphasis is on 'we' rather than 'I'. Flexibility, however, can be associated with weak uncertainty avoidance, small power distance and individualism.

Conservatism versus optimism

Conservatism could be linked to uncertainty avoidance. In these societies one is more conservative with regard to profit recognition and asset measurement. Conservatism is an important value for accountants, especially in continental Europe where financial reporting is more creditor oriented and where there is a strong link between accounting income and taxable income.

Secrecy versus transparency

Secrecy implies a preference for confidentiality. Secrecy can be linked to uncertainty avoidance, but also to societies with large power distances. Information asymmetry will then reinforce inequalities and power relations between the different parties. Secrecy will have a direct impact on the level of information disclosure by companies.

The most important economic and cultural elements cited in the literature as causes for differences between national accounting systems have now been discussed. Other factors also listed in the literature as contributors to those differences are, for example, the level of economic development in a country, the degree of industrialization, inflation levels, the adherence to accounting theory (e.g. in the Netherlands income determination and valuation is inspired by the theory of Limperg, financial reporting in Germany was inspired by the theory of Schmalenbach).

In the next part of the chapter we will analyse how these different economic and cultural factors shaped financial reporting practices and standards in each individual country. The causes for differentiation had their influence on the existing accounting system in a country.

Differences in accounting systems

Since accounting responds to its environment, different cultural, economic, legal and political environments produce different accounting systems, while similar environments produce similar accounting systems.

In this section we focus on these differences in accounting systems. In the next section, the emphasis lies on the different sets of domestic generally accepted accounting principles (GAAP). Under the heading of accounting systems we discuss two elements that characterize accounting systems, namely the organization of accounting regulation and the organization of the accounting profession.

Types of accounting regulation

When shareholders are the main providers of capital we expect them to have great interest in the way in which companies communicate their financial information. The shareholders will definitely want to have a hand in the communication process, including the financial reporting process. The shareholders are mainly trying to achieve this objective by hiring professional accountants who check on their behalf the communication process and its outcome within a company. In order to be able to fulfill their task properly the accountants started to play a major role in the standard-setting process of those countries.

Activity 2.6

Consider Tables 2.1 and 2.2, which provide information on the different sources of finance in each country and the existing legal system. What kind of accounting regulation would you expect in those countries?

Activity feedback

If we consider Tables 2.1 and 2.2 again, we observe to a certain extent a correlation between the provision of finance (debt versus equity) and the legal system in place (code law/common law). In most countries with active equity markets the legal system is the common law system. This is in favour of the private sector developing financial reporting rules or standards.

In countries in which companies are financed to a large extent through debt, the code law system is present as the legal system. In those countries creditor protection is high on the agenda. Because large creditors such as banks are able to obtain inside information from the companies, they are less in need of financial information published by these companies. In these countries accounting regulation is in the hands of the government.

We observe that in those countries with a code law system and a creditor orientation the government often makes use of financial reporting for their own purposes. First of all, in those countries the annual accounts are often used for tax purposes which serves the government. Second, the financial statements may be used for specific information needs of the government (e.g. in Belgium, the social balance sheet [a document containing employment statistics, e.g. number of employees, breakdown into different categories, change in the workforce, use of government incentives for the creation of employment] must be included in the financial statements by Royal Decree of 1996. It mainly serves the need of the government for information with regard to employment in order to evaluate the effectiveness of their governmental employment policies). Financial reporting in those countries essentially comes down to compliance with legal requirements and tax laws.

These observations show that there are two types of accounting regulation, each of which is embedded in a different economic and legal environment. First of all, there are countries in which accounting regulation is in the hands of the private sector: the UK, the USA, Australia and the Netherlands. In these countries private standard setting goes together with a shareholder orientation of the financial information published and, in most countries, a common law system. Second, there are countries in which the government plays a major part in accounting regulation. This system is observed in many continental European countries. In those countries detailed accounting rules are embodied in the law, normally the company law. Financial information has mainly a creditor orientation in those countries and they are further characterized by a code law system.

Differences in the organization of the accounting profession

When companies are financed by equity capital and if this equity capital is in the hands of a widespread group of small shareholders, these shareholders are in need of a well-organized control system with regard to the quality and reliability of the information provided by the financial statements. The strength and size of the accounting profession is directly influenced by the need for the external control mechanisms or audit of the published financial information. Table 2.4 illustrates that in those countries with active capital markets the profession developed earlier than in countries where companies are more financed by debt.

In countries with a well organized accounting profession we observe that the influence of that profession on local accounting practices and on national GAAP is larger than in countries with smaller and later developed professional organizations.

Characteristics and differences in national GAAP

Economical and environmental differences lead to differences in accounting systems (e.g. regulation). These accounting systems produce different national or domestic

Table 2.4 Dates of establishment of professional accountancy bodies

Country	Professional body	Founding date (founding date of predecessor)
Austria		
Belgium	Instituut der Bedrijfsrevisoren/Institut des Reviseurs d'Entreprises	1953
England and Wales	Institute of Chartered Accountants in England and Wales	1880 (1870)
Denmark	Foreningen af Statsautoriserede Revisorer	1912
Finland	KHT-yhdistys	1925 (1911)
France	Ordre des Experts Comptables	1942
Germany	Institut der Wirtschaftsprüfer	1932
Ireland	Institute of Chartered Accountants of Ireland	1888
Italy	Consiglio Nazionale dei Dottori Commercialisti	1924
	Collegio dei Ragionieri e Periti Commerciali	1906
Japan	Japanese Institute of Certified Public Accountants	1948 (1927)
Norway	Den norske Revisorforening	1999 (1930)
Portugal	Sociedade Portuguesa de Contabilidade	1930
Scotland	Institute of Chartered Accountants of Scotland	1951 (1854)
Spain	Institut of Sworn Auditors of Accounts	1943
Sweden	Föreningen Auktoriserade Revisorer (FAR)	1923
	Svenska Revisorsamfundet (SRS)	1899
Netherlands	Nederlands Instituut voor Registeraccountants	1967 (1895)
New Zealand	New Zealand Society of Accountants	1909 (1894)
United States	American Institute of Certified Public Accountants	1887

Source: Alexander and Nobes (2004), Nobes and Parker (2003) and Ordelheide and KPMG (2001)

accounting standards. The following illustrates several differences in financial reporting characteristics. Although they are presented as separate items, they are linked together.

Shareholder orientation versus stakeholder orientation

In countries with widespread ownership there is a need for high-quality published financial information. As companies have to rely to a large extent on the capital market, information disclosure becomes extremely important because existing and potential shareholders do not have access to internal information in order to assess the financial situation of the company they might want to invest in or increase their investment in. In those countries the pressure for disclosure is much greater than in countries where providers of finance have the power to obtain internal information. Besides the need for more disclosure and more auditing the debt versus equity orientation also has a direct influence on valuation issues.

In equity-oriented countries financial reporting is aimed at communicating the performance and efficiency of the business to existing and potential shareholders. Profit measurement is very important and reported profit data will be used to make predictions about the future earnings, cash flow and financial position of the company. In countries where companies are financed through debt, financial statements serve the information needs of many different stakeholders, especially creditors, and also the government.

Their information needs are concerned with the underlying assets of the company and the determination of taxable income. The debt/equity orientation lies at the origin of the different reporting and principles described next.

Fairness versus legality

In common law countries the aim of financial reporting is a fair representation of the financial situation of the company. In the UK this is translated into the 'true and fair view' concept. In code law countries financial reporting is focused on compliance with the legal requirements and tax laws. This often leads the 'legal form' to dominate 'the substance'. The most cited example in this respect is the accounting treatment of a lease contract. In countries with strong shareholder orientation and emphasis on fairness, lease contracts are accounted for on the balance sheet although the company is not the legal owner of the assets (e.g. UK and USA). In countries where the legal form prevails these assets used by the company are kept off balance sheet as the company is not the legal owner (e.g., until recently, France). This difference can have a major impact on the debt/equity ratio of companies (for example Euro Disney SCA, see Chapter 26).

Conservatism versus accruals

In countries in which financial reporting is more creditor oriented and used for tax purposes, valuation rules will be more conservative or prudent than in countries with a shareholder orientation. Adherence to conservatism versus accruals will lead to a different choice in valuation rules and accounting practices. For example, with regard to depreciation, the declining balance method will be used more often than the straight line method, if conservatism is an important characteristic in financial reporting. Further, more use will be made of provisions in these countries, especially when provisions are tax deductible. Conservative accounting is often regarded as a system in which lower profits are reported than under a system driven by accrual accounting. However, with the use of extensive depreciation and creation of provisions, those companies are also able to increase results in periods with weak economic performance.

Much research is currently being undertaken with regard to the quality of earnings reported under conservative accounting. With quality of accounting information one refers to the use of accounting data for the prediction of future performance (value relevance of accounting information). The results of these studies reveal that information provided under conservative accounting practices is less value relevant (see, for example, Basu, 1997; Pope and Walker, 1999; Penman and Zhang, 2002).

Uniformity, accounting plans and formats

In code law countries we observe that the regulator attaches importance to uniformity. Compliance with prescribed accounting plans (France, Spain and Belgium) and detailed formats for the balance sheet and the profit and loss account are a result of this drive for uniformity. When regulation is in the hands of the government the layout of the balance sheet, profit and loss accounts and notes is much more detailed.

The schemes for balance sheet and profit and loss account put forward by the Fourth and Seventh Directives of the European Union are more detailed than the layout presented by the IASB.

Consolidated accounts

In countries where financial reporting has a strong shareholder orientation, the practice of preparing and publishing consolidated financial statements emerged much earlier. Preparing consolidated financial statements was already common practice at the beginning of the 20th century in the USA (in the 1920s). In the UK and the Netherlands consolidation became common practice in the 1930s. In typical creditor orientation countries, which are usually also code law countries, consolidation was introduced by law. This was done in the late second half of the 20th century (Germany, 1965, *Aktiengesetz* for public companies; France, 1985, a law which obliged listed companies to publish consolidated accounts; Belgium, the Royal Decree of March 1990, in Italy consolidation became compulsory in the early 1990s).

Deferred taxation

In countries with no direct link between tax income and accounting income the practice of recording deferred taxes on the balance sheet is well established and common practice. For countries in which there is a strong link between accounting income and tax income the practice of recording and calculating deferred taxes is relatively new. Further, in the individual accounts of companies in those countries the amounts recorded under deferred taxes will be rather small.

Country classification

Research into the possible causes to explain the observed differences in national accounting practices reveal several moderating or intervening variables (e.g. providers of finance, legal system, cultural differences and taxation). These variables shape the existing accounting systems in the different countries (accounting regulation and organization of the profession), accounting values and financial reporting practices.

These different factors are used by researchers as cluster variables in order to classify different countries into separate more homogeneous groups according to their characteristics. These classification exercises were very popular in the 1970s and the 1980s. Examples can be found in the following publications Hatfield (1966), Mueller (1967), Seidler (1967), American Accounting Association (1977), Da Costa, Bourgeois and Lawson (1978), Frank (1979) and Nair and Frank (1980). The most cited classification pattern of countries is that of Nobes (1980).

To illustrate these country classification exercises, we now look at the classification system of Nobes. The popularity of classification attempts based purely on observed differences dropped in the 1990s, although Nobes' classification scheme still figures in many textbooks.

Nobes based his classification research on the financial reporting practices of public companies in the western world. The date of classification was 1980, that is, before the enactments in EU countries of the Fourth Directive on company law and before the emergence of IAS. Nobes selected the following nine discriminating variables:

1 type of user of the published accounts of listed companies
2 degree to which law or standards prescribe in detail and exclude judgement
3 importance of tax rules in measurement
4 conservatism/prudence
5 strictness of application of historical cost
6 susceptibility to replacement cost adjustments in main or supplementary accounts
7 consolidation practices
8 ability to be generous with provisions and to smooth income
9 uniformity between companies in application of rules.

Some of the discriminating factors relate to explanatory variables (for example factors one and two) while other variables relate more to valuation practices (for example, four and eight) (see Figure 2.1).

In the 1990s less pure classification attempts were carried out. From those that have been undertaken, we observe that the clusters move to each other and that more countries are now clustered into one group.

So far in this chapter we have explained how an existing accounting system in a specific country (financial reporting standards and practices, type of accounting regulator and strength of the accounting profession) is a result of national or local characteristics or influences. There are countries, however, in which the accounting systems in place do not result from national characteristics but are 'exported' to them or 'economically' or 'politically' imposed on them.

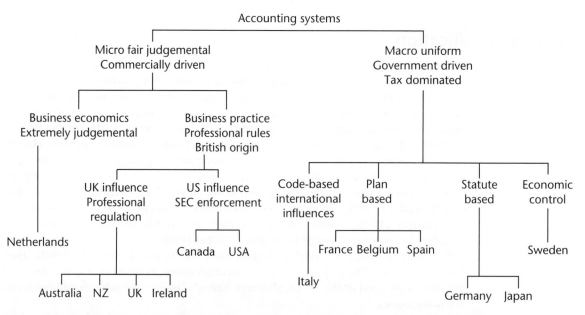

Figure 2.1 Suggested classification of accounting 'systems' in some developed countries
Source: Nobes (1980)

Western countries have exported their accounting systems to their colonies in the past. For example the accounting system in place in Singapore and the local GAAP are very similar to the British system and UK GAAP. In some countries in Africa, which were former French colonies a uniform chart of accounts (similar to the French *plan comptable*) is in use.

A more recent phenomenon is that standards are imposed on countries in the wake of globalization and economic progress. For example, countries in eastern Europe are now moving fast towards the adoption of IAS. However, some less developed countries have adopted IAS and one can wonder whether the local economies there are in need of a set of such technical accounting standards.

Classification issues: more recent evolutions

As mentioned earlier in this chapter, classification exercises that attempted to cluster countries in homogeneous groups became less popular in the 1990s. In the 1980s through the enactment of the Fourth Directive in EU countries and in the 1990s under the pressure of the globalization of capital markets, national accounting practices started slowly to move towards each other. This development is still going on and some differences have already become less noticeable or have almost disappeared for certain categories of companies or for certain items of the financial statement. A few examples of this evolution will now be discussed.

In the classification of Nobes, for example, Japan is classified in the same cluster as Germany. Although Japanese accounting and tax laws have been inspired by the German system, Japanese accounting standards are influenced by US GAAP. Japanese listed companies find inspiration in US GAAP for the preparation of their consolidated accounts. So in more recent classification exercises Japan has moved away from Germany.

Spain is classified in the cluster tax-based, continental macro uniform. Together with the implementation of the EU directives in Spain the link between the commercial accounts and the tax accounts has been loosened (Gonzalo and Gallizo, 1992).

With respect to the number of standards that are now in use in the USA and UK, these countries evolve also towards a situation in which many detailed rules come to exist. So with regard to the level of detailed regulations these countries start to move towards the situation of detailed rules that exists in the code law countries.

One country, the Netherlands, is a cluster on its own in the traditional classification exercises. This is due to a large extent to the adherence of business economics concepts for the determination of valuation practices (e.g. theory of Limperg). However, the valuation method of current value accounting is increasingly being abandoned and valuation practices and rules are now in line with other European countries and in recent cluster exercises the Netherlands has moved closer to the rest of Europe.

In the 1980s listed companies were, to a large extent, listed on only one stock exchange, often the national one. From the late 1980s on more and more companies sought dual listings. Many European multinationals went to capital markets abroad, especially to the US. In Germany, for example, at that time Daimler-Benz started to publish two sets of annual accounts, i.e. annual accounts presented according to German GAAP and annual accounts presented according to US GAAP. At that time the differences between equity and earnings presented according to US GAAP and the

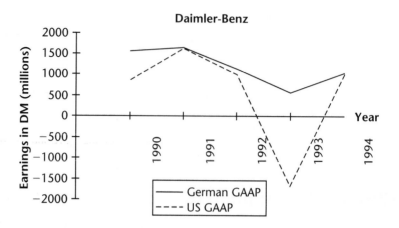

Figure 2.2 Earnings evolution of Daimler-Benz, 1989–1994
Source: Annual reports of Daimler-Benz (1989–1994)

equity and earnings presented according to German GAAP surprised many. Figure 2.2 became world famous.

Figure 2.2 provides clear evidence of the impact of conservative accounting practices on the reported result. In 1993 the US GAAP result of Daimler-Benz is much lower: conservative accounting leads to a kind of smoothing. Through conservative valuation rules earnings are decreased in 'good' years, but at times of weak economic performance results can be increased.

Differences in reported results and reported equity do not only arise between so-called conservative accounting GAAP and accruals-based GAAP. They can also arise between sets of GAAP with similar orientation. As an example, Table 2.5 shows the results and the equity of British Airways and Ryanair presented according to UK and to US GAAP.

Many Swiss, German and Scandinavian multinationals switched to IAS in the 1990s. In France a number of listed companies prepared their consolidated accounts using US GAAP (e.g. Total Fina, Suez) or IAS (e.g. Eutelsat, Rémy Cointreau, Renault). Academics started to study the reaction of the capital market to these voluntary switches of companies from 'conservative or low-quality' accounting standards to a set of 'higher quality' accounting standards. Empirical research results show that capital markets react positively to the switch, since capital markets perceive the switch as a reduction in information asymmetry between firms and investors. As a result the cost of capital drops (see, for example, Leuz and Verrechia, 2000).

This evolution resulted in the emergence of two groups of companies in most countries. The first group consists of companies that made an appeal to the international capital market for funds and then started to apply accounting rules that would lead to an increase of comparability of their financial information worldwide. This group started to use 'high-quality' accounting standards such as IAS/IFRS, US GAAP, UK GAAP, whereby 'high-quality' standards are defined as follows: 'Financial reporting quality relates to the usefulness of financial statements for contracting, monitoring, valuation and other decision making by investors, creditors, managers and all other

Table 2.5 Comparative data on equity and net income of Ryanair and British Airways according to UK and US GAAP

Ryanair (€ 000)	1998	1999	2000	2001	2002	2003	2004
Net income UK GAAP	45 525	57 471	72 518	104 483	150 375	239 398	206 611
Net income US GAAP before cumulative	36 693	61 771					
effect of accounting change		23 122			155 549	241 810	215 430
Net income US GAAP	36 693	84 893	71 866	112 388	1 002 274	1 241 728	1 455 288
Equity UK GAAP	133 472	250 964	441 357	669 898	1 019 607	1 177 187	1 356 281
Equity US GAAP	102 696	249 912	439 340	674 386			

British Airways (million £)	1998	1999	2000	2001	2002	2003	2004
Net income UK GAAP	460	206	−21	114	−142	72	130
Net income US GAAP	654	104	−451	226	−119	−128	396
Equity UK GAAP	3 321	3 355	3 147	3 215	2 016	2 058	2 218
Equity US GAAP	3 044	3 198	2 389	2 334	2 081	1 932	2 381

Source: Annual reports of British Airways and Ryanair

parties contracting with the firm' (Ball and Shivakumar, 2002). The other large group consisting of non-listed domestic companies, predominantly small and medium sized, would continue to apply national GAAP.

It seemed that for these large companies seeking capital worldwide, their location no longer played a significant role in the choice of the accounting rules or principles to be applied in their annual accounts. Much more important was the fact that these companies wanted to make an appeal on the international capital market. In recent years this appeal to the capital market and the fact that a company is operating internationally or globally became important factors in explaining reporting behaviour. Also non-listed global players started to use IAS or US GAAP for their annual accounts. Another important element is the industry to which a company belongs. In some industries, certain reporting practices prevail and are followed by companies worldwide without the enforcement of a legal or stock exchange authority. For example, companies active in the software industry all seem to opt for US GAAP, which has become the dominating GAAP in that industry.

Due to the drive towards global harmonization of reporting practices, one might expect that national influences on reporting behaviour would soon vanish. Although the location of the company no longer solely explains the reporting behaviour of a company, it is still a major influencing factor.

National differences: will they still play a role in the future?

So for large companies the location of the company is no longer the sole influencing factor on the reporting behaviour of a company. Next to the country the characteristics of the company such as industry, dimension, operating internationally, listed on international stock markets also became important in the explanation of reporting behaviour. This does not mean, however, that the role of the national environment has become insignificant as we will now see.

Even when all companies comply with US GAAP or IAS/IFRS, national influences still play a role. Current empirical research provides us with evidence of this influence, and this is another reason why we have paid so much attention to such national variables in this chapter.

The variables pointed out by researchers in the 1970s and 1980s as causes that might explain and have led to differences in national accounting systems and national GAAP are now used in empirical multi-country studies in which different aspects of the financial reporting practices of companies are researched. These studies focus, among other things, on the value relevance of accounting information, on earnings management practices and on characteristics of the audit market and audit process. A few examples of these empirical studies will be presented here together with their research results.

Ali and Hwang (2000) found that the value relevance of accounting information is lower for countries with bank-oriented (as opposed to market-oriented) financial systems. Value relevance was specified in terms of explanatory power of accounting variables (earnings and book value of equity) for security returns. Their results indicate further that value relevance of accounting income is lower for countries where private sector bodies are not involved in the standard-setting process. This finding is consistent with the premise that government standard setters use financial accounting rules to satisfy their own regulatory needs such as computing income taxes or demonstrating compliance with the national government policies and macroeconomic plans (Choi and Mueller, 1992). The research provides further evidence for the fact that value relevance is lower for continental model countries than for British–American model countries, besides the value relevance is lower when there is a strong link between accounting results and tax results and finally they find that value relevance is higher when more is spent on external auditing services.

Ball, Kothari and Robin (2000) investigated two properties of accounting income (conservatism and timeliness) and the influence of international institutional factors on accounting income. The property timeliness is defined as the extent to which current period accounting income incorporates current period economic income. Conservatism has been used in this study using the definition of Basu (1997), which regards conservatism as the extent to which current period income asymetrically incorporates economic losses, relative to economic gains. Their central result is that accounting income in common law countries is significantly more timely that in code law countries, due entirely to quicker incorporation of economic losses which means more income conservatism.

Guenther and Young (2000) investigated how cross-country differences in legal systems, differences in legal protection for external shareholders, and differences in the degree of tax conformity affect the relation between financial accounting earnings and real economic value-relevant events that underlie those earnings. The results provide evidence that the association between financial accounting earnings and real economic activity in a country is related in predictable ways to the legal and economic systems that underlie financial accounting standard setting and the demand for financial accounting standards. The high association for the UK and the USA and the low association for France and Germany are consistent with expectations that accounting earnings in common law countries, countries with legal systems that protect external shareholder rights, countries with market-oriented (rather than bank-oriented) capital markets and countries where financial accounting rules are independent of tax rules better reflect underlying economic activity. Not only the traditional elements of differentiation (provision of capital, legal system, link with taxation) seem to be relevant, but also elements such as risk of litigation, investor protection and enforcement of accounting rules are important factors that explain differences in reporting behaviour.

Leuz, Nanda and Wysocki (2003) found that the quality of financial reports increased in countries where investor protection is stronger. They found support for their 'diversion hypothesis', which implies that earnings management decreases when outside legal protection is high. Their findings suggest an important link between legal institutions and the quality of financial information provided to market participants worldwide. The legal rights accorded to the outside investors and the quality of their enforcement are both associated with the properties of firms' accounting earnings. Their study indicated further that a switch to high-quality standards alone was not a guarantee for high-quality financial information. Other academics had also put forward this issue. For example, Schipper (2000) stated that: 'Reporting quality is not only a function of the set of standards applied. High-quality standards implemented in a defective manner will not result in high-quality financial reports.' Without adequate enforcement, even the best accounting standards will be inconsequential.

Maijoor and Vanstraelen (2002) in their study put forward the idea that the international comparability of earnings reported depends not only on the set of accepted accounting standards, but also on the national quality of audits and the constraints imposed on earnings management by the national audit environment. In their research they studied earnings management in France, Germany, the Netherlands and the United Kingdom. Although companies in all four countries engage in earnings management, its magnitude is not uniform across the four.

Summary

In this chapter we outlined the major influencing factors which led to differences in the development of national accounting environments and national reporting practices from the 18th century until almost the end of the 20th century. Empirical research conducted in the 1970s and the 1980s indicated the following variables as important determinants of those differences: provision of finance, the legal system, the link between accounting and taxation and cultural values.

From the 1970s on a movement towards harmonization of financial reporting started slowly to emerge. From the 1990s on under pressure from multinational companies, seeking dual listings to attract capital, the request for one set of GAAP to be applied worldwide emerged. Whether this goal will be obtained in the near future is the subject of part of Chapter 3. Meanwhile, as attempts for worldwide harmonization and standardization are undertaken, national institutional differences still influence, to some extent, the output of the financial reporting process.

✔ 1 Discuss whether, in essence, accounting is law based or economics based.

✔ 2 If accounting is culture based and national, indeed local, cultures are different, international harmonization will obviously be impossible. Discuss.

3 In this chapter several causes are discussed which had some influence on existing accounting systems. Which of the causes listed played a significant role in your country? Discuss.

4 If you take Hofstede's (1984) framework for describing cultural differences, how would you describe your own country in relation to these constructs?

5 Do you notice in your country an evolution in the existing accounting system? What would you suggest are the driving forces? Explain.

6 If you consider Gray's (1988) adaptation of Hofstede's framework in relation to accounting values, could you describe which accounting values are prevalent in your country?

7 Is Gray's (1988) adaptation of the Hofstede (1984) framework of cultural differences able to explain the observed differences concerning voluntary disclosures made to the financial statements?

The process of harmonization

After studying this chapter you should be able to:
☐ outline the role of the European Union in the development of accounting harmonization
☐ outline the history and changing role of the International Accounting Standards Committee/Board in the development of accounting harmonization
☐ understand current developments and their implications (current when you read the chapter!).

Introduction

Chapter 2 gave some idea of the very real historical differences between accounting thinking and practice across the world. Since accounting is essentially a communication process, such differences are not helpful in the context of multinational and international business. Either reporting enterprises need to prepare multiple sets of financial statements under different bases or users have to familiarize themselves with, and understand, a variety of different accounting preparation systems. Both alternatives are time consuming and costly, and can easily lead to confusion and error.

Reduction in such differences, and ideally, the elimination of such differences, is desirable. It is also extremely difficult, because of the deep-seated causes discussed in Chapter 2. A number of attempts have been made on a regional basis, of which that of the European Union is perhaps the most significant, to reduce country differences and the International Accounting Standards Board has become increasingly significant at the global level. We discuss these two attempts in some detail, starting with the European Union (EU). In the early years, the EU had a much greater effect than the IASC, so we look at the EU first. Now, however, its influence relative to the IASB has declined.

A note on terminology, which can be very confusing, is necessary. 'Harmonization' is a process of increasing the compatibility of accounting practices by setting bounds to their degree of variation. 'Standardization' appears to imply the imposition of a more rigid and narrow set of rules. However, within accounting these two words have almost become technical terms and one cannot rely on the normal difference in their meanings. Harmonization is a word that tends to be associated with the supranational legislation promulgated in the European Union, while standardization is a word often associated with the International Accounting Standards Committee. In practice, the words are often used interchangeably.

It is possible to distinguish between de jure harmonization (that of rules, standards, etc.) and de facto harmonization (that of corporate financial reporting practices). For any particular topic or set of countries, it is possible to have one of these two forms of harmonization without the other. For example, countries or companies may ignore the harmonized rules of standard setters or even lawmakers. By contrast, market forces persuade many companies in France or Switzerland to produce English-language financial reports that approximately follow Anglo-American practice.

EU Directives

For many years the major method of engendering change across the EU has been by means of Directives. Once agreed (a process that can take and has taken over 20 years), a Directive is a binding agreement by all the member states of the EU that they will introduce national legislation. It is important to clarify precisely what this means and what it does not mean. It does mean that all member states are required to implement the Directives. It does not mean that citizens or institutions within a member state are required to follow the Directive, unless and until the contents of the Directive are enacted by legislation within the state. Another important point is that each Directive exists not merely in one language version, but in each of the official EU languages. It is the language version applicable to a particular member state that is to be enacted into the law of that country. There may not be perfect semantic equivalence between different language versions of the Directives. Furthermore, where the contents of the national legislation following from a Directive differs from that Directive (either by restricting allowed options or by going against the terms of the Directive itself), only European legal procedures can be used to enforce the Directive requirements.

The fundamental EU Directive relating to financial reporting is the Fourth Company Law Directive of 25 July 1978. This relates to the annual accounts of limited companies. It was followed by the Seventh Company Law Directive of 13 June 1983, which extended the principles of the Fourth Directive to the preparation of consolidated (group) accounts. The Fourth Directive seeks to provide a minimum of coordination of national provisions for the content and presentation of annual financial accounts and reports, of the valuation methods used within them and of the rules for publication. It applies to 'certain companies with limited liability' – broadly, all those above defined minimum size criteria – and aims to ensure that annual accounts disclose comparable and equivalent information.

It is important to place the Fourth Directive into its historical context. It was drafted and debated over a period of some ten years, beginning when the EU had six members and ending when it had ten. The pre-Directive national characteristics of the accounting practices of the member states were significantly different, both in degree of sophistication and in direction. When appraising the success (or otherwise) of this Directive we must measure its achievements against those, at times, startlingly diverse existing practices.

Crucial to the content of the Fourth Directive is the requirement that published accounts should show a 'true and fair view'. The implications and origin of the phrase are discussed in some detail in Chapter 8. Briefly, however, this is a classic example of the cultural divide between the common law tradition and the tradition of codified law. In the former, definitions of such concepts are typically provided by courts in relation to specific situations, rather than by legislative texts intended to apply to many different situations. In the latter, the converse is true; the courts have a role of interpretation and clarification of legislative texts, but not of providing situationally appropriate legal definitions. Thus, the tradition of economic liberalism of the English-speaking countries, the faith in markets and the suspicion of technocracy, go hand in hand with an essentially pragmatic common law tradition and a belief that the accounting profession can largely lay down its own rules in the form of 'generally accepted accounting principles'. By contrast, the countries of continental Europe have less historical attachment to economic liberalism, more faith in technocracy and a preference for explicit legal texts, which extends to the framing of accounting rules. Harmonization of accounting within the EU has involved bringing these two traditions into some degree of harmony and it is in this respect that the inclusion of the 'true and fair' requirement in the Fourth Directive was both crucial and controversial.

By the early 1990s it had become clear, even to the European Commission, that directives were too cumbersome and slow to achieve further useful harmonization. The Fourth Directive, agreed in 1978, did not cover several topics and it had been too complicated to amend it often. Furthermore, global harmonization had become more relevant than regional harmonization.

It had also become clear that, for large European companies, voluntary harmonization might focus on US rules over which the European Commission and other Europeans have no influence. Consequently, from the middle of the 1990s, the European Commission began to support the increasingly important efforts of the IASC.

International Accounting Standards

The IASC was created in 1973. Its creation was related to that of the International Federation of Accountants (IFAC), which is the worldwide umbrella organization of accountancy bodies. It is independent of government or pseudo-government control. Its stated purpose is to develop and enhance a coordinated worldwide accountancy profession with harmonized standards. All members of the IFAC were, under the old IASC constitution, automatically members of the IASC.

IASC's description of itself as an 'independent private sector body' is accurate and revealing. It was, in essence, a private club, with no formal authority. This is in contrast to national regulatory or standard-setting bodies, which operate within a national jurisdiction and some form of legal and governmental framework that delineates, defines and provides a level of authority. The IASC, however, operated throughout its existence in the knowledge that in the last resort, it and its standards have no formal authority. It therefore always had to rely on persuasion and the quality of its analysis and argument. This can be seen to have had two major effects. First, the quality of logic and discussion in its publications was generally high and its conclusions were – if sometimes debatable – feasible and clearly articulated. Second, however, the conclusions and recommendations of many of the earlier published IAS documents often had to accommodate two or more alternative acceptable treatments, simply because both or all were already being practised in countries that were members of IASC and were too significant to be ignored.

The disadvantages of this state of affairs are obvious and were well recognized by the IASC itself. Toward the end of the 1980s the IASC decided it would attempt a more proactive approach and early in 1989 it published an exposure draft (E32) on the comparability of financial statements. This proposed the elimination of certain treatments permitted by particular IASs and the expression of a clear preference for one particular treatment, even where two alternatives were still to be regarded as acceptable.

This 'comparability project' led to a large number of revised standards operative from the mid-1990s, which did indeed considerably narrow the degree of optionality compared with the earlier versions of the standards issued in the 1970s and 1980s. The comparability project, therefore, can be said to have made the set of IASs more meaningful and significant. Of course, it did nothing to increase the formal authority of the IASC.

In 1995, as the next stage in its development, IASC entered into an agreement with the International Organization of Securities Commissions (IOSCO) to complete a 'core set' of IASs by 1999. With regard to the agreement, IOSCO's Technical Committee stated that completion of 'comprehensive core standards acceptable to the Technical Committee' would allow it to 'recommend endorsement' of those standards for 'cross-border capital raising in all global markets'. The significance of this agreement is great. It would mean that one set of financial statements, properly prepared in accordance with IAS GAAP, would automatically be acceptable for listing purposes without amendment and without any reconciliation to national (i.e. local) GAAP on each and all of the world's important stock exchanges. This would save huge resources at the international and multinational level, both for preparers and for users and analysts. The role of national standard setters, except arguably for small and medium-sized enterprises, would simply disappear, if enforcement were left to other bodies.

From the IAS viewpoint, successful implementation of this process would provide the de facto authority that it needs and craves. Any enterprise failing to accept the authority of IAS would know that its shares would be likely to be de-listed.

This, of course, raises the issue of effective enforcement, for which IASB is dependent on securities regulators and other bodies with the power to impose de-listing and other sanctions and on a mechanism for bringing breaches of IASs to the attention of such bodies.

In December 1998 the then IASC completed its 'core standards' programme with the approval of IAS 39, *Financial Instruments Recognition and Measurement*. Following the publication of the report of IASC's Strategic Working Party, *Recommendations on Shaping IASC for the Future*, in November 1999, the board of IASC approved proposals in December 1999 to make significant changes to IASC's structure, in order to prepare it for an enhanced role as a global accounting standard setter.

Following these preparations, the year 2000 was a momentous one for IASC. In May the proposed structural changes were approved by IASC's membership. (The results of these changes are outlined in the following section.) Also in May, IOSCO formally accepted the IASC's 'core standards' as a basis for cross-border securities-listing purposes worldwide (although for certain countries, notably the United States, reconciliations of items such as earnings and stockholders' equity to national GAAP would still be required). In June, the European Commission issued a Communication proposing that all listed companies in the European Union would be required to prepare their consolidated financial statements using IASs, a proposal that has since been adopted.

It is apparent, however, that acceptance of IASs by the SEC, for the financial reporting of foreign registrants for US listing, is a crucial element in the new IASB's acceptance as the global accounting standard setter. This is discussed further later.

It is important to note that International Standards, although they do not apply to 'immaterial items', are mostly explicitly intended to apply to all enterprises, in all types of economy and of all sizes. This is unlike, for example, the US Standards which only apply to listed enterprises. This universality of IAS application is increasingly being questioned, especially as the direction of US and EU influence is likely to push IASs further towards a large enterprise multinational focus. The relevance of this focus to small or medium-sized enterprises (SMEs) or to developing economies is debatable.

Given the position and role of IASB and the widely differing practices and attitudes of its constituents, is it really valid to talk of generally accepted accounting principles in the IASB context? Is IAS GAAP the same species of animal as, say, US GAAP, distinguished only by minor genetic individualities? Or is it of a different species or even genus?

One difference is clear, at least at the time of writing and at the time of the issuance of the International Accounting Standards described and discussed in this volume. IAS GAAP (we continue to use the term, if only for convenience) is, inevitably, designed to be 'generally accepted' in a variety of different legal and cultural contexts. US GAAP, UK GAAP, German regulation and other national systems have no need for this consideration. This may sound like a weakness of IAS GAAP. From a national standpoint, perhaps, it is, but national standpoints are no longer entirely valid. The very reason for the existence of the IASB is that financial reports must be comprehensible across countries, across jurisdictions and across cultures. Country X may justifiably be able to say that its own national GAAP, as applied in its own national context, is 'better' than IAS GAAP as applied in the *same* national context. But that is no longer the point. In a global market, the relevance of the national context is hugely reduced.

New structure of the IASB

Like the Financial Accounting Standards Board (FASB) in 1972 and the UK Accounting Standards Board in 1990, which replaced the APB and the ASC, respectively, the new IASB differs from its predecessor by having a two-tier structure, based on an organ of governance not involved in standard setting (the trustees) and a standard-setting board. According to Clause 6 of the new Constitution:

> The governance of IASC shall rest with the Trustees and the Board and such other governing organs as may be appointed by the Trustees or the Board in accordance with the provisions of this Constitution. The Trustees shall use their best endeavours to ensure that the requirements of this Constitution are observed; however, they are empowered to make minor variations [in the Constitution] in the interest of feasibility of operation if such variations are agreed by 75% of all the Trustees.

The new structure is the one proposed in the Strategic Working Party's November 1999 report, *Recommendations on Shaping IASC for the Future*. There are 19 trustees, of whom six are from North America, six from Europe, four from the Asia/Pacific region and three from any area, subject to establishing 'overall geographical balance'. The new board differs significantly from its predecessor (the committee) by having 12 full-time members as well as two part-time members. Moreover, its members are chosen for their technical expertise and background experience and (in contrast to the trustees) not on the basis of geographical representation. However, seven of the full-time members have 'formal liaison responsibilities with national standard setters in order to promote convergence ... but shall not be voting members of the national standard setters' (Constitution, Clause 27). The seven countries with whose national standard setters such liaison arrangements have been set up in the first board are Australia with New Zealand, Canada, France, Germany, Japan, the United Kingdom and the United States (see Figure 3.1).

A minimum of five members of the board must have a background as practising auditors, at least three must have a background as preparers of financial statements, at least three a background as users of financial statements and at least one must have an academic background. Each member has one vote and most decisions are to be made by a simple majority of members attending in person or by a telecommunications link, with a quorum being such attendance by 'at least 60% of the members' and the chairman having a casting vote. The publication of an exposure draft, final IAS, or final interpretation of the Standing Interpretations Committee requires approval by at least eight members of the board. This change to majority voting is significant, as the old IASC required a 75% majority.

The first chairman of the IASC trustees is Paul A. Volcker, former Chairman of the US Federal Reserve Board. The first chairman of the new board is Sir David Tweedie, who moved from being chairman of the UK Accounting Standards Board and was formerly UK technical partner for KPMG, after an academic career in Scotland.

As well as the trustees and the board, the new structure includes a Standing Interpretations Committee (SIC – similar to its predecessor in the previous structure)

19 trustees with diverse geographic and
functional backgrounds, who:

- appoint the Members of the Board, the Standing Interpretations Committee and the Standards Advisory Council
- monitor IASB's effectiveness
- raise its funds
- approve IASB's budget
- have responsibility for constitutional change

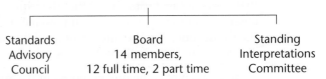

| Standards Advisory Council | Board 14 members, 12 full time, 2 part time | Standing Interpretations Committee |

Figure 3.1 Structure of the IASB

and a Standards Advisory Council; the members of both these bodies are appointed by the trustees. The name of the SIC has been changed to the International Financial Reporting Interpretations Committee (IFRIC) and for Standards issued by IASB the term 'International Financial Reporting Standard' (IFRS) is used.

The Standards Advisory Council, with 49 members, provides a forum for participation by organizations and individuals with an interest in international financial reporting and having diverse geographic and functional backgrounds, with the objective of giving advice to the board on agenda decisions and priorities, informing the board of the view of members of the Council on major standard-setting projects and giving other advice to the board or the trustees. The Council is chaired by the chairman of the board.

In addition to the seven 'liaison' members, the other seven members of the new board are citizens of South Africa, Switzerland, the United Kingdom and the United States, albeit with substantial international experience. Thus, the only 'emerging economy' country that has one of its citizens on the board is South Africa. One purpose of the Standards Advisory Council may be to give a greater voice to such countries. The orientation of the IASB towards global capital markets has left accountants in such countries (both practitioners and academics) feeling that their needs are not receiving sufficient attention and, in some cases, these feelings amount to bitterly expressed resentment. The outgoing board of IASC expressed some concern for the needs of small enterprises and constituents in developing countries. These needs do not seem to be high on the list of the IASB's priorities. However, a project group on small and medium enterprises (SMEs) has been set up, which produced a preliminary discussion paper in the summer of 2004. Early signs are that simplification will not be carried to excess(!).

The future?

It is important to realize that international accounting harmonization, like many important issues, is a very political process. At the time of writing, i.e. autumn 2004, the position is approximately as follows. The IASB is fully established and a stream of proposed new and revised Standards is expected to emerge over the next couple of years. The American SEC, despite its involvement in the IOSCO board acceptance of the IASC's final set of standards, is very much qualifying its support and insisting on continuation of a compulsory reconciliation for companies listed in the US from IAS to US GAAP.

The European Union proposal to require IAS Standards for listed European enterprises is now definitive. The EU has given final approval to its regulation on the application of International Accounting Standards. Unlike an EU Directive, the Regulation has the force of law and no further action is required by member states before the Regulation comes into effect. The Regulation applies in all member states plus Iceland, Norway and Liechtenstein. This includes the ten new accession countries that joined the EU in 2004.

The Regulation requires all listed companies within the European Economic Area to publish IAS consolidated financial statements for accounting periods beginning on or after 1 January 2005. The term IAS encompasses all standards and interpretations issued or adopted by the International Accounting Standards Board. Member states may allow a two-year extension for companies that have their securities publicly traded outside the EU and which, for that purpose, had already been using internationally accepted standards (in practice, US GAAP) since a financial year that started before the regulation was published. Member states may also allow a two-year extension for companies that have only debt securities listed on a regulated market.

While the regulation requires the publication of IAS consolidated financial statements, the European Commission is required to decide on the applicability of individual IASs within the EU. It may adopt an IAS only if:

- It is not contrary to the principles of the EU Fourth and Seventh Directives.
- It is conductive to the European public good.
- It meets the criteria of understandability, relevance, reliability and comparability required of financial information needed for making economic decisions and assessing stewardship of management.

At the time of writing (autumn of 2004), the position regarding this EU 'endorsement' process is complicated and rather confused. First of all, all the old IASC standards were endorsed, except for IAS 32 and 39 relating to financial instruments. Many of these standards have since been revised to a greater or lesser extent, and endorsement of these revisions seems to require a considerable time lag. Further, political interference and lobbying by European banks anxious to maintain secretive traditions have so far prevented endorsement of IAS 32 or 39, despite significant conciliatory amendments made by IASB. Legalistically speaking, considerable difficulties could result if the EU authorities continue to allow or facilitate such interference (a practice they have learnt from US Congress). In early 2005 the European Commission confirmed the adoption of IAS 39 in Europe minus two (significant) sections. The story will, however, have moved on by the time you read this.

Member states have the option of extending the application of the regulation to unlisted companies and to legal entity, rather than consolidated, financial statements.

The EU has also updated the Fourth and Seventh Directives to make them more receptive to the International Standards. Major amendments:

- Empower member states to allow or require a cash flow statement.
- Bring the definition of parent and subsidiary fully into line with IAS 27 (see Chapter 24).
- Require the consolidation of all subsidiaries, even those with dissimilar activities.
- Achieve consistency between the formal requirements for the financial statements and IAS requirements.
- Allow for likely IAS requirements on performance reporting.
- Allow the revaluation of intangible assets and any other class of assets.
- Extend the disclosures about environmental and social aspects of a business.
- Modify the format and content of the audit report to reflect current best practice and achieve harmonization.

Major changes, potentially very significant, are also taking place in the USA. The collapse of Enron and subsequent further 'scandals' have shaken the complacency of American regulation to the core. Early accusations against Enron did not accuse the company of not following US GAAP, merely of following it in an inappropriate manner. This has led to the suggestion, which the IASB was very quick to take up, that the US desire for evermore detailed standards has been demonstrated to be unhelpful. Rather, standards based on general principles, as International (and also UK) standards generally are, would perhaps be more effective. The European Union (and not merely the UK) is strongly behind the IASB on this issue.

At almost the same time, a new chairman was appointed to the US Financial Accounting Standards Board (FASB), Robert Herz. Herz was one of the two half-time appointments to the new IASB and can be expected to be an active supporter of convergence between the USA and IAS, and of a more principles-based, rather than detail-based, approach for US standards, which would obviously make such convergence easier.

This is not to say that practical convergence will be simple. There is a real need, again strongly expressed from the USA, for visible enforcement and adequately uniform application of international standards. The people applying those standards will come from many different countries with many different native languages. Their attitudes will inevitably be influenced by all the historical and cultural baggage inherent in our discussion in Chapter 2. The precise outcome is uncertain. But the future is going to be interesting!

Activity 3.1

By means of the IASB website (http://www.iasb.org.uk), websites of regulatory and professional accounting organizations in your own country and any other convenient sources, update this chapter for yourself.

Activity feedback

Up to you, of course. Think about the political dimension as well as about the pure accounting issues.

Summary

This chapter has provided a background of history and understanding behind the current international accounting developments, with an emphasis on the increasing importance of the IASB. You should update it for yourself.

EXERCISES
(✔ indicates answers are available on page 718)

✔ 1 The European Commission has handed over accounting regulation in Europe to the IASB. Discuss.

2 The European Commission, through its 2005 requirement, has given the IASB authority that it could never have achieved by itself. Discuss.

3 Global accounting ignores the needs of developing economies. Discuss.

Economic valuation concepts

After studying this chapter you should be able to:
- [ ] provide an overview and context of the asset valuation debate
- [ ] explain definitions and interrelationships of income, capital and value
- [ ] describe the variety of alternatives that need to be explored within the parameters of the valuation debate
- [ ] outline the concepts of income developed by Fisher (1930) and Hicks (1946)
- [ ] contrast *ex ante* and *ex post* economic income
- [ ] outline the scope of economic thinking in this area.

Introduction

This chapter is the first of a series that explores the whole area of asset valuation and income measurement. A number of separated research traditions have grown up, some over several centuries, often associated with particular individuals. There is a tendency in the English-speaking world to think that most of the important ideas involved were invented by Anglo-Saxons, but this is far from the truth. Nevertheless, since, as we have shown in Chapter 2, IASB capital market-driven accounting has largely developed from Anglo-Saxon thinking (very broadly defined), it is suitable to present the analysis in something of what in the old nationalistic days would have been regarded as an Anglo-Saxon context. We briefly relate the ideas to a number of other research traditions at the end of Chapter 7. It is also important to realize that the principles underlying much of this theoretical debate are directly applicable to regulatory issues and debates considered in Parts Two and Three.

More pertinently, it is important to accept that we are here concerned with theoretical analysis, i.e. with what *could* be done, and what appear to be the advantages and disadvantages of doing it. Practical traditions are, again, outlined at the end of Chapter 7.

The basic equation

We have already established that a well-behaved balance sheet does not balance just because accountants are good at adding up. It balances because it is *defined* in such a way that it *must* balance. Following from the business entity convention, capital is the balancing figure. Capital is the liability of the business entity to the ownership entity. The business owns a collection of assets, and owes a collection of borrowings to lenders and unpaid suppliers of goods and services. Deducting these borrowings from the assets enables us to say that the business owns a collection of net assets. So the owners own the business and the business owns the net assets. Therefore the owners' investment in the business – i.e. the capital – *must* equal the net assets.

That much is couched in static terms. But we can easily modify the wording to allow for profit or income. To avoid possible confusion, we use profit and income as, in the accounting context, completely synonymous terms. Profit (income) means the positive difference between revenues and expenses for a given period. If a business makes a profit then money or money's worth received or to be received increases by more than money or money's worth consumed. This is a complicated way of saying that its net assets go up by the amount of the profit. But in logic and in bookkeeping profit represents an increase in capital. Profit is attributable to owners, is owned by owners and is therefore owed by the business to the owners.

So the amount of profit equals the amount of the increase in the net assets, which, in turn, equals the amount of the increase in the capital. In practice, drawings or dividends are likely to occur. These obviously represent a withdrawal of money or money's worth and therefore a reduction in net assets. They also mean that the business has paid the owners some of what is owed to them. There is therefore a reduction in what remains owing to them, i.e. a reduction in capital. If drawings in a period equal profits for the period then capital (and net assets) is maintained at its original level. If profit exceeds drawings in a period capital (and net assets) increase.

This can usefully be summarized schematically. Let W_1 be the opening wealth (net assets of the business) and W_2 be the closing net assets. Let P be the profit for the period and D be the (net) drawings. Then:

$$W_1 + P - D = W_2$$

Or in more purely accounting terms:

Opening capital plus profit minus drawings equals closing capital

It is obvious that the $W_1 + P - D = W_2$ equation fits our traditional accounting model. But it is in no way restricted to that model. It is expressed in the most general of terms. It can be reduced to:

What you had
+ What you've added to it
− What you've removed from it
= What you've got

This is a truism, mere tautology. The unit of measurement could be absolutely anything. But in accounting we take a particular view. First, we measure the elements in money terms. Second, we traditionally measure the sums of money in a particular way, following the concepts we considered in Chapter 1. We record assets using the historic cost convention and we recognize revenue and net asset increases following the realization and accrual conventions. We are so used to this procedure that we tend to do it automatically, without considering the alternatives. We tend to accept normal practice out of sheer habit. Such acceptance will not do.

Income and capital

Activity 4.1

Go to a library and look up the words 'income' (or 'profit') and 'capital' in **(a)** a number of accounting texts, **(b)** a number of economics texts, **(c)** general dictionaries and encyclopaedia.

Record book titles under these three subheadings and summarize the definitions given.

Record book titles that fail to include definitions of either concept (you may wish to avoid these in the future).

Does a clear consensus and a clear understanding emerge?

Activity feedback

You may have more luck than we did, but likely conclusions are:

1   The terms have a wide variety of different meanings
2   clear definition is extremely difficult
3   many accounting texts evade the difficulties by talking in purely bookkeeping terms.

A useful starting point is the work of the economist Irving Fisher (1930). He defines capital thus: 'Capital is a stock of wealth at an instant in time.' In contrast to this, we can say that: Income is a flow of benefits or services arising through time. This is quite consistent with our earlier tautological equation. What you had (capital, stock) plus additions (income, flow) less withdrawals equals what you have got.

Capital is a stock of wealth that generates income. Income is the enjoyment from the use of capital. These seem like circular and therefore inadequate definitions. The way round this difficulty is to distinguish between *capital*, on the one hand, and *the value of capital*, on the other. *Capital* is a stock of assets capable of generating future services. *The value of capital* is dependent on the value of those future services. For example, a field is a stock of wealth, a field is capital. The value of the field, the value of the capital, is dependent on the (net) value of crops to be grown on the field, i.e. on the income.

All this makes income and the value of capital sound like forward-looking concepts. Perhaps they are!

Wealth and value

It should be clear by now that we can talk about evaluating the assets of an entity, we can talk about evaluating the wealth of an entity and we can talk about evaluating the capital of an entity. Each of these descriptions amounts to exactly the same thing. It amounts to an evaluation of what the entity 'has got'. Whichever way we look at this problem, whichever word we wish to use, the key point is the obvious need for evaluation. We noticed earlier that *any* measuring unit will do. But there must *be* a measuring unit – certainly a generally understandable one and preferably one generally accepted as a means of exchange (i.e. acceptable as 'money'). You are already familiar with the ways in which accountants usually evaluate different assets in a balance sheet. You are familiar, at least intuitively, with ideas of the 'A is better off than B' or 'this car is worth more than that one' variety. Try the next activity – it may be both more fun and more productive if you try it in a group, but if this is not possible think it over for half an hour while doing something else and then summarize your ideas.

Activity 4.2

A brief case study

We have an asset, for example a briefcase, and we wish to evaluate it, to attach a monetary value to it. List and describe all the possible ways of doing this you can think of. Illustrate each possible way by making up some simple figures. Which is the best method?

Activity feedback

One of the purposes of this activity is simply the realization that there is a very large number of possible answers. Here are some possibilities:

1   We could take as our basic figure the amount of money we originally paid for the briefcase:
   (a)   We could simply use this base figure as being our 'value'.
   (b)   We could reduce it according to the life of the item. Thus, if the briefcase cost €10, is expected to last for ten years and is now eight years old, we could retain the figure of €10 as giving the 'value', but it arguably makes more sense to say that since the briefcase is eight-tenths 'used up', then eight-tenths of the €10 has been 'used up' and therefore the remaining 'value' is €2.
2   We could take as our basic figure the amount of money we would now have to pay to buy the briefcase. Again there are several specific possibilities arising from this basis:
   (a)   We could take the cost, today, of buying a new briefcase.
   (b)   We could take the cost, today, of buying a second-hand briefcase in this particular condition.
   (c)   We could take the cost, today, of buying a new briefcase and reduce it according to the life of our briefcase. Thus, if a new briefcase costs €20, the second-hand cost of an old one is €3 and other information is as before, the alternative figures under this basis would be (a) €20; (b) €3; (c) eight-tenths of €20, i.e. €4.
   A variant of this basis is not to consider the cost of replacing the asset, but rather to consider the cost of replacing its function. Thus, in our example, we would consider the cost of enabling me to carry my bits and pieces if my briefcase were lost, rather than the cost of replacing my briefcase. In situations of rapid technology change, this variant may be the only practical possibility, as the original assets are no longer available.
3   We could take as our basic figure the amount of money we would get if we sold the briefcase in its existing condition – say, €1. This should be the net figure after deducting any selling expenses.
4   We could take as our basic figure an evaluation of the future usefulness to us of the briefcase if we keep it and use it. We might say that the value of the use we shall get from the briefcase in the two final years of its life is €3 and €2, respectively. This does not mean that our basic figure would be $3 + 2 = €5$. The question is not: what is

the sum of the valuations of the usefulness in each year over the remaining life of the briefcase, but rather: what is the value today of the receipts of usefulness expected in the future. Thus, in our example, we need to find the value today of receiving a benefit of €3 in one year's time and a further €2 in two year's time. (Strictly, this assumes that the whole of a year's benefit or usefulness occurs on the last day of the year.)

The essence of this problem can be considered as follows. Suppose I owe you €80. If I say, 'Would you prefer €80 now or €90 in one year?', you would probably say you would take €80 now. If I were to say, 'Would you prefer €80 now or €150 in one year?', however, you would probably prefer the €150 in one year.

There will be some point between 90 and 150 at which you are completely indifferent as between the €80 and the higher figure in one year.

If that point occurs at €100, i.e., you are completely indifferent between €80 now and €100 in one year, then the rate of discount is 25% (25% × 80 = 20; 100 − 20 = 80).

This enables us to say that €100 expense in one year is the equivalent of €80 expense today and, equally, that €100 benefit in one year is only 'worth' €80 benefit today.

Suppose a project involves expenses of €100 pa for three years and then benefits of €200 for a further two years. At a 25% discount rate the present 'value' of this project is found as follows:

End year				
1 − 100 × 80% =				− 80
2 − 100 × 80% =	80 × 80% =			− 64
3 − 100 × 80% =	80 × 80% =	64 × 80% =		− 51
4 + 200 × 80% =	160 × 80% =	128 × 80% =		
		102 × 80% =		+ 80
5 + 200 × 80% =	160 × 80% =	128 × 80% =		
		102 × 80% =		
		80 × 80% =		+ 64
				€ − 51

Therefore, the project, involving net cash inflow of €100 (2 × 200) − (3 × 100), has a net present 'value' (discounted value) of −51 and is not worth pursuing (unless all available alternatives give even greater negative present values).

The problem, of course, is finding the rate of discount, which is influenced by alternative uses of the resource (e.g. interest on money) and by future expectations, which are of necessity subjective. Even if a discount rate as of now can be found, the implied assumption used here, that the rate remains constant, is almost certainly false.

If we take the same 25% discount factor as in the example, then €3 in one year will be evaluated at 80% of €3 today, i.e. €2.40, and €2 in two years will be evaluated at 80% of 80% of €2, i.e. €1.28. Thus, the value today of the future usefulness to us of the briefcase would, under these assumptions, be €2.40 + €1.28 = €3.68.

We can label these four evaluation approaches:

1 historic cost
2 replacement cost
3 net realizable value
4 net present value or economic value.

You may, of course, have thought of other ideas or other combinations. Our suggestions are restricted in at least two ways. First, we have thought purely in *monetary* terms. Second, we have assumed that money is a perfectly acceptable measuring unit – that we know exactly what one euro means. Both these assumptions require critical consideration.

Activity 4.3

Analyse and summarize the thought process that made you decide this book was worth buying.

Activity feedback

These suggestions make the assumption, not necessarily valid, that you did actually buy it. Whatever the price you paid, we can logically deduce that you considered that having the book was worth more to you than having the money. But you do not want the book in order to have the book. You bought the book in order to read it, to learn from it, to enjoy and savour its every word. This cannot be precisely evaluated. Equally, if you had not bought the book it would not be because you wanted to have the money. It would be because you wanted to spend the money on something else *even more advantageous* than ownership of your own copy. This also would not mean that you had evaluated the benefits of this alternative with any precision. There is no need to *evaluate* the benefits of these alternative courses of action, merely to *rank* them. So in order to take this significant investment decision it is not obvious that we can necessarily restrict our thinking to the financially quantifiable. This idea is further explored in Chapter 10.

Activity 4.4

Obtain a pencil, a measuring rule and an elastic band. Now attempt to measure the length of the pencil **(a)** with the rule and **(b)** with the elastic band.

Activity feedback

Quite! Stupid, isn't it? A centimetre is a precisely defined concept. But the idea of measuring a length with an elastic band is nonsensical because, of course, we do not know how far we have stretched it – it is continually changing by unknown amounts.

But a euro is as elastic a concept as an elastic band! In relative terms, for example in relation to the US dollar, the euro keeps changing, as published exchange rates tell us. Even more importantly, the euro keeps changing in absolute terms – indeed, is undefinable in absolute terms – as published inflation rates confirm. The value of a euro is neither clearly defined nor constant. Yet accountants use it as if it were both. This is another idea requiring detailed analysis and we return to it in Chapter 7.

An array of value concepts

A fuller explanation of some possible value concepts is given in a book that every accounting student should read (Edwards and Bell, 1961). We are asked to consider a semi-finished asset, i.e. part-way through the production process, to enumerate the various dimensions through which we can describe this asset and thus to calculate and define all possible permutations arising from this multidimensional consideration. Three dimensions are suggested:

1 the form (and place) of the thing being valued
2 the date of the price used in valuation
3 the market from which the price is obtained.

The form can be of three types. First, the asset could be described and valued in its present form, e.g. a frame for a chair. Second, it could be described and valued in terms of the list of inputs – wood, labour, etc., its initial form. Third, it could be described and valued as the expected output, less the additional inputs necessary to reach that stage – a chair less a padded seat, for example: its ultimate form.

The date of the price used in valuation, when applied to any of these three forms, gives rise to three possibilities – past, current and future. We can talk about past costs, current costs or future costs of the initial inputs. We can talk about past costs of the present form (i.e. what we *could* have bought it for in the past as bought-in work in progress), about current costs of the present form or about future costs of the present form. Finally, the prices assigned to the asset in its ultimate form (and to the inputs which must be deducted) could also bear past, current or future dates.

This now yields nine possible alternatives for our asset. But we have still to consider the third dimension – the market from which the price is obtained. Two basic types of market need to be distinguished, the market in which the firm could *buy* the asset in its specified form at the specified time, giving entry prices, and the market in which the firm could *sell* the asset in its specified form at the specified time, giving exit prices. Adding this third dimension with its two possibilities leads to a total of 18 possible alternatives for the asset. Edwards and Bell summarize this in Table 4.1.

Table 4.1 An array of value concepts

Value date, market	Initial inputs	Form and place of asset Present form	Ultimate form
Past, entry	*Historic costs*	Discarded alternatives	Irrelevant
Past, exit	Discarded alternatives	Discarded alternatives	Irrelevant
Current, entry	*Current costs*	*Present costs*	Irrelevant
Current, exit	Irrelevant	*Opportunity costs*	*Current values*
Future, entry	Possible replacement costs	Possible replacement costs	Irrelevant
Future, exit	Irrelevant	Possible selling values	*Expected values*

Activity 4.5

Articulate and explain the meaning of each of the 18 alternatives shown in Table 4.1.

Activity feedback

Your words will undoubtedly be different from ours but your ideas should be somewhat on the following lines.

Initial inputs

Past, entry	original costs of raw inputs
Past, exit	past selling prices of those raw inputs in their raw form
Current, entry	cost of those raw inputs today
Current, exit	today's potential selling price of those raw inputs if still in their original form (which they are not)
Future, entry	expected future costs of those same raw inputs in their original form
Future, exit	the expected future selling price of those raw inputs if still in their original form (which they are not)

Present form

Past, entry	the past cost at which the product could have been purchased in its present partially completed form (it was not)
Past, exit	past selling prices at which the product could have been sold in its present partially completed form (but it was not)
Current, entry	the cost at the present time of buying the asset in its present partially completed form
Current, exit	today's selling price of the product in its present partially completed form
Future, entry	the expected future cost of buying the asset directly from a supplier in its present partially completed form
Future, exit	the expected future selling price of the product in its present partially completed form

Ultimate form

Past, entry	the past cost at which the product could have been purchased directly from a supplier in its final fully completed form (but it was not)
Past, exit	the past selling price at which the product could have been sold in its final fully completed form (if we had had the product in that form, which we did not)
Current, entry	the cost at the present time of buying the product in its final fully completed form (which we did not)
Current, exit	today's selling price of the product in its final fully completed form
Future, entry	the expected future cost of buying the product directly from a supplier in its final fully completed form
Future, exit	the expected future selling price of the product in its final fully completed form

Activity 4.6

You may have found Activity 4.5 rather mind bending! It is a good example of the type of mental flexibility required if we are going to analyse from first principles without being influenced by prior experience. Now a rather easier task. Select the six alternatives from the total of 18 that you think are most likely to lead to the provision of useful information.

Table 4.2 Edwards and Bell's useful valuation possibilities

Exit values

1 *Expected values* (ultimate, future, exit) – values expected to be received in the future for output sold according to the firm's planned course of action
2 *Current values* (ultimate, current, exit) – values actually realized during the current period for goods or services sold
3 *Opportunity costs* (present, current, exist) – values that could currently be realized if assets (whether finished goods, semi-finished goods or raw materials) were sold (without further processing) outside the firm at the best prices immediately obtainable

Entry values

1 *Present costs* (present, current, entry) – the cost currently of acquiring the asset being valued
2 *Current cost* (initial, current, entry) – the cost currently of acquiring the inputs which the firm used to produce the asset being valued
3 *Historic cost* (initial, past, entry) – the cost at time of acquisition of the inputs which the firm in fact used to produce the asset being valued

Activity feedback

The six as selected and defined by Edwards and Bell (1961) themselves are shown in Table 4.2. It is clear from the feedback to Activity 4.5 that not all the other tasks are totally irrelevant (although some of them obviously are). So you may have included one or two different ones. Satisfy yourself, however, that you at least agree that the six alternatives selected in Table 4.2 will indeed provide useful information for decision-making purposes. These six ideas, as developed by later thinking, are all explored in subsequent chapters.

Economic value

We have already met the idea of this in our brief case study (Activity 4.2). It is mentioned again here in order to point out that the Edwards and Bell exposition of the array of value concepts is clearly incomplete in that it excludes the economic value possibility. To extend their own illustration, one possible course of action with a partly completed chair is to complete it and hire it out for rental or use it oneself by sitting on it, in either case producing returns over a number of periods capable of being evaluated using the discounting process. Economic value, too, requires proper exploration in a later chapter.

Capital maintenance

We established with our tautology that profit is increase in capital. Turning the argument around, we can suggest that profit is the increase in the closing capital *after having maintained the original capital*. This provides a different but often useful way of looking at problems of income measurement. For each and every *value* concept that we can define, with its corresponding income concept, there is also a clearly definable capital maintenance concept.

Activity 4.7

Under traditional accounting conventions, based on historical cost, what precisely is the definition of capital that has to be maintained before a profit is reported?

Activity feedback

Traditionally, profit is the numerical quantity of money units generated by the business for the owners over a period. If opening money capital is 100 and closing money capital 103, then (ignoring dividends and capital infusions) profit is 3. Profit is the excess after having maintained the original 100, so it is the original money capital, the number of euros originally invested, which has to be maintained under this traditional thinking. If the 100 were in 1896 and the 103 in 2006, this statement still applies!

We shall return to the idea of capital maintenance for each of the methods we consider in detail. It will help considerably in appraising the usefulness of the various alternatives. It is also an important element in the IASB conceptual framework discussed in Chapter 8.

Criteria for appraising alternative valuation concepts

We discussed the definition and role of accounting together with suggested characteristics of useful information. In essence, accounting communicates useful information for decision making. We need to analyze each valuation concept to be considered so as to understand in detail the meaning and significance of the information it gives. Different users face different decisions. Users are asking a number of questions. An array of valuation bases are providing a number of answers. If we can match up question with answer then we are being useful. Many valuation bases may be useful, but for different purposes. The question is generally not 'which is the best valuation concept?', but 'which is the best valuation concept to answer this question or help this decision?'. Appraisal is a way of analyzing and a way of thinking, never an absolute.

Activity 4.8

What are the questions, what are the decisions, for which traditional historical cost accounting as outlined in Chapter 3 appears to provide the relevant information?

Activity feedback

One safe answer, following from our discussion on capital maintenance, is that it tells us our gain, our profit, after ensuring the retention of the number of euros we originally invested. It does not seem obvious, however, that this is very useful information. Investment and expansion decisions as regards future activity require projections into the future based on today's euros. Reports on past activity related to euros of the day the business started seem a pretty illogical substitute. But you may, of course, have other ideas!

Fisher and psychic income

The implication of Activity 4.3 was that people buy something, not because of the object itself, but because of what they can do with it. This idea leads us into Fisher's concept of psychic income. People do things because of the satisfaction they derive from so doing. Satisfaction is a mental occurrence, an event of the mind. It is a psychic rather than a physical happening. People act, and make decisions about actions, so as to maximize their personal, mental or psychic satisfaction. Fisher (1930) puts the argument as follows:

> For each individual only those events which come within the purview of his experience are of direct concern. It is these events – the psychic experiences of the individual mind – which constitute ultimate income for that individual. The outside events have significance for that individual only in so far as they are the means to these inner events of the mind. The human nervous system is, like a radio, a great receiving instrument. Our brains serve to transform into the stream of our psychic life those outside events which happen to us and stimulate our nervous system.
>
> Directors and managers providing income for thousands of people sometimes think of their corporation merely as a great money-making machine. In their eyes its one purpose is to earn money dividends for the stock-holders, money interest for the bond-holders, money wages and money salaries for the employees. What happens after these payments are made seems too private a matter to concern them. Yet that is the nub of the whole arrangement. It is only what we carry out of the market place into our homes and our private lives which really counts. Money is of no use to us until it is spent. The ultimate wages are not paid in terms of money but in the enjoyments it buys. The dividend cheque becomes income in the ultimate sense only when we eat the food, wear the clothes, or ride in the automobile which are bought with the cheque.

The essence of this proposition seems to us to be obviously correct. How do we decide whether to work overtime and earn an extra €20 or to go for a walk in the sunshine? We shall take the decision that, we believe (possibly wrongly, of course), will lead to the greater pleasure. Clearly the pleasure to be derived from spending the €20 is relevant in this equation. Equally obviously, such pleasure or satisfaction – enjoyment income as Fisher terms it – cannot be measured directly or objectively. He proposes a series of approximations. The first approximation he calls real income. This involves physical events and material things. A litre of milk and a daily newspaper are both examples of real income. Real income consists of:

> those final physical events in the outer world which give us our inner enjoyments. This real income includes the shelter of house, the music of a radio, the use of clothes, the eating of food.

In one sense real income is measurable – litre is an objective term (although 'milk' is less so!). But there is no additivity – no standard measuring unit or common denominator. To achieve this we need to move to a second approximation, which Fisher calls the cost of living. This consists of the money paid to obtain the real income – the cost of the litre of milk and the daily newspaper. Fisher's exposition of the argument has something of a period flavour:

> So, just as we went behind an individual's enjoyment income to his real income, we now go behind his real income, or his living, to his cost of living, the money measure of real income. You cannot measure in dollars either the inner event of your enjoyment while eating your dinner or the outer event of eating it, but you can find out definitely how much money that dinner cost you. In the same way, you cannot measure your enjoyment at the cinema, but you do know what your house shelter is really worth to you, you can tell how much you pay for your rent, or what is a fair equivalent for your rent if you happen to live in your own house. You cannot measure what it is worth to wear an evening suit, but you can find out what it costs to hire one, or a fair equivalent of its hire if, perchance, the suit belongs to you. Deducing such equivalents is an accountant's job.
>
> The total cost of living, in the sense of money payments, is a negative item, being outgo rather than income; but it is our best practical measure of the positive items of real income for which those payments are made.

The problem with this as Fisher himself recognizes is that money paid out (outgo) does not seem to make much sense as a measure of income in money terms. We therefore move to a third approximation, that of money income:

> All money received and readily available and intended to be used for spending is money income.

We can illustrate Fisher's arguments by considering eating a meal. If we wish to eat, we have to go out and earn some money. This means that we have a money income – in this case, wages. This money income, of course, is the idea that corresponds to the everyday use of the words 'income' or 'earnings'. Having some money, we go out to a restaurant where we eat, and pay for, a meal. Here we have real income. We have the 'final physical event', namely the actual eating of the food. This is approximately measured by the 'cost of living', i.e. by the cost of the meal – the amount we pay the restaurant. This idea of taking a cost-based approach is clearly not a new one to an accountant.

But this is not the end of the story. Fisher argues further. We did not eat a meal for the sake of it, we ate a meal to receive the satisfaction, the pleasure of having eaten (or to avoid the unpleasantness, the pain, of feeling hungry). This satisfaction, this pleasure, is the 'enjoyment' or 'psychic' income. It may be unmeasurable, at least in a manner that can be recorded, but it is still, argues Fisher, the most important. After all, if it did not exist, we would have had no reason to buy the meal. And without a reason to buy the meal, we have no reason to earn the wages.

Fisher thus distinguishes three successive stages, or aspects, of a person's income:

1 *enjoyment* or psychic income, consisting of agreeable sensations and experiences
2 *real income* 'measured' by the cost of living
3 *money income*, consisting of the money received by someone for meeting their costs of living.

The last – money income – is most commonly called income; and the first – enjoyment income – is the most fundamental. But for accounting purposes real income, as measured by the cost of living, is the most practical.

This last statement may seem surprising, Fisher dismisses money income as being unimportant (enjoyment income is the most important, the cost of living is the most practical).

Notice again the definition he gives of money income, emphasis now added:

> All money received and readily available and *intended* to be used for spending is money income.

So if we receive a salary of $10 000 (Fisher's figures, writing in 1930!), save $4000 and put $6000 as available for spending, the significant figure to Fisher is the $6000, not the $10 000. Real income as measured by the cost of living may be more or less than money income. Real income is a closer approximation to ultimate reality (i.e. psychic satisfaction) than money income, so real income is the preferable concept:

> A definition of income which satisfies both theory and practice, in both economics and accountancy, must reckon as income in the most basic sense all those uses, services, or living for which the cost of living is expended even though such expenditure may exceed the money income.

What this all boils down to is that Fisher's definitions of income *do not involve a concept of capital maintenance*. It is this point that distinguishes Fisher's ideas from the mainstream of both accounting and economic thinking. Fisher's measure of income is really a measure of *consumption*.

Hicks and capital maintenance

We have already seen (Activity 4.2) that in very general terms economic value is based on a current evaluation of future streams of (net) receipts. It is also obvious that in our earlier equation $W_1 + P - D = W_2$ capital maintenance requires that W_2 is at least equal to W_1. Another way of putting this is that D ($=$ drawing or consumption) cannot exceed P ($=$ profit or income). The classic analysis of the implications of this thinking is by Hicks (1946). The opening of the following quote makes it clear just how fundamental he feels capital maintenance to be:

> The purpose of income calculations in practical affairs is to give people an indication of the amount which they can consume without impoverishing themselves. Following out this idea, it would seem that we ought to define a man's income as the maximum value which he can consume during a week, and still expect to be as well off at the end of the week as he was at the beginning. Thus, when a person saves, he plans to be better off in the future; when he lives beyond his income, he plans to be worse off. Remembering that the practical purpose of income is to serve as a guide for prudent conduct, I think it is fairly clear that this is what the central meaning must be.
>
> However, business men and economists alike are usually content to employ one or other of a series of approximations to the central meaning. Let us consider some of these approximations in turn.

Hicks moves on to attempt to operationalize this 'central meaning'. Like Fisher, Hicks is obviously adopting a forward-looking approach to valuation and income measurement. We have seen in Activity 4.2 that we can operationalize such an approach (once we have invented the raw figures!) by calculating net present value figures for expected receipts. Putting these two ideas together, we can regard capital, wealth, 'well-offness' as being the net present value of expected receipts. If we put this notion into the original definition in place of the vague 'as well off', we arrive at a first approximation:

> Income No. 1 is thus the maximum amount which can be spent during a period if there is to be an expectation of maintaining intact the capital value of prospective receipts (in money terms). This is probably the definition which most people do implicitly use in their private affairs; but it is far from being in all circumstances a good approximation to the central concept.

Activity 4.9

Suppose that at the beginning of the week our individual possesses property worth €10 010 and no other source of income. If the rate of interest were one-tenth per cent per week, income would be €10 for the week. For if €10 were spent, €10 000 would be left to be reinvested; and in one week this would have accumulated to €10 010 – the original sum. This is income No. 1. But suppose that the rate of interest per week for a loan of one week is one-tenth per cent, that the corresponding rate expected to rule in the second week from now is one-fifth per cent and that this higher rate is expected to continue indefinitely afterwards. What is the individual's income for: **(a)** week 1, **(b)** week 2?

Activity feedback

At the beginning of week 1 the individual is bound to spend no more than €10 in the current week, if he is to expect to have €10 010 again at his disposal at the end of the week; but if he desires to have the same sum available at the end of the second week, he will be able to spend nearly €120 in the second week, not €10 only. The same sum (€10 010) available at the beginning of the first week makes possible a stream of expenditures:

€10, €20, €20, €20, ...

while if it is available at the beginning of the second week it makes possible a stream:

€20, €20, €20, €20, ...

It is obvious that these two alternative possible expenditure streams do not give equal well-offness. One is worth more than the other. If we put the income as €10 for week 1 and €20 for week 2, then we are not 'maintaining intact the capital value of prospective receipts (in money terms)'. The amount the individual can spend each week while still maintaining well-offness intact *must*, under these conditions, be the same in week 1 and in week 2 (and subsequent weeks):

> This leads us to the definition of Income No. 2. We now define income as the maximum amount the individual can spend this week, and still expect to be able to spend the same amount in each ensuing week. So long as the rate of interest is not expected to change, this definition comes to the same thing as

the first; but when the rate of interest is expected to change, they cease to be identical. Income No. 2 is then a closer approximation to the central concept than Income No. 1 is.

There are several problems with this as an operational concept. First, interest rates may change. The second problem is that prices may be expected to change. In principle we can deal with this easily by a small addition to the wording:

> Income No. 3 must be defined as the maximum amount of money which the individual can spend this week, and still expect to be able to spend the same amount in real terms in each ensuing week. If prices are expected to rise, then an individual who plans to spend €10 in the present and each ensuing week must expect to be less well off at the end of the week than he is at the beginning. At each date he can look forward to the opportunity of spending €10 in each future week; but at the first date one of the €10s will be spent in a week when prices are relatively low. An opportunity of spending on favourable terms is present in the first case, but absent in the second.
>
> Thus, if €10 is to be his income for this week, according to definition No. 3 he will have to expect to be able to spend in each future week not €10, but a sum greater or less than €10 by the extent to which prices have risen or fallen in that week above or below their level in the first week.

In practice, of course, the apparent simplicity of this change is false. We need expectations of price changes for every individual for every commodity of projected purchase for every need of each anticipated expenditure!

In addition to this practical difficulty Income No. 3 also has the problem of how to deal with long-term assets, i.e. fixed assets or 'durable consumption goods':

> Strictly speaking, saving is not the difference between income and expenditure, it is the difference between income and consumption. Income is not the maximum amount the individual can spend while expecting to be as well off as before at the end of the week; it is the maximum amount he can consume. If some part of his expenditure goes on durable consumption goods, that will tend to make his expenditure exceed his consumption; if some part of his consumption is consumption of durable consumption goods, already bought in the past, that tends to make consumption exceed expenditure.

It should be noted that we have now come full circle back to an emphasis on consumption. But Hicks is concerned with consumption and capital maintenance, whereas Fisher is only concerned with consumption. We can summarize the basic difference between Fisher and Hicks by realizing that while Fisher is concerned with consumption, Hicks is concerned with the capacity to consume. This is clearly a long-run concept. To take an obvious example, consider the farmer's seed corn. This is the basis of next year's crops. It is available now and it could be eaten (consumed). But if it *is* eaten now there will be no crop next year and therefore no possibility of consumption next year. Therefore, if we wish to maintain the capacity to consume next year, the seed corn must not be consumed now. In other words it must be saved. This is, to put it mildly, useful information.

Calculation of economic income

One way of summarizing what we have just looked at is to say that for Fisher:

$$Income = Consumption$$

But for Hicks:

$$Income = Consumption \ and \ Saving$$

which can be expressed as:

$$Y = C + S$$

Savings can be expressed as $(K_e - K_s)$ where:

$$K_e = \text{value of capital at the end of a period}$$
$$K_s = \text{value of capital at the start of the period}$$

Thus:

$$Y = C + (K_e - K_s)$$

For example, if income = €100, capital at the end of the period = €280 and capital at the beginning of the period was €300, then: €100 = 120 + (280 − 300).

This tells us that consumption has exceeded income by €20, because of dis-saving of €20. 'Well-offness' has not been maintained.

In the business world rather than the personal consumption world, C is redefined as the realized cash flows of the period. We will illustrate this as simply as possible.

Activity 4.10

An investment on 1 January year 1 has expected receipts on 31 December each year of £1000 for three years. The discount rate to reflect the time value of money is 10%. Calculate the capital as at 1 January for each of the years 1, 2 and 3.

Activity feedback

On 1 January year 1 the expected receipt on 31 December year 1 needs to be discounted back by one year, the expected receipt on 31 December year 2 needs to be discounted back by two years and the expected receipt on 31 December year 3 needs to be discounted back by three years.

Thus capital at 1 January year 1 is:

$$\frac{1000}{1.1} + \frac{1000}{(1.1)^2} + \frac{1000}{(1.1)^3}$$

$$= 909 + 826 + 751 = €2486$$

On 1 January year 2 the receipt on 31 December year 1 is now irrelevant. The expected receipt on 31 December year 2 now needs to be discounted back to 1 January year 2, i.e. by *one* year and the expected receipt on 31 December 03 also needs to be discounted back to 1 January 02, i.e. by *two* years. Similarly, on 1 January 03 only the expected receipt on 31 December year 3 is of any relevance and this needs to be discounted back to 1 January year 3, i.e. by *one* year. Thus capital at 1 January year 2 is:

$$\frac{1000}{1.1} + \frac{1000}{(1.1)^2}$$

$$= 909 + 826 = €1735$$

and capital at 1 January 03 is:

$$\frac{1000}{1.1} = €909$$

Activity 4.11

Considering the investment in the previous activity, now suppose that the actual cost of the investment, on 1 January year 1, is €2486. According to the Hicksian way of thinking, what is the income for each year?

Activity feedback

Our formula was:

$$Y = C + (K_e - K_s)$$

So in year 1:

$$Y = 1000 + (1735 - 2486)$$
$$= 1000 - 751$$
$$= €249$$

In year 2:

$$Y = 1000 + (909 - 1735)$$
$$= 1000 - 826$$
$$= €174$$

In year 3:

$$Y = 1000 + (0 - 909)$$
$$= 1000 - 909$$
$$= €91$$

In year 1, the cash receipts are €1000, but the income is stated as €249. The difference (€751) needs to be reinvested (saved), in order to facilitate *future* spending. This reinvestment of €751 on 1 January year 2 will by itself earn 10% in the year 2, i.e. €75. So total income in year 2 is €174, from the original investment, plus €75 from the reinvestment, i.e. again €249.

In year 2, the cash receipts from the original investment are €1000, but the income is stated as €174. The difference (€826) again needs to be reinvested. This investment of

€826 will itself earn €83 in year 3, giving total cash receipts in that year of €91 from the original investment, €75 from the first reinvestment and €83 from the second reinvestment, i.e. €249 once again. Similarly in year 3, cash receipts will be €1000, but the income is stated as €91. The difference (€909) will be reinvested at 10%, earning itself €91 in each year. Total cash receipts in year 4, all from reinvestments, will therefore be $75 + 83 + 91 = €249$ and similarly in year 5 onwards. This of course satisfies our original conditions. The income of year 1 is the amount 'that can be spent while still enabling the income of all future periods to be the same amount'. This has been shown to be €249 under the given assumptions. These results are summarized in Table 4.3.

The present value of an annual income stream of €249, to infinity, at a 10% discount rate is €2490. This, allowing for rounding errors, gives us our original 'capital' figure of €2486, which of course is what it should do. So the answer may possibly have come as no surprise. But you should still make sure you understand all the logic involved.

Table 4.3 Hick's economic income model

	1	2	3	4	5	6	7	8	9
Year	C	K_e	K_s	Y	Reinvestment	Cumulative reinvestment	Total reinvestment	Income from reinvestments	Total economic income
0	0	2486	0	0	0	0	2486	0	0
1	1000	1735	2486	249	751	751	2486	0	249
2	1000	909	1735	174	826	1577	2486	75	249
3	1000	0	909	91	909	2486	2486	158	249
4	0	0	0	0	0	2486	2486	249	249

Notes: $4 = 1 + 2 - 3$
$5 = 1 - 4$
$7 = 2 + 6$
$9 = 4 + 8$

Income *ex ante* and income *ex post*

We have assumed that we are in a world of perfect knowledge and perfect foresight – an ideal world in fact. The economic income devised under these assumptions is known as ideal income. It is obviously an unreal oversimplification. We can, however, extend our analysis to allow for estimates of future events and this leads to two further models, income *ex ante* and income *ex post*. Income *ex ante* means income measured before the event; income *ex post* means income measured after the event.

Two possibilities for changes exist: in the timing and/or amount of forecast cash flow and in the appropriate discount rate.

Formally, income *ex ante* can be expressed as:

$$Y = C_1 + (K_e^1 - K_s)$$

where C_1 is the expected realized cash flow for the period anticipated at the beginning of the period, K_e^1 is the closing capital as measured (estimated) at the beginning of the period, and K_s is the capital at the beginning of the period as measured (estimated) at the beginning of the period.

Activity 4.12

Assume the same original information as in the previous two activities. Now suppose that at the end of year 2, the expected return from the investment in the year 3 increases to €1100. Using an *ex ante* approach consider the effects on the calculations for each of the years.

Activity feedback

Using an *ex ante* approach the effects will be:

Year 1 – No change

Year 2 – Still no change. The calculations for the year 2 are based on expectations as at the beginning of the year 2 and they had not altered at that time

Year 3 – The opening capital K_s will no longer be the same as the closing capital K_e at the end of year 2. It will now be:

$$K_s = \frac{1100}{1.1} = €1000$$

This compares with the corresponding figure of €909 for K_s in year 3 under the ideal income calculations. There is therefore a windfall gain of €91 appearing under the *ex ante* way of thinking in year 3.

Income *ex post* can be expressed correspondingly, as:

$$Y = C + (K_e - K_s^1)$$

where C is the actual realized cash flow of the period, K_e is the closing capital measured (estimated) at the end of the period and K_s^1 is the opening capital measured (estimated) at the end of the period.

Activity 4.13

Given all the information of the previous activity, reconsider the effects of the change in expectations which occurs at the end of year 2.

Activity feedback

Again there will be no change in year 1 but, using an *ex post* approach, there will be a change in the calculations for year 2, because at the end of year 2 our expectations had already altered. Capital at 1 January year 2, based on expectations as at the end of year 2, is:

$$\frac{1000}{1.1} + \frac{1100}{(1.1)^2}$$

$$K_s = 909 + 909 = €1818$$

This compares with the corresponding figure of €1735 for K_s in year 2 under the ideal income calculations, giving rise to a windfall gain of €83 appearing in year 2.

For present purposes, it is not considered necessary to pursue the calculations any further as regards recalculation of reinvestment amounts and so on. However, several points should be noted:

1 Income *ex post* is measured after the event, but it is still based on expectations of the future, income *ex post* for year 2 is derived from the expectations held as at the end of year 2, but these expectations relate to years 3, 4 and so on to infinity. Economic income *ex post* is therefore just as subjective as economic income *ex ante*.

2 Is the windfall gain realized? This is relatively straightforward. The gain becomes realized as the cash flow whose estimation gave rise to it is actually received.

3 Is the windfall gain income or capital, i.e. should it be saved (reinvested) or can it be spent? This is not so clear cut, as it depends on where we consider our starting point to be. Taking our original example, if our original, and permanent, intention is to maintain the capacity to consume €249 each year to infinity, then it is clear that we have already achieved that requirement without taking account of the windfall gain. The gain is, therefore, 'spare', it need not be reinvested and so it is available for immediate consumption. Notice carefully that the windfall gain is available for consumption as soon as it is recognized, *whether or not it has been realized*, i.e. in year 2 under the *ex post* method and in year 3 under the *ex ante* method. Thus the windfall gain could be regarded as a simple one-off increase in possible consumption (do not forget it could be a windfall loss, leading to a one-off decrease in possible consumption).

   However, the change in expectations might cause us to amend the permanent annual consumption requirement in some way. We might, for example, wish to redo the complete calculations taking year 2 as a new starting point, giving 2 years of cash flow only. Here the windfall gain would not, or not necessarily, be spendable at all (even if it is already realized!).

It is, of course, possible, taking the original ideal income scenario as our starting point, to consider an almost infinite number of changes in expectations, variable as to timing of the change in expectations, changes in the expected timing of receipts, changes in the expected amounts of receipts and changes in discount rates. In every case, under both *ex ante* and *ex post* thinking, we need to establish whether the effect of the change is on income or on capital before we can attempt to rework all the calculations and this depends entirely on the intentions of the decision maker concerned. If these intentions remain unaltered despite the change in expectations then the windfall will be income.

Refer back to the Hicks' Income No. 3 definition: the maximum amount of money the individual can spend this week and still expect to be able to spend the same amount in real terms in each ensuing week. If 'this week' is and remains week 1, then the windfall is income. But if 'this week' means 'the current week', e.g. the week when expectations change, then the windfall affects capital and requires that a new permanently spendable weekly consumption be calculated.

Summary

Income, capital and value are interrelated concepts. Value can be defined and enumerated in a variety of ways and detailed description, analysis and appraisal of the alternatives is required.

It is suggested that the economic ideas outlined in this chapter are:

1 theoretically sound and logically sensible
2 highly subjective in application as regards
  (a) size of future cash flows
  (b) timing of future cash flows
  (c) discount rate to apply to future cash flows
3 problematic as regards windfall gains and losses
4 and therefore, as far as accounting is concerned, they probably represent an unattainable ideal.

EXERCISES
(✔ indicates answers are available on page 718)

1 Obtain three sets of published accounts of quoted companies. Look carefully at the consolidated balance sheets and notes thereto and read the 'accounting policies'. Taking each item in the balance sheet separately describe how the item is evaluated. Are these evaluations consistent?, i.e. in mathematical terms, do we have genuine additivity?

✔ 2 Two retail businesses, A and B, run a similar trade from similar shops in similar areas. A bought its shop in 1950 for €5000 and B bought its shop in 1990 for €105 000. Both businesses consistently prepare their accounts on historic cost principles and they have identical operating profits. To what extent do the resulting accounts give a true (and fair) representation of the relative performance of the two businesses?

✔ 3 It is never possible to define capital or income, only to define capital *and* income. Do you agree?

4 (a) Outline Fisher's thinking on the concept of income.
  (b) Outline Hick's thinking on this topic.
  (c) Relate and compare the two.

5 Explain the principles of economic income, carefully distinguishing income *ex ante* and income *ex post*.

6 'Economic income is an unattainable ideal.' Consider and discuss.

7 Spock purchased a space invader entertainment machine at the beginning of year 1 for €1000. He expects to receive at annual intervals the following receipts; at the end of year 1 €400; end of year 2 €500; end of year 3 €600. At the end of year 3 he expects to sell the machine for €400.

Spock could receive a return of 10% on the next best investment. The present value of €1 receivable at the end of a period discounted at 10% is as follows:

End of year 1	0.909
End of year 2	0.826
End of year 3	0.751

Required:
Calculate the ideal economic income, ignoring taxation, and working to the nearest whole euro.

Your answer should show that Spock's capital is maintained throughout the period and that his income is constant.

(ACCA – adapted)

5

Current entry value

After studying this chapter you should be able to:
- ☐ explain the effects and implications of using current entry values to record the possession and usage of economic resources
- ☐ carry out the necessary technical manipulation
- ☐ explain the strengths, usefulness and weaknesses of the resulting information.

Introduction

The ideas of the previous chapter are of fundamental importance. But they are inherently highly subjective to apply. Of crucial importance from the point of view of accounting thinking, they are far removed from the marketplace. All 18 of the value concepts considered by Edwards and Bell (1961) (see Chapter 4) relate directly to actual or expected market values. One of these, past entry values, i.e. the historical cost (HC) of the initial inputs, is the traditional process which we summarized in Chapter 3.

Four of the remaining five are current values, two being current entry values and two current exit values. We look first at current entry values. Remember that entry values represent a market buying price, i.e. current entry values represent a *cost-based* process (but not a *historical* cost-based process).

Back to basics

Activity 5.1

On 1 January, Mr Jones starts off in business with 100 cents. His transactions are as follows:

2 January   Buys one bag of sugar for   40c
4 January   Sells one bag of sugar for   50c
5 January   Buys one bag of sugar for   44c

Prepare balance sheets on 2 January and on 6 January and a P&L account for the intervening period.

Activity feedback

This should not present major problems.

Balance sheet 2 January

Inventory	40	Capital	100
Cash	60		
	100c		100c

Balance sheet 6 January

Inventory	44	Capital	110
Cash	66		
	110c		110c

Profit and loss

Sales	50
Cost of sales	40
	10c

In terms of our very general equation, $W_1 + P - D = W_2$:

$$100 + 10 - 0 = 110$$

So Jones has made a profit of 10c. This, of course, is the usual accounting approach. But it is important to notice that there are really two stages in the progress from 2 January to 6 January. Between 2 January and the evening of 4 January, after the sale was made, Jones has turned 100c into 110c. On 4 January he actually has physically 110c and nothing else. Then between the evening of 4 January and 6 January he has changed 110c plus nothing into 66c plus a bag of sugar. Since the second bag of sugar cost 44c and we are recording all our resources at original, or historical, cost it necessarily follows that we show total resources of 110c on both 4 January and 6 January. The 4 January balance sheet was as follows:

Balance sheet 4 January

Cash	110	Capital	110
	110c		110c

Comparing this 4 January position with the 2 January and 6 January balance sheets confirms that:

1 A profit of 10c was made between 2 January and 4 January.
2 No profit or loss at all was made between 4 January and 6 January.

Jones, of course, is running a business. He also has to live. So he decides to withdraw the business profit for his own spending purposes.

If he takes 10c out then, by the accountant's definition, he has still left in all the money originally put in. This 10c must therefore be genuine gain, so it can obviously be withdrawn from the business without in any way reducing the resources of the business. So we can rewrite our 6 January sheet, after the withdrawal, as follows:

Balance sheet 6 January

Inventory	44	Capital	100
Cash	56		
	100c		100c

Our equation now becomes:

$$100 + 10 - 10 = 100$$

Activity 5.2

Compare the *physical* possessions of Jones' business on 2 January with those on 5 January, assuming still that Jones withdraws his 10c profit.

Activity feedback

In physical terms the business possesses:

On 2 January:

1 one bag of sugar
2 a pile of 60 shiny bright 1c pieces.

On 6 January:

1 one bag of sugar
2 a pile of 56 shiny bright 1c pieces.

Now, by simple subtraction, we can compare the physical position between 2 January and 6 January in terms both of sugar and of shiny bright 1c pieces. In terms of sugar, we are comparing one bag with one bag. There is no difference. In terms of bags of sugar, the business is exactly the same size as it was before. In terms of shiny bright 1c pieces, the business had 60 on 2 January and 56 on 6 January. There is therefore a reduction of four shiny bright 1c pieces. In terms of shiny bright 1c pieces the business has got smaller by four pieces.

Something must be wrong somewhere. The accountant has shown us that there is a 'genuine gain' of 10c over and above the original 100c capital put in. Jones has therefore withdrawn the 10c, and yet the result is *not* that the business is 'back where it started'. The result is that the business has *got smaller* to the tune of 4c.

Surely, either the physical comparison is wrong or the profit and loss statement prepared in Activity 5.1 is wrong. If the physical comparison is correct (try it yourself) then the 'genuine gain' of 10% mentioned is quite simply not genuine! Further thinking is needed. On 4 January we had, in physical terms, as we have already seen, a pile of 110 shiny bright 1c pieces. We have also already seen that the profit of 10c was made by 4 January. It therefore follows that the accountant's statement at 4 January is identical with the actual physical position at that date. The accountant says cash is 110c and profit is 10c. The physical position shows a pile of 110 shiny bright 1c pieces. It is obvious that since the physical position and the accounting position were identical as at 4 January the divergence, the difference between the two, must have occurred after 4 January. But only one event has happened *after* 4 January. This was the purchase of the second bag of sugar on 5 January. So the problem *must* be something to do with the accounting treatment of the second bag.

Question: Why did Jones have to buy a second bag of sugar for 44c? The answer is because he has sold the first bag of sugar (for 50c). He would not have bought the second bag of sugar had he not sold the first one. It seems, therefore, that the selling of the first bag of sugar and the buying of the second bag of sugar are really two parts of one complete action. If he does not sell the first bag of sugar and does not buy the second bag of sugar, he obviously ends up with the same amount of cash on 6 January as he had on 2 January, i.e. 60c. If he does sell the first bag of sugar for 50c and *does* buy the second bag of sugar for 44c, he will end up with 6c more cash on 6 January than he had on 2 January. So the result of selling bag 1 and buying bag 2, *as compared with doing neither*, is a gain of 6c.

We can show this as follows:

Sales	50c
Costs incurred as a direct result of making sale	44c
Profit	6c

We are now suggesting a profit of 6c, as compared with the earlier suggestion of 10c. This will presumably reduce the maximum drawing payable by 10c − 6c = 4c. And remember, we argued earlier that the error, the difference between the original accountant's calculations and physical reality, the amount by which Jones' business had unintentionally 'got smaller' was 4c. We seem to have corrected the error exactly. We have produced an accounting calculation that agrees with actual physical events:

$$W_1 + P - D = W_2$$
$$100 + 6 - 6 = 100$$

The business itself

It is essential to remember the purpose and nature of Jones' business. It is a sugar-selling business. The essence of our conclusion is a very simple one. It is that the cost of sales figure that we should relate to any particular sale should be calculated as equal to the *cost of the resulting replacement*, assuming that the replacement occurs immediately. The cost of sales figure should not be related to the cost of the item actually sold. This raises a difficulty. In order to be able to transfer this higher replacement figure out of the balance sheet and into the profit and loss calculation, the higher replacement figure must obviously first be recorded in the balance sheet. The complete picture is most easily seen by a series of balance sheets:

1 January

Cash	100	Capital	100
	100c		100c

2 January

Sugar	40	Capital	100
Cash	60		
	100c		100c

3 January

Sugar (1st bag)	44	Capital	100
Cash	60	Gain	4
	104c		104c

4 January

Cash	110	Capital	100
		Gain	4
		Profit	6
	110c		110c

5 January

Sugar (2nd bag)	44	Capital	100
		Gain	4
Cash	66	Profit	6
	110c		110c

Now, we must choose our words carefully. It is perfectly correct to say that Jones began his business on 1 January with 100c. But that is not the point. The point is that Jones began the business on 1 January with *60c plus the capacity to buy a bag of sugar*. Jones is setting up in business for the purpose of acquiring and selling bags of sugar. Therefore, we need to evaluate his position at any time in terms of his capacity, his ability, to carry out his purpose. In other words, his capacity to acquire and sell sugar.

So on 1 January Jones had the capacity to buy one bag of sugar (for 40c) plus also 60c. On 4 January Jones had 110c. More usefully, we can say that on 4 January Jones had the capacity to buy one bag of sugar (for 44c), plus also 66c. Comparing the 4 January position with the 1 January position clearly shows that Jones has:

1 maintained his capacity to buy one bag of sugar
2 and gained 6 shiny bright 1c pieces.

This calculation agrees with the real physical events. Jones has:

1 6 more shiny bright 1c pieces
2 and a statement from his accountant giving a figure for profit of 6c.

On the assumptions that Jones wishes to carry on selling and buying bags of sugar this is obviously the correct answer.

We have solved a major problem. We have shown the accountant how to produce a profit figure that actually makes physical sense and that Jones can actually believe. But we have created another difficulty. The statement from the accountant showed not only a *profit* of 6c, but also a separate, different *gain* of 4c. This gain of 4c occurred earlier than the profit. The gain was included in the balance sheet of 3 January and the profit did not appear until 4 January. We know that this 'gain' is not the same as profit – the whole point of all this is that the 'total' profit, i.e. the total increase in the capacity of the business to do things, is only 6c. So if the 'gain' is not profit, what on earth is it?

In the most simple of terms it is the double-entry for an increase in the recorded figure for an item of inventory.

Activity 5.3

Open individual accounts to reflect Jones' balance sheet on 2 January (as before). Record in these and any other necessary accounts the increase in inventory figure leading to the 3 January balance sheet, then the full effect of the sales transaction on 4 January.

Activity feedback

We have on 2 January, the inventory T account shows a debit of 40c and on 3 January, a total debit of 44c. In full we have on 2 January:

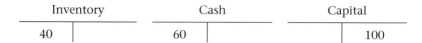

Inventory		Cash		Capital	
40		60			100

On 3 January we increase the inventory so as to bring the recorded figure up to the current level of replacement cost (RC). Thus there is a debit of 4c to inventory and a credit of 4c somewhere else. This credit cannot be to cash, neither can it be to capital, so it must be to a new T account. Now this 4c represents a gain that has arisen as a result of *holding* our inventory over a period of time. We did not sell it, but we *held* it over a period during which the replacement cost rose. We shall more formally refer to this gain as a holding gain. So on 3 January:

	Inventory				Cash	
Bal b/f	40			Bal b/f 60		
Holding gain	4	44 Bal c/d				
	44	44				
Bal b/f	44					

	Capital			Holding gain	
	100 Bal b/f				4 Inventory

This enables us to show on 4 January:

Inventory			Cash		
Bal b/f 44	44 to P&L		Bal b/f	60	
			To P&L	50	

Capital			Holding gain	
	100 Bal b/f			4 Bal b/f

P&L account			
Inventory sold	44	50 Cash sales	
Bal c/d	6		
	50	50	
		6 Bal b/f	

Capital maintenance

Given that we are considering a different profit concept from the traditional historic profit, we are necessarily implying also a different capital maintenance concept from that discussed in Activity 4.7.

Activity 5.4

Define clearly the capital maintenance concept implied by the T account calculations just examined.

Activity feedback

Profit could here be defined as the amount generated by the business over and above that necessary to replace the assets. The capital maintenance concept could therefore be said to be the maintenance of the capacity to replace the resources of the business.

A more rigorous analysis

If an item of inventory is bought for €10, held until its buying price increases to €12, and then sold for €15 then the HC profit is €15 − €10 = €5. But we know from the previous discussion that this can be split into two parts as follows.

During the time the inventory is held, the cost price rises from €10 to €12. There is therefore a holding gain of €2, giving a recorded inventory figure immediately before the sale of €12. When the inventory is sold, an asset of €12 (inventory) is transformed into an asset of (cash) giving rise to a profit from operating of €3. Clearly we have split the HC profit into two elements, namely the operating profit (revenue minus current replacement cost) and the holding gain (current replacement cost minus original purchase cost). In these circumstances both elements would be regarded as 'realized' (see Chapter 1).

More normally, both realized and unrealized gains will be involved, as in the following example:

1 October 20X1	Buy 2 at €30
1 November 20X1	Sell 1 at €50, when RC is €35
31 December 20X1	RC is €38
31 January 20X2	Sell 1 at €60, when RC is €40

The HC profits are:

Year 1   50 − 30 = €20
Year 2   60 − 30 = €30

A fuller analysis gives the following:

1 Between 1 October and 1 November, there has been a holding gain of $2 \times (35 - 30) = €10$.
2 On 1 November one of the items is sold; therefore on 1 November:
   (a) half of the holding gain becomes realized (i.e. $1 \times [35 - 30]$), as the item to which it relates has been sold.
   (b) there is a (realized) operating profit of 50 − 35 = €15.

3 On 31 December there is an additional holding gain of $38 - 35 = €3$. This will be unrealized as the item is still unsold. Between 31 December 20X1 and 31 January 20X2 there has been a holding gain of $40 - 38 = €2$.

4 On 31 January the second item is sold and therefore:

   (a) there is a (realized) operating gain of $60 - 40 = €20$

   (b) all the unrealized holding gain related to the second item becomes realized.

To summarize, for year 1 we have:

Operating profit	€15
Realized holding gain	€5
Unrealized holding gain	€8 ($5 + 3$ or $38 - 30$)

For year 2 we have:

Operating profit	€20
Realized holding gain	€10
Unrealized holding gain	€0

Note carefully that the €10 holding gain realized in the year 2 includes the €8 holding gain that was *recognized* and *recorded* in year 1, but which had not become realized in year 1, as well as the €2 of holding gain recognized in year 2.

These figures demonstrate that the HC profit consists of two of the three elements involved:

$$\text{HC profit} = \text{Operating profit} + \text{Realized holding gains}$$

In year 1 $€20 = 15 + 5$

In year 2 $€30 = 20 + 10$

Notice that we include all the holding gains realized in the year, whether or not they have been recognized and recorded (as unrealized) in earlier years.

Edwards and Bell (1961) referred to the reported results under a RC system as business income, which they defined as follows:

$$\text{Business income} = \begin{cases} \text{Operating profit} + \text{Realized holding gain recognized in the} \\ \text{period} + \text{Unrealized holding gains recognized in the period} \end{cases}$$

Thus business income in year 1 is:

$$15 + 5 + 8 = €28$$

And in year 2 is:

$$20 + 2 + 0 = €22$$

Observe that the proportion of the realized holding gain in year 2 which had already been included in business income of year 1 (as an unrealized holding gain) is not included in year 2. To do so would, of course, involve double counting.

Examination will show that the differences between accounting (HC) income and business income are caused by different elements of the holding gains being included.

Activity 5.5

Derive the formal relationship between accounting income and business income and apply it to the preceding situation.

Activity feedback

Accounting income includes:

1 realized holding gains of the period recognized in the period
2 plus realized holding gains of the period recognized in previous periods.

Business income includes:

3 realized holding gains of the period recognized in the period
4 plus unrealized holding gains recognized in the period.
   Since **1** and **3** are the same, it follows that:

$$\text{Accounting income} - 2 = \text{Business income} - 4$$

Or:

$$\text{Accounting income} = \text{Business income} - 4 + 2$$

(as defined earlier).

For the year 1   €20 = 28 − 8 + 0
For the year 2   €30 = 22 − 0 + 8

The important thing about all this analysis is that it enables us to discuss and decide which elements we wish to include in our own preferred definition of income. Edwards and Bell, arguing in favour of a current entry (RC) approach, include all the holding gains *recognized* in the period as being included in income. This has been criticized on two grounds. First, it is suggested that no unrealized gains should be included, as this would lack prudence. Second, and more importantly, it is suggested that all the holding gains, whether realized or unrealized, need to be retained in the business in order to enable it to replace resources as they are used. Using the terminology we developed earlier the operating profit is the gain after having retained sufficient resources to enable us to do those things that we originally had the capacity to do. If we ask the question: 'How much profit can I remove without impairing the substance, the operating capability of the business?' then the answer is the operating profit. Only the operating profit should be regarded and reported as income. Holding gains, whether realized or not, should be excluded. This objection to the Edwards and Bell conclusion is generally regarded as a valid one and most authors argue that the central profit figure under a current entry value system should consist of the operating profit alone.

Remember the capital maintenance concept as we defined it in Activity 5.4, i.e. the maintenance of the capacity to replace the resources of the business. The holding gains represent reserves – i.e. ownership claims on resources – corresponding to the resources which will have to be used in addition to replace existing assets if they are replaced at current prices. Income, within this capital maintenance requirement, therefore excludes all such holding gains.

In practice, the changes in cost levels are likely to be approximated to by the use of appropriate price indices. Activity 5.6 provides an example of the application of this mechanism to the principles already discussed. Study the activity carefully and try to at least rough out a solution before you work through the feedback which follows.

Activity 5.6

Chaplin Ltd's balance sheet on 31 December, year 1, after one year's trading was as follows:

	€		€	€
Capital – €1		Land and buildings at cost		110 000
ordinary shares	200 000	Plant and equipment at cost	40 000	
Profit	26 000	*less* Depreciation	4 000	36 000
	226 000			146 000
Creditors	50 000	Inventory	90 000	
Loan	50 000	Debtors	90 000	
				180 000
	326 000			326 000

1 The capital and loan had been contributed in cash and the land and buildings, plant and equipment and opening inventory of €60 000 had been purchased on 1 January.
2 Transactions took place evenly during the year. The situation may therefore be treated as if all opening balances were held from 1 January until 30 June, as if all transactions took place on 30 June and as if all closing balances were held from 30 June until 31 December.
3 Price indices were as follows:

	General inflation	Plant	Inventory
1 January	100	100	100
30 June	110	105	115
31 December	120	110	130

4 The land and buildings were professionally valued at 31 December at €135 000.

Prepare a closing balance sheet on RC lines.

Activity feedback

Chaplin Ltd – RC solution
HC profit   26 000
less Adjustments:

Depreciation	$4\,000 \times \dfrac{(110 - 100)}{100}$	400	
Inventory	$60\,000 \times \dfrac{(115 - 100)}{100}$	9 000	9 400

Current operating profit			16 600
add Holding gains:			
Inventory: realized as previously			9 000
unrealized	$90\,000 \times \dfrac{(130 - 115)}{115}$	11 740	
Plant and equipment: realized as previously		400	
unrealized	$40\,000 \times \dfrac{(110 - 100)}{100} - 400$	3 600	
Land and buildings:			
unrealized	$135\,000 - 110\,000$	25 000	49 740
Business income			€66 300

The general view today is that the holding gains should be shown separately as holding gains, rather than combining all gains of every sort as 'business income'. This leads to the following balance sheet:

		€	€
Fixed assets			
Land and building			135 000
Plant and equipment	$40\,000 \times \dfrac{110}{100}$	44 000	
less Depreciation	$4\,000 \times \dfrac{110}{100}$	4 400	39 600
			174 600

		€	€
Current assets			
Inventory	$90\,000 \times \dfrac{130}{115}$	101 740	
Debtors		90 000	191 740
			€366 340

	€
Share capital	200 000
Holding gain reserve	49 740
P&L account	16 600
	266 340
Loan	50 000
Creditors	50 000
	€366 340

In checking through Activity 5.6 note the treatment of the inventory gains; it is assumed that the opening inventory was all sold on 30 June, so the relevant holding gain is realized, the €90 000 closing inventory is treated as being purchased on 30 June and held ever since. Check that you understand the usage of all the index adjustments (and note the irrelevance of the general inflation index here). As regards the distinction between realized and unrealized holding gains, note that *only the current operating profit* can be distributed without impairing the ability to replace physical assets.

Replacement cost accounting and depreciation

Activity 5.7

There is one particular problem with replacement cost (RC) accounting and depreciation that is not revealed by the Chaplin illustration. Consider the following:

> A fixed asset costs €100, has an expected useful life of four years, with zero scrap value and the RC of a new asset rises by €20 each year. Calculate the profit and loss (P&L) account charge and show the balance sheet position, for each of the first two years, under RC.

Activity feedback

The year 1 position is simple enough. We have:

Cost (RC)	€120
Depreciation (25%) (in P&L a/c)	30
Balance sheet	€90

But year 2 is problematic. From a P&L account viewpoint we have an RC figure of €140 and we have had 25% of the benefit, therefore we should have an expense to match of 25% of 140 = €35. This leaves total accumulated depreciation of €65 and a balance sheet figure of €75 (140 − 65). But taking a balance sheet view we have an asset with an RC of €140 that is exactly half used up. Therefore, again following the matching convention, we should have accumulated depreciation of exactly half of €140, leaving a balance sheet figure also of exactly half of €140 to carry forward for future matching. This implies an expense figure in year 2 of €40 (closing depreciation balance 70, opening balance 30, therefore necessary charge for this year €40).

We are obviously in trouble. In year 2 we need a €35 charge in the P&L account (25% × 140) and at the same time a deduction of €40 (70 − 30) in the balance sheet. From a double-entry viewpoint this is somewhat disturbing. This problem is usually solved by the idea of backlog depreciation. The year 2 balance sheet deduction is regarded as consisting of two elements:

1 the proper annual charge (€35)
2 the extra figure necessary to bring the accumulated depreciation at the beginning of year 2 up to what it would have been if the current (end of year 2) RC had been prevailing earlier (€5).

Thus we have a credit of €40 to depreciation provision, a debit of €35 to P&L account and a debit of €5 to – well, where?

Since the €5 relates in effect to the correction of what we now know with hindsight to have been under-depreciation in earlier years, one possibility would seem to be to reduce the accumulated revenue reserves figure brought forward – like a prior year adjustment. By the same token, the earlier years' accounts were certainly correct at that time with the matching convention properly applied in the then current circumstances. It could be argued that the problem of this backlog adjustment is covered by the existence and recording of holdings gains. Therefore the €5 could be 'charged to' holding gain account. This last argument is usually followed. This would give year 2 balance sheet entries as follows in our example:

Fixed asset	RC		140
	Depreciation		70
	(Net book value) NBV		70
Holding gain reserve	b/f	20	
	add	20	
	less	5	35

Current entry values: preliminary appraisal

Activity 5.8

Prepare a list, in point form, of advantages and disadvantages which you think could reasonably be said to apply to current entry value accounting.

Activity feedback

Possible, but not necessarily exhaustive, suggestions are as follows:

Advantages
1 It provides more information in that it splits the total profit into holding gains and operating profit. This permits better appraisal of earlier actions and provides more useful data for decision-making purposes.
2 By permitting holding gains to be excluded from reported profit, it allows for a proper maintenance of operating capacity – the 'business substance'.
3 It provides a balance sheet based on current value, on figures relevant to the date of the balance sheet.
4 It is consistent with accounting concepts – if holding gains are excluded from reported profit it is more prudent than HC.
5 Holding gains are recognized and reported when they occur.
6 Comparisons over time, and performance analysis, are more valid and meaningful.
7 It is practicable, it has been shown to be feasible in practical application.

Disadvantages
1 It requires more subjectivity (or arbitrary choice between different available indices). It is therefore less 'auditable'.
2 It requires the use of replacement cost figures for assets that the firm does not intend, or perhaps could not possibly, replace.

3 It still fails to give an indication either of the current market value of most assets in their present state or of the business as a whole.

4 It fails to take account of general inflation, of changes in the purchasing power of money.

You may recall from the array of value concepts analysed by Edwards and Bell that they suggested that two different concepts of current entry value were worthy of more detailed consideration. They named and defined these as:

1 *Present cost* – the cost currently of acquiring the asset being valued.
2 *Current cost* – the cost currently of acquiring the inputs which the firm used to produce the asset being valued.

So far in this chapter we have ignored this distinction. We would suggest, broadly following the thinking of Edwards and Bell themselves, that the route to making a rational choice between them lies in remembering the underlying arguments for using current entry values in the first place. As we saw in Activity 5.4 we are seeking the maintenance of the capacity to replace the resources of the business. We are therefore seeking to ensure the continued long-run operation of the business. The approach we need to adopt, therefore, is that which accords with the expected operations of the firm in the ordinary course of its business. Given that the going concern convention applies and given that the firm is going to continue operations in the long run, it is clear that current cost rather than present cost (both as defined earlier) will better reflect the reality of transactions and economic events in most cases. To a firm in business to manufacture motorcars and aiming for long-run operations as a manufacturer of motorcars, it is the cost of the replacement inputs which it needs to manufacture motorcars which is the relevant datum to ensure the maintenance of operating capacity. The cost to a manufacturer of motorcars of buying in complete motorcars (at present cost) is not normally an operationally relevant figure.

So it is argued that current cost is normally the appropriate current entry value to use, on the grounds of its relevance to normal ongoing business operations. It follows, however, that where this justification ceases to be true, because, for example, the inputs are no longer available, then the conclusion may well no longer be correct. If the firm would as a matter of expected action (not merely should as a matter of efficient management) replace an asset in a more complete state than with the previous raw components, then the appropriate present cost should be used instead.

It could be suggested that in arguing for the relevance of current cost as a useful entry value measure leading to the practical maintenance of operational capability, we are failing to follow properly the logic of the arguments put forward. The essence of the whole thinking is that a firm should charge as an expense the costs of replacing the resources used or consumed. Past (historical) costs are useless for this purpose. But what is theoretically needed is obviously the amount that *will* have to be paid for the replacement items at the time when they are replaced. The *current* cost may or may not be identical to the actual cost when replacement eventually occurs. In many cases current cost will be the same as expected actual cost. But if it is not, should we make some adjustment?

Theoretically, at least from the viewpoint of the income statement and capital maintenance in the operating sense, the answer seems to be yes. But there are at least two arguments against this. The first is the essentially practical one that a considerably greater degree of subjectivity is introduced which may more than outweigh the theoretical advantages. The second argument is that there are perhaps implications for the matching principle and the balance sheet. A current entry value balance sheet can be argued as being consistent within itself, giving proper additivity in the mathematical sense. But a future entry value balance sheet, with the timing implications of the word future being different for different items, is of more suspect validity. And since today's asset figure affects next period's results there are possible implications for future periods too.

Summary

In this chapter we have explored the logic of using current entry values for the preparation of accounting results, analyzed the effects and usefulness of the additional information derived, related the approach to capital maintenance and prepared and interpreted current entry value information.

The main advantages of current entry value accounting lie in its effects on the profit and loss account information given. It can be argued as giving more effective application of the matching and accruals conventions (*current* costs against current revenues) and, through its long-run economically rational capital maintenance concept, of the going concern convention. It provides important information, at minimum, about those elements of historical cost profit which do not represent increases in economic wealth (given continuing operation). As regards the balance sheet it gives figures based on up-to-date market numbers. However, the approach is still clearly to determine profit and loss figures and then to 'stick what is left' in the balance sheet. The balance sheet is still essentially a statement of unexpired expenses, not a list of marketable assets at valuation.

EXERCISES (✔ indicates answers are available on pages 718–719)

    1 Explain and demonstrate how replacement cost accounting affects reported profit as compared with historical cost accounting.

✔ **2** Is replacement cost accounting more or less prudent than historical cost accounting?

    3 Under a replacement cost accounting system, which holding gains should be reported as:
      (a) realized
      (b) part of profit
      (c) distributable?
      Why?

    4 In general, replacement cost accounting produces reported profit figures which are a better indication of long-run future performance than historical cost accounting does. Discuss.

    5 A replacement cost balance sheet is just as useless as a historical cost balance sheet. Discuss.

✔ **6** I.M. Confused, computer dealer.
      From the following information compute
      (a) Profit and loss accounts and closing balance sheets for each of the years 20X1 and 20X2 under historical cost principles.
      (b) Profit and loss accounts and closing balance sheets for each of the years 20X1 and 20X2 under current replacement cost principles.

Comment briefly on the significance of the results.

Date	Event relating to trading in computers	'Wealth' Computers	€cash
01/01/X1	Set up business with €10 000 in the bank		10 000
02/01/X1	Buy six computers for €1000 each	6	4 000
01/05/X1	Sell two for €1500 each (RC = €1100)	4	7 000
01/09/X1	Buy two computers for €1200 each	6	4 600
01/10/X1	Pay annual rent of €600	6	4 000
31/12/X1	Financial year-end. Pay tax of €200	6	3 800
03/03/X2	Sell two computers for €1800 each (RC = €1300)	4	7 400
01/10/X2	Pay annual rent €700	4	6 700
01/11/X2	Buy two computers for €1400 each	6	3 900
31/12/X2	Financial year-end. Pay tax €450	6	3 450

7 Mallard Co. was formed on 1 January 20X1 with 10 000 issued €1 ordinary shares. The same day they obtained a 12% loan of €8000 and bought fixed assets for €9000. During 20X1 their purchases and sales of widgets were as follows:

	Purchases		Sales	
3 January	100 at €80	8 000		
1 February			60 at €120	7 200
1 April	110 at €75	8 250		
1 May			90 at €120	10 800
1 July	100 at €85	8 500		
1 August			130 at €120	15 600
1 October	120 at €90	10 800		
1 November			110 at €130	14 300

(a) Purchases and sales were all paid for in cash.

(b) The loan interest was paid early in the following year (20X2).

(c) The buying price of weidgets changed on 1 March, 1 June, 1 September and on 1 December (when it was €100).

(d) The fixed assets are to be depreciated at 10% p.a. At 31 December 20X1 their buying price was €12 600.

(e) General expenses during the year were €13 200.

  (i) prepare a balance sheet as at 31 December, 20X1 together with a trading profit and loss account for the year to 31 December 20X1, on replacement cost lines.

  (ii) What are holding gains? in what circumstances are they distributable?

8 *L and H*

On 1 January, L and H each started a business by investing €100 in cash, and then immediately purchasing one widget.

L sold her widget on 3 March for €110, but on 1 April discovered that she needed to pay this to buy another, which she did.

On 30 June this was sold for €120, and a new one bought in July for €120.

On 29 September this was sold for €130, and a replacement purchased on 30 September for €130.

H had been less active and had merely kept his first widget and read the newpaper. Both have decided to adopt 30 September as their accounting date, and come to you for accounting services.

(a) How would the above appear under

  (i) historic cost

  (ii) replacement cost.

Which results make more sense, and why?

6

Current exit value and mixed values

After studying this chapter you should be able to:
- □ explain the effects and implications of using current exit values to record the possession and usage of economic resources
- □ outline the implications of using an ad hoc mixture of valuation methods
- □ define and explain the effects and implications of deprival values as the basis of recording the possession and usage of economic resources
- □ discuss the overall relevance of current values
- □ outline the concept of fair value.

Introduction

In this chapter we look first of all at remaining current values worthy of consideration, current output or exit values. We then explore the possibility of using a combination of different valuation methods in preparing financial reports and, in particular, the concept of deprival value. In each case, as in earlier chapters, we seek to investigate both the techniques and logic of calculation and the meaning and usefulness of the resulting information.

Current exit value accounting

Edwards and Bell suggested two current exit value concepts as worthy of consideration (see p. 58). These were current values and opportunity costs. Current values they defined as 'values actually realized during the current period for goods or services sold'. On reflection, however, it quickly becomes apparent that the idea of substituting current values so defined into our basic equation of $W_1 + P - D = W_2$ does not make a great deal of sense. Values actually realized for goods and services already sold cannot obviously be argued as relevant to resources still possessed at the date or dates under consideration. Rather, of course, these realized values are the basis of revenue flows.

It is the second concept, that of opportunity costs, which we need to develop. Edwards and Bell (1961) defined this as 'values that could currently be realized if assets were sold (without further processing) outside the firm at the best prices immediately obtainable'. This is certainly a concept relevant to the resources possessed at the date under consideration. It shows the amount of money we could derive immediately (currently) from the resources held, or to take the alternative viewpoint it shows the amount of money we choose not to derive immediately if we retain the resources for any reason. We can adapt the application of the definition slightly to allow for further unavoidable processing or expenses of disposal and consider the concept of net realizable value (NRV), i.e. the proceeds after deducting these additional unavoidable expenses of disposal. These ideas are explored further in this chapter.

We intend to base our valuation figure on the current market selling price, more precisely, on NRV. So if an asset could be sold for €250, but the sale would involve €10 of selling expenses, the NRV is €240. The income under this method is based on the difference between the NRV of all resources at the two chosen dates. Following Edwards and Bell, it is often referred to as realizable income. It can be defined as follows:

$$Y_r = D + (R_e - R_s)$$

where Y_r is the exit value income, D is the distributions (less new capital inputs), R_e is the NRV of the assets at the end of the period and R_s is the NRV of the assets at the start of the period.

In practice, several possibilities exist as to exactly what we mean by NRV.

Activity 6.1

Consider an item of work in progress that has an NRV today of €10 in its existing state. The finished product (which would require a further €4 of expenses) has an NRV today of €20, but by the time the actual item of current work in progress is finished and sold, it is expected to have an NRV of €22. On a forced sale (e.g. if all the assets have to be sold off at once by a liquidator), the item in its existing state would realize €6.

Suggest possible figures for the exit value and which one you would normally find most useful.

Activity feedback

Possible figures for the exit value would seem to include €6, €10, €(20 − 4) and €(22 − 4). It is generally agreed that exit values should refer to assets in their existing state, on the assumption that they are sold in an orderly manner, i.e. in the normal course of business. Thus in our example the exit value for the work in progress would be €10.

It is clear that the exit value capital (R) at any particular date shows the amount of money that the business *could* obtain from its assets as on that date. Turning this round, exit value is seen as an opportunity cost concept – it shows the amount of cash that the business could obtain if it did not keep the asset. The opportunity cost of having an asset is the amount of cash the business sacrifices by retaining the asset instead. Advocates of exit value accounting argue that it is necessary to know the cash resources tied up in a business in order to measure efficiency. The amount of cash potentially available – the 'current cash equivalent' of the resources of a business – also provides a genuinely common measuring unit when comparing different businesses.

It is often argued – indeed often merely stated – that exit value accounting does not conform to the going concern convention. Its advocates argue that it is not intended to show what will happen, rather it is intended to show the results of what could happen, in order to assist decision making and internal appraisal.

We can usefully divide the exit value income (Y_r) into four elements:

$$Y_r = \text{realized operating gains}$$
$$+ \text{unrealized operating gains} \quad\Big\} \quad \text{i.e. on assets held for resale}$$
$$+ \text{realized non-operating gains}$$
$$+ \text{unrealized non-operating gains} \quad\Big\} \quad \text{i.e. on assets held for use}$$

Before looking at an example, it is important to understand the effect of exit value accounting on the P&L account. Since the opening and closing balance sheets are now value based, and not cost based, it necessarily follows that the P&L account is also value based and not cost based. For example 'depreciation' is no longer a process of cost allocation under the matching convention. It simply becomes the loss in value of the asset in the period. This is such a fundamental change that it would be better to invent a different word, but unfortunately nobody has yet done so.

Now work through the following example. Remember particularly that an unrealized gain in year 1, reported as such, will become a realized gain in a later year and will need to be reported as a realized gain. Care is needed to ensure that gains are not reported twice, as both unrealized and realized. This of course would be double counting.

Example

A company commences business with capital in cash of €15 000. It buys a fixed asset for €10 000. The following information is available:

	Year 1		Year 2	
	€		€	
NRV of fixed asset	6 000		4 000	
Sales	20 000		25 000	
Cost of sales	11 000		12 000	
Closing inventory: cost	2 000		3 000	
NRV	2 500		3 800	
Exit value revenue statements				
Sales	20 000		25 000	
Cost of sales	11 000		12 000	
	9 000		13 000	
'Depreciation'	4 000	(1)	2 000	(2)
	5 000		11 000	
less Operating gain included in previous year	–		500	(3)
	5 000		10 500	
add Unrealized operating gain	500	(4)	800	(5)
Realizable income	5 500		11 300	

Exit value balance sheets

Fixed assets	6 000		4 000	
Inventory	2 500		3 800	
Cash	12 000	(6)	24 000	(7)
	20 500		31 800	
Capital	15 000		15 000	
Realizable income	5 500		16 800	
	20 500		31 800	

Notes

1 10 000 – 6000
2 6000 – 4000
3 Included as realized in the 11 000, but already included, as unrealized, in the 5500 for year 1
4 2500 – 2000
5 3800 – 3000
6 15 000 – 10 000 + 20 000 – (11 000 + 2000)
7 12 000 + 25 000 – (12 000 + 1000)

The unrealized gain on inventory is here calculated on an annual basis, inventory during the year being left at cost. It would be possible, although more complicated, to record such unrealized gains more frequently – even daily if desired. Care must be taken, however, to ensure that a previously recorded unrealized gain is not again added into 'realizable income' when it is realized.

Now try the following activity, making a proper attempt before looking at the feedback which follows.

Activity 6.2

Bonds plc commenced business on 1 January year 7. Let us assume all transactions are by cheque and no credit is given or taken and that Bonds plc deals only in one type of item of inventory.

1 January Year 7
Introduced capital of €25 000 and purchased a machine for €9000.
Purchased 500 items of inventory for €15 each.

31 December Year 7
Sold 300 items of inventory for €30 each.
Paid rent for the year of €1000.
Paid other expenses for the year of €1000.

1 January Year 8
Purchased 400 items of inventory for €17 each.

31 December Year 8
Sold 500 items of inventory for €33 each.
Paid rent for the year of €1100.
Paid expenses for the year of €1200.

The following information relates to the machine:

	31.12.7	31.12.8
	€	€
Replacement cost	10 000	12 000
Realizable value	8 000	6 000
Cost of realization	1 000	1 000

Required   Produce a set of realizable value accounts for years 7 and 8.

Activity feedback

Bonds plc Trading and P&L account for the year ended 31 December

		31.12.7		31.12.8
		€		€
Sales		9 000		16 500
Less cost of sales		(4 500)		(8 100)
Gross profit		4 500		8 400
Rent	1 000		1 100	
Expenses	1 000		1 200	
Depreciation (note 2)	2 000		2 000	
		(4 000)		(4 300)
Gross profit		500		4 100
Holding gain (note 3)		3 000		(1 400)
		3 500		2 700

Balance sheet as at 31 December

		31.12.7		31.12.8
		€		€
Fixed assets				
Machine at NRV		7 000		5 000
Current assets				
Inventory at NRV (note 1)	6 000		3 300	
Bank	15 500		22 900	
		21 500		26 200
		28 500		31 200
Share capital		25 000		25 000
Profit		3 500		6 200
		28 500		31 200

Notes

1 The inventory is also brought into the balance sheet at the end of each year at its net realizable value.

31.12.7   200 units × €30 = €6000
31.12.8   100 units × €33 = €3300

2 *Depreciation.* The depreciation is the difference between the NRV of the asset at the end of each year less the NRV of the asset at the beginning of the year. Note that the NRV is after deducting the costs of realizing the asset.

Year 1   €7000   €9000
Year 2   €5000   €7000

3 *Holding gain.* In year 7 the holding gain is the unrealized holding gain on the closing inventory:

$$200 \text{ units} \times €15 \text{ (i.e. } €30 - €15) = €3000$$

In year 8 the holding gain of year 7 has now been realized (and therefore included in the trading account for year 8) while there is an unrealized holding gain on the closing stock of:

$$100 \text{ units} \times €16 \text{ (i.e. } €33 - €17) = €1600$$

Therefore, in year 8 the holding gain (loss) is:

	€
Unrealized holding gain in year 8	1 600
less: unrealized holding gain from year 7 now realized in year 8	3 000
	(1 400)

In effect we have a holding loss.

Current exit values: preliminary appraisal

Activity 6.3

Prepare a list, in point form, of advantages and disadvantages which you think could reasonably be said to apply to current exit value accounting.

Activity feedback

Advantages
1 It follows the economic 'opportunity cost' principle. It reveals the money sacrifice being made by *keeping* an asset. This permits rational decision making on the alternative uses of resources.
2 Exit values facilitate comparisons. They provide a genuinely common measure for the value of assets – cash or current cash equivalent.
3 The concept of realizable value is easy for the non-accountant to understand.
4 Useful information about assets is provided to outsiders, e.g. creditors.
5 It is already widely used, e.g. debtors, inventory at lower of historical cost (HC) and NRV, revaluation of land and buildings.

Disadvantages
1 It is highly subjective. Arguably more so than replacement cost (RC) accounting.
2 It fails to follow the going concern assumption, fails to recognize that firms do not usually sell all their assets (the proponents of exit value accounting explicitly deny this charge, arguing that it makes no assumptions either way, it merely provides useful information).

3 It fails to concentrate attention on long-run operational effectiveness.

4 It fails to give realistic information about the internal usefulness of assets – particularly of highly specialized assets that could have a very low NRV on the general market.

You may, of course, have some slightly different views. One point we should certainly consider is the possible relevance of expected values, which Edwards and Bell (1961) suggested to be a concept worth further exploration. They defined expected values (see Table 4.2) as 'values expected to be received in the future for output sold according to the firm's planned course of action'. Expected values are therefore a future exit rather than a current exit way of thinking. Expected values defined in this way certainly give useful information. In fact they form the raw material for the preparation of both cash and revenue budget statements. However, our essential purpose here is to prepare statements of current position and similar arguments apply to those already considered in relation to future entry values. To use future exit values would introduce greater subjectivity, greater possible inconsistency of evaluation and could be argued as failing to reflect current reality. Current exit values are suggested as a more useful concept.

It is essential to remember that exit value NRV accounting tends to focus on the balance sheet to a considerably greater extent that current entry value RC accounting. Profit or gain is very much determined by a consideration of changes in output values of resources. The balance sheet under NRV can be regarded as a consistent statement, with all figures on the same basis and as at the same date. This balance sheet is not just a list of 'balances left over' in the sense that a current entry value balance sheet is (see Chapter 5). However, it follows from this that it is the profit and loss calculation which in a sense picks up and contains 'the figures lying around'. Current exit value is essentially a short-run concept. It provides valuable information about market values of business resources and therefore about short-term alternatives and possibilities. This is clearly seen in the capital maintenance concept associated with NRV. This could be expressed as: the maintenance of the NRV, the current cash equivalent, of the resources of the business. But exit value accounting information does not provide us with the information necessary for management to seek to ensure the long-run operational capability of the business.

Mixed values – ad hoc methods

As we shall see in detail later on, companies following IAS, and also some national systems, may have a great deal of flexibility in practice as regards the valuation policy they wish to adopt. There is no requirement for any consistency of approach as between one asset and another. It is in fact extremely common for businesses that broadly follow historical cost accounting principles to revalue some of their fixed assets at intervals (not necessarily annually), sometimes then depreciating on the revalued figure, sometimes not depreciating at all. This may well lead to the provision of more useful information as regards particular resources. For example, a current or recent valuation of land or factory is surely more useful than a 50-year-old cost figure. But, of course, it further increases the inconsistencies within the accounting reports as a whole, making the balance sheet as a statement of resources and the sources thereof ever more difficult to understand, usually influencing the size of expense figures charged and certainly influencing any interpretational ratios relating return with the source base being employed.

Mixed values – deprival value

A much more theoretically defensible approach to the idea of using different valuation bases for different assets or more accurately for using different valuation bases for assets in different circumstances is the concept of deprival value.

Assume that a business owns an asset. What is that asset 'worth' to the business? The deprival value (DV) approach says that the DV of an asset is the loss that the rational businessman or businesswoman would suffer if he or she were deprived of the asset. This loss will depend on what would rationally have been done with the asset if he or she had not lost (been deprived of) it.

Activity 6.4

Six people, A to F, are possessors and owners of six assets, U to Z, respectively. The various monetary evaluations (in €) of each asset by its owner are shown in the following table.

Person	Asset	HC	RC	NRV	EV
A	U	1	2	3	4
B	V	5	6	8	7
C	W	9	12	10	11
D	X	16	15	14	13
E	Y	17	19	20	18
F	Z	23	22	21	24

All six people signed a contract with an insurance agent, Miss Prue Dential, under which they shall be reimbursed, in the event of loss of their assets, by 'the amount of money a rationally acting person will actually have lost as a result of losing the asset'.

Put yourself in the position of the rationally acting person, decide what *action* you would take in each circumstance and then calculate the net effect on your monetary position.

Activity feedback

In each situation the first question to ask is: Would the rationally acting businessman or businesswoman replace the asset or not? He or she will replace it if the proceeds of *either* selling it (NRV) *or* using it (economic value, EV) are higher than the costs of replacing it. If it is going to be replaced, then the loss suffered is clearly the cost of replacement. Thus, in situations where the rationally acting businessman or businesswoman would replace the asset, DV is RC. If he or she would not replace it, the loss suffered is given by the value of the benefits that *would have derived* from the asset but which he or she will now never receive. Being rational, the intention must have been to act so as to derive the highest possible return, i.e. the higher of NRV and economic value (EV). Therefore, in situations where the rationally acting businessman or businesswoman would not replace the asset if deprived of it, DV is the higher of NRV and EV. This last element, the higher of NRV and EV, is known as the 'recoverable amount'.

So we can formally state that DV is the lower of RC and recoverable amount, where recoverable amount is the higher of NRV and EV (see Figure 6.1). Given three different concepts (RC, NRV and EV) there are in fact only six possible different rankings:

EV	>	NRV	>	RC
NRV	>	EV	>	RC
RC	>	EV	>	NRV
RC	>	NRV	>	EV
NRV	>	RC	>	EV
EV	>	RC	>	NRV

The example contains all six of these alternatives. The DV in each situation is as follows:

Person	DV	Reason
A	2	Cost of replacement
B	6	Cost of replacement
C	11	EV not received
D	14	Realizable value not received
E	19	Cost of replacement
F	22	Cost of replacement

Make sure that you understand why, in the context of the logic of the DV definition (and notice the irrelevance of the HC figures).

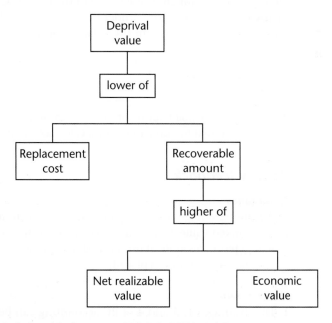

Figure 6.1 Relationship between DV, RC, NRV and EV

Deprival value (DV): appraisal

Deprival value has a clearly definable concept of capital maintenance. Profit is here being regarded as the excess after maintaining the 'value to the business' of its assets. The value to the business is clearly seen to be related to actual operations (what the business would do). Following from this, we can say that DV seeks to maintain the business' capacity to do things, usually expressed as the *operating capacity* or *operating capability*. We saw earlier that in four of the six possible rankings, DV equals RC. In the practical business situation, the chances of replacement cost being higher than both NRV and EV will generally be relatively small, so the other two rankings will in practice not occur frequently. This means that in a practical business context, DV usually comes back to RC.

Theoretically, therefore, it can be suggested that deprival value provides an improvement and refinement on current replacement cost accounting. It reduces itself to replacement cost when the economically logical action is to replace and uses the more relevant benefit foregone figure in those situations where replacement would logically not occur. Notice, of course, that it is not strictly a completely *current* concept at all, as the EV possibility is a future orientation. Another way to look at the implications of the previous discussions would be to take the more practical line of arguing that deprival value shows that replacement cost is relevant most of the time. In other words, deprival value thinking positively explores the possibilities of refining replacement cost thinking and shows that in most situations the refinements introduce difficulty and subjectivity, for very little benefit in terms of extra relevance of information.

As a final thought, what about additivity? Is deprival value a separate concept, leading to a balance sheet consistently valued in deprival terms? Or is deprival value merely a formula for choosing which of the three (RC, NRV, EV) valuation bases to use in any particular situation? Under the latter way of thinking deprival value obviously leads to a variety of bases in the balance sheet and therefore to a lack of additivity.

Activity 6.5

Prepare a list, in point form, of advantages and disadvantages which you think could reasonably be said to apply to deprival value accounting.

Activity feedback

Advantages
1 All the advantages of RC accounting can be claimed here also.
2 As a 'mixed value' system it is more realistic and relevant than either RC or NRV. It values resources at RC if it is profitable to replace them and at the expected proceeds if they would not be replaced.

Disadvantages
1 Disadvantages 1, 3 and 4 of RC accounting can be claimed here too.
2 It is more subjective than RC.

3 If the balance sheet is expressed in 'mixed values', what do the asset and capital employed totals mean? Can mixed values be validly added at all?

4 Firms are not in practice being continually deprived of their assets.

Fair values

The concept of fair value seems to have become popular in recent years. It is very important to be careful how you use the phrase and even more important to work out very carefully how another author has used it when you come across it. It seems sometimes to be used loosely and vaguely to mean 'current value' or 'market value'. It appears in US regulations from around the early 1980s, but apparently with a slightly different meaning from that discussed here.

We take fair value, here, as having the general IASB definition, used in a number of Standards and in the IASB glossary of terms:

> Fair value is the amount for which an asset could be exchanged, or a liability settled, between knowledgeable willing parties in an arm's length transaction.

The concept of fair value in IAS regulations has emerged gradually over the last 20 years or so. Comparing IAS 41 (*Agriculture*, issued in 2001) with IAS 40 (*Investment Properties*, issued in 2000) it is clear that the concept is still developing. It is also very important to note that IAS requirements based on the fair value concept do not necessarily require the actual recorded figure (carrying value) to *be* fair value as defined in the relevant standard. Details are discussed in the appropriate chapters in Part Two. Fair value is also closely related to the idea of asset impairment, discussed in several places in Part Two, especially Chapter 13. The general points to note are:

- Fair value may not necessarily be defined or operationalized identically in all situations.
- Carrying value may differ from fair value (and for different reasons) under particular Standards.

Here we are concerned only to attempt an understanding and analysis of the central concept. This has its difficulties. IASB seems to be working backwards from the pronouncements in its Standards and is now recognizing the need to clarify fair value as a theoretical concept and we are forced to follow the same process. Creating the concept clearly, before applying it, would be a more valid scientific process.

Activity 6.6

S takes a product to market, incurring transport costs of €2 and exchanges it with B, in an arm's length (i.e. independent) transaction at an agreed exchange price of €30. B takes the product to his own enterprise, incurring transport costs of €3. Calculate each of the following within the limits of the given data:

(a) S's selling price.
(b) S's net realizable value.
(c) B's buying price.
(d) B's historical cost.

(e) B's current replacement cost.
(f) Fair value to S before the sale.
(g) Fair value to B after the sale.

Activity feedback

Answers would seem to be as follows:

(a) S's selling price	€30.
(b) S's net realizable value	€28.
(c) B's buying price	€30.
(d) B's historical cost	€33.
(e) B's current replacement cost	€33.
(f) Fair value to S before sale	€30.
(g) Fair value to B after purchase	€30.

A number of points emerge: **(a)** and **(c)** are necessarily equal, **(f)** and **(g)** are necessarily equal at least instantaneously before and after the transaction. Further **(a)**, **(c)**, **(f)** and **(g)** are all necessarily equal. Third, **(b)** < **(c)** < **(e)**, i.e. in the general case where disposal and acquisition costs are not nil:

$$NRV < Fair\ value < CRC$$

So, is fair value an entry value, an exit value, both or neither?

The short answer seems to be that nobody is quite sure. We suggest that two propositions can safely be made. First, from a theoretical perspective, taking the definition at face value and ignoring transaction costs, fair value is both entry and exit value at the same time. Since it is the *agreed* price between buyer and seller, there can be no other answer.

Second, from a practical point of view and allowing for the reality of transaction costs, it is arguably neither, being in between NRV (an operational exit value) and CRC (an operational entry value), as Activity 6.6 illustrates.

These two propositions taken together arguably suggest that the fair value concept as defined by IASB breaks down on rigorous examination and can neither be rationally analyzed and positioned within the analysis of alternatives created in these chapters nor operationalized without the introduction of market costs, with which the definition is incompatible. When you come across this fair value concept in the context of particular applications and IASs, as you will a number of times in Part Two, try to relate the application to the general issues discussed here. The implications of the fair value concept, both theoretically and in practice, have not yet been fully explored. But the IASB's enthusiasm for fair value is still increasing.

Current values: some overall thoughts

In Chapter 1 we revised and developed the traditional historical cost model. This is backwards looking and relatively objective (remember the relatively!). In Chapter 4 we considered the thinking of important economists in this area, the psychic theories of Fisher – unmeasurable in money terms by very definition but properly recognizing that only human beings take decisions and that they are the ultimate consumers – and the more quantifiable work of Hicks with its important capital maintenance implications. These economic-based ideas are properly forward looking and logically relevant to the decision-making process, but they are highly subjective. Current values lie in the middle of this spectrum both in terms of their time relationship (in between past and future) and in terms of their degrees of objectivity/subjectivity. In this sense they are clearly worth exploring as a compromise between relevance and verifiability.

There are stronger claims that can be made, however. The usual financial reporting statements essentially claim to report on the position at a (current) date and on the results ending on that date. Current values can properly claim to provide information consistent with this approach. The question follows, of course, which current value? The discussions in this and the previous chapter suggest that each of the suggested bases has particular merits. All provide useful information. All give good and relevant answers to *some* questions. One obvious suggestion to follow from this is that the preferable method in any situation depends on the particular situation itself – in other words, the abstract question 'Which is the best method?' has no answer and indeed is simply a silly question. We should be prepared to use different valuation methods and different reporting methods for different purposes.

A second suggestion is an idea for you to take away and think about. The practice and application of double-entry channel us unthinkingly into the assumption that the balance sheet and the income statement are two elements in the same system and that they therefore have to be fully compatible with each other. But our basic purpose is to produce meaningful reports and there is no logical reason why they should be in any way constrained by data-recording systems. Perhaps we should consider producing smaller more ad hoc statements, using *combinations* of valuation bases depending on the purpose of each statement.

Summary

In this chapter we have analyzed the logic and implications of current exit value accounting and prepared accounting statements on a current exit (NRV) basis. We then explored the possibility of ad hoc mixtures within the framework of traditional accounting reports and analyzed the logic and implications of deprival value accounting and of fair values. Finally, we asked ourselves to consider the usefulness of current values generally and individually.

EXERCISES   (✔ indicates answers are available on pages 719–721)

   1 Explain the principles of exit value accounting, providing a simple made-up illustration.
   2 Explain the principles of deprival value accounting, providing a simple made-up illustration.
✔ 3 Discuss the proposition that businesses should be required to publish their P&L statement on replacement cost lines and their balance sheet on net realizable value lines.
   4 Deprival value removes significant disadvantages of replacement cost, while retaining its advantages. Discuss.

5 (a) Provide a definition of the deprival value of an asset.
  (b) For a particular asset, suppose the three bases of valuation relevant to the calculation of its deprival value are (in thousands of euros): €12, €10 and €8. Construct a matrix of columns and rows showing all the possible alternative situations and, in each case, indicate the appropriate deprival value.
  (c) Justify the use of deprival value as a method of asset valuation, using the matrix in (b) to illustrate your answer.

✔ 6 Steward plc commences business on 1 January year 1. Let us assume all transactions are by cheque and no credit is given nor taken and that Steward deals only in one type of item of inventory.

1 January Year 1
Introduced capital of €30 000.
Purchased machine for €10 000.
Purchased 1000 items of inventory for €10 each.

31 December Year 1
Sold 800 items of inventory for €15 each.
Paid expenses for the year of €1000.
The NRV of the machine is €9000.

1 January Year 2
Purchased 800 items of inventory for €13 each.

31 December Year 2
Sold 500 items of inventory for €20 each.
Paid expenses for the year of €1200.
The NRV of the machine is €8000.

Produce profit and loss accounts and balance sheets relating to years 1 and 2 using NRV accounting.

7 On 1 January, Stan and Oliver each started a business by investing €100 in cash, and then immediately purchasing one widget, which at that date could have been resold for €120.

Stan sold his widget on 31 March for €130, but on 1 April discovered that he needed to pay €115 to buy another, which he did.

On 30 June this was sold for €140, and a new one bought on 1 July for €125.

On 29 September this was sold for €150, and a replacement purchased on 30 September for €130, on which date the new one could have been sold for €160.

Oliver had been less active and had merely kept his first widget and read the newspaper.

Both have decided to adopt 30 September as their accounting date, and come to you for accounting services.

All widgets are identical.

Replacement costs changed on 31 March, 30 June, 29 September.

How would the above appear under:
(a) historic cost
(b) replacement cost
(c) net realizable value
Note: You may find it helpful to do this by using a table with each date on the left and columns for Cash, Inventory, Profit, Holding Gains, etc. across the top.

Current purchasing power accounting

After studying this chapter you should be able to:
- [ ] explain the concept of general inflation and its implications for accounting measurement
- [ ] explain the mechanisms for taking account of general inflation in financial reporting especially, but not exclusively, in the context of historical cost accounting
- [ ] discuss theoretical arguments, and practical considerations, for and against current purchasing power accounting
- [ ] outline present attitudes to the whole changing prices and inflation debate.

Introduction

In our discussion so far we have considered various methods of 'putting a monetary figure on something'. There are many ways of deriving a figure with a € sign in front that we must consider and appraise. But we have not yet stopped to consider what we mean by the € sign. What is a euro? It is a unit of money – and money is of no use by itself. Money has no intrinsic value. Its value is related to what we can get with it, what we can do with it. When most prices are rising, then we can obtain gradually less and less with any given number of euros. This means that if, under any particular valuation basis, we have maintained our capital appropriately defined in terms of numbers of euros, we have not necessarily maintained our capital in terms of the purchasing power of those euros. *Current purchasing power* (CPP) accounting attempts to take account of this.

The measuring unit problem

There are many examples of difficulties with measuring units. Litres and gallons or inches and centimetres are classic examples. But in these cases the use of different measuring units may be a nuisance, but the problems are capable of rapid and objective solution. An inch has a precise or standard specification. A centimetre has a precise or standard specification. It follows, of course, that the relationship between the two also has a precise or standard specification. We can very exactly convert one to the other and, even more significantly, the conversion factor is fixed and constant between different people, between different places and between different times.

None of this is true of money as a measuring unit. A unit of money is an artificial construct. It is related to spending power and spending patterns, and these are personal and individual. It follows that a unit of money is not fixed as between different people, is not fixed between different places and, crucially for accounting, it is not fixed between different times. We need a conversion factor between our altering measuring units. But since our units (euros) are not fixed in inherent valuation, it follows that the conversion factor cannot be fixed either. The solution (or evasion) which current purchasing power provides to this problem is to use averages as an approximate surrogate for the theoretically unique conversion factor required. The euro is converted, or adjusted, by means of general indices.

Current purchasing power

It is vital to understand that current purchasing power (CPP) is a general purchasing power concept. We are concerned with general inflation, usually expressed as the average rise in the cost of living, i.e. with inflation in the politicians' sense. If inflation in the last year is 10%, then €100 last year has the same general (i.e. average) purchasing power as €110 this year. This means that in order to know what we are talking about we have to 'date' all our euros. Euros at different dates can no longer be regarded as the same, as a common measuring unit. In order to return to the position, essential for proper comparison, of having a common measuring unit, we have to convert euros of one date's purchasing power into euros of the other date's purchasing power. This needs illustrating!

Basic figures (all at 31 December) are:

20.1   €200
20.2   €250

The general inflation index stood at 300 in 20.1 and 330 in 20.2 (i.e. inflation in the year was 10%).

Over the year $200_{20.1}$ euros have been changed into $250_{20.2}$ euros. How much better off are we?

Activity 7.1

Well. How much better off are we?

Activity feedback

To answer this, we need to calculate the equivalent in $€_{20.2}$, of $€_{20.1}$ 200. In terms of general purchasing power this will be:

$$200 \times \frac{330}{300} = €_{20.2} \ 220$$

So in terms of a common measuring unit ($€_{20.2}$) we have an increase in well-offness of $250 - 220 = €_{20.2} \ 30$.

The description 'basic figure' is deliberately vague. The idea of CPP adjustments can be superimposed on *any* valuation basis. The practical proposals made in recent years for the introduction of CPP have generally assumed a HC basis and for the present we will discuss and illustrate the ideas under this assumption.

It is important to distinguish, when considering CPP accounting, between monetary and non-monetary items. Monetary items are items fixed by contract, custom or statute in terms of numbers of euros, regardless of changes in the general price level and the purchasing power of the euros. Examples are cash, debtors and creditors and longer term loans. Non-monetary items are all items not so fixed in terms of number of euros, for example land, buildings, plant, inventory, shares held as investments.

Suppose I held a monetary asset in 20.1 of €200 (i.e. €$_{20.1}$ 200). If I still hold this asset, untouched and unchanged, a year later, it will be worth €200. It might even be a pile of 200 physical € coins, although it could equally be a debtor or a loan. But in 20.2 what sort of euro is it worth 200 of? The answer is 20.2 euros. By definition the item is fixed in terms of number of euros. So I have turned €$_{20.1}$ 200 into €$_{20.2}$ 200. But we know that in terms of general purchasing power €$_{20.2}$ is worth less than €$_{20.1}$ was. Therefore, in maintaining my position in terms of the number of euros of my monetary asset, I have failed to maintain my position in terms of purchasing power.

Contrariwise, suppose we borrow €100 in 20.1 and repay the loan, €100, one year later. We have borrowed €$_{20.1}$ 100 and repaid €$_{20.2}$ 100. We have repaid the same number of euros that we borrowed, but each euro is of lower purchasing power. Therefore, in terms of (general) purchasing power we have repaid less than we borrowed, so we have gained. (We shall also have to pay interest of course, which may have attempted to take account of the effects of inflation.) These gains and losses on monetary items are an important part of the argument in favour of CPP accounting – it is suggested that such gains and losses should be calculated and reported.

With monetary items, then, when considering two sets of accounts at different dates, no *adjustment* to the € figure reported is needed, but care must be taken in interpretation. However, when *comparing* two sets of accounts of the same business at different dates it is necessary to adjust *all* the contents of one balance sheet into the measuring unit (dated euro) of that of the other. The question may be: what is the current (today) purchasing power of the €100 I held one year ago (and still hold)? The answer is 100 of today's euros. But the question might be: If I have €200 today and I had €100 one year ago, how much better off am I in terms of purchasing power? The answer, in terms of today's euros is:

$$200 - 100 \times \frac{(\text{RPI today})}{(\text{RPI 1 year ago})}$$

For example:

$$200 - 100 \times \frac{(330)}{(300)}$$
$$= 200 - 110$$
$$= \text{€ today } 90$$

This process leads to a good deal of confusion. Study the following example carefully.

Example

Given: All the information of Chaplin Ltd, as on p. 80
Prepare: A closing balance sheet under CPP principles.

Chaplin Ltd – CPP solution

		€	€
Capital	$200\,000 \times \dfrac{120}{100}$		240 000
Operating profit			21 382
			261 382
Gain on net monetary liabilities			2 000
			263 382
Loan			50 000
Creditors			50 000
			363 382
Land and buildings	$110\,000 \times \dfrac{120}{100}$		132 000
Plant and equipment: cost	$40\,000 \times \dfrac{120}{100}$	48 000	
depreciation	$4\,000 \times \dfrac{120}{100}$	4 800	43 200
Inventory	$90\,000 \times \dfrac{120}{110}$	98 182	175 200
Debtors		90 000	188 182
			363 382

Notes

1 *Operating profit*. Balancing figure or provable as follows:

Per HC results		26 000
less Depreciation adj.	$4\,000 \times \dfrac{110 - 100}{100}$	400
Inventory sold adj.	$60\,000 \times \dfrac{110 - 100}{100}$	6 000
Adjusted profit as *30 June prices*		19 600
Adjusted profit at 31 December prices	$19\,600 \times \dfrac{120}{110}$	€21 382

2 *Gain on net monetary liabilities*.
  (a) In total this is easily provable as follows:
      Net monetary liabilities 1 January €10 000 (loan 50 000 less cash 40 000).
      Net monetary liabilities 31 December €10 000 (loan 50 000 plus creditors 50 000 less debtors 90 000).

      Therefore gain is $10\,000 \left(1 - \dfrac{120}{110}\right) = €2\,000$ (at 31 December prices).

(b) More generally, however, the figures should be considered individually:

Debtors — arose on 30 June, remained until 31 December:

$$90\,000 \left(1 - \frac{120}{100}\right) = \text{Loss} \qquad\qquad €8\,181$$

Creditors – arose on 30 June, remained until 31 December:

$$50\,000 \left(1 - \frac{120}{110}\right) = \text{Gain} \qquad\qquad €4\,545$$

Loan – arose on 1 January, remained until 31 December:

$$50\,000 \left(1 - \frac{120}{100}\right) = \text{Gain} \qquad\qquad €10\,000$$

Cash – arose on 1 January, remained until 30 June:

$$40\,000 \left(1 - \frac{110}{100}\right) = \text{Loss} \qquad\qquad €4\,000$$

But this loss on holding cash is expressed in 30 June euros. This figure must be converted to 31 December euros i.e.:

$$4\,000 \times \frac{120}{110} = \text{Loss} \qquad\qquad €4\,364$$

So in summary, we have:

Losses of 8 181 + 4 364	€12 545
Gains of 4 545 + 10 000	€14 545
Giving a net gain on net monetary liabilities of:	€2 000

Is this €2000 gain distributable? Is it realized? In fact as the practical businessman or businesswoman might say, where is it?

3 *Indices used*. Study carefully which index number is used where and make sure you see why. Remember the simplifying assumption that all sales, purchases and associated payments occurred on 30 June and also that monetary items need no adjustment for balance sheet purposes. Note the irrelevance of the plant and inventory indices.

4 *Complexity*. This example is highly simplified yet the numbers and, more important, the logic, are not at all easy.

5 *Comparatives*. Next year this balance sheet will be used as a comparative for next year's results. For this purpose it will need, next year, to be multiplied by:

$$\frac{\text{(RPI at 31 December next year)}}{120}$$

This will need to be done to every figure, whether monetary or non-monetary. Thus, for example, the loan figure at the end of the year 2 will be 50 000 year 2 euros. If the RPI is then 150, then the comparative figure from year 1, as updated to year 2 euros will be:

$$50\,000 \times \frac{150}{120} = €62\,500$$

This cannot, of course, mean that the loan has been reduced in monetary amount by €12 500. What it does mean is that the loan has reduced in value in terms of year 2 euros (i.e. there has been another gain on monetary liabilities).

Now try the following activity. Our solution follows, but we strongly suggest that you make a serious attempt at your own solution first.

Activity 7.2

Mushroom Ltd was established on 1 January 20X4. Its opening balance sheet (on this date) was as follows:

	€
	€
Land	6 000
Equipment	4 000
Inventory	2 000
Equity	12 000

During 20X4, the company made the following transactions:

(a) purchased extra inventory €10 000
(b) sold inventory for €11 000 cash, which had an historical cost value of €9000
(c) closing inventory on 31 December 20X4 had an historical cost of €3000 and was bought when the RPI index was 115 (average)
(d) the equipment has an expected life of four years and nil residual value. The straight line method of depreciation is used
(e) the general price index stood at:

100 on 1 January 20X4
110 on 30 June 20X4
120 on 31 December 20X4

You should assume that purchases and receipts occur evenly throughout the year. There are no debtors or creditors.

Required   Calculate the CPP profit for 20X4 and prepare the CPP balance sheet as at 31 December 20X4.

Activity feedback

		€CPP	€CPP
Sales	11 000 × 120/110		12 000
Opening inventory	2 000 × 120/100	2 400	
Add purchases	10 000 × 120/110	10 909	
		13 309	
less Closing inventory	(3 000 × 120/115)	3 130	
			10 179
			1 821
less Depreciation			1 200
			621
Loss on holding monetary assets (cash)*			91
CPP profit			530

* If cash accrues evenly over the year, the loss is

$$€(1000 \times 120/110) - €1000 = €91$$

The historical cost profit (€11 000 – €9000 – €1000 for depreciation = €1000) and the CPP profit can be reconciled as follows:

	€
Historical cost profit	1 000

Inventory
Additional charge based on restating the cost of inventory at the beginning and end of the year in euros of current purchasing power, thus taking the inflationary element out of the profit on the sale of inventory. Opening inventory + 400 – closing inventory – 130   (270)

Depreciation
Additional depreciation based on cost, measured in euros of current purchasing power of fixed assets €1200 – €1 000   (200)

Monetary items
Net loss in purchasing power resulting from the effects of inflation on the company's net monetary assets   (91)

Sales, purchases and all other costs*
These are increased by the change in the index between the average date at which they occurred and the end of the year. This adjustment increases profit as sales exceed the costs included in this heading   91

CPP profit   530

* The historical cost profit is based on:

	€	$€_{CPP}$	€
Sales	11 000	12 000	1 000
Purchases	10 000	10 909	(909)
Net difference			91

Calculation of balance sheet items, and reconciliation of profit figure with balance sheet:

1 Value of equity, 1 January 20X4   €12 000
    Revalued in terms of $€_{CPP}$ at 31 December 20X4
        (€12 000 × 120/100) $€_{CPP}$14 400

2 Mushroom Ltd
    CPP balance sheet as at 31 December 20X4

		$€_{CPP}$	$€_{CPP}$
Land	6 000 × 120/100		7 200
Equipment	4 000 × 120/100	4 800	
less Depreciation	1 000 × 120/100	1 200	
			3 600
			10 800
Inventory	3 000 × 120/115	3 130	
Cash	(11 000 – 10 000)	1 000	
			4 130
			14 930
Financed by equity and reserves			14 930
CPP profit – €CPP (14 930 – 14 400) =		$€_{CPP}$	530

Combination of methods

As already stated, CPP thinking can be applied to any valuation basis, not just historical costs. It is often suggested that CPP adjustments could and indeed should be applied to replacement cost calculations. It is important to remember that:

1 RC accounting deals with *specific* price rises only
2 CPP accounting deals with *general* price rises only
3 both types of change are in fact occurring at the same time.

Thus to take the simplest of examples, if HC = 10 and a year later RC = 13, there is a holding gain of €3. But if the GI has increased by 10% then $(10 \times 110/100) = €1$ of that holding gain of 3 (closing date) euros is not 'real' because it cannot be translated into increased purchasing power. The 'real' holding gain is arguably only 2 $(3-1)$ (closing date) euros. This combined approach, known as *stabilized accounting*, is shown for Chaplin Ltd in the following example.

Example

Chaplin Ltd – stabilized (RC plus CPP) solution

	€
Capital (per CPP answer)	240 000
Operating profit	18 328
	258 328
Real holding gain	8 012
	266 340
Loan	50 000
Creditors	50 000
	366 340
Land and building (per RC answer)	135 000
Plant and equipment (per RC answer)	39 600
Inventory (per RC answer)	101 740
Debtors	90 000
	366 340

Notes

1 *Operating profit.*

Per HC answer	$26\,000 \times \dfrac{120}{110}$	=	28 364
Depreciation RC 30 June	4 200		
Depreciation *less* HC	4 000		
	$200 \times \dfrac{120}{110}$	=	(218)
Cost of sales (per RC answer)	$9\,000 \times \dfrac{120}{110}$	=	(9 818)
			18 328

2 *Real holding gain.*

Gain on net monetary items (per CPP answer)			2 000
Land and buildings	$110\,000 \times \left(\frac{135}{110} - \frac{120}{100}\right)$	=	3 000

Plant and equipment:

Cost	$40\,000 \times \left(\frac{115}{100} - \frac{120}{100}\right)$	=	(4 000)	
Depreciation	$\left(400 \times \frac{105}{100}\right) \times \left(\frac{110}{105} - \frac{120}{100}\right)$	=	182	(3 818)
				1 181

Cost of sales:

Opening inventory	$\left(60\,000 \times \left(\frac{115}{110} - \frac{110}{100}\right)\right) \times \frac{120}{110}$	=	3 273	
Closing inventory	$90\,000 \times \left(\frac{130}{115} - \frac{120}{110}\right)$	=	3 557	6 830
				€8 012

Current purchasing power – what does it really mean?

It is most important when thinking about CPP accounting to be fully aware of exactly what it is doing and what it is not doing. The crucial point is that it is not producing a current valuation of the term concerned in any sense. What it is doing, in general terms, is to re-express in terms of current euros, the figures as originally calculated under the original measurement basis, whatever that was. It does not alter the basis of valuation. It alters the measuring unit which is being applied to the original basis of valuation.

Activity 7.3

Look at the figure of €132 000 for land and buildings shown in the Chaplin CPP example on p. 104 and think about it carefully. What does it mean?

Activity feedback

We would suggest it means something like: the number of current euros that would have to be spent today to buy the land and buildings if all economic circumstances were exactly unaltered from when the original purchase was made. Since all economic circumstances will most certainly not be unaltered from when the original purchase was made, it is not obvious that this is particularly useful information.

The other point that could be made concerns the assumption that a *general* adjustment to purchasing power is of relevance even when viewed in measuring unit terms to the *particular* user of the *particular* set of accounts of the *particular* business being considered. Can the spending or purchasing power of one euro be equated as between a retail shop and a chemical manufacturer? Can the spending or purchasing power of one euro be equated as between a non-smoking pensioner and a smoking teenager? Is general purchasing power so general that it is not really relevant to any particular user?

Activity 7.4

Prepare a list, in point form, of advantages and disadvantages which you think could reasonably be said to apply to current purchasing power accounting.

Activity feedback

Advantages

1 All necessary figures are stated or restated in terms of a common measuring unit (CPP units). This facilitates proper comparison.
2 It distinguishes between gains or losses on monetary liabilities and assets, on the one hand, and 'real' gains or losses through trading activities, on the other.
3 It requires only a simple objective adjustment to HC accounts. Easily auditable.

Disadvantages

1 It is not clear what CPP units are. They are not the same as monetary units.
2 *General* purchasing power, by definition, has no direct relevance to any *particular* person or situation.
3 When CPP is applied to HC-based accounts, the resulting figures necessarily contain all the disadvantages of the original HC accounts.
4 It fails to give any sort of meaningful 'value' to balance sheet items, although it gives the impression to non-accountants that it has done precisely that.
5 It is extremely difficult to understand and interpret.

Some European practices and traditions

No attempt is made here to replicate a full coverage of either national research traditions or of national practices. Readers wishing to investigate the story as it applies in their own country should look elsewhere. We merely present a brief sketch and overview.

A significant starting point is the publication of a French *ordinance* (law) in 1673 and an authorized (by Royal Decree) commentary on it published in 1675 by Jacques Savary. Savary argued that an annual inventory – which we would now call balance sheet – had two functions. The first function is to give an indication of the position of the business as a performing (and continuing) operation. This function logically requires that assets are measured on a cost basis if not yet sold. The second function is an indication of debt coverage, i.e. to give an indication of the risk of bankruptcy. This function logically requires that assets are measured on a net realizable value basis.

These two functions, and the resulting balance sheets, later become known as dynamic and static respectively. These are the terms used in the German tradition, developed to considerable sophistication by theorists in the early years of the 20th century. Schmalenbach wrote *Dynamische Bilanz*, in several editions to 1926 (also available in English), which argues for a reporting system based on historical costs together with general indexation adjustment. This is in contrast with Schmidt, who supported the essentially static view (in the sense already described) that current values should be used, actually current entry (replacement cost) figures under his proposals.

The Dutch academic Theodor Limperg broadly followed and developed the Schmidt approach in the years to 1940, see for example Mey (1966). The essential argument is that replacement cost is the sacrificed value for production resources used. Distributable income is then logically defined as the difference between revenue and the value sacrificed in order to obtain that revenue, i.e. profit is revenue less replacement cost of consumption.

A connection into the English-speaking world was made through the publication by Sweeney of *Stabilized Accounting* (1936). Sweeney had access to the German literature and was strongly influenced by Schmidt. Sweeney went further, however, and demonstrates in detail the feasibility of a full-scale combination of replacement cost measurement in combination with general indication, i.e. RC + CPP at the same time.

The 'resources sacrificed' approach, essentially an opportunity cost philosophy, can be traced into *The Valuation of Property*, by Bonbright, published in the USA in 1937. It was this book that provided the foundations for the development of the concept of deprival value, already discussed.

Practice since the middle of the 20th century bears little resemblance to the earlier research developments. The general middle European practical approach, influenced by the factors discussed in Chapter 2, has been a strict adherence to historical costs. The same is true in the USA, although perhaps more for reasons of objectivity (and fear of the power of lawyers) than for reasons of prudence. The UK (and also the Netherlands) have adopted a more flexible approach, both in law and in practice. The large Dutch company, Phillips, used a broadly Limpergian reporting system for several decades.

In the 1970s the UK experimented with a compulsory supplementary *Current Purchasing Power System* (SSAP 7, 1974). Following the government-sponsored (and influenced) Sandilands Report (1975), an expanded (and excessively complicated) development of deprival value, known as *Current Cost Accounting* (SSAP 16, 1980) was required (without general indexation). Neither lasted very long. But the timing of these events strongly influenced the content and wording of the Fourth European Directive on the accounts of limited companies, published in 1978 and still very much with us today. This Directive allows a very wide variety of different approaches.

In terms of the future, general inflation adjustments are regularly employed in hyperinflationary economies, such as some South American countries and supported by requirements in IAS 29, discussed in Chapter 21. Specific price change adjustments are not generally in fashion at present, but as trends of price rise tend to increase, then the debate is likely to return. Any such system in practice is not likely to be more complicated than the system briefly operated in the UK in the 1980s, which had four major elements. The last two of these, the monetary working capital adjustment and the gearing adjustment, raise important conceptual issues. Either of them could be dropped from a practical system without affecting the other. As an exposition of the issues involved, we discuss the requirements of this former Standard here. It is never likely to be reintroduced, in this form, in any jurisdiction, but the issues and arguments are permanent ones.

The profit calculation is divided into two stages. The first stage is to arrive at the current cost operating profit. This is calculated by starting from the historical cost profit and then making three adjustments. These are the depreciation and cost of sales adjustments and the monetary working capital adjustment. All three will usually, although not universally, be debits.

The second stage is to calculate the current cost profit attributable to shareholders. This is calculated by starting from the current cost operating profit and then making the gearing adjustment. This will normally be a credit.

The methodology of the depreciation adjustment and the cost of sales adjustment will be exactly the same as for replacement cost accounting as considered earlier (see Chapter 5). The only difference is that the calculations will be based on the 'value to the business', which is usually the replacement cost, rather than on the replacement cost, which, of course, is always the replacement cost. The other two adjustments require more detailed consideration.

Monetary working capital adjustment

If profit is revenue less expenses and the HC profit is correctly calculated to include all expenses, then adjustments for cost of sales and depreciation would seem to be all that is necessary to update the reported profit figure. Incidental expenses can reasonably be assumed to be 'current' already (e.g. administrative wages, the telephone bill and so on). An alternative argument, however, points out that rising costs will, other things being equal, have an effect on working capital needs as a whole, not just on inventory. Rising costs of inputs will lead to higher cash payments and these cash payments are not replaced in cash terms until the debtors resulting from the eventual sale actually pay. Therefore, the amount of cash the firm needs to finance from its own resources is increased because of the rise in the replacement cost of the inputs. Rising costs therefore lead to an increased burden because of rising debtors. Conversely, creditors will tend to protect the business to some extent because the business will lag behind current prices in its rate of payment.

For example, if inventory costing €100 is bought and not paid for and then inventory costing €110 is bought and not paid for, but the first inventory is now paid for, then the business has not, at this point, had to pay any extra money because of the rise in cost levels. The amount of extra finance needed to support the level of activity has arguably not increased. Therefore the unfavourable inventory (cost of sales) adjustment of €10 can be offset by a favourable monetary working capital adjustment (MWCA) of €10.

There are several problems arising from this idea:

1 How do we determine which monetary items are part of monetary *working* capital? It should include trade creditors, trade debtors, cash floats necessary in operating the business, any items of inventory not included in the cost of sales adjustment (COSA) and any part of bank balances or overdrafts relating to fluctuations in inventory, debtors or creditors. It should not include loans, idle money or any 'non-operating' items. In practice, this obviously leads to difficult distinctions.

2 Which index should be used? It is usually argued that a specific cost index is often used as for the COSA. However, it could be argued that a selling price index should be used – if selling price goes up 15% and input costs go up 10% then the money tied up in debtors, the money the firm would have already had if debtors had paid immediately, has gone up by 15% not 10%. Alternatively, it could be suggested that a general index should be used on the grounds that money is by definition available for any purpose and anything other than a general index makes unjustified assumptions about intentions.

3 Why regard an 'amount of money' as an expense? The MWCA does not reduce profit by the cost of the extra finance. It reduces profit by the *amount* of the extra finance. It could therefore be suggested that it confuses expenses with increases in necessary

investment. This, of course, brings us back to the capital maintenance concept of operating capability.

MWCA is a difficult concept and opinions differ as to its desirability. Both elements of this statement are even more true of the gearing adjustment.

Gearing adjustment

In essence, the argument for a gearing adjustment can be stated very simply. The depreciation and COSAs and the MWCA if present, have, by definition, related to the business as a whole. The depreciation entries relate to all the fixed assets, and so on. This is obviously necessary, as the whole point of the operation is to maintain the operating capability (of the business as a whole). But for the gearing adjustment we take a different standpoint.

We consider how the total assets of the business (regarding net working capital as 'an asset' for this purpose) have been financed. The assets have generally been financed from two sources:

1 shareholders equity – capital and reserves of all kinds
2 loans and borrowings from non-shareholders.

So, we have adjusted (generally reduced) profit by a series of adjustments that relate to all the assets. But we are reporting primarily to shareholders and, therefore, what we *should* be doing is adjusting profit by adjustments that relate to those assets financed by the shareholders. Therefore we have over-adjusted and we need to 'add a bit back again' – to adjust the adjustments, in fact!

To calculate the gearing adjustment the basic procedure is as follows:

1 Add the adjustments made in arriving at current cost operating profit.
2 Calculate the gearing proportion. The gearing proportion is the relationship between the average net borrowing (L) and the average total capital employed figure (the ordinary shareholders' equity $S + L$), i.e.:

$$\text{Gearing proportion} = \frac{L}{L + S}$$

3 Multiply the total arrived at in **1** by the proportion arrived at in **2**.

This procedure arrives at the gearing adjustment, which then reduces the effect of the 'operating' adjustments. In the general case where the operating adjustments reduce profit (i.e. are debits) the gearing adjustment will be a credit. Using the terminology of SSAP 16, we have:

HC profit		X
less Depreciation adjustment	X	
COSA	X	
MWCA	X̲	
	X	
CC operating profit		X
plus Gearing adjustment		X̲
CC profit attributable to shareholders		X̲

The double-entry for these adjustments goes into the revaluation reserve, now called *current* cost *reserve*, on the balance sheet.

The following example shows the replacement cost (RC) solution to Chaplin, reworked to include a MWCA and a gearing adjustment. Study it carefully.

Example

Chaplin – SSAP 16 accounts

	€	€
HC profit		26 000
less Adjustments		
Depreciation	400	
Inventory	9 000	
MWCA	4 615	14 015
CC operating profit		11 985
add back gearing adjustment		
(not applicable to shareholders)		
$18\% \times 14\,015$		2 524
CC profit attributable to shareholders		14 509

Balance sheet

	€		€
Share capital	200 000	Assets (per RC answer)	366 340
Profit	14 509		
Holding gains	51 831		
	266 340		
Loan	50 000		
Creditors	50 000		
	366 340		366 340

		€
Holding gains	Per RC answer	49 740
	+MWCA	4 615
	less Gearing	(2 524)
		51 831

Notes

1 *Calculation of MWCA.*

	Actual		Mid year €
Opening MWC	$0 \times \dfrac{115}{100}$	$=$	0
Closing MWC	$40\,000 \times \dfrac{115}{130}$	$=$	35 385
Increase	40 000		35 385

This mid-year increase is the 'real' increase, therefore the 'price effect' increase must be $40\,000 - 35\,385 = €4615$.

2 *Calculation of gearing adjustment.*

Closing capital, on a current cost basis, equals closing assets on a current cost basis less closing liabilities:

$$\begin{array}{ll} 366\,340 & \text{(as RC solution)} \\ \underline{-\,100\,000} & (50\,000+50\,000) \\ €266\,340 & \end{array}$$

Opening capital $=€200\,000$

$$\text{Average capital} = \frac{200\,000 + 266\,340}{2} = €233\,170$$

$$\text{Gearing proportion} = \frac{50\,000}{50\,000 + 233\,170} = 18\%$$

The idea of the gearing adjustment is difficult and controversial. If we look at the business as a whole, as an entity in itself, then a gearing adjustment seems unnecessary. This is known as the 'entity view'. In order to maintain the operating capability and assuming that the assumptions made in calculating value to the business adjustments are valid, *all* the appropriate operating adjustments must be made to HC profit. Gains on borrowing are not represented by cash inflows to the business and they are not available for distribution as dividends without reducing the business's 'well-offness'.

This means that the 'CC profit attributable to shareholders' does *not* generally show the amount that can be paid out as dividends without reducing the operating capacity of the business. This maximum amount of dividend that can be paid out without defeating the stated capital maintenance concept of operating capacity is given by the CC operating profit.

Alternatively, we can take what is known as the 'proprietary view'. This suggests that we should look at the company through the eyes of the shareholders; we should look at the business as it affects the shareholders and not as an entity in itself. This would seem to support the idea of a gearing adjustment. It is additionally argued by supporters of this viewpoint that the business, although admittedly unable to distribute the gearing adjustment from its own resources, can always borrow the additional cash necessary for this distribution without increasing (worsening) the gearing proportion. This argument is technically correct, but the relevance of a *financing* argument to a *profit* calculation is not universally accepted. A second major problem is that the gearing adjustment as illustrated here is closely related to the operating adjustments and the logic of this can be criticized. First, it can be criticized as being too conservative. Consider the treatment of the plant and equipment in the Chaplin CC accounts (p. 114). The CC reserve has been increased by €4 000, the debit being to the balance sheet. Arising from this, €400 has been deducted from profit as depreciation adjustment, the credit being to the balance sheet. This €400 adjustment is usually regarded as realized. Our gearing adjustment has increased profit attributable to shareholders by the gearing proportion of the (realized) depreciation adjustment, i.e. by 18% of the €400. But the total gain is €4 000. Since 18% of this 4 000 can clearly be deemed to be financed by borrowing, why not increase profit attributable to shareholders by 18% of the whole €4 000? Certainly it cannot be argued as being realized, but remember that even 'realized' gains are not necessarily distributable anyway.

Additionally, remember that what the gearing adjustment does is to 'do something about monetary items'. We have argued earlier that gains or losses on monetary items are perhaps best measured in terms of purchasing power – the fall in the value of money. This implies the use of a *general* index and that any gearing adjustment must be calculated completely independently of the operating adjustments. If we are focusing our attention on the assets, which are financed by borrowing, perhaps a specific asset index is suggested. If we are focusing our attention on the borrowings of the business and on opportunity costs and future effects, perhaps a general index is indicated.

Summary

In this chapter we have explored the concept of general inflation and current purchasing power adjustments and seen how the figures are calculated. Finally, we attempted to consider the meaning and usefulness of the resulting accounts and statements and to explore some national and practical developments.

EXERCISES	(✔ indicates answers are available on pages 721–724)

✔ 1 What do CPP adjustments do and how do they do it?

2 Are general indices more or less useful in financial reporting than specific price changes?

3 Look at the figure of €240 000 for capital shown in the Chaplin CPP example on p. 103 and think about it carefully. What does it mean?

4 To what extent do current purchasing power adjustments to historical cost figures lead to up-to-date valuations in a balance sheet?

5 Current purchasing power adjustments are simple to apply, but hard to explain and interpret. Discuss.

6 From the following historic cost accounts of Page plc, prepare a set of CPP accounts for the year-ended 31.12.8.

			31.12.7			31.12.8
			€000			€000
Fixed assets						
Cost (purchased 1.1.5)			500			500
less depreciation			300			400
			200			100
Current assets						
Inventory (purchased 31.10)	100			150		
Debtors	200			300		
Bank	150			350		
	450			800		
less Current liabilities	300			400		
			150			400
			350			500
Share capital			100			100
Reserves			250			400
			350			500

Profit and loss account for the year-ended 31 December year 8:

		€000
Sales		1850
Cost of goods sold		
opening inventory	100	
purchases	1350	
	1450	
less closing inventory	150	
		1300
		550
Gross profit		
Expenses	300	
Depreciation	100	
		400
Net profit		150

The movement on the retail price index has been as follows:

1 January year 5	180
1 January year 7	200
Average for year 7	210
31 October year 7	215
31 December year 7	220
Average for year 8	230
31 October year 8	235
31 December year 8	240

Assume all sales, purchases and expenses accrue evenly throughout the year.

✔ 7 From the following information produce a set of current cost accounts as per SSAP 16. Calgary plc had the following historic cost profit and loss account for the year-ended 30 June:

		Year 4
		€000
Sales		7000
Profit before interest and taxation		1560
Interest	140	
Taxation	300	
		440
Profit attributable to shareholders		1120
Dividends		300
Retained profit for the year		820
Balance brought forward		1420
Balance carried forward		2240

Balance sheet as at 30 June:

	Year 3	Year 4
	€000	€000
Fixed assets		
Land at cost	1500	1500
(purchased 1 July year 2)		

Plant and machinery at cost (purchased 1 July year 2)		1200	1200
Less depreciation		(240)	(480)
		2460	2220
Current assets			
Inventory (purchased 30 April)	650		900
Debtors	830		1300
Bank	10		620
	1490		2820
Less Current liabilities			
Creditors	790		1060
		700	1760
		3160	3980
Share capital		1040	1040
Profit and loss		1420	2240
		2460	3280
Loan capital		700	700
		3160	3980

The following index numbers are applicable.

	RPI	Land	Inventory	Plant and machinery
1 July year 2	120	213	412	610
30 April year 3	125	232	423	639
30 June year 3	131	241	431	649
31 December year 3	139	263	442	661
30 April year 4	148	278	456	678
30 June year 4	158	289	462	691

8 You are the management accountant of a manufacturing company where production is capital-intensive using machinery that is estimated to have a five-year life. The present machinery is now approximately three years old. Whilst raw material stocks have a low turnover due to supply problems, finished goods are turned over rapidly and there is minimal work-in-progress at any one time. The technology incorporated in the means of production is thought to be stable.

In recent years, it has not been possible to increase the price of the company's outputs beyond the rate of general inflation without diminishing market share, due to keen competition in this sector. The company does not consider that it has cash-flow problems. The company is all equity financed. Although a bank overdraft is a permanent feature of the balance sheet this is primarily due to customers being given a 60-day credit period, whilst most suppliers are paid within 30 days. There is always a positive balance of short-term monetary assets.

In the previous financial year, net profit after taxation on a strict historic cost basis was considered very healthy, and the directors felt that they could prudently distribute a major portion of this by way of dividend. The directors are considering whether, and if so how, to reflect price-level changes in their financial statements. They are concerned that this would affect their profit figure and therefore the amount they could distribute as dividend.

The following price-level changes have been brought to the attention of the directors:

	Retail price index	Index for company's machinery	Raw materials stock index
3 years previously	100	100	100
2 years previously	104	116	102
1 year previously	107	125	108
Present	112	140	120

You are required to prepare a report for your directors setting out in general terms how to explain to the shareholders the likely impact on the historic cost profit of possible methods of accounting for price-level changes.

(CIMA – adapted)

Accounting theory and conceptual frameworks

After studying this chapter you should be able to:
☐ explain what accounting theory is
☐ describe the main attempts at constructing an accounting theory
☐ appraise current developments in the area
☐ describe and discuss the contents of the IASB Framework
☐ appraise the quality and usefulness of the IASB Framework in the context of its self-declared purposes
☐ describe and discuss the parts of IAS 1 relating to accounting concepts and policies
☐ appraise the overall effect of the Framework and comparable parts of IAS 1.

Introduction

This chapter is about to deal with something that many people believe does not exist – a single generally accepted accounting theory. There is no generally accepted accounting theory at this time even though many attempts have been made to formulate one. According to Eldon S. Hendriksen in *Accounting Theory* (1977):

> Theory as it applies to accounting is the coherent set of hypothetical, conceptual and pragmatic principles forming the general frame of reference for a field of inquiry. Thus accounting theory may be defined as logical reasoning in the form of a set of broad principles that
>
> 1 Provide a general frame of reference by which accounting practices can be evaluated and
> 2 Guide the development of new practices and procedures.
>
> Accounting theory may also be used to explain existing practices to obtain a better understanding of them. But the most important goal of accounting theory should be to provide a coherent set of logical principles that form the general frame of reference for the evaluation and development of sound accounting practices.

Let us compare this with what many believe is the accounting framework, the IASC Framework for the Preparation and Presentation of Financial Statements. This Framework purports to:

1 assist the board of IASC in the development of standards and review of existing standards
2 provide a basis for reducing the number of permitted alternative accounting treatments
3 assist preparers in dealing with topics that have yet to form the subject of a standard.

This certainly sounds like an accounting theory. But if it is, then this theory would clearly determine how we should provide information to users and different practices would not prevail. The primary purpose of an accounting theory should be to provide a basis for the prediction and explanation of accounting behaviour and events.

Is an accounting theory possible?

According to both Hendriksen (1977) and McDonald (1972) the development of an accounting theory should be possible. McDonald argues that a theory must have three elements:

1 encoding of phenomena to symbolic representation
2 manipulation or combination according to rules
3 translation back to real-world phenomena.

Activity 8.1

Do the three elements that McDonald states are necessary for a theory exist in accounting?

Activity feedback

The first obviously exists as we have the symbols of 'debits and credits' and we have also developed accounting terminology e.g. depreciation, accruals, matching, current cost, revaluation etc. all unique to accounting.

The second also exists as we have a wealth of rules and regulations for manipulating or combining these debits and credits.

Translation is evidenced in how we present these debits and credits to users in the form of financial reports.

Approaches to the formulation of accounting theory

If it *is* possible to develop an accounting theory (Hendriksen and McDonald), how do we approach its development? Research in this area has centred on traditional approaches, regulatory approaches and what have come to be regarded as new approaches. We will look briefly at each type.

Traditional approaches

Traditional approaches cover:

- non-theoretical
- theoretical.

Non-theoretical approaches to accounting theory are concerned with developing a theory or accounting techniques and principles that will be useful to users, particularly decision makers. This approach can be developed in a pragmatic or authoritarian way. In essence, this is the approach the accounting profession has used in the past to develop an accounting theory and it is fairly apparent it has not been able to resolve conflict in accounting practices or principles. Theoretical approaches to the development of an accounting theory are many but Belkaoui, in his text *Accounting Theory*, categorizes these as:

- deductive
- inductive
- ethical
- sociological
- economic
- eclectic.

Deductive approach

This approach involves developing a theory from basic propositions, premises and assumptions that results in accounting principles that are logical conclusions about the subject. The theory is tested by determining whether its results are acceptable in practice. Edwards and Bell (1961) are deductive theorists (Chapter 4) and historical cost accounting was also derived from a deductive approach.

Inductive approach

For this approach we start with observed phenomena and move towards generalized conclusions. The approach requires empirical testing, i.e. the theory must be supported by sufficient instances/observations that support the derived conclusions. Quite often the deductive and inductive approaches are mixed as researchers use their knowledge of accounting practices. As Belkaoui states: General propositions are formulated through an inductive process, but the principles and techniques are derived by a deductive approach. He also observes that when an inductive theorist, Littleton (1953), collaborates with a deductive theorist, Paton (1922), a hybrid results showing compromise between the two approaches.

Ethical approach

Activity 8.2

Identify concepts that could be at the core of the ethical approach to an accounting theory.

Activity feedback

Basically, this approach consists of the concepts of 'true and fair'. These concepts have, of course, been taken on board by the EU in the Fourth Directive.

Writers/researchers in this area are D. R. Scott (1941) and Yu (1976).

Sociological approach

This is actually an ethical approach that centres on social welfare. In other words, accounting principles and techniques are evaluated for acceptance after considering all effects on all groups in society. Thus within this approach we would need to be able to account for a business entity's effect on its social environment. We consider this type of reporting in Chapter 10.

Economic approach

This approach focuses on general economic welfare. Thus accounting principles and techniques are evaluated for acceptance depending on their impact on the national economy. Sweden, in its national GAAP, uses an economic approach to its development. The IASB in developing its standards does tend to take an economic approach into account. For example, the current discussion on accounting for leases focuses on the effect that a standard requiring the capitalization of all leases, whether finance or operating, might have on the economy or business in general. Traditionally, accounting standards have been set without considering economic consequences but lobby pressures from groups who perceive themselves as being affected can be strong.

Eclectic approach

This is perhaps our current approach where we have a combination of all the approaches already identified appearing in our accounting theory. This approach has come about more by accident than as a deliberate attempt, due to the interference in the development of accounting theory by professionals, governmental bodies (including the EU) and individuals. This eclectic approach has also led to the development of new approaches to accounting theory.

Regulatory approaches

Many would regard this as the approach we currently have to accounting theory. They hold this view because to them it does not appear that standards, even those of the IASB, are based on broad, relevant theories but are developed as solutions to current conflicts that emerge in our attempts to provide useful information to users. Indeed, they might argue that new standards are only developed when a particular user complains about misinformation or non-information. But there are questions to consider if we do adopt this approach to the development of accounting theory. In the main these questions centre on whether we should adopt a freemarket approach to the regulation, a private sector regulatory approach or public sector regulatory approach.

This regulatory approach is also one that tends to identify solutions to difficulties that have occurred in our reporting rather than providing us with a theory that anticipates the issues.

New approaches

These attempt to use both conceptual and empirical reasoning to formulate and verify an accounting framework (Belkaoui, *Accounting Theory*, Chapter 10). The approaches are:

- events
- behavioural
- human information processing
- predictive
- positive.

Events approach

The events approach was developed in 1969 by George Sorter and was defined as 'providing information about relevant economic events that might be useful in a variety of decision models'. The events approach leaves the user to aggregate and assign weights and values to the event. The accountant would only provide information on the economic event to the user, he would not assume a decision model. Thus, for example, the event approach income statement would not indicate financial performance in a period but would communicate events that occurred during the period without any attempt to determine a bottom line.

Activity 8.3

Identify advantages and disadvantages of the events approach to the development of an accounting theory.

Activity feedback

1 Research has shown that structured/aggregate reports are preferable for high-analytic decision makers but not for low-analytic decision makers. Thus, the success of the events approach is dependent on the analytical skills of the user.
2 Users, in attempting to evaluate all information provided, may reach 'information overload'.
3 No criteria have yet been developed for the choice of events to be reported.
4 It will probably prove difficult to measure all characteristics of an event.

Behavioural approach

The behavioural approach attempts to take into account human behaviour as it relates to decision making in accounting. Devine (1960) stated the following:

> On balance it seems fair to conclude that accountants seem to have waded through their relationships to the intricate psychological network of human activity with a heavy handed crudity that is beyond belief. Some degree of crudity may be excused in a new discipline, but failure to recognise that much of what passes as accounting theory is hopelessly entwined with unsupported behaviour assumptions is unforgiveable.

This to us seems fair comment. Given that financial reporting is about communicating information to users to enable them to make decisions, a lack of consideration of how that information influences their behaviour is indeed unforgivable. Studies in this area have tended to concentrate on:

- the adequacy of disclosure
- usefulness of financial statement data
- attitudes about corporate reporting practices
- materiality judgements
- decision effects of alternative accounting practices.

In one of these areas, materiality, it was discovered that users' assessment of materiality was individualistic and that the provider of the information was not in the best position to determine materiality for a user. There is much work still to do within the behavioural approach.

Human information processing approach

This is similar to a behavioural approach in that it focuses on how users interpret and use the information provided.

Predictive approach

This approach attempts to formulate an accounting theory by focusing on the predictive nature/ability of a particular method of reporting an event that would be of use to the user. Such approaches are most prevalent in what could be regarded as management accounting. Efficient market hypothesis, Beta models, chaos theory are all examples of this approach.

Positive approach

This can be best explained by quoting Jensen (1976), who called for the:

> development of a positive theory of accounting which will explain why accounting is what it is, why accountants do what they do, and what effects these phenomena have on people and resource utilisation.

The approach is based on the proposition that managers, shareholders and regulators are rational and that they attempt to maximize their utility. The theory became known as 'the Rochester school of accounting'. The positive approach is completely opposite to the normative approach and attempts to explain why accounting procedures and policies are as they are, whereas the normative approach attempts to prescribe the accounting procedures and policies to be implemented.

The future of theory

This section has been very brief and has mainly merely listed the approaches to the development of an accounting theory that exist in the current literature. For an in-depth study of this area we recommend *Accounting Theory* by Belkaoui.

This does, however, leave us with several questions:

- Can we develop an all-encompassing accounting theory?
- Would such a theory be useful to users?

- Should any theory be global in aspect and take into account behavioural aspects?
- Do researchers need to take into account their own underlying cultural beliefs and behaviour when developing an accounting theory?

As Glen Lehman states in *Accounting Forum* (2001) in his editorial:

> Accounting might benefit by exploring its direction and future. Accounting must improve 'community usefulness' and not just simply expand into other fields such as information technology if it is to remain committed to the public interest. The technology of accounting might benefit through consideration of the relationships between regulation and construction of community virtues. Accountants have been criticised for assuming that if the 'figures' are constructed in line with current mandatory and legislative requirements, then the accounts are true and fair. Yet what is reported often bears little relation to a reasonable view of the true financial health of the enterprise. Future accounting research might work toward explaining the means through which corporations might be enabled to act in the interests of the communities they serve.

This statement is particularly pertinent given the Enron and Worldcom disasters in the USA.

The IASB conceptual framework

We have already outlined some of the fundamental general concepts of accounting in Chapter 1. We quickly noted that they are not always compatible between themselves and that they do not necessarily provide a prescriptive solution to a given problem. They do not, therefore, provide a rational coherent basis, which can be applied, in a scientific sense, to solve problems in ways which are likely to be themselves consistent and compatible. They are not true 'theories' in the sense discussed earlier.

A number of attempts have been made since the 1970s to create some form of more coherent conceptual framework. The IASB version, known as the Framework for the Preparation and Presentation of Financial Statements, was issued in 1989. It belongs to the family of conceptual frameworks for financial reporting that have been developed by accounting standard setters in a number of countries where accounting standard setting is carried out by a private sector body. On one level, such conceptual frameworks may be considered attempts to assemble a body of accounting theory (or interrelated concepts) as a guide to standard setting, so that standards are (as far as possible) formulated on a consistent basis and not in an ad hoc manner. On another, but complementary, level, they may be thought of as devices to confer legitimacy and authority on a private sector standard setter that lacks the legal authority of a public body. The IASB, as a private sector standard setter, shares these reasons for developing a conceptual framework.

Conceptual frameworks developed by accounting standard setters are essentially based on identification of 'good practice' from which principles are derived inductively. The criteria for identifying 'good practice' are related to the assumed objectives of financial reporting. At the same time, attention is paid to conceptual coherence, and the development process typically involves 'conceptual tidying up'. Conceptual frameworks may be written in a prescriptive style or a descriptive style, or a mixture of the

↓ make rule.

two. In any event, they are essentially *normative*, since they seek to provide a set of principles as a guide to setting and interpreting accounting standards. Such guidance, however, does not necessarily preclude a standard being issued that, for compelling pragmatic reasons, departs from a principle set out in the applicable conceptual framework.

The IASB's Framework is written in a descriptive style (in fact, it is IASB policy to use the word 'should' only in Standards) and seeks to avoid being excessively prescriptive. One principal reason for this is that it needs to have broad international applicability. In the final paragraph of the Framework, the IASB states:

> This Framework is applicable to a range of accounting models and provides guidance on preparing and presenting the financial statements constructed under the chosen model. At the present time [1989], it is not the intention of the Board of IASB to prescribe a particular model other than in exceptional circumstances, such as ... a hyperinflationary economy.

The Framework was intended to be separate from the IASs and to avoid binding the IASB to particular accounting treatments in IASs. It was approved and issued in April 1989 and has not been revised since that time, although the need to update it is now clearly recognized by the new board.

However, the Framework has been quite influential in the recent development of IASs and in major revisions. For example, its definitions (and especially those of assets and liabilities) were highly influential in the preparation of IAS 22, *Business Combinations*; IAS 37, *Provisions, Contingent Liabilities and Contingent Assets*; IAS 38, *Intangible Assets* and IAS 39, *Financial Instruments: Recognition and Measurement*.

The Framework is not an IAS and does not override any specific IAS; in case of conflict between it and an IAS, the requirements of the latter prevail. *One may, however, consider the Framework as embodying IAS GAAP in respect of issues that are not dealt with in any IAS.* This is apparent from the way in which the purpose and status of the Framework are described (see points 4 and 5 in the following list). For example, in the case of topics that have not yet been the subject of an IAS, the purpose of the Framework is to assist preparers in dealing with such topics. Moreover, the IASB will be guided by the Framework in the development of future IASs and in reviewing existing ones, so that the number of cases of conflict between the Framework and IASs are likely to diminish over time. The Framework itself will be subject to revision in the light of experience. A revision can be expected over the next few years as part of the new board's development programme.

The IASB Framework

As indicated earlier, the Framework does not have the status of an IAS, does not override any specific IAS and, in case of conflict between the Framework and an IAS, the latter prevails (paras 2–3). The purpose of the Framework is stated as follows (para. 1):

1. To assist the Board of IASC in the development of future IASs and in its review of existing IASs;
2. To assist the Board of IASC in promoting harmonization of regulations, accounting standards and procedures relating to the presentation of

financial statements by providing a basis for reducing the number of alternative accounting treatments permitted by IASs;

3 To assist national standard-setting bodies in developing national standards;

4 To assist preparers of financial statements in applying IASs and in dealing with topics that have yet to form the subject of an IAS;

5 To assist auditors in forming an opinion as to whether financial statements conform with IASs;

6 To assist users of financial statements in interpreting the information contained in financial statements prepared in conformity with IASs;

7 To provide those who are interested in the work of the IASC with information about its approach to the formulation of accounting standards.

The overall scope of the document covers:

1 objectives of financial statements
2 qualitative characteristics that determine the usefulness of financial statement information
3 definition, recognition and measurement of financial statement elements
4 concepts of capital and capital maintenance.

The Framework is concerned with 'general purpose financial statements', including consolidated financial statements. These are described as being prepared and presented at least annually and being directed toward the common information needs of a range of users. They do not include special purpose reports such as prospectuses and tax computations (para. 6).

The Framework applies to the financial statements of all commercial, industrial and business reporting enterprises, whether in the private or public sectors (para. 8).

The Framework first of all outlines the users of accounting information in a manner broadly similar to our discussion in Chapter 1:

- *Investors*. The providers of risk capital and their advisers are concerned with the risk inherent in and return provided by, their investments. They need information to help them determine whether they should buy, hold or sell. Shareholders are also interested in information which enables them to assess the ability of the enterprise to pay dividends.

- *Employees*. Employees and their representative groups are interested in information about the stability and profitability of their employers. They are also interested in information which enables them to assess the ability of the enterprise to provide remuneration, retirement benefits and employment opportunities.

- *Lenders*. Lenders are interested in information that enables them to determine whether their loans, and the interest attaching to them, will be paid when due.

- *Suppliers and other trade creditors*. Suppliers and other creditors are interested in information that enables them to determine whether amounts owing to them will be paid when due. Trade creditors are likely to be interested in an enterprise over a shorter period than lenders unless they are dependent on the continuation of the enterprise as a major customer.

- *Customers*. Customers have an interest in information about the continuance of an enterprise, especially when they have a long-term involvement with, or are dependent on, the enterprise.

■ *Governments and their agencies.* Governments and their agencies are interested in the allocation of resources and, therefore, the activities of enterprises. They also require information in order to regulate the activities of enterprises, determine taxation policies and as the basis for national income and similar statistics.

■ *Public.* Enterprises affect members of the public in a variety of ways. For example, enterprises may make a substantial contribution to the local economy in many ways including the number of people they employ and their patronage of local suppliers. Financial statements may assist the public by providing information about the trends and recent developments in the prosperity of the enterprise and the range of its activities.

Para. 10 states the following:

> While all of the information needs of these users cannot be met by financial statements, there are needs which are common to all users. As investors are providers of risk capital to the enterprise, the provision of financial statements that meet their needs will also meet most of the needs of other users that financial statements can satisfy.

Activity 8.4

Does the last sentence of para. 10 follow logically?

Activity feedback

As a matter of *logic*, the answer is definitely not. The suggestion that *because* investors are providers of risk capital, information meeting the needs of investors will also meet most of the needs of, say, employees is clearly nonsense. Nevertheless, as an empirical pragmatic issue, the emphasis on investors, or at least an emphasis on providers of finance generally, may have some validity. Either way it is widely accepted in practice.

The Framework then goes on to summarize the overall objectives of financial statements. This is pretty standard stuff and can be briefly extracted here:

12 The objective of financial statements is to provide information about the financial position, performance and changes in financial position of an enterprise that is useful to a wide range of users in making economic decisions.

13 Financial statements prepared for this purpose meet the common needs of most users. However, financial statements do not provide all the information that users may need to make economic decisions since they largely portray the financial effects of past events and do not necessarily provide non-financial information.

15 The economic decisions that are taken by users of financial statements require an evaluation of the ability of an enterprise to generate cash and cash equivalents and of the timing and certainty of their generation. This ability ultimately determines, for example, the capacity of an enterprise to pay its employees and suppliers, meet interest payments, repay loans and

make distributions to its owners. Users are better able to evaluate this ability to generate cash and cash equivalents if they are provided with information that focuses on the financial position, performance and changes in financial position of an enterprise.

19 Information about financial position is primarily provided in a balance sheet. Information about performance is primarily provided in an income statement. Information about changes in financial position is provided in the financial statements by means of a separate statement.

20 The component parts of the financial statements interrelate because they reflect different aspects of the same transactions or other events. Although each statement provides information that is different from the others, none is likely to serve only a single purpose or provide all the information necessary for particular needs of users. For example, an income statement provides an incomplete picture of performance unless it is used in conjunction with the balance sheet and the statement of changes in financial position.

Next the Framework discusses the various 'assumptions and characteristics' of accounting statements. These correspond closely to the conventions and characteristics of Chapter 1, but they are arranged in a series of subgroups with various headings and subheadings, which give interesting nuances of degrees of relative significance and importance. In order to give the full flavour of this the Framework is quoted here at some length.

Underlying assumptions

Accrual basis

22 In order to meet their objectives, financial statements are prepared on the accrual basis of accounting. Under this basis, the effects of transactions and other events are recognized when they occur (and not as cash or its equivalent is received or paid) and they are recorded in the accounting records and reported in the financial statements of the periods to which they relate. Financial statements prepared on the accrual basis inform users not only of past transactions involving the payment and receipt of cash but also of obligations to pay cash in the future and of resources that represent cash to be received in the future. Hence, they provide the type of information about past transactions and other events that is most useful to users in making economic decisions.

Going concern

23 The financial statements are normally prepared on the assumption that an enterprise is a going concern and will continue in operation for the foreseeable future. Hence it is assumed that the enterprise has neither the intention nor the need to liquidate or curtail materially the scale of its operations; if such an intention or need exists, the financial statement may have to be prepared on a different basis and, if so, the basis used is disclosed.

Qualitative characteristics of financial statements

24 Qualitative characteristics are the attributes that make the information provided in financial statements useful to users. The four principal qualitative characteristics are understandability, relevance, reliability and comparability.

Understandability

25 An essential quality of the information provided in financial statements is that is it readily understandable by users. For this purpose, users are assumed to have a reasonable knowledge of business and economic activities and accounting and a willingness to study the information with reasonable diligence. However, information about complex matters that should be included in the financial statements because of its relevance to the economic decision-making needs of users should not be excluded merely on the grounds that it may be too difficult for certain users to understand.

Relevance

26 To be useful, information must be relevant to the decision-making needs of users. Information has the quality of relevance when it influences the economic decisions of users by helping them to evaluate past, present or future events or confirming, or correcting, their past evaluations.

27 The predictive and confirmatory roles of information are interrelated. For example, information about the current level and structure of asset holdings has value to users when they endeavour to predict the ability of the enterprise to take advantage of opportunities and its ability to react to adverse situations. The same information plays a confirmatory role in respect of past predictions about, for example, the way in which the enterprise would be structured or the outcome of planned operations.

28 Information about financial position and past performance is frequently used as the basis for predicting future financial position and performance and other matters in which users are directly interested, such as dividend and wage payments, security price movements and the ability of the enterprise to meet its commitments as they fall due. To have predictive value, information need not be in the form of an explicit forecast. The ability to make predictions from financial statements is enhanced, however, by the manner in which information on past transactions and events is displayed. For example, the predictive value of the income statement is enhanced if unusual, abnormal and infrequent items of income or expense are separately disclosed.

Materiality

29 The relevance of information is affected by its nature and materiality. In some cases, the nature of information alone is sufficient to determine its relevance. For example, the reporting of a new segment may affect the assessment of the risks and opportunities facing the enterprise irrespective of the materiality of the results achieved by the new segment in the

reporting period. In other cases, both the nature and materiality are important, for example, the amounts of inventories held in each of the main categories that are appropriate to the business.

30 Information is material if its omission or misstatement could influence the economic decisions of users taken on the basis of the financial statements. Materiality depends on the size of the item or error judged in the particular circumstances of its omission or misstatement. Thus, materiality provides a threshold or cut-off point rather than being a primary qualitative characteristic which information must have if it is to be useful.

Reliability

31 To be useful, information must also be reliable. Information has the quality of reliability when it is free from material error and bias and can be depended on by users to represent faithfully that which it either purports to represent or could reasonably be expected to represent.

32 Information may be relevant but so unreliable in nature or representation that its recognition may be potentially misleading. For example, if the validity and amount of a claim for damages under a legal action are disputed, it may be inappropriate for the enterprise to recognize the full amount of the claim in the balance sheet, although it may be appropriate to disclose the amount and circumstances of the claim.

Faithful representation

33 To be reliable, information must represent faithfully the transactions and other events it either purports to represent or could reasonable be expected to represent. Thus, for example, a balance sheet should represent faithfully the transactions and other events that result in assets, liabilities and equity of the enterprise at the reporting date which meet the recognition criteria.

34 Most financial information is subject to some risk of being less than a faithful representation of that which it purports to portray. This is not due to bias, but rather to inherent difficulties either in identifying the transactions and other events to be measured or in devising and applying measurement and presentation techniques that can convey messages that correspond with those transactions and events. In certain cases, the measurement of the financial effects of items could be so uncertain that enterprises generally would not recognize them in the financial statements; for example, although most enterprises generate goodwill internally over time, it is usually difficult to identify or measure that goodwill reliably. In other cases, however, it may be relevant to recognize items and to disclose the risk of error surrounding their recognition and measurement.

Substance over form

35 If information is to represent faithfully transactions and other events that it purports to represent, it is necessary that they are accounted for and presented in accordance with their substance and economic reality and not merely their legal form. The substances of transactions or other events is not always consistent with that which is apparent from their legal or

contrived form. For example, an enterprise may dispose of an asset to another party in such a way that the documentation purports to pass legal ownership to that party; nevertheless, agreements may exist that ensure that the enterprise continues to enjoy the future economic benefits embodied in the asset. In such circumstances, the reporting of a sale would not represent faithfully the transaction entered into (if indeed there was a transaction).

Neutrality

36 To be reliable, the information contained in financial statements must be neutral, that is, free from bias. Financial statements are not neutral if, by the selection or presentation of information, they influence the making of a decision or judgement in order to achieve a pre-determined result or outcome.

Prudence

37 The preparers of financial statements do, however, have to contend with the uncertainties that inevitably surround many events and circumstances, such as the collectability of doubtful receivables, the probable useful life of plant and equipment and the number of warranty claims that may occur. Such uncertainties are recognized by the disclosure of their nature and extent and by the exercise of prudence in the preparation of the financial statements. Prudence is the inclusion of a degree of caution in the exercise of the judgements needed in making the estimates required under conditions of uncertainty, such that assets or income are not overstated and liabilities or expenses are not understated. However, the exercise of prudence does not allow, for example, the creation of hidden reserves or excessive provisions, the deliberate understatement of assets or income or the deliberate overstatement of liabilities or expenses, because the financial statements would not be neutral and, therefore, not have the quality of reliability.

Completeness

38 To be reliable, the information in financial statements must be complete within the bounds of materiality and cost. An omission can cause information to be false or misleading and thus unreliable and deficient in terms of its relevance.

Comparability

39 Users must be able to compare the financial statements of an enterprise through time in order to identify trends in its financial position and performance. Users must also be able to compare the financial statements of different enterprises in order to evaluate their relative financial position, performance and changes in financial position. Hence, the measurement and display of the financial effect of like transactions and other events must be carried out in a consistent way throughout an enterprise and over time for that enterprise and in a consistent way for different enterprises.

40 An important implication of the qualitative characteristic of comparability is that users be informed of the accounting policies employed in the preparation of the financial statements, any changes in those policies and the effects of such changes. Users need to be able to identify differences between the accounting policies for like transactions and other events used by the same enterprise from period to period and by different enterprises. Compliance with International Accounting Standards, including the disclosure of the accounting policies used by the enterprise, helps to achieve comparability.

41 The need for comparability should not be confused with mere uniformity and should not be allowed to become an impediment to the introduction of improved accounting standards. It is not appropriate for an enterprise to continue accounting in the same manner for a transaction or other event if the policy adopted is not in keeping with the qualitative characteristics of relevance and reliability. It is also inappropriate for an enterprise to leave its accounting policies unchanged when more relevant and reliable alternatives exist.

42 Because users wish to compare the financial position, performance and changes in financial position of an enterprise over time, it is important that the financial statements show corresponding information for the preceding periods.

Constraints on relevant and reliable information

Timeliness

43 If there is undue delay in the reporting of information it may lose its relevance. Management may need to balance the relative merits of timely reporting and the provision of reliable information. To provide information in a timely basis it may often be necessary to report before all aspects of a transaction or other event are known, thus impairing reliability. Conversely, if reporting is delayed until all aspects are known, the information may be highly reliable but of little use to users who have had to make decisions in the interim. In achieving a balance between relevance and reliability, the overriding consideration is how best to satisfy the economic decision-making needs of users.

Balance between benefit and cost

44 The balance between benefit and cost is a pervasive constraint rather than a qualitative characteristic. The benefits derived from information should exceed the cost of providing it. The evaluation of benefits and costs is, however, substantially a judgemental process. Furthermore, the costs do not necessarily fall on those users who enjoy the benefits. Benefits may also be enjoyed by users other than those for whom the information is prepared; for example, the provision of further information to lenders may reduce the borrowing costs of an enterprise. For these reasons, it is

THE IASB CONCEPTUAL FRAMEWORK

difficult to apply a cost benefit test in any particular case. Nevertheless, standard setters in particular, as well as the preparers and users of financial statements, should be aware of this constraint.

Balance between qualitative characteristics

45 In practice a balancing, or trade-off, between qualitative characteristics is often necessary. Generally the aim is to achieve an appropriate balance among the characteristics in order to meet the objective of financial statements. The relative importance of the characteristics in different cases is a matter of professional judgement.

True and fair view/fair presentation

46 Financial statements are frequently described as showing a true and fair view of, or as presenting fairly, the financial position, performance and changes in financial position of an enterprise. Although this framework does not deal directly with such concepts, the application of the principal qualitative characteristics and of appropriate accounting standards normally results in financial statements that convey what is generally understood as a true and fair view of or as presenting fairly such information.

This last paragraph concerning fair presentation has been rather overtaken by events, and is effectively superseded by IAS 1, discussed next.

It is worth emphasizing the suggested interrelationships between these various notions. There are two, and only two, *underlying assumptions*, the accrual basis and the going concern assumption. There are four *principal qualitative characteristics*, some with related sub-characteristics, as shown in Table 8.1.

There are a number of peculiarities about these suggested relationships. Not every national tradition would accept them. Note that the importance of prudence is significantly downgraded, to the lowest level. Neither is it at all obvious how prudence (which is hardly 'neutral') is necessary for 'reliability', however important one may think prudence is in itself.

Table 8.1 Assumptions and characteristics of accounting statements

Principal characteristic	Sub-characteristic
Understandability	
Relevance	Materiality
Reliability	Faithful representation
	Substance over form
	Neutrality
	Prudence
	Completeness
Comparability	

Elements of financial statements

The section of the Framework concerning the elements of financial statements (paras 47–80) consists essentially of definitions of the elements of financial statements as identified by the Framework. The definitions given in this section, and especially those of assets and liabilities, are the core of the Framework as a prescriptive basis for standard setting. The section on 'Recognition of Elements' (paras 82–98) acts to reinforce this core. In particular:

1 The Framework defines income and expenses in terms of increases and decreases in economic benefits that are equated with changes in assets and liabilities;
2 The latter are defined in terms of 'resources controlled' and 'present obligations' to exclude some of the types of items that have been recognized as assets or liabilities (accruals and deferrals) in the name of 'matching' expenses and revenues.

In other words, the definitions of assets and liability are the starting point for the entire edifice, putting the focus on balance sheet items, not on profit (revenue and expense) calculation.

The elements considered to be 'directly related to the measurement of financial position' are assets, liabilities and equity, which are defined as follows (para. 49):

1 An asset is a resource
 (a) controlled by the enterprise,
 (b) as a result of past events, and
 (c) from which future economic benefits are expected to flow to the enterprise.

Recognition as an asset thus requires that all three components of the definition, (a), (b) and (c), be satisfied.

2 A liability is
 (a) a present obligation of the enterprise,
 (b) arising out of past events,
 (c) the settlement of which is expected to result in an outflow from the enterprise of resources embodying economic benefits.

Recognition as a liability thus requires that all three components of the definition, (a), (b) and (c), be satisfied.

3 Equity is defined as the residual interest in the assets of the enterprise after deducting all its liabilities.

Merely satisfying these definitions does not entail recognition, since the recognition criteria in paras 82–98 must also be satisfied and also the principle of 'substance over form' must be respected. For example, this principle requires fixed assets held under finance leases to be recognized by the lessee as fixed assets (with corresponding leasing liabilities), while the lessor recognizes a financial asset (paras 50–51).

Balance sheets drawn up in accordance with 'current' [in 1989] IASs may include items the treatment of which does not satisfy these definitions, but the definitions will underlie 'future' reviews of existing standards and the formulation of new ones (para. 52). As noted earlier, the IASB has acted accordingly and it would be unusual to find an item whose treatment according to a recently issued IAS would conflict with the definitions.

Assets

The 'future economic benefit embodied in an asset' is defined as 'the potential to contribute, directly or indirectly, to the flow of cash and cash equivalents to the enterprise', including 'a capability to reduce cash outflows'. In case that definition should leave the status of cash itself as an asset unclear, it is stated that cash satisfies this definition, because it 'renders a service to the enterprise because of its command over other resources'. Assets embody future economic benefits that may flow to the enterprise by having one or more of the following capabilities:

- being exchanged for other assets
- being used to settle a liability
- or being distributed to the enterprise's owners.

Cash conspicuously possesses these three capabilities; as well as that of being used singly or in combination with other assets in the production of goods and services to be sold by the enterprise (paras 53–55).

Neither having physical form nor being the object of a right of ownership is an essential attribute of an asset. Intangible items such as patents and copyrights may satisfy the definition of an asset, as may a fixed asset held under a finance lease (by virtue of which it is a resource controlled though not owned by the enterprise and from which future benefits are expected to flow). Moreover, knowledge obtained from development activity may meet the definition of an asset (capitalized development costs) even though neither physical form nor legal ownership is involved, provided there is de facto control such that, by keeping the knowledge secret, the enterprise controls the benefits that are expected to flow from it (paras 56–57).

Assets may result from various types of past transactions and other past events. Normally, these are purchase transactions and the events associated with production, but they may include donation (for example, by way of a government grant) or discovery (as in the case of mineral deposits). Expected future transactions or events do not give rise to assets; for example, a binding contract by an enterprise to purchase inventory does not cause the inventory in question to meet the definition of an asset of that enterprise until the purchase transaction that fulfils the contract has occurred. While expenditure is a common way to acquire or generate an asset, expenditure undertaken with a view to generating future economic benefits may fail to result in an asset, for example, if the intended economic benefits cannot be expected or are not controlled by the enterprise (paras 58–59).

Activity 8.5

Consider whether each of the following are assets, giving reasons for your answers.

1 A heap of rusty metal worth €10 as scrap but costing €20 to transport to the scrap dealer.

2 A municipal or trades union social or welfare centre outside the factory that substantially improves the overall working conditions of a firm's employees.

3 The benefits derived from next year's sales.

Activity feedback

None of these is an asset because:

1 has no probable future benefit

2 is not possessed or controlled by the business

3 contains no earlier transaction or event.

Assets are always divided into *fixed assets* and *current assets*. The definition of fixed assets is often misunderstood. A fixed asset is not an asset with a long life. The essential criterion is the *intention* of the owner, the intended *use* of the asset. A fixed asset is an asset that the firm intends to *use* within the business, over an extended period, in order to assist its daily operating activities. A current asset, by way of contrast, is usually defined in terms of time. A current asset is an asset likely to change its form, i.e. likely to undergo some transaction, usually within 12 months. Consider two firms, *A* and *B*. Firm *A* is a motor trader. It possesses some motor vehicles that it is attempting to sell, and it also possesses some desks used by the sales staff, management and so on. Firm *B* is a furniture dealer. It possesses some desks that it is attempting to sell and it also possesses some motor vehicles used by the sales staff and for delivery purposes. In the accounts of *A*, the motor vehicles are current assets and the desks are fixed assets. In the accounts of *B*, the motor vehicles are fixed assets and the desks are current assets. Note incidentally that a fixed asset, which, after several years' use, is about to be sold for scrap, remains in the fixed asset part of the accounts even though it is about to change its form.

These two definitions, because they are based on different criteria (one on use and one on time), are not mutually exclusive. It is possible to think of assets that do not conveniently appear to be either fixed or current. Investments, for example, or goodwill.

Liabilities

An essential characteristic of (or necessary condition for) a liability is that the enterprise should have a 'present obligation'. An obligation is 'a duty or responsibility to act or perform in a certain way'. The duty or responsibility may arise from the law, for example, the law of contract; or it may arise from normal business practice, which leads to legitimate expectations that the enterprise will act or perform in a certain way (that is, a constructive obligation). An example of the latter is a constructive obligation to extend the benefits of a warranty for some period beyond the contractual warranty period, because this is an established practice (para. 60).

A present obligation (in the relevant sense) is not the same as a future commitment. An enterprise may have a commitment to purchase an asset in the future at an agreed price; however, this does not entail a net outflow of resources. The commitment does not give rise to a liability, which arises only when the purchase has actually taken place and title in the asset has passed to the enterprise, leaving the latter with an obligation to pay for it. (In the case of a cash transaction, no liability would arise (para. 61).)

There are a number of ways in which a liability may be settled or discharged, which include replacement by another obligation, conversion into equity and the creditor waiving or forfeiting his rights. There are also various types of 'past transactions or past events' from which liabilities may result (paras 62–63). If a provision involves a present obligation and satisfies the rest of the definition of a liability given in the Framework, it is a liability even if the amount has to be estimated (para. 64). Paragraph 64 does not emphasize the equally important point that a provision that fails to satisfy the criterion of being an *obligation* arising from a past transaction or past event is not a liability. This point, however, was crucial in arriving at the requirements for recognition of provisions in IAS 22, *Business Combinations* (now IFRS 3) and IAS 37, *Provisions, Contingent Liabilities and Contingent Assets* (see Chapters 18 and 24).

Equity

Paras 65–68 are concerned with equity. The fact that equity is defined as a residual interest (assets minus liabilities) does not mean that it cannot be meaningfully divided into sub-classifications that are shown separately in the balance sheet. Examples are the difference among the following:

- paid-in capital (capital stock and paid-in surplus)
- retained earnings
- reserves representing appropriations of retained earnings
- reserves representing the amounts required to be retained in order to maintain 'real' capital, that is, either real financial capital or (real) physical capital (para. 65).

There are various legal, tax and valuation considerations that affect equity, such as requirements for legal reserves and whether or not the enterprise is incorporated. It is emphasized that transfers to legal, statutory and tax reserves are appropriations of retained earnings and not expenses. (Likewise, releases from such reserves are credits to retained earnings and not income, but this is not spelled out.) The rather obvious point is made that the amount at which equity is shown in the balance sheet is not intended to be a measure of the market value of the enterprise, either as a going concern or in a piecemeal disposal. It is stated that the definition and treatment of equity in the Framework are appropriate for unincorporated enterprises, even if the legal considerations are different.

Performance

Paras 69–81 contain the section of the Framework in which definitions of the financial statement elements relating to performance are given. 'Profit is frequently used as a measure of performance or as the basis for other measures, such as return on investment and earnings per share' (para. 69). However, this section of the Framework does not discuss the relationship between the elements of performance and the profit measure, except to say that 'the recognition and measurement of income and expenses, and hence profit, depends in part on the concepts of capital and capital maintenance used by the enterprise in preparing its financial statements'. The determination of profit and related issues are discussed in a later section of the Framework (paras 102–110).

The elements of income and expenses are defined as follows:

1 Income is increases in economic benefits during the accounting period in the form of inflows or enhancements of assets or decreases of liabilities that result in increases in equity, other than those relating to contributions from equity participants.
2 Expenses are decreases in economic benefits during the accounting period in the form of outflows or depletions of assets or incurrences of liabilities that result in decreases in equity, other than those relating to distributions to equity participants (para. 70).

These definitions identify the essential features of income and expenses but do not attempt to specify their recognition criteria (para. 71). The definition makes it clear that the Framework's approach treats the definitions of assets and liabilities as *logically prior to* those of income and expenses. This is sometime characterized as a 'balance sheet approach' to the relationship between financial statements. This term is potentially misleading, however. The Framework's approach should certainly not be understood as implying the subordination of the income statements to the balance sheet from an *informational* perspective.

Income

The Framework's definition of income encompasses both revenue and gains. Revenue is described as arising in the course of the ordinary activities of an enterprise and includes sales, fees, interest, royalties and rent. Gains may or may not arise in the course of ordinary activities. Gains may arise on the disposal of non-current assets and also include unrealized gains such as those arising on the revaluation of marketable securities and from increases in the carrying amount of long-term assets. Gains, when recognized in the income statements, are usually displayed separately because their economic significance tends to differ from that of revenue, and they are often reported net of related expenses (paras 74–77).

The counterpart entry corresponding to a credit for income may be to various asset accounts (not only cash or receivables) or to a liability account such as when a loan is discharged by the provision of goods or services (para. 77).

Expenses

The Framework's definition of expenses encompasses losses as well as expenses that arise in the course of the ordinary activities of the enterprise. Examples given of expenses that arise in the course of ordinary activities are cost of sales, wages and depreciation. They usually take the form (that is, are the accounting counterpart) of an outflow or depletion of assets such as cash and cash equivalents, inventory, property or plant and equipment (para. 78).

Losses represent items that may or may not arise in the course of ordinary activities. They include those that result from such disasters as fire or flood, as well as those arising on the disposal of non-current assets and also encompass unrealized losses, such as those arising from the effects of adverse currency exchange rate movements on financial assets or liabilities. Losses, when recognized in the income statement, are usually displayed separately because their economic significance tends to differ from that of other expenses and they are often reported net of related income (paras 79–80).

Recognition of the elements of financial statements

Recognition issues are dealt with in paras 82–98. Recognition is described as 'the process of incorporating in the balance sheet or [the] income statement an item that meets the definition of an element and satisfies the criteria for recognition set out in paragraph 83'. (The statement of changes in financial position is not mentioned because its elements consist of those that are also elements of financial position or performance.) Failure to recognize *in the main financial statements* items that satisfy the relevant definition and recognition criteria is not rectified by disclosure of the accounting policies used or by use of notes or other explanatory material.

The recognition criteria set out in para. 83 are that an item that meets the definition of an element should be recognized if:

1 It is probable that any future economic benefit associated with the item will flow to or from the enterprise; and
2 The item has a cost or value that can be measured with reliability.

Recognition is subject to materiality. Accounting interrelationships are also significant, since recognition in the financial statements of an item that meets the definition and recognition criteria for a particular element, for example an asset, entails the recognition of another (counterpart) element, such as income or a liability (para. 84). (This refers, strictly speaking, to the initial recognition of an item. However, a similar point could be made about the implications of re-measurement or valuation adjustments.)

Probability of future economic benefit

The concept of *probability* is used in the recognition criteria 'to refer to the degree of uncertainty [as to whether] the future economic benefits associated with the time will flow to or from the enterprise . . . in keeping with the uncertainty that characterizes the environment in which an enterprise operates'. Assessments of such uncertainty are made on the basis of the evidence available when the financial statements are prepared. In regard to receivables, for example, for a large population of accounts, some statistical evidence will usually be available regarding collectability (para. 85).

Reliability of measurement

Reliability, the second recognition criterion, was discussed earlier in the section on qualitative characteristics of financial statements. If an item does not possess a cost or value that can be measured with reliability (so that the information has that qualitative characteristic), then it is not appropriate to recognize it. However, in many cases, cost or (more particularly) value must be estimated; indeed, the use of reasonable estimates is an essential part of the financial reporting process and need not undermine reliability. In cases where an item satisfied the definition of an element but not the recognition criteria, it will not be recognized in the financial statements themselves, but its relevance is likely to require its disclosure in the notes to the financial statements or in other supplementary disclosures. This applies when the item meets the probability criterion of recognition but not the reliability criterion, but may also apply to an item that meets the definition of an element when neither recognition criterion is met. The key issue here is whether the item is considered to be relevant to the evaluation of financial position, performance or changes in financial position. An item that does not satisfy the recognition criteria for an asset or a liability at one time may do so later, if more information relevant to estimating its probability, cost or value becomes available (paras 86–88).

It is important to note that 'probable' and 'reliability' are both relative and subjective concepts. The Framework does not pretend otherwise. Professional judgement is required in the context of the particular situation in which the enterprise concerned operates.

Recognition of assets

An asset is recognized in the balance sheet when it is probable that future economic benefits will flow to the enterprise (as a result of its control of the asset) and the asset's cost or value can be measured reliably. When expenditure has been incurred but it is not considered probable that economic benefits will flow to the enterprise beyond the current accounting period, this expenditure will be recognized as an expense, not as an asset. The intention of management in undertaking the expenditure is irrelevant (paras 89–90).

Recognition of liabilities

A liability is recognized in the balance sheet when it is probable that an outflow of resources embodying economic benefits will result from the settlement of a present obligation and the amount of that settlement can be measured reliably. Obligations under executory contracts, that is, non-cancellable contracts that are equally proportionately unperformed (such as the amount that will be a liability when inventory ordered and awaiting delivery is received), are not generally recognized as liabilities in the balance sheet, neither are the related assets recognized in the balance sheet. In some cases, however, recognition may be required (para. 91).

Recognition of income

Recognition of income occurs simultaneously with the recognition of increases in assets or decreases in liabilities (or a combination of the two). The normal recognition procedures used in practice are applications of the Framework's recognition criteria. An example is the requirement that revenue should be earned (that is, it should be associated with a simultaneous increase in assets or decrease in liabilities). These procedures are concerned with restricting the recognition of income to items that, in effect, meet the Framework's recognition criteria of *probability* (a sufficient degree of certainty that an economic benefit has flowed or will flow to the enterprise) and *reliability* of measurement (paras 92–93).

Recognition of expenses

Recognition of expenses occurs simultaneously with the recognition of an increase in liabilities or a decrease in assets (or a combination of the two). Expenses are commonly recognized in the income statement on the basis of an association (matching) between the incurrence of costs and the earning of specific items of revenue, that result directly and jointly from the same transactions or other events. An example is the matching of the cost of goods sold with the associated sales revenue. However, the Framework does not permit the application of the matching procedure to result in the recognition of items in the balance sheet that do not meet the definition of assets or liabilities (paras 94–95).

Measurement of the elements of the financial statements

Paras 99–101 deal with measurement issues, insofar as these are covered in the Framework. The treatment here is descriptive and avoids being prescriptive. Measurement is described as 'the process of determining the monetary amounts at which the elements of the financial statements are to be recognized and carried in the balance sheet and income statement'. It involves the selection of a particular basis of measurement.

Four different measurement bases are specifically mentioned and described (without any claim to exhaustiveness): historical cost, current cost (of replacement or settlement), realizable or (for liabilities) settlement value and present value. Historical cost is mentioned as the measurement basis most commonly adopted by enterprises in preparing their financial statements, usually in combination with other measurement bases. An example of the latter is the carrying of inventories at the lower of historical cost and net realizable value. Marketable securities may be carried at market value and pension liabilities are carried at their present value. Current cost may be used as a means of taking account of the effects of changing prices of non-monetary assets.

Concepts of capital and capital maintenance

Concepts of capital

The Framework identifies two main concepts of capital: the financial concept and the physical concept. The financial concept of capital may take two forms: invested money (nominal financial) capital or invested purchasing power (real financial) capital. In either case, capital is identified with the equity of the enterprise (in either nominal or real financial terms) and with its net assets measured in those terms. The physical concept of capital is based on the notion of the productive capacity or operating capability of the enterprise, as embodied in its net assets. Most enterprises adopt a financial concept of capital, normally (in the absence of severe inflation) nominal financial capital (para. 102).

Capital maintenance and the determination of profit

Choice of a concept of capital is related to the concept of capital maintenance that is most meaningful, given the implications of the choice for profit measurement and the needs of the users of the financial statements in that regard, as follows:

1 *Maintenance of nominal financial capital.* Under this concept a profit is earned only if the money amount of the net assets at the end of the period exceeds the money amount of the net assets at the beginning of the period, after excluding any distributions to, and contributions from, equity owners during the period.

2 *Maintenance of real financial capital.* Under this concept a profit is earned only if the money amount of the net assets at the end of the period exceeds the money amount of the net assets at the beginning of the period, restated in units of the same purchasing power, after excluding distributions to, and contributions from, owners. Normally, the units of purchasing power employed are those of the currency at the end of the

period, into which the net assets at the beginning of the period are restated.

3 *Maintenance of real physical capital.* Under this concept a profit is earned only if the operating capability embodied in the net assets at the end of the period exceeds the operating capability embodied in the net assets at the beginning of the period, after excluding distributions to, and contributions from, owners. Operating capability embodied in assets may, in principle, be measured by employing the current cost basis of measurement

(paras 103–106).

The main difference among the three concepts of capital maintenance is the treatment of the effects of changes in the carrying amounts of the enterprise's assets and liabilities. Under nominal financial capital maintenance, increases in the money-carrying amounts of assets held over the period (to the extent that they are recognized as gains) are part of profit.

Under real financial capital maintenance, such increases are part of profit only if they are 'real' increases, that is, increases that remain after money-carrying amounts have been restated in units of the same purchasing power. The total amount of the restatement is known as a 'capital maintenance adjustment' and is transferred to a capital maintenance reserve, which is part of equity (but not of retained profits). Real financial capital maintenance may be used in conjunction with historical cost as a measurement basis but would more normally be used in conjunction with the current cost basis.

Under real physical capital maintenance, changes in the money prices at current costs of assets and liabilities held over the period are considered not to affect the amount of operating capability embodied in those items and therefore the total amount of those changes is treated as a capital maintenance adjustment and excluded from profit.

Illustration

Let us assume that a company begins with capital stock of €100 and cash of €100. At the beginning of the year, one item of inventory is bought for €100. The item of inventory is sold at the end of the year for €150, its replacement cost at that time is €120 and general inflation throughout the year is 10%. Profit measured using each of the capital maintenance concepts mentioned earlier would be as shown:

	Nominal financial capital maintenance	Real financial capital maintenance	Real physical capital maintenance
Sales	€150	€150	€150
less Cost of sales	(100)	(100)	(120)
Operating profit	50	50	30
less Inflation adjustment	–	(10)	–
Total gain	€50	€40	€30
Capital maintenance adjustment	€0	€10	€20

Column 1 shows the gain after ensuring the maintenance of the stockholders' opening capital measured as a sum of money. Column 2 shows the gain after ensuring the maintenance of the stockholders' opening capital measured as a block of purchasing power. Both of these are concerned, under different definitions, with the maintenance of financial capital – in terms either of its money amount or of its general purchasing power. Column 3 shows the gain after ensuring the maintenance of the company's initial operating capacity and is therefore of a completely different nature.

Different combinations of measurement bases and capital maintenance concepts provide different accounting models, between which management should choose, taking into account relevance and reliability. Readers should be very familiar with the concepts underlying these alternatives, which have been fully discussed in Chapters 4–7.

IAS 1 Presentation of Financial Statements

It is most important to remember that the Framework has not been revised since 1989 and is now, as the IASB is well aware, in need of further development. However, to complicate the situation further, a revised version of IAS 1, *Presentation of Financial Statements*, was issued in 1997 and this covers some of the topics discussed in the Framework. As a full Standard, IAS 1 automatically takes priority over the Framework where there is any overlap or conflict. A further revision was finalized in 2004, effective from 1 January 2005, with earlier adoption being 'encouraged'. It is this version that we discuss here.

Presentation of Financial Statements represents an attempt to cover several important aspects. The objective of the Standard is to prescribe the basis for presentation of general purpose financial statements, in order to ensure comparability both with the entity's own financial statements of previous periods and with the financial statements of other enterprises. To achieve this objective, the Standard sets out overall considerations for the presentation of financial statements, guidelines for their structure and minimum requirements for the content of financial statements.

In principle, therefore, IAS 1 applies to all aspects of all businesses. Many aspects of financial reporting are covered additionally by other more specific International Accounting Standards, as detailed elsewhere in this volume. However, some other aspects are not further developed and IAS 1 therefore comprises the IAS GAAP in those respects. For example, disclosure of fixed assets is discussed in IAS 16, *Property Plant and Equipment* (see Chapter 12), but disclosure of current assets has no additional Standard, except for component parts such as inventories, covered by IAS 2, *Inventories* (see Chapter 15).

Broadly speaking, IAS 1 consists of two parts. Part 1 discusses a number of 'overall considerations' consisting of general principles, conventions and requirements. Much of Part 1 is a restatement of aspects of the Framework, as discussed already. Part 2 discusses in some detail the required contents of general purpose financial statements. It is worth noting that most national accounting standards operate, and are designed to operate, within the context of national legislation, especially for corporations. There is, of course, no single international company or corporation statute. To some extent, IAS 1 provides a minimal filling in of this lacuna.

Consistent with our chapter structure in this book, the first part of IAS 1 is discussed here. Part 2 is covered in Chapter 9.

Scope

The scope and applicability of IAS 1 revised (hereafter IAS 1) is very wide. It should be applied in the presentation of all general purpose financial statements prepared and presented in accordance with International Accounting Standards.

General purpose financial statements are those intended to meet the needs of users who are not in a position to demand reports tailored to meet their specific information needs. They include statements presented separately or those within another public document such as an annual report or prospectus.

IAS 1 does not apply to condensed interim financial information, but it must be applied in full to all general purpose statements as already described which claim to be in accordance with International Accounting Standards. This includes banks and insurance companies and IAS 1 notes that IAS 30, *Disclosures in the Financial Statements of Banks and Similar Financial Institutions*, contains additional requirements which are 'consistent with the requirements of' IAS 1. Not-for-profit organizations can also apply the Standard (and IAS GAAP generally) by amending item descriptions in the financial statements as appropriate.

IAS 1 repeats the objective of general purpose financial statements from the Framework, as being to provide information about the financial position, performance and cash flows of an entity that is useful to a wide range of users in making economic decisions. Financial statements also show the results of management's stewardship of the resources entrusted to it. Financial statements provide information about an entity's (para. 5):

- assets
- liabilities
- equity
- income and expenses, including gains and losses
- other changes in equity
- cash flows.

A complete set of financial statements therefore includes the following components (para. 8):

1 Balance sheet.
2 Income statement.
3 A statement showing either:
    (a) all changes in equity
    (b) or changes in equity other than those arising from transactions with equity holders acting in their capacity as equity holders.
4 Cash flow statements.
5 Accounting policies and explanatory notes.

Item 3 may be a new concept in some jurisdictions. To deal with users' demands for more comprehensive information on 'performance', measured more broadly than the 'profit' shown in the income statement, the Standard establishes a new requirement for a primary financial statement showing those gains and losses not presented in the income statement. (This is discussed and illustrated in more detail in Chapter 9.)

IAS 1 encourages, but does not require, the additional presentation, 'outside the financial statements', of a management report about the financial performance and financial position of the enterprise and about its environment, risks and uncertainties. Brief suggestions as to coverage are made in paragraph 9, but none of the suggestions is mandatory. Further additional statements and reports, for example on environmental matters, are also encouraged.

Fair presentation and compliance with International Accounting Standards

The first substantive part of IAS 1 concerns the vexed question of the override. The issue at stake is whether or not the detailed regulations, i.e. the Standards in this case, are always and automatically both necessary and sufficient conditions for the preparation of adequate financial statements or whether some more fundamental overriding criterion, such as the provision of a true and fair view, a requirement to present fairly or a requirement not to mislead users is, when a clash occurs, the determining requirement (hence 'overriding' the Standards). IAS 1 recognizes that compliance with the International Standards may be insufficient or inadequate 'in extremely rare circumstances'.

Entities which comply with IASs should say so. This requires that they comply with *all* applicable aspects of all applicable Standards and with all applicable interpretations of the Standing Interpretations Committee. However, the overall requirement is that financial statements should present fairly the financial position, financial performance and cash flows of an entity. The appropriate application of International Accounting Standards, with additional disclosure when necessary, results, in 'virtually all circumstances', in financial statements that achieve a fair presentation.

In the extremely rare circumstances when management concludes that compliance with a requirement in a Standard would be misleading and therefore that departure from a requirement is necessary to achieve a fair presentation, an entity should (not may) depart from that requirement 'if the relevant regulatory framework requires, or otherwise does not prohibit, such a departure' (para 17).

When an entity departs from a requirement of a Standard or an Interpretation in accordance with paragraph 17, it shall disclose:

(a) that management has concluded that the finanical statements present fairly the entity's financial position, financial performance and cash flows;

(b) that it has complied with applicable Standards and Interpretations, except that it has departed from a particular requirement to achieve a fair presentation;

(c) that title of the Standard or Interpretation from which the entity has departed, the nature of the departure, including the treatment that the Standard or Interpretation would require, the reason why that treatment would be so misleading in the circumstances that it would conflict with the objective of financial statements set out in the Framework, and the treatment adopted; and

(d) for each period presented, the financial impact of the departure on each item in the financial statements that would have been reported in complying with the requirement.

The question of terminology and national positions here is both important and potentially confusing. The US requirement to present fairly in accordance with (US) GAAP means to follow GAAP, at least as far as accounting standards are concerned, although the situation is slightly less clear as regards US auditing standards. The UK requirement to give a true and fair view equally clearly means to follow Standards where suitable, but to depart from them if a true and fair view requires it. The UK position in essence found its way into the European Union Fourth Directive and hence, subject to varying degrees of bastardization, into other European countries. IAS 1 follows the US *wording* but the UK/EU philosophy. Table 8.2 makes this clear.

This is not to imply that the override is likely to be used in similar ways or in similar volumes in the various jurisdictions where it exists. We predict that its usage under the IASB will indeed be rare. But an important issue of principle is at stake. Can the qualitative characteristics required of financial reporting be ensured by *compliance* with a set of (static) rules, or is some *professional judgement* involved which may, in principle, entail departure from one or more rules?

Although no attempt to define 'fair presentation' is provided (rightly in our view), the presumption 'in virtually all circumstances' is that a fair presentation is achieved by compliance in all material respects with applicable International Accounting Standards. A fair presentation requires (para. 15):

1 Selecting and applying accounting policies as described later.
2 Presenting information, including accounting policies, in a manner which provides relevant, reliable, comparable and understandable information.
3 Providing additional disclosures when the requirements in International Standards are insufficient to enable users to understand the impact of particular transactions or events on the enterprise's financial position and financial performance.

In extremely rare circumstances, application of a specific requirement in an International Accounting Standard might result in misleading financial statements. In such circumstances departure from the Standard is required. IASB is at pains to minimize the likelihood of this happening. The override can only be applied when following the Standard plus providing additional information would not give a fair presentation (i.e., presumably, would mislead). The existence of national regulations which conflict with IASB Standards is not an adequate reason for departing from an

Table 8.2 Terminology versus philosophy

Jurisdiction	Terminology	Overriding
UK	True and fair view	Yes
European Union	True and fair view	Yes
USA	Fair presentation	No
IASB	Fair presentation	Yes

International Standard. IAS 1 requires in addition, as detailed earlier, if the override is employed, that full details of the departure are given in the financial statements, sufficient to enable users to make an informed judgement on whether the departure is necessary and to calculate the adjustments that would be required to comply with the Standard.

Accounting policies

The actual process of selecting accounting policies by a particular entity was discussed in the 1997 version of IAS 1, but in 2004 was transferred to the new version of IAS 8. This is discussed in Chapter 23. However, IAS 1 proceeds to incorporate and discuss some, but not all, of the assumptions and qualitative characteristics of financial statements included in the Framework. The two 'underlying assumptions' are going concern and the accrual basis of accounting. The going concern assumption means that it is assumed that the entity will continue in operation for the foreseeable future. Financial statements should be prepared on a going concern basis unless management either intends to liquidate the entity or to cease trading or has no realistic alternative but to do so. When management is aware, in making its assessment, of material uncertainties related to events or conditions which may cast significant doubt on the entity's ability to continue as a going concern, those uncertainties should be disclosed. When the financial statements are not prepared on a going concern basis, that fact should be disclosed, together with the basis on which the financial statements are prepared and the reason why the entity is not considered to be a going concern. When the financial statements are prepared on the going concern basis it is not necessary to say so. Judgement, and in uncertain cases detailed investigation, may be required.

The accrual basis of accounting (except for cash flow statements) is also an automatic assumption that need not be explicitly stated. Under the accrual basis of accounting, transactions and events are recognized when they occur (and not as cash or its equivalent is received or paid) and they are recorded in the accounting records and reported in the financial statements of the periods to which they relate.

The actual wording indicates that the application of the matching concept in IAS GAAP does not allow the recognition of items in the balance sheet which do not meet the IAS definition of assets or liabilities.

The Framework states, however, that financial statements may include items not falling within these definitions if specific Standards require their recognition. Some other Standards do so require, e.g. with regard to the deferral of government grants (IAS 20, see Chapter 12) and the deferral of income and expenses relating to operating leases (IAS 17, Chapter 14). Although there seems to be conflict between the Framework and IAS 1 on this point, standards, explicitly, override the Framework.

IAS 1 also incorporates the principle of consistency from para. 39 of the Framework, but, oddly, only as regards presentation. A change in presentation and classification of items in financial statements between one period and another is permitted only when it results in a more appropriate presentation (which is expected to continue) or is required by a specific International Standard or interpretation. The Framework principle continues to relate, of course, to recognition and measurement.

The issue of materiality and aggregation raises some important considerations. Each material item should be presented separately in the financial statements. Immaterial amounts should be aggregated with amounts of a similar nature or function and need not be presented separately. In this context, information is material if its non-disclosure could influence the economic decisions of users taken on the basis of the financial statements. Materiality depends on the size and nature of the item judged in the particular circumstances of its omission. In deciding whether an item or an aggregate of items is material, the nature and the size of the item are evaluated together. Depending on the circumstances, either the nature or the size of the item could be the determining factor. For example, evidence of breaking the law causing a fine could be significant in principle, even if the amount is small. But similar items should be aggregated together however large they or the resulting total are in relation to the enterprise as a whole.

It is important that both assets and liabilities, and income and expenses, when material, are reported separately. Offsetting in either the income statement or the balance sheet, except when offsetting reflects the substance of the transaction or event, would detract from the ability of users to understand the transactions undertaken and to assess the future cash flows of the enterprise. Assets and liabilities, and income and expenses, should not be offset except when offsetting is required or permitted by another International Accounting Standard.

It is often not fully appreciated that the prevention of offsetting between assets and liabilities and between income and expenses is not at all the same thing as the prevention of netting out between debits and credits in a bookkeeping sense. Receipts and payments in relation to the purchase of one asset, for example, involve the netting out of debits and credits and are not examples of offsetting as discussed in IAS 1.

It should also be noted that there are several examples where other International Accounting Standards do 'require or permit' offsetting. One such example is IAS 11 (see Chapter 15), where contract costs plus recognized profits less losses are offset against progress billings to give a net figure of amount due from customers.

It is explicitly stated that the specific disclosure requirements of International Accounting Standards need not be met if the resulting information is not material. It thus follows that full compliance with IAS GAAP requires the following of complete IAS GAAP except for immaterial disclosure requirements, not the following of complete IAS GAAP period.

The 'presentation' section of IAS 1 concludes with requirements about comparative figures. Unless a Standard or Interpretation permits or requires otherwise, comparative information should be disclosed in respect of the previous period for all numerical information in the financial statements. Comparative narrative and descriptive information should be included when it is relevant to an understanding of the current period's financial statements.

Comparative information should be restated if necessary if the presentation or classification of items in the current financial statements is altered, unless it is impractical to do so, in which case the reason for not reclassifying should be disclosed together with 'the nature of the adjustments that would have been made if the amounts had been reclassified'. Five- or ten-year summaries should logically be changed as well, although IAS 1 does not consider this point.

It should be noted that IAS 8, *Accounting Policies, Changes in Accounting Estimates and Errors*, applies if changes constitute a change in accounting policy as discussed in that Standard (see Chapter 23).

As already indicated, the remainder of IAS 1 relates to the structure and content of published financial statements, which is dealt with in the next chapter.

Summary

This chapter began with an outline of 'theories about theories' in the accounting context. We then looked at the nearest that accounting seems to have got to a generally agreed theory, as illustrated by the IASB Framework and relevant parts of IAS 1. These documents, however, seem far removed from theory in a scientific sense.

EXERCISES	(✔ indicates answers are available on pages 724–725)

✔ **1** To what extent is financial reporting a suitable subject for theorizing about?

✔ **2** Positive research is a necessary starting point on the road to normative thinking, but can never be enough by itself. Discuss.

3 Is the IASB Framework useful in its present form? How could it be improved?

4 Accounting standards and regulations should aim to state how to deal with all situations. Discuss.

5 Rework question 9 from Chapter 1, specifically by applying the IASB Framework. Does it alter or improve your original answer? Does IAS 1 make any difference?

Structure of published financial statements

After studying this chapter you should be able to:
☐ describe and apply the format requirements of the EU Fourth Directive
☐ describe and apply the format and disclosure requirements of IAS 1
☐ discuss the adequacy of the disclosure requirements of IAS 1 and the EU Fourth Directive and to suggest and appraise possible alterations thereto.

Introduction

There has been an increasing tendency over recent decades to regulate not only the *contents* of published financial statements, but also the precise layout and format in which those contents must be presented. Former country traditions in this respect varied considerably, as Chapter 2 should have made you expect. The central European countries usually had a much higher degree of precise specification than the UK- and US-influenced regions of the world.

There are two non-nationalistic influences of importance on the structure and contents of published financial statements. The first one chronologically, and in some way the most detailed, is the Fourth Directive of the European Union. This obviously only directly affects those countries that are members of the EU and also those trying to join. The more recent influence, and the more general one, but soon to become the more pervasive, is the IASB, as represented by IAS 1, *Presentation of Financial Statements*, issued in its current form in 2004.

The requirements from these sources are presented in this chapter in logical rather than chronological order. Thus, the IAS 1 requirements, both more general and more wide ranging in the countries they are likely to influence, are presented first in each section, followed by EU Directive considerations.

IAS 1 requires that financial statements that claim to follow IASs should be clearly distinguished from any other information that is included in the same published document. Figures, components and separate pages must be fully and clearly described. Financial statements should be presented at least annually, normally for a 12-month period and any exceptions (such as a change in reporting date following an acquisition by another enterprise) should be clearly explained.

Balance sheets

It is usual in Europe (and required by the Fourth Directive even though not at present by IAS 1) for a balance sheet to present current and non-current (fixed) assets and current and non-current liabilities, as separate classifications on the face of the balance sheet. When an enterprise chooses not to make this analysis, assets and liabilities should still be presented broadly in order of their liquidity, although, under the 2004 revision of IAS 1, this alternative is only allowed when it would lead to information that is 'reliable and more relevant'. In such circumstances, the IAS does not specify 'which way up' the liquidity analysis should go. For example, it is European practice for assets to end with cash (which is required by the Directive), whereas it is North American, Japanese and Australian practice to start with cash. Whichever method of presentation is adopted, an enterprise should disclose the amounts included in each item that are expected to be recovered or settled before and after 12 months.

Where, as is usually the case, the current/non-current classification is followed, then IAS GAAP specifies the distinctions as now described. IAS 1 deals with assets first, by defining a current asset.

An asset should be classified as a current asset when it (para. 57):

1   Is expected to be realized in or is held for sale or consumption in the entity's normal operating cycle.
2   Is held primarily for trading purposes or expected to be realized within 12 months of the balance sheet date.
3   Is cash or a cash equivalent which is not restricted in its use.

All other assets should be classified as non-current assets.

This definition of a current asset requires careful consideration. Only one of the three conditions needs to be met for classification as a current asset to be required. Thus, an asset which meets condition 1 in a business which has a two-year operating cycle is a current asset even if it is not expected to be realized within 12 months.

Although the wording on the matter is perhaps not as clear as it might be, a non-current asset remains non-current throughout its useful life to the enterprise, as it is not held primarily for trading purposes. It does not eventually become 'current' merely because its expected disposal is within less than 12 months. The IASB definition also implies that the currently due portion of a long-term non-trading receivable is similarly not to be reclassified as current.

The classification of liabilities, when undertaken by the reporting enterprise, must follow a comparable distinction. A liability should be classified as current when it satisfies any of the following criteria:

1   it is expected to be settled in the entity's normal operating cycle
2   it is held primarily for the purpose of being traded
3   it is due to be settled within 12 months after the balance sheet date
4   or the entity does not have an unconditional right to defer settlement of the liability for at least 12 months after the balance sheet date.

All other liabilities shall be classified as non-current.

Items 2 and 4 in this list are new specifications in the 2004 version of IAS 1.

Again, only one of these criteria needs to apply, so a long operating cycle could lead to the classification as current liabilities of items due to be settled in more than 12 months. In the case of liabilities the 'current' (i.e. due within 12 months) portion of long-term interest-bearing liabilities *is* to be classified as 'current' in most cases. Further, in a direct change from the 1997 version, the 2004 version of IAS 1 now requires (para. 63) that an entity classifies its financial liabilities as current when they are due to be settled within 12 months after the balance sheet date, even if:

- the original terms were for a period longer than 12 months and
- an agreement to refinance, or to reschedule payments, on a long-term basis is completed after the balance sheet date and before the financial statements are authorized for issue.

It is common for loan agreements to contain clauses such that, in the event of defined undertakings by the borrower not being satisfied (e.g. maintenance of an agreed maximum leverage ratio), the liability becomes payable on demand. If this happens, then the liability would in general immediately become 'current' under IAS GAAP. The liability would continue to be classified as non-current, however, if the lender has agreed, before the approval of the financial statements, not to demand payment within 12 months of the balance sheet date.

As a minimum, the face of the balance sheet (i.e. not the notes to the balance sheet) should include separate line items that present the following amounts (para. 68):

1 property, plant and equipment
2 investment property
3 intangible assets
4 financial assets (excluding amounts shown under 5, 8 and 9)
5 investments accounted for using the equity method
6 biological assets
7 inventories
8 trade and other receivables
9 cash and cash equivalents
10 trade and other payables
11 tax liabilities and assets (current and deferred separately) as required by IAS 12, *Income Taxes* (see Chapter 19)
12 financial liabilities (excluding amounts shown under 10 and 11)
13 provisions
14 minority interest, presented within equity
15 issued capital and reserves.

Logically, following from our earlier discussion of materiality, these separate line items are required only if 'material'. Disclosures are also required of assets, and liabilities, classified separately as 'held for sale' under IFRS 5 (see Chapter 23).

This list represents a minimum. Additional line items, headings and subtotals should also be presented on the face of the balance sheet when such presentation is relevant to an understanding of the entity's financial position.

IAS 1 states that the use of different measurement bases for different classes of assets suggests that their nature or function differs and, therefore, that they should be presented as separate line items. It gives as an example the carrying of certain classes of property, plant, and equipment at cost, and other classes at revalued amounts, under IAS 16, *Property, Plant, and Equipment* (see Chapter 12).

It seems to us that this proposition, or at least the example given, is not logical. The recording of different subsets of property, plant and machinery under different valuation bases does not necessarily suggest any difference in nature or function. Further disclosure *in the notes* may well be desirable, as discussed later, but that is a separate matter. A more logical example might be the different treatments allowed for investment properties (see Chapter 12), where the function of the property may affect the accounting treatment.

A third category of required disclosure relating to the balance sheet can be presented either on the face of the balance sheet or in the notes. Further sub-classifications of the line items should be presented, classified in a manner appropriate to the entity's operations.

The detail provided in sub-classifications, either on the face of the balance sheet or in the notes, depends on the requirements of International Standards and the size, nature and function of the amounts involved. In some cases, other International Standards provide requirements (subject always to the materiality consideration). Tangible assets, for example, are classified by class as required by IAS 16, *Property, Plant and Equipment* (see Chapter 12) and inventories are sub-classified in accordance with IAS 2, *Inventories* (see Chapter 15). Other applications will be more subjective.

Extensive detailed disclosure regarding owner's equity is required, either on the face of the balance sheet or in the notes, as follows (para. 76):

1 For each class of share capital:
   (a) the number of shares authorized
   (b) the number of shares issued and fully paid and issued but not fully paid
   (c) par value per share or that the shares have no par value
   (d) a reconciliation of the number of shares outstanding at the beginning and at the end of the year
   (e) the rights, preferences, and restrictions attaching to that class, including restrictions on the distribution of dividends and the repayment of capital
   (f) shares in the entity held by the entity itself or by subsidiaries or associates of the entity
   (g) shares reserved for issue under options and sales contracts, including the terms and amounts.
2 A description of the nature and purpose of each reserve within equity.

Entities without share capital are required to present equivalent information showing details and movements of each category of equity interest.

The Fourth Directive sets out considerably more detail in its specifications regarding balance sheets. It requires that all member states should prescribe one or both of the layouts specified by its Articles 9 and 10. Article 9, reproduced in Table 9.1, gives a 'horizontal' format with the debits on one side and the credits on the other, following the general continental European tradition. Article 10, reproduced in Table 9.2, gives a 'vertical' format of the type more traditional in the UK. Companies are required to show the items in these tables in the order specified, except that the headings preceded by Arabic numbers may be combined or taken to the notes.

Table 9.1 Fourth Directive: horizontal balance sheet format

Assets

A **Subscribed capital unpaid**
B **Formation expenses**
C **Fixed assets**
 I *Intangible assets*
  1 Costs of research and development
  2 Concessions, patents, licences, trade marks and similar rights and assets
  3 Goodwill, to the extent that it was acquired for valuable consideration
  4 Payments on account
 II *Tangible assets*
  1 Land and buildings
  2 Plant and machinery
  3 Other fixtures and fittings, tools and equipment
  4 Payments on account and tangible assets in course of construction
 III *Financial assets*
  1 Shares in affiliated undertakings
  2 Loans in affiliated undertakings
  3 Participating interests
  4 Loans to undertakings with which the company is linked by virtue of participating interests
  5 Investments held as fixed assets
  6 Other loans
  7 Own shares
D **Current assets**
 I *Stocks*
  1 Raw materials and consumables
  2 Work in progress
  3 Finished goods and goods for resale
  4 Payments on account
 II *Debtors*
  (Amounts becoming due and payable after more than one year must be shown separately for each item.)
  1 Trade debtors
  2 Amounts owed by affiliated undertakings
  3 Amounts owed by undertakings with which the company is linked by virtue of participating interests
  4 Other debtors
  5 Subscribed capital called but not paid
  6 Prepayments and accrued income
 III *Investments*
  1 Shares in affiliated undertakings
  2 Own shares
  3 Other investments
 IV *Cash at bank and in hand*
E **Prepayments and accrued income**
F **Loss for the financial year**

Table 9.1   *(continued)*

Liabilities

A   **Capital and reserves**
   I   *Subscribed capital*
   II   *Share premium account*
   III   *Revaluation reserve*
   IV   *Reserves*
      1   Legal reserve
      2   Reserve for own shares
      3   Reserves provided for by the articles of association
      4   Other reserves
   V   *Profit or loss brought forward*
   VI   *Profit or loss for the financial year*
B   **Provisions for liabilities and charges**
      1   Provisions for pensions and similar obligations
      2   Provisions for taxation
      3   Other provisions
C   **Creditors**
   (Amounts becoming due and payable within one year and amounts becoming due and payable after more than one year must be shown separately for each item and for the aggregate of these items.)
      1   Debenture loans, showing convertible loans separately
      2   Amounts owed to credit institutions
      3   Payments received on account of orders in so far as they are now shown separately as deductions from stocks
      4   Trade creditors
      5   Bills of exchange payable
      6   Amounts owed to affiliated undertakings
      7   Amounts owed to undertakings with which the company is linked by virtue of participating interests
      8   Other creditors including tax and social security
      9   Accruals and deferred income
D   **Accruals and deferred income**
E   **Profit for the financial year**

In the European Union, companies that fall below a given size limit, which is updated as circumstances change, may be permitted by the laws of member states to produce abridged accounts. As far as the balance sheet is concerned these would consist of only those items preceded by letters and roman numerals in Tables 9.1 and 9.2.

Income statements

As with the balance sheet, IAS 1 requires certain disclosures on the face of the income statement and other disclosures either on the face of the income statement or in the notes, at the discretion of the entity. As a minimum, the face of the income statement should include line items that present the following amounts (paras 81–3).

Table 9.2 Fourth Directive: vertical balance sheet format

A Subscribed capital unpaid

B Formation expenses

C Fixed assets

   I *Intangible assets*

      1 Costs of research and development

      2 Concessions, patents, licences, trade marks and similar rights and assets

      3 Goodwill, to the extent that it was acquired for valuable consideration

      4 Payments on account

   II *Tangible assets*

      1 Land and buildings

      2 Plant and machinery

      3 Other fixtures and fittings, tools and equipment

      4 Payments on account and tangible assets in course of construction

   III *Financial assets*

      1 Shares in affiliated undertakings

      2 Loans to affiliated undertakings

      3 Participating interests

      4 Loans to undertakings with which the company is linked by virtue of participating interests

      5 Investments held as fixed assets

      6 Other loans

      7 Own shares

D Current assets

   I *Stocks*

      1 Raw materials and consumables

      2 Work in progress

      3 Finished goods and goods for resale

      4 Payments on account

   II *Debtors*

   (Amounts becoming due and payable after more than one year must be shown separately for each item.)

      1 Trade debtors

      2 Amounts owed by affiliated undertakings

      3 Amounts owed by undertakings with which the company is linked by virtue of participating interests

      4 Other debtors

      5 Subscribed capital called but not paid

      6 Prepayments and accrued income

   III *Investments*

      1 Shares in affiliated undertakings

      2 Own shares

      3 Other investments

   IV *Cash at bank and in hand*

E Prepayments and accrued income

F Creditors: amounts becoming due and payable within one year

      1 Debenture loans, showing convertible loans separately

      2 Amounts owed to credit institutions

      3 Payments received on account of orders in so far as they are not shown separately as deductions from stocks

Table 9.2 *(continued)*

    4 Trade creditors
    5 Bills of exchange payable
    6 Amounts owed to affiliated undertakings
    7 Amounts owed to undertakings with which the company is linked by virtue of participating interests
    8 Other creditors including tax and social security
    9 Accrual and deferred income

G Net current assets/liabilities

H Total assets less current liabilities

I Creditors: amounts becoming due and payable after more than one year
    1 Debenture loans, showing convertible loans separately
    2 Amounts owed to credit institutions
    3 Payments received on account of orders in so far as they are not shown separately as deductions from stocks
    4 Trade creditors
    5 Bills of exchange payable
    6 Amounts owed to affiliated undertakings
    7 Amounts owed to undertakings with which the company is linked by virtue of participating interests
    8 Other creditors including tax and social security
    9 Accruals and deferred income

J Provisions for liabilities and charges
    1 Provisions for pensions and similar obligations
    2 Provisions for taxation
    3 Other provisions

K Accruals and deferred income

L Capital and reserves
    I   *Subscribed capital*
    II *Share premium account*
    III *Revaluation reserve*
    IV *Reserves*
        1 Legal reserve
        2 Reserve for own shares
        3 Reserves provided for by the articles of association
        4 Other reserves
    V *Profit or loss brought forward*
    VI *Profit or loss for the financial year*

As a minimum, the face of the income statement shall include line items that present the following amounts for the period:

    (a) revenue;
    (b) finance costs;
    (c) share of the profit or loss of associates and joint ventures accounted for using the equity method;
    (d) tax expenses;
    (e) a single amount comprising the total of (i) the post-tax profit or loss of discontinued operations and (ii) the post-tax gain or loss recognised on the

measurement to fair value less costs to sell or on the disposal of the assets or disposal group(s) constituting the discontinued operation; and

(f) profit or loss.

The following items shall be disclosed on the face of the income statement as allocations of profit or loss for the period:

(a) profit or loss attributable to minority interest; and
(b) profit or loss attributable to equity holders of the parent.

Additional line items, headings and subtotals shall be presented on the face of the income statement when such presentation is relevant to an understanding of the entity's financial performance.

It is important to note that no line item for 'extraordinary items' is required. Indeed, in a significant change from earlier requirements, IAS 1 explicitly states that

Table 9.3 Fourth Directive: vertical profit and loss account by nature

Item	Description
1	Net turnover
2	Variation in stocks of finished goods and in work in progress
3	Work performed by the undertaking for its own purposes and capitalized
4	Other operating income
5	(a) Raw materials and consumables
	(b) Other external charges
6	*Staff costs*
	(a) wages and salaries
	(b) social security costs with a separate indication of those relating to pensions
7	(a) Value adjustments in respect of formation expenses and of tangible and intangible fixed assets
	(b) Value adjustments in respect of current assets, to the extent that they exceed the amount of value adjustments which are normal in the undertaking concerned
8	Other operating charges
9	Income from participating interests, with a separate indication of that derived from affiliated undertakings
10	Income from other investments and loans forming part of the fixed assets, with a separate indication of that derived from affiliated undertakings
11	Other interest receivable and similar income, with a separate indication of that derived from affiliated undertakings
12	Value adjustments in respect of financial assets and of investments held as current assets
13	Interest payable and similar charges, with a separate indication of those concerning affiliated undertakings
14	Tax on profit or loss on ordinary activities
15	Profit or loss on ordinary activities after taxation
16	Extraordinary income
17	Extraordinary charges
18	Extraordinary profit or loss
19	Tax on extraordinary profit or loss
20	Other taxes not shown under the above items
21	Profit or loss for the financial year

such a category is now forbidden, whether on the fact of the income statements or in the notes. IAS 33, *Earnings per Share*, requires the disclosure of earnings per share data on the face of the income statement (see Chapter 23). IAS 1 explicitly accepts that considerations of materiality and the nature of an entity's operations may require addition to, deletions from, or amendments of descriptions within, the list. The ordering of items may be changed from that given 'when this is necessary to explain the elements of performance' (which seems likely to occur only very rarely).

The requirement for further disclosure is drawn widely and in general terms. An entity should present, either on the face of the income statement, which is encouraged but not obligatory or in the notes to the income statement, an analysis of expenses using a classification based on either the nature of expenses or their function within the entity. The implications of this distinction between classification by nature and classification by function are conveniently illustrated by turning to the Fourth Directive's specifications for the income statement. The Directive requires that member states allow one or more of the four layouts in its Articles 23 to 26.

These four layouts are necessary to accommodate the possibility of following either an analysis by nature or an analysis by function combined with either a horizontal-type presentation or a vertical-type presentation. Table 9.3 classifies the expense items by nature showing, for example, staff costs as a single separate figure. Table 9.4 classifies by function. Thus for example staff costs as a total are not shown,

Table 9.4 Fourth Directive: vertical profit and loss account by function

Item	Description
1	Net turnover
2	Cost of sales (including value adjustments)
3	Gross profit or loss
4	Distribution costs (including value adjustments)
5	Administrative expenses (including value adjustments)
6	Other operating income
7	Income from participating interests, with a separate indication of that derived from affiliated undertakings
8	Income from other investments and loans forming part of the fixed assets, with a separate indication of that derived from affiliated undertakings
9	Other interest receivable and similar income, with a separate indication of that derived from affiliated undertakings
10	Value adjustments in respect of financial assets and of investments held as current assets
11	Interest payable and similar charges, with a separate indication of those concerning affiliated undertakings
12	Tax on profit or loss on ordinary activities
13	Profit or loss on ordinary activities after taxation
14	Extraordinary income
15	Extraordinary charges
16	Extraordinary profit or loss
17	Tax on extraordinary profit or loss
18	Other taxes not shown under the above items
19	Profit or loss for the financial year

being split up between the various functional heads related to staff activity, such as distribution and administration.

The formats in Tables 9.3 and 9.4 are vertical in style, treating the revenues (credits) as pluses and the expenses (debits) as minuses. However, the Directive allows a horizontal double-entry style of income statement. Table 9.5 shows the horizontal version of the by nature format, i.e. a rearrangement of Table 9.3. Although the Directive also allows a horizontal by function format this is not used in practice and is not illustrated here.

Activity 9.1

Consider the relative advantages and usefulness of the four Directive formats for the income statement.

Activity feedback

As regards the financial reports of large listed enterprises there is no doubt that the vertical presentations are increasingly predominant. As between the by nature and by function classification, both methods have advantages. Showing expenses by nature requires less analysis and less judgement, but is arguably less informative. It shows the amount *incurred* on production for the period, but does not highlight the total *expenses* under the accruals convention. It fails to reveal the cost of sales, and therefore the gross profit and it has the logical disadvantage that it might seem to imply (see Tables 9.3 or 9.5) that changes in inventory are an expense or a revenue in their own right, which they are not. They are logically an adjustment to purchases.

However, because information on the nature of expenses is regarded as useful in predicting future cash flows, IAS 1 and the Directive require additional disclosure on the nature of expenses, including depreciation and amortization expenses and staff costs, when the by function classification is used.

Changes in equity

IAS 1 requires the inclusion in financial statements of what in many jurisdictions will be an unfamiliar concept, a separate and distinct primary statement to record changes in equity. The requirements relating to this are divided into two sections, numbers 1–4 and 5–7 as defined in the following. An entity shall present a statement of changes in equity showing on the face of the statement (para. 96):

1 profit or loss for the period;
2 each item of income and expense for the period that, as required by other Standards or by Interpretations, is recognized directly in equity, and the total of these items;
3 total income and expense for the period (calculated as the sum of (1) and (2), showing separately the total amounts attributable to equity holders of the parent and to minority interest; and
4 for each component of equity, the effects of changes in accounting policies, and of corrections of errors, recognised in accordance with IAS 8.

Table 9.5 Fourth Directive: horizontal profit and loss account by nature

Item	Description

A Charges
   1 Reduction in stocks of finished goods and in work in progress
   2 (a) Raw materials and consumables
      (b) Other external charges
   3 *Staff costs*
      (a) wages and salaries
      (b) social security costs with a separate indication of those relating to pensions
   4 (a) Value adjustments in respect of formation expenses and of tangible and intangible fixed assets
      (b) Value adjustments in respect of current assets, to the extent that they exceed the amount of value adjustments which are normal in the undertaking concerned
   5 Other operating charges
   6 Value adjustments in respect of financial assets and of investments held as current assets
   7 Interest payable and similar charges, with a separate indication of those concerning affiliated undertakings
   8 Tax on profit or loss on ordinary activities
   9 Profit or loss on ordinary activities after taxation
   10 Extraordinary charges
   11 Tax on extraordinary profit or loss
   12 Other taxes not shown under the above items
   13 Profit or loss for the financial year

B Income
   1 Net turnover
   2 Increase in stocks of finished goods and in work in progress
   3 Work performed by the undertaking for its own purposes and capitalized
   4 Other operating income
   5 Income from participating interests, with a separate indication of that derived from affiliated undertakings
   6 Income from other investments and loans forming part of the fixed assets, with a separate indication of that derived from affiliated undertakings
   7 Other interest receivable and similar income, with a separate indication of that derived from affiliated undertakings
   8 Profit or loss on ordinary activities after taxation
   9 Extraordinary income
   10 Profit or loss for the financial year

An entity shall also present either on the face of the statement of changes in equity or in the notes (para. 97):

   5 the amounts of transactions with equity holders acting in their capacity as equity holders, showing separately distributions to equity holders;

6 the balance of retained earnings (i.e. accumulated profit or loss) at the beginning of the period and at the balance sheet date, and the changes during the period; and

7 a reconciliation between the carrying amount of each class of contributed equity and each reserve at the beginning and the end of the period, separately disclosing each change.

The implications of this are best explained by illustration. Table 9.6 presents a pro forma layout giving all seven items on the face of the statement (note that for simplicity we present Table 9.6 for one year only; in practice the complete set of information would also need to be included for the previous year). Table 9.7 presents a pro forma layout covering items 1–4 only. If the format of Table 9.7 were used, then full disclosure relating to items 5–7 would also be needed in the notes.

The essential difference between either of these statements, as illustrated in Tables 9.6 and 9.7, and the income statement is, of course, that the income statement is restricted to the inclusion of items recognized as revenues or expenses, whereas gains and losses are included in these separate primary statements whether or not they are recognized as part of income. Both of the suggested formats include the net result from the income statement as a separate line item.

Table 9.6 XYZ Group – statement of changes in equity for the year ended 31 December 20–2

	Attributable to equity holders of the parent					Minority interest	Total equity
	Share capital	Other reserve*	Translation reserve	Retained earnings	Total		
Balance at 31 December 20–1 bought forward	X	X	(X)	X	X	X	X
Changes in equity for 20–2							
Loss on property revaluation		(X)			(X)	(X)	(X)
Available-for-sale investments:							
Valuation gains/(losses) taken to equity		(X)			(X)		(X)
Transferred to profit or loss on sale		X			X		X
Cash flow hedges:							
Gains/(losses) taken to equity		X			X	X	X
Transferred to profit or loss for the period		(X)			(X)	(X)	(X)
Transferred to initial carrying amount of hedged items		(X)			(X)		(X)
Exchange differences on translating foreign operations			(X)		(X)	(X)	(X)
Tax on items taken directly to or transferred from equity		X	X		X	X	X
Net income recognized directly in equity		(X)	(X)		(X)	(X)	(X)
Profit for the period				X	X	X	X
Total recognized income and expense for the period		(X)	(X)	X	X	X	X
Dividends				(X)	(X)	(X)	(X)
Issue of share capital	X				X		X
Balance at 31 December 20–2	X	X	(X)	X	X	X	X

*Other reserves are analysed into their components, if material.

Table 9.7 XYZ Group – statement of recognized income and expense for the year ended 31 December 20–2

	20–2	20–1
Gain/(loss on revaluation of properties	(X)	X
Available-for-sale investments:		
Valuation gains/(losses) taken to equity	(X)	(X)
Transferred to profit or loss on sale	X	(X)
Cash flow hedges:		
Gains/(losses) taken to equity	X	X
Transferred to profit or loss for the period	(X)	X
Transferred to the initial carrying amount of hedged items	(X)	(X)
Exchange differences on translation of foreign operations	(X)	(X)
Tax on items taken directly to or transferred from equity	X	(X)
Net income recognized directly in equity	(X)	X
Profit for the period	X	X
Total recognized income and expense for the period	X	X
Attributable to:		
Equity holders of the parent	X	X
Minority interest	X	X
	X	X
Effect of changes in accounting policy:		
Equity holders of the parent		(X)
Minority interest		(X)
		(X)

The whole issue of the appropriate format for presentation of these aspects of financial performance is in something of a state of flux. Much debate is underway within and between the world's major standard-setting bodies. There are two important questions. One concerns the question of what is known as recycling. Suppose an unrealized gain is recorded, outside the income statement, in year 1. In year 2 this gain becomes realized and now meets the criteria for inclusion in the income statement. How, *if at all*, should this be recorded in year 2? At the time of writing, to give two examples under IAS GAAP, IAS 16, *Property, Plant and Equipment*, requires in para. 41 that a transfer from revaluation surplus to retained earnings, on realization, 'is not made through the income statement', (see Chapter 12). However IAS 21, *The Effects of Changes in Foreign Exchange Rates* requires in para. 37 that, when a foreign entity is disposed of, related cumulative deferred exchange differences 'should be recognised as income or as expenses' in the period in which the gain or loss is recognized (see Chapter 25). The issue requires clarification as a matter of general principle.

The other major question, not entirely unrelated to the first, concerns the very idea of the separation of the two statements (i.e. of income and of gains/losses in equity). Because the second is an extension of the first or the first is merely a detailed breakdown of one element (net profit) of the second, why require separation at all?

The idea of a single statement sounds quite simple in one sense, but it carries the fundamental implication, objectionable to some, that the sanctity of the realization convention regarding the income statement would be downgraded or defiled. Nevertheless, there are signs of possible moves in this direction. This debate is ongoing. The precise outcome is unclear, but we expect to see further developments and changes to IAS 1 in the future.

Cash flow statements

The widespread inclusion of cash flow statements in annual financial reporting packages is a relatively recent phenomenon in some countries. There was no mention at all in the EU directives of the possibility or need to provide such statements. This formal regulatory position as regards the reporting of cash flows may seem rather surprising given the demonstrable importance of cash availability and cash flows in the management of an enterprise. This is presumably because at the time of the creation of the directives there was no general practice of any such thing in the major countries involved. The effect was that when national governments came to enact national legislation derived from the directives, there was usually still no mention of any such statement.

Nevertheless the rise of the cash flow statement as a necessary part of a comprehensive reporting package has been rapid. Something like it became a standard requirement in the UK in 1975, in IASs in 1977 and eventually in German law, for listed companies in 1998. There have been a number of developments in the format – and indeed, in the underlying principles – of such statements and there have been two different versions of an International Accounting Standard in the area, IAS 7. This is dealt with in full in Chapter 22.

Notes to the financial statements

In one sense, the notes to the financial statements are 'where everything else goes'. IAS 1 summarizes the functions of the notes as being to (para. 91):

1 Present information about the basis of preparation of the financial statements and the specific accounting policies selected and applied for significant transactions and events.
2 Disclose the information required by International Standards that is not presented elsewhere in the financial statements.
3 Provide additional information which is not presented on the face of the financial statements but that is relevant to an understanding of those statements.

Notes to the financial statements should be presented in a systematic manner. Each item on the face of the balance sheet, income statement and cash flow statement should be cross-referenced to any related information in the notes.

The Standard suggests that notes 'are normally' presented in the following order:

1 statement of compliance with International Standards
2 measurement basis (or bases) used in preparing the financial statements

3 each specific accounting policy that is necessary for a proper understanding of the financial statements

4 supporting information for items presented on the face of each financial statement in the order in which each line item and each financial statement is presented

5 other disclosures, including:

(a) contingencies, commitments and other financial disclosures

(b) non-financial disclosures.

Measurement basis refers to the valuation method, for example, historical cost, fair value. The Standard gives a long list of areas of accounting policy that an enterprise 'might consider presenting'.

Many of the areas specifically require mention under the terms of the relevant IAS, but all significant policies (not the same as policies for all significant amounts) should be clearly disclosed. In addition, an entity shall disclose in the notes:

- the amount of dividends proposed or declared before the financial statements were authorized for issue but not recognized as a distribution to equity holders during the period and the related amount per share
- the amount of any cumulative preference dividends not recognized.

Finally, additional disclosures are required, if not disclosed elsewhere in information published with the financial statements of:

1 The domicile and legal form of the enterprise, its country of incorporation, and the address of the registered office (or principal place of business, if different from the registered office).

2 A description of the nature of the enterprise's operations and its principal activities.

3 The name of the parent enterprise and the ultimate parent enterprise of the group.

4 Either the number of employees at the end of the period or the average for the period.

Summary

This chapter has described and discussed the requirements of the EU Fourth Directive and IAS 1 in relation to the structure of published financial statements.

EXERCISES   (✔ indicates answers are available on page 725)

---

1 Are fixed formats for the key financial statements a good thing? If they are, why are several different ones allowed?

✔ 2 It is important that revenues as determined under the realization convention are reported in a separate statement from any other gains and asset increases. Discuss.

3 The accountant is entitled to assume that readers of financial statements will read and understand all the notes to the accounts. Discuss.

Additional disclosure statements

After studying this chapter you should be able to:
☐ identify the need for additional statements to be included in a reporting package
☐ outline, and comment on the importance of, a variety of possible additional statements and reports which could be included in a reporting package.

Introduction

Earlier chapters have considered a wide range of alternative ways of evaluating financial events. However, in terms of the basic statements that are to be used for presentation to the users of accounting information nothing fundamentally new has been discussed. It has been implicitly assumed throughout that two essential statements are to be created:

■ some form of position statement (balance sheet)
■ some form of income statement.

Several possible extensions or alternatives have been suggested in recent years and we will consider some of these here.

Need for additional statements

All the varied analysis of the last few chapters has been based on the concepts of income and value. We have been thinking about different ways of producing a statement of wealth and about different ways of producing a statement of income, i.e. a change in wealth over time. All of these methods and methodologies, even when reporting on past periods, contain significant assumptions and estimates, and it can be argued that this makes them all less than satisfactory.

Even the traditional accounting process is, as we have seen, an uncertain and complex process. Not only is profit determination complex, it is potentially misleading. In any accounting year, there will be a mixture of complete and incomplete transactions. Transactions are complete when they have led to a final cash settlement and these cause no profit measurement difficulties. However, considerable problems arise in dealing with incomplete transactions, where the profit or loss figure can only be determined by means of the accruals concept. Thus, the profit for the past year is dependent on the validity of many assumptions about the future. The greater the volume of incomplete transactions, the greater the degree of estimation and, accordingly, the greater the risk that investors could turn out to have been misled if actual outcomes deviate from estimates.

Thus, one possible extension to the accounting framework would be to provide information on cash inflows and outflows for an enterprise. This is considered further in Chapter 22. Another possible extension would be to provide information on individual segments within an enterprise. It is quite possible for one particular segment of an enterprise to earn all the profit and the others to provide none. The information provided on segments would allow us to assess the risks inherent in the enterprise. We will look at segmental reports in Chapter 23.

However, if users wish to make decisions on the stewardship of the enterprise's management and to make their own economic decisions on investing either their cash and/or employee skills in the enterprise, they arguably need further information.

Possible additional statements

Activity 10.1

Make a list of further information additional to the income statement, balance sheet and some form of cash statement that might be significantly useful to one or more of the user groups involved in an enterprise.

Activity feedback

(a) A statement showing how the benefits of the efforts of an enterprise are shared between employees, providers of capital, the state and reinvestment. This statement will assist users to evaluate the economic performance of the entity. It is generally known as a 'value added statement'.

(b) Users will need to assess the performance of the enterprise in relation to employees. A report showing the size and composition of the workforce relying on the enterprise for its livelihood, the work contribution of employees and the benefits earned would be useful. This is often known as an employment report.

(c) Users may wish to assess the relationship between the enterprise and the state. Thus a statement of money exchanges with government will assist users to assess the economic function of the enterprise in relation to society.

(d) A statement of future prospects, showing likely future profit, employment and investment levels. This statement will assist users to evaluate the future prospects of the entity and assess managerial performance.

(e) A statement of corporate objectives showing management policy and medium term strategic targets. This statement will assist users to evaluate managerial performance, efficiency and objectives.

(f) A statement of the social and environmental impact of the enterprise on the society surrounding it.

(g) A statement on the 'risks' inherent in the enterprise. Providing information on the potential risks associated with an enterprise's activities may enable users to assess the possible consequence of materialization of that risk and whether suitable measures have been taken to mitigate it.

(h) Past trends in key financial figures and ratios, key financial highlights and stock trend data.

(i) Information in respect of innovations in the organization which will develop tangible and intangible capital/assets in the future.

You may not have identified all of these but we hope you identified some of them. In the rest of this chapter we will discuss all of them.

Value added statements

Value added is the wealth that an enterprise has been able to create by its own and its employees' efforts. It is defined as 'sales income less materials and services purchased'. In rough and ready terms then, it consists of the sales proceeds, reduced by resources given to other parties not connected with the enterprise. In this context, employees, providers of capital and the government are regarded as connected to the business. This thinking enables the second half of the statement to show how the total value added is shared between employees, providers of capital, the state, and finally the business itself for reinvestment. The statement will show how value added has been used to pay those contributing to its creation. An example of a value added statement is given in Table 10.1 taken from Bayer's annual report 2001.

Note that depreciation is not shown as providing for the maintenance of assets as retained profit does but is shown as a deduction from turnover. Thus the value added shown is an indicator of wealth created over and above that required for current maintenance.

Activity 10.2

Identify information in the value added statement in Table 10.1 that is not provided in the published financial statements.

Activity feedback

Rather difficult to do as a value added statement does not give any information that is not already in traditional published accounts. What it does do is to rearrange the information and present it from a different perspective. The emphasis on shareholders inherent in the income statement is removed and instead attention is focused on the wealth created by the business as a whole and on how that created wealth has been split up for various subgroups of the community. It is therefore arguable that a much more rounded picture is presented both of the business as a whole and of the inter-relationships between the various essential inputs that make the business operations possible.

There are no formal requirements from any source on the necessity to include a value added statement in the reporting package, but in spite of this many enterprises do publish a statement of this type.

Table 10.1 Value added by continuing operations

Source			Distribution		
Million euros	2001	Change in %	Million euros	2001	Share in %
Net sales	28 938	+1.1	Stockholders	657	6.7
Other income	701	−22.5	Employees	7 576	77.1
Total operating performance	29 639	+0.4	Governments	826	8.4
Cost of materials	11 057	+10.1	Lenders	463	4.7
Depreciation	2 403	+20.8	Earnings retention	304	3.1
Other expenses	6 353	+0.5			
Value added	9 826	−10.1	Value added	9 826	100.0

Employment report

Employees are obviously closely involved in business. They have to make many important decisions for themselves that will be heavily influenced by the activities, actions and prospects of business organizations. It could be argued that they have much more to lose than many shareholders or lenders, particularly as they are unable to spread their risk. Employees almost always have to put their faith in one business, they cannot involve themselves with large numbers, as investors or lenders can.

Employees certainly need some indication of future profitability, as do other users, but they also need additional information. Some of this may be financial e.g. relating to the profitability of their own particular plant, but much of it will not be best presented in financial terms at all. In spite of this, many accountants would regard the provision of information useful to employees as being a necessary component of the total reporting package.

Employment reports could contain the following information:

- numbers employed, average for the financial year and actual on the first and last day
- broad reasons for changes in the numbers employed
- age distribution and sex of employees
- functions of employees
- geographical location of major employment centres
- major plant and site closures, disposals and acquisitions during the period
- hours scheduled and worked by employees giving as much detail as possible concerning the differences between groups of employees
- employment costs including fringe benefits
- costs and benefits associated with pension schemes and the ability of such schemes to meet future commitments
- cost and time involved in training
- names of unions recognized by the entity for the purpose of collective bargaining and membership figures where available or the fact that this information has not been made available by the unions concerned
- information concerning safety and health including the frequency and severity of accidents and occupational diseases
- selected ratios relating to employment.

Some of this information can be found in the current management reports that are provided by most enterprises in Europe. These management reports are additional to the financial statements but are generally consistent with them. In general auditors when reporting on the financial statements also report on the management report: 'In our opinion, the management report provides, on the whole, a fair understanding of the group's position and adequately presents the risks related to its future development' (extract from auditor's report Bayer annual report, 2001).

Statement of money exchanges with government

Part of the purpose of this idea is to emphasize the extent to which businesses provide governments with money and therefore to show the importance of business organizations to the community as a whole:

> The purpose of the statement is to present the direct flow of money between the enterprise and the government with the object of demonstrating the degree of interdependence between the enterprise and the state. It does not purport to reflect the full extent of the direct and indirect benefits derived by entities from social services and public facilities provided by government.
>
> (corporate report, 1975, UK ASC)

Statement of future prospects

Two points are absolutely clear. First, many users want to assess an enterprise's future prospects. Second, any such assessment of future prospects involves a high degree of uncertainty. Forecasts of future prospects do not predict the future but they do set out in a logical and systematic manner the future implications of past and present known facts adjusted by reference to estimates of likely future developments. These projections will have different degrees of probability attached to them that the user will need to judge. It is the certainty of uncertainty that makes enterprises unwilling to make public projections, although all those acquainted with such exercises are perfectly familiar with the limits on reliability that are inherent in them.

Activity 10.3

Identify three objections to publishing such forecasts.

Activity feedback

- Forecasts are concerned with the future and are therefore inherently uncertain. Unless carefully presented users may regard forecasts as presenting facts rather than best estimates.
- Management will be judged by how well it has met its forecasts and may be encouraged to lower its targets by publishing only conservative forecasts it knows are wholly attainable and to accept results that meet those forecasts.
- The provision of forecasts by enterprises suffering from financial difficulties may result in the withdrawal of support and thus precipitate an otherwise avoidable collapse.

However, such forecasts are certainly desired by users and competitors and, in general, management and accountants are likely to be able to make better and more rational projections which can then be reported than the external users can make for themselves. Forecast statements could include information covering:

- future profit levels
- future employment levels and prospects
- future investment levels.

It should be remembered that these forecasts will be highly subjective and based on various management assumptions. The following 'Further prospects/forecast' is taken from the management report of Beiersdorf AR, 2000:

> In the financial year 2001 Beiersdorf will implement the announced changes in the structure of the business. In April 2001, the Tesa business was hived-off as an independent corporation with retrospective effect from 1 January. This gives Tesa the organisational and legal structures appropriate to the requirements of the market and form the basis for further successful development in the future. The joint venture BSN medical GmbH & Co. HG has also commenced operations, beginning 1 April. This company brings together the professional businesses of Beiersdorf and Smith & Nephew in the field of conventional wound care. With annual sales of around 490 million Euros, BS medical will occupy a leading position worldwide in its competence areas: professional wound care, casting, bandages and compression stockings.
>
> These two projects have high priority for Beiersdorf. We are confident that with these changes we have taken the right steps to ensure successful development of Medical's professional business and Tesa's business in the future.
>
> In our core business we will concentrate entirely on retail consumer sales of big brands. We expect 2001 to bring a worldwide continuation of the generally good economic situation. In Germany and Western Europe, however, the growth of our sales markets will be slow. We also expect a slackening of the pace of growth in North America. International competition and trend to concentration among our customers will continue to increase. We will counteract these developments by focusing on our strong brands. This will further increase our attractiveness as a strong partner for the distributive trade. In 2001 we plan to increase our sales by some 8 to 10% to around 4500 million euros. These figures include 50% of sales by BSN medical and also take account of the sale of the advanced wound care business to Smith & Nephew. We also expect that, after allowing for all remaining restructuring measures, we will achieve an EBIT operating result of around 450 million euros. The profit for the year will come to about 270 million euros. Thus Beiersdorf will probably achieve a net return on sales of 6% in 2001.

It is not until the last paragraph of this forecast that we see some quantitative information.

Statement of corporate objectives

It can be argued that the objectives being pursued by a business need to be publicized for two reasons. First, so that users can see the extent to which management objectives differ from their own and, second, so that management's ability to achieve the stated objectives can be assessed.

Activity 10.4

Identify policy areas where information could usefully be reported under this heading.

Activity feedback

Such policy areas could cover:

- sales
- added value
- profitability
- investment and finance
- dividends
- employment
- consumer issues
- environmental matters
- other relevant social issues.

Again, of course, there is a distinct danger that management will declare objectives that it feels it can be almost certain of achieving.

Other information

Many enterprises provide information in their annual reports that they believe investors will find useful. Such information covers:

- Stock data where share prices, market capitalizations, number of shares traded in a period and dividends are tracked for a number of years.
- Balance sheet ratios where the traditional ratios of return on capital employed etc., are tracked. Bayer 2001 shows information as seen in Table 10.2.
- Financial highlights where the enterprise identifies key changes from one to the next in such items as sales, capital expenditure, personnel expenses, research and development expenses etc.

Table 10.2 Balance sheet ratios tracking ROCE etc.

	2001	2000
Non-current assets/total assets %	58.6	55.8
Depreciation/capital expenditure %	94.2	80.2
Net sales/inventories	5.2	5.1
Net sales/trade accounts receivable	5.6	5.0
Stockholders' equity/total assets %	45.7	44.3
Stockholders' equity/non current assets %	78.0	79.3
Short-term liabilities/total liabilities %	51.9	53.8

- Ten-year summary information of sales, assets, financial obligations etc.
- Risk management issues where enterprises report, as part of best practice within corporate governance, on the potential risks associated with their activities, the assessment of the possible consequences of their materialization and measures available to mitigate them.

Activity 10.5

Does the additional information just examined provide useful information to users?

Activity feedback

The additional information is certainly relevant and probably understandable to several type of user but questions remain over its comparability to similar information from other enterprises and its reliability.

Social accounting

Social accounting has been defined as:

> The process of communicating the social and environmental effects of organisations' economic activities to particular interest groups within society at large. As such, it involves extending the accountability of organisations, beyond the traditional role of providing a financial account to the owners of capital, in particular, shareholders. Such an extension is predicated upon the assumption that companies do have wider responsibilities than simply to make money for their shareholders.
>
> (Gray, Owen and Adams, 1996)

As long ago as 1975 social accounting was suggested in the UK via the corporate report.

Through legislation, both country and EU based, society is imposing duties on enterprises to comply with anti-pollution, safety and health and other socially beneficial requirements. Legislation of this type will continue to increase in the future. Such legislation imposes costs on enterprises that were previously borne by the community at large and there is therefore good reason to require such expenditure, both compulsory and voluntary expenditure, to be reported. If enterprises do disclose information on their impact on social and environmental effects then we will, of course, need generally agreed measurement and recognition criteria for such impacts. Much work has been done, in the USA and Europe, to measure environmental costs. An attempt was made to measure pollution costs caused by employees driving to work. However, quite often in such studies, the costs and benefits of interest are not always quantifiable in money terms. This does not mean that such attempts at recognition and measurement should not be considered but does mean that we might have to design radically different measuring tools if we wish to provide useful information in this area to users. The attention of the community is increasingly focused on the 'quality of life' rather than money and if accountants do not attempt to produce useful information in this area then someone else will.

The last ten years or so have seen an extensive growth in environmental reporting and legislation, which has forced enterprises to begin to assess their environmental liabilities and risks. Shell plc discovered the pressure that environmental groups can assert, as they were forced to abandon their attempts to dump the *Brent Spar* oil platform at sea. Users of Shell's financial statements may now demand a great deal more information in respect of Shell's environmental risks and liabilities.

Several research initiatives into social and environmental reporting have been established, in particular a centre has been established at the University of Dundee in the UK and the Canadian Institute of Accountants has produced a discussion paper.

Social and environmental reporting is gaining in importance politically, for example the EU has produced a regulation – Community Eco-management and Audit Schemes (EMAS) – where participating enterprises must establish environmental goals and report on their performance in meeting those goals. These reports will require external verification, surely a job for accountants as auditors. Environmental auditing was defined by the Canadian Institute as 'a systematic process of objectively obtaining and evaluating evidence regarding a verifiable assertion about activities and events to ascertain the degree of correspondence between the assertion and established criteria and then communicating the results to interested users'.

Most environmental reporting tends to be narrative and descriptive with enterprises using the document as a public relations exercise rather than as a true measure of the environmental risks and liabilities they carry. This is due to the inherent difficulties of measurement of environmental factors and of applying accounting concepts to these factors.

Activity 10.6

Traditionally, accounting was based around the concepts of money measurement, going concern, and accruals. Identify whether environmental issues are taken into account in the application of these concepts to a business and, if not, why not.

Activity feedback

Money measurement requires that only those facts that can be recorded in monetary terms with some objectivity are taken into account even if other facts are extremely relevant. Environmental factors are very difficult to measure in monetary terms. How, for example, do you place a monetary measure on the damage being done to the environment through car exhaust emissions of employees travelling to work?

The going concern convention requires that in the absence of evidence to the contrary it is assumed that the enterprise will continue into the future. This concept is principally concerned with solvency and financial performance, not with the impact of environmental factors. For example, in assessing going concern for Shell, little regard was had as to whether pressure groups could ever force them out of business.

Accruals requires a matching of expenses used up in generating revenues. However, enterprises make no assessment of the expense of environmental factors such as their contribution to global warming through the emission of carbon dioxide or to acid rain from the emission of sulphur and nitrogen oxides.

Environmental information is, however, becoming essential for many businesses and its users. Indeed some organizations, which see environmental issues as important, are becoming market leaders, for example Body Shop. Businesses are becoming 'greener' and we must develop accounting systems to enable environmental performance reporting to take place.

The international scene in respect of environmental reporting is developing. FEE, the Fédération des Experts Comptables Européens, established an environmental taskforce to review the current body of IASs and to recommend improvements in those standards. A report by the United Nations Conference on Trade and Environment (UNCTAD) Secretariat; *Environmental Financial Accounting and Reporting at the Corporate Level*, was also issued on 19 November 1997. The report aimed to identify best practice for reporting and communicating environmental performance both in terms of reporting costs of environmental risks and in presenting non-financial information. The report was actually synthesized from two others:

- accounting and reporting for environmental liabilities and costs within the existing financial reporting framework (David Moore, Canadian Institute of Chartered Accountants, 1997)
- making environmental and financial performance: a survey of best practice techniques (Roger Adams, ACCA, 1997).

The findings of the report were that financial sector investors were placing increasing importance on environmental data in forming their decisions, although no obvious causal mechanism could be identified.

The EC has also urged greater corporate social responsibility (CSR) in Europe through a green paper promoting a European framework for CSR. The aim of the paper is to trigger debate on all aspects of CSR and views on it were requested by 31 December 2001. When the paper was launched two commissioners, Diamantopouilou and Liikanen stated: 'More and more firms are realising the link between profitability and best ethical and environmental practice. Conscientious firms not only attract and retain best workers, they can also get ahead in the technology game, vital for that all-important competitive edge.'

The debate on CSR is also influenced by the Commission's proposals for a European strategy on sustainable development endorsed at the Gothenburg Summit in June 2001. At this stage it might be useful to identify for you the meaning of several terms used in the environmental debate.

- CSR is about enterprises taking account of the social and environmental impact of their decisions when making business decisions. Enterprises who voluntarily do this will be seen as 'good corporate citizens'.
- Sustainable development is about ensuring that business decisions taken by enterprises now do not limit the range of economic, social and environmental options available to others in the future. In other words we must ensure that enterprises do not 'rape the planet'.
- Socially responsible investing – SRI – is a phenomenon that has grown in recent years. Many investors now take account of how enterprises impact on society as well as their financial performance when making investment decisions. There is currently a growth in 'ethical' investment funds.

■ Triple bottom line (TBL) is a concept whereby companies voluntarily take on board social, environmental and economic issues and report on them. The EC endorses this triple bottom approach in its green paper and suggests that all the elements, social, environmental and economic can, taken together, create more productive and profitable business. Under the TBL approach information is provided on:
  – economic – covering financial and non-financial information as we currently have in annual reports
  – environmental – effect of the products or services on the environment
  – social – covering values, ethics and relationships with various stakeholders.

Activity 10.7

Identify reasons why European enterprises should take CSR accounting seriously.

Activity feedback

The list is probably endless and we identify only a few here:

■ The growth of SRI means enterprises will have to report on their social and environmental impact or risk losing investors.
■ Environmental disasters caused by enterprises are now widely reported through the global media and enterprises are thus under greater scrutiny and pressure to disclose information.
■ An enterprise's value in the market can be damaged if it does not take on board social and environmental risk factors. Its brand and reputation are likely to be damaged.
■ An enterprise's reputation as a good 'corporate citizen' can have a positive effect on employee recruitment and retention.
■ Good corporate citizenship can also generate customers and forge better links with suppliers.

Shell in its annual report 2000 made the following statement:

Sustainable development underlies our strategy and is being integrated into everything Shell companies do – in oil and gas as much as renewables. We have to do business in the real world, with all its complexities. We look to governments to create conditions that foster social and economic development but some lack the means. We believe responsible business promotes development. We support Kofi Annan's Global Compact and the Global Sullivan Principles.

Bayer in its 2000 annual report pack included a booklet entitled 'Shaping the future' and it is to this we have to turn to find any mention of CSR:

Bayer is a diversified, international health care and chemicals group. We offer our customers a wide variety of products and services in areas ranging from pharmaceuticals and crop protection to plastics and speciality chemicals. Bayer is research-based and aims for technological leadership in its core activities. Our goals are to steadily increase corporate value and generate a high value added for the benefit of our stockholders, our employees and the community in every country in which we operate. We believe that our technical and commercial expertise involves a responsibility to work for the common good and contribute to sustainable development. Bayer: success through Expertise with Responsibility.

This statement, however, does seem to indicate a commitment to increasing corporate value before any contribution to sustainable development. However, page 51 of the brochure references Bayer's standing in the area of ecology and economy in harmony as follows:

The Bayer group's long standing commitment to environmental protection is acknowledged all over the world, as illustrated by the distinguished honours we have been awarded during the year under review:

■ U.S. President Bill Clinton presented Bayer Corporation with the coveted Presidential Green Chemistry Challenge Award for the development of water-soluble coatings systems.
■ Thanks to the company's sustainable and forward-looking business approach, Bayer AG's listing in the Dow Jones Sustainability Group index was reaffirmed.
■ The leading Scandinavian financial services company Storebrand Investments, which only invests in companies with a responsible attitude to the environment, rated Bayer's performance above average in six out of seven criteria.

There is some information available in current annual reports on an enterprise's impact in social and environmental terms but much of it is discursive rather than quantitative. However, the European Environmental Agency (EEA) in partnership with the World Business Council on Sustainable Development (WBCSD) did manage to produce 'environmental headline indicators' in 1999, which have since been adopted and developed by the EU.

Activity 10.8

Identify key criteria for CSR in order for it to be useful to users.

Activity feedback

■ Continuity – in that the same methods and metrics are used year after year.
■ Comparability – to allow for benchmarking and assessing progress.
■ Credibility – to ensure that the information provides a 'true and fair' picture of the company's environmental performance.

You could, of course have listed understandability, comparability, relevance and reliability just as easily.

In conclusion to the discussion on CSR we return to Hicks and his theory of capital maintenance that we dealt with in Chapter 4. Remember the quote: 'The purpose of income calculations in practical affairs is to give people an indication of the amount which they can consume without impoverishing themselves.'

This can be applied to the environment because if we continue to consume the environment we will impoverish perhaps not ourselves, but certainly future generations. Economic activity affects the environment as natural resources are depleted or polluted through for example usage, the effects of global warming and acid rain. There is a need to look forward, as the theory of capital maintenance does, to ensure natural wealth – the environment – is maintained and therefore a system of stewardship and maintenance of this natural wealth is a necessity. Reporting in respect of stewardship and maintenance of assets is the accountant's domain. If the objective of financial statements is to provide useful information to users in order for them to assess the stewardship of management and for making economic decisions then, in the view of many, financial statements will need to incorporate the issue, certainly, of environmental reporting and possibly CSR to meet this objective. This will not be an easy task as systems will be difficult to design, but, through their training, accountants are ideally placed to play a leading role in this area.

Other extension frameworks

Throughout the accounting world examples of different (better) reporting are being considered. In the UK in 2000 the Institute of Chartered Accountants produced an exemplar report for a fictitious company, Prototype plc. This suggested that future reporting would consist of a core document of summary information supported by additional reports of financial and economic information, people report, sustainability report and supply chain report.

Perhaps it is also worth considering the adoption of a 'balanced scorecard' (Kaplan and Norton, Harvard Business Press, 1996) approach to company reporting.

From work in the field of human asset accounting the idea of intellectual capital accounts (ICAs) has developed. Edvinsson, who in 1991 was appointed Director of Intellectual Capital at Skandia Assurance and Financial Services stated that the difference between the market value of a firm and its financial or book value is represented by the firm's stock of intellectual capital. He defined intellectual capital as 'the process of knowledge, applied experience, organisational technology, customer relationships, and the professional skills that provide an enterprise with a competitive edge in the market'.

He makes a fundamental distinction between human capital and structural capital. Structural capital is composed of customer, image, innovation, process and IT capital. Carl Bro Group, a Danish company, provides their users with ICAs but they are not subject to audit. Carl Bro Group has also attempted to identify performance indicators in this area.

Activity 10.9

Suggest possible performance indicators for human, customer, image, innovation, process and IT capital within the ICAs model.

Activity feedback

- Human – number of staff, age distribution, training costs, staff satisfaction surveys etc.
- Customer – customer satisfaction index, turnover by customer, largest customer's share of turnover etc.
- Image – among executives and students, surveys of enterprise as potential future employer.
- Innovation – number of development projects, number of first time sales of new products, innovation rate per employer etc.
- Process – gross sales, interdisciplinary projects, shared knowledge documents on the internet.
- IT – cost per employee, size of shared knowledge bases, employees with option of teleworking etc.

There is much development work to do in the area of ICAs.

Summary

There is a school of thought that more information is always, provided it is properly presented, a good thing. The list of possibilities is almost endless as we have hopefully indicated in this chapter. But there is a danger that the purpose of the whole operation becomes lost. We need to provide information that is useful to the typical user. What evidence there is tends to suggest that many users are not able to understand the information they are already getting. It could be argued that the priority for accountants should be to improve their ability to communicate understanding, rather than to increase the detail and complexity of their reports. Is the graph or the pie chart more useful than the beautifully balanced balance sheet? Is the 'chatty' chairman's statement of more use than the precisely detailed and carefully audited accounts and voluminous notes? Is the CSR report or TBL report of more use than the segmental report even if they do lack a degree of reliability? And how can we audit this CSR and TBL report? These are all questions that the profession will need to answer.

In this chapter we have outlined a wide variety of possible developments and extensions to the accounting framework and reporting practice. All involve additional effort and therefore additional cost. But if the advantages to some users or potential users outweigh those costs then we should perhaps produce them.

EXERCISES   (✔ indicates answers are available on page 725)

1 Using the annual report of any enterprise of your choice discuss whether the information provided therein is of use to users.
2 For the same enterprise identify what, if any, additional information you as a potential shareholder would have wished to be available and what use you would make of the information.

3 Using the information given in Activity 10.2 in respect of Bayer's value added statement identify possible conclusions that could be drawn in respect of Bayer's performance for the year and any caveats you would place on these conclusions.

4 Using the management report from any enterprise of your choice identify all information it contains relevant to employees and discuss the importance of this information to the employees of the enterprise.

5 Critically appraise the following statement: *All information provided by enterprise in addition to that required by country law is potentially misleading to users.*

✔ 6 Discuss the need for enterprises to provide additional information to users.

✔ 7 Identify the potential drawbacks of enterprises providing additional information and suggest possible means of overcoming these drawbacks.

8 In the last analysis, financial reporting is about numbers. Discuss.

9 *When users are asked what they want from corporate environmental statements, there appears to be the usual mix of that which is deliverable, that which would be nice if only the accountants could find a way of delivering it and that which will never be deliverable – available or not – because of commercial sensitivity* [Roger Adams, *Accountancy Age*, May 1994, p. 16]. Is this pessimistic or realistic today? Discuss and illustrate.

Quo vadis?

After studying this chapter you should be able to:
□ critically discuss the adequacy of accounting principles and processes in an international context.

Introduction

Where is accounting going? This is by no means an easy question to answer. The first requirement is to make sure that we have some fairly clear ideas as to where accounting has come from. The essential point is that accounting developed as a *practical* response to *local* needs. What we are now trying to do, we being academics, practitioners and regulators, is to provide a conceptual logic and consistency for our discipline and a global harmonization and consistency for our practices.

The difficulties of achieving these twin aims can be summed up in one word: people. First, the people who wish to use financial statements have different purposes, which create different and often conflicting implications. Desirable attributes of the principles and practices of financial reporting are therefore often conflicting. Second, citizens of different countries and cultures have different 'typical' ways of thinking. The same words, even the same numbers, will be interpreted differently in different parts of the world. It follows from all this that there are limits to the degree of coherence, consistency and harmonization that can be achieved.

The future

Much progress has been made. The conceptual framework developments of the last quarter of the 20th century have done much to improve thinking and understanding of what accounting can and does do – and also, even more importantly, have done much to improve our understanding of what accounting does not and cannot do.

Determined efforts to tackle the international harmonization issue began more recently. They are still very much ongoing. Considerable progress and development can be expected over the next few years. The IASB is set to consolidate its position, although progress is not likely to be smooth. Regional cooperation – Europe, North America, Asia-Pacific – is also set to develop further. But, as with the conceptual issues, there are, in our view, very real limits to the extent that harmonization can and will be achieved. Only with a common context, a common economic system and stage of development and a common culture, is true harmonization possible. Such commonality is unlikely and, arguably, thoroughly undesirable from a broader perspective.

In such an unclear and imprecise situation, one minimal requirement is absolutely unavoidable. This is that, as regards both the conceptual accounting issues and the regulatory internationalization issues, a real understanding of *alternatives* is essential. That is why Part One of this book needs to be studied and understood before the significance of the problems and regulations discussed in Parts Two and Three can be appreciated and understood. That is why it is not adequate just to 'learn the regulations'.

It is also why accounting, in general and financial reporting, in particular, are so interesting. They will continue to change and develop and will therefore continue to be interesting subjects of study for many years to come. We hope that you will read the rest of this book in that spirit. And we hope that you will end up with the same enthusiasm that we have.

EXERCISE

1 Where *is* accounting going?

Part Two

Annual Financial Statements

In this part we look in detail at the international rules that accountants have created for themselves to govern financial reporting. In each case, we explore the underlying issues involved, applying the principles developed in Part One, and consider the International Standard requirements. Do these Standards achieve what they are setting out to do when considered individually? Do they make sense, when looked at as a whole? As with Part One, you are invited to form your own opinion on 'the story so far'.

Fixed (non-current) tangible assets

After studying this chapter you should be able to:
- ☐ discuss and apply the principles, concepts and major methods of providing for depreciation
- ☐ explain what depreciation does and does not do
- ☐ explain the issues involved in determining appropriate treatments for government grants
- ☐ describe, apply and appraise the requirements of IAS 20, relating to government grants
- ☐ explain the issues involved in determining appropriate treatments for borrowing costs
- ☐ describe, apply and appraise the requirements of IAS 23 relating to borrowing costs
- ☐ describe, apply and appraise the requirements of IAS 16, property, plant and equipment
- ☐ discuss alternative treatments for investment properties
- ☐ describe, apply and appraise the requirements of IAS 40 related to investment properties.

Introduction

Assets have been defined (in Chapter 8) as follows: (Framework para. 49a):

An asset is a resource controlled by the enterprise as a result of past events and from which future economic benefits are expected to flow.

Assets are divided into fixed assets and current assets. The IAS terms are non-current assets and current assets respectively. The distinction is formally defined in IAS 1 (para. 57), as discussed in more detail in Chapter 9.

An asset should be classified as a current asset when it:

1 is expected to be realized in, or is held for sale or consumption in, the normal course of the entity's operating cycle
2 is held primarily for trading purposes or for the short term and expected to be realized within 12 months of the balance sheet date
3 or is cash or a cash equivalent asset which is not restricted in its use.

All other assets should be classified as non-current assets.

The definition of non-current assets is often misunderstood. A non-current asset is not an asset with a long life. The essential criterion is the *intention* of the owner, the intended *use* of the asset. A non-current asset is an asset that the firm intends to use within the business, over an extended period, in order to assist its daily operating activities. A current asset, by way of contrast, is usually defined in terms of time. A current asset is an asset likely to change its form, i.e. likely to undergo some transaction, within 12 months.

Activity 12.1

Consider two firms, A and B. Firm A is a motor trader. It possesses some motor vehicles that it is attempting to sell and it also possesses some desks used by the sales staff, management and so on. Firm B is a furniture dealer. It possesses some desks that it is attempting to sell and it also possesses some motor vehicles used by the sales staff and for delivery purposes. How are these items treated in each case?

Activity feedback

In the accounts of A, the motor vehicles are current assets and the desks are non-current assets. In the accounts of B, the motor vehicles are non-current assets and the desks are current assets. Note incidentally that a fixed asset which, after several years' use, is about to be sold for scrap, remains in the fixed asset part of the accounts even though it is about to change its form.

Principles of accounting for depreciation

The first major problem with depreciation, perhaps surprisingly, is to agree on what it is and what it is for. The generally agreed view nowadays is that it is in essence a straightforward application of the matching, or accruals, convention. With a non-current asset the benefit from the asset is spread over several years. The matching convention requires that the corresponding expense be matched with the benefit in each accounting period. This does not simply mean that the total expense for the asset's life is spread over the total beneficial life. It means, more specifically, that the total expense for the asset's life is spread over the total beneficial life *in proportion to the pattern of benefit.* Thus, to take a simple example, if a non-current asset gives half of its benefit, or usefulness, in year 1, one-third in year 2 and one-sixth in year 3 and the total expenses arising are €1200, then the matching convention requires the charging of €600 in year 1, €400 in year 2, and €200 in year 3, in the annual profit calculation. This charge is known as the *depreciation charge.*

In order to calculate a figure for this charge it is necessary to answer four basic questions:

1 What is the cost of the asset?
2 What is the estimated useful life of the asset to the business? (This may be equal to, or may be considerably less than, its technical or physical useful life.)
3 What is the estimated residual selling value ('scrap value') of the asset at the end of the useful life as estimated?

4   What is the pattern of benefit or usefulness derived from the asset likely to be (not the *amount* of the benefit)?

It is perfectly obvious that the second, third and fourth of these involve a good deal of uncertainty and subjectivity. The 'appropriate' figures are all dependent on future plans and future actions. It is important to realize that even if the first figure, the cost of the fixed asset, is known precisely and objectively, the basis of the depreciation calculation as a whole is always uncertain, estimated and subjective.

The estimates should, as usual, be reasonable, fair and prudent (whatever precisely this implies!).

But the first figure is often not at all precise and objective, for several reasons.

Activity 12.2

Suggest reasons why the cost of a particular fixed asset may be difficult to determine with precision.

Activity feedback

Possible reasons include the following:

1   Incidental expenses associated with making the asset workable should be included, e.g. installation costs carried out by the business's own staff, probably including some overhead costs.
2   The non-current asset may be constructed within the business by its own workforce, giving rise to all the usual costing problems of overhead definition and overhead allocation.
3   Depending on the accounting policies used by the firm generally, the 'basic' figure for the fixed asset may be revalued periodically. Additionally, if land is not depreciated but the building on the land is, then this requires a split of the total cost (or value) figure for the land and buildings together into two possibly somewhat arbitrary parts.
4   Major alterations/improvements may be made to the asset part way through its life. If these appear to increase the benefit from the asset over the remaining useful life and perhaps also to increase the number of years of the remaining useful life, and are material, then the costs of these improvements should also be capitalized (i.e. treated as part of the non-current asset from then on). However, maintenance costs, including a major overhaul that does not occur frequently, are 'running' expenses and should be charged to the income statement as incurred. In practice, this distinction can be difficult to make.
5   Accounting policies in relation to government grants receivable and to capitalization of borrowing costs, may influence the figures. These two issues are the subjects of separate International Standards. They are considered later in the chapter.

The total figure to be depreciated, known as the *depreciable amount*, will consist of the cost of the asset less the scrap value. This depreciable amount needs to be spread over the useful life in proportion to the pattern of benefit. Once the depreciable amount has been found, with revision if necessary to take account of material improvements, several recognized methods exist for spreading, or allocating, this amount to the various years concerned. The more important possibilities are outlined next. It is essential to understand the implicit assumption that each method makes about the pattern of benefit arising and therefore about the appropriate pattern of expense allocation.

Methods of calculating depreciation

Straight line method

The depreciable amount is allocated on a straight line basis, i.e. an equal amount is allocated to each year of the useful life. If an asset is revalued or materially improved then the new depreciable amount will be allocated equally over the remaining, possibly extended, useful life.

Activity 12.3

Using the straight line method calculate the annual depreciation charge from the following data:

Cost ('basic' value figure)	€12 000
Useful life	4 years
Scrap value	€2 000

Activity feedback

$$\text{Annual charge} = \frac{€12\,000 - €2\,000}{4}$$

$$= €2\,500$$

This is by far the most common method. It is the easiest to apply and also the preparation of periodic, e.g. monthly, accounts for internal purposes is facilitated. This method assumes, within the limits of materiality, that the asset is equally useful, or beneficial, each year. Whether this assumption is as frequently justified as the common usage of the method suggests, is an open question.

Reducing balance method

Under this method, depreciation each year is calculated by applying a constant percentage to the net book value (NBV) brought forward from the previous year. (Note that this percentage is based on the cost less depreciation to date.) Given the cost (or valuation) starting figure and the useful life and 'scrap' value figures, the appropriate percentage needed to make the NBV at the end of the useful life exactly equal to the scrap value can be found from a formula:

$$d = \sqrt[n]{S/C}$$

where d is the depreciation percentage, n is the life in years, S is the scrap value and C is the cost (or basic value).

This formula is rarely used. In practice, when this method is used a standard 'round' figure is usually taken, shown by experience to be vaguely satisfactory for the particular type of asset under consideration. Notice, incidentally, that the formula fails to work when the scrap value is zero and produces an extreme and possibly distorted allocation of expense when the scrap value is very small.

Activity 12.4

Using the data from the previous activity and assuming a depreciation percentage of 40%, calculate the depreciation charge for each of the four years using the reducing balance method.

Activity feedback

Year 1	Cost	€12 000
	Depreciation 40%	4 800
Year 2	NBV	7 200
	Depreciation 40%	2 880
Year 3	NBV	4 320
	Depreciation 40%	1 728
Year 4	NBV	2 592
	Depreciation 40%	1 037
	NBV	€1 555

If the estimated scrap value turns out to be correct, then a 'profit' on disposal of 445 would be recorded also in year 4. This is an example of a reducing charge method or of an accelerated depreciation method. The charge is highest in the first year and gradually reduces over the asset's life.

Activity 12.5

Compare.

Suggest, and critically appraise, arguments in favour of using the reducing balance method rather than the straight line method.

Activity feedback

1 It better reflects the typical benefit pattern, at least of some assets.
2 It could be argued that, where the pattern of benefit is assumed to be effectively constant, the appropriate 'expense', which needs to be correspondingly evenly matched, is not the pure depreciation element, but the sum of:
   (a) the pure depreciation element
   (b) and the maintenance and repair costs.
   Because **(b)** will tend to increase as the asset gets older, it is necessary for **(a)** to be reduced as the asset gets older, in the hope that the total of the two will remain more or less constant. This may be a valid argument in the most general of terms, but of course there is no reason why an arbitrary percentage applied in one direction should even approximately compensate for flexible and 'chancy' repair costs in the other.

3 It better reflects the probable fact that the value (i.e. the market or resale value) of the asset falls more sharply in the earlier years. This argument, often advanced, is questionable in principle. Depreciation is concerned with appropriate allocation of expense, applying the matching convention. It is not concerned with an annual revaluation of the fixed assets, so whether or not a particular method is good or bad from this viewpoint is, or should be, irrelevant. So long as the original estimate of future benefit is still valid, the fact that current market value is small, at an intermediate time, is not of concern.

4 Since it frontloads the depreciation expense charge in the earlier years of the useful life, it is consistent with the prudence principle. It is indeed true that prudence can be said to support the reducing balance method rather than the straight line method. What is not clear is whether this a valid *advantage*. This is a particular example of the general debate concerning the relative importance of the prudence principle, discussed in Chapter 3.

A particular variant found in practice in some countries is known as the double-declining balance method. This involves calculating the appropriate 'straight line' depreciation percentage, then doubling it and applying the resulting percentage on the reducing balance basis.

Sum of the digits method

This is another example of a reducing charge method. It is based on a convenient 'rule of thumb' and produces a pattern of depreciation charge somewhat similar to the reducing balance method.

Using the same figures as before, we give the four years weights of 4, 3, 2 and 1, respectively and sum the total weights. In general terms we give the n years weights of $n, n - 1, \ldots, 1$ respectively, and sum the total weights, the sum being $n(n + 1)/2$. The depreciable amount is then allocated over the years in the proportion that each year's weighting bears to the total.

Activity 12.6

Use the sum of the digits method to calculate annual depreciation charges for the data in the previous activities.

Activity feedback

$4 + 3 + 2 + 1 = 10$ (the 'sum' of the 'digits')
Depreciable amount $= €12\,000 - €2\,000 = €10\,000$

Depreciation charges are:

Year 1	$4/10 \times 10\,000 = €4\,000$
Year 2	$3/10 \times 10\,000 = €3\,000$
Year 3	$2/10 \times 10\,000 = €2\,000$
Year 4	$1/10 \times 10\,000 = €1\,000$

This gives NBV figures in the balance sheet of €8000, €5000, €3000 and €2000 for year ends 1–4, respectively.

Output or usage method

This is particularly suitable for assets where the rate of usage or rate of output can be easily measured. For example, a motor vehicle might be regarded as having a life of 100 000 miles, rather than a life of four years. The depreciable amount can then be allocated to each year in proportion to the recorded mileage, e.g. if 30 000 miles are covered in year 1, then 3/10 of the depreciable amount will be charged in year 1. The life of a machine could be defined in terms of machine hours. The annual charge would then be:

$$\text{Depreciable amount} \times \frac{\text{Machine hours used in the year}}{\text{Total estimated life in machine hours}}$$

Revaluation or arbitrary valuation

This approach is occasionally used with minor items such as loose tools. An estimated or perhaps purely arbitrary figure for the value of the items (in total) is chosen at the end of each year. Depreciation is then the difference between this figure and the figure from the previous year. Strictly, of course, this is not a method of depreciation at all, but a lazy alternative to it.

All these methods can be criticized on the grounds that they ignore the fact that the resources 'tied up' in the fixed asset concerned have an actual cost to the business in terms of interest paid or an implied (opportunity) cost in terms of interest foregone. This could well be regarded as an essential expense that should be matched appropriately against the benefit from the asset. The 'actuarial' methods that attempt to take account of interest expense are complicated to apply and in financial accounting are hardly ever used.

Some misconceptions underlined

The process of depreciation calculation is not designed to produce balance sheet numbers that are either particularly meaningful or particularly useful, as measurements of value; in fact, they are measurements of unexpired costs.

It must be remembered that depreciation is a process of matching expenses in proportion to benefits. Given that the depreciable amount has been agreed, the annual charge is based on actual or implied assumptions as to the pattern of benefit being derived and nothing else. In simple bookkeeping terms, all that is happening is that a transfer is being made from the non-current assets section in the balance sheet to the expenses section in the income statement. And it is the expense that is being positively calculated, not the reduction in the asset figure. It follows from this that:

1 The asset figure for an intermediate year has no very obvious or useful meaning. It can only be defined in a roundabout way. For example, under historical cost (HC) accounting, it is the amount of the original cost not yet deemed to have been used, or not yet allocated. This intermediate figure is often called 'net book value' but it is *not* a value at all within the proper meaning of the word.

2 Depreciation has nothing to do with ensuring that the business can 'afford' to buy another asset when the first one becomes useless. This is true even if we ignore the likelihood of rising price levels. Depreciation does not increase the amount of any particular asset, cash or otherwise.

3 However, depreciation, like any other expense figure, does have the effect of retaining *resources* (or total assets) in the business. By reducing profit we reduce the maximum dividend payable (which would reduce resources) and therefore increase the 'minimum resources remaining' figure. This is, in fact, a particular illustration of the idea of capital maintenance discussed in Chapter 4.

Determining the cost of a fixed asset

In this section, we look at two particular problem areas regarding cost determination, i.e. government grants and interest capitalization. Before that, as a check on your understanding of general principles, try the following activity.

Activity 12.7

In the year to 31 December, Hans bought a new fixed asset and made the following payments in relation to it:

	€	€
Cost as per supplier's list	12 000	
less Agreed discount	1 000	11 000
Delivery charge ✓		100
Erection charge ✓		200
Maintenance charge		300
Additional component to increase capacity ✓		400
Replacement parts		250

Required

(a) State and justify the cost figure which should be used as the basis for depreciation.
(b) What does depreciation do and why is it necessary?
(c) Briefly explain, without numerical illustration, how the straight line and reducing balance methods of depreciation work. What different assumptions does each method make?
(d) Explain the term objectivity as used by accountants. To what extent is depreciation objective?
(e) It is common practice in published accounts in Germany to use the reducing balance method for a fixed asset in the early years of its life, and then to change to the straight line method as soon as this would give a higher annual charge.

What do you think of this practice? Refer to relevant accounting conventions in your answer.

Activity feedback

1 This figure should be the total cost of making the fixed asset usable, excluding all costs of actually using it. Therefore:

$$11\,000 + 100 + 200 + 400 = €11\,700$$

The additional component is cost of machine as it enhances the revenue earning capacity of the asset but the replacement parts are cost of using machine – hence the difference in treatment between the two. Maintenance is obviously a cost of usage.

2   Depreciation spreads the cost (or value) of an item over its useful life, in appropriate proportion to the benefit (usefulness). It is necessary in accordance with the matching convention – allocating expense against corresponding benefit, as part of the profit calculation.

3   The straight line method charges a constant percentage of the cost (or value) each year. The reducing balance method charges a constant percentage of the net book value (cost less accumulated depreciation brought forward). Thus the straight line method has a constant charge but the reducing balance method has a charge reducing each year of the asset life. The two methods therefore make different assumptions about the usefulness, the trend or pattern of benefit, of the fixed asset concerned.

4   Objectivity implies lack of bias. It removes the need for and the possibility of subjectivity, of personal opinion. For an accounting figure to be objective, it must be expected that all accountants would arrive at the same figure. Clearly, the figure stated on an invoice has a high degree of objectivity. However, the calculation of depreciation is based on estimates of future life and future usefulness and is therefore highly subjective.

5   This practice can claim the advantage of greater prudence, as the expense is always the higher of the two possibilities. However, it seems to lack consistency. Perhaps more importantly, it obviously fails to attempt to follow the matching convention. It makes no attempt to make the trend of expenses consistent with the trend of benefit or usefulness.

Government grants

Enterprises which receive a material amount of assistance from government or state sources are clearly in a different economic position from otherwise comparable enterprises which receive no such assistance. In order to allow proper appraisal of the results of the enterprise activities and to facilitate comparisons, disclosure of this government assistance in as much detail as practicable is necessary.

More specifically, government *grants* are usually easily quantifiable and the general principle of transparency requires that they are both properly accounted for and clearly disclosed. Government grants typically represent a reduction in net cash outflows and, therefore, at least ultimately, an increase in enterprise earnings.

Suppose a government grant is paid to an enterprise because, and under the condition that, the enterprise purchases a depreciable non-current asset. The figures concerned are as follows:

Purchase price of asset	€12 000
Expected useful life	4 years
Expected residual value	Nil
Government grant	€2 000
Annual profits before depreciation, and grants relating to the asset	€20 000

It is possible to suggest at least four possible different ways of treating the grant:

1 to credit the total amount of the grant immediately to the income statement
2 to credit the amount of the grant to a non-distributable reserve
3 to credit the amount of the grant to revenue over the useful life of the asset by:
   (a) reducing the cost of the acquisition of the non-current asset by the amount of the grant
   (b) or treating the amount of the grant as a deferred credit, a portion of which is transferred to revenue annually.

Activity 12.8

Which of these methods do you prefer? Give reasons.

Activity feedback

The first two methods may be rejected on the ground that they provide no correlation between the accounting treatment of the grant and the accounting treatment of the expenditure to which the grant relates. The first method would increase the profits in the first year by the entire amount of the grant, failing to associate the grant with the useful life of the asset. It thus ignores both the prudence convention and the matching convention. The second method means that the grant will *never* affect the profit figure. It also therefore ignores the matching convention and, additionally, leaves the 'non-distributable reserve' in the balance sheet, presumably for ever, i.e. it is treated as paid-in surplus.

The third and fourth methods both follow and apply the matching convention. They both have exactly the same effect on reported annual profits, the differences only being concerned with balance sheet presentation.

Illustration of different accounting treatments

Using the data just given, the two 'acceptable' methods give the following results.

Method 3(a)	€	€	€	€
Profit before depreciation etc.	20 000	20 000	20 000	20 000
Depreciation	(2 500)	(2 500)	(2 500)	(2 500)
Profit	17 500	17 500	17 500	17 500
Balance sheet extract at year end				
Non-current asset at (net) cost	10 000	10 000	10 000	10 000
Depreciation	2 500	5 000	7 500	10 000
Carrying amount	7 500	5 000	2 500	0
Method 3(b)				
Profit before depreciation etc.	20 000	20 000	20 000	20 000
Depreciation	(3 000)	(3 000)	(3 000)	(3 000)
Grant released	500	500	500	500
Profit	17 500	17 500	17 500	17 500

Balance sheet extract at year end	€	€	€	€
Non-current asset at cost	12 000	12 000	12 000	12 000
Depreciation	3 000	6 000	9 000	12 000
Carrying amount	9 000	6 000	3 000	0
Deferred credit				
Government grant	1 500	1 000	500	0

Thus method (a) shows assets of 7500, 5000, 2500 and 0 over the four years and method (b) shows assets of 9000, 6000, 3000 and 0 together with 'liabilities' of 1500, 1000, 500 and 0.

From a pragmatic point of view, method (a) has the obvious advantage of simplicity. No entries and no thought are required in the second and subsequent years. However, method (b) has the advantage that assets acquired at different times and locations are recorded on a uniform basis regardless of changes in governmental policy. But what *is* the cost of the asset? Is it 12 000 or is it 10 000? IAS 16, *Property, Plant and Equipment* (see later) states that cost is the amount of cash or cash equivalents paid, net of any trade discounts and rebates. This statement does not seem to categorically resolve the question. The government grant is not a trade discount. It is not a *trade* rebate, but it is a rebate. This would seem to imply that the cost in the sense of IAS 16 is 10 000. This is surely the net outflow arising because of the purchase. Yet IAS 20, as discussed in detail later, allows both methods.

A difficult conceptual problem arises with the deferred credit under method (b), e.g. the 1500 at the end of year 1. We described it earlier as a 'liability'. As discussed in Chapter 8, IASB defines a liability as a present obligation of the enterprise arising from past events, the settlement of which is expected to result in an outflow of resources embodying economic benefits. On the assumption that the grant cannot be reclaimed by the governmental body concerned (the usual situation), the 1500 is clearly *not* a liability as no outflow of resources is foreseeable. It is more logically either a reserve (not yet realized) or a contra-asset. It could be suggested that this leads to a different possible treatment, i.e. regular inclusion in the balance sheet as a visible contra-asset, i.e. included as a negative balance among the 'assets' instead of as a positive balance among the liabilities. This would raise its own problems – not least the lack of user friendliness involved in the concept of a negative asset. Such conceptual difficulties do not appear to worry either IASB or other national regulators.

The IASB requirements relating to government grants are contained in IAS 20, effective since 1984. The full title of IAS 20 is *Accounting for Government Grants and Disclosure of Government Assistance*. Its coverage therefore extends beyond the area of fixed assets, but for completeness we deal with all aspects of IAS 20 here. Where IAS 41, *Agriculture*, applies, government grants are to be treated under IAS 41 (see appendix), not under IAS 20.

Key concepts introduced in IAS 20 are as follows.

Government assistance is action by government designed to provide an economic benefit specific to an enterprise or range of enterprises qualifying under certain criteria. Government assistance for the purpose of this Standard does not include benefits provided only indirectly through action affecting general trading conditions, such as the provision of infrastructure in development areas or the imposition of trading constraints on competitors.

A specific subset of government assistance is government grants. *Government grants* are assistance by government in the form of transfers of resources to an entity in return for past or future compliance with certain conditions relating to the operating activities of the entity. They exclude those forms of government assistance that cannot reasonably have a value placed on them and transactions with government that cannot be distinguished from the normal trading transactions of the entity.

The notion of government is to be interpreted broadly. *Government* refers to government, government agencies and similar bodies whether local, national or international.

Government grants may be related to revenue/expense items, such as repayment of 10% of the wages bill, or to capital/asset items, such as repayment of 10% of the cost of a machine. These two types are formally distinguished by IAS 20:

- *Grants related to assets* are government grants whose primary condition is that an enterprise qualifying for them should purchase, construct or otherwise acquire long-term assets. Subsidiary conditions may also be attached restricting the type or location of the assets or the periods during which they are to be acquired or held.
- *Grants related to income* are government grants other than those related to assets.

The Standard gives two other definitions, including the familiar fair value.

- *Forgivable loans* are loans that the lender undertakes to waive repayment of under certain prescribed conditions.
- *Fair value* is the amount for which an asset could be exchanged between a knowledgeable, willing buyer and a knowledgeable, willing seller in an arm's length transaction.

Government assistance

Despite the inclusion of government assistance in the title of IAS 20, the statements about it are brief and rather obscure. The definitions given suggest, in effect, that government grants are government assistance that is distinguishable and quantifiable. Turning this round, references to government assistance in the Standard are to government activities that cannot be quantified or clearly distinguished. It follows, of course, that government assistance in this sense cannot be included numerically in the financial statements.

Examples of assistance that cannot reasonably have a value placed on it are free technical or marketing advice and the provision of guarantees. An example of assistance that cannot be distinguished from the normal trading transactions of the enterprise is a government procurement policy that is responsible for a portion of the enterprise's sales. The existence of the benefit might be unquestioned but any attempt to segregate the trading activities from government assistance could well be arbitrary.

The significance of the benefit in the examples just presented may be such that disclosure of the nature, extent and duration of the assistance is necessary in order that the financial statements may not be misleading (para. 36). The Standard explicitly states (para. 37) that while loans at nil or low interest rates are a form of government assistance, the 'benefit is not quantified by the imputation of interest'.

The disclosure requirement implied in this seems rather weakly stated. Non-quantified government support, which explicitly includes loans at low or zero interest, need not be disclosed at all unless its omission would be so serious as to be 'misleading'.

Treatment of government grants

The major portion of IAS 20 is concerned with the treatment of government grants. The first issue to deal with is the timing of recognition. The IAS requirement (para. 7) is that government grants, including non-monetary grants at fair value, should not be recognized until there is reasonable assurance that the entity will comply with the conditions attaching to them and that the grants will be received. Receipt of a grant does not of itself provide conclusive evidence that the conditions attaching to the grant have been or will be fulfilled.

'Reasonable assurance' is not, of course, definable or defined, but it is clearly less rigorous or demanding than, for example, 'virtual certainty' or 'beyond all reasonable doubt'. The Standard confirms (para. 10) that a forgivable loan (as defined earlier) is treated as a government grant when there is reasonable assurance that the enterprise will meet the terms for forgiveness of the loan. Once a government grant is recognized, any related contingency would be treated in accordance with International Accounting Standard IAS 37, *Provisions, Contingent Liabilities and Contingent Assets* (see Chapter 18).

The key requirement of the Standard (para. 12) is that government grants should be recognized as income over the periods necessary to match them with the related costs they are intended to compensate, on a systematic basis, i.e. following method 3a or b as discussed at the beginning of this chapter. They should not be credited directly to shareholders' interests. SIC 10, *Government Assistance – No Specific Relation to Operating Activities*, effective from 1 August 1998, has confirmed that government assistance to entities is a grant under IAS 20, even if granted generally to all entities within certain regions or industry sectors.

The matching principle will usually be simple to apply, as illustrated earlier in this chapter. Grants related to non-depreciable assets may also require the fulfilment of certain obligations and would then be recognized as income over the periods that bear the cost of meeting the obligations. As an example, a grant of land may be conditional on the erection of a building on the site and it may be appropriate to recognize it as income over the life of the building. A government grant that becomes receivable as compensation for expenses or losses already incurred or for the purpose of giving immediate financial support to the entity with no future related costs should be recognized as income of the period in which it becomes receivable. Separate disclosure and explanation may be required.

Usually, a careful reading of the contract with the governmental body will determine the appropriate accounting treatment, although an intelligent appraisal of the in-substance thrust of the contract may be required. For example, a grant towards building a factory, stipulates that the factory must remain operating and employing at least 30 people for at least three years, is clearly in essence a grant towards building a factory, not a revenue grant towards reducing net wage costs. However, where a grant clearly relates in material terms to both specific capital and specific revenue items, the Standard is silent on appropriate treatment. Accounting common sense obviously requires an apportionment in such cases.

The Standard is surprisingly vague about non-monetary government grants, such as land donated by a government. IAS 20 merely notes (para. 23) that:

> It is usual to assess the fair value of the non-monetary asset and to account for both grant and asset at that fair value. An alternative course that is sometimes followed is to record both asset and grant at a nominal amount.

This is worded as a description, not as a requirement, although the preference is clear enough. Our view is that merely to record the event at nominal amount lacks transparency to an unacceptable degree. Also it is not consistent with the substance over form principle and would lead to an inconsistent treatment of assets affecting both inter-enterprise and intra-enterprise comparisons.

Presentation of government grants

Regarding the presentation of grants related to assets, IAS 20 allows both methods (a) and (b) as discussed and illustrated earlier. Thus, government grants related to assets, including non-monetary grants at fair value, should (paras 24–28) be presented in the balance sheet either by setting up the grant as deferred income or by deducting the grant in arriving at the carrying amount of the asset. The Standard spells out that separate disclosure of the gross cash flows in the cash flow statement is likely to be necessary, whatever treatment is followed in the balance sheet. IAS 7, *Cash Flow Statements* (see Chapter 22), is more explicit in making this grossing up of cash flows a requirement.

Regarding the presentation of grants related to income, the Standard again accepts either of two alternatives (paras 29–31). It states, with approval, that grants related to income are sometimes presented as a credit in the income statement, either separately or under a general heading such as 'Other income'; alternatively, they are deducted in reporting the related expense.

A proper understanding of the financial statements may require separate disclosure of the grant and of its effects on particular items of income or expense.

Repayment of government grants

A grant to which conditions were attached may have been properly recognized under the 'reasonable assurance' criterion discussed earlier. However, it may still become repayable in whole or in part if, in fact, the conditions are not met. IAS 20 requires (para. 32) that such a grant, as soon as the repayment becomes foreseeable (which might be significantly earlier than when the repayment actually occurs) should be accounted for as a revision to an accounting estimate, under IAS 8, *Accounting Policies, Changes in Accounting Estimates and Errors* (see Chapter 23). This essentially requires that the entries be made in the financial statements of the year concerned. Repayment of a grant related to income should be applied first against any unamortized deferred credit set up in respect of the grant. To the extent that the repayment exceeds any such deferred credit, or where no deferred credit exists, the repayment should be recognized immediately as an expense. Repayment of a grant related to an asset should be recorded by increasing the carrying amount of the asset or reducing the deferred balance by the amount repayable. The cumulative additional depreciation that would have been recognized to date as an expense in the absence of the grant should be recognized immediately as an expense. Circumstances giving rise to repayment of a grant related to an asset may require consideration to be given to the possible impairment of the new carrying amount of the asset (see IAS 36, *Impairment of Assets*, discussed in Chapter 13).

Disclosure

Key disclosure requirements are as follows:

- the accounting policy adopted for government grants, including the methods of presentation adopted in the financial statements
- the nature and extent of government grants recognized in the financial statements and an indication of other forms of government assistance from which the enterprise has directly benefited
- unfulfilled conditions and other contingencies attaching to government assistance that has been recognized.

National requirements

US GAAP, or at least promulgated US GAAP, appears to be silent on this whole area. FAS 116, *Accounting for Contributions Received and Contributions Made*, applies to not-for-profit organizations and explicitly excludes transfer of assets from governments to businesses. The US promulgated GAAP for the treatment of investment tax credits, perhaps analogous, permits either deferral and gradual release of the benefit to income or instant release to income.

UK GAAP in SSAP 4 does not permit the netting out of capital grants in the balance sheet and allows only the treatment retaining a separate deferred income balance. This is under the stated, but mistaken, belief that UK law, following European Directive wording, prohibits such setting off. UK (and European) legal requirements forbid the netting out of assets and liabilities, but of course deferred income is not a liability, as already discussed, so therefore netting would be perfectly legal!

Borrowing costs (IAS 23)

The second particular problem area related to the cost of fixed assets is that of interest costs. In the general case, interest cost is a straightforward periodic expense, it should be charged against revenues in proportion to the benefit received, i.e. on a time basis. This is a normal application of the matching principle. The benefit is the existence of the loan and the expense is the interest cost, allocated proportionate to the size of the borrowing.

However, there are circumstances in which accounting theory seems to rationalize an alternative argument. We pointed out in our feedback to Activity 12.2, that 'cost of an asset' includes any item which is necessary to obtain the asset and make it workable. Suppose a loan is necessary in order to obtain the funds without which the asset cannot be obtained. Can it be argued that the cost of the loan (i.e. the interest) is part of the 'cost of the asset'? Clearly, once the asset is workable, i.e. able to function and generate revenues, then there can be no question of this argument justifying non-expensing of interest. But can interest be capitalized as part of the cost of an asset *during* the period of its creation or construction?

Activity 12.9

From your knowledge of accounting principles, what do you think the answer to this question should be?

Activity feedback

As far as it goes, the logic of the 'cost' argument seems inescapable. With a typical self-constructed asset, all direct costs and in some circumstances some allocable indirect costs are properly regarded as part of the total historical cost. It follows that any borrowing costs that can be directly linked to the financing of the asset concerned are also logically part of the total historical cost, as an application of the matching principle.

However, it is not difficult to find arguments which point in a different direction. It is clearly not very prudent to avoid the immediate expensing of interest payments that undeniably relate to periodic costs of the accounting period in question. Further, is not the economic argument, i.e. that the cost of necessary finance is part of the cost of production, true *whether or not* a separate source of finance related to the particular asset can be distinguished? If it is true, as we would certainly suggest that it is, then an imputed interest charge should be included even if not supported by any payments or external documentation. This arguably departs much too far from the traditional function of accounting as the recording of transactions. A problem of consistency in asset cost calculations thus arises if some interest costs are capitalized (relatable to specific loans) and others are not.

IAS 23 Borrowing costs

The IASB has issued two versions of IAS 23, the more recent in 1994. The IASB attempted a significant tightening up of the degree of optionality allowed, as part of its E32 comparability project of the early 1990s (see Chapter 3), but was less successful than intended.

Borrowing costs are defined (para. 4) as interest and other costs incurred by an entity in connection with the borrowing of funds. IAS GAAP take a broad view of what constitutes borrowing costs and include such items as amortization of ancillary costs incurred in connection with borrowings and preferred stock dividends if the preferred stock is classified as a liability in the balance sheet. By contrast, the imputed cost of financial instruments classed as equity capital is strictly excluded.

The benchmark treatment of IAS 23 is that borrowing costs should all be recognized as an expense of the period in which they are incurred (para. 7). This, of course, is very straightforward. However, an allowed alternative treatment also exists. This is that borrowing costs that are *directly attributable* to the acquisition, construction, or production of a *qualifying asset* should be capitalized as part of the cost of that asset when they can be measured reliably and when it is probable that they will result in future economic benefits to the enterprise. Borrowing costs that do not meet these conditions should be recognized as an expense of the period in which they are incurred (IAS 23, paras 10–12). This alternative treatment may not be applied selectively; it must be applied to all qualifying assets or to none at all, as required by IAS 8 (see Chapter 23).

A *qualifying asset* (for the purposes of the 'alternative' treatment) is an asset that necessarily takes a substantial period of time to get ready for its intended use or sale. Examples of qualifying assets given in the standard are inventories that require a substantial period of time to bring them to a saleable condition, manufacturing plants, power generation facilities and investment properties (IAS 23, paras 5–6). Examples of inventory items that would be qualifying assets include wine and spirits being aged, ships and aircraft being built and long-term construction contracts in general. Intangibles such as capitalized development costs and other internally generated intangibles that meet the recognition criteria of IAS 38 (see Chapter 13) may also be qualifying assets.

Borrowing costs that are directly attributable to obtaining a qualifying asset are those borrowing costs that would have been avoided if the expenditure on the qualifying asset had not been made. This is straightforward when funds are borrowed specifically for the purpose of obtaining a particular qualifying asset. In that case, the amount of borrowing costs eligible for capitalization as part of the cost of that asset for the period are the actual costs of that borrowing during the period, less any investment income from temporary investment of the funds borrowed (IAS 23, paras 13–15).

In other circumstances, the determination of the amount of borrowing costs that are directly attributable to obtaining a qualifying asset may be difficult, and judgement may need to be exercised. To the extent that funds that have been borrowed for general purposes are used for obtaining a qualifying asset, the amount of borrowing costs that are eligible for capitalization should be determined by applying a capitalization rate to the expenditures on that asset. This capitalization rate should be calculated as the weighted average of the borrowing costs applicable to the *general borrowings* of the enterprise during the period (any borrowings made specifically for the purpose of obtaining a qualifying asset are by definition not part of 'general borrowings').

Thus, borrowing costs capitalizable in respect of a qualifying asset should be identified, first, as those of any borrowings made specifically for the purpose of obtaining the asset. If there were no specific borrowings or these account for less than all of the expenditure on the asset, then 'general borrowings' should be applied to the balance of the expenditure on the asset.

The amount of borrowing costs capitalized during a period should not exceed the total amount of borrowing costs incurred during that period, thus confirming that imputed interest cannot be capitalized. Capitalization of interest costs, if the allowed alternative treatment is followed for qualifying assets, should begin when:

1 expenditures on the qualifying asset are being incurred
2 borrowing costs are being incurred
3 activities that are necessary to prepare the asset for its intended use or sale are in progress.

'Necessary activities' include technical, administrative and legal work (as well as aging or maturing certain types of inventory), but simply holding an asset (such as development land or other property or finished items in inventory) does not allow attributable borrowing costs to be capitalized (IAS 23, paras 20–22). Moreover, during extended periods in which necessary activities are interrupted, *suspension* of capitalization is required.

Capitalization of borrowing costs should *cease* when *substantially all* the activities necessary to prepare the qualifying asset for its intended sale or use are complete (IAS 23, para. 25).

An enterprise should disclose in the notes to its financial statements:

1 the accounting policy adopted for borrowing costs
2 in the case of the allowed alternative treatment:
  (a) the amount of borrowing costs capitalized during the period
  (b) the capitalization rate (or rates) used to determine the amount of borrowing (IAS 23, para. 29).

National considerations

The main differences between IAS GAAP and US GAAP are the following:

1 US GAAP (FAS 34) *require* borrowing costs to be capitalized when the relevant conditions are met, namely, when the borrowing costs are part of the expenditures normally incurred in readying an asset for use and are thus part of the asset's acquisition cost. In IAS GAAP, this is *permitted* as the 'alternative' treatment, but the 'benchmark' treatment is to expense all borrowing costs.
2 US GAAP (FAS 58) treat as qualifying assets equity investments in, and loans and advances to, investees accounted for under the equity method, if the latter are themselves acquiring qualifying assets as part of activities necessary to start their planned principal operations. IAS GAAP exclude from qualifying assets all investments except investment properties and the qualifying assets of an investee accounted for using proportionate consolidation.
3 FAS 34 considers borrowing costs to consist of interest costs actually incurred. IAS GAAP include in borrowing costs the effects of changes in exchange rates on the effective cost of borrowing in foreign currencies. These effects would not be recognized in US GAAP as borrowing costs for the purpose of capitalization.

UK GAAP, in FRS 15, *Tangible Fixed Assets*, broadly follows the IAS approach. It states that an entity need not capitalize finance costs, but if it does adopt a policy of capitalization of finance costs, then the policy should be applied consistently to all relevant tangible fixed assets.

Property, plant and equipment

We are now, at last, in a position to look at the central requirements of IAS GAAP in relation to accounting for fixed assets. Even now, four different aspects and four different IASs need to be considered, i.e. property, plant and equipment; investment properties; intangibles; and finally the whole question of impairment of fixed assets. Although there are relationships and interlinking between all of these, it will aid understanding to explore them separately. We begin with property, plant and equipment, IAS 16, which is the general standard regarding the treatment of fixed (non-current) assets. We deal only with the latest version of IAS 16, as revised in 2004, applicable from 1 January 2005, earlier adoption being encouraged.

The Standard notes that the general definition and recognition criteria for an asset given in the Framework for the Preparation and Presentation of Financial Statements (discussed in Chapter 8) must be satisfied before IAS 16 applies. Subject to that, IAS 16 applies to accounting for all property, plant and equipment except when another IAS requires or permits a different accounting treatment (para. 2).

There are, in fact, a number of exclusions. It is explicitly stated (para. 2) that IAS 16 does not apply to biological assets related to agricultural activity (to which IAS 41 applies; see appendix) or to mineral rights, the exploration for and extraction of minerals, oil, natural gas and similar non-regenerative resources. However, it does apply to property, plant and equipment used to develop or maintain these activities or assets but separable from those activities or assets. IAS 16 also does not apply to property, plant and equipment classified as held for sale in accordance with IFRS 5, *Non-current Assets Held for Sale and Discontinued Operations* (see Chapter 23).

An enterprise applies IAS 40, *Investment Property*, rather than IAS 16, to its investment property (see later). IAS 16 applies to property being constructed or developed for future use as an investment property, but on its completion IAS 40 would apply. IAS 40 also applies to existing investment property being redeveloped for future continued use as investment property.

If any other IAS permits a particular approach to the initial recognition of the carrying amount of property, plant and equipment, then that Standard will prevail as regards this initial carrying value, but IAS 16 would then apply to all other aspects, including depreciation. An example of this would be IFRS 3, *Business Combinations*, which requires property, plant and equipment acquired in a business combination to be measured initially at fair value (see Chapter 24).

The Standard then gives a number of key definitions as follows:

- *Property, plant and equipment* are tangible items that:
  - **(a)** are held for use in the production or supply of goods or services, for rental to others, or for administrative purposes, and
  - **(b)** are expected to be used during more than one period.
- *Depreciation* is the systematic allocation of the depreciable amount of an asset over its useful life.
- *Depreciable amount* is the cost of an asset, or other amount substituted for cost, less its residual value.
- *Useful life* is:
  - **(a)** the period of time over which an asset is expected to be used by an entity
  - **(b)** or the number of production or similar units expected to be obtained from the asset by an entity.
- *Cost* is the amount of cash or cash equivalents paid or the fair value of the other consideration given to acquire an asset at the time of its acquisition or construction or, where applicable, the amount attributed to that asset when initially recognized in accordance with the specific requirements of other IFRSs, e.g. IFRS 2, *Share-based Payment*.
- The *residual value* of an asset is the estimated amount that an entity would currently obtain from disposal of the asset, after deducting the estimated costs of disposal, if the asset were already of the age and in the condition expected at the end of its useful life.

- *Entity-specific value* is the present value of the cash flows an entity expects to arise from the continuing use of an asset and from its disposal at the end of its useful life, or expects to incur when settling liability.
- *Recoverable amount* is the higher of an asset's net selling price and its value in use.
- *Fair value* is the amount for which an asset could be exchanged between knowledgeable, willing parties in an arm's length transaction.
- An *impairment loss* is the amount by which the carrying amount of an asset exceeds its recoverable amount.
- *Carrying amount* is the amount at which an asset is recognized after deducting any accumulated depreciation and accumulated impairment losses.

These definitions contain no real surprises and confirm the general earnings calculation focus of the depreciation process.

The first issue to deal with is the issue of when an item of PPE should be recorded, i.e. *recognized*, in the financial statements.

An item of property, plant and equipment should be recognized (para. 7) as an asset if, and only if:

1 it is probable that future economic benefits associated with the item will flow to the entity and
2 the cost of the item to the entity can be measured reliably.

In determining whether an item satisfies the first criterion for recognition, an entity needs to assess the degree of certainty attaching to the flow of future economic benefits on the basis of the available evidence at the time of initial recognition. Existence of sufficient certainty that the future economic benefits will flow to the entity necessitates an assurance that the entity will receive the rewards attaching to the asset and will undertake the associated risks. The second criterion for recognition is usually readily satisfied because the exchange transaction evidencing the purchase of the asset identifies its cost.

IAS 16 allows for the aggregation of items which may individually be insignificant (para. 9), giving 'moulds, tools and dies' as an example. The aggregation is then treated as '*an asset*' if the recognition criteria are met. Conversely, when it is clear that, although an asset may initially be acquired as a whole, significant components of it will have significantly different useful lives, then the expenditure on the asset should be allocated to the component parts and each part should be accounted for as a separate item. An aircraft and its engines are given as a likely example. This separate treatment allows depreciation figures to properly reflect the different consumption patterns of the various components.

Subsequent costs

The first and obvious point is that costs of day-to-day servicing of an item of property, plant and equipment, often described as 'repairs and maintenance', are expenses, not additions to costs. However, major parts of some items of property, plant and equipment may require replacement at regular intervals. For example, a furnace may require relining after a specified number of hours of use; aircraft interiors such as seats and galleys may require replacement several time during the life of the airframe.

Items of property, plant and equipment may also be acquired to make a less frequently recurring replacement, such as replacing the interior walls of a building or to make a non-recurring replacement. Under the recognition principle in para. 7, an entity recognizes in the carrying amount of an item of property, plant and equipment the cost of replacing such a part of an item when that cost is incurred if the recognition criteria are met. The carrying amount of those parts that are replaced is derecognized in accordance with the derecognition provisions of the Standard.

Note that in order to facilitate this, the component parts of the original item need to have been accounted for separately in the first place.

A major inspection or refit, even if it does not 'improve' the original item, may logically be treated the same way. Thus (para. 14) notes that a condition of continuing to operate an item of property, plant and equipment (for example, an aircraft) may be performing regular major inspections for faults regardless of whether parts of the item are replaced. When each major inspection is performed, its cost is recognized in the carrying amount of the item of property, plant and equipment as a replacement of the recognition criteria are satisfied. Any remaining carrying amount of the cost of the previous inspection (as distinct from physical parts) is derecognized. This occurs regardless of whether the cost of the previous inspection was identified in the transaction in which the item was acquired or constructed. If necessary, the estimated cost of a future similar inspection may be used as an indication of what the cost of the existing inspection component was when the item was acquired or constructed.

Once the criteria for recognition have been met, the issue of measurement arises. This is considered in two stages: initial measurement and subsequent remeasurement.

Initial measurement

The essential requirement is straightforward and can be simply stated (para. 15). An item of property, plant and equipment that qualifies for recognition as an asset should initially be measured at its cost. The cost of an item of property, plant and equipment comprises its purchase price, including import duties and non-refundable purchase taxes and any directly attributable costs of bringing the asset to working condition for its intended use; any trade discounts and rebates are deducted in arriving at the purchase price. Examples of directly attributable costs are:

- cost of site preparation
- initial delivery and handling costs
- installation costs
- professional fees such as for architects and engineers
- the estimated cost of dismantling and removing the asset and restoring the site, to the extent that it is recognized as a provision under IAS 37, *Provisions, Contingent Liabilities and Contingent Assets* (see Chapter 18).

In practice, however, a number of complications are likely to arise. The Standard goes into some detail about several aspects (para. 18–28). It notes that in cases where payment is deferred beyond normal credit terms, defined or imputed interest must be removed from the total of the payments, thus reducing the cost to the cash purchase price equivalent. General and administration overheads are not likely to be 'directly attributable costs' as the term was used earlier, but, for example, pension costs of direct labour could be.

The question of what is an essential cost of 'bringing the asset to working condition' is likely to be difficult and subjective.

The basic principle is that recognition of costs in the carrying amount of an item of property, plant and equipment ceases when the item is in the location and condition necessary for it to be capable of operating in the manner intended by management. For example, the following costs are not included in the carrying amount of an item of property, plant and equipment:

- costs incurred while an item capable of operating in the manner intended by management has yet to be brought into use or is operated at less than full capacity
- initial operating losses, such as those incurred while demand for the item's output builds up
- costs of relocating or reorganizing part or all of an entity's operations
- costs of opening a new facility
- costs of introducing a new product or service (including costs of advertising and promotional activities)
- costs of conducting business in a new location or with a new class of customer (including costs of staff training)
- administration and other general overhead costs.

Measurement subsequent to initial recognition

The IASB has always operated on the basis that a strict adherence to historical cost is not required and, indeed, has recognized the possibility of rejecting historical cost accounting as the normal basis (see Chapter 8). Consistent with this approach, two alternative approaches to subsequent measurement are allowed under IAS 16 (paras 30 and 31). The first is described as the cost model and is simply stated:

> After recognition as an asset, an item of property, plant and equipment shall be carried at its cost less any accumulated depreciation and any accumulated impairment losses.

The second is the revaluation model.

> After recognition as an asset, an item of property, plant and equipment whose fair value can be measured reliably shall be carried at a revalued amount, being its fair value at the date of revaluation less any subsequent accumulated depreciation and subsequent accumulated impairment losses. Revaluations shall be made with sufficient regularity to ensure that the carrying amount does not differ materially from that which would be determined using fair value at the balance sheet date.

In the previous version of IAS 16, these were presented as the benchmark treatment and the alternative treatment, respectively. However, they are now presented simply as two alternatives.

The fair value of land and buildings will usually be its market value as determined by professional qualified valuers. It is the fair value on the open market which should be used, and note again that fair value is likely to be higher than net realizable value.

When there is no evidence of market value because of the specialized nature of the plant and equipment and because these items are rarely sold, except as part of a continuing business, they are valued at their depreciated replacement cost. Appropriate specific price indices may if necessary be used to determine replacement cost.

IAS 16, para. 35 discusses the treatment of accumulated depreciation. The wording is obscure and we quote the paragraph in full:

> When an item of property, plant and equipment is revalued, any accumulated depreciation at the date of the revaluation is treated in one of the following ways:
>
> **(a)** restated proportionately with the change in the gross carrying amount of the asset so that the carrying amount of the asset after revaluation equals its revalued amount. This method is often used when an asset is revalued by means of an index to its depreciated replacement cost; or
> **(b)** eliminated against the gross carrying amount of the asset and the net amount restated to the revalued amount of the asset. This method is often used for buildings.
>
> The amount of the adjustment arising on the restatement or elimination of accumulated depreciation forms part of the increase or decrease in carrying amount that is accounted for in accordance with paragraphs 39 and 40.

Activity 12.10

Suppose we have an asset to which IAS 16 applies, cost 10 000, useful life 5 years, estimated residual value nil, now 3 years old. The asset is then revalued to a new gross figure of 15 000, that is the new 'cost' is 15 000, for the purpose of treatment (a). Alternatively the asset is now revalued to a current fair value *in its existing state* of 6000, for the purpose of treatment (b). Show the implications of each of these two treatments.

Activity feedback

(a) suggests the following:

Cost	Depreciation	Carrying amount
10 000	6 000	4 000

The asset is now revalued, by index or otherwise, to a new gross figure of 15 000, i.e. the new 'cost' is 15 000. The depreciation is now 'restated proportionately', i.e. it is also increased by 50%. We thus end up with:

Gross revaluation	Depreciation	Carrying amount
15 000	9 000	6 000

This increase in carrying amount of 2000 is then dealt with as discussed later.

(b) suggests a different sequence. Suppose the asset is again recorded before revaluation:

Cost	Depreciation	Carrying amount
10 000	6 000	4 000

The new carrying value is to be 6000. Other balances will need to be altered or eliminated as shown.

Asset revaluation
Account

Transfer of cost	10 000	6 000	Transfer of depreciation
Surplus (calculated)	2 000	6 000	New carrying value (given)
	12 000	12 000	

As already indicated, the treatment of increases and decreases arising on revaluation is dealt with in IAS 16 paras 39 and 40. On the first revaluation after initial recognition:

■ Decreases are charged to the income statement as an expense.
■ Surpluses are credited directly to equity, under the heading of revaluation surplus.

At subsequent revaluations (to the extent that there is a previous revaluation surplus in respect of the same asset held in equity) a decrease should be charged against it, but any excess of deficit over that previous surplus should be expensed to the income statement. Where a previous revaluation gave a deficit in respect of the same asset that was charged to expense, a subsequent revaluation surplus should be recognized as income to the extent of the previous deficit; any excess should be credited to equity.

Such a revaluation surplus reserve is not 'realized', and is therefore not 'earned' and not available for dividend. However it is likely to become realized over time. Such revaluation surplus included in equity may be transferred directly to retained earnings when the surplus is realized. The whole surplus may be realized on the retirement or disposal of the asset. However, some of the surplus may be realized as the asset is used by the enterprise; in such a case, the amount of the surplus realized is the difference between depreciation based on the revalued carrying amount of the asset and depreciation based on the asset's original cost.

It is noteworthy that the word 'may' is used three times in the last three sentences. The increase in carrying amount may be transferred to retained earnings eventually when the asset is disposed of or gradually over the remaining useful life – thus, in effect, offsetting in the retained earnings balance the effect of 'extra' depreciation. Note that in neither case is there any effect on the income statement for any year; this will be charged in full with the new depreciation expense. Alternatively, it appears that the increase could be left in revaluation surplus for ever. Under a historical cost accounting philosophy this last possibility seems illogical, though under a current cost philosophy it would be logically correct (see Chapter 7).

The Interpretations Committee issued IFRIC 1 in May 2004, effective for annual periods beginning on or after 1 September 2004, earlier application being encouraged. IFRIC 1, *Changes in Existing Decommissioning, Restoration and Similar Liabilities*, provides guidance on how to account for the effect of changes in the measurement of existing such liabilities. The details of IFRIC 1 are complicated, pedantic, and common sense.

Depreciation

The formal requirement of IAS 16 for the calculation of depreciation should by now have a familiar ring (para. 50).

The depreciable amount of an item of property, plant and equipment should be allocated on a systematic basis over its useful life. The depreciation method used should reflect the pattern in which the asset's economic benefits are consumed by the enterprise. The depreciation charge for each period should be recognized as an expense unless it is included in the carrying amount of another asset (e.g. as part of the manufacturing cost of inventories).

The Standard goes into detail about a number of aspects. The residual value and the useful life of an asset shall be reviewed at least at each financial year end and, if expectations differ from previous estimates, the change(s) shall be accounted for as a change in an accounting estimate in accordance with IAS 8, *Accounting Policies, Changes in Accounting Estimates and Errors*.

Depreciation is recognized even if the fair value of the asset exceeds its carrying amount, as long as the asset's residual value does not exceed its carrying amount. Repair and maintenance of an asset do not negate the need to depreciate it. The depreciable amount of an asset is determined after deducting its residual value. In practice, the residual value of an asset is often insignificant and therefore immaterial in the calculation of the depreciable amount. The residual value of an asset may increase to an amount equal to or greater than the asset's carrying amount. If it does, the asset's depreciation charge is zero unless and until its residual value subsequently decreases to an amount below the asset's carrying amount. This last point is rather significant. It recognizes and confirms that, while a depreciation charge is *required* for all items of property, plant and machinery, the correctly calculated charge may well be zero.

Land and buildings are separable assets with different accounting characteristics and should be considered separately, even if acquired as a single purchase.

The Standard mentions three depreciation methods by name: straight line, reducing (or diminishing) balance and the units of production (usage) method (para. 62). This list is neither exhaustive nor in order of preference. The method used for an asset is selected based on the expected pattern of economic benefits and is consistently applied from period to period unless there is a change in the expected pattern of economic benefits from that asset. This implies that for any particular asset, with its own particular expected pattern of economic benefits, there is one particular appropriate method. Once the method has been chosen, consistency is required.

Activity 12.11

It is sometimes argued, for example in the case of hotels, that depreciation of the building is not necessary, on the grounds that its fair value is being maintained by the incurrence of expensive maintenance costs which are being charged as expenses. To charge depreciation as well could appear to be 'double-counting'. What do you think of this argument?

Activity feedback

Standard setters generally are at pains to counter this argument. It is not valid to argue that maintenance increases residual value at the end of economic life, so in principle the proposition is invalid, although maintenance is certainly a factor in determining the *length* of the economic life. However, the useful life could, it must be remembered, be significantly shorter than the economic life. It certainly seems theoretically valid for a hotel owner to argue that expected residual value at the end of the expected useful life (to him) is equal to or greater than the initial carrying value. This would suggest that, while depreciation needs to be provided, the 'correct' figure will be nil! Auditors may be suspicious of this argument although, as discussed earlier, IAS 16 now recognizes its possible legitimacy.

The depreciation method applied to an asset shall be reviewed at least at each financial year end and, if there has been a significant change in the expected pattern of consumption of the future economic benefits embodied in the asset, the method shall be changed to reflect the changed pattern. Such a change shall be accounted for as a change in an accounting estimate in accordance with IAS 8.

It is necessary to determine whether or not an item of property, plant and equipment has become impaired. This area is covered by IAS 36, *Impairment of Assets* (see Chapter 13). Impairments or losses of items of property, plant and equipment, related claims for or payments of compensation from third parties and any subsequent purchase or construction of replacement assets are separate economic events and are accounted for separately as follows:

- impairments of items of property, plant and equipment are recognized in accordance with IAS 36
- derecognition of items of property, plant and equipment retired or disposed of is determined in accordance with IAS 16
- compensation from third parties for items of property, plant and equipment that were impaired, lost or given up is included in determining profit or loss when it becomes receivable
- the cost of items of property, plant and equipment restored, purchased or constructed as replacements is determined in accordance with IAS 16.

Derecognition

The carrying amount of an item of property, plant and equipment shall be derecognized:

- on disposal
- or when no future economic benefits are expected from its use or disposal.

The gain or loss arising from the derecognition of an item of property, plant and equipment shall be determined as the difference between the net disposal proceeds, if any, and the carrying amount of the item. The gain or loss is to be included in profit or loss when the item is derecognized (unless IAS 17 requires otherwise on a sale and leaseback). Gains shall not be classified as revenue.

This confirms that any element of revaluation reserve relating to the item will not pass through the income statement.

The disposal of an item of property, plant and equipment may occur in a variety of ways (e.g. by sale, by entering into a finance lease or by donations). In determining the date of disposal of an item, an entity applies the criteria in IAS 18, *Revenue*, for recognizing revenue from the sale of goods. IAS 17 applies to disposal by a sale and leaseback.

Disclosure

The disclosure requirements under IAS 16 are lengthy and incapable of effective summarization. In general, full details and reconciliations of movements concerning additions, disposals, impairments and revaluations are required.

Accounting for investment properties

Principles and definitions

Activity 12.12

We have seen that, under IAS, a non-current asset is any asset other than a current asset, where a current asset is an asset which, (IAS 1, para. 57) is:

- expected to be realized in, or is intended for sale or consumption in, the entity's normal operating cycle
- held primarily for trading purposes or expected to be realized within 12 months of the balance sheet date
- or cash or a cash equivalent asset which is not restricted in its use.

If an enterprise owns a property which it intends to hire out in the short to medium term and eventually sell or possibly to sell in the short to medium term, consider:

(i) whether it is a non-current or current asset
(ii) whether the economic substance of the situation implies a need for annual depreciation.

Activity feedback

The answer to (i) seems to depend on the particular situation. If the enterprise is actually trading in properties as an operating activity, then the property does seem to be a current asset. In this case, the question of depreciation does not arise, either logically under the matching principle, or in legal or regulatory terms under EC directives or IAS GAAP.

If the enterprise is intending to hold the property for a number of accounting periods, for rental and/or capital gain, then the current/non-current distinction is less clear, although perhaps non-current better reflects the substance. However, the property is still *not* being consumed in supporting the operating activities of the enterprise. Further, the key information of relevance to stakeholders should accord with the expected future outcomes, i.e. some kind of rental income and an eventual profitable disposal, not the wearing out of the asset. Arguably, therefore, depreciation is neither logical nor relevant, although this can raise legal and regulatory issues. This whole area needs separate discussion.

The classic perception of a non-current asset is that of a long-term resource that is necessary to support the day-to-day operational activities of a business. It is used in production or administration, but is not itself sold. It generally wears out, as its use value, or service potential, is consumed, in recognition of which depreciation is charged in the annual profit calculation. The classic perception of an investment is that of an asset held so that the asset itself will earn positive returns, either through regular inflows such as interest, dividend, or rent or through capital appreciation. With an investment, the key issue is impairment or capital appreciation, rather than consumption of use value or service potential.

The specific problem with properties is that they can be held for either purpose or for both purposes at different times. Because of a general tendency, over the long term, for property prices to rise significantly in nominal terms, the distinction in practice is often particularly significant.

Until at least the 1970s, property held as an investment was generally treated for accounting purposes like any other property, with or without the possibility of revaluation and with or without the possibility of non-depreciation, depending on the jurisdiction. This approach began to be challenged, notably in the United Kingdom. It was argued that if a property is held as an investment then:

1 The matching convention is arguably not relevant, as no service potential is being used up.
2 The current values of such investments and any change therein are of prime importance and relevance.

IAS 25, *Accounting for Investments*, effective from 1 January 1987 until 31 December 2000, was constructed to allow, but not to require, the treatment of an investment property as a long-term investment under IAS 25, rather than as property under IAS 16, *Property, Plant and Equipment*. Even under IAS 25, such a property could be carried at either cost or revalued amount. Thus there was a great deal of choice involved.

The IASB issued an exposure draft on investment properties, E64, in July 1999. This proposed a mandatory fair value model for investment properties. However, in the resulting debate, IAS was forced to backtrack and the Standard, IAS 40, gives a choice.

Investment property, as defined later, can be treated in either of two ways. Entities can choose between a fair value model and a cost model. The fair value model is the model proposed in E64: investment property should be measured at fair value and changes in fair value should be recognized in the income statement.

The cost model is as defined in IAS 16, *Property, Plant and Equipment*: investment property should be measured at depreciated cost (less any accumulated impairment losses). An entity that chooses the cost model should additionally disclose the fair value of its investment property in the notes to the financial statements.

IAS 40 gives the following key definitions:

- *Investment property* is property (land or a building or part of a building – or both) held (by the owner or by the lessee under a finance lease) to earn rentals or for capital appreciation or both, rather than for:
  - use in the production or supply of goods or services or for administrative purposes, or
  - sale in the ordinary course of business.
- *Owner-occupied property* is property held (by the owner or by the lessee under a finance lease) for use in the production or supply of goods or services or for administrative purposes.

It follows from the definition of investment property that an investment property will generate cash flows 'largely independently' of other assets held by an enterprise. It is this which distinguishes investment property from owner-occupied property, as owner-occupied property only generates cash flows in conjunction with other operating assets necessary for the production or supply process.

An investment property within the definition should be recognized as an asset when, and only when:

1 It is probable that the future economic benefits that are associated with the investment property will flow to the entity.
2 The cost of the investment property can be measured reliably.

Figure 12.1 summarizes the various alternatives for treating a property under IAS GAAP (based on a figure in the appendix to the 2000 version of IAS 40).

Activity 12.13

Consider each of the assets described in (a) to (i) and indicate whether they are or are not investment properties as defined in IAS 40:

(a) Land held for long-term capital appreciation rather than for short-term sale in the ordinary course of business.
(b) Land held for a currently undetermined future use.
(c) Property that is being constructed or developed for future use as investment property.
(d) A building owned by the entity (or held by the entity under a finance lease) and leased out under one or more operating leases.
(e) A building that is vacant but is held to be leased out under one or more operating leases.
(f) Property intended for sale in the ordinary course of business, for example, property held for trading by property traders or for development and resale by property developers.
(g) Property being constructed for third parties.
(h) Owner-occupied property.
(i) Property that is leased to another entity under a finance lease.

Activity feedback

(a), **(d)**, and **(e)** are clearly held for investment purposes and are investment properties. **(b)** cannot really be regarded as other than a speculative purchase at the time it was acquired and so is an investment property unless and until, presumably, it eventually becomes part of an owner-occupied property. **(c)**, however, does not at present meet the definition; it is property under construction, and IAS 16 would apply. None of the final four is an investment property and IAS 40 would not apply to them. **(f)** would be dealt with as inventory under IAS 2 (see Chapter 15), **(g)** as a construction contract under IAS 11 (see Chapter 15), **(h)** and **(i)** as property, plant and equipment under IAS 16.

Note that in marginal cases, judgement will be needed in distinguishing investment properties from owner-occupied properties. For example, an owner-managed hotel is essentially concerned with the provision of services to guests, so it is not an investment property. However, the owner of a building which is managed as a hotel by a third

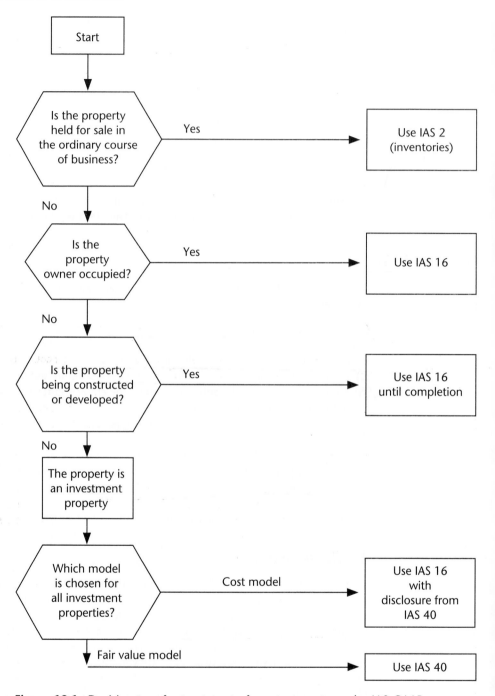

Figure 12.1 Decision tree for treatment of most property under IAS GAAP

party is in the position of holding an investment, with 'largely independent' cash flows arising, hence creating an investment property. In complex intermediate situations, the substance of the situation and the balance of emphasis should be followed. Disclosure of the criteria used is required when classification is difficult.

A new introduction in the 2004 version of IAS 40 concerns property interests under operating leases. It was widely suggested that, in substance, given the long life of most property, these should be treatable similarly to finance leases. Accordingly (para. 6), a property interest that is held by a lessee under an operating lease may be classified and accounted for as investment property if, and only if, the property would otherwise meet the definition of an investment property and the lessee uses the fair value model for the asset recognized. This classification alternative is available on a property-by-property basis. However, once this classification alternative is selected for one such property interest held under an operating lease, all property classified as investment property shall be accounted for using the fair value model. When this classification alternative is selected, any interest so classified is included in the disclosures required. Note that this is an option, not a requirement.

Measurement

The initial measurement of a newly acquired investment property under IAS 40 is reasonably simple, but the issue of subsequent measurement is much more complicated. An investment property should be measured initially at its cost, which is the fair value of the consideration given for it. Transaction costs are included in the initial measurement. The cost of a purchased investment property comprises its purchase price and any directly attributable expenditure. Directly attributable expenditure includes, for example, professional fees for legal services and property transfer taxes.

When an investment property has already been recognized, subsequent expenditure on that investment property should be recognized as an expense when it is incurred unless it is probable that this expenditure will enable the asset to generate future economic benefits in excess of its originally assessed standard of performance and the expenditure can be measured and attributed to the asset reliably.

The initial cost of a property interest held under a lease and classified as an investment property shall be as prescribed for a finance lease by para. 20 of IAS 17, i.e. the asset shall be recognized at the lower of the fair value of the property and the present value of the minimum lease payments. An equivalent amount shall be recognized as a liability in accordance with that same paragraph. Note that this applies both to finance leases and to property interests under operating leases treated as investment properties under the option introduced in para. 6.

As suggested, the question of measurement subsequent to the initial measurement is more complicated. As already outlined, two models are available: the fair value model and the cost model. An enterprise has a choice between these two models under IAS and should apply the chosen model to all of its investment property. Although the choice given in IAS 40 between these two models is a free one, and there is no stated 'benchmark' treatment, it is very clear that the preference indicated in E64 for a fair value model remains. Fair value has to be determined in *all* cases – for measurement in the financial statements if the fair value model is used and for disclosure in the notes if the cost model is used. The Standard notes that IAS 8 (see Chapter 23) states that a voluntary change in accounting policy should be made only if the change will result in a more appropriate presentation of events or transactions in the financial statements of the enterprise. IAS 40 explicitly states that it is highly unlikely that a change from the fair value model to the cost model will result in a more appropriate presentation.

Some insurers and other entities operate an internal property fund that issues notional units, with some units held by investors in linked contracts and others held by the entity. A newly introduced para. (32A) states that an entity may:

(a) choose either the fair value model or the cost model for all investment property backing liabilities that pay a return linked directly to the fair value of, or returns from, specified assets including that investment property; and

(b) choose either the fair value model or the cost model for all other investment property, regardless of the choice made in **(a)**.

After initial recognition, an enterprise that chooses the cost model should measure all its investment property using the benchmark treatment in IAS 16, that is, at cost less any accumulated depreciation and any accumulated impairment losses. In other words, if choosing the cost model, an enterprise proceeds, in measurement (but not disclosure) terms to follow IAS 16 as if IAS 40 did not exist.

However, investment properties that meet the criteria to be classified as held for sale (or are included in a disposal group that is classified as held for sale) shall be measured in accordance with IFRS 5 (see Chapter 23).

There is a rebuttable presumption that an enterprise will be able to determine the fair value of an investment property reliably on a continuing basis. After initial recognition, an enterprise that chooses the fair value model should measure all its investment property at its fair value, unless this presumption is not valid.

A gain or loss arising from a change in the fair value of investment property should be included in net profit or loss for the period in which it arises. The standard makes it absolutely explicit that changes in fair value are to be taken directly to earnings and not taken to or from reserves.

We have discussed the concept of fair value elsewhere (see Chapter 7). Fair value is the amount for which an asset could be exchanged between knowledgeable, willing parties in an arm's length transaction. Note that the fair value figure used in a balance sheet should reflect the actual market state and circumstances as of the balance sheet date, not as of either a past or a future date. It follows, for example, that the cost of any anticipated future capital expenditure that will enhance the property and any related expected increase in benefits are both omitted from the estimation of fair value at the current date.

The best evidence of fair value is normally given by current prices on an active market for similar property in the same location and condition and subject to similar lease and other contracts. In the absence of current prices on an active market, an entity considers information from a variety of surrogate sources, including different properties, less active markets adjusted as appropriated and net present value calculations.

In the rare situations in which fair value measurement proves impossible for a particular property, the entity should measure that investment property using the cost model treatment in IAS 16. The residual value of the investment property should be assumed to be zero. The entity should continue to apply IAS 16 until the disposal of the investment property. In such circumstances, the entity measures all its other investment properties at fair value. IAS 40 requires that once an entity has begun measuring an investment property at fair value, it should continue to do so, even if the measurements subsequently become less reliable.

Transfers and disposals

Under IAS 40, transfers to or from investment property should be made only when there is a clearly evidenced change of use. When the cost model is being used for investment properties, transfers between investment property, owner-occupied property and inventories do not change the carrying amount of the property transferred and they do not change the cost of that property for measurement or disclosure purposes. The Standard does not remind us, but we should note, that the fair value of investment properties measured under the cost model has to be disclosed in the notes, a requirement that does not extend to owner-occupied property or to inventory.

A transfer to or from investment properties which are being carried at fair value obviously has potentially very significant effects on the measurement process and the carrying amount of an asset. If an investment property carried at fair value becomes an owner-occupied property or is transferred to inventory, then the property's cost for subsequent accounting purposes is its fair value as at the date of the change in use.

If an owner-occupied property becomes an investment property carried at fair value, then IAS 16 should be applied up to the date of the change of use, i.e. the entity continues to depreciate the property and to recognize any impairment losses. A difference between the carrying amount of the asset under IAS 16 at the date of the change of use and the fair value at that date is dealt with in the same way as a revaluation under IAS 16.

If a property classed as inventory is transferred to become an investment property carried at fair value, then the treatment is consistent with that of a sale of inventory under IAS 2. A difference between the fair value of the property at that date and its previous carrying amount is therefore part of net profit or loss for the period. Similarly, a self-constructed investment property that will be carried at fair value will give rise, on completion, to an effect on reported net profit or loss for the period equal to the difference between the fair value on the completion date and its previous (cost-based) carrying amount.

Activity 12.14

Read the immediately preceding paragraph again. Does it meet the ⸱⸱irement in IAS 1 and the underlying concept in the IAS Framework to be prudent?

Activity feedback

There is, certainly in comparison with what many wou' apparent lack of prudence, and of strict adherence to inherent in the previous paragraph. However, this is the w concept. There is, by definition, reliable evidence to dete market-based concept and therefore it follows logically sale, that a gain relating to operating processes has been 'made'. Anybody who regards only a completed transaction as providing adequate evidence for fair value should reject the whole notion of fair value accounting.

An investment property should be eliminated from the balance sheet (derecognized) on disposal. The disposal of an investment property may occur by sale or by entering into a finance lease. In determining the date of disposal for investment property, an enterprise applies the criteria in IAS 18, for recognizing revenue from the sale of goods (see Chapter 17). IAS 17 applies on a disposal by entering into a finance lease or by a sale and leaseback (see Chapter 14). An investment property must also be derecognized when it is permanently withdrawn from use and no further economic benefits are expected from its disposal. Gains and losses arising on derecognition, i.e. the difference between the net disposal proceeds and the carrying amount, are recognized as income or expense in the income statement, unless IAS 17 requires otherwise in the case of a sale and leaseback. This is, of course, consistent with the treatment of annual changes in fair value of a retained investment property, which are likewise taken directly to the income statement.

IAS 40 gives extensive and detailed disclosure requirements. The crucial point to remember is that if the cost model is used, then disclosure of fair values, by way of note, is still required.

Some national considerations

Broadly speaking, the treatment of investment properties in important accounting jurisdictions mirrors the general characteristics of those jurisdictions, as discussed in Chapter 2. It may be suggested that the attitude to investment properties often illustrates these characteristics quite strongly. It is generally argued that the Fourth EU Directive, as agreed in 1978, does not allow non-depreciation of property, although of course the true and fair override in Article 2 can be used to justify departure from this, at least in those countries that believe in the override anyway. National practice in 'continental' European countries would be, at least up to the present, to use the cost model.

The so-called Anglo-Saxons are clearly split on the matter. At the time of writing, UK Standards *require* investment properties to be evaluated on a broadly fair value basis, in SSAP 19. US GAAP, as currently constituted (ARB 43, APB 6), require that investment properties be treated the same way as any other properties and are, therefore, squarely inconsistent with the original E64 proposals and with the UK requirements.

It is important to note, however, that although at first sight IAS 40 seems to be a compromise in that it allows both the UK to use fair values and the US to forbid them, this is over simplistic. There is in fact a major difference between the UK and IAS. SSAP 19 in the UK, at para. 13, requires that changes in the market value of investment properties should not be taken to the income statements but should be taken to the statement of total recognized gains and losses (being a movement on an investment revaluation reserve), unless a deficit (or its reversal) on an individual property is expected to be permanent, in which case it should be charged (or credited) in the profit and loss account of the period.

This is in sharp contrast to the IAS 40 requirements, which, as discussed earlier, generally require such changes in market value to be taken directly to annual reported earnings. As regards the important concept of reported earnings, therefore, current UK GAAP is significantly more prudent than the requirements of the fair value alternative in IAS GAAP.

It should also be noted that IAS 40 has gone out of its way to give the impression that it is a stepping stone towards an eventual compulsory fair value model for investment properties. Time will tell.

Activity 12.15

An extract from the financial statements of the British Land Company PLC for the year to 31 March 2001 is shown in Table 12.1.

Included in the leasehold properties is an amount of £13.0m, in respect of property occupied by the Group.

The historical cost of properties held by investment subsidiaries was £5 221.7m (2000 – £5 317.1m).

Comment on the major differences which will arise between applying UK GAAP, US GAAP, IAS 40 fair value basis and IAS 40 cost basis to this information.

Table 12.1 Extract from financial statements of the British Land Company plc for the year to 31 March 2001

	Freehold £m	Long leasehold £m	Short leasehold £m	Total £m
Investment and development properties				
Valuation and cost 1 April 2000	6 548.2	229.6		6 777.8
Additions	244.4	0.9		245.3
Disposals	(348.6)	(56.4)		(405.0)
Reallocations	(8.6)	8.6		
Exchange fluctuations	3.9			3.9
Revaluation	526.6	1.8		528.4
Valuation and cost 31 March 2001	6 965.9	184.5		7 150.4
Trading properties				
At lower of cost and net realizable value 31 March 2001	48.9	2.2	2.2	53.3
External valuation surplus on development and trading properties				130.3
Total investment, development and trading properties				7 334.0

	£m
Total external valuation surplus on development and trading properties	
Development and trading properties	130.3
Share of joint ventures	19.1
	149.4

Activity feedback

The key points are that under UK GAAP, as shown, the investment properties are regularly revalued. The surplus on revaluation in the year, of over £500 million, will *not* be taken to the income statement. Under US GAAP, all the properties would be recorded at historical cost, i.e. some £1700 million less than in Table 12.1, further reduced by accumulated depreciation. The depreciation charge for the year would be included in the income statement.

Under IAS 40, if the cost model is used, then the position will be similar to the US GAAP situation. If the fair value model is used, then the balance sheet position will be broadly similar to Table 12.1, but the £500 + million annual revaluation *would* be taken to the income statement.

In other words, there are some very material differences!

Summary

In this long chapter we have explored a number of aspects of IAS thinking in relation to the accounting treatment of fixed (non-current) assets. We looked at problems of cost determination, in particular IAS 20 on government grants and IAS 23 on borrowing costs and on the recognition and measurement of property, plant and equipment (IAS 16), including alternative methods of depreciation calculation. We also exposed alternative views on the treatment of investment properties, and the IAS requirements on this in IAS 40.

EXERCISES	(✔ indicates answers are available on page 725)

1 What are fixed (non-current) assets?

2 Outline four different depreciation methods and appraise them in the context of the definition and objectives of depreciation.

3 Are government grants related to the purchase of fixed assets by an enterprise a reduction in cost of acquisition?

4 Can the receipt of a government grant create a liability?

5 In what circumstances, if at all, should borrowing costs be capitalized, in your opinion?

6 IAS 23 gives a choice of accounting policy in relation to borrowing costs. Is a choice acceptable? If not, how should IAS 23 be altered?

✔ 7 Should land be allowed to be, or required to be, revalued?

✔ 8 Should buildings be allowed to be, or required to be, revalued?

9 In what circumstances, if any, do you think that regulation should allow the non-depreciation of owned buildings?

10 IAS 40 gives a choice of accounting policy in relation to investment properties. Is a choice acceptable? If not, how should IAS 40 be altered?

11 IAS 23 *Borrowing Costs* has a benchmark treatment that requires borrowing costs to be recognised as an expense in the period in which they are incurred. It also permits an allowed alternative treatment for certain borrowing costs to be capitalised as part of the cost of a qualifying asset.

Required:

(i) Discuss the arguments in favour of, and those against, the capitalisation of borrowing costs as part of the cost of an asset.

On 1 April 20X2, Webster commenced the construction of a large development consisting of several separate retail premises. It has a policy of capitalising borrowing costs where this is permissible under IAS 23. At 31 March 20X3 the amount of expenditure on the development totalled $12 million. These expenditures can be taken to have been incurred evenly throughout the year. The development is being financed from funds generally borrowed for the construction of similar development projects. Webster's cost of capital on these funds can be calculated from the following:

$2 million overdraft at 15% per annum

$3 million 5 year secured 8% loan note

$5 million 5 year unsecured 10% loan note

Construction of the development was halted twice during the accounting period to 31 March 20X3. The first occasion, for a two-week period, was due to the discovery of ancient artefacts unearthed during excavation work. The second, an extended period of two months, was due to an industrial relations dispute.

Required:

(ii) Calculate the amount of finance costs that Webster should capitalise for the period to 31 March 20X3. (ACCA June 03)

Intangible assets and impairment of assets

After studying this chapter you should be able to:
- ☐ define and distinguish intangible assets, and goodwill
- ☐ describe, apply and appraise the requirements of IAS 38 relating to intangible assets
- ☐ discuss alternative possible treatments for purchased goodwill
- ☐ describe, apply and appraise the requirements of IAS 22 relating to purchased goodwill
- ☐ describe, apply and appraise the requirements of IAS 36 relating to impairment of assets.

Introduction

The accounting treatment of goodwill and intangible assets has caused great difficulty and confusion over the years. Part of the trouble was a failure to distinguish clearly between the two. Much of the confusion has been removed by recent international developments, but the future treatment of goodwill is under active consideration and discussion, as regulators move further towards an acceptance of the use of fair values.

In the 'bad old days' goodwill was often very loosely regarded as a conglomerate figure for all unrecorded net asset values. In other words, if a business were bought for €1 million and the recorded net assets had 'book values' of €600 000, then the difference of €400 000 was considered to be goodwill. This adherence to book values, which are by definition largely meaningless in market terms, is now generally unacceptable. IASB now defines goodwill (IFRS3, Appendix A) as follows:

> Future economic benefits arising from assets that are not capable of being individually identified and separately recognized.

In principle, goodwill is in existence all the time. Its value is different to define, and is constantly changing. Its value can, of course, be negative. But goodwill is always there, it is inherent in the business. This is often referred to as *inherent goodwill*, *non-purchased goodwill* or *internally generated goodwill*. It is contrasted with purchased goodwill. This contrast is not for reasons of principle, but purely for the practical reason that purchased goodwill has a convenient cost figure. There has been a transaction, the cost convention can be applied, we have a figure capable of being audited. If we buy a business for €100 000 and the net separable assets have fair value of €60 000 then we can certainly say that goodwill is, or at least at that instant was, worth €40 000.

The accounting treatment for purchased goodwill is regarded as an aspect of accounting for business combinations. IASB covers this in IFRS 3 and we discuss purchased goodwill separately in the next section. We first consider in detail the problems of accounting for intangibles other than purchased goodwill; this is covered by IAS 38, *Intangible Assets*.

The concluding part of this chapter looks at the whole issue of impairment of assets. This applies generally to all the types of asset discussed in both this and the previous chapter and may, in rare circumstances, apply to other assets as well.

Intangible assets

In IAS GAAP, an intangible asset is defined as an *'identifiable* non-monetary asset without physical substance'. This excludes goodwill, which is by definition non-identifiable.

Identifiability in IAS GAAP does not equal separability, since an asset of an enterprise is defined as 'a *resource* [that is] (a) *controlled* by the enterprise as a result of past events; and (b) from which future economic benefits are expected to flow to the enterprise'. For an intangible asset to be recognized, the future economic benefits must be 'probable', and it must be possible to measure the cost of the asset reliably. 'Control' encompasses both the right to obtain the benefits and the ability to restrict access to them by others. It is not necessarily considered to imply the ability to sell the item separately from other assets of the enterprise. These criteria thus permit the recognition as assets, in appropriate circumstances, of non-separable items such as development costs that have not been converted into (separable) patents. They do not permit the recognition of internally generated goodwill.

IAS 38 is a relatively recent standard. At its original creation in 1998 the IASB decided to include the requirements on research and development (R&D) costs, originally separately stated in IAS 9, with those on other intangibles because R&D costs are intangible in nature, any value attributable to them being due to the know-how embodied in them rather than to physical items such as prototypes. The IASB was concerned to achieve, as far as possible, uniformity of treatment for all long-term non-financial assets, whether tangible or intangible, and for intangibles whether internally generated or acquired. This concern is manifested in IAS 38 in the following ways:

- many of the paragraphs of IAS 38 are similar in wording and in places virtually identical, to paragraphs of IAS 16, *Property, Plant and Equipment*
- the recognition as assets of internally generated intangibles is allowed, subject to stringent and cumbersome criteria.

Although the principle is that any intangibles that meet the asset recognition criteria should be recognized (except in the case of the 'alternative treatment' discussed later), it remains to be seen whether the effect of these criteria acts as a deterrent to a reporting entity from so doing, in the absence of a powerful reason.

The treatment of R&D costs has been the subject of particular controversy internationally. While there is general (but not universal, e.g. Norwegian law explicitly states the opposite) agreement that research does not give rise to intangible values that can be recognized as assets, there is disagreement as to whether development may do so, subject to certain criteria. In its 1993 revision of IAS 9, *Research and Development Costs*, the IASB changed its preferred (benchmark) treatment from that proposed in its Exposure Drafts E32 and E47, namely, the immediate expensing of all development costs, to capitalization (i.e. recognition as an asset), provided certain criteria were met. It was thought that this was more consistent with the concept of an asset as set out in the IASB's Framework. In IAS 38, capitalization is maintained, but the criteria for recognition have been tightened up; immediate expensing is not allowed as an alternative treatment if these criteria are met.

Another area of controversy has been the treatment of brands. Here, however, the IASB has felt able to take a firm line: internally generated brands are not to be recognized as assets. Brands acquired in a business combination are not considered to be separately identifiable assets and are thus part of goodwill.

The new version of IAS 38, applicable from 1 January 2005, makes various amendments and clarifications and, in a major development, requires the non-depreciation of intangible assets with indefinite lines, as defined, requiring regular impairment tests instead.

Scope of IAS 38

The scope of IAS 38 is clarified in paras 2 and 3 by stating which categories of item are not included, namely:

  (a) intangible assets that are within the scope of another Standard;
  (b) financial assets, as defined in IAS 39, *Financial Instruments: Recognition and Measurement*; and
  (c) mineral rights and expenditure on the exploration for, or development and extraction of, minerals, oil, natural gas and similar non-regenerative resources.

If another Standard prescribes the accounting for a specific type of intangible asset, an entity applies that Standard instead of IAS 38. For example:

(a) intangible assets held by an entity for sale in the ordinary course of business (see IAS 2, *Inventories*, and IAS 11 *Construction Contracts*)
(b) deferred tax assets (see IAS 12, *Income Taxes*)
(c) leases that are within the scope of IAS 17, *Leases*
(d) assets arising from employee benefits (see IAS 19, *Employee Benefits*)
(e) financial assets as defined in IAS 39; recognition and measurement of some financial assets are covered by IAS 27, *Consolidated and Separate Financial Statements*, IAS 28, *Investments in Associates*, and IAS 31, *Interests in Joint Ventures*
(f) goodwill acquired in a business combination (see IFRS 3, *Business Combinations*).
(g) deferred acquisition costs, and intangible assets, arising from an insurer's contractual rights under insurance contracts within the scope of IFRS 4, *Insurance Contracts*
(h) non-current intangible assets classified as held for sale (or included in a disposal group that is classified as held for sale) in accordance with IFRS 5, *Non-current Assets Held for Sale and Discontinued Operations*.

The term *intangible assets* raises the major issue of which intangible items should be recognized as assets and which should not. Hence, IAS 38 mentions numerous items of expenditure on what may be termed *intangible resources*, many of which do not meet its asset recognition criteria. These items include expenditure on advertising, training, start-up, research and development activities, and computer software, patents, copyrights, motion picture films. A good number of these do not qualify for recognition as assets in terms of the criteria set out in the IASB's Framework and one of the main purposes of IAS 38 is to distinguish between those that do and those that do not. Examples of expenditure that do not meet these criteria are start-ups, research, training, advertising and/or promotion and relocation or reorganization. Para. 63 adds internally generated brands, mastheads, publishing titles, customer lists and items similar in substance as items not qualifying for recognition as assets.

According to IAS 38, para. 6, an intangible asset held by a lessee under a finance lease is considered, after initial recognition, to be an asset falling within the scope of IAS 38.

Recognition under IAS 38

Three criteria need to be satisfied before an item should be recognized as an intangible asset under IAS 38. These are identifiability, control and reliable measurability.

Identifiability (IAS 38, paras 10–12 and 17) is necessary in order to distinguish an intangible asset from goodwill. Separability is a sufficient condition for identifiability, but in IAS GAAP not a necessary one. An asset is separable if the enterprise could rent, sell, exchange or distribute the specific future economic benefits attributable to the asset without also disposing of other assets or future economic benefits that flow from them. (Future economic benefits include both revenues and cost savings.)

An enterprise, however, may be able to identify an intangible asset in some other way. If an intangible asset is acquired together with a set of other assets, it may be separately identifiable by virtue of separate legal rights attaching to it. An internally generated intangible asset may also result from an internal project that gives rise to legal rights for the enterprise. Nevertheless, usually legal rights are transferable, so that such assets are separable (an exception is rights resulting from a legal duty on employees to maintain confidentiality). But identifiability in IAS GAAP can be achieved even if an asset generates future economic benefits only in combination with other assets, that is, it is not separable, provided the enterprise can identify the future economic benefits that will flow from the asset. In that case, however, the second criterion, control, is particularly crucial.

Control (IAS 38, paras 13–16) is exercised by an enterprise over an asset if the enterprise:

- has the power to obtain the future economic benefits flowing from the underlying resource
- can also restrict the access of others to such benefits.

The resource itself is not recognizable as an asset unless the criterion of control (as well as that of identifiability) is met. Control will generally result from legal rights enforceable in law and such rights provide a sufficient condition for control. IAS GAAP do not exclude the possibility that control over the future economic benefits could be exercised in some other way, but give no examples of this.

In the case of such intangible resources as benefits arising from a team of skilled staff and from training, even if the identifiability criterion can be satisfied, the criterion of controllability will most likely not be met in the absence of protection by legal rights. The same is true for customer lists or market shares. Such intangible resources therefore do not usually qualify for recognition as intangible assets.

Reliable measurability is also a necessary precondition for the recognition of intangible assets.

IAS 38, paragraphs 21 and 24, state that an intangible asset (that has met the other recognition criteria) should be recognized only if its cost can be measured reliably and that it should be measured initially at that cost.

For the purpose of determining cost, four different modes of acquisition are considered (paras 25–47): separate acquisition; acquisition as part of a business combination; acquisition by way of a government grant; and acquisition by exchange of assets. Little needs to be said in explanation of this.

In the case of separate acquisition, the rules for determining cost are the same as those for assets generally, discussed in Chapter 12. The rules for determining cost in the case of acquisition as part of a business combination are given in IFRS 3 (see Chapter 24). In the case of acquisition by way of a government grant, the rules in IAS 20 are applicable (see Chapter 12).

In general, exchanges of assets are accounted for at fair value, the fair value of the asset given being treated as the cost of the asset acquired, subject to any necessary adjustments for any other partial consideration such as cash. In the case of an intangible asset that is exchanged for an equity interest in a similar asset (such as a share in a research and development joint venture), the cost of the new asset is the carrying amount of the asset given up, with no gain or loss being recognized on the transaction, unless the fair value of the asset received is less than the carrying amount of the asset given up.

Internally generated intangible assets

Note that internally generated goodwill cannot be an intangible asset within the terms of IAS 38 and so cannot be capitalized. In order to assess whether an internally generated intangible resource meets the criteria for recognition as an asset, IAS 38 set out the following methodology (paras 52–62).

The enterprise, first, classifies the internal project resulting in the generation of the resource into two phases: a research phase and a development phase. If this distinction cannot be made for the internal project, then the entire project should be considered as a research phase.

Research is defined as original and planned investigation undertaken with the prospect of gaining new scientific or technical knowledge and understanding. Development is the application of research findings or other knowledge to a plan or design for the production of new or substantially improved materials, devices, products, processes, systems or services before the start of commercial production or use (IAS 38, para. 8).

It is worth pausing at this point to remind ourselves about the general principles involved here. It is obvious that the management of an enterprise will authorize the expenditure of money and resources on either research or development only if there is in some sense or other an expectation of benefit to the enterprise. It can be argued that an expectation of future benefit from a past event automatically creates the expectation of an asset now. However, the IAS definition of an asset needs to be remembered in full, i.e. an asset is a resource:

- controlled by an enterprise as a result of past events
- and from which future economic benefits are expected to flow.

Activity 13.1

From your knowledge of the IASB Framework and general accounting concepts, suggest briefly, with justification, how expenditure in the research and development phases should be treated.

Activity feedback

In essence, the matching convention argues in favour of capitalization now, in order to permit expensing later against resulting benefit. The asset figure will need to be charged to the P&L account over the period of benefits, in approximate proportion to the benefit pattern. In effect, we would have a fixed asset that would require depreciating. And since there is likely to be a gap, perhaps of several years, between expenditure and eventual benefit in terms of production and sales, it follows that the expense or depreciation may be zero for one or more accounting periods. If the benefit has not begun to appear yet, then under the matching convention we should not yet begin to write off the asset as an expense.

It can be suggested that this treatment is inconsistent with the prudence convention. Research and development expenditure is by definition speculative and, particularly with more basic investigation, the outcome is highly uncertain. It is perhaps difficult to argue that the existence of future benefit, of greater amount than the expenditure, can be established with 'reasonable certainty'. It is even harder to argue that the *relationship* to the revenue or benefit in any particular future period can be established with 'reasonable certainty'. It must also be remembered that a successful profitable outcome is crucially dependent on the validity of the going concern convention.

There is clearly a tension regarding research and development expenditure between matching and prudence. Whatever detailed views an individual holds, it is obvious that research is significantly more speculative than development and that development expenditure becomes less speculative and more reasonably predictable in its outcome, as actual production and sale of the product comes nearer. The IASB solution is to forbid the capitalization of all research and development expenditure, except for development phase items which meet specified conditions, in which case they are required (not just permitted) to be capitalized.

Thus under IAS 38, no intangible asset should be recognized as resulting from research or from the research phase of an internal project. Expenditure on research should be recognized as an expense when incurred.

An intangible resource arising from development (or from the development phase of an internal project) should be recognized as an intangible asset if, and only if, an enterprise can demonstrate all the following:

- the technical feasibility of completing the intangible asset so that it will be available for use or sale
- its intention to complete the intangible asset and use or sell it
- its ability to use or sell it
- how the intangible asset will generate probable future economic benefits. Among other things, the following should be demonstrated: the existence of a market for the intangible asset or its output or, if it is to be used internally, its usefulness to the enterprise
- the availability of adequate technical, financial and other resources to complete the development and to use or sell the intangible asset, which may be demonstrated by an appropriate business plan
- the enterprise's ability to measure reliably the expenditure attributable to the intangible asset during its development, for example, by means of the enterprise's costing system.

To demonstrate how an intangible asset will generate probable future economic benefits, the principles set out in IAS 36, *Impairment of Assets*, especially paras 30–57 on value in use should be applied. If the asset will generate economic benefits only in combination with other assets, the principles for 'cash-generating units' set out in IAS 36 should be followed (IAS 36 is discussed later).

As discussed above, under the 'Scope' heading, IAS 38 names a number of items that do not meet these criteria.

The cost of an internally generated asset is the sum of the expenditure incurred from the date when the intangible asset first meets the recognition criteria set out earlier. Cost includes all expenditure that is either directly attributable to generating the asset or has been allocated on a reasonable and consistent basis to the activity of generating it. Allocations of overheads should follow the principles set out in IAS 2, *Inventories* (see Chapter 15). With regard to the recognition of interest as a cost, IAS 23, *Borrowing Costs* (see Chapter 12) sets out the applicable principles.

Expenditure that is not part of the cost of the intangible asset includes that on selling, administration and training staff to operate the asset. Expenditure on an intangible resource that was initially recognized as an expense in previous financial statements or reports (for example, expenditure during the 'research phase' of an internal project) should not be recognized as part of the cost of an intangible asset at a later date (IAS 38, para. 71).

Any expenditure that is not part of the cost of an intangible asset properly recognizable as defined and discussed earlier is, naturally, to be recognized as an expense when incurred (unless the expenditure is part of the cost of a business acquisition, when IFRS 3 applies as already stated).

Subsequent expenditure

The view taken in IAS 38 is that only rarely will expenditure incurred after the initial recognition of a purchased intangible asset or after the completion of an internally generated intangible asset result in an addition to the amount of its capitalized cost. This is because it is generally difficult:

- to attribute such expenditure to a particular intangible asset rather than to the business as a whole
- and even when that difficulty does not arise, to determine whether such expenditure will enhance, rather than merely maintain, the probable economic benefits that will flow from the asset.

Consequently, subsequent expenditure should be recognized as an expense, except in the rare cases where:

- probable enhancement of the economic benefits that will flow from the asset can be demonstrated
- the expenditure can be measured and attributed to the asset reliably (IAS 38, paras 18–20).

Measurement subsequent to initial recognition

Two treatments are available, the cost model and the revaluation model. In the 1998 version of IAS 38 these were characterized as 'benchmark' and 'alternative' treatments, respectively. These terms have been removed and the new IAS 38 gives the two alternatives ostensibly equal weighting.

The cost model is that an intangible asset should be carried at cost less any accumulated depreciation and (if any) accumulated impairment losses (IAS 38, para. 63).

The revaluation model is to carry the intangible asset at a revalued amount. The revalued amount should be the fair value of the asset at the date of revaluation less any subsequent accumulated depreciation and (if any) subsequent accumulated impairment losses (IAS 38, para. 75). This alternative treatment can only be applied *after* initial recognition, i.e. all the conditions and requirements stated earlier must previously have been fully satisfied.

If an intangible asset is revalued, revaluation of all the other assets in its class should also be carried out (i.e. those of similar nature and use within the enterprise's operations), except those for which there is no active market, which should be carried at cost less accumulated amortization and impairment losses.

Fair value should be determined by reference to an active market and revaluations should be made with sufficient regularity so that the carrying amount does not diverge materially from the fair value at the balance sheet date. An active market is defined as one in which all the following conditions exist:

- the items traded within it are homogeneous
- willing buyers and sellers can normally be found at any time (within reason)
- prices are public information (IAS 38, para. 8).

It is considered unlikely that such an active market would exist for an intangible asset (IAS 38, para. 67), although there may be exceptions to this generalization; for example, there may be active markets in freely transferable taxi licences, fishing licences, production quotas or airport takeoff and landing 'slots'. If an active market is not available, the revaluation model cannot be used.

The revaluation model cannot apply to initial recognition, which should be at cost, or to intangible resources that were not previously recognized as assets. However, if only part of the cost of an intangible resource was recognized as an asset because it did not meet the criteria for recognition until part of the way through an internal project, the alternative treatment may be applied to the whole of the asset and not just to that proportion of it that would be represented by the amount recognized as its cost. The alternative treatment may also be applied to an intangible asset received by way of a government grant and initially recognized at a nominal amount (IAS 38, para. 77).

An active market that has existed for an intangible asset may cease to exist. In that case, if the asset has been accounted for by using the alternative treatment, then its carrying amount should be its revalued amount at the date of the last revaluation by reference to the formerly active market less any accumulated depreciation and impairment losses. The cessation of the active market may be an indication of possible impairment of the asset's value and this should be tested in accordance with IAS 36, *Impairment of Assets* (see later). If, at a subsequent measurement date, an active market is available again so that the fair value of the asset can be determined, the asset should be revalued at its fair value as of that date.

Recognition of revaluation gains and losses

The usual prudence and realization conventions prevail. Increases in an intangible asset's carrying amount (gains) should be credited directly to equity under the heading of revaluation surplus, except to the extent that the increase is a reversal of a previous revaluation decrease (loss) recognized as an expense in respect of the same asset, in which case the amount of the reversal is recognized as income.

Revaluation decreases (losses) are recognized as expenses except to the extent that the decrease is a reversal of a revaluation increase (gain) that was previously credited to revaluation surplus in respect of the same asset, in which case the amount of the reversal should be charged against the revaluation surplus (IAS 38, paras 73–77).

According to IAS 38, para. 87, the cumulative revaluation surplus 'may' be transferred directly to retained earnings when the surplus is realized. Realization of the surplus may occur through retirement or disposal of the asset or through the process of using up the asset, insofar as the amortization based on the revalued carrying amount exceeds that which would have been calculated on the basis of the asset's historical cost. The transfer from revaluation surplus to retained earnings is not made through the income statement, but directly in the balance sheet, i.e. it does not affect reported earnings in the year the transfer is made.

Amortization and depreciation

IAS 38 uses the terms *amortization* and *depreciation* interchangeably with reference to intangible assets to refer to the process of systematic allocation of an asset's cost or revalued amount, less any residual value, over its useful life. The residual value should be assumed to be zero, unless:

■ either there is a commitment by a third party to purchase the asset at the end of its estimated useful life to the enterprise (i.e. the period of time over which it is being depreciated)

- or there is an active market for the asset, such that the asset's residual value can be determined by reference to that market and it is probable that the market will exist at the end of asset's estimated useful life to the enterprise.

An estimate of an asset's residual value is based on the amount recoverable from disposal using prices prevailing at the date of the estimate for the sale of a similar asset that has reached the end of its useful life and has operated under conditions similar to those in which the asset will be used. The residual value is reviewed at least at each financial year end. A change in the asset's residual value is accounted for as a change in an accounting estimate in accordance with IAS 8, *Accounting Policies, Changes in Accounting Estimates and Errors*.

Useful life

The previous (1998) version of IAS 38 contained a 'rebuttable assumption' that the useful life for an intangible asset could not exceed 20 years, and, in all cases, required amortization. The new version makes very significant changes. IAS 38 now requires (paras 88–9) that an entity shall assess whether the useful life of an intangible asset is finite or indefinite and, if finite, the length of, or number of production or similar units constituting, that useful life. An intangible asset shall be regarded by the entity as having an indefinite useful life when, based on an analysis of all the relevant factors, there is no foreseeable limit to the period over which the asset is expected to generate net cash inflows for the entity.

The accounting for an intangible asset is based on its useful life. An intangible asset with a finite useful life is amortized and an intangible asset with an indefinite useful life is not.

Factors that need to be considered in estimating an intangible asset's useful life include the following (IAS 38, paras 90 and 94):

1 The expected usage of the asset by the entity and whether the asset could be efficiently managed by another management team.
2 Typical product life cycles for the asset and public information on estimates of useful lives for similar assets that are used in a similar way.
3 Technical, technological, commercial or other types of obsolescence.
4 The stability of the industry in which the asset operates and changes in the market demand for the outputs of the asset.
5 Expected actions by competitors or potential competitors.
6 The level of maintenance expenditure required to obtain the expected future economic benefits from the asset and the entity's intent and ability to spend such amounts.
7 The entity's period of control over the asset and legal and similar limits on control or use, such as the expiration dates of related leases. If control over the future economic benefits from the asset is achieved though legal rights that have been granted for a finite period, the useful life of the asset should not exceed the duration of the legal rights unless they are renewable and renewal is virtually certain.
8 Whether the asset's useful life is dependent on that of other assets of the enterprise.

The term 'indefinite' does not mean 'infinite'. The useful life of an intangible asset reflects only that level of future maintenance expenditure required to maintain the asset at its standard of performance assessed at the time of estimating the asset's useful life and the entity's ability and intention to reach such a level. A conclusion that the useful life of an intangible asset is indefinite should not depend on planned future expenditure in excess of that required to maintain the asset at that standard of performance.

Intangible assets with finite useful lives

The depreciable amount of an intangible asset with a finite useful life shall be allocated on a systematic basis over its useful life. Amortization shall begin when the asset is available for use, i.e. when it is in the location and condition necessary for it to be capable of operating in the manner intended by management. Amortization shall cease at the earlier of the date that the asset is classified as held for sale (or included in a disposal group that is classified as held for sale) in accordance with IFRS 5, *Non-current Assets Held for Sale and Discontinued Operations*, and the date that the asset is derecognized. The amortization method used shall reflect the pattern in which the asset's future economic benefits are expected to be consumed by the entity. If the pattern cannot be reliably determined, the straight line method shall be used. The amortization charge for each period shall be recognized in profit or loss unless IAS 38 or another Standard permits or requires it to be included in the carrying amount of another asset.

IAS 38 envisages a variety of amortization methods that may be used to allocate systematically the depreciable amount of an intangible asset over the periods making up its useful life. The standard mentions the straight line, diminishing balance and units of production methods. The straight line method should be used unless the time pattern of consumption of the asset's economic benefits can be determined reliably and clearly indicates that one of the other methods is more suitable. There will rarely, if ever, be persuasive evidence to support a method for intangible assets that is less conservative (that is, results in a lower amount of accumulated depreciation) than the straight line method (IAS 38, paras 88–90).

The amortization period and method should be reviewed at least at each financial year end and the amortization period should be changed if the expected useful life of the asset is significantly different from previous estimates (IAS 38, para. 104). If the expected time pattern of economic benefits has changed, the amortization method should be changed accordingly. Such changes should be accounted for as changes in accounting estimates under IAS 8 (see Chapter 23).

In addition to all of the above, the requirements of IAS 36, *Impairment of Assets* (discussed later), will apply.

Intangible assets with indefinite useful lives

The essential treatment is very simple. Such assets are not depreciated (i.e. shall not be, not need not be). IAS 36 is applied and an impairment test is carried out annually *and* whenever there is an indication that the intangible asset may be impaired. This will lead to reductions in carrying value to the recoverable amount at the date of the impairment test.

Retirements and disposals

An intangible asset shall be derecognized:

- on disposal
- or when no future economic benefits are expected from its use or disposal.

The gain or loss arising from the derecognition of an intangible asset shall be determined as the difference between the net disposal proceeds, if any, and the carrying amount of the asset. It shall be recognized in profit or loss when the asset is derecognized (unless IAS 17, *Leases*, requires otherwise on a sale and leaseback). Gains shall not be classified as revenue.

Amortization of an intangible asset with a finite useful life does not cease when the intangible asset is no longer used, unless the asset has been fully depreciated or is classified as held for sale (or included in a disposal group that is classified as held for sale) in accordance with IFRS 5.

Disclosure

The disclosure requirements are, as usual, long and detailed. Full details of balances, movements over the year and any revaluations or impairment losses are specified.

International differences

The main differences between IAS GAAP and US GAAP regarding intangibles are the following:

1   With the exception of certain software development costs, which are required to be capitalized in accordance with FAS 86, *Accounting for the Costs of Computer Software to be Sold, Leased or Otherwise Marketed*, US GAAP (FAS 2) require all R&D costs to be immediately expensed. Under IAS GAAP, the required treatment of development costs is that they should be capitalized if certain recognition criteria are met.
2   IAS GAAP permit the restatement of intangible assets to their fair values, provided fair value can be determined by reference to an active market for that type of asset. This is not permitted by US GAAP.
3   US GAAP permit useful lives of identified intangibles to have a duration of up to 40 years, like goodwill acquired in a business combination.

UK GAAP is difficult to map onto the IASB requirements. FRS 10 goes out of its way to treat both intangible assets and purchased goodwill in the same standard and as consistently as possible. However, research and development expenditure is regulated separately, in SSAP 13 issued long ago. SSAP 13 is notable for specifying the same six criteria as IAS 38 related to the capitalization of development expenditure, but saying that if they are all met then the expenditure 'may' be capitalized. Such a weak politically inspired compromise must surely soon be removed.

European practices in this area are historically variable. The general emphasis on prudence would suggest reluctance to capitalize, for example, development expenditure. Paradoxically, however, formation expenses, which require immediate write off under IAS, are commonly capitalized and written off over five years as explicitly allowed by the Fourth European Directive.

Accounting for purchased goodwill

As we discussed earlier, purchased goodwill is regulated under IAS by IFRS 3 on business combinations, not by IAS 38 on intangible assets. Nevertheless the basic issues involved in its treatment are asset/expense questions, not principles of consolidations, and it is appropriate to deal with its treatment here.

As already noted, goodwill is defined (IFRS 3, Appendix A) as follows:

> Future economic benefits arising from assets that are not capable of being individually identified and separately recognized.

It could be suggested that this rather strange wording (future economic benefits *arising from* assets...) implies that goodwill is not, itself, an asset.

Activity 13.2

Does goodwill on acquisition meet the IASB's own definition of an asset?

Activity feedback

An asset (Framework, para. 49a) is a resource controlled by the enterprise as a result of past events and from which future economic benefits are expected to flow. There is certainly a past event and there must logically be an expectation of future economic benefits in the eyes of the management of the acquirer. But is there a 'resource controlled' by the enterprise? Remember that, by definition, no 'identifiable asset' is involved. The issue is a complicated theoretical one and general opinion seems to be that goodwill on acquisition is certainly not a normal asset, but is at least sufficiently asset-like to be treated as if it was one.

A variety of ways can be suggested for how goodwill on acquisition might be treated after recognition. Here are seven:

1 carry it as an asset and amortize it over its estimated useful life through the profit and loss account
2 carry it as an asset and amortize it over its estimated useful life by writing off against reserves
3 eliminate it against reserves immediately on acquisition
4 retain it in the accounts indefinitely, unless a permanent reduction in its value becomes evident, when impairment is recognized
5 charge it as an expense against profits in the period when it is acquired
6 show it as a deduction from shareholder's equity (and either amortize it or carry it indefinitely)
7 Revalue it annually to incorporate later non-purchased goodwill.

Activity 13.3

Comment on each of these possible treatments, in relation to rational justification and usefulness.

Activity feedback

Here are some thoughts, which you may or may not completely agree with:

1 is a straightforward application of matching the acquisition 'cost' in proportion to the benefit

2 seems illogical; amortization represents an expense and therefore should appear in the profit and loss account

3 this solves the problem as if the item had never existed. It implies that no asset exists, and that equity must face the 'loss' immediately

4 this is rational if it is accepted that purchased goodwill can be maintained, as a building can. Arguably, however, the reality is that purchased goodwill is gradually being replaced by non-purchased goodwill. It can also be suggested that the costs of maintaining the goodwill are being expended as they occur and that to charge amortization as well would usually be simple double counting

5 seems illogical and excessively prudent

6 also seems illogical, and potentially confusing, being essentially a misrepresentation of either **1** or **4**

7 would be consistent with the trend towards fair value generally, but highly subjective (and inconsistent with legal restrictions in many countries).

We are now in a position to explore the formal requirements of IFRS 3 in relation to goodwill on acquisition.

Goodwill and IFRS 3

Goodwill in IAS GAAP is the difference between the fair value of the purchase consideration given and the aggregate fair values of the identifiable assets and liabilities of the acquiree that are recognized on acquisition, as discussed earlier. What is recognized as goodwill on acquisition is therefore a function of the recognition criteria and valuation rules applied to the identifiable assets and liabilities (and notably those in IASs 36, 37, 38 and 39). As such, it is therefore not itself an identifiable asset or liability but a residual amount. Nevertheless, IAS GAAP require it to be shown as an asset.

Goodwill on acquisition is calculated through the following process (paras 36–7).

The acquirer shall, at the acquisition date, allocate the cost of a business combination by recognizing the acquiree's identifiable assets, liabilities and contingent liabilities that satisfy the recognition criteria in paragraph 37 at their fair values at that date, except for non-current assets (or disposal groups) that are classified as held for sale in accordance with IFRS 5, *Non-current Assets Held for Sales and Discontinued Operations*, which shall be recognized at fair value less costs to sell. Any difference between the cost of the business combination and the acquirer's interest in the net fair value of the identifiable assets, liabilities and contingent liabilities so recognized shall be accounted for as goodwill.

The acquirer shall recognize separately the acquiree's identifiable assets, liabilities and contingent liabilities at the acquisition date only if they satisfy the following criteria at that date:

■ in the case of an asset other than an intangible asset, it is probable that any associated future economic benefits will flow to the acquirer and its fair value can be measured reliably

■ in the case of a liability other than a contingent liability, it is probable that an outflow of resources embodying economic benefits will be required to settle the obligation and its fair value can be measured reliably

- in the case of an intangible asset or a contingent liability, its fair value can be measured reliably.

The excess of cost over the net fair value of the identified intangible assets is the goodwill on acquisition figure. The acquirer is required to treat such goodwill as follows (paras 51–2):

The acquirer shall, at the acquisition date:

(a) recognize goodwill acquired in a business combination as an asset; and
(b) initially measure that goodwill at its cost, being the excess of the cost of the business combination over the acquirer's interest in the net fair value of the identifiable assets, liabilities and contingent liabilities recognized in accordance with paragraph 36.

Goodwill acquired in a business combination represents a payment made by the acquirer in anticipation of future economic benefits from assets that are not capable of being individually identified and separately recognized. Goodwill acquired in a business combination shall not be amortized. Instead, the acquirer shall test it for impairment annually, or more frequently if events or changes in circumstances indicate that it might be impaired, in accordance with IAS 36, *Impairment of Assets.*

Note that this treatment is exactly consistent with the requirements for identifiable intangible assets with indefinite lives, as discussed earlier in relation to IAS 38.

It is, of course, possible for the calculated goodwill figure to be negative. IFRS 3 studiously avoids calling this negative goodwill, stating that if the acquirer's interest in the net fair value of the identifiable assets, liabilities and contingent liabilities recognized in accordance with para. 36, exceeds the cost of the business combination, the acquirer shall:

- reassess the identification and measurement of the acquiree's identifiable assets, liabilities and contingent liabilities and the measurement of the cost of the combination
- recognize immediately in profit or loss any excess remaining after that reassessment.

It follows that, in future, negative goodwill, under that or any other label, will not appear in IAS group balance sheets. This is a major change. Any negative goodwill brought forward under previous IASB standards is to be derecognized and transferred to retained earnings.

International developments

Many different methods have been used over the years. The previous IAS requirement was essentially our suggested method **1**, with compulsory impairment reviews added on in the case of a useful life over 20 years. The current IAS requirement is essentially our method **4**. US GAAP allowed a useful life of up to 40 years until recently. Method **3** was common for many years in the UK and may still be found in a number of European national systems. UK GAAP now allows, in effect, a choice between methods **1** and **4**. There is a presumption that useful life will not normally exceed 20 years (requiring method 1); impairment reviews at intervals are specified. A longer useful life or an unlimited life with no annual amortization both require annual impairment reviews. US GAAP has now moved to annual impairment reviews, with amortization prohibited. Harmonization is getting closer, but has not yet been reached.

Impairment of assets

The problem

Reference to impairment of assets has been made at a number of points in this and the previous chapters. In very simple terms, the principle of deferring charges to future periods under the matching principle means, of course, that such deferred charges appear in an intermediate balance sheet as assets.

Activity 13.4

If there is a reasonable expectation of future revenues associated with the past expenditure being greater than the deferred expenses, does any other circumstance, such as a low current market value for the asset, lead to a need for immediate write off down to this lower figure?

Activity feedback

Prudence and the informational needs of lenders with a short-term focus might both suggest an argument for such an immediate expense charge and reduction in the balance sheet carrying value of the asset (i.e. the deferred expense). However, matching and the informational needs of investors suggest the opposite. Long-term assets should be appraised in a long-term context, it can be argued. The IASB generally takes this second argument.

Very broadly speaking, purchase transactions are recorded in accounting terms first by including the purchased item as an asset at its cost price, then by expensing the item over one or a number of accounting periods according to its usage or consumption pattern. The going concern convention supports this treatment as it explicitly assumes that there will be future operational accounting periods in which present assets can be transferred to expenses.

Strictly, this means that there is no need, at an intermediate stage in this process, to compare the temporary balance sheet number with any form of value – using the word *value* in its proper sense of monetary benefit to be derived. This would not be in accordance with the prudence convention, however, and would arguably be dangerously misleading to creditors and lenders. Over the years accounting has dealt with the inherent tension and conflict here in a variety of ways, all more or less ad hoc, depending on the accounting issue involved (and often depending also on the country involved).

The IASB has quite properly attempted to provide a general Standard, IAS 36, *Impairment of Assets*, to provide consistency and coherence to this whole matter. The principle of the Standard is clear and simple. First, the carrying amount of an asset is determined in accordance with accounting principles and other relevant International

Standards. Second, the 'recoverable amount' of the asset is determined as of that date, being the *higher* of fair value less costs to sell and the asset's value in use (to the existing enterprise). If the recoverable amount is lower than the carrying value as recorded, then an impairment loss must be recognized immediately, that is, the carrying value is lowered to the recoverable amount. Otherwise, no impairment loss is required. It is important to emphasize that recoverable amount is a very different concept from fair value and, for non-current assets, will often be significantly higher than fair value. IAS 36 does not require assets within its scope to be recorded at the lower of cost and market or fair value.

The question of which assets IAS 36 does apply to is rather complicated and the following section on scope should be read carefully. Unfortunately, although the principle of IAS 36 is simply stated, the IASB, perhaps influenced by American tradition, found it necessary to specify considerable operational detail in relation to its application. We examine these details later, to the extent that we consider it necessary. However, we are writing a textbook, not a manual for practitioners, and IAS 36 is very much a technical 'how to do it' Standard. It would be unhelpful to attempt to cover all this technical specification here.

A revised version of IAS 36 is effective from 31 March 2004 (not 1 April 2004). The only major changes of principle relate to impairment tests for goodwill and are linked with contemporaneous changes introduced by IFRS 3, *Business Combinations* (see earlier).

However, the opportunity has been taken to amend and clarify (and make more complex) much of the detailed specification. A further more fundamental reconsideration of the whole impairment area is ongoing; any resulting changes are not likely to appear in the short term.

Scope and coverage

The essential objective of IAS 36 is to ensure that assets are not carried at a figure greater than their recoverable amount. The Standard itself says nothing about possible or normal methods of arriving at carrying value. The Standard applies whatever the underlying basis of valuation of the asset is.

The Standard begins by saying that it applied to all assets except . . . and then gives a significant number of exceptions (para. 1). These are generally items that are covered in detail by other International Accounting Standards. Thus IAS 36 does not apply to:

1 inventories (see IAS 2, *Inventories*, discussed in Chapter 15)
2 assets arising from construction contracts (see IAS 11, *Construction Contracts*, discussed in Chapter 15)
3 deferred tax assets (see IAS 12, *Income Taxes*, discussed in Chapter 19)
4 assets arising from employee benefits (see IAS 19, *Employee Benefits*, discussed in Chapter 20)
5 financial assets that are included in the scope of IAS 39, *Financial Instruments: Recognition and Measurement* (see Chapter 16)
6 investment property that is measured at fair value (see IAS 40, *Investment Property*, Chapter 12)
7 biological assets related to agricultural activity that are measured at fair value less estimated point-of-sale costs (see IAS 40, *Agriculture*, website appendix)

8 deferred acquisition costs, and intangible assets, arising from an insurer's contractual rights under insurance contracts within the scope of IFRS 4, *Insurance Contracts* (see Chapter 16)

9 non-current assets (or disposal groups) classified as held for sale in accordance with IFRS 5, *Non-current Assets Held for Sale and Discontinued Operations* (see Chapter 23).

In relation to point 5, it must be noted that financial assets excluded from IAS 39 are automatically excluded from the exclusion! Thus, investments in:

1 subsidiaries, as defined in IAS 27, *Consolidated Financial Statements and Accounting for Investments in Subsidiaries*

2 associates, as defined in IAS 28, *Accounting for Investments in Associates*

3 and joint ventures, as defined in IAS 31, *Financial Reporting of Interests in Joint Ventures*

are financial assets but are excluded from the scope of IAS 39. Therefore, IAS 36 applies to such investments. Note carefully that the Standard very deliberately describes itself as dealing with impairment of assets, not with impairment of non-current assets. However, it then excludes inventories and construction contracts (IAS 2 and IAS 11) and accounts receivable and cash (both covered by IAS 39). In many if not most businesses, this will mean that all current assets are excluded from consideration under IAS 36. However, the IAS definition of current assets (discussed in Chapter 9) is more generally expressed and IAS 36 could be applicable to certain current assets in special cases.

Terminology

IAS 36 gives a number of definitions of key terms. Many of these definitions are interrelated, one term being used in the definition of another (para. 6).

An *impairment loss* is the amount by which the carrying amount of an asset or a cash-generating unit exceeds its recoverable amount.

Carrying amount is the amount at which an asset is recognized after deducting any accumulated depreciation (amortization) and accumulated impairment losses thereon.

Depreciation (amortization) is the systematic allocation of the depreciable amount of an asset over its useful life.

Depreciable amount is the cost of an asset or other amount substituted for cost in the financial statements, less its residual value.

Useful life is:

- either the period of time over which an asset is expected to be used by the entity
- or the number of production or similar units expected to be obtained from the asset by the entity.

Fair value less costs to sell is the amount obtainable from the sale of an asset or cash-generating unit in an arm's length transaction between knowledgeable, willing parties, less the costs of disposal.

Costs of disposal are incremental costs directly attributable to the disposal of an asset or cash-generating unit, excluding finance costs and income tax expense.

Value in use is the present value of the future cash flows expected to be derived from an asset or cash-generating unit.

The *agreement date* for a business combination is the date that a substantive agreement between the combining parties is reached and, in the case of publicly listed entities, announced to the public. In the case of a hostile takeover, the earliest date that a substantive agreement between the combining parties is reached is the date that a sufficient number of the acquiree's owners have accepted the acquirer's offer for the acquirer to obtain control of the acquiree.

An *active market* is a market in which all the following conditions exist:

- the items traded within the market are homogeneous
- willing buyers and sellers can normally be found at any time
- prices are available to the public.

Most of these terms should be fairly easy to understand, but they can be difficult to calculate. Two further definitions are given, as follows:

A *cash-generating unit* is the smallest identifiable group of assets that generates cash inflows that are largely independent of the cash inflows from other assets or groups of assets.

Corporate assets are assets other than goodwill that contribute to the future cash flows of both the cash-generating unit under review and other cash-generating units.

When several assets are interrelated in their usage in a way which makes it impossible meaningfully to attribute cash inflows to each individual asset, they are to be considered together as a single cash-generating unit as just defined. In effect, therefore, a cash-generating unit is 'an asset' for the purposes of IAS 36. Corporate assets do not generate their own cash flows, but, as described earlier, are necessary for the generation of cash flows by other units. Special considerations, discussed later, apply to such assets.

Identifying an asset that may be impaired

It is important to be clear that IAS 36 does not require that the recoverable amount of all assets must be determined annually in order to test for impairment. Rather, it postulates a two-stage process. The first stage is to assess, at each balance sheet date, whether there is any indication that an asset may be impaired. If any such indication exists, the enterprise should estimate the recoverable amount of the asset.

These are two different formal requirements. The first relates to all assets (para. 9). This is that an entity should assess at each reporting date whether there is any indication that an asset may be impaired. If such an indication exists, the entity should estimate the recoverable amount of the asset. The second is more stringent, but relates only to certain intangible assets. This is that (para. 10), irrespective of whether there is any indication of impairment, an entity shall also:

- test an intangible asset with an indefinite useful life or an intangible asset not yet available for use for impairment annually by comparing its carrying amount with its recoverable amount; this impairment test may be performed at any time during an annual period, provided it is performed at the same time every year; different intangible assets may be tested for impairment at different times, however, if such an intangible asset was initially recognized during the current annual period, that intangible asset shall be tested for impairment before the end of the current annual period

■ test goodwill acquired in a business combination for impairment annually in accordance with paras 80–99, as described later.

The concept of materiality applies to the general requirement in para. 9, but not to the specific requirement of para. 10, which, in its defined circumstances, is absolute.

Activity 13.5

Suggest situations that may indicate that an asset has been impaired.

Activity feedback

IAS 36 suggests that, when assessing whether there is any indication that an asset may be impaired, an enterprise should consider, *as a minimum*, the following indications (para. 9):

External sources of information:

1 During the period, an asset's market value has declined significantly more than would be expected as a result of the passage of time or normal use.
2 Significant changes with an adverse effect on the entity have taken place during the period or will take place in the near future in the technological, market, economic or legal environment in which the entity operates or in the market to which an asset is dedicated.
3 Market interest rates or other market rates of return on investments have increased during the period and those increases are likely to affect the discount rate used in calculating an asset's value in use and decrease the asset's recoverable amount materially.
4 The carrying amount of the net assets of the reporting enterprise is more than its market capitalization.

Internal sources of information:

1 Evidence is available of obsolescence or physical damage of an asset.
2 Significant changes with an adverse effect on the entity have taken place during the period or are expected to take place in the near future in the extent to which, or manner in which, an asset is used or is expected to be used. These changes include the asset becoming idle, plans to discontinue or restructure the operation to which an asset belongs, plans to dispose of an asset before the previously expected date and reassessing the useful life of an asset as finite rather than indefinite.
3 Evidence is available from internal reporting that indicates that the economic performance of an asset is, or will be, worse than expected.

Only if such an indication of likely impairment exists do we need, in the general case, to move on to the second stage and actually measure the recoverable amount.

Several of these considerations require some comment. Items 1 and 2 (under external sources of information) are fairly obviously indicators of a possible fall in recoverable amount, relating directly to net selling price and value in use, respectively. In neither case, however, does a low or lower recoverable amount *necessarily* follow, as recoverable amount is the *higher* of fair value less costs to sell and value in use. The relevance of item 3 is that value in use, as defined earlier, is the *present value* of future cash flows. Discounting is thus central to the calculation or recoverable amount and an increase in discount rate may significantly reduce the value in use of an asset, as defined, if the new discount rate is regarded as relevant in the long term. Item 4, again, is a fairly obvious indicator that something is widely perceived as being wrong somewhere, although not, of course, that every, or any one particular, asset is impaired.

Measurement of recoverable amount

IAS 36 devotes no fewer than 39 paragraphs to the measurement of recoverable amount, not including another 42 paragraphs on cash-generating units, and sets out detailed computations. Nevertheless, a number of simplifications may be justified. If either fair value less costs to sell or value in use exceeds the asset's carrying amount, then the other figure need not be determined at all. If fair value less costs to sell is unobtainable even by reliable estimate, because of the absence of an active market, then the recoverable amount can be taken as equal to value in use. Conversely, the recoverable amount may be taken or given by fair value less costs to sell if the nature of the asset or the nature of its usage by enterprise is such that value in use is unlikely to differ materially from fair value less costs to sell, which will usually be the case with active and competitive factor markers (i.e. in developed economies).

Fair value less costs to sell

This will often be straightforward to determine, being fair value less any incremental costs that would be directly attributable to the disposal of the asset. Fair value may need to be estimated by reference to comparable transactions. Costs of disposal, other than those that have already been recognized as liabilities, are deducted in determining net selling price. Examples of such costs are legal costs, stamp duty and similar transaction taxes, costs of removing the asset and direct incremental costs to bring an asset into condition for its sale. However, termination benefits (as defined in IAS 19, *Employee Benefits* see Chapter 20) and costs associated with reducing or reorganizing a business after the disposal of an asset are not direct incremental costs to dispose of the asset (see IAS 37, *Provisions, Contingent Liabilities and Contingent Assets*, discussed in Chapter 18).

Value in use

Estimating the value in use in a realistic way is often likely to be rather more difficult. It involves the following steps (para. 31):

1 estimating the future cash inflows and outflows to be derived from continuing use of the asset and from its ultimate disposal
2 applying the appropriate discount rate to these future cash flows.

Estimates of future cash flows should include:

1 projections of cash inflows from the continuing use of the asset, net of projections of cash outflows that are necessarily incurred to generate the cash inflows (including cash outflows to prepare the asset for use) and that can be directly attributed, or allocated on a reasonable and consistent basis, to the asset

2 net cash flows, if any, to be received (or paid) for the disposal of the asset at the end of its useful life.

Future cash flows should be estimated for the asset in its current condition. It follows that estimates of future cash flows should not include estimated future cash inflows or outflows that are expected to arise from:

1 a future restructuring to which an entity is not yet committed
2 or future (uncommitted) capital expenditure that will improve or enhance the asset in excess of its originally assessed standard of performance.

The issue of when an enterprise is 'committed to a future restructuring' is discussed in IAS 37, *Provisions, Contingent Liabilities and Contingent Assets* (see Chapter 18). If it is so committed, then obviously the related cash inflows and outflows *are* to be included.

The estimate of net cash flows to be received (or paid) for the disposal of an asset at the end of its useful life is determined in a similar way to an asset's fair value less costs to sell, except that, in estimating those net cash flows:

1 an entity uses prices prevailing at the date of the estimate for similar assets that have reached the end of their useful life and that have operated under conditions similar to those in which the asset will be used
2 those prices are adjusted for the effect of both future price increases due to general inflation and specific future price increases (decreases). However, if estimates of future cash flows from the asset's continuing use and the discount rate exclude the effect of general inflation, this effect is also excluded from the estimate of net cash flows on disposal.

Discount rate

The key points can be very briefly stated. The discount rate (or rates) should be a pre-tax rate (or rates) that reflect(s) current market assessments of the time value of money and risks specific to the asset (para. 55). The discount rate(s) should not reflect risks for which future cash flow estimates have been adjusted, as this would involve double counting. The standard rightly makes no attempt to argue that this process is other than subjective. It does try to suggest a suitable thought process (Appendix A).

As a starting point, the entity may take into account the following rates:

1 the entity's weighted average cost of capital determined using techniques such as the capital asset pricing model
2 the entity's incremental borrowing rate
3 other market borrowing rates.

These rates are adjusted:

1 to reflect the way that the market would assess the specific risks associated with the projected cash flows
2 to exclude risks that are not relevant to the projected cash flows.

Consideration is given to such risks as country risk, currency risk, price risk and cash flow risk.

This makes it clear, for example, that the appropriate discount rate may be different for different types of asset or different circumstances, within the same entity. What is crucial, above all else except basic rationality and common sense, is that the chosen method should be applied consistently.

Recognition and measurement of impairment losses

After all the subjectivity, complexity, and detail of earlier sections of IAS 36 it is easy to lose sight of the importance of those paragraphs dealing with recognition and measurement of impairment losses. This is the point and purpose of the entire Standard. The Standard requires that if, and only if, the recoverable amount of an asset is less than its carrying amount, the carrying amount of the asset should be reduced to its recoverable amount. That reduction is an impairment loss (para. 59).

An impairment loss should be recognized immediately as an expense in the income statement, unless the asset is carried at revalued amount under another Standard (for example, under IAS 16, *Property, Plant and Equipment* (see Chapter 12)). Any impairment loss of a revalued asset should be treated as a revaluation decrease under the other Standard.

In the general case, if the estimated impairment loss is greater than the carrying value of the relevant asset, the asset is simply reduced to nil, with a corresponding expense. Only if so required by another Standard should a liability be recognized.

Common sense indicates, but the standard feels it necessary to state, that after the impairment loss has been recognized, the depreciation charge for the asset should be adjusted to allocate the revised carrying amount, net of any expected residual value, on a systematic basis over its remaining useful life.

This is all very well when 'an asset' means 'an asset'. But when 'an asset' means 'a cash-generating unit', as discussed earlier, the treatment is not so easy in practice – as the Standard's need for over 40 paragraphs on the topic would suggest. If it is not possible to estimate the recoverable amount of an individual asset, an enterprise should determine the recoverable amount of the cash-generating unit to which the asset belongs (the asset's cash-generating unit) (para. 66). Identification of an asset's cash-generating unit involves judgement. If the recoverable amount cannot be determined for an individual asset, an enterprise identifies the lowest aggregation of assets that generate largely independent cash inflows from continuing use.

In other words, an asset's cash-generating unit is the smallest group of assets that includes the asset and that generates cash inflows from continuing use that are largely independent of the cash inflows from other assets or groups of assets.

Perhaps inevitably, the standard resorts to a series of examples in order to try and indicate more precisely how the analysis of any particular situation should proceed. Common sense and economic substance are perhaps the key watchwords. Thus if an active market exists for the output produced by an asset or a group of assets, this asset or group of assets should be identified as a cash-generating unit, even if some or all of the output is used internally. If this is the case, management's best estimate of future market prices for the output should be used (para. 70):

1 in determining the value in use of this cash-generating unit, when estimating the future cash inflows that relate to the internal use of the output
2 in determining the value in use of other cash-generating units of the reporting entity, when estimating the future cash outflows that relate to the internal use of the output.

As an indicative illustration, the example given by IAS 36 in relation to this specification follows.

Illustration

A significant raw material used for plant Y's final production is an intermediate product bought from plant X of the same entity. X's products are sold to Y at a transfer price that passes all margins to X. 80 per cent of Y's final production is sold to customers outside the reporting entity. 60% of X's final production is sold to Y and the remaining 40% is sold to customers outside the reporting entity.

For each of the following cases, what are the cash-generating units for X and Y?

Case 1: X could sell the products it sells to Y in an active market. Internal transfer prices are higher than market prices.

Case 2: There is no active market for the products X sells to Y.

Case 1

X could sell its products on an active market and so generate cash inflows that would be largely independent of the cash inflows from Y. Therefore, it is likely that X is a separate cash-generating unit, although part of its production is used by Y.

It is likely that Y is also a separate cash-generating unit. Y sells 80% of its products to customers outside the reporting entity. Therefore, its cash inflows can be considered to be largely independent.

Internal transfer prices do not reflect market prices for X's output. Therefore, in determining value in use of both X and Y, the entity adjusts financial budgets/forecasts to reflect management's best estimate of future arm's length market prices for those of X's products that are used internally (see para. 70 of IAS 36).

Case 2

It is likely that the recoverable amount of each plant cannot be assessed independently from the recoverable amount of the other plant because:

1 The majority of X's production is used internally and could not be sold in an active market. So, cash inflows of X depend on demand for Y's products. Therefore, X cannot be considered to generate cash inflows that are largely independent from those of Y.

2 The two plants are managed together.

As a consequence, it is likely that X and Y together is the smallest group of assets that generates cash inflows from continuing use that are largely independent.

Once the cash-generating unit has been defined, the next step is to determine and compare the recoverable amount and carrying amount of that unit. It should go without saying, but the standard reminds us, that the carrying amount of a cash-generating unit should be determined consistently with the way the recoverable amount of the cash-generating unit is determined.

This means, for example, that the carrying amount of a cash-generating unit includes the carrying amount of only those assets that can be attributed directly or allocated on a reasonable and consistent basis to the cash-generating unit and that will generate the future cash inflows estimated in determining the cash-generating unit's value in use and does not include the carrying amount of any recognized liability, unless the recoverable amount of the cash-generating unit cannot be determined without consideration of this liability. However, the Standard notes that in practice the recoverable amount of a cash-generating unit may be considered either including or excluding assets or liabilities that are not part of the cash-generating unit – for example a net selling price of a business segment might be determined on the assumption that either the vendor or the purchaser accepts certain obligations. Consistency requires that if the obligation is included in the evaluation of recoverable amount, it is the *net* carrying value with which this recoverable amount must be compared in determining whether an impairment loss exists.

There are two problems that need special consideration, namely goodwill and corporate assets (as already defined). In essence these two problems are related.

Goodwill, by definition, does not generate cash flows independently from other assets or groups of assets and, therefore, the recoverable amount of goodwill as an individual asset cannot be determined. As a consequence, if there is an indication that goodwill may be impaired, the recoverable amount is determined for the cash-generating unit to which the goodwill belongs. This amount is then compared to the carrying amount of this cash-generating unit and any impairment loss is recognized, attributed first to the goodwill as discussed later.

It is particularly in relation to the treatment of possible impairment of goodwill that the new version of IAS 36 has been made much more detailed (and therefore, at least apparently, more complex). The previous version of IAS 36 required goodwill acquired in a business combination to be tested for impairment as part of impairment testing of the cash-generating unit(s) to which it related. It employed a 'bottom-up/top-down' approach under which the goodwill was, in effect, tested for impairment by allocating its carrying amount to each cash-generating unit or smallest group of cash-generating units to which a portion of that carrying amount could be allocated on a reasonable and consistent basis. The Standard now similarly requires goodwill acquired in a business combination to be tested for impairment as part of impairment testing the cash-generating unit(s) to which it relates. However, IAS 36 now clarifies that:

1 the goodwill should, from the acquisition date, be allocated to each of the acquirer's cash-generating units, or groups of cash-generating units, that are expected to benefit from the synergies of the business combination, irrespective of whether other assets or liabilities of the acquiree are assigned to those units or groups of units
2 each unit or group of units to which the goodwill is allocated should:
   (i) represent the lowest level within the entity at which the goodwill is monitored for internal management purposes
   (ii) not be larger than a segment based on either the entity's primary or the entity's secondary reporting format determined in accordance with IAS 14, *Segment Reporting*
3 if the initial allocation of goodwill acquired in a business combination cannot be completed before the end of the annual period in which the business combination

occurs, that initial allocation should be completed before the end of the annual period beginning after the acquisition date

4 when an entity disposes of an operation within a cash-generating unit (group of units) to which goodwill has been allocated, the goodwill associated with that operation should be:

   (i) included in the carrying amount of the operation when determining the gain or loss on disposal

   (ii) measured on the basis of the relative values of the operation disposed of and the portion of the cash-generating unit (group of units) retained, unless the entity can demonstrate that some other method better reflects the goodwill associated with the operation disposed of

5 when an entity reorganizes its reporting structure in a manner that changes the composition of cash-generating units (groups of units) to which goodwill has been allocated, the goodwill should be reallocated to the units (groups of units) affected. This reallocation should be performed using a relative value approach similar to that used when an entity disposes of an operation within a cash-generating unit (group of units), unless the entity can demonstrate that some other method better reflects the goodwill associated with the reorganized units (groups of units).

By way of example, to illustrate point 4, suppose that an entity sells for 100 an operation that was part of a cash-generating unit to which goodwill has been allocated. The goodwill allocated to the unit cannot be identified or associated with an asset group at a level lower than that unit, except arbitrarily. The recoverable amount of the portion of the cash-generating unit retained is €300. Because the goodwill allocated to the cash-generating unit cannot be non-arbitrarily identified or associated with an asset group at a level lower than that unit, the goodwill associated with the operation disposed of is measured on the basis of the relative values of the operation disposed of and the portion of the unit retained. Therefore 25% of the goodwill allocated to the cash-generating unit is included in the carrying amount of the operation that is sold and 75% is left in the retained portion.

The Standard permits (not requires) the annual impairment test for a cash-generating unit (group of units) to which the goodwill has been allocated to be performed at any time during an annual reporting period, provided that the test is performed at the same time every year and different cash-generating units (groups of units) to be tested for impairment at different times. However, if some of the goodwill allocated to a cash-generating unit (group of units) was acquired in a business combination during the current annual period, the Standard requires that unit (group of units) to be tested for impairment before the end of the current period.

The Standard also permits the most recent detailed calculation made in a preceding period of the recoverable amount of a cash-generating unit (group of units) to which goodwill has been allocated to be used in the impairment test for that unit (group of units) in the current period, provided specified criteria are met, as follows:

- the assets and liabilities making up the unit have not changed significantly since the most recent recoverable amount calculation
- the most recent recoverable amount calculation resulted in an amount that exceeded the carrying amount of the unit by a substantial margin

- based on an analysis of events that have occurred and circumstances that have changed since the most recent recoverable amount calculation, the likelihood that a current recoverable amount determination would be less than the current carrying amount of the unit is remote.

Similarly, corporate assets, also by definition, do not generate independent cash flows and, again, recoverable amount is determined by reference to the cash-generating unit to which the corporate asset belongs. In testing a cash-generating unit for impairment, an entity shall identify all the corporate assets that relate to the cash-generating unit under review. If a portion of the carrying amount of a corporate asset can be allocated on a reasonable and consistent basis to that unit, the entity shall compare the carrying amount of the unit, including the portion of the carrying amount of the corporate asset allocated to the unit, with its recoverable amount. Any impairment loss shall be recognized in accordance with para. 104, discussed later. If a portion cannot be allocated on a reasonable and consistent basis to that unit, the entity shall:

1 compare the carrying amount of the unit, excluding the corporate asset, with its recoverable amount and recognize any impairment loss in accordance with para. 104
2 identify the smallest group of cash-generating units that includes the cash-generating unit under review and to which a portion of the carrying amount of the corporate asset can be allocated in a reasonable and consistent basis
3 compare the carrying amount of that group of cash-generating units, including the portion of the carrying amount of the corporate asset allocated to that group of units, with the recoverable amount of the group of units. Any impairment loss shall be recognized in accordance with para. 104.

An amazingly lengthy illustrative example (No. 8) is given in an accompaniment to the Standard.

Once the impairment loss for a cash-generating unit has been determined, it has to be deducted from the carrying amounts of specific assets that are part of that unit, in some systematic manner. IAS 36 specifies its requirements with precision (paras 104 and 105).

An impairment loss should be recognized for a cash-generating unit if, and only if, its recoverable amount is less than its carrying amount. The impairment loss should be allocated to reduce the carrying amount of the assets of the unit in the following order:

1 first, to goodwill allocated to the cash-generating unit (if any)
2 then, to the other assets of the unit on a pro rata basis based on the carrying amount of each asset in the unit.

In allocating an impairment loss the carrying amount of an asset should not be reduced below the *highest* of:

1 its fair value less costs to sell (if determinable)
2 its value in use (if determinable)
3 zero.

The amount of the impairment loss that would otherwise have been allocated to the asset should be allocated to the other assets of the unit on a pro rata basis. A liability should be recognized for any remaining amount of an impairment loss for a cash-generating unit, if, and only if, that is required by other International Accounting Standards.

The effect of this is, first, to eliminate goodwill, but then to ensure that the carrying amount of any individual asset is not reduced so far as to produce a figure not economically relevant to that asset.

Reversal of an impairment loss

The whole point, in a sense, of impairment losses is that they represent unusual or 'extra' reductions in asset numbers (carrying values) as used in financial statements. If regular depreciation is a downward slope, then an impairment loss is a step downward. The basic cause of this downward step is something unusual and/or extraneous to the asset and its regular accounting treatment. It follows that this cause, this unusual or extraneous factor, may be removed over time. In such a situation, as explained and defined in IAS 36, the original impairment loss *must* be reversed; *except* for goodwill.

As with impairment losses, we again have a two-stage process. An enterprise first checks to see whether there is any *indication* that an impairment loss recognized in earlier years may have decreased significantly. IAS 36 spells out a series of likely indicators (para. 111) that mirror those discussed earlier under 'identifying an asset that may be impaired'.

The formal requirement for reversing impairment losses for an asset other than goodwill (para. 114) is that an impairment loss recognized for an asset in prior years must be reversed if, and only if, there has been a change in the estimates used to determine the asset's recoverable amount since the last impairment loss was recognized. If this is the case, the carrying amount of the asset should be increased to its recoverable amount. That increase is a reversal of an impairment loss. It is important to note that an asset's value in use may become greater than the asset's carrying amount simply because the present value of future cash inflows increases as they become closer. However, the service potential of the asset has not increased. Therefore, such an impairment loss is not reversed, even if the recoverable amount of the asset becomes higher than its carrying amount.

The reversal of an impairment loss should in no circumstances increase the carrying value of an asset above what it would have been at this balance sheet date if no impairment loss had been recognized in prior years. This means, in particular, that the carrying value of assets subject to depreciation cannot be increased above the figure which the pre-impairment depreciation policy applied to the pre-impairment recoverable amount would have given at this balance sheet date, that is, the amount of the reversal will be less than the amount of the original impairment. The new carrying value forms the basis for a systematic depreciation policy to allocate the carrying value, less estimated residual value if any, over the remaining useful life.

A reversal of an impairment loss for an asset as above should be recognized as income immediately in the income statement, unless the asset is carried at revalued amount under another International Accounting Standard (for example, under the allowed alternative treatment in IAS 16, *Property, Plant and Equipment* (see Chapter 12). Any reversal of an impairment loss on a revalued asset should be treated as a revaluation increase under that other Standard.

A reversal of an impairment loss for a cash-generating unit should be allocated to increase the carrying amount of the assets of the unit on a pro rata basis based on the carrying amount of each asset in the unit and then to goodwill allocated to the cash-generating unit.

In allocating a reversal of an impairment loss for a cash-generating unit, the carrying amount of an asset should not be increased above the *lower* of:

1 the recoverable amount (if determinable)
2 the carrying amount that would have been determined (net of amortization or depreciation) had no impairment loss been recognized for the asset in prior years.

The amount of the reversal of the impairment loss that would otherwise have been allocated to the asset should be allocated to the other assets of the unit, except for goodwill, on a pro rata basis.

The treatment of a reversal of an impairment loss for goodwill has changed significantly in the new version of IAS 36 (i.e. with effect from 31 March 2004) as compared with the earlier version. The previous version of IAS 36 required an impairment loss recognized for goodwill in a previous period to be reversed when the impairment loss was caused by a specific external event of an exceptional nature that was not expected to recur and subsequent external events have occurred that reverse the effect of that event. The Standard now completely prohibits the recognition of reversals of impairment losses for goodwill.

The rationale for prohibiting the reversal of impairment losses for goodwill is presented by the IASB as follows. The key point is that IAS 38, *Intangible Assets* (see above) prohibits the recognition of internally generated goodwill. This prohibition is theoretically debatable, but is undoubtedly widely supported, and is consistent with national laws in many countries including the whole of the European Union, following the Fourth Directive.

Given this prohibition, there is still no *theoretical* problem in arguing, supported by analogy with other assets, that *previously purchased* goodwill that has been subsequently impaired because of a circumstance now reversed should have the impairment loss reversed. However, there is a *practical* problem in distinguishing, numerically as well as conceptually, between a reversal of a previous impairment to previously purchased goodwill, on the one hand, and the appearance of new internally generated goodwill, which cannot be recognized, on the other. It is because of this practical impossibility, and the resulting 'danger' of effectively capitalizing internally generated goodwill that the change to an outright prohibition of the recognition of a reversal of an impairment loss for goodwill has been introduced.

The IASB notes that internally generated goodwill may in fact be involved at an earlier stage in the whole impairment process, in that purchased goodwill may not be impaired in the first place because its recoverable amount is kept up through the creation of new goodwill to replace the old, but also notes that, again on purely practical grounds, such a position cannot be numerically demonstrated and therefore cannot be prevented.

Disclosure

The disclosure requirements of IAS 36, like much else in the Standard, are extensive. They are also quite straightforward, requiring detailed numerical, explanatory and background information.

Summary

This chapter has completed the coverage, began in Chapter 12, of the accounting treatment of fixed (non-current) assets. We looked at the problems of accounting for intangible assets and the requirements of IAS 38. We also considered accounting for purchased goodwill and the requirements of IFRS 3 relating to goodwill. Finally, we looked in some detail at the issue of impairment of assets in general and of fixed assets in particular and at the contents of IAS 36.

EXERCISES	(✔ indicates answers are available on page 726)

✔ **1** Is goodwill an asset?

   2 Identifiable intangible assets should be treated, for all accounting purposes, identically with tangible assets. Discuss.

   3 Outline five different ways of treating goodwill in financial statements, discussing arguments for and against each one.

   4 If depreciation is done properly, impairment adjustments will not arise. Discuss.

   5 What is 'recoverable amount' as the phrase is used in IAS 36? How does it relate to the alternative valuation bases discussed at length in Part One of this book?

✔ **6** A cash-generating unit was reviewed for impairment at 31 May 20X3 as required by IAS 36 – *Impairment of assets*. The impairment review revealed that the cash-generating unit has a value in use of $25 million and a net realisable value of $23 million.

   The carrying values of the net assets of the cash-generating unit immediately prior to the impairment review were as follows:

	$000
Goodwill	5 000
Property, plant and equipment	18 000
Net current assets	4 000
	27 000

The review indicated that an item of plant (included in the above figure of $18 million) with a carrying value of $1 million had been severely damaged and was virtually worthless.

   There was no other evidence of obvious impairment to specific assets.

   What is carrying value of the goodwill relating to the unit immediately after the results of the impairment review have been reflected in accordance with IAS 36?

A	$1 million
B	$2 million
C	$3 million
D	$4 million

(CIMA Nov 03)

7 On 31 December 20X1, U purchased 100% of the equity share capital of V and V became a subsidiary of U on that date. U paid $110 million for the shares, and the fair value of the net assets of V at 31 December 20X1 was $100 million. Goodwill on consolidation is written off over 10 years, starting in 20X2. At 31 December 20X2, the balance sheet of V showed the following balances:

	$million
Property, plant and equipment:	
Land and buildings	50
Plant and machinery	30
Net current assets	15
	95

On 31 December 20X2, the directors of U carried out an impairment review in which V was treated as a single cash-generating until. The recoverable amount of the cash-generating unit at 31 December 20X2 was computed as $96 million. No assets within the cash-generating unit had suffered obvious impairment.

What is the reduction in the consolidated reserves of U as a result of the impairment review of V (not including the normal annual write-off of goodwill)?

A $1 million
B $5 million
C $8 million
D $9 million

(CIMA May 03)

8 (a) IAS 36 *Impairment of Assets* was published in June 1998. Its primary objective is to ensure that an asset is not carried on the balance sheet at a value that is greater than its recoverable amount. The Standard does not apply to inventories (including construction contracts). It replaces guidance given in several other International Financial Reporting Standards.

Required:
(i) Describe the circumstances where an impairment loss is deemed to have occurred and explain when companies should perform an impairment review of tangible and intangible assets;
(ii) Describe the matters to be considered in assessing whether an asset may be impaired.

(b) Avendus is preparing its financial statements to 30 September 20X3. It has identified the following issues:
(i) Avendus owns and operates an item of plate that had a carrying value of $400 000 and an estimated remaining life of 5 years. It has just been damaged due to incorrect operation by an employee. It is not economic to repair the plant but it still operates in a limited capacity although it is now no longer expected to last for 5 years. As the plant is damaged it could only be sold for $50 000. The cost of replacing the plant is $1 million. The plant does not generate cash flows independently and is part of a group of assets that have a carrying value of $5 million and an estimated recoverable amount of $7 million.

Required:
Explain how the above item of plant should be treated in the financial statements of Avendus for the year to 30 September 20X3. Your answer should consider the situations where the plant continues to be used and where it would be replaced.

(ii) Avendus owns an investment property which has a remaining useful economic life of five years. The property has a carrying value of $200 000 on 30 September 20X3. It is currently let to Marchant at an annual rental of $50 000 per annum. A surveyor has estimated that Avendus could expect net proceeds of $165 000 from sale of the property. The lease and the rental are due for renegotiation on 1 October 20X3. There is currently a surplus of rental properties and this has affected rental incomes and selling prices considerably. Aware of this, Marchant has offered to rent the property for a further five years, but for an annual rental, payable in advance, of only $40 000. The rental would be payable in full on 1 October each year. The current cost of capital of Avendus is 10% per annum, but current market assessments of a widely expected increase in interest rates means this will soon rise to 12% per annum. Avendus uses the cost method in IAS 40 *Investment Property*. The following information can be taken as correct:

	10%	12%
Interest rate	10%	12%
Present value of 4 year annuity	3.2	3.0
Present value of 5 year annuity	3.8	3.6

Required:
Explain how the above investment property should be treated in the financial statements of Avendus for the year to 30 September 20X3.
Your answer should be supported with numerical calculations.

(iii) Avendus recently acquired a company called Fishright, a small fishing and fish processing company for $2 million. Avendus allocated the purchase consideration as follows:

	$000
Goodwill	240
Fishing quotas	400
Fishing boats (2 of equal value)	1 000
Other fishing equipment	100
Fish processing plant	200
Net current assets	60
	2 000

Shortly after the acquisition, one of the fishing boats sank in a storm and this has halved the fishing capacity. Due to this reduction in capacity, the value in use of the fishing business as a going concern is estimated at only $1.2 million. The fishing quotas now represent a greater volume than one boat can fish and it is not possible to replace the lost boat as it was rather old and no equivalent boats are available. However, the fishing quotas are much in demand and could be sold for $600 000. Avendus has been offered $250 000 for the fish processing plant. The net current assets consist of accounts receivable and payable.

Required:
Calculated the amounts that would appear in the consolidated financial statements of Avendus in respect of Fishright's assets after accounting for the impairment loss.

(ACCA Dec 03)

Leases

After studying this chapter you should be able to:
- ☐ explain the issues underlying the accounting treatment of leases
- ☐ discuss alternative accounting treatments for leases of various types
- ☐ describe, apply and appraise the requirements of IAS 17 in relation to leased assets for lessor and lessee
- ☐ understand, and contribute to, ongoing debates concerning the treatment of leases in financial statements.

Introduction

A lease is an agreement that conveys to one party (the lessee) the right to use property, but does not convey legal ownership of that property. It follows that if an asset is defined as something which is legally owned (i.e. that has been acquired in an exchange transaction), then leases will not give rise to an asset in the financial statements of the lessee. It also follows that if nothing has been 'acquired', then nothing is unpaid for, that is, the lease agreement will also not give rise to a liability in the financial statements of the lessee.

If, however, the lease agreement allows the lessee to use the property for all or most of its useful life, requires the lessee to pay total amounts close to and possibly greater than the normal buying price of the item and requires or assumes that the lessee will look after the item as if the item belonged to it (e.g. insurance, repairs and maintenance), then it is clear that in substance the lessee would be in the same position, both economically and in terms of production and operating capacity, *as if* the lessee actually owned the asset. Furthermore, a contractual requirement to make future payments greater than the net cost of a straightforward purchase of the item means that the lessee is in the same position *as if* it had taken out a loan under agreed regular repayment terms and at an agreed rate of interest. Thus, in such circumstances, the economic substance of the situation is that the lessee has an asset and a liability, although the legal form of the agreement makes it quite clear that the legal ownership of the item remains with the other party (the lessor).

Activity 14.1

A company obtains the use of two identical assets costing €100 000 by obtaining one asset on a credit sale agreement and the other on a lease. Assuming fixed assets are only recorded on a company's balance sheet when it has legal ownership, show the adjustments that would be necessary to the company's accounts and identify the problems, if any, with this method of accounting.

Activity feedback

	€
Fixed assets	100 000
Creditors	100 000

Under this method of accounting only one asset would be shown under fixed assets and only the liability to pay for one asset would be shown. The fact that the company has the use of another fixed asset and that they have the liability outstanding for lease payments is not shown and this could be considered misleading to shareholders and to other potential lenders.

If the two assets are obtained in these different ways by two different companies then the difference will be even more obvious. If the assets are being used equally profitably, then one company will appear to be using significantly fewer resources and significantly less finance than the other one, to achieve comparable operating activities. This apparent economic (and managerial) efficiency of the company which leases the asset is not logically justified and, in addition, unavoidable obligations are not being recorded as liabilities.

The general principle of substance over form discussed in Chapter 8 requires that, in such circumstances, the lessee *does* record an asset and a liability in its balance sheet and also that the lessor records a sale and a debtor in its financial statements.

In broad terms, the whole issue of accounting for leases can be summarized very simply. If a lease agreement essentially gives the parties rights and obligations similar to those arising from a legal purchase, then the accounting proceeds as if it *were* a legal purchase. This gives rise to a fixed asset and an obligation. If, by way of contrast, a lease agreement is, in the context of the particular characteristics of the object in question, essentially a short-term rental, then the accounting treats it as such, giving rise in the books of the lessee to a simple expense, normally allocated on a time basis.

Unfortunately, this simple division masks a considerable amount of practical difficulty. There are problems involved in creating a clear demarcation line between the two situations and a number of particular issues and problems have arisen over the years which IASB and various national Standards have tried to tackle.

As an introduction to the accounting principles involved, consider the following activity.

Activity 14.2

A company signs a lease agreement under which it will pay €2000 at the end of each of years 1–6 inclusive. The purchase cost of the asset concerned is €10 000 and the asset is expected to be worthless after six years. Discuss what the accounting entries in year 1 should be.

Activity feedback

In substance, this transaction is clearly a purchase on deferred credit terms. There should be an immediate recording of an asset of €10 000 on day 1, with an equal liability. At the end of year 1, a payment of €2000 is recorded, i.e. a credit. The double-entry for this payment will need to be split two ways. There is a total interest cost of €2000 over the 6-year period ($(2000 \times 6) - 10\,000$) and some of the €2000 payment at the end of year 1 will be the payment of the interest relating to year 1, say X^i. This will be an expense of year 1 and the remainder of this payment, i.e. $(2000 - X^i)$ will be a partial settlement of the liability. There will also be a depreciation charge made at the end of year 1, of €1667 if the straight line basis is used. This gives entries as follows:

Leasehold asset

1/1/1 cost	10 000	1 667 depreciation	31/12/1

Lease liability

		10 000	1/1/1
		$(2000 - X^i)$	31/12/1

Profit and loss

31/12/1 interest	X^i	
31/12/1 depreciation	1 667	

In year 2 the payment, interest and depreciation entries will be repeated, but the interest expense of X^{ii} should be less than X^i, because the liability during year 2 was lower than that during year 1. This follows the basic matching principle by allocating the total interest charge of €2000 over the six years pro rata to the benefit, thus the annual interest charge reduces as the amount borrowed reduces.

We first of all explore the considerable number of definitions given by IAS 17, the key standard on this issue, and consider the whole issue of the classification of leases into two distinct types, i.e. those that are, in substance, creating fixed assets and long-term debt and those that are not. We then look separately at accounting requirements for lessees, and lessors. Finally, we look at an actual case study and consider possible future developments. IAS 17 was originally issued in 1982, as *Accounting for Leases*, but was replaced by a new standard, *Leases*, issued in 1997 but standard from 1 January 1999. A further revision appeared in March 2004, effective for annual periods beginning on or after 1 January 2005, with earlier application encouraged. The main (but limited) objective of this revision was to clarify the classification of a lease of land and buildings and to eliminate accounting alternatives for initial direct costs in the financial statements of lessors.

Definitions of IAS 17

- A *lease* is an agreement whereby the lessor conveys to the lessee in return for a payment or series of payments the right to use an asset for an agreed period of time.

- A *finance lease* is a lease that transfers substantially all the risks and rewards incidental to ownership of an asset. Title may or may not eventually be transferred.
- An *operating lease* is a lease other than a finance lease.

The risks of ownership relating to a finance lease are those of breakdown, damage, wear and tear, theft, obsolescence and so on. The rewards of ownership are extracted by using the asset for substantially all its productive usefulness, that is, its economic life, and by receiving its residual value at the time of its disposal.

- *Economic life* is either:
  - the period over which an asset is expected to be economically usable by one or more users
  - or the number of production or similar units expected to be obtained from the asset by one or more users.
- *Useful life* is the estimated remaining period, from the commencement of the lease term, without limitation by the lease term, over which the economic benefits embodied in the asset are expected to be consumed by the entity.

Note that the useful life relates to the expected situation for the lessee. The economic life relates to the asset, whether or not the current lessee is the only presumed user. Thus, although the useful life can exceed the lease term, the useful life cannot exceed the economic life.

- The *lease term* is the non-cancellable period for which the lessee has contracted to lease the asset together with any further terms for which the lessee has the option to continue to lease the asset, with or without further payment, when, at the inception of the lease, it is reasonably certain that the lessee will exercise the option.
- A *non-cancellable lease* is a lease that is cancellable only in one of the following four circumstances:
  - on the occurrence of some remote contingency
  - with the permission of the lessor
  - if the lessee enters into a new lease for the same or an equivalent asset with the same lessor
  - on payment by the lessee of an additional amount such that, at inception, continuation of the lease is reasonably certain.
- The *inception of the lease* is the earlier of the date of the lease agreement and the date of commitment by the parties to the principal provisions of the lease. As at this date:
  - a lease is classified as either an operating or a finance lease
  - and, in the case of a finance lease, the amounts to be recognized at the commencement of the lease term are determined.
- The *commencement of the lease term* is the date from which the lessee is entitled to exercise its right to use the leased asset. It is the date of initial recognition of the lease (i.e. the recognition of the assets, liabilities, income or expenses resulting from the lease, as appropriate).

One of the major criteria for deciding whether or not a finance lease exists is the total amount or more accurately the total minimum amount payable under the lease contract. This leads to a set of related terms, as follows:

- *Minimum lease payments* are the payments over the lease term that the lessee is, or can be, required to make excluding contingent rent, costs for services and taxes

to be paid by and reimbursed to the lessor, together with:
- in the case of the lessee, any amounts guaranteed by the lessee or by a party related to the lessee
- or in the case of the lessor, any residual value guaranteed to the lessor by either:
  1 the lessee
  2 a party related to the lessee
  3 or a third party unrelated to the lessor that is financially capable of discharging the obligations under the gurantee.

However, if the lessee has an option to purchase the asset at a price that is expected to be sufficiently lower than the fair value at the date when the option becomes exercisable so that, at the inception of the lease, it is reasonably certain to be exercised, that is, a 'bargain purchase option' exists, then the minimum lease payments comprise the minimum payments payable over the lease term and the payment required to exercise this purchase option.

- *Fair value* is the amount for which an asset could be exchanged or a liability settled, between knowledgeable, willing parties in an arm's length transaction.
- From the viewpoint of the lessee, the *guaranteed residual value* is that part of the residual value which is guaranteed by the lessee or by a party related to the lessee (the amount of the guarantee being the maximum amount that could, in any event, become payable).
- From the viewpoint of the lessor, the *guaranteed residual value* is that part of the residual value which is guaranteed by the lessee or by a third party unrelated to the lessor who is financially capable of discharging the obligations under the guarante.
- *Unguaranteed residual value* is that portion of the residual value of the leased asset, the realization of which by the lessor is not assured or is guaranteed solely by a party related to the lessor.
- The lessor's *gross investment in the lease* is the aggregate of the minimum lease payments receivable by the lessor under a finance lease and any unguaranteed residual value accruing to the lessor.
- *Net investment in the lease* is the gross investment in the lease discounted at the interest rate implicit in the lease.
- *Unearned finance income* is the difference between:
  - the gross investment in the lease
  - and the net investment in the lease.

Some of the greatest technical difficulties are caused by the need, at least theoretically, to calculate backwards the interest rates implicitly included in arriving at the total payments under the lease.

- The *interest rate implicit in the lease* is the discount rate that, at the inception of the lease, causes the aggregate present value of (a) the minimum lease payments and (b) the unguaranteed residual value to be equal to the sum of fair value of the leased asset and any initial direct costs of the lessor.
- The *lessee's incremental borrowing rate of interest* is the rate of interest the lessee would have to pay on a similar lease or, if that is not determinable, the rate that, at the inception of the lease, the lessee would incur to borrow over a similar term, and with a similar security, the funds necessary to purchase the asset.

- *Contingent rent* is that portion of the lease payments that is not fixed in amount but is based on the future amount of a factor that changes other than with the passage of time (e.g. percentage of sales, amount of usage, future price indices, future market rates of interest).

Activity 14.3

A lessee leases an asset on a non-cancellable lease contract with a primary term of five years from 1 January 20X1. The rental is €650 per quarter payable in advance. The lessee has the right to continue to lease the asset after the end of the primary period for as long as they wish at a nominal rent. In addition, the lessee is required to pay all maintenance and insurance costs, as they arise. The leased asset could have been purchased for cash at the start of the lease for €10 000 and has a useful life of eight years.

Calculate the interest rate implicit in the lease.

Activity feedback

From the definition of 'interest rate implicit in the lease' we can state that:

1 €10 000 (fair value) = the present value at implicit interest rate of 20 quarterly rentals payable in advance of €650
2 the present value of the first rental payable is €650 as it is paid now
3 thus €9350 = the present value at implicit interest rate of 19 rentals of €650
4 therefore 9350/650 = 14.385 = present value at implicit interest rate of 19 rentals of €1
5 using discount tables we can determine the interest rate as 2.95%.

In principle, IAS 17 and the definitions just given apply to all leases when IAS GAAP is to be followed. However, a number of exceptions are given. IAS 17 does not apply to:

- lease agreements to explore for or use minerals, oils, natural gas and similar non-regenerative resources
- or licensing agreements for items such as motion pictures, video recordings, plays, manuscripts, patents and copyrights.
  Additionally, IAS 17 should not be applied to the measurement by:
- lessees of investment property held under finance leases (see IAS 40, *Investment Property*, Chapter 12)
- lessors of investment property leased out under operating leases (see IAS 40)
- lessees of biological assets held under finance leases (see IAS 41, *Agriculture*, Appendix)
- lessors of biological assets leased out under operating leases (see IAS 41).

Lease classification

As already indicated, the form of words which determines the classification of a lease as either a finance lease or an operating lease is very simple. A lease is classified as a finance lease if it transfers substantially all the risks and rewards incidental to ownership. A lease is classified as an operating lease if it does not transfer substantially all the risks and rewards incidental to ownership. Because the transaction between a lessor and a lessee is based on a lease agreement common to both parties, it is appropriate to use consistent definitions. The application of these definitions to the differing circumstances of the two parties, however, may sometimes result in the same lease being classified differently by lessor and lessee.

The Standard makes no attempt to define 'substantially all'. Some national GAAPs take a much more numerical approach to this question, for example requiring the present value of the minimum lease payments to be 90% or more of the fair value of the asset at the inception of the lease (e.g. USA, Germany). Others, such as the UK, suggest that 90% gives a 'presumption' of a finance lease, but make it clear that the determining factor is 'substantially all', not 90%.

What IAS 17 does do is to give a number of examples of situations that 'would normally' (1 to 5) or that 'could', (6 to 8) point to a lease being properly classified as a finance lease. These are as follows (paras 10 and 11):

1 The lease transfers ownership of the asset to the lessee by the end of the lease term.
2 The lessee has the option to purchase the asset at a price that is expected to be sufficiently lower than the fair value at the date the option becomes exercisable such that, at the inception of the lease, it is reasonably certain that the option will be exercised (i.e. a bargain purchase option exists).
3 The lease term is for the major part of the economic life of the asset even if title is not transferred.
4 At the inception of the lease the present value of the minimum lease payments amounts to at least substantially all of the fair value of the leased asset.
5 The leased assets are of a specialized nature such that only the lessee can use them without major modifications being made.
6 If the lessee cancels the lease, the lessor's losses associated with the cancellation are borne by the lessee.
7 Gains or losses from the fluctuation in the fair value of the residual accrue to the lessee (for example in the form of a rent rebate equalling most of the residual sales proceeds at the end of the lease).
8 The lessee has the ability to continue the lease for a secondary period at a rent which is substantially lower than market rent (i.e. a bargain rental option).

Activity 14.4

Explain briefly in your own words why each of these situations points towards a finance lease.

Activity feedback

Our suggested wording is as follows. Because, under situations 1 and 2 the lessee ends up with legal ownership, the validity of a finance lease classification is obvious. Situation 3 assumes, reasonably enough, that a major part of the economic life (measured in years) must imply transfer of substantially all the risks and rewards of ownership (measured in money). Situation 4 argues that payment of substantially all the purchase price, after discounting to present value, must again imply that the substance of the transaction is a purchase on credit terms and situation 5 indicates by definition that only the lessee can derive 'rewards' from possession of the particular items. The remaining three situations, 6, 7, and 8, while perhaps less definitive, all clearly point to the likelihood of the lessee being in the in-substance ownership position of deriving the benefits and 'paying the price'.

The US prescriptive approach is continued in other respects. For example, the US version of situation 3 specifies that for a finance lease the lease term is 75% or more of the economic life of the asset. The UK leasing Standard contains no similar consideration at all, relying on the 'substantially all the risks and rewards' criterion.

Note that the lease classification is to be made at the inception of the lease.

Activity 14.5

Costa uses three identical pieces of machinery in its factory. These were all acquired for use on the same date by the following means:

1 Machine 1 rented from Brava at a cost of €250 per month payable in advance and terminable at any time by either party.
2 Machine 2 rented from Blanca at a cost of eight half-yearly payments in advance of €1500.
3 Machine 3 rented from Sol at a cost of six half-yearly payment in advance of €1200.

The cash price of this type of machine is €8000 and its estimated life is four years. Are the three machines rented by operating or finance leases?

Activity feedback

Machine 1 is held on an operating lease as there is no transfer of the risks or rewards of ownership. Machine 2 involves a total payment of €12 000. In present value terms this will almost certainly be more than the €8000 fair value of the asset and therefore clearly more than 'substantially all of the fair value of the leased asset' (see our earlier situation 4). Machine 2 is therefore held on a finance lease. Machine 3 involves a total payment of €7200, the present value of which will be significantly less than €8000, so that situation 4 will not apply. The question is whether or not situation 3 applies, that is, whether or not three years is a 'major part of the economic life' of the machine (which is four years). Under US GAAP, which specifies an arbitrary 75% ratio here, this would be a finance lease under situation 3 (in which circumstance the lease agreement would probably have been changed before signing in order to be a week or two shorter). Under UK GAAP, which focuses more exclusively on situation 4, machine 3 would, on the available information, be an operating lease. Our interpretation of IAS 17 would be that situation 3 does not apply to machine 3, i.e. that this would be treated as an operating lease under IAS GAAP. This example well illustrates the practical difficulties which may arise in lease classification.

Activity 14.6

Do you think the use of numerical specifications in the finance/operating lease distinction is beneficial?

Activity feedback

The desirability of creating a precise numerical distinction is very much open to question. It has the obvious surface advantage of apparent objectivity and precision. However, the chosen figure is purely arbitrary. More importantly, the creation of a definitive numerical distinction allows, and arguably encourages, business enterprises to structure lease contracts so that they fall just marginally below the chosen criterion, even though the whole purpose may, quite visibly, be, in substance, to finance the 'purchase' of major resources by borrowing. The use of a fixed numerical boundary may substantially reduce subjectivity for the accountant and the auditor, but it may at the same time substantially increase creative accounting and the likelihood of misleading or unfair financial statements.

The latest (2004) revision has added a number of detailed requirements relating to leases of land and buildings (paras 14–19). The essential point is that the land and buildings elements of a lease of land and buildings are considered separately for the purposes of lease classification. If title to both elements is expected to pass to the lessee by the end of the lease term, both elements are classified as a finance lease, whether analyzed as one lease or as two leases, unless it is clear from other features that the lease does not transfer substantially all risks and rewards incidental to ownership of one or both elements. When the land has an indefinite economic life, the land element is normally classified as an operating lease unless title is expected to pass to the lessee by the end of the lease term. The buildings element is classified as a finance or operating lease in accordance with the above specifications.

Separate measurement of the land and buildings elements is not required when the lessee's interest in both land and buildings is classified as an investment property in accordance with IAS 40 and the fair value model is adopted. Detailed calculations are required for this assessment only if the classification of one or both elements is otherwise uncertain. In accordance with IAS 40, it is possible for a lessee to classify a property interest held under an operating lease as an investment property. If it does, the property interest is accounted for as if it were a finance lease and, in addition, the fair value model is used for the asset recognized. The lessee should continue to account for the lease as a finance lease, even if a subsequent event changes the nature of the lessee's property interest so that it is no longer classified as investment property.

Accounting and reporting by lessees – finance leases

In the case of finance leases, the substance and financial reality are that the lessee acquires the economic benefits of the use of the leased asset for the major part of its economic life in return for entering into an obligation to pay for that right an amount approximating to the fair value of the asset and the related finance charge.

Lessees should recognize finance leases as assets and liabilities in their balance sheets at amounts equal at the inception of the lease to the fair value of the leased property or, if lower, at the present value of the minimum lease payments (para. 20). In calculating the present value of the minimum lease payments, the discount factor is the interest rate implicit in the lease, if this is practicable to determine; if not, the lessee's incremental borrowing rate should be used. At the inception of the lease, the asset and the liability for the future lease payments are recognized in the balance sheet at the same amounts.

During the lease term, each lease payment should be allocated between a reduction of the obligation and the finance charge so as to produce a constant periodic rate of interest on the remaining balance of the obligation over the amortization period, in the manner illustrated earlier. The asset initially recorded is depreciated in a manner consistent with that used by the lessee for owned assets.

If the circumstances described in situations 1 or 2 earlier are present, that is a transfer of ownership is clearly foreseeable, then depreciation is usually based on the economic life of the leased asset; otherwise, it is based on the shorter of economic life and lease term. Contingent rentals are generally not included in the minimum lease payments and are not accounted for as part of the capitalized lease. They should be charged to expense in the period to which they relate.

Activity 14.7

Using the information given in Activity 14.3, assuming the asset has a nil residual value and assuming the asset is leased for a further two years after the primary period, show the accounting entries over the life of the lease required in the lessee's books by IAS 17.

Activity feedback

The lease falls within the definition of a finance lease, therefore the 'rights in the lease' will be capitalized at fair value of €10 000 and the obligation under the lease of €10 000 will be shown as a liability:

		€	€
1.1.XI	Fixed asset	10 000	
	Creditors (lessor)		10 000

The minimum lease payments amount to $20 \times €650 = €13\,000$, the cash price was €10 000, hence the total finance charge will be €3000.

Remembering that this total finance charge should be allocated to accounting periods during the lease so as to produce a constant periodic rate of charge on the remaining balance of the obligation for each accounting period, then an appropriate method of allocation would be the actuarial method as follows:

Period	Capital sum at start of period €	Rental paid €	Capital sum during period €	Finance charge (2.95% per quarter)* €	Capital sum at end of period €
1/X1	10 000	650	9 350	276	9 626
2/X1	9 626	650	8 976	265	9 241
3/X1	9 241	650	8 591	254	8 845
4/X1	8 845	650	8 195	242	8 437
				1 037	
1/X2	8 437	650	7 787	230	8 017
2/X2	8 017	650	7 367	217	7 584

3/X2	7 584	650	6 934	205	7 139
4/X2	7 139	650	6 489	191	6 680
				843	
1/X3	6 680	650	6 030	178	6 208
2/X3	6 208	650	5 558	164	5 722
3/X3	5 722	650	5 072	150	5 222
4/X3	5 222	650	4 572	135	4 707
				627	
1/X4	4 707	650	4 057	120	4 177
2/X4	4 177	650	3 527	104	3 631
3/X4	3 631	650	2 981	88	3 069
4/X4	3 069	650	2 419	71	2 490
				383	
1/X5	2 490	650	1 840	54	1 894
2/X5	1 894	650	1 244	37	1 281
3/X5	1 281	650	631	19	650
4/X5	650	650	–	–	–
				110	
		13 000		3 000	

We can now apportion the annual rental of €2600 (i.e. $4 \times €650$) between a finance charge and a capital repayment as follows:

	Total rental	Finance charge	Capital repayments
	€	€	€
X1	2 600	1 037*	1 563
X2	2 600	843	1 757
X3	2 600	627	1 973
X4	2 600	383	2 217
X5	2 600	110	2 490
	13 000	3 000	10 000
	(a)	(b)	(a) − (b)

* as calculated using actuarial method

We also need to calculate a depreciation charge. The period for depreciation will be seven years as this is the lesser of economic life (eight years) and lease period (seven years). The annual depreciation charge on a straight line basis is therefore:

$$€10\,000 \div 7 = €1\,429$$

The accounting entries in the lessee's books will be as follows assuming year end as 31 December.

Profit and loss account charges

	Depreciation	Finance charge	Total
X1	1 429	1 037	2 466
X2	1 429	843	2 272
X3	1 429	627	2 056

X4	1 429	383	1 812
X5	1 428	110	1 538
X6	1 428	–	1 428
X7	1 428	–	1 428
	10 000	3 000	13 000

Balance sheet entries

Assets held under finance leases

	Cost		Accumulated depreciation		Net book value of assets held under finance leases
	€		€		€
31.12.X1	10 000	–	1 429	=	8 571
31.12.X2	10 000	–	2 858	=	7 142
31.12.X3	10 000	–	4 287	=	5 713
31.12.X4	10 000	–	5 716	=	4 284
31.12.X5	10 000	–	7 145	=	2 855
31.12.X6	10 000	–	8 574	=	1 426
31.12.X7	10 000	–	10 000	=	–

Obligations under finance leases (i.e. the capital element of future rentals payable)

	Obligations under finance leases outstanding at start of year		Capital repayment		Obligations under finance leases outstanding at year end
	€		€		€
31.12.X1	10 000	–	1 563	=	8 437
31.12.X2	8 437	–	1 757	=	6 680
31.12.X3	6 680	–	1 973	=	4 707
31.12.X4	4 707	–	2 217	=	2 490
31.12.X5	2 490	–	2 490	=	–
31.12.X6					–
31.12.X7					–

Accounting and reporting by lessees – operating leases

Lease payments under an operating lease should be recognized as an expense in the income statement on a straight line basis over the lease term unless another systematic basis is more representative of the time pattern of the user's benefit (para. 33). Note that the pattern of payment is not relevant. Remember that contingent rent, as defined earlier, is not included in the original calculations. It therefore follows that the rental expense for any year will consist of:

1 the minimum rent under the lease divided equally over the number of years
2 plus any contingent rent relating to that year.

Activity 14.8

If the lease in Activity 14.6 were to be treated as an operating lease, show the entries in the lessee's books.

Activity feedback

The only entries in the lessee's books would be the following annual entry:

Rental expense (4 × 650)   2 600
        Creditors (4 × 650)   2 600

During the negotiation of a new operating lease or the renewal of an existing one, the lessee may receive incentives to sign the agreement from the lessor. Incentives take many forms, including rent-free periods, reduced rents for a period of time, leasehold improvements on the lessor's account or a cash signing fee. IAS 17 is silent on this matter, but the Standing Interpretations Committee has clarified the position in SIC 15, *Incentives in an Operating Lease*. This requires that the benefit of such incentives be recognized at the inception of the lease and treated as a reduction of rental expense over the term of the lease. The benefit is recognized on a straight line basis, unless another systematic basis is more representative of the time pattern in which benefit is derived from the leased asset.

Accounting and reporting by lessors – finance leases

As is the case with the financial statements of lessees, the approach is to follow and record the substance of the situation. From the viewpoint of the lessor, the substance is that the lessor has an amount receivable, much of it usually non-current, due from the lessee. In direct relation to the lease contract, the lessor has no other assets or liabilities. The amounts received from the lessee will embrace two elements, i.e. a repayment of 'loan' and an interest revenue.

Lessors should recognize assets held under a finance lease in their balance sheets and present them as a receivable at an amount equal to the net investment in the lease (paras 36–41). A lessor aims to allocate finance income over the lease term on a systematic and rational basis. This income allocation is based on a pattern reflecting a constant periodic return on the lessor's net investment outstanding in respect of the finance lease. Lease payments relating to the accounting period, excluding costs for services, are applied against the gross investment in the lease to reduce both the principal and the unearned finance income.

Estimated unguaranteed residual values used in computing the lessor's gross investment in a lease are reviewed regularly. If there has been a reduction in the estimated unguaranteed residual value, the income allocation over the lease term is reviewed and any reduction in respect of amounts already accrued is recognized immediately.

Initial direct costs are often incurred by lessors and include amounts such as commissions, legal fees and internal costs that are incremental and directly attributable to negotiating and arranging a lease. They exclude general overheads such as those incurred by a sales and marketing team. For finance leases other than those involving manufacturer or dealer lessors, initial direct costs are included in the initial measurement of the finance lease receivable and reduce the amount of income recognized over the lease term. The interest rate implicit in the lease is defined in such a way that the initial direct costs are included automatically in the finance lease receivable; there is no need to add them separately. Costs incurred by manufacturer or dealer lessors in connection with negotiating and arranging a lease are excluded from the definition of initial direct costs. As a result, they are excluded from the net investment in the lease and are recognized as an expense when the selling profit is recognized, which for a finance lease is normally at the commencement of the lease term.

An asset under a finance lease that is classified as held for sale (or included in a disposal group that is classified as held for sale) in accordance with IFRS 5, *Non-current Assets Held for Sale and Discontinued Operations*, shall be accounted for in accordance with that IFRS (see Chapter 23).

Finance leasing by manufacturers or dealers

The manufacturer or dealer may be the person who actually provides the asset, as well as the finance. A finance lease of an asset by a manufacturer or dealer lessor gives rise to two types of income:

1 the profit or loss equivalent to the profit or loss resulting from an outright sale of the asset being leased, at normal selling prices, reflecting any applicable volume or trade discounts
2 the finance income over the lease term.

The sales revenue recorded at the commencement of a finance lease term by a manufacturer or dealer lessor is the fair value of the asset or, if lower, the present value of the minimum lease payments accruing to the lessor, computed at a commercial rate of interest (para. 44). The cost of sale recognized at the commencement of the lease term is the cost, or carrying amount if different, of the leased property less the present value of the unguaranteed residual value. The difference between the sales revenue and the cost of sale is the selling profit, which is recognized in accordance with the policy followed by the enterprise for sales which will be consistent with IAS 18 (see Chapter 17).

Manufacturer or dealer lessors sometimes quote artificially low rates of interest in order to attract customers. The use of such a rate would result in an excessive portion of the total income from the transaction being recognized at the time of sale. If artificially low rates of interest are quoted, selling profit must be restricted to that which would apply if a commercial rate of interest were charged. Initial direct costs should be charged as expenses at the inception of the lease.

Activity 14.9

A lessor leases out an asset on terms which constitute a finance lease. The primary period is five years commencing 1 July 20X0, and the rental payable is €3000 per annum (in arrears). The lessee has the right to continue the lease after the five-year period referred to for an indefinite period at a nominal rent. The cash price of the asset in question at 1 July 20X0 was €11 372, and the rate of interest implicit in the lease can be calculated to be 10%.

Show the entries in the lessor books.

Activity feedback

The finance charge is simply the difference between the fair value of the asset (in this case being the cash price of the new asset) and the rental payments over the lease period, i.e. of €15 000 less €11 372 or €3628.

Using the actuarial method with an interest rate of 10%, the allocation of the finance charge will be as follows:

Year ended 30 June	Balance b/f		Finance charge (10%)	Rental		Balance c/f (in year end balance sheet)
	€		€	€		€
20X1	11 372	+	1 137	−(3 000)	=	9 509
20X2	9 509	+	951	−(3 000)	=	7 460
20X3	7 460	+	746	−(3 000)	=	5 206
20X4	5 206	+	521	−(3 000)	=	2 727
20X5	2 727	+	273	−(3 000)	=	0
			€3 628	€15 000		

The relevant extracts from the income statements of the years in question will thus appear as follows:

	20X1	20X2	20X3	20X4	20X5	Total
Rentals	3 000	3 000	3 000	3 000	3 000	15 000
less Capital repayments	1 863	2 049	2 254	2 479	2 727	11 372
Finance charges	1 137	951	746	521	273	3 628
Interest payable	(x)	(x)	(x)	(x)	(x)	
Overheads	(x)	(x)	(x)	(x)	(x)	

The relevant balance sheets will appear as follows:

	Year ended June 30			
	20X1	20X2	20X3	20X4
Net investment in finance lease				
Current	2 049	2 254	2 479	2 727
Non-current	7 460	5 206	2 727	−
	9 509	7 460	5 296	2 727

Accounting and reporting by lessors – operating leases

As IAS 17 (para. 49) unsurprisingly says, lessors should present assets subject to operating leases according to the nature of the asset. The asset subject to the operating lease is, in substance as well as in form, a non-current asset of the lessor. Such an asset should be depreciated on a basis consistent with the lessor's policy for similar assets. IAS 16, *Property, Plant and Equipment*, or IAS 38, *Intangible Assets*, will apply (see Chapter 12). In addition IAS 36, *Impairment of Assets*, will need to be considered (see Chapter 13).

Costs, including depreciation, incurred in earning the lease income are recognized as an expense. Lease income (excluding receipts for services provided such as insurance and maintenance) is recognized in income on a straight line basis over the lease term even if the receipts are not on such a basis, unless another systematic basis is more representative of the time pattern in which use benefit derived from the leased asset is diminished. By definition, no element of selling profit can arise.

Initial direct costs incurred specifically to earn revenues from an operating lease are added to the carrying amount of the leased asset and recognized as an expense over the lease term on the same basis as the lease income.

Disclosure

The disclosure requirements are extensive for both lessors and lessees. Leases are a form of financial instrument and disclosure requirements relating to financial instruments generally will apply to leases. IAS 17 specifies detailed additional requirements. These include details designed to give a clear indication of the timing of future cash movements and of future expected expense and revenue outcomes.

Sale and leaseback transactions

A sale and leaseback transaction involves the sale of an asset by the vendor and the leasing of the same asset back to the vendor. The lease payment and the sale price are usually interdependent as they are negotiated as a package. The accounting treatment of a sale and leaseback transaction depends on the type of lease involved. Again, the principle of substance over form is fundamental.

If the leaseback is an operating lease and the lease payments and the sale price are established at fair value, there has in effect been a normal sale transaction and any profit or loss is recognized immediately. If the sale price is below fair value, any profit or loss should be recognized immediately except that, if the loss is compensated by future lease payments at below market price, it should be deferred and amortized in proportion to the lease payments over the period for which the asset is expected to be used. If the sale price is above fair value, the excess over fair value should be deferred and amortized over the period for which the asset is expected to be used. Also, for operating leases, if the fair value at the time of a sale and leaseback transaction is less than the carrying amount of the asset, a loss equal to the amount of the difference between the carrying amount and fair value should be recognized immediately.

If the leaseback is a finance lease, the transaction is a means whereby the lessor provides finance to the lessee, with the asset as security. For this reason it is not appropriate to regard an excess of sales proceeds over the carrying amount as income because there has, in substance, been no sale. Such excess is deferred and amortized over the lease term. For finance leases, if the fair value at the time of the sale and leaseback transaction is less than the carrying amount of the asset, then no recognition of the difference between the two is necessary (again, because there has in substance not been a sale). However, such a difference might indicate an impairment in accordance with IAS 36, *Impairment of Assets*, which Standard would then be applied (see Chapter 13).

SIC 27 extends the principles of the sale and leaseback discussion earlier to situations of linked multiple transactions in general. The principle of following the substance of the overall situation remains crucial.

Case study

The published consolidated financial statements of Euro Disney SCA for the year to 30 September 2000 provide a sharp illustration of how significant the leasing question can be. Broadly speaking, this is a consolidation of the French part of the worldwide Disney organization. It is published in English, but is explicitly stated to follow 'French accounting principles' in the audit report and 'French GAAP' elsewhere. Most of the land and property utilized by Euro Disney is owned, through complicated relationships, by financing companies. Under French GAAP, the leases involved are operating leases and the financing companies are not consolidated. The effect is that major obligations are not revealed. However, a detailed reconciliation is given to US GAAP which, in broad terms, has the same effect as using IAS GAAP as regards the relevant leases.

Four reconciliations are now given.

Reconciliation of net income (loss)

	30 September	
(€ *in millions*)	**2000**	**1999**
Net income, as reported under French GAAP	38.7	23.6
Lease and interest adjustments	(106.0)	(74.5)
Other	1.1	1.0
Net loss under US GAAP	**(66.2)**	**(49.9)**

Reconciliation of shareholders' equity

	30 September	
(€ *in millions*)	**2000**	**1999**
Shareholders' equity, as reported under French GAAP	1 247.5	1 140.8
Cumulative lease and interest adjustments	(1 172.9)	(1 067.0)
Effect of revaluing the ORAs and sale/leaseback transactions	178.1	26.7
Other	(14.6)	(15.6)
Shareholders' equity under US GAAP	**238.1**	**84.9**

Reconciliation of borrowings

	30 September	
(€ *in millions*)	**2000**	**1999**
Total borrowings, as reported under French GAAP*	873.8	941.4
Unconsolidated Phase 1 SNCs debt	1 245.4	1 249.6
Lease financing arrangements with TWDC	236.9	236.9

Borrowings including unconsolidated Financing *Companies*	2 356.1	2 427.9
US GAAP adjustments to revalue lease financing arrangements and ORAs	(6.3)	(8.5)
Total US GAAP borrowings*	**2 349.8**	**2 419.4**

*(excluding accrued interest)

Balance sheet under US GAAP

	30 September	
(€ *in millions*)	**2000**	**1999**
Cash and short-term investments	452.9	347.6
Receivables	203.2	184.6
Fixed assets	2 493.3	2 455.5
Other assets	169.4	161.4
Total assets	**3 318.8**	**3 149.1**
Accounts payable and other liabilities	730.9	644.8
Borrowings*	2 349.8	2 419.4
Shareholders' equity	238.1	84.9
Total liabilities and equity	**3 318.8**	**3 149.1**

*(excluding accrued interest)

Total assets under French GAAP were 2793.8 for 2000 and 2518.8 for 1999

Activity 14.10

Calculate the following ratios, within the limits of the given information, under (a) French GAAP and under (b) US GAAP and comment.

$$\frac{\text{net income}}{\text{shareholders' equity}}$$

$$\frac{\text{borrowings}}{\text{equity} + \text{borrowings}}$$

$$\frac{\text{net income}}{\text{total assets}}$$

Activity feedback

(a) *French GAAP*

	2000		1999	
$\dfrac{\text{net income}}{\text{shareholders' equity}}$	$\dfrac{38.7}{1\,247.5}$	$= 3\%$	$\dfrac{23.6}{1\,140}$	$= 2\%$
$\dfrac{\text{borrowings}}{\text{equity} + \text{borrowings}}$	$\dfrac{873.8}{873.8 + 1247.5}$	$= 41\%$	$\dfrac{941.4}{941.4 + 1140.8}$	$= 45\%$

net income / total assets	$\dfrac{38.7}{2\,793.8}$	$=1\%$	$\dfrac{23.6}{2\,518.8}$	$=1\%$

(b) *US GAAP*

net income / shareholders' equity	$\dfrac{(66.2)}{238.1}$	$=-28\%$	$\dfrac{(49.9)}{84.9}$	$=-58\%$
borrowings / equity + borrowings	$\dfrac{2349.8}{2349.8 + 231.8}$	$=91\%$	$\dfrac{2419.4}{2419.4 + 84.9}$	$=97\%$
net income / total assets	$\dfrac{(66.2)}{3\,318.8}$	$=-2\%$	$\dfrac{(49.9)}{3\,149.1}$	$=-2\%$

To state the obvious, a very different picture is given. When the substance of the situation is recorded and the contracted (legally as well as economically) liabilities related to the operations are involved, the whole enterprise is shown to be very highly geared (leveraged), as well as unprofitable. Can both sets of figures be validly regarded as equally fairly presenting the position to readers of the financial statements?

Possible future developments

In December 1999 the IASC published a discussion paper on the subject of leases entitled *Leases: Implementation of a New Approach*. The paper had been developed by the G4 + 1 group. This group consisted of representatives of accounting standard setters from Australia, Canada, New Zealand, UK and USA working with the IASC.

The essential, and apparently very radical, proposal is that the arbitrary distinction between operating and finance leases is unsatisfactory and should be abolished, to be replaced by an approach that applies the same regulations for all leases. The IASC note in the paper that many analysts recast financial statements by applying the same approach to operating and finance leases. G4 + 1 believe that recognition in a lessee's balance sheet of material assets and liabilities arising from operating leases should take place:

> The general effect of the approach proposed is that the amounts recognized as an asset and a liability by a lessee in respect of a lease of a given item would vary in amount depending on the nature of the lease.

The financial statements would thus reflect the extent to which differing lease arrangements result in financial obligations and provide financial flexibility.

Table 14.1 provides an overview of the items that would be included in the liabilities of a lessee and reported at the beginning of the lease with an asset and those that would not according to the discussion paper (p. 13).

The discussion paper debates the issue of recognition and measurement in relation to those leases to be included on the balance sheet.

For a lease contract the recognition point could be:

- signing a contract to lease
- purchase or manufacture by the lessor of the specific item of property that is the subject of the lease
- delivery of the property to the lessee
- rental payments falling due during the lease term.

Table 14.1 Lessee's liabilities and items excluded

Items included in initial assets and liabilities	Item excluded from initial assets and liabilities
Minimum payments required by lease	
Amounts payable in respect of obtaining renewal options	Rentals relating to optional renewal periods
Contingent rentals that represent consideration for the fair value of rights conveyed to lessee	Contingent rentals relating to optional additional usage
Fair value of residual value guarantees	Residual values guaranteed where transfer of economic benefits in settlement is not probable

The discussion paper suggests that recognition take place at delivery of the property to the lessee.

For measurement of a lease we have to remember the principle that assuming an arm's length transaction the cost of an acquired asset is normally measured by fair value of the consideration given. Thus the objective is to record at the beginning of the lease term the fair value of the rights and obligations that are conveyed by the lease.

Activity 14.11

A lessee agrees to hire a piece of equipment for three years at an annual rental of £10 000. The lessee returns the equipment to the lessor at end of the three-year period. Rights and obligations of the lessee are thus:

- right to use for three years
- obligation to pay £10 000 per annum for three years
- obligation to return the equipment to lessor after three years.

At which point should the lessee recognize an asset and at what value in accordance with the discussion paper?

Activity feedback

When the equipment is delivered to the lessee he should recognize an asset equivalent to the present value of three annual payments of £10 000 and a corresponding liability. The asset would subsequently require depreciation and impairment.

The discussion paper works through even more complicated examples involving lessee interest in residual values and various optional features, e.g. lease payments that vary with price changes and considers the measurement problems involved. It then moves on to the issue of discount rates. Recording fair value of rights and obligations in a lease requires the discounting of future payments, thus there is a need to settle on a discount rate. The rate suggested by the discussion paper is the rate at which the lessee could borrow money for the term of the lease and with similar security to that of the lease.

The paper also proposes significant changes to lessor accounting practices. Lessors would report financial assets (representing amounts receivable from the lessee) and residual interests as separate assets. In the group's view, this would be a marked improvement in lessor accounting because a lessor's investment in a leased asset has two distinct elements, receivables and residual interest, which are subject to quite different risks.

The IASB has been too busy dealing with a multitude of urgent matters relevant to the 1 January 2005 deadline for implementation of many new Standards to devote much attention to these radical proposals. But they have not been removed from the longer term agenda.

Summary

This chapter has explored the accounting measurement and disclosure problems relating to leases in the financial statements of both lessors and lessees. The requirements of IAS 17 have been explored and illustrated. Finally, suggestions that the distinction between finance and operating leases should be abolished have been considered.

EXERCISES   (✔ indicates answers are available on pages 726–727)

✔ **1** Explain the theoretical distinction between finance leases and operating leases.

2 IAS 17 fails to give a clear definitional distinction between finance and operating leases. Discuss.

3 IAS 17 states that a particular lease which is a finance lease for the lessee need not automatically be a finance lease as regards the lessor. Can this make sense?

4 The need to account for lease transactions in a useful way proves that the principle of substance over form is essential. Discuss.

5 All unavoidable obligations relating to all lease contracts should be shown in the balance sheet of published financial statements. Discuss.

6 The following figures have been extracted from the accounting records of Lavalamp on 30 September 20X3:

	$000	$000
Sales revenue		112 500
Cost of sales (note (i))	78 300	
Operating expenses	11 400	
Lease rentals (note (iii))	2 000	
Loan interest paid	1 000	
Dividends paid	1 200	
Leasehold (20 years) factory at cost (note (ii))	25 000	
Plant and equipment at cost	34 800	
Depreciation 1 October 20X2 – leasehold		6 250
– plant and equipment		12 400
Accounts receivable	25 550	
Inventory – 30 September 20X3	21 800	
Cash and bank		4 000
Accounts payable		7 300

Ordinary shares of $1 each	20 000
Share premium	10 000
8% Loan note (issued in 20X0)	25 000
Accumulated profits – 1 October 20X2	3 600
201 050	201 050

The following notes are relevant:

(i) Lavalamp has spent $6 million (included in the cost of sales) during the year developing and marketing a new brand of soft drink called Lavaflow. Of this amount $1 million is for advertising and the remainder is the development costs. A firm of consultants has been reviewing the sales of the new product and based on this, it has valued the brand name of Lavaflow at $10 million and expects the life of the brand to be 10 years. Lavalamp wishes to capitalise the maximum amount of intangible assets permitted under International Financial Reporting Standards.

(ii) Due to a sharp increase in the values of properties, Lavalamp had its leasehold property revalued on 1 October 20X2 with the intention of restating its carrying value. A firm of surveyors contracted to value the property found that it had suffered some damaged which will cost $1.5 million to rectify. They gave a valuation of $24 million for the property on the assumption that the repairs are carried out. Lavalamp has informed Capitalrent, the owner of the property, of the repairs needed. Capitalrent has since sent their own surveyors to inspect the property and have informed Lavalamp that they believe the damage is due to the type of machinery being used in the building and accordingly have requested that Lavalamp pay for the repairs. Lavalamp has taken professional advice on this matter which concluded that the property was not in good condition when it was originally leased, but the use of the plant is making the damage worse. Lavalamp has offered to share the cost of the repairs with Capitalrent, but it has not yet had a reply.

(iii) Included in the income statement charge of $2 million for lease rentals is a payment of $600 000 in respect of a five-year lease of an item of plant (requiring ten payments in total). The payment was made on 1 April 20X3. The fair value of this plant at the date is was leased (1 April 20X3) was $5 million. Information obtained from the finance department confirms that this is a finance lease with an implicit interest rate of 10% per annum. The company depreciates plant used under finance leases on a straight-line basis (with time apportionment) over the life of the lease. Other plant is depreciated at 20% per annum on cost. The remaining payments were confirmed as being for operating leases of office equipment.

(iv) A provision for income tax for the year to 30 September 20X3 of $3 470 000 is required.

(v) Lavalamp made and accounted for a rights issue on 1 October 2002 of 1 new share for every 4 held at a price of $1.60 per share. The issue was fully subscribed.

Required:
Prepare the financial statements for the year to 30 September 20X3 for Lavalamp in accordance with International Financial Reporting Standards as far as the information permits. They should include:

(a) An Income Statement;
(b) A Statement of Changes in Equity; and
(c) A Balance Sheet.

Other than for item (ii) above, notes to the financial statements are NOT required, nor is a calculation of earnings per share. Ignore deferred tax.   (ACCA Dec 03)

✔ **7** (i) Different accounting practices for leases are an area that, without a robust accounting standard, can be used to manipulate a company's financial statements. IAS 17 *Leases* was revised in 1999 and has as its objective to prescribe the appropriate accounting policies and disclosures for financial and operating leases.

Required:

Summarise the effect on the financial statements of a lessee treating a lease as an operating lease as opposed to a finance lease; and describe the factors that normally indicate a lease is a finance lease.

(ii) Gemini leased an item of plant on 1 April 20X1 for a 5 year period. Annual rentals in advance were $60 000. The cash price (fair value) of the asset on 1 April 20X1 was $260 000. The company's depreciation policy for this type of plant is 25% per annum on the reducing balance.

Required:

Assuming the lease is a finance lease and the interest rate implicit in the lease is 8%, prepare extracts of the financial statements of Gemini for the year to 31 March 20X3.

(ACCA Dec 03)

Inventories and construction contracts

After studying this chapter you should be able to:
- □ explain the composition of inventories
- □ describe five inventory cost assumptions, i.e. unit cost, first in first out (FIFO), last in, first out (LIFO), weighted average and base inventory
- □ show the effect on annual profit and profit trends of using different inventory cost assumptions
- □ discuss IAS 2 requirements relating to inventories
- □ define construction contracts, attributable profit and foreseeable losses
- □ appraise IAS 11 requirements relating to construction contracts
- □ calculate amounts to be disclosed in financial statements relating to construction contracts
- □ compare IAS 2 and 11 with other GAAP requirements
- □ identify the disclosure requirements of IAS 2 and 11.

Introduction

Inventories, including work in progress, present several problems to the accountant. First, we have to determine the cost of the item. Second, we have to apply prudence as currently appropriate. Third, we have to determine the revenue recognition (sale) point, and apply the matching convention correspondingly. These problems are particularly difficult in the case of construction contracts – a single contract lasting several years – and it is useful, as the Standards do, to treat these separately. We consider first inventories and work in progress other than construction contracts. The valuation of inventories requires care as it is a key determinant of cost of goods sold and therefore in determining net income.

Inventories

These comprise:

1 goods or other assets purchased for resale
2 consumable stores
3 raw materials and components purchased for incorporation into products for sale
4 products and services in intermediate stages of completion
5 finished goods.

The 'cost' of each item at each of these stages is the key to determining the costs of goods sold and the cost of inventory still left in the business, the closing inventory, which will presumably appear as a current asset on the balance sheet.

In determining the cost of such inventory, we will need to consider not only the cost of the raw materials but also the cost of converting raw materials into products and services for sale. Thus, we need to include in our valuation of inventory costs of purchase and costs of conversion including both direct and indirect overhead costs.

A moment's reflection will make it obvious that there are practical problems here. 'Direct' items should present no difficulties as figures can be related 'directly' by definition. But overhead allocation necessarily introduces assumptions and approximations – what is the normal level of activity taking one year with another? – can overheads be clearly classified according to function? – which other (non-production) overheads are 'attributable' to the present position and location of an item of inventory? So for any item of inventory that is not still in its original purchased state, it is a problem to determine the cost of a unit or even of a batch. Methods in common use include job, process, batch and standard costing. All include more or less arbitrary overhead allocations.

Once we have found a figure for unit cost 'in its present location and position', the next difficulty will arise when we have to select an appropriate method for calculating the related cost where several identical items have been purchased or made at different times and therefore at different unit costs.

Consider the following transactions:

Purchases:	January	10 units at €25 each
	February	15 units at €30 each
	April	20 units at €35 each
Sales:	March	15 units at €50 each
	May	18 units at €60 each

How do we calculate inventory, cost of sales and gross profit? There are several ways of doing this, based on different assumptions as to which unit has been sold or which unit is deemed to have been sold.

Inventory cost assumptions

Five possibilities are now discussed.

Unit cost

Here we assume that we know the actual physical units that have moved in or out. Each unit must be individually distinguishable, e.g. by serial numbers. In these circumstances, impractical in most cases, we simply add up the recorded costs of those units sold to give cost of sales and of those units left to give stock. This needs no detailed illustration.

First in, first out (FIFO)

Here it is assumed that the units moving out are the ones that have been in the longest (i.e. came in first). The units remaining will therefore be regarded as representing the latest units purchased.

Activity 15.1

Calculate the cost of sales and gross profit based on FIFO inventory cost assumption from the data on page 280.

Activity feedback

			€	Cost of sales €
January	10 at €25	=	250	
February	15 at €30	=	450	
February total	25		700	
March	− 10 at €25 (Jan.)	=	250	
	− 5 at €30 (Feb.)	=	150	400
March total	10		300	
April	+ 20 at €35	=	700	
April total	30		1 000	
May	− 10 at €30 (Feb.)	=	300	
	− 8 at €35 (Apr.)	=	280	580
May total	12 at €35		420	
				980

Sales are 750 + 1080 = €1830
Purchases are 250 + 450 + 700 = €1400

This gives:	Sales		1 830
	Purchases	1 400	
	Closing inventory	420	
	Cost of sales		980
	Gross profit		850

Last in, first out (LIFO)
Here we reverse the assumption. We act as if the units moving out are the ones which came in most recently. The units remaining will therefore be regarded as representing the earliest units purchased.

Activity 15.2

Calculate the cost of sales and gross profit based on LIFO inventory cost assumption using the data on page 271.

Activity feedback

			€	Cost of sales €
January	10 at €25	=	250	
February	15 at €30	=	450	
February total	25		700	
March	− 15 at €30 (Feb.)	=	450	450
March total	10	=	250	

(continued from previous page)

April	+20 at €35	=	700	
April total	30		950	
May	−18 at €35 (Apr.)	=	630	630
	− 2 at €35 & 10		320	
	at €25			1 080
This gives:	Sales		1 830	
	Purchases	1 400		
	Closing inventory	320		
	Cost of sales		1 080	
	Gross profit		750	

Weighted average

Here we apply the average cost, weighted according to the different proportions at the different cost levels, to the items in inventory. The illustration that follows shows the fully worked out method, involving continuous calculations. In practice, an average cost of purchases figure is often used rather than an average cost of inventory figure. This approximation reduces the need for calculation to a periodic, maybe even annual, requirement.

Activity 15.3

Calculate the cost of sales and gross profit based on weighted average inventory cost assumption.

Activity feedback

			€	*Cost of sales €*
January	10 at €25	=	250	
February	15 at €80	=	450	
February total	25 at €28*	=	700	
March	−15 at €28	=	420	420
March total	10 at €28	=	280	
April	+20 at €35	=	700	
April total	30 at €32⅔**	=	980	
May	−18 at €32⅔	=	588	588
May total	12 at €32⅔	=	392	
				1 008

Working: $\dfrac{(10 \times 25) + (15 \times 30)}{(10 + 15)} = 28^{*}$

$\dfrac{(10 \times 28) + (20 \times 35)}{(10 + 20)} = 32\tfrac{2}{3}^{**}$

This gives:	Sales		1 830
	Purchases	1 400	
	Closing inventory	392	
	Cost of sales		1 008
	Gross profit		822

Base inventory

This approach is based on the argument that a certain minimum level of inventory is necessary in order to remain in business at all. Thus, it can be argued that some of the inventory viewed in the aggregate, is not really available for sale and should therefore be regarded as a fixed asset. This minimum level defined by management, remains at its original cost and the remainder of the inventory above this level is treated, as inventory, by one of the other methods. In our example, the minimum level might be ten units.

Activity 15.4

Calculate the cost of sales and gross profit based on a minimum inventory level of ten units and using FIFO.

Activity feedback

January purchase of base stock: 10 at €25 = €250

			€	Cost of sales €
February	15 at €30	=	450	
March	− 15 at €30	=	450	450
March total	0		0	
April	+ 20 at €35	=	700	
April total	20	=	700	
May	− 18 at €35	=	630	630
May total	2 at €35	=	70	
				1 080
This gives:	Sales			1 830
	Purchases		1 150	
	Closing inventory		70	
	Cost of sales			1 080
	Gross profit			750

In this particular case, the gross profit is the same with this method (base inventory + FIFO) as with LIFO. Can you work out why? This will not generally be the case.

So which approach or approaches are preferable or acceptable?

In selecting a method management presumably must exercise judgement to ensure that the methods chosen provide the fairest practicable approximation to cost. If standard costs are used to value inventory they will need to be reviewed frequently to ensure that they bear a reasonable relationship to actual costs obtaining during the period. Methods such as base stock and LIFO often result in inventories being stated in the balance sheet at amounts that bear little relationship to recent cost levels. When this happens, not only can the presentation of current assets be misleading, but there is potential distortion of subsequent results if inventory levels reduce and out of date costs are drawn into the income statement. However, the method of arriving at cost by applying the FIFO method could be as unacceptable in principle because it is not necessarily the same as actual cost and, in times of rising prices, will result in the taking of a profit which has not been realized. To amplify, consider the cost of sales figure for the May sales in the earlier FIFO and LIFO calculations. Is it preferable to match an April cost level against an April revenue (LIFO) or, partially at least, to match a February cost level against an April revenue level (FIFO)? From a balance sheet viewpoint, however, the criticism of LIFO perhaps makes more sense. The balance sheet total under both LIFO and base stock is likely to be badly out of date. Applying the latest purchase price level to all units, sometimes called next in first out (NIFO), could also be rejected in principle for the same reason as LIFO.

Before we consider IAS 2 and how it attempts to answer this puzzle there is another problem to consider. In the activities so far we have virtually been able to match an inventory item with its sale but this is not the general case.

Inventory systems

Periodic systems

Within this system inventory is determined by a physical count at a specific date. As long as the count is made frequently enough for reporting purposes, it is not necessary to maintain extensive inventory records. The inventory shown in the balance sheet is determined by the physical count and is priced in accordance with the inventory method used. The net charge between the beginning and ending inventories enters into the computation of costs of goods sold.

Perpetual system

In a perpetual system, inventory records are maintained and updated continuously as items are purchased and sold. The system has the advantage of providing inventory information on a timely basis but requires the maintenance of a full set of inventory records. Audit practice will certainly require that a physical check of perpetual inventory records be made periodically.

IAS requirements for inventory

It is now quite clear that the calculation of the appropriate inventory at 'cost' figure is by no means clear cut. Assumptions in two respects have to be made, the cost of the unit and how these costs are matched with the items sold. The actual 'standard accounting practice' requirement itself is very brief and ignores all these difficulties. It is as follows: 'Inventories shall be measured at the lower of cost and net realizable value' (NRV) (para. 9, IAS 2).

The scope of the Standard has been changed by the IASB's improvement project. Previously IAS 2 (1993) covered financial statements prepared in the context of the historical cost system. This was assumed by some readers to imply that the standard applied only under a historical cost system and permitted entities the choice of applying other measurement bases, for example fair value. To clarify that the standard applied to all inventories, regardless of measurement base, the phrase was deleted.

Definitions

Three definitions are given in the Standard, in para. 6:

1 *Inventories* are assets:
   (a) held for sale in the ordinary course of the business;
   (b) in the process of production for such sale; or
   (c) in the form of materials or supplies to be consumed in the production process or in the rendering of services.
2 *Net realizable value* is the estimated selling price in the ordinary course of business less the estimated costs of completion and the estimated costs necessary to make the sale.
3 *Fair value* is the amount for which an asset could be exchanged, or a liability settled, between knowledgeable, willing parties in an arm's length transaction.

Para. 8 of the IAS also states that inventories are 'goods purchased and held for resale including, for example, merchandise purchased by a retailer and held for resale or land and other property held for resale. They also encompass finished goods produced or work in progress being produced by the enterprise and include materials and supplies awaiting use in the production process. In the case of a service provider, inventories include the costs of the service for which the enterprise has not yet recognized the related revenue.'

Separate items

Returning to the heart of the matter, that inventories must be measured at the lower of cost and NRV it is obvious that for each separate item of inventory we need to determine:

1 cost
2 NRV.

The separate item point is significant and this is shown in the following activity.

Activity 15.5

An enterprise has three products in its inventory with values as follows:

Product	Cost	NRV
A	10	12
B	11	15
C	12	9
Total	**33**	**36**

At what value should the inventory be stated in the balance sheet in accordance with IAS 2?

Activity feedback

If the inventory is not separated into each type then we would value at the lower of cost of 33 and NRV of 36. The answer is 33. However, IAS 2 requires us to value each type of inventory separately and therefore the lower in each case is A 10, B 11 and C 9 giving us an inventory valuation of 30.

Cost of inventory

The improved Standard gives guidance on cost of inventories as follows (para. 10):

> The cost of inventories should comprise all costs of purchase, costs of conversion and other costs incurred in bringing the inventories to their present location and condition.

Further amplification of cost is given in para. 11 as follows:

> **11** The costs of purchase of inventories comprise the purchase price, import duties and other taxes (other than those subsequently recoverable by the enterprise from the taxing authority) and transport, handling and other costs directly attributable to the acquisition of finished goods, materials and services. Trade discounts, rebates and other similar items are deducted in determining the costs of purchase.

It must be noted here that the improved IAS 2 does *not* permit exchange differences arising directly on the recent acquisition of inventories invoiced in a foreign currency to be included in the costs of purchase of inventories. This change is because the improved IAS 21 has eliminated the allowed alternative treatment of capitalizing certain exchange differences.

Costs of conversion explanation covers three paragraphs 12, 13 and 14, indicating the associated problems. Costs of conversion include direct labour and the systematic allocation of fixed production overheads, e.g. depreciation, maintenance charges and variable production overheads e.g. indirect materials and labour. (Remember here that fixed overheads are those indirect costs of production that remain relatively constant regardless of volume of production whereas variable overheads are those that vary directly or nearly with volume of production.)

The allocation of fixed overheads is based on the normal capacity of production facilities, taking into account the loss of capacity resulting from planned maintenance and that of variable overheads on the actual use of production facilities. Where joint products are concerned a rational basis for allocation of costs of conversion between them needs to be found.

The Standard suggests the use of relative sale value or gross contribution margin as rational and consistent bases. This can be seen as somewhat arbitrary and subjective but nevertheless is at least a consistent, if not entirely logical, method for dealing with a difficult issue.

Activity 15.6

Determine the valuation of inventory items A and B from the following data:

	A	B
Direct labour charge per item	2	4

Fixed production overheads total €50 000 and normal capacity of production is 5200 of A and 10 200 of B but this is reduced by 200 A and 200 B for planned maintenance. The target of production was 6000 A and 12 000 B. It is estimated that B will sell at twice the value of A. Variable production overheads are calculated as €10 000 in total and are to be allocated on a machine hour basis. Each A item takes two hours of machine time and each B one hour.

Activity feedback

Fixed production overheads will be charged over 5000 A and 10 000 B as normal capacity is after planned maintenance allowance. The target of production is irrelevant in the calculation unless this high production level is actually achieved in which case the fixed overheads to each unit will be decreased so as not to measure the item above cost.

	A	B
Direct labour	2	4
Fixed overheads (allocated in ratio of 1:2 and on number of items)	2	4
Variable overheads (0.5 per hour)	$\underline{1}$	$\underline{0.5}$
	$\underline{5}$	$\underline{8.5}$

Activity 15.7

Calculate the cost of inventories in accordance with IAS 2 from the following data relating to Unipoly Company for the year ended 31 May 20X7.

	€
Direct cost of can opener per unit	1
Direct labour cost of can opener unit	1
Direct expenses cost of can opener unit	1
Production overheads per year	600 000
Administration overheads per year	200 000
Selling overheads per year	300 000
Interest payments per year	100 000

There were 250 000 units in finished goods at the year end. You may assume that there were no finished goods at the start of the year and that there was no work in progress. The normal annual level of production is 750 000 can openers, but in the year ended 31 May 20X7 only 450 000 were produced because of a labour dispute.

Activity feedback

The direct costs of the inventory are straightforward to calculate as follows:

	€
250 000 units at €1 direct material cost	250 000
250 000 units at €1 direct labour cost	250 000
250 000 units at direct €1 expenses cost	$\underline{250\,000}$
	$\underline{750\,000}$

IAS 2 only permits the inclusion of production overheads in the valuation of inventories and therefore the administration, selling and interest costs (unless interest costs meet the requirements identified in the alternative treatment permitted under IAS 23, *Borrowing Costs*) (see Chapter 12) are not relevant here.

Production overheads $600\,000 \times 250\,000/750\,000 = 200\,000$. The abnormal costs associated with the labour dispute will be charged as an expense in the period they are incurred.

$$\text{Cost of finished inventory} = €950\,000$$

Activity 15.8

Which of the following costs can be included in the cost of inventory in accordance with IAS 2? Reference to paras 9–20 of IAS 2 will help in completing this activity.

Discounts on purchase price
Travel expenses of buyers
Import duties
Transport insurance
Commission and brokerage costs
Storage costs after receiving materials that are necessary in the
    production process
Salaries of sales department
Warranty cost
Research for new products
Audit and tax consultation fees

Activity feedback

Discounts on purchase price	yes
Travel expenses of buyers	no
Import duties	yes
Transport insurance	yes
Commission and brokerage costs	yes
Storage costs after receiving materials that are necessary in the production process	yes
Salaries of sales department	no
Warranty cost	no
Research for new products	no
Audit and tax consultation fees	no

Techniques for the measurement of cost

The Standard permits the use of the standard cost method where normal levels of materials, supplies, labour, efficiency and capacity utilization will be used to calculate a standard cost. These standard costs have to be reviewed regularly if this method is used.

The Standard also permits the use of the retail method. The retail method is generally used in the retail industry where there are large numbers of rapidly changing items that have similar margins. The cost of the inventory is determined by reducing the sales value of the inventory by the appropriate gross profit margin. Problems occur with this method when a retailer deals in products of widely differing profit margins or discounts slow moving items.

Cost formulas

The cost of inventories of items that are not ordinarily interchangeable and goods or services produced and segregated for specific projects should be assigned by using specific identification of their individual costs (para. 23).

If specific costs cannot be attributed to an identified item of inventory (and this rarely occurs in an enterprise) then IAS 2 advocates the use of FIFO or weighted average cost formula. The 1993 version of IAS 2 permitted the allowed alternative of using the LIFO method. The improvement project has eliminated this alternative because LIFO lacks 'representational faithfulness of inventory flows'.

Remember the use of LIFO in a period of rising costs will reduce profits and value inventory on the balance sheet at older costs whereas FIFO shows inventory on the balance sheet at newer costs and what many would regard as a more relevant cost.

The elimination, however, does not rule out specific cost methods that reflect inventory flows that are similar to LIFO. For example, when stock bins of coal, cement etc. are replenished by 'topping up', then LIFO may reflect the actual physical flow of inventories.

Comparison with other GAAPs

US GAAP – inventory is carried at lower of cost or market with market generally meaning replacement cost.

Otherwise, in general, the UK and US GAAPs are comparable to IAS.

Disclosure requirements

According to IAS 2, financial statements have to disclose:

- the accounting policies adopted in measuring inventories, including the cost formulas used
- the total carrying amount of inventories and the carrying amount in classifications appropriate to the enterprise
- the carrying amount of inventories carried at fair value less costs to sell
- the amount of any write down of inventories recognized as an expense in the period in accordance with para. 34
- the carrying amount of inventories pledged as security for liabilities
- the cost of inventories recognized as an expense during the period
- the amount of any reversal of any write down that is recognized as a reduction in the amount of inventories recognized as an expense in the period in accordance with para. 34
- the circumstances or events that led to the reversal of a write down of inventories in accordance with para. 34.

The following example of disclosure requirements under IAS 2 is taken from Bayer's financial report 2000.

Raw materials, supplies and goods purchased for resale are valued at the cost of acquisition; work in process and finished goods are valued at the cost of production. If the inventory values are lower at the closing date because of a drop in market prices, for example, the lower amounts are shown. Of the €6095 million in inventories carried as of 31 December 2000, €431 million represents those included at their net realizable value. Inventories are normally valued by the weighted average method.

The cost of production comprises the direct cost of materials, direct manufacturing expenses, appropriate allocations of materials and manufacturing overheads and an appropriate share of the depreciation and write downs of assets used for production.

It also includes the shares of expenses for company pension plans and discretionary employee benefits that are attributable to production. Administrative costs are included where they are attributable to production.

Work in progress and finished goods are grouped together in light of the production sequences characteristic of the chemical industry.

Inventories are comprised as shown in Table 15.1.

Table 15.1 Inventory composition in the chemical industry

€ million	31 December 2000	31 December 1999
Raw materials and supplies	1 041	978
Work in process, finished goods and goods purchased for resale	5 046	4 006
Advance payments	8	8
	6 095	4 992

Construction contracts

Introduction

Construction contracts generally last over a long period of time, certainly longer than one accounting period. Such contracts involve all the difficulties discussed earlier in the context of inventories, with one major addition. This is the question of profit allocation over the various accounting periods. If a contract extends over, say, three years, should the contribution to profits be 0%, 0% and 100%, respectively, for the three years? Can we make profits on something before we have finished it? The realization convention might seem to argue against doing so and the old idea of prudence would certainly argue against it too. But would this give a 'fair presentation' of the results for each period? And would it be of any use? All the various users want regular information on business progress. Remember the desirability of timeliness of information. Can we not argue that we can be 'reasonably certain' during the contract, of at least some profit – and if we can then surely the matching principle is more important than an excessive slavishness to prudence? This discussion has led to two basic methods of dealing with construction contracts, completed-contract method and percentage-of-completion method. This latter method requires allocation over accounting periods of the total profit on the contract while the former delays profit recognition until completion.

Activity 15.9

Zen enterprise is contracted to Alpha for $2 m to construct a building. The following data are available in relation to the contract:

	20X5	20X6	20X7
Costs incurred during year	500 000	700 000	300 000
Year end estimate costs to complete	1 000 000	300 000	
Bills raised during year	400 000	700 000	900 000
Cash received during year	200 000	500 000	1 200 000

Show the profit to be included in the accounts under both the percentage-of-completion method and completed-contract method assuming that degree of completion is based on costs incurred.

Activity feedback

Under the completed-contract method the profit of 500 000 will not be recognized until 20X7 whereas under the percentage-of-completion method it will be allocated to each accounting year as follows:

$$20X5 \ \frac{500\,000}{1\,500\,000} \times 500\,000 - \text{previously recognized (0)} \quad 166\,667$$

$$20X6 \ \frac{1\,200\,000}{1\,500\,000} \times 500\,000 - 166\,667 \quad\quad\quad\quad 233\,333$$

$$20X7 \ \frac{1\,500\,000}{1\,500\,000} \times 500\,000 - 233\,333 - 166\,667 \quad \frac{100\,000}{500\,000}$$

Having decided on the use of percentage-of-completion method our next problem is to determine how this profit and indeed any sale and therefore resulting contract work in progress should be shown in the accounts. If the contract work in progress is shown as a current asset with its attributable profit, as implied by the percentage-of-completion method then this is in direct conflict with the requirement to show inventories at cost or NRV, whichever is the lower.

IAS 11

IAS 11 was issued in 1978 and revised in 1993 and was not included in the IASB's improvement project. IAS 11 requires the percentage-of-completion method to be used. It also determines how contract revenue and contract costs will be shown in the accounts.

The stage of completion of a contract is determined by the method that measures reliably the work performed and this could be:

- proportion that costs incurred for work performed to date bear to total estimated costs
- surveys of work performed
- or completion of a physical proportion of the contract work.

Definitions

Within the Standard we have three definitions:

> A *construction contract* is a contract specifically negotiated for the construction of an asset or a combination of assets that are closely interrelated or inter-dependent in terms of their design, technology and function or their ultimate purpose or use.
>
> A *fixed price contract* is a construction contract in which the contractor agrees to a fixed contract price or a fixed rate per unit of output, which in some cases is subject to cost escalation clauses.
>
> A *cost plus contract* is a construction contract in which the contractor is reimbursed for allowable or otherwise defined costs, plus a percentage of these costs or a fixed fee.

From these definitions we can see that construction contracts can take one of two forms, either fixed price or cost plus according to the IASB. However, the type of contract is not always so clear cut and many have characteristics of both types. It is also worth noting that there is no definition given for 'contractor' which appears to be used in a general sense in the Standard.

The Standard also covers a separability issue. Many contracts can cover the construction of a number of assets and in these cases each asset must be treated as a separate contract if:

- separate proposals have been submitted for each asset
- each asset has been subject to separate negotiations and the contractor and customer have been able to accept or reject that part of the contract relating to each asset
- the costs and revenues of each asset can be identified.

Conversely, a group of contracts may in substance be a single construction contract and is required to be treated as such when:

- the group of contracts is negotiated as a single package
- the contracts are so clearly interrelated that they are in effect part of a single project with an overall profit margin
- the contracts are performed concurrently or in a continuous sequence.

After these definitions and explanations the Standard finally arrives at the heart of the problem in para. 11.

> Contract revenue should comprise:
> (a) the initial amount of revenue agreed in the contract; and
> (b) variations in contract work claims and incentive payments:
>   (i) to the extent that it is probable that they will result in revenue; and
>   (ii) they are capable of being reliably measured.

Para. 16 identifies contract costs as comprising:

- costs that relate directly to the specific contract
- costs that are attributable to contract activity in general and can be allocated to the contract
- such other costs as are specifically chargeable to the customer under the terms of the contract.

Thus, in determining appropriate figures for construction contracts, first we calculate total costs attaching to the contract to date, including appropriate production overheads, which could include borrowing costs. Second, we calculate revenue attributable to the contract to date and therefore attributable profit.

The Standard provides lists of costs that may and may not be charged to a specific contract.

Activity 15.10

Identify four costs that could be charged to a specific contract and four that may not.

Activity feedback

Para. 16 of the Standard gives a number of items, as follows:
Costs that may be charged are:

- site labour costs
- materials used in construction
- depreciation of assets used on construction
- costs of moving assets to and from the site
- hire charges
- design and technical assistance that is directly related
- estimated costs of rectification and guarantee work, including warranty costs
- claims from third parties
- insurance
- construction overheads.

Costs that may not be charged are:

- general administration costs not specified in the contract
- selling costs
- research and development costs not specified
- depreciation of idle assets not used on a specific contract.

Activity 15.11

The following data are available in respect of a construction contract:

Costs to date	$2 m
Total contract revenue expected	$2 m
Further costs to completion	$0.5 m

How should this contract be treated in the accounts?

Activity feedback

The problem here is that the contract is forecast to make a loss of $0.5 m and we need to determine how much of this loss should be recognized at the current stage of completion. Percentage of completion method might imply we should recognize $2/2.5 \times 0.5 = 0.4$ but prudence would suggest we should recognize all the foreseeable loss immediately it becomes apparent.

IAS 11 requires that, 'an expected loss should be recognized as an expense immediately'. It also requires that the gross amount due from customers for contract work should be shown as an asset and gross amount due to customers for contract work as a liability. The gross amount due from customers is defined as the net amount of:

$$\text{costs incurred} + \text{recognized profits} - \text{the sum of recognized}$$
$$\text{losses and progress billings}$$

for all contracts in progress for which costs incurred plus recognized profits (less recognized losses) exceeds progress billings.

The gross amount due to is defined as the net amount of:

$$\text{costs incurred} + \text{recognized profits} - \text{the sum of recognized}$$
$$\text{losses and progress billings}$$

for all contracts in progress for which progress billings exceed costs incurred plus recognized profits (less recognized losses).

The following activity should demonstrate these requirements.

Activity 15.12

The following data are available in respect of five contracts in progress at the end of year 1 by Gamma Enterprise. Identify how each contract should be shown in the accounts in accordance with IAS 11.

	Contracts					Total
	A	B	C	D	E	
Contract revenue recognized	145	520	380	200	55	1 300
Contract expenses recognized	110	450	350	250	55	1 215
Expected losses				40	30	70
Contract costs incurred in period	110	510	450	250	100	1 420
Contract costs recognized as contract expenses	110	450	350	250	55	1 215
Contract costs relating to future activity		60	100		45	205
Progress billings	100	520	380	180	55	1 235
Payments in advance of billings		80	20		25	125

Activity feedback

We will explain the treatment of each contract separately.

Contract A
Income statement

Shown as contract revenue	145
Shown as contract expenses	110
Gross profit	35

Balance sheet
The amount to be included in current assets under amounts due from customers calculated as follows:

Cumulative revenue	145
less Cumulative billings	100
Amounts due from customers	45

This can also be calculated as:

Costs incurred, 110 plus recognized profits, 35 less progress billings, 100 = 45.
In this case all the costs incurred to date relate to the contract activity recorded as revenue and are transferred to income statement as contract expenses leaving a zero balance.

Contract B
Income statement

Shown as contract revenue	520
Shown as contract expenses	450
Gross profit	70

Balance sheet
As cumulative billings are greater than revenue there is a credit balance, calculated as follows:

Cumulative revenue	520
Billing plus advances	600
Advances received (shown under current liabilities)	80

Contract costs incurred to date	510
Contract expenses	450
Amounts due from customers, current assets	60
(also calculated as 510 + 70 − 520)	

Contract C

Contract revenue	380
Contract expenses	350
Gross profit	30

Balance sheet

As with contract B cumulative billings and payments in advance are greater than contract revenue and there is a credit balance calculated as follows:

Contract revenue	380
Billings plus advances	400
Advances received – current liabilities	20

The amount to be included in current assets is calculated as follows:

Contract costs incurred to date	450
Contract expenses	350
Amounts due from customers – current asset	100
(also calculated as 450 + 30 − 380)	

Contract D

Income statement

Contract revenue	200
Contract expenses (costs 250 + loss 40)	290
Gross loss	90

Balance sheet

The amount to be included in current assets is calculated as follows:

Cumulative revenue	200
Billings	180
Balance	20

However, there is also a foreseeable loss credit balance sitting in the accounts and this 40 is transferred to the balance creating a liability of 20 – amounts due to customers. This can also be calculated via costs incurred 250, less foreseeable losses 90, less billings, 180 = (20)

Contract E

Income statement

Contract revenue	55
Contract expenses (costs incurred 55 + loss 30)	85
Gross loss	30

Balance sheet

As cumulative billings are greater than contract revenue there is a credit balance calculated as follows:

Contract revenue	55
Billings plus advances	80
Advance payment – current liabilities	25

Contract costs incurred	100
Contract expenses	85
Due from customers – current asset	15
(also calculated as 100 − 30 − 55)	

Thus, in total for contracts A to E, we have:

Contract revenue		1 300
Contract expenses	1 215	
Expected losses	70	1285
Profit		15

Payments in advance shown as creditor $(0+80+20+0+25)$	125
Payments due from customers shown as current asset $(45+60+100+0+15)$	220
Payments due to customers shown as liability (contract D)	20

To test your understanding of Activity 15.12 we include a further activity for you which is slightly easier.

Activity 15.13

Show how the following information for two construction contracts should be recorded in the financial statements.

	Contract X	Contract Y
Contract revenue	500	350
Contract expenses	450	400
Billings	500	200
Payments in advance of billings	25	–
Contract costs incurred	600	400
Foreseeable additional losses	–	60

Activity feedback

Contract X

Contract revenue			Contract costs incurred			
P&L 500$_{(2)}$	Debtors 500$_{(1)}$		Costs incur.	600	P&L	450$_{(3)}$
					Bal.c/d	150
				600		600
			Bal.b/d	150		

Bal.b/d 150 is shown as due from customers under current assets on BS (also calculated as $600 + 50 - 500$)

Income statement				Debtors		
Contract expenses 450$_{(3)}$	Contract revenue 500$_{(2)}$			Revenue 500	Billing 500	
Profit 50						

Billings		
Debtor 500	Payments 525	
Bal. pays in advance 25		

Contract Y

	Contract revenue			Contract costs incurred	
P&L 350$_{(2)}$	Debtors 350$_{(1)}$		Costs incur. 400	P&L	400$_{(3)}$

	Income statement			Debtors	
Contract costs 400$_{(3)}$ Prov. for	Contract rev 350$_{(2)}$		Contract rev 350	Billing	200
losses 60$_{(4)}$	Loss 110			Bal.c/d	150
			350		350
		Bal.b/d	150	Prov.loss	60$_{(5)}$
	Prov. for loss account			Bal.c/d	90
			150		150
Debtors 60$_{(5)}$	P&L 60$_{(4)}$	Bal.b/d	90		

Bal.b/d 90 shown as due from customers under current assets $(400 - 110 - 200)$

(1) raise the contract revenue
(2) transfer contract revenue to income statement
(3) transfer proportion of contract costs incurred to date to income statement or contract expenses
(4) raise provision for foreseeable losses
(5) transfer provision to debtors

In total, the contracts will be shown as follows:

Income statement
Contract revenue $(500 + 350)$ 850
Contract expenses $(450 + 460)$ 910
Loss   60
Balance sheet
Current assets
Due from customers construction contracts $(90 + 150)$ 240
Current liabilities
Payments in advance construction contracts   25

So far we have dealt with construction contracts where the outcome can be reliably estimated. For those contracts that cannot be reliably estimated the Standard requires that revenue should be recognized only to the extent of contract costs incurred that it is probable will be recoverable and contract costs should be recognized as an expense immediately.

Activity 15.14

An enterprise is involved in two construction contracts the outcome of which cannot be assessed with reliability for which the following data are available:

Contract A   contract costs incurred 30 000 all probably recoverable

Contract B   contract costs incurred 100 000, similar contracts have shown a loss of 15% on contract sale price due to pending legislation affecting the construction. Contract sale price 1m.

Identify how these two contracts should be treated in the accounts of the enterprise.

Activity feedback

Contract A	Contract revenue	30 000
	Contract costs	30 000
Contract B	Contract revenue	0
	Contract costs recognized as expense	150 000

Disclosure requirements

These are detailed at paras 39–45 of the Standard and cover such items as:

- amount recognized as revenue in the period
- method used to determine revenue and stage of completion
- aggregate amounts relating to costs and profits recognized, advances received and retentions.

In addition, amounts due to and from customers must be presented as a current asset and liability respectively.

Activity 15.15

Using the data from the feedback to Activity 15.13 show, as far as possible, the disclosure requirements for contracts X and Y in accordance with IAS 11.

Activity feedback

Contract revenue recognized as revenue in period	850
Contract costs incurred and recognized profits less losses	
600 + 400 + 50 − 110	940
Advances received	25
Amounts due from customers (150 + 90)	240

Comparison with different GAAPs

UK GAAP in SSAP 9, *Stocks and Long-term Contracts*, is similar to IAS 11 except for some differences in the offset of final balances on the contracts.

US GAAP – if an enterprise cannot determine contract revenue or costs, estimated costs to completion or the stage of completion then the completed contract method is required. IAS 11 prohibits the use of the completed-contract method.

Summary

This chapter has defined inventories and construction contracts and identified the accounting requirements for them in accordance with IAS 2 and 11. Valuation of inventories using the unit cost, FIFO, LIFO, weighted average and base inventory are all possible but all lead to a different profit figure and asset figure. Remember the improved IAS 2 has now eliminated the use of LIFO.

It should be clear to you that valuation of inventories is by no means a straightforward task and it requires management to make several judgements.

EXERCISES   (✔ indicates answers are available on pages 727–729)

✔ 1 P Forte commences business on 1 January buying and selling pianos. He sells two standard types, upright and grand, and his transactions for the year are given in the table below.

	Upright		Grand	
	Buy	Sell	Buy	Sell
1 January	2 at €400		2 at €600	
31 March		1 at €600		
30 April	1 at €350		1 at €700	
30 June		1 at €600		1 at €1 000
31 July	2 at €300		1 at €800	
30 September		3 at €500		2 at €1 100
30 November	1 at €250		1 at €900	

You observe that the cost to P Forte of the pianos is changed on 1 April, 1 July and 1 October and will not change again until 1 January following.

Required:

(a) Prepare a statement showing gross profit and closing inventory valuation, separately for each type of piano, under each of the following assumptions:

  (i) FIFO

  (ii) LIFO

  (iii) weighted average

  (iv) RC.

(b) At time of rising prices, (i.e. using the grand pianos as an example) comment on the usefulness of each of the methods.

2 Using any information you wish from exercise 1 illustrate and discuss the effects on the income statement and balance sheet from using the different cost assumptions available to value closing inventory.

3 Critically appraise the different cost assumptions underlying the valuation of closing inventory.

4 Discuss the solution offered by IAS2 to the valuation of inventories.

5 IAS 11 uses the percentage-of-completion method for the valuation of construction contracts. Discuss the advantages and disadvantages of this method and appraise whether it results in useful information for users.

✔ 6 Explain the rationale behind the prohibition of the completed-contract method for valuing construction contracts by IAS 11 given that US GAAP permits this option under certain circumstances.

7 The inventory of Base at 30 September 200X was valued at cost €28.5 million. This included €4.5 million of slow-moving stock that Base had been trying to sell to another retailer. The best price Base has been offered for this slow moving stock is €2 million. Identify how Base should record its inventory in its year end accounts at 30 September 200X.

8 Gear Software, a public limited company, develops and sells computer games software. The revenue of Gear Software for the year ended 31 May 2003 is $5 million, the balance sheet total is $4 million and it has 40 employees. There are several elements in the financial statements for the year ended 31 May 2003 on which the directors of Gear require advice.

(i) Gear has two cost centres relating to the development and sale of the computer games. The indirect overhead costs attributable to the two cost centres were allocated in the year to 31 May 2002 in the ratio 60:40 respectively. Also in that financial year, the direct labour costs and attributable overhead costs incurred on the development of original games software were carried forward as work-in-progress and included with the balance sheet total for inventory of computer games. Inventory of computer games includes directly attributable overheads. In the year to 31 May 2003, Gear has allocated indirect overhead costs in the ratio 50:50 to the two cost centres and has written the direct labour and overhead costs incurred on the development of the games off to the income statement. Gear has stated that it cannot quantify the effect of this write off on the current year's income statement. Further, it proposes to show the overhead costs relating to the sale of computer games within distribution costs. In prior years these costs were shown in cost of sales.

(ii) In prior years, Gear has charged interest incurred on the construction of computer hardware as part of cost of sales. It now proposes to capitalise such interest and to change the method of depreciation from the straight-line method over four years to the reducing balance method at 30% per year. Depreciation will now be charged as cost of sales rather than administrative expenses as in previous years. Gear currently recognises revenue on contracts in proportion to the progression and activity on the contract. The normal accounting practice within the industrial sector is to recognise revenue when the product is shipped to customers. The effect of any change in accounting policy to bring the company in line with accounting practice in the industrial sector would be to increase revenue for the year by $500 000.

The directors have requested advice on the changes in accounting practice for inventories and tangible non-current assets that they have proposed. (ACCA June 03)

9 At 30 September 2003 Bowtock had included in its draft balance sheet inventory $250 000 valued at cost. Up to 5 November 2003, Bowtock had sold $100 000 of this inventory for $150 000. On this date new government legislation (enacted after the year end) came into force which meant that the unsold inventory could no longer be marketed and was worthless.

Bowtock is part way through the construction of a housing development. It has prepared its financial statements to 30 September 2003 in accordance with IAS 11 'Construction Contracts' and included a proportionate amount of the total estimated profit on this contract. The same legislation referred to above (in force from 5 November 2003) now requires modifications to the way the houses within this development have to be built. The cost of these modifications will be $500 000 and will reduce the estimated total profit on the contract by that amount, although the contract is still expected to be profitable.

Required:

Assuming the amounts are material, state how the information above should be reflected in the financial statements of Bowtock for the year ended 30 September 2003.

(ACCA Dec 03)

10 (a) (i) Linnet is a large public listed company involved in the construction industry. Accounting standards normally require construction contracts to be accounted for using the percentage (stage) of completion basis. However under certain circumstances they should be accounted for using the completed contracts basis.

Required:

Discuss the principles that underlie each of the two methods and describe the circumstances in which their use is appropriate.

(ii) Linnet is part way through a contract to build a new football stadium at a contracted price of $300 million. Details of the progress of this contract at 1 April 2003 are shown below:

	$ million
Cumulative sales revenue invoiced	150
Cumulative cost of sales to date	112
Profit to date	38

The following information has been extracted from the accounting records at 31 March 2004:

	$ million
Total progress payment received for work certified at 29 February 2004	180
Total costs incurred to date (excluding rectification costs below)	195
Rectification costs	17

Linnet has received progress payments of 90% of the work certified at 29 February 2004. Linnet's surveyor has estimated the sales value of the further work completed during March 2004 was $20 million.

At 31 March 2004 the estimated remaining costs to complete the contract were $45 million.

The rectification costs are the costs incurred in widening access roads to the stadium. This was the result of an error by Linnet's architect when he made his initial drawings.

Linnet calculates the percentage of completion of its contracts as the proportion of sales value earned to date compared to the contract price.

All estimates can be taken as being reliable.

Required:

Prepare extracts of the financial statements for Linnet for the above contract for the year to 31 March 2004.   (ACCA June 04)

Accounting for financial instruments

After studying this chapter you should be able to:
- [ ] describe a financial instrument
- [ ] identify the need to account for them
- [ ] outline the history of accounting for financial instruments
- [ ] define the scope of IASs regarding financial instruments
- [ ] identify and explain the requirements of the IASB for financial instruments
- [ ] critically appraise these current requirements
- [ ] identify and appraise current international accounting requirements for insurance contracts – IFRS 4.

Introduction

Financial instruments, which include such things as interest rate swaps, Treasury bond options, credit swaps, equity swaps, bonds, receivables, loans, shares etc., have become more complex over the past 20 years. This complexity has led to difficulties in recognizing, measuring, presenting and disclosure of such instruments in the financial statements of an enterprise. The international work on accounting for financial instruments began in 1988 but it was in 1995 that a Standard was issued on presentation and disclosure and 1998 for a Standard on recognition and measurement.

The complexity of the whole issue had led to the decision by the IASC to split the project on financial instruments into two parts, first, presentation and disclosure and, second, recognition and measurement. The real stumbling block in the entire debate on financial instruments is around the issue of whether the financial assets and liabilities involved should be valued at fair value.

IAS 39, *Financial Instruments: Recognition and Measurement* first issued 1998 and revised 2000, was seen as an interim solution to accounting for financial instruments. Its publication was driven by the need for the IASB to have a set of core standards available for approval by IOSCO by early 1999. The Standard was further revised as part of the improvement project and it is this extant version of 2004 that we consider here.

The complexity of the whole area was further demonstrated by the fact that the IASB decided there was a need to issue guidance on IAS 39 in the form of questions and answers. This guidance was included in a publication from the IASB entitled *Accounting for Financial Instruments – Standards, Interpretations and Implementation Guidance*. Several

SICs have also been issued: SIC 5, *Classification of Financial Instruments – Contingent Settlement Provisions*; SIC 16, *Share Capital – Reacquired Own Equity Instruments*; SIC 17 *Equity – Costs of an Equity Transaction*. The new Standard 2004 supersedes the previous interpretations and implementation guidance as these are now included in the Standard as Implementation Guidance. SIC 5 is also now withdrawn and superseded by the revised IAS 32, as are SIC 16 and 17.

This chapter, as you can imagine from the outline, is highly complex and, on many issues, controversial. We advise you to work through the chapter methodically, completing all the activities as you go.

History of accounting for financial instruments

The IASC's work on financial instruments began in 1988 following an OECD symposium on the issue. Even at this early stage the most difficult issue to deal with concerned the valuation of the instruments and whether this should be at fair value or not. The first Draft Statement of Principle was issued in March 1990 and this advocated fair value measurement for financial assets and liabilities held for trading but not for others. The DSOP was approved by the IASC in November 1990.

In June 1991 E40 was issued. It advocated a benchmark treatment consisting of fair value for trading items and cost for others and an allowed alternative of fair value for all items; a compromise solution.

An agreement had also been made between the IASC and the Canadian Institute of Chartered Accountants (CICA) to cooperate on the development of the IASC Standard on financial instruments. However, in 1991 the CICA issued an exposure draft which did not allow fair value accounting for other than trading items. The two drafts were also at odds over the criteria for designation of a hedge. Both IASC and CICA published revised exposure drafts in 1994 and after consultation with standard-setting bodies in 20 countries the IASC decided to split its work on financial instruments into two stages. The first stage was to deal with presentation and disclosure and the second with recognition and measurement. The time scales set for these two stages were optimistic but IAS 32 was published in March 1995 on time. For recognition and measurement the IASC had to establish a further steering group which issued a discussion paper jointly with CICA in March 1997. Even at this stage, however, consensus could not be reached on whether to use fair values and where the resulting unrealized recognized gains and losses should be reported. Events then speeded up, as the IASC had to produce a core set of Standards by early 1999 to meet the IOSCO agreement. One of these core Standards had to deal with financial instruments. IAS 39 was issued in March 1999 and it took a cautious approach to fair value accounting. This cautious approach gave rise to complex requirements for hedging. The standard was so complex that guidance notes in the form of questions and answers were issued during 2000.

However, the Standards produced in 2000 were not universally accepted. A working group of standard setters and professional organizations from several countries produced draft revisions to the Standard on financial instruments, in December 2000, which proposed radical changes. One of their proposals was that virtually all financial instruments should be measured at fair value. The improvement project to IAS 32 and IAS 39 took this proposal up and fair value is now an option under IAS 39. However, such has been the controversy surrounding the new Standard, with uncertainty surrounding its adoption by several countries as well as Europe, that the IASB has issued further exposure drafts. It also set up (in September 2004) a further working party to analyze accounting issues relating to financial instruments. In the meantime, partial (as opposed to full) adoption of IAS 39 by Europe could cause long-term damage to the credibility and quality of financial reporting in Europe.

Problems identified

Information available

The growth in the variety of financial instruments available over the past 20 years had given rise to a lack of understanding by users of financial statements of the significance of such instruments on an enterprise's financial performance, position and cash flows. Many of the instruments were carried off balance sheet and the user was unable to access the effect of these unless there was adequate presentation and disclosure. In addition, an enterprise, by the use of financial instruments, can significantly change its financial risk profile resulting in excessive gains or losses depending on whether prices of such instruments move in favour of or against the enterprise.

Measurement practice

Measuring financial instruments at historical cost does not always provide the most relevant or consistent information for users. Throughout the programme of work on financial instruments the view grew that using fair values for such assets and liabilities could provide more relevant information.

However, the use of fair values then raises the question of where the unrealized gain or loss should be reported in the income statement or as a change in equity. Historically the principal driver in the recognition of gains was 'realization' but this may have less relevance in a situation where enterprises are trading underlying risks. Careful consideration would need to be given to information derived by measuring financial instruments at fair value and recognizing that gain or loss in the income statement as compared with valuation at historical cost.

Illustration

Enterprise *A* enters into an interest swap with *B*. The notional amount of the swap is €1m but this amount is not exchanged. *A* pays interest to *B* at three month intervals at 7% and *B* pays interest to *A* at London Interbank Offered Rate (LIBOR). If LIBOR moves above 7% then *A* gains on the deal, otherwise he loses. On a historical cost basis no asset or liability would be recorded by either party and interest payments would be shown through the income statement. It could be the case that at a year end, if LIBOR has moved to 10%, the fair value of this interest swap is €50 000. If fair value accounting is used then the interest rate swap would be recorded at €50 000 and presumably this gain would be shown in the income statement. In six months' time the fair value of this

> swap could have dropped to €10 000. Which method of accounting for the swap would provide relevant and reliable information to the user? We leave this question for you to debate.

What is a financial instrument?

IAS 32 and 39 define a financial instrument as 'any contract that gives rise to a financial asset of one enterprise and a financial liability or equity instrument of another enterprise'.

A financial asset is any asset that is:

(a) cash;
(b) a contractual right to receive cash or another financial asset from another enterprise;
(c) a contractual right to exchange financial instruments with another enterprise under conditions that are potentially favourable; or
(d) an equity instrument of another enterprise.

A financial liability is any liability that is a contractual obligation:

(a) to deliver cash or another financial asset to another enterprise; or
(b) to exchange financial instruments with another enterprise under conditions that are potentially unfavourable.

From these definitions we can assert that a financial instrument is the contract, not the asset or liability and thus we must be clear what is meant by contract, contractual right and obligation. Neither Standard defines these terms but IAS 32 does state that 'contract' and 'contractual' refer to an agreement between two or more parties that has clear economic consequences that the parties have little, if any, chance of avoiding, because generally the agreement is enforceable in law. Contracts need not, however, be in writing.

Activity 16.1

Identify which of the following are financial instruments:

- cash
- gold bullion
- debtors
- creditors
- loans
- bank deposits
- debentures
- a promissory note payable in government bonds
- ordinary shares
- preference shares

- plant and equipment previously bought and paid for by the enterprise
- pre-payments for goods or services.

Activity feedback

Clearly, the last two are not financial instruments as there is no contract to settle anything in cash or another financial instrument.

Cash is clearly not a financial instrument but it *is* a financial asset. Gold bullion, contrariwise, is a commodity or physical asset as there is no contractual right to receive cash or other financial asset.

Debtors are financial assets but *not* financial instruments as they cannot be described as a contract although they quite possibly arose from a contract. Creditors are likewise a financial liability. Loans, bank deposits and debentures are financial assets of one enterprise and liabilities of another but it is debatable whether they are actually a financial instrument as this requires a contract. Presumably there is a contract behind these assets and liabilities and it should be this that is the financial instrument. The Standard tends to confuse the terms financial assets, financial instruments and financial liabilities.

A promissory note payable in government bonds *is* a financial instrument as the note is the contract that gives the holder the contractual right to receive and the issuer the contractual obligation to deliver government bonds. The bonds themselves are financial assets of one enterprise and liabilities of another. Ordinary and preference shares can also be regarded as financial instruments if we regard them as a contract that will ultimately result in the enterprise paying cash to the holder. The Standard defines an equity instrument as any contract that evidences a residual interest in the assets of an enterprise after deducting all of its liabilities.

This activity is somewhat tortuous given that the Standard uses the terms financial instrument, financial asset and financial liability rather loosely.

Other examples of financial instruments given in the standards are derivatives such as financial options, futures and forwards, interest rate swaps and currency swaps. The Standard gives further examples of contracts that do not give rise to financial instruments as they do not involve the transfer of a financial asset. For example, an operating lease for the use of a physical asset can be settled only by the receipt and delivery of services and is therefore *not* a financial instrument.

Finance leases are, however, financial instruments as they are contracts which result in a financial asset of one enterprise and a financial liability of another. (Finance leases are outside the scope of IAS 32 and 39 as they are subject to IAS 17, *Leases*.)

A derivative is defined in the Standards as:

a financial instrument:

(a) whose value changes in response to the change in a specified interest rate, security price, commodity price, foreign exchange rate, index of prices or rates, a credit rating or credit index or similar variable (underlying);

(b) that requires no initial net investment or little initial net investment relative to other types of contracts that have a similar response to changes in market conditions; and

(c) that is settled at a future date.

Activity 16.2

Are the following contracts financial instruments?

1 Enterprise *A* enters into both derivatives and an interest rate swap with another, *B*, that requires *A* to pay a fixed rate of 7% and receive a variable amount based on a three-month LIBOR. The notional amount of the swap is 1 million euros but this amount is not exchanged. *A* pays or receives a net cash amount each quarter based on the difference between 7% and LIBOR.

2 *A* also enters into a pay fixed, receive variable interest swap with *C*. The notional amount is for 100 million euros and fixed rate 10%. The variable rate is based on a three-month LIBOR. *A* prepays its fixed interest rate obligation as 100m × 10% × 5 years discounted at market interest rates at inception of the swap.

3 *A* enters into a contract to pay 10 million if X shares increase by 5% or more during a six-month period and to receive 10 million if share price decreases by 5% or more in the same period. No payment is made if the price swing is less than 5% up or down.

Activity feedback

1 There is no initial net investment, settlement occurs at a future date and its value changes based on changes in LIBOR, the underlying, therefore this is a financial instrument as it meets the definition of a derivative.

2 This is also a derivative and therefore a financial instrument even though there is an initial net investment. The payment of the fixed interest at inception will be regarded as 'little' compared with other similar contracts such as a variable rate bond where the notional amount of 100m would be paid over.

3 There is no initial net investment, settlement occurs at a future date and the underlying is the share price. This is a derivative and therefore a financial instrument.

Categories of financial asset/liability

The Standard categorizes financial assets/liabilities as:

- held for trading
- held to maturity investments
- loans and receivables
- available for sale.

Held for trading asset is one, regardless of why it was acquired, which is part of a portfolio for which there is evidence of short-term profit taking or was initially acquired for purposes of generating a profit through short term fluctuations in price or dealer's margins.

Held to maturity investments are financial assets with fixed or determinable payments and fixed maturity that an enterprise has the positive intent and ability to hold to maturity. The Standard subsequently defines what it means by 'positive intent' and 'ability to hold to maturity' in an appendix at paras AG 16–AG 25.

Loans and receivables originated by the enterprise are financial assets created by the enterprise by providing money, goods, or services directly to a debtor.

Available for sale are those that are not loans and receivables originated by the enterprise, held to maturity or held for trading.

Activity 16.3

Which categories of financial asset/liability do the following fit into:

1 a non-derivative financial asset acquired with the intent to hold for a long period irrespective of short-term fluctuations in price
2 a bond purchased at original issuance where funds are transferred directly to the issuer?

Activity feedback

1 held for maturity
2 originated loan.

These definitions are very important as the Standard requires available for sale and held for trading to be measured at fair value and the loans and receivables and held to maturity to be measured at amortized cost using the effective interest method. In addition, any financial asset that does not have a quoted market price in an active market and whose fair value cannot be reliably measured is measured at amortized cost.

Measurement of financial instruments

From the preceding paragraph it becomes apparent that we need a definition of amortized cost and effective interest method.

The Standard defines these as follows:

Amortized cost is the amount at which the financial asset or liability was measured at initial recognition minus principal repayments, plus or minus the cumulative amortization of any difference between the initial amount and the maturity amount, and minus any write-down for impairment or uncollectability.

Effective interest method is a method of calculating amortization using the effective rate of a financial asset or liability. The effective interest rate is the rate that exactly discounts the expected stream of future cash payments through maturity or the next market-based repricing date to the current net carrying amount of the financial asset or liability. That computation should include all fees and points paid or received between parties to the contract. The effective interest rate is sometimes termed the level yield to maturity or to next repricing date and is the internal rate of return of the financial asset or liability for that period.

Any financial asset or financial liability can be designated as at fair value through the profit and loss account. This option overrides the other measurement requirements of IAS 39 such that any financial asset or liability so designated will be revalued to fair value at each accounting period date. As this facility is an option any financial asset or financial liability not designated as at fair value through the profit and loss account will be initially recognized and subsequently measured in accordance with IAS39 (see summary at end of chapter). Fair value of the consideration is generally estimated as the sum of all future cash payments or receipts discounted using prevailing market rate of interest for a similar instrument of an issuer with a similar credit rating. Transaction costs are also included in the initial measurement of all financial assets and liabilities. Transaction costs include fees and commissions and costs of issuing debt.

Illustration

On 1 January 2000, an enterprise acquires €100 000 par value 9% bonds of Paper Co. priced to yield 10% with a maturity date of 31.12.2004. The value of the bonds on acquisition is

	€
Present value of interest payments	
9% of €100 000 for five years discounted at 10%	
= 9 000 × 3.79079 (annuity factor at 10% for 5 years)	34 117
Present value of maturity value = 100 000 × 0.62092	
(annuity factor at 10% in 5 years)	62 092
Market value	96 209
Discount from par value therefore is	3 791
Par value	100 000
Thus the bonds are initially recognized at	€96 209

Subsequent recognition of the bonds each year requires amortization using the effective interest rate method. Thus, we need to amortize the discount from par value over the five years recognizing this together with interest received as interest income.

Table 16.1 shows the carrying amount (amortized cost) (column E) of the instrument each year and the interest income (column A).

Table 16.1 Amortization of bonds

Year	Interest income CA × 10% A	Cash received B	Discount amortized C	Discount remaining D	Carrying amount E
1.1.00				3 791	96 209
31.12.00	9 621	9 000	621	3 170	96 830
31.12.01	9 683	9 000	683	2 487	97 513
31.12.02	9 751	9 000	751	1 736	98 264
31.12.02	9 826	9 000	826	910	99 090
31.12.04	9 910	9 000	910		100 000

Fair value is defined by the Standard as the amount for which an asset could be exchanged or a liability settled, between knowledgeable, willing parties in an arm's length transaction. If the fair value of the instrument cannot be reliably measured then the instrument is carried at amortized cost if it has a fixed maturity and at cost if no fixed maturity.

Activity 16.4

Identify three situations in which the fair value of a financial instrument (FI) could be reliably measured and one in which it might not.

Activity feedback

Reliable measurement:

- a financial instrument for which there is a published price quoted in an active public securities market for the instrument
- a debt instrument that has been rated by an independent rating agency and whose cash flows can be reasonably estimated
- a financial instrument for which there is an appropriate valuation model and for which the data inputs to that model can be measured reliably because the data come from active markets.

Unreliable measurement of fair value:

- no quoted market price available in an active market and for which other methods of reasonable estimation of fair value are unworkable.

Activity 16.5

Company A holds 15% of the share capital of B which is publicly traded in an active method. Quoted price is 100 and the daily trading volume is 0.1% of outstanding shares. Company A believes that if it sold its shares in B in one lot it would obtain greater than the quoted market price. Several independent estimates have confirmed this and suggested a price about 105. At what value should A record its holding?

Activity feedback

The holding needs to be measured at fair value as it is an instrument held for trading. Fair value is the current quoted price 100; 105 will not be regarded as the fair value unless company A has entered into a contract to sell at that price.

Gains and losses on remeasurement to fair value

The Standard requires that a gain or loss from a change in fair value of a financial instrument (FI) held for trading should be included in net profit or loss for the period but a similar gain or loss on an FI available for sale is recognized directly in equity except for impairment losses and foreign exchange gains and losses, which are both recognized in profit or loss. Note here that this is one of the changes made by the improvement to IAS 39 as previously entities had a choice of where they recognized the gain or loss – profit or loss or equity. This choice had a marked effect on profits!

Once the available for sale Financial Instrument is derecognized the cumulative gain or loss is moved from equity to profit or loss.

All financial instruments have to be reviewed for impairment at each balance sheet date. For loans and receivables and held-to-maturity investments carried at amortized cost the impairment loss is measured as the difference between the asset's carrying amount and the present value of future estimated future cash flows.

Initial recognition

According to the Standard an enterprise should only recognize a financial asset or liability on its balance sheet when it becomes a party to the contractual provisions of the instrument. Put simply this means that even where a firm commitment to buy or sell goods exists this would not be recognized until the goods have been shipped, delivered or services rendered and that planned future transactions, no matter how likely, are not recognized. However, a forward contract which is a commitment to purchase or sell a specified FI or commodity on a future date at a specified price is recognized on the commitment date rather than the closing date.

The Standard (and this is rather confusing so take your time reading this) then deals with something called 'regular way contracts'.

Regular way contracts are those for the purchase or sale of financial assets that require delivery of the assets within the timeframe generally established by regulation or convention in the market concerned. For these contracts recognition is permitted at either trade date or settlement date but the policy chosen must be applied consistently.

Settlement date accounting, when applied, does, however, require the enterprise to recognize any change in the fair value of the asset that occurs between the trade and settlement date. This is a somewhat strange requirement given that the financial asset itself is not yet recognized. Regular way contracts actually meet the definition of a derivative as they are forward contracts but are not recognized as derivatives because of the short duration of the commitment.

An example of a regular way contract is where a bank makes a loan commitment at a specified rate of interest and then takes a commitment period to enable it to complete its underwriting and to provide time for the borrower to execute the transaction that is the subject of the loan. This commitment period would have to be of a normal duration for such an agreement. The loan, once recognized at either trade date or settlement date, would be carried at amortized cost.

Activity 16.6

On 29 December 20X1 an enterprise commits to buy a financial asset for €1000 which is its fair value on commitment date (trade date). On 31.12.X1 and 4.1.X2, the settlement date, the fair value of the asset is 1002 and 1003 respectively.

Show the amounts to be recorded for the asset at 29.12.X1, 31.12.X1 and 4.1.X2 using both settlement and trade date accounting and identify where any change in value will be recognized. Note you do not know whether this asset is held to maturity or available for sale.

Activity feedback

There is a lot to sort out in this question.

If the asset is held to maturity then it will be carried at amortized cost but if available for sale it will need to be remeasured to fair value. On remeasurement to fair value the change is taken to equity. We also have to choose between initial recognition at trade (Table 16.2) or settlement date (Table 16.3).

Table 16.2 Trade date accounting

Date of balance	Held to maturity	Available for sale
29.12.X1		
Financial asset	1 000	1 000
Liability	(1 000)	(1 000) Note 1
31.12.X1		
Financial asset	1 000	1 002
Liability	(1 000)	(1 000)
P&L	Note 2	
Equity		(2)
4.01.X2		
Financial asset	1 000	1 003
Liability	Note 3	
P&L		
Equity		(1) in addition to the previous 2

Note 1: At this stage in the recognition we have both a financial asset that we have purchased and the liability outstanding to pay for this asset

Note 2: We still haven't settled this transaction so the liability still remains and as it is held for maturity we carry at amortized cost

Note 3: Settlement date is now reached so the liability is removed but note that other assets, perhaps cash, would be reduced

Note 4: Only the value of the financial asset changes to fair value, not that of the liability

Table 16.3 Settlement date accounting

Date of balance	Held to maturity	Available for sale
29.12.X1	–	–
31.12.X1		
Financial asset	–	2 Note 5
Liability	–	
P&L	–	
Equity	–	(2)
4.1.X2		
Financial asset	1 000	3
Liability		
P&L		
Equity		(1) in addition to the previous 2

Note 5: In both cases here we need to recognize the change in fair value that has occurred between trade and settlement date even though the full financial asset is not yet recognized

Derecognition

17 An entity shall derecognize a financial asset when and only when:
(a) The contractual rights to the cash flows from the financial assets expires; or
(b) It transfers the financial asset as set out in paragraphs 18 and 19 and the transfer qualifies for derecognition in accordance with paragraph 20.

18 An entity transfers a financial asset if, and only if, it either:
(a) Transfers the contractual rights to receive the cash flows of the financial asset; or
(b) Retains the contractual rights to receive the cash flows of the financial asset, but assumes a contractual obligation to pay the cash flows to one or more recipients in an arrangement that meets the conditions in paragraph 19.

19 When an entity retains the contractual rights to receive the cash flows of a financial asset (the 'original asset'), but assumes a contractual obligation to pay those cash flows to one or more entities (the 'eventual recipient'), the entity treats the transaction as a transfer of financial asset if, and only if, all of the following three conditions are met:
(a) The entity has no obligation to pay amounts to the eventual recipient unless it collects equivalent amounts for the original asset. Short-term advances by the entity with the right of full recovery of the amount lent plus accrued interest at market rates do not violate this condition.
(b) The entity is prohibited by the terms of the transfer contract from selling or pledging the original asset other than as security to the eventual recipients for the obligation to pay them cash flows.
(c) The entity has an obligation to remit any cash flows it collects on behalf of the eventual recipients without material delay. In addition, the entity is not entitled to reinvest such cash flows, except for investment in cash or cash equivalents (as defined in IAS 7, *Cash Flow Statements*) during the short settlement period from the collection date to the date of required remittance to the eventual recipients, and interest earned on such investments is passed to the eventual recipients.

20 When an entity transfers a financial asset (see paragraph 18) it shall evaluate the extent to which it retains the risks and rewards of ownership of the financial asset. In this case:
(a) If the entity transfers substantially all the risks and rewards of ownership of the financial asset, the entity shall derecognize the financial asset and recognize separately as assets or liabilities any rights and obligations created or retained in the transfer;
(b) If the entity retains substantially all the risks and rewards of ownership of the financial asset, the entity shall continue to recognize the financial asset;
(c) If the entity neither transfers nor retains substantially all the risks and rewards of ownership of the financial asset, the entity shall determine whether it has retained control of the financial asset. In this case:
(i) If the entity has not retained control, it shall derecognize the financial asset and recognize separately as assets or liabilities any rights and obligations created or retained in the transfer,

(ii) If the entity has retained control, it shall continue to recognize the financial asset to the extent of its continuing involvement in the financial asset (see paragraph 30).

Derecognition is used by the IASB as a term meaning 'to remove from the balance sheet'. This area is again complex, given that derecognition of a portion of the asset is permitted and there is the possibility of repurchase options or other derivatives being involved. From, the paragraphs above it is apparent that the issue of derecognition involves determination of whether an enterprise has lost control of the financial asset; has the transferor given the rights to obtain benefits from the financial asset to the transferee?

Activity 16.7

In each of the following cases state, with reasons, whether the financial asset should be derecognized in the books of enterprise A.

1 A transfers a loan it holds to a bank but stipulates that the bank cannot sell or pledge the loan (this is to protect the customer to whom the loan was originally made).
2 A transfers a financial asset to B on terms that stipulate that A can repurchase the asset before the expiry of a specific period and that repurchase is at the value at transfer date plus interest at a market rate on that value.
3 A transfers a financial asset to B on terms that stipulate that A must repurchase the asset before the expiry of a specific period at market value at the date of repurchase.
4 A sells receivables to B and provides a guarantee with that sale to pay for any credit losses that may be incurred on the receivables as a result of the failure of the debtor to pay when due. All other substantive risks and rewards of the receivables are transferred to B.

Activity feedback

1 Even though the transferee, the bank, cannot sell or pledge the loan it does receive all other benefits from holding the loan and therefore A would derecognize this financial asset. However, A would also need to show the separate forward commitment to repurchase the loan.
2 This is in effect similar to B making a loan to A secured on the financial asset. A does not lose control of any risks or rewards in the financial asset and therefore the asset remains recognized throughout the period in A's books. No derecognition.
3 This might seem similar to example 2 but it isn't. In this case, the risks and rewards associated with the asset have been transferred to B as he will bear the loss if the market value falls and the gain if it increases. The asset will be derecognized by A and recognized when it is repurchased.
4 A derecognizes these receivables. A has lost control of the financial asset and his risk is limited to a credit risk in the case of default. This credit risk would need to be recognized by A as a financial liability, a separate financial instrument.

Derecognition accounting treatment

The accounting treatment on derecognition requires the enterprise to recognize in the net profit or loss for the period the difference between the carrying amount of the asset, or portion, transferred to another party and the sum of the proceeds received or receivable and any prior adjustment to reflect the fair value of that asset that had been reported in equity.

Partial derecognition

Derecognition of part of a financial asset is again complex. Para. 27 of IAS 39 requires that if an enterprise transfers a part of a financial asset to others and retains the other part, then the part transferred/sold must be derecognized. To do this the carrying amount of the financial asset must be allocated between the part sold and the part retained based on their relative fair values at the date of sale. The gain or loss recognized is based on the proceeds for the part sold.

Illustration

(Adapted from IAS 39 implementation guide.)

A purchases €100 of bonds in the marketplace with an effective yield of 11%. An 80% portion of the principal amounts of these bonds is sold on to investors. The investors purchase 80% of the bonds at par at interest of 6%. The 80% of the bonds transferred need to be derecognized and to do so we need to allocate the carrying amount of the bonds based on their fair values at date of sale. At the date of sale A estimates that the present value of the cash flows from the 20% it retains is equal to 25% of the principal amount of the bonds, i.e. €25. The fair value of the portion sold is €80 as that was what the investors paid. The carrying amount of the asset, €100, needs allocating to the portion retained and portion sold based on fair values at date of sale.

Carrying amount is €100
Fair value of portion sold €80
Fair value of 100% of bonds is €105 (80 + 25)
Carrying amount allocated to sold portion is $100 \times 80/105 = 76.19$
Profit on sale is therefore €3.81

Occasionally, it could be the case that an enterprise is unable to estimate reliably the fair value of the portion of the asset retained. In this case para. 47 of the Standard requires us to allocate zero value to the portion retained and to allocate the entire carrying amount to the portion sold/derecognized.

Activity 16.8

Enterprise A with receivables in its books at a carrying amount of €100 sells them for €90. The enterprise continues to service the receivables even after they have been sold for a fee, which is expected to exceed the cost of servicing. The fair value of this fee cannot be reliably estimated. How should this transaction be shown in the books of A?

Activity feedback

The receivables are derecognized from A's books and a loss of €10 shown in the net profit and loss account. The servicing asset would be recorded at zero.

A more complicated example is given in Activity 16.9 below.

Activity 16.9

A holds originated loans of €1000 yielding 10% interest p.a. for their nine-year life. The loans are sold to B enterprise at €1000 with an interest rate of 8% pa. A continues to service the loans at a fee equivalent to half of the interest not sold. The other half of the interest not sold is to be regarded as an interest-only strip receivable. The fair value of the loan plus servicing at date of transfer is €1100 including fair value of servicing and interest-only strip as €40 and €60 respectively. Identify the treatment of this transaction in A's books.

Activity feedback

The loans will be derecognized and a servicing asset and an interest-only strip receivable will be recognized in the balance sheet.

The €1000 carrying amount of the loan is allocated as follows:

	Fair value	%	Carrying amount
Loans sold	1 000	91	910
Servicing asset	40	3.6	36
Interest-only strip receivable	60	5.4	54
	1 100	100.0	1 000

Thus a gain of €90 (1000 − 910) will be shown in the net profit and loss account on the sale of the loan, the servicing asset will be recorded at €36 in the balance sheet and interest-only strip receivable at €54.

Derecognition coupled with new asset or liability

Quite often asset derecognition is coupled with the recognition of a new financial asset or liability. When this occurs IAS 39 requires recognition of the new financial asset or liability at fair value and the recognition of a gain or loss on the transaction based on the difference between:

- the proceeds
- and the carrying amount of the financial asset sold plus the fair value of any new financial liability assumed, minus the fair value of any new financial asset acquired and plus or minus any adjustment that had been previously reported in equity to reflect the fair value of that asset.

Derecognition of a financial liability

Derecognition of a financial liability is also relatively straightforward. We remove the financial liability from the balance sheet when the obligation specified in the contract is discharged, cancelled or expires. Occasionally, one financial liability will be exchanged for a similar one with the same lender, if the terms of the new agreement are substantially different from the old then the old is derecognized and the new recognized. The problem with this requirement from the Standard, para. 61, is that we need to set boundaries to 'substantially'. The Application Guidance to the Standard at para. 62 states the following:

> The terms are substantially different if the discounted present value of the cash flows, under the new terms, including any fees paid net of any fees received, is at least 10% different from the discounted present value of the remaining cash flows of the original debt instrument.

Hedging

The Standard takes 30 paragraphs to deal with this issue and we recommend you read the Standard in detail if you want complete information on this issue. Hedging is about offsetting the loss or potential loss on one item against the gain or potential gain on another. The loss or gain on the hedging arises from changes in fair values or cash flows. The rules in relation to hedging are complex because IAS 39 does not require all financial instruments to be carried at fair value. Remember loans and receivables originated by the enterprise and held to maturity as investments are carried at amortized cost. Only financial assets and liabilities held for trading and available for sale, financial assets and derivatives are carried at fair value. Thus, the Standard permits the use of hedging where derivatives are designated as the hedge instrument but only permits non-derivatives to hedge a foreign currency risk. The hedging relationship only qualifies for the special accounting arrangements in IAS 39 if:

- formal documentation of the detail of the hedge relationship exists
- the hedge is expected to be highly effective or highly probable
- the effectiveness of the hedge can be reliably measured.

These requirements need full expansion in the standard to ensure consistency and comparability in the application of the hedging allowance. This expansion covers numerous detailed paragraphs.

Hedged relationships are of three types:

1 fair value hedge where the change in fair value of the asset or liability is hedged
2 cash flow hedge where the variability to cash flows in the hedged item is hedged
3 foreign currency hedge, which we consider in Chapter 25.

Fair value hedges

For fair value hedges the gain or loss from remeasuring the hedging instrument at fair value is recognized immediately in net profit or loss and the gain or loss on the hedged item is recognized immediately in net profit or loss.

Activity 16.10

On 1 January 20X0 a fixed interest debt security is purchased by an enterprise for $100. Its current fair value at 31 December 20X0 is $110. The investment is regarded as an available for sale financial asset and the enterprise adopts the policy of equity accounting on remeasurement. The enterprise acquires a derivative asset on 31 December 20X0. By 31 December 20X1 the fair value of the derivative has increased by $4 but the security has reduced to $105.

Show the accounting entries if:

1 no hedging is designated
2 the derivative is designated as a hedge as from 1 January 20X1.

Activity feedback

1 The investment would be shown at fair value at 31.12.X0 and 31.12.X1 as $110 and $105 respectively. The first-year gain of $10 and second-year loss of $5 would both be taken to equity. The increase in the fair value of the derivative would also be taken to equity. Thus at 31.12.X1 the balance sheet will show an investment at $105, a derivative at $4 and over the two years a change in equity year 1 of $10 and year 2 of $1.
2 For the first year the increase in fair value of the investment will be taken to equity as before and the balance sheet will record a fair value of $110. For the second year the loss on the investment of $5 will be taken to net profit and loss and hedged by the increase from the derivative of $4. At 31.12.X1 the balance sheet will show an investment at $105, a derivative at $4, and a −$1 effect on the net profit or loss.

The hedging accounting rules force the gains or losses on the FIs through the profit or loss account but these are offset by the loss or gain on the hedge.

Cash flow hedges

For cash flow hedges that portion of the gain or loss on the hedging instrument which is determined to be an effective hedge should be recognized directly in equity, as follows: the component of equity associated with the hedged item should be adjusted to the lower of (a) the fair value of the cumulative change in expected future cash flows of the hedged item from the inception of the hedge and (b) the cumulative gain or loss on the hedging instrument needed to offset the cumulative change in expected cash flows of the hedged item from the inception of the hedge. Any remaining gain or loss on the hedging instrument constitutes the ineffective portion and should be reported (a) if the hedging instrument is a derivative, immediately in net profit or loss, and (b) if the hedging instrument is not a derivative, in accordance with the requirement for reporting fair value remeasurement gains and losses for the type of instrument involved.

The following should help to illustrate the difference in treatment between a fair value hedge and a cash flow hedge.

> ## Illustration
>
> An export sale is made at a price denominated in foreign currency for which an account receivable is raised payable in 90 days. In addition a 90-day foreign exchange contract to hedge the foreign currency exposure is taken out. The hedge can be designated as either a fair value or a cash flow hedge.
>
> Under normal foreign currency transaction rules the sale will be recorded at the spot rate at the day of sale and the receivable will be restated during the 90-day period with any difference being taken to net profit or loss.
>
> However, if the foreign exchange contract is designated as a fair value hedge, then the gain or loss from remeasuring the forward exchange contract at fair value is also recognized in the net profit or loss thereby offsetting the gain or loss on the receivable.
>
> If the foreign exchange contract is designated as a cash flow hedge then the portion of the gain or loss that is determined to be an effective hedge is recognized directly in equity and the ineffective portion in net profit and loss. When the receivable remeasurement gain or loss is recognized in net profit and loss then the effective portion of the hedge is transferred from equity to profit.

Activity 16.11

1 An enterprise plans to issue a fixed rate debt in six months. The forecasted issue is hedged by a eurodollar future derivative. At the end of the six months the derivative has losses of $2m and the forecasted debt issuance has accumulated $1.8m of positive expected future cash flows at fair value (i.e. after discounting).

2 On 4.1.X0 the enterprise has a forecasted sale of 500 tonnes of wheat, cost £1m, which is expected to occur on 31.12.X0. On 4.1.X0 a hedge is designated against the cash flows of the forecasted sale. The hedge is a future contract (derivative) to sell 500 tonnes at £1.1m on 31.12.X0. On 31.12.X0 the derivative has a fair value of £25 000 and is closed. The inventory is sold by the enterprise at £1 075 000 on 31.12.X0.

Show how both these cash flow hedges should be accounted for.

Activity feedback

1 The ineffective part of the hedge, $200 000, will be recognized as a loss immediately. The remainder of the hedged loss of $1.8m is recognized in equity. When the debt is issued and the hedge cleared the $1.8m is transferred out of equity and recorded as a reduction to the debt. Thus the debt is recorded as issued at a discount.

2 The wheat future is entered in the books at £25 000 as an asset with the gain of £25 000 taken to equity. This gain remains in equity until the forecasted sale takes place. When the inventory sale occurs on 31.12.X0, £75 000 profit will be shown in the net profit and loss. At the same time £25 000 will be transferred from equity to profit making a total profit of £100 000. The total cash flow will be £1.1m, £1 075 000 from the sale and £25 000 from the hedge as cash is received from the hedge on 31.12.X0.

All of this is quite complicated and requires judgement as to the effectiveness of the hedge at the outset. This 'effectiveness' also needs to be kept under review throughout the life of the hedge and the accounting changed if it is no longer effective. A hedge is normally regarded as effective if expected changes in the hedged item are almost fully offset by changes in the hedging instrument. The actual results need to be in the range of 80% to 125%.

Foreign entity investment hedges

Hedges of a net investment in a foreign entity are accounted for in a similar fashion to cash flow hedges. Thus the gain or loss on the hedging instrument is recognized immediately in equity. On recognition of the foreign currency translation gain or loss the hedging gain or loss will be recognized in the same manner.

Presentation and disclosure

The presentation and disclosure requirements in relation to financial instruments are detailed in IAS 32, which was revised in 1998 and further revised under the Board's improvement project, and are added to in relation to hedging by those of IAS 39. IAS 32 covers 100 paragraphs and has 40 paragraphs of Application Guidance, so we advise you to read it in detail. The requirements for presentation and disclosure cover:

- classification of the FI as a liability or equity using substance over form
- separate classification of component parts of the FI in equity and liabilities
- reporting of interest, dividends, losses and gains from a FI
- offsetting of a financial asset and a financial liability that can only occur if there is a legally enforceable right to offset or if the enterprise intends to settle on a net basis or to realize the asset and settle the liability simultaneously
- disclosure such that understanding of the significance of on balance sheet and off balance sheet FIs on an enterprise's financial position, performance and cash flows is given to users
- disclosure of risk management policies of an enterprise including its policy for hedging
- disclosure of terms, conditions and accounting policies in relation to all financial assets, financial liabilities and equity
- exposure to interest rate risk and credit risk in all financial assets and financial liabilities
- information on fair values for example method used to determine fair value
- description of hedging instruments.

Possible revisions to IAS 39

IAS 39 as it now stands permits users the option of designating all financial assets and liabilities at fair value with gains and losses recognized in the profit or loss. The IASB is now preparing to change this option as it is possible that it might be used inappropriately. The proposal would limit the fair value option to five specified cases with an additional restriction that the fair value should be verifiable. The five specified cases are:

1 financial assets and liabilities that contain embedded derivatives
2 financial liabilities whose cash flows are contractually linked to the performance of assets measured at fair value

3 case when the exposure to changes in the fair value of the financial asset or liability is substantially offset by the exposure to the changes in the fair value of another asset or financial liability

4 financial assets other than loans and receivables

5 items for which other standards allow the option to be applied.

For the verifiable test the IASB are proposing that this would be met if the variability in the range of reasonable fair value estimates made in accordance with IAS 39 is low. Let us hope that we receive some clarification of 'low' in the final Standard.

One issue you might like to debate in relation to FIs is that of realization. Historically, the principal driver of recognition of gains has been the realization concept, but perhaps this is unrealistic in a marketplace involving complex financial instruments that trade on the basis of their underlying risks.

IFRS 4, *Insurance contracts*

Introduction

Before the issue of IFRS 4, *Insurance Contracts*, in March 2004 there was no International Accounting Standard to deal with the diverse practices of insurance contract accounting. The IASC had established a steering committee in 1997 to investigate the issues surrounding insurance contracts but the IASB did not really discuss the matter until 2001. As with many other controversial issues, the IASB has split the project for insurance contracts into two:

> *Phase I* **(a)** to make limited improvements to accounting practices for insurance contracts without requiring major changes that may need to be reversed in phase II
>
> **(b)** to require disclosure that (i) identifies and explains the amounts in an insurer's financial statements arising from insurance contracts and (ii) helps users of those financial statements understand the amount, timing and uncertainty of future cash flows from insurance contracts. Phase I resulted in IFRS 4, which is basically a presentation and disclosure Standard.
>
> *Phase II* will be concerned with the recognition and measurement of an insurance contract.

The basic issue with an insurance contract is determining the risks and rewards in the contract and who in substance owns them and in addition how to treat payments received and made within the contract.

Insurance contract

As defined by IFRS 4, this is a contract under which one party (the insurer) accepts significant insurance risk from another party (the policyholder) by agreeing to compensate the policyholder if a specified uncertain future event (the insured event) adversely affects the policyholder.

Several terms used in the above definition are also defined in IFRS 4:

> *Insurance risk:* risk, other than financial risk, transferred from the holder of a contract to the issuer

Insured event: an uncertain future event that is covered by an insurance contract and creates insurance risk.

Risk is the essence of an insurance contract and as such at least one of the following will be uncertain at the inception of the contract:

1 whether an insured event will occur
2 when it will occur
3 and how much the insurer will need to pay if it occurs.

For example, insurance against theft or damage to property is an insurance contract as 1) and 2) above are uncertain and the contract will compensate the policyholder for the loss or damage, albeit generally to a limited amount. Life insurance is also deemed an insurance contract under IFRS 4, as, although death is certain, the timing is uncertain.

Activity 16.12

Identify which of the following are insurance contracts:

(a) compensation in cash or kind to contract holders for losses suffered while travelling
(b) financial guarantee contract that requires payment even if the holder has not insured a loss on the failure of the debtor to make payments when due
(c) deferred annuity contract where holder will receive or can elect to receive a life contingent annuity at rates prevailing when the annuity begins
(d) a contract that requires specified payments to reimburse the holder for a loss it incurs because a specified debtor fails to make payment when due
(e) a catastrophe bond in which principal, interest payments or both are reduced significantly if a specified triggering event occurs and the triggering event includes a condition that the issuer of the bond suffered a loss
(f) loan contract containing a pre-payment fee that is waived if pre-payment results from the borrower's death.

Activity feedback

(a), (d) and (e) are insurance contracts.

In (b) there is no specified uncertain future event, the payment is required whatever happens to the debt. In (c) the insurer can reprice the mortality risk. It will become an insurance contract only when the annuity rate is fixed. Before the contract in (f), the borrower faced no risk corresponding to the pre-payment fee thus no risk has been transferred.

Disclosure

IFRS 4 requires disclosure of:

1 information that identifies and explains the amounts in its financial statements arising from insurance contracts
2 information that helps users to understand the amount, timing and uncertainty of future cash flows from insurance contracts.

Under 1 accounting policies, recognized assets, liabilities, income and expense will be disclosed as well as processes used to determine assumptions within these amounts and the effects of changes in these assumptions. Under 2 terms and conditions of the insurance contract that have a material effect on the cash flows of the insurer, and actual claims compared with previous estimates, will be disclosed.

Unbundling of deposit components

Some insurance contracts contain both an insurance component and a deposit component. A deposit component is defined by IFRS 4 as:

> A contractual component that is not accounted for as a derivative under IAS 39 and would be within the scope of IAS 39 if it were a separate instrument. This requirement ensures that assets and liabilities are not omitted from the balance sheet.

Illustration

A policyholder pays premiums of €100 every year for 5 years. The policy provider establishes an experience account equal to 90% of the cumulative premiums (including additional payments as below) less 90% of cumulative claims. If the experience account is negative (claims exceed premiums) the policyholder has to pay an additional payment equal to the experience account balance divided by the number of years left to run on the contract. At the end of the contract if the experience account is positive (premiums exceed claims) it is refunded to the policyholder; if the balance is negative that amount is paid to the insurer. Other terms of the contract are that it cannot be cancelled before maturity and maximum loss of the insurer in any one period is €2000.

This contract is obviously an insurance contract as significant risk is transferred to the insurer and there is uncertainty in respect of the experience account as the claims are uncertain. Let us assume that in the above case there are no claims by the policyholder during the five-year period, then at the end of the five years the policyholder will receive €450 (90% of cumulative premiums of €500). In substance, the policyholder has made a loan to the insurer, which is repaid in one instalment in year five, thus we need to unbundle the loan and the insurance contract. We therefore need to measure the loan advance each year at fair value in accordance with IAS 39. Assuming a discount rate of 10%, and that the insurance premium is equal in each year, then each payment of €100 is made up of a loan advance of €67 (see data that follow) and premium of €33.

Year	Opening balance	10% interest	advance	Closing balance
0	0	0	67	67
1	67	6.7	67	140.7
2	140.7	14.1	67	221.8
3	221.8	22.2	67	311
4	311	31.1	67	409.1
5	409.1	40.9	(450)	–
Total		**115**	**(115)**	

Other main features of IFRS 4 are:

1 The standard exempts an insurer temporarily (until Phase II of the project is complete) from some requirements of other IFRSs.
2 Permits an insurer to change its accounting policies but only if the resulting financial statements would be more relevant but no less reliable or vice versa.
3 Permits insurers to introduce an accounting policy that would see the insurance liabilities in each period reflected at market interest rates.
4 Does not require the insurer to change its accounting policies even if they are excessively prudent.
5 When an insurer changes its accounting policies for insurance liabilities, it may reclassify some or all financial assets as 'at fair value through profit or loss', i.e. at the date of change the financial asset is measured at fair value with any gain or loss from the carrying amount reflected in profit or loss.

Summary

A complicated chapter.

Table 16.4, summarizing the current major requirements of IAS 39 (excluding hedged items) might be useful for you. The table clearly shows that full fair value

Table 16.4 Summary of current major requirements of IAS 39

	Loans and receivables originated by the enterprise	Held to maturity investments	Financial assets held for trading	Available for sale financial assets	Financial liabilities held for trading	Financial asset or financial liability at fair value through profit or loss account (option)
Recognition	When becomes a party to the transaction					
Derecognition	When loses control of contractual rights				When obligation discharged, cancelled or expired	When loses control of contractual rights
Gain or loss on derecognition	To net profit for period					
Initial measurement	Cost equals fair value of consideration given or received					
Subsequent measurement	At cost less amortization	At cost less amortization	At fair value subject to rebuttable assumption re reliable estimation	At fair value subject to rebuttable assumption re reliable estimation	At fair value with minor exceptions	At fair value subject to rebuttable assumption re relative estimation
Gain or loss on remeasurement	N/A	N/A	To income	To equity	To income	To income

accounting for financial assets and liabilities is still not a requirement of IAS 39 on initial recognition. In addition, IAS 39 has introduced an option whereby entities can designate a financial asset or liability as 'at fair value through profit or loss account' and measure it at fair value for the whole period of its recognition.

Derivatives are always assumed to be held for trading, unless specifically designated as effective hedges. The information required to be kept and disclosed in respect of hedging instruments is substantial. Hedging instruments, if they are not effective hedges, will increase the volatility of earnings as the ineffective hedge will be recorded immediately in earnings. Remember that hedge accounting has the effect that an asset or liability that would otherwise be measured on a cost basis is measured on a fair value basis and the gain or loss is taken to profit and loss either immediately or via recycling at a later date.

IFRS 4 fills a gap in international accounting standards but it is a stopgap until Phase II of the project on insurance contracts is complete. This is not expected until 2007 at the very earliest. IFRS 4 has not eliminated the diverse practices in accounting for insurance contracts, but it has ensured there will be more disclosure to improve comparability and provide risk information. However, IFRS 4 has defined an insurance contract, this definition it is intended will continue into Phase II of the project, which will provide more consistency. The biggest challenge for Phase II of the project is the decision whether or not to apply fair value measurement to insurance liabilities. Given the problems this fair value measurement has presented in IAS 39, the IASB will need to tread carefully and consult widely to ensure the result provides useful information to users that has the characteristics of relevance, reliability, comparability and understandability.

EXERCISES

(✔ indicates answers are available on page 729)

  ✔ **1** Discuss the problems faced by users of financial reports if financial instruments are kept off balance sheet.

  2 What is a financial instrument?

  3 How does the IASB determine differentiation between financial instruments and other assets and liabilities?

  4 What is a derivative?

  5 Discuss the IASB's metholodgy for the recognition of gains and losses on remeasurement of financial instruments to fair value and illustrate the effects on the income statement.

  6 Appraise the effect of using settlement date accounting as opposed to trade date accounting for regular way contracts.

  7 Discuss the proposal by the IASB to move to full fair value accounting for financial instruments and identify the effects this move would have on an enterprise's income statement and balance sheet.

  ✔ **8** It is unrealistic to apply the realization concept to complex financial instruments. Discuss.

Revenue

After studying this chapter you should be able to:
- □ define revenue and what type of transactions it arises from
- □ determine when it should be recognized by an enterprise
- □ explain how it should be measured
- □ critically appraise IAS 18 in relation to revenue recognition and measurement
- □ identify the disclosure requirements in respect of revenue in accordance with IAS 18
- □ compare IAS GAAP with other GAAPs.

Introduction

The income statement reports the profit of an enterprise by matching expenses to revenues, but before we can carry out this matching we need to define revenues and expenses and identify at what point we should recognize them. Many standards that we have already considered are about the expense side of these issues but as yet we have given very little consideration to the revenue.

Chapter 8 dealt with the general principles in respect of revenue but this chapter will consider them in more detail and also IAS 18, *Revenue*. IAS 18 was originally issued in 1982 and revised in 1993 and is effective for financial statements covering periods beginning on or after 1 January 1995. It is worth noting at this point that neither the US nor the UK has a specific standard on 'revenue'.

What is revenue?

The Framework for the Preparation and Presentation of Financial Statements defines income as increases in economic benefits during the accounting period in the form of inflows or enhancements of assets or decreases of liabilities that result in increases in equity, other than those relating to contributions from equity participants. It further states that income encompasses both revenues and gains. Revenues are further described as arising in the course of the ordinary activities of an enterprise. So what is this revenue and how do we distinguish it from other gains?

Revenue is regarded by many as simply the cash that you are paid for selling things and this simple idea also implies exchange – cash for things. We have also carried this idea of exchange through to the balance sheet. Consider the simple exchange of selling an item of inventory for cash, the accounting entries would be to derecognize the item of inventory in the balance sheet and recognize the asset of cash. The asset of cash would qualify as revenue and against this we would match relevant expenses to determine profit. Traditionally, we have not regarded the item of inventory as revenue until it is sold or at least until we have exchanged it for another asset, perhaps a debtor. This approach seems to equate revenue with economic activity involving exchange with a customer and ignores other items such as gains on assets that are revalued or carried at current value.

IAS 18 (para. 7) defines revenue as:

> The gross inflow of economic benefits during the period arising in the course of the ordinary activities of an enterprise when those inflows result in increases in equity, other than increases relating to contributions from equity participants.

There are several important notions in this definition.

1 Revenue is the *gross inflow*, i.e. before the deduction of any expenses. We must also presume that this gross inflow is to the enterprise although it isn't specifically stated in the definition.
2 Revenue results from ordinary activities. This notion distinguishes revenue from other gains. Gains are defined in the framework as 'other items that meet the definition of income and may, or may not, arise in the ordinary activities of an enterprise'.
3 Revenue gives rise to an increase in equity.

Activity 17.1

An enterprise receives €100 for the sale of an item of inventory. This amount includes a sales tax at 25% on cost which is payable to the tax authorities. The enterprise also sells another item of inventory on behalf of an agent for which it only retains a 10% commission charge on sale price. Identify the revenue to the enterprise in both cases in accordance with the IAS 18 definition.

Activity feedback

The first item of inventory only results in an increase in equity of €80, the other €20 is paid directly to the tax authorities and is effectively collected by us on their behalf.

The second item of inventory has only generated revenue and subsequent increase in equity to the enterprise of €10. The other €90 is collected on behalf of the agent.

Activity 17.2

Two enterprises both sell an item of real estate (cost €1m) for €2m. One enterprise operates in the chemical industry; the other is a property development company. Identify the revenue for both enterprises.

Activity feedback

For the chemical enterprise the income of €2m will be regarded as a gain as the sale of real estate is not regarded as part of the ordinary activities. For the property development company the income of €2m would be regarded as revenue.

Activity 17.3

The following transactions occur in an accounting period for A enterprise:

■ 1m €1 shares are issued at a premium on nominal value of €2
■ property is sold for €2m
■ the enterprise deals in the retail of widgets and makes sales of €150 000, 50% of which are on credit.

Identify the revenue for the enterprise in accordance with IAS 18 for the period.

Activity feedback

All these transactions give rise to an increase in equity but only the last is regarded as revenue. The share issue is income received from equity participants and the second is not part of the ordinary activities of the enterprise.

What does revenue arise from?

So far we have defined revenue as arising from exchange transactions that give rise to gross inflows from ordinary activities. However, exchange transactions, as we have already seen, can take many forms and we need to consider whether all of them or only some give rise to revenue.

Exchange transactions can be viewed as contracts between a seller and a buyer but would we regard interest received and royalties as part of such an exchange contract and therefore revenue?

Interest received results from the use by another of enterprise cash or cash equivalent and thus we have an exchange contract that gives rise to an increase in equity, and therefore the interest can be regarded as revenue. Note that when the principal element of the loan is repaid this will not be regarded as revenue as it will not result in an increase in equity, only an asset of cash replacing the debt. Royalties are similar, as they are charges for the use of long-term assets of the enterprise such as copyrights, patents, trademarks etc.

IAS 18 states that revenue arises from three types of transaction and event:

■ the sale of goods
■ the rendering of service
■ the use by others of enterprise assets yielding interest, royalties and dividends.

There is some revenue that the Standard does not deal with and this is generally that which is dealt with by another standard e.g. construction contracts, leases, dividends from associated companies, changes in the fair value of financial assets and liabilities or their disposal (dealt with under financial instruments). Changes in other non-current assets, extraction of mineral ores, insurance contracts of insurance enterprises and natural increases in herds, agricultural and forestry products are also outside the scope of IAS 18.

In determining whether or not a sale has been made or a service has been rendered the Standard requires us to determine whether certain conditions have been met before we recognize revenue.

Recognition

Activity 17.4

An enterprise transfers assets to a customer as follows:

- €2000 of bottles of wine in exchange for €2000 cash with the option for the customer to return as many of the bottles, unopened, within seven days and claim a refund of the cash paid for each.
- €200 of glasses in exchange for €50 cash where the customer is required to return all glasses within seven days or pay the full price for them.

Identify in each case whether a sale has occurred and therefore whether revenue should be recognized.

Activity feedback

The answer here involves us looking at the substance of the transactions and deciding whether the customer, on receipt of the asset, has acquired the associated risks and rewards of the asset.

In the case of the wine it would seem that the customer has received the risks and rewards associated with it, but do we recognize all the €2000 or do we only recognize 90% of it, assuming it is normal that 10% is returned. Alternatively, we could delay the recognition of the revenue until the return time has expired.

In the case of the glasses the customer is not acquiring all the risks and rewards associated with them, only a very limited proportion of them. Indeed, the enterprise retains effective control over them.

Sale of goods
IAS 18 identifies several criteria that must be met before revenue can be recognized on sale of goods as follows:

- the enterprise has transferred to the buyer the significant risks and rewards of ownership of the goods
- the enterprise retains neither continuing managerial involvement to the degree usually associated with ownership nor effective control over the goods sold
- the amount of revenue can be measured reliably
- it is probable that the economic benefits associated with the transaction will flow to the enterprise
- the costs incurred or to be incurred in respect of the transaction can be measured reliably.

Activity 17.5

Identify, for the following transactions, if and when the risks and rewards associated with the transaction have passed between the parties concerned:

1 A publisher sells books to a retailer on sale or return. If the books are not sold the retailer returns them to the publisher for a refund. It is impossible to estimate reliably how many books will remain unsold.

2 A retailer offers a 12-month guarantee on all its products whereby a customer can return the product for whatever reason and have a full refund. In the normal course of business it has been found that 1% per annum of sales are subject to such refunds.

3 A software house develops a customized finance system for a customer. Title to the software passes to the customer on a given date but included in the agreement is a three-month warranty period beyond this date to cover the need for any amendments or debugging of the system. It is impossible to estimate the potential for these costs.

4 A piece of machinery is sold by Alpha enterprise to Beta for €100 000. In addition Beta is required to pay €75 000 to Alpha for the installation of the machinery. The machinery is inoperable without installation.

5 Alpha sells another machine to Gamma but under an agreement that allows Gamma to return the machine if a contract Gamma is seeking, and for which it needs the machine, is not won. No information is available on the likelihood of Gamma's winning the contract.

Activity feedback

1 In this example, the receipt of revenue to the publisher is dependent on the derivation of revenue by the retailer from the sale of the goods and thus the risks and rewards do not pass until the retailer has sold the books. This would not be regarded as a sale and revenue would only be recognized when the books are sold by the retailer.

2 In this case the retailer retains very little risk associated with the products and therefore revenue should be recognized when the sale is made and an accrual made for the expected returns.

3 Legal title has passed to the customer but the risks and rewards still remain with the developer until the end of the three-month period. Revenue will not be recognized until the end of the three-month period.

4 This sale will not be completed until the installation, which is a material part of the cost, is complete. Revenue will be recognized on completion of installation.

5 Revenue cannot be recognized by Alpha until and if Gamma wins the contract.

The Standard provides other examples of when to recognize revenue on sale of goods in an appendix. This covers such things as 'bill and hold' sale – where the buyer accepts the billing for the product but the products are left with the seller until the buyer requests delivery – goods shipped subject to conditions, lay away sales, orders when payment is received in advance, sale and repurchase agreements, sales to intermediate parties, subscription sales, instalment sales and real estate sales.

It is worth noting at this stage that the recognition of revenue on sale of goods involves management in a subjective decision, i.e. revenue is recognized when significant risks and rewards have been transferred to the buyer.

Rendering of services

Criteria for recognition are also required for rendering of services.

Activity 17.6

Suggest criteria for the recognition of revenue from services rendered.

Activity feedback

The criteria are quite similar to those for sale of goods:

- The amount of revenue can be measured reliably.
- It is probable that the economic benefits associated with the transaction will flow to the enterprise.
- The stage of completion of the transaction at the balance sheet date can be measured reliably.
- The costs incurred for the transaction and the costs to complete the transaction can be measured reliably.

The stage of completion criterion is most important here.

Illustration

Alpha has a contract with Beta to provide daily security services for a period of three years. The contract involves payment by Beta of €10 000 per annum and commences at Alpha's opening balance sheet date.

At each balance sheet date Alpha will recognize revenue of €10 000 for the period of three years as this is in line with the performance of the service.

Illustration

A recruitment agency has a contract with Gamma to seek and appoint a new chief executive. The contract is for a period of 18 months. On the appointment of the CE the agency will receive a payment of €25 000.

This revenue will not be recognized by the agency until the service is actually rendered, that is, the CE is appointed. The specific act of finding the CE is the significant factor that results in revenue and therefore this service would not be recognized on a straight line basis over the period of the contract.

This stage of completion recognition of revenue is often referred to as percentage-of-completion method (see Chapter 15). The percentage of completion can be estimated by one of several methods but management must choose the most reliable. The methods available are:

- surveys of work performed
- services performed to date as a percentage of total services to be performed

■ the proportion that costs incurred to date bear to the estimated total costs of the transaction.

If the revenue cannot be measured reliably for a service then revenue should only be recognized to the extent that costs incurred can be recovered. If the costs cannot be recovered then these are recognized as an expense.

Interest, royalties and dividends
The criteria for recognition of these are:

■ It is probable that the economic benefits associated with the transaction will flow to the enterprise.
■ The amount of revenue can be measured reliably.

IAS 18 also specifies the period over which these amounts are recognized: 'Interest should be recognized on a time proportion basis that takes into account the effective yield on the asset.' The effective yield is the rate of interest required to discount the stream of future cash receipts expected over the life of the asset to the initial carrying amount of the asset. An example of this is given in Activity 17.9.

'Royalties should be recognized on an accrual basis in accordance with the substance of the relevant agreement.' Generally, royalty payments are based on time or sales. If it is time based then the revenue should be recognized on the same time base. If sales based then revenue is recognized, say, on the budgeted sales with an adjustment to reflect actual sales at the year end.

'Dividends should be recognized when the shareholder's right to receive payment is established.' This means that the revenue in this case is recognized in accordance with legal form rather than substance.

How should it be measured?

'Revenue is measured at the fair value of the consideration received or receivable' (IAS 18, para. 9). This sounds simple enough and as fair value is the amount for which an asset could be exchanged or a liability settled between knowledgeable, willing partners in an arm's length transaction then we would measure the revenue after trade discounts, early payment discounts or volume rebates.

A problem does arise, however, in the case where revenue is not received by the seller for a period of time. In this case, the consideration eventually received, due to the time value of money, will be less than that originally agreed. It is therefore necessary for the nominal amount of revenue to be discounted where there would be a material difference in the amount received due to the time value of money. The question then needing an answer is 'what discount rate should be used?' The Standard answers as follows:

The imputed rate of interest is the more clearly determinable of either:

■ the prevailing rate for a similar instrument of an issuer with a similar credit rating; or
■ a rate of interest that discounts the nominal amount of the instrument to the current cash sales price of the goods or services.

Activity 17.7

An enterprise sells a product to another under an agreement that allows for payment to be made by a series of annual instalments of €4000 for four years. The product generally sells for cash €16 000. The buyer would, under normal circumstances, be able to obtain finance at a cost of 10% per annum. (Note the buyer is acquiring the product under a 0% financing agreement.) Identify the revenue to be recognized at the outset by the seller and any other accounting entries to be made over the five-year period.

Activity feedback

The revenue must be recognized at fair value which equates to discounting the cash payments made at 10%. The buyer has received the product at a discounted price from normal sale value of €10 000. A corresponding debtor would be raised at the date of sale. As the instalments are received these will be split between the principal amount which reduces the debt and an amount of interest which will be recognized as revenue.

It is often the case that goods or services are swapped, not for cash, but for other goods and/or services. These swaps, barter transactions, can occur of both like and dissimilar products. We need to determine whether or not these barter transactions should be treated as revenue and, if they are, how that revenue should be measured.

Where the products are alike, which generally occurs for commodities such as milk, gas or oil where suppliers exchange inventories in different locations to fulfil demand, then the exchange is not regarded as one which generates revenue by IAS 18. Where products are dissimilar then, according to IAS 18, revenue is generated and should be measured at the fair value of the goods or services received or, if this cannot be reliably measured, then at the fair value of the goods or services given up.

Activity 17.8

Explain the basis of the logic used by IAS 18 in accounting for barter transactions.

Activity feedback

IAS 18 defines revenue as a gross inflow of economic benefits that should be recognized when an enterprise has transferred to the buyer the significant risks and rewards of ownership of the goods.

In a barter transaction involving the exchange of oil in Saudi Arabia for oil in Russia, barter of similar products, then the enterprises involved are not in a substantially different position to that before the exchange assuming that the barter was a fair exchange. Each will still have the same risks associated with the oil and neither party will actually have been rewarded. There is no revenue, because, in substance there is no sale.

In the situation involving different products then the barter will result in each enterprise placing itself in a different position in its operating cycle. Each enterprise has reached the end of the operating cycle in relation to its product and dispensed with the risks and rewards associated with that product. In exchange they have started on the operating cycle in relation to the new product and are now subject to the new risks and rewards associated with it. So revenue does exist and will be measured by each enterprise at the fair value of the goods it has received.

In relation to barter transactions involving advertising a specific SIC, SIC 31, Barter *Transactions Involving Advertising Services*, has been issued. The SIC is concerned with the fair value of the revenue and states that:

> The revenue in these transactions can only be reliably measured by reference to non-barter transactions that:
>
> - involve advertising similar to the advertising in the barter transaction;
> - occur frequently;
> - represent a predominant number of transactions and amount when compared to non-barter transactions to provide advertising that is similar to the advertising in barter transactions;
> - involve cash and/or another form of consideration (e.g. marketable securities) that has a reliably measurable fair value; and
> - do not involve the same counterparty as in the barter transaction.

Transactions made up of parts

Transactions can often be made up of several components and to identify their substance we will need to unbundle them and recognize the revenue on the separate parts and perhaps at different times.

Activity 17.9

An enterprise sells a product plus a servicing agreement for three years for €15 000. The product without the servicing could be sold at fair value of €9000. At what point should any revenue be recognized?

Activity feedback

At the initial point of sale €9000 will be recognized as revenue, always assuming all other criteria have been met for recognition. The servicing revenue will be deferred and only be recognized when that service is rendered.

The following activity should test your understanding of this chapter.

Activity 17.10

Identify when the revenue, if indeed there is such, in the following transactions should be recognized:

1 commitment fees received by an enterprise to originate or purchase a loan
2 advertising media commissions carried out for a client where inflows will be received when the advert is exposed in the media
3 tuition fees paid to a training enterprise

4 servicing fees included in the price of a product sold by an enterprise
5 an enterprise sells all its inventory of wine to the bank with the option to repurchase the wine at any time it wishes and at a price that increases by 5% per annum on the original sale price.

Activity feedback

1 If it is unlikely that a specific loan agreement will be entered into then the commitment fee will be recognized on a time basis over the commitment period. Otherwise, the commitment fee will be recognized when both parties legally agree to the loan.
2 These will be recognized when the advertisement is seen by the public.
3 Revenue will need to be recognized over the period of tuition.
4 The servicing amount included in the price of the product is separated out and deferred and recognized as revenue over the period of service generally on a straight line basis.
5 In this case it seems apparent that the seller has not transferred the risks and rewards associated with the wine to the bank. In fact, the substance of the transaction is that of a loan guaranteed on the value of the wine. No revenue will be recognized in this case, as it is a financing arrangement.

Disclosure requirements

The disclosure requirements of IAS 18 are quite straightforward and what we would expect. They cover accounting policy adopted to recognize revenue, method of determining stage of completion of services, the amount of significant revenue from sale of goods, rendering of services, interest, royalties and dividends and the amount of revenue recognized from exchanges of goods or services.

GAAP comparisons

IAS is the only GAAP to have a specific Standard for revenue recognition. The IAS Framework defines income as including revenues and gains. The Standard defines revenues as the gross inflows of economic benefits during the period arising from the ordinary activities of an enterprise when the inflows result in an increase in equity, other than increases relating to contributions from equity participants.

All three frameworks, i.e. IASB, FASB and UK ASB, require measurement of revenues at fair value of consideration received or receivable and both IAS and UK permit discounting to present value where inflows are deferred. US GAAP does not permit this discounting.

UK GAAP does not define revenue but the Statement of Principles requires that a gain must be recognized if there is sufficient evidence that an asset has been created and the asset can be measured with sufficient reliability. Recognition occurs when a critical event in the operating cycle is reached, e.g. delivery of goods or services. It also states that in some cases it might be appropriate to recognize revenue earlier. In July 2001 the UK ASB issued a discussion paper entitled *Revenue Recognition* with the intention of provoking discussion, and with the longer term aim of establishing a framework within which to consistently address revenue issues that arise in different contexts.

US GAAP focuses on realization of revenue. Realization occurs when the transaction is converted into cash or cash equivalents or the likelihood of its receipt is reasonably certain.

Summary

We have seen throughout this chapter that the recognition of revenue, which is key in the determination of profit of an enterprise, is dependent on several factors. These factors also require judgements to be made by management, many of which will require subjectivity. Management has to take decisions on:

- What constitutes the ordinary activities of the enterprise.
- Whether or not significant risks and rewards of ownership have been transferred to a buyer.
- Whether the amount of revenue involved can be measured reliably, i.e. can its fair value be determined.
- If it is probable that economic benefits associated with the transaction (sale) will flow to the enterprise.
- Whether the costs in respect of the transaction can be measured reliably.
- What stage a particular service has reached in its delivery.

We have also seen that revenue is distinguished from income, which incorporates gains as well as revenue. Gains are generally seen as being those items that result from activities outside the ordinary activities of the enterprise, e.g. gains from the sale of non-current assets or upward revaluations of non-current assets.

All of this ensures that the revenue that is recognized in financial statements is reliable and prudent but it may not be very relevant in a business world where most production is sold. Currently, we do not recognize gains on stocks of goods for sale but it is arguable that this information would be relevant to users. All we provide them with is information on the cost of the product (or NRV, whichever is the lower) not information on what the asset of stock could be sold for assuming a reasonable marketplace.

Several commentators on IAS 18 believe it leaves substantial scope for interpretation, due to its 'principles base'. For several industrial sectors, neither the Standard nor its appendices includes any specific examples, e.g. telecoms, software. Currently, the IASB is working to replace IAS 18 but an exposure draft is unlikely to be ready before 2006.

EXERCISES   (✔ indicates answers are available on page 730)

  ✔ **1** What is revenue? Distinguish it from other gains.

    2 Useful information is provided to users by restricting the definition of revenue to that arising from ordinary activities only. Discuss.

  ✔ **3** IAS 18 is based on substance over form. Discuss.

4 Financial reports prepared under IAS 18 are irrelevant and unreliable. Discuss.

5 The IAS 18 method of revenue recognition proves that accountants are prudent. Discuss.

6 Explain the relationship between revenue recognition and asset valuation.

7 Analyse the need to discount deferred inflows to an enterprise as permitted by IAS 18.

✔ 8 Recognition of revenue in accordance with IAS 18 is objective. Discuss.

9 (a) Revenue recognition is the process by which companies decide when and how much income should be included in the income statement. It is a topical area of great debate in the accounting profession. The IASB looks at revenue recognition from conceptual and substance points of view. There are occasions where a more traditional approach to revenue recognition does not entirely conform to the IASB guidance; indeed neither do some International Accounting Standards.

Required:

Explain the implications that the IASB's Framework for the Preparation and Presentation of Financial Statements (Framework) and the application of substance over form have on the recognition of income. Give examples of how this may conflict with traditional practice and some accounting standards.

(b) Derringdo sells good supplied by Gungho. The goods are classed as A grade (perfect quality) or B grade, having slight faults. Derringdo sells the A grade goods acting as an agent for Gungho at a fixed price calculated to yield a gross profit margin of 50%. Derringdo receives a commission of 12.5% of the sales it achieves for these goods. The arrangement for B grade goods is that they are sold by Gungho to Derringdo and Derringdo sells them at a gross profit margin of 25%. The following information has been obtained from Derringdo's financial records:

		$000
Inventory held on premises 1 April 2002	– A grade	2 400
	– B grade	1 000
Goods from Gungho year to 31 March 2003	– A grade	18 000
	– B grade	8 800
Inventory held on premises 31 March 2003	– A grade	2 000
	– B grade	1 250

Required:

Prepare the income statement extracts for Derringdo for the year to 31 March 2003 reflecting the above information.   (ACCA June 03)

Provisions, contingent liabilities and contingent assets

After studying this chapter you should be able to:
- describe the issues IAS 37 attempts to address
- define provisions and contingencies
- account for provisions and contingencies in accordance with IAS 37
- appraise the recognition and measurement criteria of IAS 37
- describe the presentation requirements in relation to provisions and contingencies.

Introduction

Financial statements of all enterprises are prepared at an arbitrary date – the balance sheet date – which is a convenient cut-off point. However, no matter how sophisticated the information systems, judgements still have to be made concerning conditions existing at the balance sheet date with uncertain outcomes. In essence, IAS 37 deals with situations where obligations from an enterprise or to an enterprise are uncertain in either existence of event and/or amount of that event. The accounting or not for such conditions can have a marked effect on both the balance sheet and income statement of an enterprise.

Problems identified

Activity 18.1

PPR enterprise, a retailer of washing machines, has a year end of 31 December. During December a washing machine was sold to a customer who carried out the plumbing himself. On 24 December the washing machine failed to operate correctly, resulting in the customer's house suffering severe damage due to flooding. The customer, together with several relatives, had to spend the festive season in an hotel as his home was uninhabitable. The customer is planning to sue PPR for a considerable amount of damages. Would you as an accountant for PPR accrue a loss for the damages pending or not?

Activity feedback

The first question to answer is, is there a liability? A liability is 'a present obligation of the enterprise arising from past events, the settlement of which is expected to result in an outflow from the enterprise of resources embodying economic benefits' (IASB Framework; para. 49(b)). The problem here is that the outcome will presumably only be confirmed when the claim for damages is settled. What view should we take of the outcome of this claim? Will we have to pay out damages? If so, how much? Should we assume the claim will be found against the enterprise and estimate how much that claim will be and accrue in the income statement or not? The decision as to whether we do or not is likely to have a profound effect on profits if the claim is substantial.

The area of provisions and contingencies has led to substantial creative accounting within accounts and has given rise to the term 'big bath accounting' which is discussed in more detail in Part Four. The following activity illustrates this term.

Activity 18.2

An enterprise with annual expected future profits of €2.5m decides to recognize a provision (on the grounds of prudence) for reorganization costs for future years of €2m in the current year when its expected profits are €4.5m. The reorganization involves decentralization of all activities relating to purchases and sales to the enterprises' outlying units from the centre.

In the event the charges for the reorganization are 0.5m next year, €0.5m the following year and thereafter no further costs arise.

Show the effect of the proposed accounting treatment for the reorganization costs on the profits for the company for the current and future years. Comment on this treatment.

Activity feedback

	Year 1	Year 2	Year 3	Year 4
Provision b/f	0	2.0	1.5	0
Expense	0	(0.5)	(0.5)	0
Income statement charge	2.0	0	(1.0)	0
Provision c/f	2.0	1.5	0	0
Profits	4.5	2.5	2.5	2.5
Provision charged to income statement	(2.0)	0	1.0	0
Profit after provision	2.5	2.5	3.5	2.5

The enterprise has been able to charge the provision for the reorganization against the profits in the first year which were higher than generally expected. In future years the enterprise has been able to charge €0.5m to the provision instead of the income statement, thus profits in these year have not been reduced. In addition, as all the provision has not been required, the excess provision has been released back to the income statement in year 3 increasing profits to €3.5m. In effect, the enterprise has taken a 'big bath' in year 1 when it had substantial profits and has protected future years' profits.

Activities 18.1 and 18.2 show the potential for creativity in the provisions area and therefore the need for a standard on the issue. If recognition of a provision is further based on the intention to incur expenditure rather than an obligation to do so then this could create even more creativity in accounting. We could have the situation arising where a provision is provided, as for the reorganization costs just given, and then if this reorganization is not carried out the whole provision might be released to next year's profits. The recognition of such a provision does not reflect a change in economic position of the enterprise, since only an external commitment can affect the financial position at the balance sheet date. Without a complete framework for accounting for and disclosure of provisions users are not presented with a true and fair view of the state of affairs.

Provisions, contingent liabilities and contingent assets

IAS 37, issued by the IASB in 1998 operative for annual financial statements beginning on, or, after 1 July 1999 updated those parts of IAS 10, *Contingencies and Events occurring after the Balance Sheet Date* (1974) relating to contingencies but issued guidance also on provisions which were not covered by IAS 10.

IAS 37 effectively bans:

- big bath accounting
- creation of provisions where no obligation to a liability exists
- the use of provisions to smooth profits

and requires greater disclosure in relation to provisions to aid the user's understanding and present a true and fair view.

Scope

IAS 37 is to be applied to all enterprises when accounting for provisions, contingent liabilities and contingent assets except for those items resulting from executory contracts except where the contract is onerous, and those covered by another IAS. Examples of items covered by another IAS are IAS 11, *Construction Contracts*, and IAS 19, *Retirement Benefits*. Executory contracts also need some explanation. These are contracts where neither party has performed any of its obligations or both parties have partially performed obligations to an equal amount. The standard does not apply to financial instruments that are within the scope of IAS 39, *Financial Instruments: Recognition and Measurement*.

Activity 18.3

Identify an executory contract within an enterprise.

Activity feedback

Such contracts generally cover delivery of future services, e.g.:

- gas, electricity; local taxes

- purchase orders
- employee contributions in respect of continued employment.

It is also worth clarifying at this point certain 'provisions' that IAS 37 does not cover. This arises because IAS 37 uses the word provisions to mean a liability of uncertain timing or amount but in the general language of accounting it is common for the word provision to be applied to:

- provision for depreciation
- provision for doubtful debts
- provision for impairment.

In these cases the 'provision' is adjusting the carrying amount of the asset; it is not a liability of uncertain timing or amount.

Objectives

The objectives of IAS 37 are fairly clear and laudable. 'To ensure that appropriate recognition criteria and measurement bases are applied to provisions, contingent liabilities and contingent assets and that sufficient information is disclosed in the notes to the financial statements to enable users to understand their nature, timing and amount.'

Definitions

We have already identified two of these for you:

A provision is a liability of uncertain timing or amount.

A liability is a present obligation of the enterprise arising from past events, the settlement of which is expected to result in the outflow from the enterprise of resources embodying economic benefits.

(IAS 37, para. 10)

One of the key words in the definition of a liability is 'obligation'. So what is an obligation? An obligation can be either legal or constructive:

A legal obligation is an obligation that derives from:

(a) a contract (through its explicit or implicit terms);
(b) legislation; or
(c) other operation of law.

A contract can become onerous and this occurs when 'the unavoidable costs of meeting the obligations under the contract exceed the economic benefits expected to be received under it.'

(IAS 37, para. 10)

A constructive obligation is an obligation that derives from an enterprise's actions where:

(a) by an established pattern of past practice, published policies or a sufficiently specific current statement, the enterprise has indicated to other parties that it will accept certain responsibilities; and

(b) as a result the enterprise has created a valid expectation on the part of those other parties that it will discharge those responsibilities.

(IAS 37, para. 10)

Activity 18.4

Identify which of the following is a constructive obligation of the enterprise:

1 A, a leisure enterprise causes severe damage to the habitat of wildlife in a country where there is no legal protection for the wildlife. The company has a high profile in the support of wildlife as it makes large contributions to the World Wildlife Fund and campaigns vigorously on its behalf. To rectify the damage to the habitat a charge of €1m is likely.
2 An enterprise in the oil industry causes severe pollution when one of its tankers grounds off a Pacific island. The enterprise has avoided costs of cleaning up such contamination in the past and pays little regard to environmental issues.

Activity feedback

1 is a constructive obligation as there is a valid expectation that the enterprise will clean up the habitat.
2 is not a constructive obligation as no valid expectation has been created by the enterprise that it will repair the damage to the ocean.

A contingent liability is:

■ a possible obligation that arises from past events and whose existence will be confirmed only by the occurrence or non-occurrence of one or more uncertain future events not wholly within the control of the enterprise
■ or a present obligation that arises from past events but is not recognized because:
  – it is not probable that an outflow of resources embodying economic benefits will be required to settle the obligation
  – or the amount of the obligation cannot be measured with sufficient reliability.

Activity 18.5

Identify, in your own words, the key differences between a provision and a contingent liability.

Activity feedback

Provisions require:

■ a present obligation from past event
■ a probable outflow of economic benefits
■ an evaluation of timing and amount.

Contingent liabilities occur when one or more of the conditions for a provision are not met, i.e. either:

- a possible obligation from past event exists
- and/or an outflow of economic benefits is not probable
- and/or a reliable estimate of outflow cannot be made.

In essence, a contingent liability is a provision where one or more of the three requirements is not met. IAS 37 provides in an appendix a useful decision tree to determine whether a provision or contingent liability exists in a given set of circumstances and we reproduce this for you (Figure 18.1).

This is all rather confusing as a provision is, in fact, a liability which is contingent as its timing or amount is uncertain; but it is called a provision not a contingent liability. A contingent liability as defined by IAS 37 is by its name a liability but is not recognized as such as it is not charged in the accounts; it is only disclosed.

IAS 37 also defines a contingent asset for us as:

> A possible asset that arises from past events and whose existence will be confirmed only by the occurrence or non-occurrence of one or more uncertain future events not wholly within the control of the enterprise.
>
> (IAS 37, para. 10)

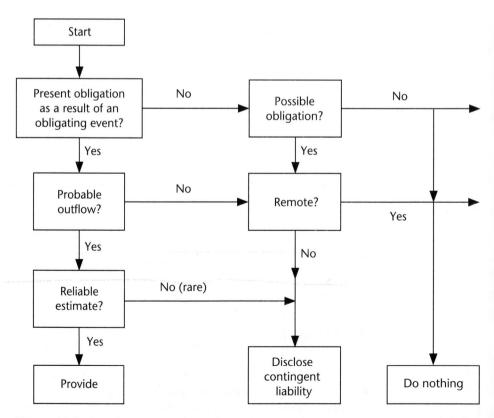

Figure 18.1 Decision tree to determine existence of provision or contingent liability

Accounting for provisions, contingent liabilities and contingent assets

If the conditions for a provision are met and a reliable estimate can be made of the amount then this amount will be recognized in the income statement for the year and shown as a provision on the balance sheet. A contingent liability is not recognized in the financial statements but it is disclosed as follows:

- a brief description of the nature
- an estimate of its financial effect
- an indication of the uncertainties relating to the amount or timing of outflow
- the possibility of any reimbursement.

A contingent asset is not recognized in the accounts but it is disclosed if the inflow of economic benefits is probable.

You should have noted by now that how we treat future inflow or outflow of economic benefits in the accounts is dependent on how we/management/experts define the words: probable, possible, remote. IAS 37 gives us no definitions of these three words. A standard English dictionary provides us with the following definitions:

probable – likely to be or to happen but not necessarily so

possible – feasible but less than probable

remote – distant, slight, faint.

Activity 18.6

Identify how the following items should be treated in the accounts of the enterprise at year end 31 December 20X1. All information is at year end 31 December 20X1 unless stated otherwise.

1 An airline enterprise is required by law to overhaul its aircraft once every three years. The aircraft were purchased a year ago.
2 An enterprise has guaranteed a loan taken out by one of its subsidiary enterprises. In March 20X1 the subsidiary placed itself in liquidation and there would appear to be insufficient funds to repay the loan.
3 An enterprise catered for a wedding reception in September 20X1. Subsequent to the wedding several people have died of food poisoning. The enterprise is disputing liability for the case brought against it by the relatives of the dead and its lawyers advise that it is probable that they will not be found liable.
4 An enterprise leases a factory under an operating lease. During the year it moves production of its products to a new factory but the old factory lease cannot be cancelled and it cannot be relet.
5 The government of the country in which an enterprise operates makes substantial changes to the health and safety legislation under which it must operate. The enterprise will have to retrain a large proportion of its staff to ensure compliance with the new legislation. No retraining has yet taken place.

6 An enterprise at the year end had discounted €600 000 bills of exchange without recourse. At 15 March 20X2 €150 000 were still outstanding and are due to mature in one month's time.

7 No bill has been received for electricity supplied in the last quarter of the year.

Activity feedback

1 At the current balance sheet date no obligation to overhaul the aircraft exists independent of the enterprise's future action. The enterprise could sell the aircraft to avoid the overhaul cost. This is not a provision neither is it a contingent liability.

2 The enterprise has an obligation to fulfil the guarantee given and it appears that an outflow of funds is probable. A provision should be recognized in the accounts.

3 There is no obligation and therefore no provision should be made. It is a contingent liability and a note should be made to the accounts unless the lawyers advise that the probability of any transfer of funds is extremely remote.

4 This is in fact an example of an onerous contract. There is a present legal obligation and a provision is required of the unavoidable lease payments in total. Prior to the contract becoming onerous it would have been treated in accordance with IAS 17, *Leases*.

5 There is no obligating event as no staff training has yet taken place and therefore no provision is recognized neither is there a contingent liability. The enterprise might need to consider whether there is a possibility it is placing itself in a situation where it will be fined for non-compliance with the new regulations and if this is the case, that is the legislation is already in force, then a provision may need to be made for the fines, if any, that could be imposed.

6 The bills of exchange are without recourse and therefore no liability falls on the enterprise.

7 This is an accrual as there is very little uncertainty in respect of the timing or the amount due.

There is an example in the Standard of an application to an offshore oilfield. In this example, an enterprise operating an oilrig has a legal obligation to remove the rig and clean up the site at the end of the oil extraction. The standard concludes that this cost should be charged as a provision at the outset of the operation. This appears to us to be in direct contrast to the example of the aircraft maintenance at point 1 in Activity 18.6. The oilrig could be sold as easily as the aircraft.

It is a requirement of IAS 37 that provisions be reviewed at each balance sheet date and adjusted where required and that the expenditure set against a provision is only that in relation to the intent of the provision. Therefore, a provision which we discover is no longer required cannot be used for the offset of other expenditure.

It is often the case that an enterprise can be reimbursed by another party for some of the expenditure in relation to a provision, e.g. insurance contracts, suppliers' warranties. In these cases the reimbursement must be treated as a separate asset and indeed only accounted for in the income statement, when the reimbursement is virtually certain.

Measurement of provisions

So far we have been concerned with the recognition of a provision or a contingent liability but we must also determine an amount. Remember a provision can only be recognized in the financial statements if a reliable estimate can be made of the amount. If no reliable estimate can be made of the amount then a contingent liability is disclosed (this will rarely occur).

IAS 37 requires that when determining a reliable estimate this should be 'the best estimate of the expenditure required to settle the present obligation at the balance sheet date' (para. 36). The best estimate is determined by the judgement of management supplemented by experience of similar transactions and/or reports from independent experts. The emphasis on present obligation in the measurement rule is deliberate and this means that the effect of future events in this measurement must be carefully evaluated. It is only where such future events are expected with some certainty and objectivity to occur that they will be taken account of.

Activity 18.7

An enterprise has a present obligation due to a past event to pay €2m to clean up a waste site. It is currently expected that technological developments that are near completion will decrease this cost to €1.5m. It has also been brought to management's attention that some research is underway, but in its infancy, that might reduce these costs further. At what value would the provision for the clean-up costs be shown in the accounts.

Activity feedback

The technological developments appear to have certainty and objectivity to them but the other research is much less objective and therefore the provision should be shown at €1.5m.

In practice the decision may not be as clear cut as we have just indicated. One future event that is not taken account of in measuring a provision is the gain on the expected disposal of a related asset. The Standard states that these gains must be dealt with in accordance with the standards dealing with the assets concerned. This is presumably because until there is a binding contract to sell the asset the management can change the decision in respect of the sale. We will deal with this issue again when we look at restructuring and provisions later in this chapter.

The best estimate of a provision can require the use of statistical methods of estimation. This can occur when a provision consists of a large population of items where possible outcomes have various probabilities attached. The method of estimation used in this case is known as 'expected value'.

If the provision relates to a single item or event or a small number of events then the expected value technique cannot be used. In this case the most 'likely outcome' is used.

> ### Illustration
>
> An enterprise sells goods under warranty. Past experience indicates that 80% of goods sold will have no defects, 15% will have minor defects and 5% major defects. If minor defects occurred in all goods sold the cost of rectification would be €5m and for major defects €15m. What is the expected value of the provision to be recorded in the financial statements of the enterprise at the balance sheet date?
>
>   The expected value is:
>
> $$80\% \times 0 + 15\% \times 5 + 5\% \times 15 = 1.5m$$

Activity 18.8

An enterprise is facing a substantial legal claim for €5m. The lawyers estimate that there is a 40% chance of successfully defending the claim. At what value should this provision be shown in the accounts?

Activity feedback

Care needs to be exercised here as the answer is not 40% × €5m. We have to use the most likely outcome technique here. The most likely outcome, 60% chance, is of an unsuccessful defence against the claim and therefore the best estimate of the provision required is €5m.

Activity 18.9

An enterprise is under warranty to replace a major component in a computer hardware system. The major component costs €0.5m to replace and five of these components are used in the system. Experience shows that there is a 45% chance of one component failing only, a 30% chance of two failing and 25% of three failures. It has never been known for more than three to fail. What is the value of the provision that should be shown in the accounts of the enterprise?

Activity feedback

At first glance the answer to the best estimate would appear to be the costs of one failure, €0.5m, as this is the most likely outcome at 45% occurrence. However, there is a 55% probability that more than one failure would occur and therefore the best estimate is €1m, that is of two failures. If the probabilities had been 25% one failure, 35% two and 40% three then the best estimate would again be €1m, two failures, as there is only a 40% chance of three failure and a 60% chance of fewer than three.

Provisions are measured before the effect of any tax consequences. The tax effect will be shown in accordance with IAS 12, *Income Taxes* (see Chapter 19).

Measurement at present value

'Where the effect of the time value of money is material, the amount of a provision should be the present value of the expenditure expected to be required to settle the obligation' (IAS 37, para. 45). This requirement of the Standard means that we must discount the expenditures required and the IAS specifies the discount rate as a pre-tax rate that reflects current market assessments of the time value of money and the risks specific to the liability. If future cash flows are adjusted to take account of risk then the discount rate used must be risk free and vice versa. This is to ensure that the risk involved in future cash flows is not allowed for twice. The best estimate measurement of the provision is becoming somewhat subjective!

Activity 18.10

The information in an earlier illustration enabled us to calculate the expected value for the provision for warranties. This provision was not discounted, even though it is expected that the time value of money will have a material effect on the provision. What type of discount rate should be applied, risk free or risk adjusted?

Activity feedback

Risk free, as the specific risk has already been accounted for in the information gathered about the number of warranties taken up.

Activity 18.11

An enterprise identifies a provision for €250 000 at the year end 31 December 20X1. The outflow of this amount is expected at year end 20X3. Specific risk associated with this provision has already been taken account of when calculating the best estimate for the provision. A suitable risk-free discount rate to use is identified as 5%.

Show the provision charged in the accounts for the year ends 20X1, 20X2 and 20X3 assuming no change takes place in the best estimate and any other related entries required.

Activity feedback

As at 20X1 the provision of 250 000 is due for payment in two years' time and therefore will need to be discounted at 5% for a period of two years:

$$250\,000 \times 0.91 = 227\,500$$

As at 20X2 the provision is now due for payment in one year's time and therefore will be charged at:

$$250\,000 \times 0.95 = 237\,500$$

As at 20X3 the provision should have been paid at 250 000 and therefore will not be required at the year end.

The problem inherent in the discounting of provisions is that the carrying amount of the provision increases as the discount unwinds. Where do we account for this unwinding? The IASB view this unwinding as a charge to interest. There is no doubt that this unwinding is a financial item but whether it should be regarded as an interest charge is debatable.

In Activity 18.11 in year ended 20X2 €10 000 would be charged to interest in the income statement and at year end 20X3 €12 500.

Specific application of recognition and measurement rules

IAS 37 identifies three specific applications of recognition and measurement of provisions:

1 *Future operating losses.* These do not meet the definition of a liability as there is no present obligation and thus no liability. The loss will be recognized as it occurs. However, the possibility of future losses should lead management to test assets for impairment.

2 *Onerous contracts.* We discussed these at Activity 18.6. IAS 37 requires us to recognize the present obligation under an onerous contract as a provision.

3 *Restructuring.*

Activity 18.12

The management board of Alex takes a decision on 24 March to close down one of its divisions. The board also agrees the detailed plan for closure put forward on 24 March. No further action is taken on the closure and the year end for Alex is 31 March. What should Alex provide in the accounts in respect of the closure?

Activity feedback

First question to ask is: is there a present obligation (legal or constructive) as a result of a past event (see Figure 18.1).

The answer is *no*. The board of Alex can change their mind in regard to the closure. A constructive obligation will only exist when the closure is communicated in detail to employees and customers. A problem does exist here, however, as the point of recognition of the constructive obligation is dependent on a subjective judgement – at what point will the company make a sufficiently specific statement as to the closure? No provision will be made in the accounts as at 31 March.

IAS 37 tells us that a constructive obligation to restructure arises only when an enterprise:

■ has a detailed formal plan for the restructuring identifying at least:
   – the business or part of a business concerned
   – the principal locations affected
   – the location, function and approximate number of employees who will be compensated for termination of their services
   – the expenditures that will be undertaken
   – when the plan will be implemented
■ and restructures by starting to implement that plan or announcing its main features to those affected by it (para. 72).

This still leaves us with a subjective judgement to make.

In addition, we have to be careful about the expenditure included in a restructuring provision as we cannot include those costs associated with ongoing activities of the enterprise. Thus, we cannot include retraining or relocation costs of continuing staff, marketing or investment in new systems and distribution networks. We can only include the direct expenditures. Also remember that gains from expected disposal of assets should not be taken account of when measuring the provision for restructuring.

Other applications

In the next activity there are a further two circumstances outlined for the application of the recognition and measurement rules of IAS 37.

Activity 18.13

1 An enterprise has for many years made a provision for repair and maintenance of its assets. Should the enterprise continue to do so now IAS 37 is effective?
2 An enterprise that operates a chain of retail outlets decides not to insure itself in respect of the risk of minor accidents to its customers but to self-insure. Based on past experience it expects to pay €100 000 a year in respect of these accidents. Should provision be made for the amount expected to arise in a normal year?

Activity feedback

1 The enterprise has no constructive or legal obligation for repairs and maintenance as a result of a past event. No provision. Charge the amount of repairs and maintenance to the income statement as actually expensed.
2 There is no present obligation as a result of a past event as no event has occurred. No provision. However, as the minor accidents occur the expenditure associated with them will be charged to the income statement.

Disclosure

The disclosure requirements are fairly extensive but are those you would expect in terms of providing relevant information to users. The following disclosure in respect of provisions, contingent liabilities and contingent assets comes from Bayer's financial report 2000:

> Other provisions
> Other provisions are valued in accordance with IAS 37 using the best estimate of the extent of the obligation. Interest-bearing provisions are discounted to fair value.

GAAP comparison

UK GAAP (FRS 12) is very similar to IAS in this area. Indeed the examples and decisions trees used in both standards are identical.

US GAAP is again similar but with some minor differences as follows:

- *Measurement*:
  - discount rate is pre-tax reflecting current market assessment of time value of money (thus no account of risk is taken).
  - where a range of estimates of the outflow are available and all are equally likely then the lowest is taken (not mid-point as per IAS).
- *Restructuring*:
  - management approval and commitment is sufficient to recognize the restructuring. Thus, under US GAAP restructuring provisions are likely to occur at an earlier point than under IAS.
- *Contingent asset*:
  - under US GAAP insurance recoveries will be recognized when probable (IAS requires virtual certainty). Thus US GAAP will recognize the contingent asset at an earlier stage than IAS.

Fourth Directive and IAS 37

There is some discrepancy between the Fourth Directive and IAS 37. The Directive requires member states to ensure that accounts are drawn up in such a way as to take account of all foreseeable and potential losses arising in the financial year (article 31(1)©(bb)). IAS 37 quite obviously does not do this. Article 31(1)(d) requires that charges relating to the financial year irrespective of date of payment must be taken into account and article 20 requires the creation of a provision to cover charges that are likely to be incurred (or certain) but where amount or timing is uncertain.

Clearly, the Fourth Directive was written at a time when prudence was a key element, even a bias, of financial reporting and since then the underlying concepts of accounting have changed. This inconsistency between the Directive and IAS 37 has been highlighted by the European Commission and we believe the new Directive takes account of this.

Activity 18.14

Felix, a commercial port operator, is uncertain how do deal with the following issues in its year end accounts:

1 Significant one-off refurbishments of operational port assets that are required in the future.
2 A decision has been taken to alter employee conditions by reducing overtime payments from twice the normal rate to 1.5 times at one port. A one-off payment will be made to all employees who accept this change of condition. Employees and unions are aware of the proposed change and have also been informed that if agreement is not given to the proposal other ways will be found to avoid the overtime.
3 Felix has a contract to purchase items at €1 per unit. Current market price of these items is 50c. The items are used in a part of the business that is profitable. The management believe the contract is onerous.

4 Felix purchased four small ports for €100m during the year; however, the Monopolies and Mergers Commission has directed Felix to sell them. No sale has been made by the year end but the best estimate of their sale value is €50m.

Activity feedback

1 There is no present obligation, either legal or obligatory, so no provision or contingent liability is shown.
2 The one-off payment is associated with future work not current and therefore no provision should be made.
3 The contract is not onerous as no loss is being made by Felix on these items as they form part of a profitable item.
4 A provision of €50m should be made in the accounts as this is a present obligation due to a past event and a reasonable estimate of the loss can be made.

Summary

You should now realize that the area of provisions, contingent liabilities and contingent assets is controversial and requires a great deal of subjective judgement. Many people would argue that IAS 37 lacks prudence in that it does not require the recognition of and accounting for all future expenses. We would not argue this, as we view prudence as a state of being free from bias, not being overly pessimistic. The issues involved in this chapter have been quite difficult and Tables 18.1 and 18.2 summarize the position of IAS 37.

Table 18.1 IAS 37: Summary of provisions and contingent liabilities

Obligation	Accounting result	Disclosure
Present obligation that probably requires outflow	Provision recognized	Amounts, nature, uncertainties, assumptions, reimbursements
Possible obligation or present obligation that may require outflow	No provision recognized Contingent liability disclosed	Nature, estimate of financial effect, uncertainties, reimbursement
Possible obligation or present obligation where outflow remote	No provision recognized No contingent liability disclosed	Nil

Table 18.2 IAS 37: Summary of contingent assets

Economic benefits	Accounting result	Disclosure
Inflow virtually certain	Asset rules apply	
Inflow probable	No asset recognized Contingent asset disclosed	Nature, financial effect
Inflow not probable	No asset recognized No contingent asset disclosed	Nil

1 Outline the recommended treatment of provisions, contingent liabilities and contingent assets in accordance with IAS 37, clearly defining and illustrating the meaning of each term.

2 Identify any other methods of accounting for provisions, contingent liabilities and contingent assets and discuss why IAS 37 rejects these methods in favour of its recommended treatment.

3 Discuss the statement that financial reports prepared under IAS 37 provide a 'true and fair view' to users.

4 Explain the terms:
- big bath accounting
- profit smoothing.
Give an illustration of each.

5 IAS 37 ensures 'consistency between enterprises in the recognition and measurement of provisions and contingencies and that sufficient information is disclosed about them to users so that they can understand their effect on current and future results'. Discuss.

✔ **6** The distinction between a provision and a contingent liability is irrelevant. Discuss.

7 Describe the accounting arrangements in accordance with IAS 37 for provisions and contingent liabilities. Comment on whether these arrangements provide useful information to users.

8 Appraise the requirement in IAS 37 to measure a provision at the 'best estimate'.

✔ **9** Debate the contention that IAS 37 lacks prudence.

10 (i) In relation to a failed acquisition, a firm of accountants has invoiced Gear for the sum of $300 000. Gear has paid $20 000 in full settlement of the debt and states that this was a reasonable sum for the advice given and is not prepared to pay any further sum. The accountants are pressing for payment of the full amount but on the advice of its solicitors, Gear is not going to settle the balance outstanding. Additionally Gear is involved in a court case concerning the plagiarism of software. Another games company has accused Gear of copying their games software and currently legal opinion seems to indicate that Gear will lose the case. Management estimates that the most likely outcome will be a payment of costs and royalties to the third party of $1 million in two years' time (approximately). The best case scenario is deemed to be a payment of $500 000 in one year's time and the worst case scenario that of a payment of $2 million in three years' time. These scenarios are based on the amount of the royalty payment and the potential duration and costs of the court case. Management has estimated that the relative likelihood of the above payments are best case – 30% chance, most likely outcome – 60% chance, and worst case – 10% chance of occurrence. The directors are unsure as to whether any provision for the above amounts should be made in the financial statements.

(ii) In the event of the worst case scenario occurring, the directors of Gear are worried about the viability of their business as the likelihood would be that current liabilities would exceed current assets and it is unlikely that in the interim period there will be sufficient funds generated from operational cash flows.

The discount rate for any present value calculations is 5%.

Required:

Write a report to the directors of Gear Software explaining the implications of the above information contained in paragraphs (i) and (ii) for the financial statements.

(ACCA June 03)

11 IAS 37 'Provisions, Contingent Liabilities and Contingent Assets' was issued in 1998. The Standard sets out the principles of accounting for these items and clarifies when provisions should and should not be made. Prior to its issue, the inappropriate use of provisions had been an area where companies had been accused of manipulating the financial statements and of creative accounting.

Required:

(a) Describe the nature of provisions and the accounting requirements for them contained in IAS 37.

(b) Explain why there is a need for an accounting standard in this area. Illustrate your answer with three practical examples of how the standard addresses controversial issues.

(c) Bodyline sells sports goods and clothing through a chain of retail outlets. It offers customers a full refund facility for any goods returned within 28 days of their purchase provided they are unused and in their original packaging. In addition, all goods carry a warranty against manufacturing defects for 12 months from their date of purchase. For most goods the manufacturer underwrites this warranty such that Bodyline is credited with the cost of the goods that are returned as faulty. Goods purchased from one manufacturer, Header, are sold to Bodyline at a negotiated discount which is designed to compensate Bodyline for manufacturing defects. No refunds are given by Header, thus Bodyline has to bear the cost of any manufacturing faults of these goods.

Bodyline makes a uniform mark up on cost of 25% on all goods it sells, except for those supplied from Header on which it makes a mark up on cost of 40%. Sales of goods manufactured by Header consistently account for 20% of all Bodyline's sales.

Sales in the last 28 days of the trading year to 30 September 2003 were $1,750,000. Past trends reliably indicate that 10% of all goods are returned under the 28-day return facility. These are not faulty goods. Of these 70% are later resold at the normal selling price and the remaining 30% are sold as 'sale' items at half the normal retail price.

In addition to the above expected returns, an estimated $160 000 (at selling price) of the goods sold during the year will have manufacturing defects and have yet to be returned by customers. Goods returned as faulty have no resale value.

Required:

Described the nature of the above warranty/return facilities and calculate the provision Bodyline is required to make at 30 September 2003:

(i) for goods subject to the 28 day returns policy; and

(ii) for goods that are likely to be faulty.

(d) Rockbuster has recently purchased an item of earth moving plant at a total cost of $24 million. The plant has an estimated life of 10 years with no residual value, however its engine will need replacing after every 5000 hours of use at an estimated cost of $7.5 million. The directors of Rockbuster intend to depreciate the plant at $2.4 million ($24 million/10 years) per annum and make a provision of $1500 ($7.5 million/5000 hours) per hour of use for the replacement of the engine.

Required:

Explain how the plant should be treated in accordance with International Accounting Standards and comment on the Director's proposed treatment.   (ACCA Dec 03)

12 Nette, a public limited company, manufactures mining equipment and extracts natural gas. The directors are uncertain about the role of the IASB's 'Framework for the Preparation and Presentation of Financial Statements' (the Framework) in corporate reporting. Their view is that accounting is based on the transactions carried out by the company and these transactions are allocated to the company's accounting period by using the matching and prudence concepts. The argument put forward by the directors is that the Framework does not take into account the business and legal constraints

within which companies operate. Further they have given a situation which has arisen in the current financial statements where they feel that the current accounting practice is inconsistent with the Framework.

Situation

Nette has recently constructed a natural gas extraction facility and commenced production one year ago (1 June 2003). There is an operating licence given to the company by the government which requires the removal of the facility at the end of its life which is estimated at 20 years. Depreciation is charged on the straight line basis. The cost of the construction of the facility was $200 million and the net present value at 1 June 2003 of the future costs to be incurred in order to return the extraction site to its original condition are estimated at $50 million (using a discount rate of 5% per annum). 80 per cent of these costs relate to the removal of the facility and 20% relate to the rectification of the damage caused through the extraction of the natural gas. The auditors have told the company that a provision for decommissioning has to be set up.

Required:

(a) Explain the importance of the 'Framework' to the reporting of corporate performance and whether it takes into account the business and legal constraints placed upon companies.

(b) (i) Explain with reasons and suitable extracts/computations the accounting treatment of the above situation in the financial statements for the year ended 31 May 2004.

   (ii) Discuss whether the treatment of the items appears consistent with the 'Framework'.   (ACCA June 04)

Income taxes

After studying this chapter you should be able to:
- [ ] explain deferred tax
- [ ] describe the arguments for and against providing for deferred tax
- [ ] identify several possible methods of accounting for deferred tax
- [ ] identify the requirements of IAS 12, *Income Taxes*
- [ ] critically appraise the IAS approach.

Introduction

The amount of tax charged against the profit in any period is an important determinant of earnings per share and thus the price earnings ratio. It also obviously has an effect on all other ratios which are calculated after tax. However, the tax charge, calculated according to a country's tax legislation, is not necessarily the same as applying the tax rate to the accounting profits. This difference arises because of the different recognition and measurement rules in tax legislation compared to accounting GAAP. The implications arising from these differences have led to a long, complicated and sometimes badly argued debate over the last three decades or more, both nationally and internationally.

The expense question

The first question to answer is 'Is tax a business expense?' At first glance your answer might be an unequivocal *yes*, but it needs further consideration. An expense is an outflow or other using up of assets or incurrences of liabilities during a period from delivering or producing goods, services etc. Expenses are also discretionary in a sense, i.e. the business could avoid them if it wished. Tax is not a charge for the exchange of goods or services and cannot be avoided by the business. Many see tax not as an expense but as a distribution of income like distributions to shareholders. This view regards the tax authorities as a stakeholder in the business. If this distribution view of tax was adopted the rest of this chapter would be irrelevant. Tax is internationally treated as an expense but the argument for doing so is not very well founded.

The deferred tax problem

In many countries the amount of tax payable by a business for a particular period often bears little relationship to profit as reported by the accountants in the income statement. It is often the case that the tax authorities take the accountant's reported profit figure as their starting point but they make all sorts of adjustments to it. One of these adjustments can be in respect of depreciation. As we have already seen in Chapter 12, the 'appropriate' charge for depreciation can be a highly uncertain, subjective amount which to many taxation authorities is unacceptable. Additionally, several national governments have felt that by specifying tax allowances (not equivalent to an accountant's depreciation figure) for capital assets against profits, which they can vary from year to year, they can provide incentives to businesses to invest more or to invest in some particular way. The first thing that such tax authorities do to the accountant's profit figure, as calculated and published, is to remove all the depreciation entries put in by the accountant. In other words, the depreciation figure, which will have been deducted in arriving at the accountant's profit figure, is simply added back again (a profit on disposal that will have been added by the accountant will of course need to be removed by deduction). From the resulting figure the tax authority now deducts whatever the tax allowance for the capital asset is and tax is levied on this taxable profit.

The following activity illustrates the difference between accounting profits and tax authority profits.

Activity 19.1

An asset attracting 25% tax allowances per annum costs Deftax Ltd €100. It has an expected life of five years at the end of which it is estimated it can be sold for €25. Taxation is payable at the rate of 33%. Complete the following (note that tax allowances apply to the reducing balance of the asset).

	Year				
	1	2	3	4	5
	€	€	€	€	€
Accounting profit (after depreciation charge)	100	100	100	100	100
Depreciation					
Tax allowance					
Taxable profit					
Profit before tax					
Taxation 33% taxable profit					
Profit after tax					
Profit before tax					
Taxation charge if calculated on accounting profits					
Profit after accounting tax					

Activity feedback

	Year				
	1	2	3	4	5
	€	€	€	€	€
Accounting profit (after depreciation charge)	100	100	100	100	100
Depreciation	15	15	15	15	15
Tax allowance	25	18	14	11	8
Taxable profit	90	97	101	104	107
Profit before tax	100	100	100	100	100
Taxation 33% taxable profit	30	32	33	34	36
Profit after tax	70	68	67	66	64
Profit before tax	100	100	100	100	100
Taxation charge if calculated on accounting profit	33	33	33	33	33
Profit after accounting tax	67	67	67	67	67

The profit after tax figures, which are used for the EPS and PE ratio (see Chapter 26) would indicate that in year 2 the performance of the company decreased and continued to do so for the next three years. But have the firm and management been less successful? Arguably not! Over the five-year period the company has made the same accounting profit with the same resources each year (excluding the problems of historical cost here). Thus, the profit after accounting tax figures provides a better guide to performance of the company.

If we look carefully at the activity feedback we note that the total tax charge is €165 over the five-year period using either method. Thus, the use of tax allowances does not alter the total tax due, only the timing of those tax payments. The difference between the depreciation charge in any year and the tax allowance for that year is referred to as the 'timing difference'. The tax allowance has the effect of deferring tax payments in year 1, €3 and year 2, €1, and then collecting these in years 4 and 5.

So we have an eventual payment that relates to year 1 and 2 and arises as a result of the transactions and results of years 1 and 2 and it is therefore arguable that there is a liability created at year 1 and increased at year 2. We are in effect suggesting that:

1 The tax charge for year 1 and year 2 should really be €33, as this is the amount that must eventually be paid as a result of the year 1 and 2 activities.
2 There is a liability of €3 at the end of year 1, in respect of tax related to year 1 but payable in later years which increases to €4 by the end of year 2.

We can easily allow for both these considerations by creating a liability account, known as a deferred tax account. This is shown below. The amount to be transferred to the credit of the deferred tax account can be formally calculated as follows.

Amount equals:

$$\text{Tax rate} \times (\text{tax allowances given} - \text{depreciation disallowed})$$

Thus for year 1:

$$33\% \times (25 - 15) = 3$$

and year 2:

$$33\% \times (18 - 15) = 1$$

	Year					
	1	2	3	4	5	Total
	€	€	€	€	€	€
Profit before tax	100	100	100	100	100	500
Taxation: payable for year	30	32	33	34	36	165
Additional charge (credit) to deferred tax account	3	1	0	(1)	(3)	0
Total tax charge	33	33	33	33	33	165
Profit after tax	67	67	67	67	67	335

Deferred tax account			
	€		€
Balance c/d 31.12.01	3	Appropriation account 31.12.01	3
	3		3
		Balance b/d 1.1.02	3
Balance c/d 31.12.02	4	Approp. acc 31.12.02	1
	4		4
Balance c/d 31.12.03	4	Balance b/d 1.1.03	4
	4		4
Approp. acc. 31.12.04	1	Balance b/d 1.1.04	4
Balance c/d 31.12.04	3		4
	4		4
Approp. acc 31.12.05	3	Balance b/d 1.1.05	3

For year 4	And year 5
$33\% \times (11 - 15) = -1$	$33\% \times (8 - 15) = -3$

So the transfer for year 4 is a debit to deferred tax account of €1 (or in effect, a credit of €1, if you will find that easier to see) and a credit of €1 to the appropriation account. For year 5 we have a debit to deferred tax account of €3 and a credit of €3 to the appropriation account.

Arguments for deferred tax

From this discussion we can note that:

1 The tax charge by including deferred tax is €67 for years 1–5, which provides a profit after-tax figure which reflects the performance of the company.
2 There is a liability balance remaining at the end of each year in respect of tax related to the current or earlier years but not yet paid or due for payment. This, we also suggested, was a desirable outcome.
3 The total position viewed over the five years as a whole remains unaltered. This is to be expected as nothing we are doing and also nothing that the tax authorities are doing, through tax allowances, alters the total tax eventually payable as a result of a year's profits.

All this appears totally logical and in accord with accounting principles. So what is the problem?

Arguments against deferred tax

A problem occurs with the previous logic if a company buys assets regularly, which is a realistic assumption as companies tend to become more capital intensive. Let us demonstrate the problem with an activity.

Activity 19.2

In addition to the information given in Activity 19.1 Deftax Ltd buys an asset in year 2 for €100, one in year 3 for €120 and one in year 4 for €220 and two in year 5 for €250 and €300, respectively. All these assets also have an expected life of five years, but unlike the first asset, all these later ones have an expected scrap value of zero. Complete the table in Activity 19.1 using the new information and show the deferred tax account over the five-year period. Comment on the results.

Activity feedback

	Year				
	1	2	3	4	5
	€	€	€	€	€
Accounting profit (after deprec. charged)	100	100	100	100	100
Depreciation	15	35	59	103	213
Tax allowance	25	43	62	103	215
Taxable profit	90	92	97	100	98
Tax charge	30	30	32	33	32
Deferred tax charge	3	3	1	0	1
Total tax	33	33	33	33	33
Profit after tax	67	67	67	67	67

To help you with the activity we provide the workings for years 2 and 3 for the calculation of depreciation and capital allowances. Years 4 and 5 follow the same pattern.

Workings
Year 2:
Asset 1 depreciation $75/5 = 15$
Asset 2 depreciation $100/5 = \underline{20}$
$\overline{35}$

Asset 1 tax allowance $25\% \times 75 = 18$
Asset 2 tax allowance $25\% \times 100 = \underline{25}$
$\overline{43}$

Year 3:
Asset 1 depreciation $= 15$
Asset 2 depreciation $= 20$
Asset 3 depreciation $120/5 = \underline{24}$
                              $\underline{\underline{59}}$

Asset 1 tax allowance $25\% \times (75 - 18) \; = 14$
Asset 2 tax allowance $25\% \times (100 - 25) = 18$
Asset 3 tax allowance $25\% \times 120 \qquad = \underline{30}$
                                           $\underline{\underline{62}}$

Deferred tax account

Balance c/d 31.12.01	$\underline{3}$	$\underline{3}$	Appropriation a/c	31.12.01
	3	3		
		3	Bal. b/d 1.1.02	
Balance c/d 31.12.02	$\underline{6}$	3	Appropriation a/c	31.12.02
	6	$\underline{3}$		
		6	Bal. b/d 1.1.03	
Bal. c/d 31.12.03	$\underline{7}$	1	Appropriation a/c	31.12.03
	7	$\underline{7}$		
		7	Bal. b/d 1.1.04	
Bal. c/d 31.12.04	$\underline{7}$	0	Appropriation a/c	31.12.04
	7	$\underline{7}$		
		7	Bal. b/d 1.1.05	
Bal. c/d 31.12.05	$\underline{8}$	1	Appropriation a/c	31.12.05
	8	$\underline{8}$		
		8	Bal. b/d 1.1.06	

Comparing the tables from Activities 19.1 and 19.2 we see that the total position over the five years is no longer the same. The total tax charge is increased by €8. This is not surprising, as it equals the liability provided for at the end of year 5 on the deferred tax account. The transfer to the deferred tax account can be seen to be the result of an amalgam of positive originating timing differences relating to depreciation. The resultant figure of profit after tax, €67 per annum, reflects the underlying profitability of the company. It does not give an impression of improved profitability because of the effect of tax allowances related to asset acquisitions. Everything appears fine so where is the problem? The problem is the €8 remaining on the deferred tax account. Does this liability actually exist?

In the long term we can suggest that:

1 If the enterprise reaches the state where it has a constant volume of fixed assets, merely replacing its existing assets as they wear out and also the price it has to pay for replacement fixed assets does not rise over time, then the balance of liability on the deferred tax account will remain a more or less constant figure.

2 If the enterprise finds that it is effectively in the position of paying gradually more and more money for fixed assets each year, then the balance of liability on the deferred tax account will gradually rise, apparently without limit.

3 Only if the monetary amount of reinvestment in fixed assets actually falls will the balance of liability on the deferred tax account start to fall.

How likely is each of these three outcomes? In general **2** will tend to be the most frequent for three reasons:

1 Enterprises have a tendency to expand.
2 Enterprises have a tendency to become more capital intensive.
3 Inflationary pressures tend to cause the amount of money paid for assets to increase over time.

So the most likely outcome, if full provision is to be made for deferred tax in this way, is of a liability figure on the balance sheet that is apparently ever increasing. But what is a liability? Informally, we can say that it is an amount to be paid out in the future. We have an account representing a liability to the tax authorities. The balance on this account is gradually getting bigger and bigger and, as far as can reasonably be foreseen, this process is going to continue. Therefore, the liability balance does not seem to be getting paid, neither in the foreseeable future is it likely to be paid. Therefore, it appears that it is not a liability at all within the meaning of the word liability! If the liability account seems all set to keep on growing, is there a probable future sacrifice?

It should be observed that one way of summarizing the two arguments as regard the liability aspect is that we can consider the position for each individual asset or we can consider the position for all assets in the aggregate. In the former case the tax deferred will all have become payable by the end of the asset's life, so deferred tax provision would seem to be necessary. In the latter case the aggregate liability is likely to go on increasing so deferred tax provision would seem to be unnecessary.

Accountants' response

Formally, three approaches have been distinguished:

1 *The flow through approach*, which accounts only for that tax payable in respect of the period in question, i.e. timing differences are ignored.
2 *Full deferral*, which accounts for the full tax effects of timing differences, i.e. tax is shown in the published accounts based on the full accounting profit and the element not immediately payable is recorded as a liability until reversal.
3 *Partial deferral*, which accounts only for those timing differences where reversal is likely to occur in aggregate terms (because, for example, replacement of assets and expansion is expected to exceed depreciation).

These alternatives are discussed and explained in the following activities.

Activity 19.3

Should the flow through approach be identified as the method to be used for accounting for tax?

Activity feedback

Arguments in favour:

- Tax is assessed on taxable profits not accounting profits. The only liability for tax for the period therefore is that accordingly assessed.
- Future years' tax depends on future events and is therefore not a present liability (see definition of liability, Chapter 18).
- Even if current events were giving rise to future tax liabilities then, as the tax charge will be based on a complex set of future transactions, it cannot be measured with reliability and therefore should not be recognized.

Arguments against:

- As tax charges can be traced to individual transactions and events then any future tax consequences arising from these should be provided for at the outset.
- Flow through method can understate an entity's liability to tax.

Activity 19.4

Should the full deferral method be adopted as the method to be used for accounting for tax?

Activity feedback

The view can be taken that the amount of tax saving should not appear as a benefit of the year for which it was granted, but should be carried forward and recredited to the profit and loss account (by way of reduction of the tax charged therein) in the year or years in which there are reversing time differences.

In effect, therefore, the full unreversed element is shown as a liability. Applying this to the circumstances of Deftax Ltd, we arrive at the position in Activity 19.2. Thus, we could well be showing a liability that will never crystallize.

Activity 19.5

Should partial deferral be the method adopted for accounting for tax?

Activity feedback

As we have seen, the one major problem with full deferral is that the balance on the deferred tax account is likely to increase continuously where there is expansion and replacement at increased prices. If, however, timing differences are regarded in aggregate terms rather than as relating to individual assets, then this could be taken as evidence that the differences were not reversing. In short, is a liability that is never likely to become payable a liability at all? In many businesses, timing differences arising from accelerated capital allowances are of a recurring nature and reversing differences are themselves offset, wholly or partially, or are exceeded, by new originating differences thereby giving rise to continuing tax reductions or the indefinite postponement of any liability attributable to the tax benefits received. It is, therefore, appropriate that in the case of accelerated capital allowances, provisions be made for deferred taxation except insofar as the tax benefit can be expected with reasonable probability to be retained in the future in consequence of recurring timing differences of the same type.

Activity 19.6

On the assumption that the directors of Deftax Ltd foresee no reversal of timing differences for some considerable time and using the information from Activity 19.2, show the taxation effect using the partial deferral method.

Activity feedback

	Year				
	1	2	3	4	5
	€	€	€	€	€
Profit before tax	100	100	100	100	100
Taxation	30	30	32	33	32
Deferred tax charge	0	0	0	0	0
	70	70	68	67	68

Deferred tax calculation

Year	Originating (O) timing difference	Reversing (R) timing difference	Net timing difference
1	10 (25 capital allowance − 15 depreciation)	–	10 (O)
2	18 (43 − 35)	–	8 (O)
3	6 (30 − 24)	3	3 (O)
4	11 (55 − 44)	11	(O)
5	28 (138 − 110)	26	2 (O)

6 onwards no net reversals

The liability for tax will never crystallize, therefore no provision for deferred tax is required. No net reversal appears ever to be expected.

Deferral v liability method

The deferred tax amount is dependent on the tax rate used. When calculating the amount we could either use:

- the tax rate applying when the timing difference originated – deferral method
- or the tax rate (or the best estimate of it) ruling when the tax will become payable – liability method.

A simple example is used to illustrate the difference.

Illustration

An enterprise purchases a non-current asset for €5 000 000 on 1.1.X0. It is depreciated on a straight line basis over five years. It attracts tax allowances of €200 000 in X0 and €150 000 in X1. The tax rate in X0 is 30% and X1 25%.

	X0	X1
Depreciation charge	100 000	100 000
Tax allowance	200 000	150 000
Timing difference	100 000	50 000

Deferred tax provided

	Deferral method		Liability method	
	X0	X1	X0	X1
	30%	25%	30%	25%
Deferred tax charge	30 000	12 500	30 000	12 500
Deferred tax balance	30 000	42 500		(5 000)
			30 000	37 500

The (5000) in X1 under the liability method adjusts the carry forward of 30 000 to 25 000 which is the timing difference of 100 000 at 25% tax rate. The 37 500 is now the best estimate of the tax payable if the timing differences reversed, whereas the 42 500 does not represent the best estimate of the likely liability.

Income statement or balance sheet view of deferred tax

When the income statement view of deferred tax is taken there is a focus on the difference between the accounting profit and taxable profit, as we described earlier at p. 359. This was the view of deferred tax taken internationally and in the UK and US until the 1990s. The balance sheet view focuses on the difference between carrying amount of assets and liabilities and their amount in tax terms and forms the basis for current IAS and US GAAP.

UK GAAP still focuses on the income statements. In some situations, it makes no difference whether we take an IS or BS view but in many it does, as the following illustration shows.

Illustration

An enterprise buys an asset for €100 depreciated over five years on a straight line basis. Tax allowances on capital assets are 50% in the first year and tax rate is 30%. Under the income statement view, known as limiting difference, the deferred tax provided for at the end of the first year is:

Tax allowance	50
Depreciation	20
Timing differences	30
Deferred tax	9

The balance sheet view, temporary difference, is:

Net book value of asset end year 1	80
Tax base (tax written down value)	50
	30
Deferred tax	9

In this example there is no difference between the two methods.

If the asset had been revalued to €200 at the end of year 1 then only the balance sheet calculation would change:

NBV	200
Tax base	50
Temporary differences	150
Deferred tax	45

The argument for providing deferred tax on this temporary difference (note there is no timing difference) is that it is presumed the revalued carrying amount of the asset will be recovered through use and will generate taxable income that will be taxable in the future and therefore there is a deferred tax liability. There is a problem with this logic, though, given the definition of a liability as 'a present obligation arising out of a past event'. The future taxable income referred to here is not a past event.

IAS 12 and tax

Introduction

IAS 12 revised was issued in 1996 and some slight changes were made in 2000. In addition there are two SICs, SIC 21 *Income Taxes – Recovery of Revalued Non-depreciable Assets* and SIC 25 *Income Taxes – Changes in the Tax Status of an Enterprise or its Shareholders*. The Standard deals with both current tax and deferred tax issues.

The current version of IAS 12 has major changes from the one first issued in 1979. This original Standard basically allowed deferred tax to be calculated based on any method available, deferral or liability method, full or partial provision, and was based on an income statement approach.

The current IAS 12 is based on a balance sheet approach and therefore a liability measurement of deferred tax together with a full provision method for all temporary differences.

Definitions

The definitions given in IAS 12 (para. 5) are now reproduced:

– Accounting profit is net profit or loss for a period before deducting tax expense.
– Taxable profit (tax loss) is the profit (loss) for a period, determined in accordance with the rules established by the taxation authorities, upon which income taxes are payable (recoverable).

- Tax expense (tax income) is the aggregate amount included in the determination of net profit or loss for the period in respect of current tax and deferred tax.
- Current tax is the amount of income taxes payable (recoverable) in respect of taxable profit (tax loss) for a period.
- Deferred tax liabilities are the amounts of income taxes payable in future periods in respect of taxable temporary differences.
- Deferred tax assets are the amounts of income taxes recoverable in future periods in respect of:
  (a) deductible temporary differences
  (b) the carryforward of unused tax losses, and
  (c) the carryforward of unused tax credits.
- Temporary differences are differences between the carrying amount of an asset or liability in the balance sheet and its tax base. Temporary differences may be either:
  (a) taxable temporary differences, which are temporary differences that will result in taxable amounts in determining taxable profit (tax loss) of future periods when the carrying amount of the asset or liability is recovered or settled; or
  (b) deductible temporary differences, which are temporary differences that will result in amounts that are deductible in determining taxable profit (tax loss) of future periods when the carrying amount of the asset or liability is recovered or settled. These lead to deferred tax assets.
- The tax base of an asset or liability is the amount attributed to that asset or liability for tax purposes.

Tax base

In many cases the tax base of an asset or liability is fairly obvious.

Activity 19.7

An enterprise buys an asset for €500 000, which it intends to depreciate equally over five years. Under tax legislation the asset attracts a 50% first-year allowance and then an equal allowance each year over the next four to write the asset down to zero.

What is the tax base of the asset (at the end of each year) and its carrying amount in the balance sheet.

Activity feedback

		Tax base	Carrying amount
End year	1	250 000	400 000
	2	187 500	300 000
	3	125 000	200 000
	4	62 500	100 000
	5	0	0

The tax base of an asset is the amount that is deducted, in tax calculations, from the tax calculated on taxable economic benefits that will flow to an enterprise when it recovers the carrying amount of the asset. If the economic benefits are not taxable then the tax base of the asset is equal to its carrying amount.

Activity 19.8

An enterprise has interest receivable of €200 and dividends receivable of €300 in its balance sheet (these amounts are thus the carrying amount of the assets.) As far as tax legislation that the enterprise is subject to is concerned the interest will be taxed in full on a cash basis but the dividends are not taxable. Identify the tax base for the interest receivable and the dividends receivable.

Activity feedback

As the interest is taxed in full there is no deduction from the economic benefit and therefore the tax base is nil. The benefit of the dividends is not subject to tax and therefore the whole €300 must have been deducted from the economic benefit and thus the tax base of €300.

In the activity note the following:

	Tax base	Carrying amount	Temp. difference
Interest receivable	0	200	200
Dividends receivable	300	300	–

Thus, deferred tax liability would need to be recognized on the interest but not the dividend receivable. A similar situation occurs in the case of liabilities where the tax base of a liability is its carrying amount less any amount that will be deductible for tax purposes in respect of that liability in future periods. For example, suppose an enterprise makes a provision in its accounts for €100 on which tax relief in full will be given when the liability is paid, then:

	Tax base	Carrying amount	Temp. difference
Provision	0	100	100

and a deferred tax asset will be required.

Activity 19.9

An enterprise has a loan of €500 repayable in five years' time. The principal repayment is not deductible for tax purposes. Identify the tax base and therefore the timing difference.

Activity feedback

	Tax base	Carrying amount	Temp. difference
Loan	500	500	0

There are several more examples of tax base calculations in the Standard.

Current tax liabilities and assets

The requirements of IAS 12 here are quite straightforward. Unpaid current tax in relation to current or earlier periods is shown as a liability and if the amount paid exceeds the amount due then the excess is recognized as an asset. In addition where the benefit from a tax loss can be carried back to recover current tax of a previous period this should also be recognized as an asset.

Recognition of deferred tax

According to IAS 12, a deferred tax liability is recognized on all taxable temporary differences except:

1 Goodwill for which amortization is not deductible for tax purposes
2 The initial recognition of an asset or liability in a transaction which is not a business combination and at the time of the transaction affects neither accounting profit nor taxable profit.

Activity 19.10

Explain the reasoning for these two exceptions to the provision of deferred tax.

Activity feedback

Goodwill is an asset and if we assume a carrying amount of €1000 then its tax base will be nil which implies a temporary difference of €1000, but if deferred tax is provided on this then the goodwill which is a function of all the net assets of the acquired business will change which will consequently change the deferred tax. This will keep occurring as we try to calculate the deferred tax and thus an exemption is made as the calculation becomes circuitous.

The second exemption can best be understood by an example.

Suppose a company buys a current asset for €100 which is not deductible for tax purposes when the asset is sold. Then:

	Tax base	Carrying amount	Temp. difference
Asset	nil	100	100

would imply a deferred tax liability should be recognized on the asset. However, the purchase of the asset had created no taxable or accounting income and therefore no timing difference and thus no need for deferred tax.

Temporary differences normally occur due to timing differences, i.e. when income or expense is recognized in an accounting profit in a different period to when it is included in taxable profit. Remember the example of depreciation here. There are, however, temporary differences that are not timing differences.

Temporary differences that are not timing differences

IAS 12 discusses five circumstances where temporary differences arise that are not timing differences. We have already discussed two of these, goodwill and initial recognition, and as we saw this temporary difference does not give rise to deferred tax as IAS 12 exempts them. The other three cases do give rise to deferred tax though as we now describe.

Business combinations

When a combination occurs under the acquisition method then the acquired assets and liabilities are revalued to fair value. However, the tax base of the asset or liability remains at its original figure within the subsidiary. (NB A group is not a taxable entity.) A temporary difference therefore arises on which a deferred tax liability is recognized.

Revaluation of assets

Where assets are revalued to fair value there may be a temporary difference. This temporary difference will arise in tax jurisdictions where the tax base of the asset is not adjusted for the revaluation. IAS 12 requires deferred tax to be recognized on this temporary difference. This does seem somewhat illogical. If the tax base of the asset is not adjusted as there is no tax effect from the revaluation then how can a liability arise? The IASB justifies the recognition of the liability on the grounds that the asset will generate future taxable income but this is again debatable as it is difficult to see how future taxable income can equal a past event! We discussed this point on p. 367.

Investment in subsidiaries, branches, associates and joint ventures

In the case of an enterprise with these types of investment the tax base of the investment is generally cost. The carrying amount of the investment, however, changes over time as undistributed profits are built up in the subsidiary, associate etc. or due to foreign currency translation or when the investment is reduced to its recoverable amount. These changes will give rise to temporary differences and IAS 12 requires deferred tax to be recognized except where:

■ the parent, investor or venturer is able to control the timing of the reversal of the difference
■ and it is probable that the difference will not reverse in the foreseeable future.

One circumstance where a parent can control the difference is the declaration of dividends from the subsidiary but the parent could not control the difference in relation to foreign currency translation.

Deferred tax asset

IAS 12 requires that a deferred tax asset is recognized for all deductible temporary differences to the extent that it is probable that taxable profit will be available against which the deductible temporary difference can be utilized. The deferred tax asset is required to be recognized on a partial basis when there is not sufficient deductible temporary difference. The meaning of 'probable' is to some extent subjective, as it is under IAS 37 *Provision, Contingent Liabilities and Contingent Assets*. There are two circumstances when a deferred tax asset should not be recognized and these are when it arises from:

■ negative goodwill that is treated as deferred income in accordance with IAS 22 *Business Combinations* or

■ the initial recognition of an asset or liability in a transaction that:
   – is not a business combination
   – at the time of the transaction affects neither accounting profit nor taxable profit (loss).

These mirror the exemptions under deferred tax liability.

Activity 19.11

An enterprise has calculated deferred tax assets of €1m which will result in deductions in tax computations for the next three years. Deferred tax liabilities of €0.5m have also been calculated in accordance with IAS 12. Taxable profits, including reversal of deferred tax liabilities, are expected to be €0.2m per annum over the next three years. How much of the deferred tax asset should be recognized?

Activity feedback

As only €0.6 of the deferred tax asset can be reversed against future taxable profits then this is the only amount that should be recognized.

Measurement of deferred tax

IAS 12 requires that deferred tax is measured by reference to tax rates and laws, as enacted or substantively enacted by the balance sheet date, that are expected to apply in the periods in which the assets and liabilities to which the deferred tax relates are realized or settled. This is the liability method discussed at p. 365.

Amount recognized in income statement

So far we have concentrated on the measurement of the asset or liability of deferred tax in the balance sheet as this is the approach adopted by IAS 12. The amount recognized in the income statement of a period is the movement in deferred tax from the opening to closing balance sheet. This difference is recognized in arriving at the net profit and loss for the period except for tax arising from:

■ a transaction or event which is recognized in any accounting period directly in equity, in which case the movement in deferred tax should be accounted for directly in equity
■ or a business combination that is accounted for as an acquisition, in which case the movement in deferred tax is included in the resulting goodwill figure.

Activity 19.12

An enterprise purchases an asset, cost €50 000, on 1.1.X1. Depreciation is on a straight line basis over its useful life of five years. The taxable allowance for the asset is straight line over four years. On 31.12.X3 the asset is revalued to €45 000 but its useful life and method of depreciation remains unchanged. The revaluation of the asset is irrelevant for tax legislation. Show the charge to the income statement for deferred tax over the life of the asset given tax rate at 30% for all years and compare it with the situation where there is no revaluation.

Activity feedback

Revaluation:

Date	Carrying amount €	Tax base	Temp. difference
31.12.X1	40 000	37 500	2 500
31.12.X2	30 000	25 000	5 000
31.12.X3	45 000	12 500	32 500
31.12.X4	22 500	0	22 500
31.12.X5	0		

When the asset was revalued €25 000 would have been transferred to revaluation reserve. The charge against this for deferred tax is at 30% = 7500. Net amount to revaluation reserve therefore €17 500.

Deferred tax liability At 30%	Movement in year	IS charge	Equity charge
750	750	750	0
1 500	750	750	0
9 750	8 250	750	7 500
6 750	(3 000)	(3 000)	(3 750)
0	(6 750)	(6 750)	(3 750)

Transfers from the equity revaluation reserve to retained earnings will be required for the excess depreciation charged over and above historical cost basis net of deferred tax in each of the final two years as follows:

Historical cost depreciation charge	10 000
Revaluation depreciation charge	22 500
Excess	12 500
Deferred tax 30%	3 750
	8 750

and therefore the €3750 will need to be credited to the revaluation reserve in the last two years.

No revaluation:

Date	Carrying amount	Tax base	Temp. diff	DT liability	Movement in year	Income statement charge
31.12.X1	40 000	37 500	2 500	750	750	750
31.12.X2	30 000	25 000	5 000	1 500	750	750
31.12.X3	20 000	12 500	7 500	2 250	750	750
31.12.X4	10 000	0	10 000	3 000	750	750
31.12.X5	0	—	0	0	(3 000)	(3 000)

Activity 19.13

An enterprise purchases shares in another enterprise, leading to a parent/subsidiary relationship. The fair value of the net assets purchased included a deferred tax liability of €50 000 being temporary differences of €125 000 at 40%. In the accounting year after the purchase it is announced that the tax rate applicable for the following year is to change to 42%. By the end of the accounting year after the year of the purchase €40 000 of the temporary difference had reversed. Show the deferred tax liability at the end of the accounting year after the year of purchase and state where any changes would be charged.

Activity feedback

In this activity the years are confusing and it is therefore easier to see the effects using a table.

Year	Tax rate	Temp. difference	DT liability
Of purchase	40%	125 000	50 000
After purchase	40%	85 000	34 000
Next year	42%		35 700

If the tax rate change had not been enacted or substantively enacted the deferred tax liability account would have remained at €34 000, but as the change is known about at the year end the deferred tax under the liability method must be accounted for at €35 700 and thus €1700 will be charged to the income statement for the year after the purchase. The charge cannot be debited to any goodwill on the acquisition as it results from a post-acquisition event.

Presentation and disclosure requirement

IAS 12 is quite prescriptive in the presentation of tax assets and liabilities in the accounts as follows:

- Tax assets and liabilities must be separated from other assets and liabilities in the balance sheet.
- Deferred tax should be distinguished from current tax.
- Deferred tax should be shown under non-current.
- Current tax assets and liabilities can be offset only where the enterprise has a legally enforceable right to do so and it intends to settle on a net basis or to realize the asset and settle the liabilities simultaneously.
- Deferred tax assets and liabilities can only be offset where the enterprise has a legally enforceable right to do so for current taxes and they relate to tax levies by the same taxation authority.

The disclosure requirements are extensive and we suggest you read the Standard in detail for these. In the main disclosure is required of the:

- separate major components of the tax charge or credit in the income statement, e.g. current tax, deferred tax, changes in either due to tax rates
- charges in respect of tax charged to equity

- tax relating to extraordinary items
- reconciliation between tax charge and that calculated by applying the tax rate to accounting profit
- detail of temporary differences of deferred tax.

Discounting

IAS 12 does not permit the discounting of deferred tax balances with one exception, unlike UK GAAP, which does permit it. IAS 12 allows discounting of deferred tax where it relates to a pre-tax amount that is itself discounted. This exception is obvious as the application of a tax rate to the discounted item will automatically result in a deferred tax charge that is discounted. Deferred tax is defined as a liability and as payment is some time in the future it is obvious that under the current regime of IAS 12 the amount shown as a liability does not reflect this deferment to the future. Discounting the deferred tax could be seen as an attempt to reflect the fair value but could also be seen as a method to reflect the time value of money. UK GAAP uses discounting to reflect the 'time value of money' effect on deferred tax but the whole issue is controversial. The IASB are reflecting on discounting but for the moment it does not permit discounting on deferred tax because:

- reliable calculation is complex and dependent on several factors not least of which is choice of discount rate and therefore if discounting was required 'reliability' would be questionable
- if discounting is permitted some enterprises would discount and others wouldn't leading to a lack of comparability.

Comparison between GAAP

US GAAP

IAS and US GAAP are fairly similar on the issue of current and deferred taxes as both require full provisioning for deferred tax based on temporary differences. There are, however, some differences in the types of temporary differences for which no deferred tax need be provided. For example, as we have seen, IAS does not require deferred tax on temporary differences arising from the initial recognition of assets or liabilities but US GAAP does.

UK GAAP

UK GAAP is based on a full provisioning for incremental timing differences (income statement approach) and IAS is based on full provisioning on a temporary difference approach (balance sheet liability method). One of the major differences ensuing from the use of these two methods is that IAS GAAP will provide for deferred tax on revalued assets whereas UK GAAP will not. IAS 12 encompasses all timing differences from UK GAAP (FRS 19), but also includes many permanent differences. However, IAS 12 requires that deferred tax should not be recognized for certain temporary differences that would be permanent differences under UK GAAP.

UK GAAP, under FRS 19, permits the use of discounting.

Examples of disclosure from IAS accounts

The following disclosure is taken from the accounts of Bayer Group for the year ended 31.12.2000:

Income taxes

This item comprises the income taxes paid or accrued in the individual countries, plus deferred taxes. Deferred taxes arise from temporary differences between the carrying amounts of assets or liabilities in the accounting and tax balance sheets, from consolidation measures and from realizable loss carryforwards. Deferred taxes are calculated at the rates which – on the basis of the statutory regulations in force, or already enacted in relation to future periods, as of the closing date – are expected to apply in the individual countries at the time of realization.

The breakdown of income taxes by origin is as follows:

€ million	2000	1999
Income taxes paid or accrued		
– Germany	442	71
– Other countries	321	429
	763	500
Deferred taxes		
– from temporary differences	383	305
– from loss carryforwards	2	13
	385	318
	1 148	818

Changes in tax rates diminished deferred tax expense for 2000 by €21 million; in 1999, such changes increased it by €41 million. The deferred taxes are allocable to the various balance sheet items as follows.

€ million	31 Dec. 2000 Deferred tax assets	31 Dec. 2000 Deferred tax liabilities	31 Dec. 1999 Deferred tax assets	31 Dec. 1999 Deferred tax liabilities
Intangible assets	87	72	101	28
Property, plant and equipment	68	1 745	18	1 409
Investments	2	79	10	40
Inventories	298	86	266	92
Receivables	116	51	76	28
Other current assets	51	132	14	74
Pension provisions	327	202	265	131
Other provisions	144	46	210	26
Other liabilities	163	40	150	32
Loss carryforwards	15	–	–	–
Changes in companies consolidated	1 271	2 453	1 110	1 806
Set-off*	858	858	703	703
	413	1 595	407	1 157

*According to IAS 12 (*Income Taxes*), deferred tax assets and deferred tax liabilities should, under certain conditions, be offset if they relate to income taxes levied by the same taxation authority.

Changes in companies consolidated in 2000 account for €122 million in deferred tax assets and €167 million in deferred tax liabilities.

Utilization of tax loss carryforwards from previous years diminished the amount of income taxes paid or accrued in 2000 by €7 million (1999: €9 million) and increased deferred tax expense by €2 million (1999: €13 million). The potential tax savings relating to tax loss carryforwards are only recognized as deferred tax income if it is sufficiently certain that this income will be realized. Tax loss carryforwards of €204 million (1999: €181 million remained untilized).

The actual income tax expense of €1148 million for 2000 is €31 million less than the €1179 million that would result from applying to the pre-tax income of the Group a tax rate of 39.5 percent (1999: 42.7 percent), which is the weighted average of the theoretical tax rates for the individual Group companies. The reconciliation of theoretical to actual income tax expense for the Group is as follows:

	2000		1999	
	€ million	%	€ million	%
Theoretical income Tax expense	1 179	100	1 212	100
Lower taxes due to tax-free income	(151)	(13)	(434)	(36)
Higher taxes due to non-tax-deductible expenses	93	8	90	7
Other tax effects	27	2	(50)	(4)
Actual income tax expense	**1 148**	**97**	**818**	**67**
Effective tax rate in %	38.4		28.8	

The income tax expense for 2000 does not include any prior-period items. The 1999 figure includes €1 million in prior-period income.

Summary

Within this chapter we have considered the principles of debate on accounting for tax and identified the regulations of IAS 12. We have seen that accounting standard-setting bodies, which all believe they are issuing standards within a conceptual framework, can view the principles of deferred tax quite differently. Our debate in this chapter has considered deferred tax from a:

- balance sheet or income statement approach
- flow through, partial or full provision method
- deferral or liability method.

We also considered the possibility of discounting deferred tax. We leave you with the question 'Does the required accounting treatment of taxation in published IAS accounts lead to a true and fair view as required by the Fourth Directive?'

1 Outline the major arguments in favour of always providing for deferred tax where the amounts are material.

2 Outline the major arguments in favour of only providing for deferred tax when it is probable that a liability will crystallize.

3 Deferred tax should be ignored when preparing financial statements. Discuss.

✔ 4 Explain and distinguish between:
- the flow through approach
- full deferral
- partial deferral.

5 Explain and distinguish between:
- the deferral method
- the liability method.

6 Comparability requires that either all enterprises provide in full for deferred tax or that it is always ignored. Discuss.

✔ 7 Explain to a non-accountant the difference between the income statement view and the balance sheet view of deferred tax.

8 Discounting deferred tax balances would provide useful information to users. Discuss.

9 Critically appraise the following statement: *The required accounting treatment of taxation in published IAS accounts does not lead to a true and fair view as required by the Fourth Directive.*

10 (i) IAS 12 'Income Tax' was issued in 1996 and revised in 2000. It details the requirements relating to the accounting treatment of deferred tax.

Required:

Explain why it is considered necessary to provide for deferred tax and briefly outline the principles of accounting for deferred tax contained in IAS 12 'Income Tax'.

(ii) Bowtock purchased an item of plant for $2 000 000 on 1 October 2000. It had an estimated life of eight years and an estimated residual value of $400 000. The plant is depreciated on straight-line basis. The tax authorities do not allow depreciation as a deductible expense. Instead a tax expense of 40% of the cost of this type of asset can be claimed against income tax in the year of purchase and 20% per annum (on a reducing balance basis) of its tax base thereafter. The rate of income tax can be taken as 25%.

Required:

In respect of the above item of plant, calculate the deferred tax charge/credit in Bowtock's income statement for the year to 30 September 2003 and the deferred tax balance in the balance sheet at that date.

Note: work to the nearest $000. (ACCA Dec 03)

11 Nette, a public limited company, manufactures mining equipment and extracts natural gas. The directors are uncertain about the role of the IASB's 'Framework for the Preparation and Presentation of Financial Statements' (the Framework) in corporate reporting. Their view is that accounting is based on the transactions carried out by the company and these transactions are allocated to the company's accounting period by using the matching and prudence concepts. The argument put forward by the directors is that the Framework does not take into account the business and legal constraints within which companies operate. Further they have given a situation which has arisen in the current financial statements where they feel that the current accounting practice is inconsistent with the Framework.

Situation

Nette purchased a building on 1 June 2003 for $10 million. The building qualified for a grant of $2 million which has been treated as a deferred credit in the financial statements. The tax allowances are reduced by the amount of the grant. There are additional temporary differences of $40 million in respect of deferred tax liabilities at the year end. Also the company has sold extraction equipment which carries a five year warranty. The directors have made a provision for the warranty of $4 million at 31 May 2004 which is deductible for tax when costs are incurred under the warranty. In addition to the warranty provision the company has unused tax losses of $70 million. The directors of the company are unsure as to whether a provision for deferred taxation is required.

(Assume that the depreciation of the building is straight line over ten years, and tax allowances of 25% on the reducing balance basis can be claimed on the building. Tax is payable at 30%.)

Required:

(a) Explain the importance of the 'Framework' to the reporting of corporate performance and whether it takes into account the business and legal constraints placed upon companies.

(b) (i) Explain with reasons and suitable extracts/computations the accounting treatment of the above situation in the financial statements for the year ended 31 May 2004.

   (ii) Discuss whether the treatment of the items appears consistent with the 'Framework'.
   (ACCA June 04)

Employee benefits

After studying this chapter you should be able to:
- □ explain how short-term employee benefits have to be accounted for
- □ explain the difference between defined contribution pension plans and defined benefit pension plans
- □ explain the purpose and function of actuarial cost or funding methods
- □ list several actuarial assumptions and discuss their impact on the pension cost and pension benefit obligation
- □ define the concept of total pension cost according to IAS 19
- □ define the concept of a defined benefit liability according to IAS 19
- □ describe what is meant by pension plan assets
- □ explain what is meant by the 'corridor' approach
- □ explain how equity-settled share-based payment transactions have to be accounted for
- □ explain how cash-settled share-based payment transactions have to be accounted for
- □ describe the contents of a pension plan report according to IAS 26.

Introduction

In every organization, people are a very important resource. Without a competent and loyal staff of personnel, an entity will usually be unsuccessful. To keep the workforce motivated and loyal most, if not all, employers provide employees with certain benefits in addition to the wages paid. Employee benefits are usually furnished by the employer in full, but some types of benefits are paid for jointly by the employer and the employee.

A benefit package may include: retirement plans; insurance plans such as hospital, dental, life and disability insurance; stock options; profit-sharing plans; recreational programmes; vacations and so on.

A number of these employee benefits have a long-term perspective, which implies that elements of uncertainty are involved. As a consequence, accounting for a number of these long-term employee benefits is not that straightforward and of a rather high technical level.

Activity 20.1

If you think of employee benefits, which benefits do you consider to be short-term benefits and which would you regard as long term-benefits?

Activity feedback

- Short-term benefits: salaries, paid holiday, bonuses, medical care.
- Long-term benefits: medical care after retirement, pension benefits.

Equity compensation benefits can be either short term or long term depending on the exercise period.

Most of the employee benefits are dealt with in IAS 19, *Employee Benefits*. One particular type of employee benefit, namely equity compensation or share-based benefits, is dealt with in IFRS 2, *Share-based Payment*. IFRS 2 describes the recognition and valuation rules when an entity undertakes a share-based payment transaction.

We will first present the definitions, recognition and measurement rules for those employee benefits that fall within the scope of IAS 19. Subsequently, we will discuss the accounting treatment of share-based compensation, which is dealt with in IFRS 2.

IAS 19 qualifies as short-term benefits wages, salaries and social security contributions, paid annual leave and paid sick leave, profit sharing and bonuses (if payable within 12 months of the end of the period) and non-monetary benefits (such as medical care, housing, cars and free or subsidized goods or services) for current employees.

Profit-sharing plans and bonus plans can be long term or short term, according to when they are payable (within 12 months or longer). Examples of long-term benefits are qualified post-employment benefits such as pensions, other retirement benefits, post-employment life insurance and post-employment medical care. Long-term employee benefits include long-service leave or sabbatical leave, jubilee or other long-service benefits and long-term disability benefits.

IAS 19 deals with further termination benefits.

If we discuss the issue of how these benefits should be accounted for then it is important to determine when a company is obliged or required to fulfil these employee benefits. The accounting treatment which IAS 19 prescribes for employee benefits is applicable if they result from:

- formal plans or other formal agreements between an enterprise and individual employees, groups of employees or their representatives
- legislative requirements, or from industry arrangements, whereby enterprises are required to contribute to national, state, industry or other multi-employer plans
- or informal practices that give rise to a constructive obligation. Informal practices give rise to a constructive obligation where the enterprise has no realistic alternative but to pay employee benefits. An example of a constructive obligation is where a change in the enterprise's informal practices would cause unacceptable damage to its relationship with employees.

Accounting for short-term employee benefits is straightforward as these elements do not include many uncertainties. We will look first at those short-term employee benefits. Then we will focus on the long-term employee benefits and, more specifically, on pension benefits.

Accounting for short-term employee benefits

Short-term benefits are salaries, paid leave, bonus plans payable within 12 months and other benefits payable. With regard to these benefits the basic valuation rule is as follows: When an employee has rendered service to an enterprise during an accounting period, the enterprise should recognize the undiscounted amount of short-term employee benefits expected to be paid in exchange for that service. The benefit will be reported as an expense, unless another International Accounting Standard requires or permits the inclusion of the benefits in the cost of an asset (see, for example, IAS 2, *Inventories*, and IAS 16, *Property, Plant and Equipment*) and as a liability (accrued expense), after deducting any amount already paid. If the amount already paid exceeds the undiscounted amount of the benefits, an enterprise should recognize that excess as an asset (prepaid expense) to the extent that the prepayment will lead to, for example, a reduction in future payments or a cash refund.

Compensated absences are short-term employee benefits. IAS 19 pays explicit attention to them. Concerning these short-term compensated absences IAS 19 makes a distinction between accumulating and non-accumulating compensated absences. The difference between the two will result in a different accounting treatment.

Activity 20.2

Can you think of some examples of paid absence? Can you distinguish between whether they arise from service rendered in the past (=accumulated absences) or whether they are not related to service rendered at work (=non-accumulated absences)?

Activity feedback

A typical example of an accumulated compensated absence is absence for vacation (holiday). According to the number of days worked an employee is entitled to a number of days of paid absence. Examples of non-accumulated absences are sickness leave, maternity and paternity leave, military service.

In the case of accumulating compensated absences the expected cost of the short-term benefit has to be recognized when the employees render the service that increases their entitlement to future compensated absences.

In the case of non-accumulating compensated absence, the benefit should be recognized when the absence occurs, as in the latter case the absence is not linked to the service rendered by the employees in a period.

Accounting for profit-sharing and bonus plans

The compensation package of many executives, but also of higher and middle management these days often includes profit-sharing plans or bonus plans. When profit-sharing or bonus plans exist executives and employees receive a variable amount as compensation on top of their salary. These bonuses can be linked to financial indicators (for example accounting numbers such as earnings before interest and taxes

(EBIT), return on assets (ROA), return on equity (ROE)) or non-financial indicators (for example customer satisfaction) or a combination of both.

The obligation to pay an amount to the employees under a profit-sharing or bonus plan results from employee service and not from a transaction with the enterprise's owners. Therefore, an enterprise has to recognize the cost of profit-sharing and bonus plans as an expense and not as a distribution of net profit (para. 21). The bonus as such qualifies as an obligation. The amount linked to it is dependent on the realized performance in relation to the indicator specified in the profit-sharing or bonus plan.

As a result the expected cost of profit-sharing and bonus payments should be recognized as an expense and as a liability when, and only when (para. 10 and 17): the enterprise has a present legal or constructive obligation to make such payments as a result of past events and a reliable estimate of the obligation can be made. A present obligation exists when, and only when, the enterprise has no realistic alternative but to make the payments.

IAS 19 in itself, unfortunately, does not require specific disclosures about short-term benefits, other International Accounting Standards, however, may require disclosures concerning these short-term benefits. For example, where required by IAS 24, *Related Party Disclosures*, an enterprise has to disclose information about employee benefits for key management personnel or IAS 1, *Presentation of Financial Statements*, requires that an enterprise should disclose staff costs.

IAS 19 does not oblige a company to provide information about the formal terms of a bonus or profit-sharing plan to external stakeholders of the company. This information disclosure is left to the voluntary disclosure policy of the firm. Since empirical research related to earnings management found evidence that these bonus plans and profit-sharing plans can create incentives to manage the reported results of a firm, it would be interesting to know the amounts paid out in respect of these plans but even more interesting to know the indicator (financial or non-financial) which drives the bonus.

This would be useful information for financial analysis purposes (for a further discussion of this item see Chapter 26). Information on the formal terms of the plan (e.g. the indicators to which the bonus is linked) can give the external user of the financial statements an idea concerning the direction in which the results possibly could have been influenced. We might hope that in the wake of the 'accounting scandals' of the year 2002, these practices become less common.

Accounting for equity compensation benefits

Bonus plans and profit-sharing plans have for a long time been the only widely used instrument to increase compensation of executives and employees. From the beginning of the 1990s stock-based compensation or share-based payment became very popular. Stock based compensation can take the form of stock options or gifts of shares for free or at lower than market values. Empirical research on incentives for earnings management also reveals that the existence of stock options might induce management to smooth reported income and to increase income upward in order to boost the share price. These elements are illustrated further in Chapter 26.

The instruments that qualify as equity-based compensation are:

(a) shares, share options and other equity instruments, issued to directors, senior executives and other employees; and

(b) cash payments, the amount of which will depend on the future market price of the reporting enterprise's shares or other equity instruments, again as part of a remuneration plan.

These instruments, without doubt, have an impact on the result, the financial position and the cash flow of an enterprise. If a company uses existing shares for the equity-based compensation plans, then the company has to buy the shares from existing shareholders. This implies a cost for the company. If a company chooses to issue extra shares (in that case employees can subscribe for new shares), there is a dilutive effect when the options are exercised (see Chapter 23).

Important elements concerning equity-based compensation are the grant date, the exercise date, the exercise price (strike price) and the vesting date. The difference between the exercise price and the market price is the key value driver of warrants/ options. Simple methods (intrinsic value) only use this difference for valuation purposes. More sophisticated methods are using valuation methods (for instance the Black and Scholes model) which incorporate additional parameters (e.g. volatility).

Relevant accounting valuation issues concerning these benefits are: How to measure the cost of compensation offered by the company to the employees? When to recognize this cost in the profit and loss account? How to account for the financial impact of stock options (e.g. if existing shares are bought, how will they be financed by the company)?

Equity-based compensation is a hot topic in accounting regulation. Previous attempts of the United States Financial Accounting Standards Board to prescribe valuation and recognition rules whereby the cost of the share-based compensation had to be charged to the profit and loss account had to be withdrawn under the pressure of the business community. So SFAS 123, *Accounting for Stock-based Compensation*, is one of the exceptional standards where preparers can make a choice whether or not to include an item on the balance sheet or account for it off balance sheet. However, since Enron the attitude of the business world is changing. In July 2002 Coca-Cola announced that it would recognize the cost of stock-based compensation in its profit and loss account from 2002 on; other companies made the same announcement.

Activity 20.3

Look at websites of several companies from different parts of Europe and worldwide and try to find information on stock-based compensation or other elements of compensation. What do you observe?

Activity feedback

Disclosure on equity-based compensation and about compensation at large differs among different countries. In the Anglo-Saxon world information on compensation has for some time found its way onto the financial statements. Compensation levels of individuals are disclosed in those financial statements. In continental Europe the presence of the value 'secrecy' (discussed in Chapter 2) probably has an impact on the amount and the way in which information is disclosed. Further a diversity of share-based compensation plans is found in the notes to the accounts of companies.

The choice left by SFAS 123 with regard to the recognition and measurement of equity-based remuneration instruments is unsatisfactory for the users of financial information. Studies by Bearn Steams and Credit Suisse First Boston show that if companies belonging to the Standards & Poor 500 had accounted for their equity-based remuneration investments on the balance sheet with the use of the fair value, the earnings of those companies would have been significantly lower.

One of the first issues the Board, in its new composition, wanted to solve is the recognition and valuation of these equity benefit compensation schemes. In the beginning of 2004 IFRS 2 *Share-based Payment* was issued. With IFRS 2, the Board has chosen for the recognition and measurement of those equity-based remuneration instruments on balance sheet. A disclosure of these benefits in the notes only and no recognition on balance sheet was no longer accepted.

The scope of IFRS 2 includes all share-based payment transactions. So IFRS 2 is applicable to more transactions than just equity-based compensation benefits. IFRS 2 defines share-based transactions as those transactions where an entity's equity instruments are transferred by its shareholder to parties that have supplied goods or services to the entity, unless the transfer is clearly for a purpose other than payment for goods or services supplied to the entity. IFRS 2 also applies to transfers of equity instruments of the entity's parent, or equity instruments of another entity in the same group as the entity, to parties that have supplied goods or services to the entity. However, an entity shall not apply this IFRS to transactions in which the entity acquires goods as part of the net assets acquired in a business combination to which IFRS 3, *Business Combinations*, applies (para. 5). A transaction with an employee (or other party) in his/her capacity as a holder of equity instruments of the entity is not considered to be a share-based payment transaction and does not fall under the scope of IFRS 2.

IFRS 2 distinguishes with regard to the nature of the share-based payment transactions between three different types of share-based transactions (para. 2):

(a) *equity-settled share-based payment transactions*, in which the entity receives goods or services as consideration for equity instruments of the entity (including shares or share options);

(b) *cash-settled share-based payment transactions*, in which the entity acquires goods or services by incurring liabilities to the supplier of those goods or services for amounts that are based on the price (or value) of the entity's shares or other equity instruments of the entity; and

(c) *share-based payment transactions with cash alternatives*, these are transactions in which the entity receives or acquires goods or services and the term of the arrangement provide either the entity or the supplier of those goods or services with a choice of whether the entity settles the transaction in cash (or other assets) or by issuing equity instruments.

Although the accounting treatment of these three types of share-based payment transaction will be different, the main objective will be that an entity should reflect in its results and in its financial position the effects of share-based payment transactions when the goods are obtained and services are received. We will now present and illustrate the definition, recognition and measurement rules of the three types of share-based payment transactions.

Equity-settled share-based payment transactions

In equity-settled share-based payment transactions an entity receives goods or services in exchange for equity instruments. For example, an entity acquires equipment from a manufacturer and uses shares as consideration. Another example is a top executive in a company who receives as part of its remuneration shares, share options or other equity instruments.

IFRS 2 (para. 10) states that for these equity-settled share-based payment transactions, the entity shall measure the goods or services received and the corresponding increase in equity, directly, at the fair value of the goods or services received, unless that fair value cannot be estimated reliably. If the entity cannot estimate reliably the fair value of the goods or services received, the entity shall measure their value, and the corresponding increase in equity, indirectly, by reference to the fair value of the equity instruments granted.

Activity 20.4

Consider the two examples just given (the acquisition of the equipment and the compensation of the top executive) and determine which amount will be used under IFRS 2 for the valuation of the transaction in the books of the entity.

Activity feedback

In case of the equipment, the market value of the equipment will be used to measure, on the one hand, the increase in the fixed assets and, on the other hand, the increase in equity. In the situation where equity instruments are used as remuneration for services rendered by employees, directors or other senior executives, it is usually not possible to measure directly the services received for particular components of the employee's remuneration package. It might also not be possible to measure the fair value of the total remuneration package independently, without measuring directly the fair value of the equity instruments granted. Furthermore, shares or share options are sometimes granted as part of a bonus arrangement, rather than as a part of the basic remuneration. By granting shares or share options, in addition to other remuneration, the entity is paying additional remuneration to obtain additional benefits. Estimating the fair value of those additional benefits is likely to be difficult. Because of the difficulty of measuring directly the fair value of the services received, the entity shall measure the fair value of the employee services received by reference to the fair value of the equity instruments granted. So the share-based remuneration will be recorded in the books of the company in the following manner. The amount of the fair value of the equity instrument will be debited on an expense remuneration account and credited on an equity account.

So IFRS 2 distinguishes with regard to the valuation of these equity-settled share-based transactions between two possibilities, namely when the fair value of the goods received and the services rendered can be measured reliably and when it is not possible to determine this value in a reliable way. In the latter situation the fair value of the equity instrument will be used for reporting purposes.

Before focusing further on the recognition and measurement issues of these equity-settled share-based payment transactions, we will explain a number of concepts that play a role in the accounting treatment of these share-based transactions. First, there is the grant date of the share-based payment transaction. This is the date at which the entity and another party (including an employee) agree to a share-based payment arrangement, being when the entity and the other contracting party have a shared understanding of the terms and conditions of the arrangement. At grant date the entity confers on the other contracting party the right to cash, other assets, or equity instruments of the entity, provided the specified vesting conditions, if any, are met. If that agreement is subject to an approval process (for example, by shareholders), grant date is the date when that approval is obtained.

In the definition of the grant date, we discover the concept of 'vesting conditions'. These are the conditions that must be satisfied for the counterparty to become entitled to receive cash, other assets or equity instruments of the entity, under a share-based payment arrangement. Vesting conditions include service conditions, which require the other party to complete a specified period of service, and performance conditions, which require specified performance targets to be met (such as a specified increase in the entity's profit over a specified period of time).

Illustration

A company, Amax, grants 50 share options to each of its 200 employees. If there is no vesting requirement the employees are entitled to receive these granted options immediately. The fair value of the share option at the grant date is €30. When the equity instruments granted vest immediately implying that the counterparty is not required to complete a specific period of service before becoming unconditionally entitled to those equity instruments, the entity shall recognize on grant date the services received in full, with a corresponding increase in equity.

In this situation the expense related to these granted share options is:

$$10\,000 \text{ options} \times €30 = €300\,000$$

This amount will be debited on an expense account and credited in an equity account.

The fair value of the equity instruments granted should be determined at the measurement date. IFRS 2 defines the measurement date as the date at which the fair value of the equity instruments are granted. For transactions with employees and others providing similar services, the measurement date is the grant date. For transactions with parties other than employees (and those providing similar services), the measurement date is the date the entity obtains the goods or the counterparty renders service.

If market prices are available they should be used as fair value of the equity instruments. If market prices are not available, valuation techniques can be used to estimate the fair value of those equity instruments on the measurement date in an at arm's length transaction between knowledgeable willing parties. In relation to share options the Black-Scholes-Merton formula might be used. When the fair value of the equity instruments cannot be measured reliably, IFRS 2 stipulates that the intrinsic value of the instrument will be used for valuation purposes. The intrinsic value of the equity instrument is defined in the appendix to IFRS 2 as the difference between the fair value of the shares the counterparty has the right to and the price (if any) the counterparty is required to pay for those shares. In many cases, transactions will have an intrinsic value of nil at the date of the grant. Therefore, IFRS 2 requires that all share-based payments measured at intrinsic value be remeasured through profit or loss at each reporting date until the transaction is settled (e.g. the exercise of options granted).

If vesting requirements exist then the grant of the equity instruments is conditional on satisfying specified vesting conditions. For example, a grant of shares or share options to an employee is typically conditional on the employee remaining in the entity's employ for a specified period of time. Suppose that company Amax still grants 50 share options to each of its 200 employees, but that each grant is conditional on the employee remaining in service over the next three years.

Vesting conditions might also take the form of performance conditions that must be satisfied, such as the entity achieving a specified growth in profit or a specified increase in the entity's share price. Suppose that company Amax grants 50 share options to each of its 200 employees, conditional on the employees' remaining in the company for a period of two years. However, the shares will only vest if at the end of year 2 the return on equity of the company will have increased with 4% over the vesting period.

The entity shall recognize an amount for the goods or services received during the vesting period based on the best available estimate of the number of equity instruments expected to vest and shall revise that estimate, if necessary, if subsequent information indicates that the number of equity instruments expected to vest differs from previous estimates. On the vesting date, the entity shall revise the estimate to equal the number of equity instruments that ultimately vested. When vesting conditions exist the amount of the services received, measured by the fair value of the equity instruments, is allocated over the vesting period.

When company Amax wants to enter its share-based transaction in its books, it needs information on the probability that the employees will remain in service. On the basis of past experience, company Amax estimates that 10% of employees will leave during the three-year period and therefore forfeit their rights to the share options. If we take the example of the share option plan that is only dependent on the vesting condition that the employee remains in service for three years we will have the following amounts to be entered in the books of company Amax. For this illustration we assume that after three years the estimates used match exactly with the reality and that the fair value of the option at grant date is €30.

Year	Calculation	Amount debited on the expense account	Amount credited on an equity account
1	10 000 options × 90% × €30 × 1/3	€90 000	€90 000
2	(10 000 options × 90% × €30 × 2/3) − 90 000	€90 000	€90 000
3	(10 000 options × 90% × €30 × 3/3) − 180 000	€90 000	€90 000

Over the vesting period an amount of €270 000 has been reported on the profit and loss account as a remuneration expense and over the same period that amount has been credited to an equity account.

After the vesting period, the entity shall not make any subsequent adjustments to its equity. IFRS 2 describes further the recognition and measurement rules on how to deal with modifications to the terms and conditions on which equity instruments were granted, including cancellations and settlements. Discussing these elements in detail would go beyond the purpose of this textbook.

Cash-settled share-based payment transactions

For cash-settled share-based payment transactions, the entity shall measure the goods or services acquired and the liability incurred at the fair value of the liability. Until the liability is settled, the entity shall remeasure the fair value of the liability at each reporting date and at the date of settlement, with any changes in fair value recognized in profit or loss for the period.

Illustration

Suppose Amax grants 50 share options to each of its 200 employees, on the condition that the employees remain in service for the next three years. The employees may choose to exercise their options at the end of year 3, year 4 or year 5. The payment will however be in cash. The amount of cash to be received will be determined by the value of the option at exercise date. During the first year eight employees leave the company, the entity estimates that 12 employees will leave the company in the next two years. During year 2 a total of eight employees leave the company and the company estimates that six employees will leave Amax in year 3. In the third year ten employees leave the company. At the end of year three the share options held by the remaining employees vest.

In the third year 30 employees exercise their options, in the fourth year another 40 employees exercise their option and in the fifth year the remaining 104 employees exercise their options.

Amax uses the following estimates for the valuation of this cash-settled share-based transaction in its books.

Year	Fair value	Intrinsic value
1	€10	
2	€11	
3	€14	€12,50
4	€17	€15,00
5		€20,00

This cash-settled share based transaction will lead to the following amounts

Year	Calculations	Expense	Liability
1	$(200 - 20) \times 50 \times €10 \times$ $1/3 = 30\,000$	30 000	30 000
2	$((200 - 22) \times 50 \times €11 \times$ $2/3) - 30\,000 = 35\,266$	35 266	65 266
3	$((200 - 26 - 30) \times 50 \times €14) -$ $65\,266 = 35\,534$ $+ 30 \times 50 \times €12{,}5 = 18\,750$	54 284	100 800
4	$((144 - 40) \times 50 \times €17) -$ $100\,800 = -12\,400$ $+ 40 \times 50 \times €15 = 30\,000$	17 600	88 400
5	$0 - 88\,400 = -88\,400$ $+ 104 \times 50 \times €20 = 104\,000$	15 600	0

The amount in the column 'Expense' represents the remuneration expense for the period and the amount in the column 'Liability' represents the amount on the liability account. In the example of the cash-settled share-based payment transaction presented above, we need to remeasure the liability at its fair value after the vesting date because not all options have been exercised. If all options are exercised at vesting date, no subsequent remeasurements are necessary.

Share-based payment transactions with cash alternatives

In relation to this third group of share-based payment transactions a distinction is made between, on the one hand, share-based payment transaction in which the terms of the arrangement provide the counterparty with a choice of settlement and, on the other, share-based payment transactions in which the terms of the arrangement provide the entity with a choice of settlement.

In the first situation where an entity has granted the counterparty the right to choose whether a share-based payment transaction is settled in cash or by issuing equity instruments, the entity has granted a compound financial instrument, which includes a debt component (i.e. the counterparty's right to demand payment in cash) and an equity component (i.e. the counterparty's right to demand settlement in equity instruments rather than in cash). For transactions with parties other than employees, in which the fair value of the goods or services received is measured directly, the entity shall measure the equity component of the compound financial instrument as the difference between the fair value of the goods or services received and the fair value of the debt component, at the date when the goods or services are received.

For other transactions, including transactions with employees, the entity shall measure the fair value of the compound financial instrument at the measurement date, taking into account the terms and conditions on which the rights to cash or equity instruments were granted.

For a share-based payment transaction in which the terms of the arrangement provide an entity with the choice of whether to settle in cash or by issuing equity instruments, the entity shall determine whether it has a present obligation to settle in cash and account for the share-based payment transaction accordingly. The entity has a present obligation to settle in cash if the choice of settlement in equity instruments has no commercial substance (e.g. because the entity is legally prohibited from issuing shares), or the entity has a past practice or a stated policy of settling in cash, or generally settles in cash whenever the counterparty asks for cash settlement.

If the entity has a present obligation to settle in cash, it shall account for the transaction in accordance with the requirements applying to cash-settled share-based payment transactions.

If no such obligation exists, the entity shall account for the transaction in accordance with the requirements applying to equity-settled share-based payment transactions, in paras 10–29. On settlement:

(a) If the entity elects to settle in cash, the cash payment shall be accounted for as the repurchase of an equity interest, i.e. as a deduction from equity, except as noted in (c) below.

(b) If the entity elects to settle by issuing equity instruments, no further accounting is required (other than a transfer from one component of equity to another, if necessary), except as noted in (c) below.

(c) If the entity elects the settlement alternative with the higher fair value, as at the date of settlement, the entity shall recognize an additional expense for the excess value given, i.e. the difference between the cash paid and the fair value of the equity instruments that would otherwise have been issued, or the difference between the fair value of the equity instruments issued and the amount of cash that would otherwise have been paid, whichever is applicable.

Disclosures

Extensive information disclosures about these share-based transactions in the notes to the accounts are required by IFRS 2. In relation to these transactions an entity shall disclose information that enables users of financial statement to:

(a) understand the nature and the extent of share-based payment arrangements that existed during the period

(b) understand how the fair value of the goods or services received, or the fair value of the equity instruments granted, during the period was determined

(c) understand the effect of share-based payment transactions on the entity's profit or loss for the period and on its financial position.

These information requirements imply that a detailed description of all share-based payment arrangements have to be disclosed (e.g. the different types of share-based arrangements and their nature and conditions, the number and weighted average exercise price of share options for the outstanding options at the beginning of the period, the ones granted, forfeited, exercised and expired during the period and the ones outstanding at the end of the period and the ones exercisable at the end of the period) a description of how the fair value is determined, details on the expenses recognized and the liabilities recorded.

Accounting for long-term employee benefits: pension benefits

The most important long-term employee benefits are pension benefits. Other long-term employee benefits, including long-service leave or sabbatical leave, jubilee or other long-service benefits, long-term disability benefits, are accounted for in a similar manner as pension benefits. Therefore, we will only discuss the recognition and valuation issues related to pension benefits extensively. We will start the discussion by defining the concept of a pension benefit and by an analysis of the impact of a company pension plan on the financial situation of the company.

Existence of different pension systems

The purpose of a pension is to grant people some money when they are retired. Worldwide three different types of 'pension systems' can be distinguished, namely state pensions, pensions received from the employer resulting from an employment contract and individual pension savings plans. So an individual can be entitled to a state pension, on top of that a retirement benefit resulting from his employment contract (if retirement benefits were included) and finally a payment from an individual pension scheme if the individual has taken the initiative to contribute to an individual savings account. The importance and presence of each type of pension system in a single country is determined by characteristics of the local or national environment. In some countries state pensions are the major source of income for retired people. In other countries initiatives such as company pension plans and individual pension schemes are stimulated by the government and are common practice, because of the lower levels of state pensions.

State pensions do not usually create any accounting problems for enterprises. The companies are collecting the premium from the employees (a deduction from the gross salary) and these amounts together with employer's contributions (if any) are paid to the government. If the premium due for an accounting period, which will be recorded as an expense is not equal to the amount transferred to the government, prepaid expenses or accrued expenses can be reported on the balance sheet. According to IAS 19 state pensions should be accounted for as multi-employer plans and these will often have the character of a defined contribution plan (this concept will be defined later). The treatment stipulated in IAS 19 concerning state pensions is usually in line with what we have already mentioned.

Individual pension schemes are totally separate from employment contracts, so IAS 19 does not focus on them. IAS 19 deals especially with company pension plans as they have an impact on the financial situation of a company.

Company pension plans

A company pension plan can be defined as an agreement between an employer and its employees, whereby the former agrees to pay benefits to the latter after their retirement. The terms of the pension plan stipulate the retirement benefit to which an employee is entitled. There are two major categories of pension schemes or pension plans, namely defined benefit plans and defined contribution plans.

Definition of a pension benefit

In a defined contribution plan the employer agrees to contribute a specific amount to the pension plan with or without a contribution from the employee. The benefits to be received by the employee at retirement are determined by the contributions transferred to the plan plus the investment return obtained on those contributions. This implies that an employee will only know the amount which he will receive as pension benefit on retirement. The contributions are usually paid into a separate entity (fund or insurance company). Further, the employee bears the risk under this type of pension plan as the amount is, in the end, dependent on the obtained investment return on the amounts contributed and invested.

A defined benefit plan is defined by IAS 19 as all plans other than defined contribution plans. If we want to describe defined benefit plans in somewhat more detail we would characterize them as those plans where the benefits promised are defined in advance, whereby the amount of pension benefit to be paid depends on the plan's benefit formula. Plans for which the pension benefit formula is based on compensation levels are called pay-related plans. The three most important types of pay-related plans are:

- the final pay plan in which the benefits are calculated as a percentage of the final salary before retirement
- the final average pay plan, where the benefits are calculated as a percentage of the average salary of the last three to five years before retirement
- the career average pay plan in which the benefits are related to the average salary someone has earned during his career.

In some defined benefit plans the state pensions are included in the benefit formula. This implies, however, that if the level of state pensions drops, the employer faces a higher cost. Plans for which the benefit formula is not based on compensation levels are called non-pay-related plans or flat benefit plans.

Organization and financing of a company pension plan

Providing retirement benefits to the employees involves many decisions. In addition to a decision about the type of pension benefit promised (defined contribution or defined benefit) decisions regarding the organization and the financing or funding patterns of these benefits have to be made as well. The choices made by companies will not only be influenced by company characteristics but also by characteristics of the national environment. The latter will be illustrated later.

When an employer provides his employees with a defined contribution plan, the finance pattern consists of the contributions, stipulated in the pension plan made to a pension account. The finance pattern and the responsibility of the employer can be determined in a very straightforward way. The pension account in which the funds are accumulated can be administered by the company or by a bank.

A defined benefit plan can be financed through the so-called pay as you go system or through a funding system. Under the pay as you go system the pensions are paid directly from the resources of the company as they fall due. The purpose of a funding system on the contrary is to make contributions through the whole employment period of the employee in order to accumulate enough funds to guarantee the pension payments. Usually actuarial cost methods (also called actuarial funding methods) are used to determine the amounts to be financed each period in order to have enough funds to pay the pension benefits when the employees retire.

If pension benefits are financed by means of a funding system two main types of organizational set-ups are possible: internal funding or external funding. In case of internal funding resources are allocated in advance for the provision of benefits, but no separation of these amounts from the other assets of the employer is made. Benefit payments when due are made directly by the employer. In some countries employers are allowed to use those funds accumulated within the enterprise for financing the operational activities of the enterprise. In other countries those funds may be kept in the enterprise but they have to be invested in certain assets. Very often these plans, financed through internal funding, are called unfunded pension plans in the Anglo-Saxon world. This term might be misleading as it may sound as if no financing arrangements have been made yet, as in the case of the pay as you go system. In fact, internally funded plans is a better way to describe this financing system.

If an employer uses external funding the resources are accumulated in a separate legal entity (i.e. there is a separate fund). In the Anglo-Saxon world these plans, which are funded externally, are called funded pension plans. This separate fund may be a unique creation for only one employer or for many employers or it may be operated by a specialist insurance company running many such schemes. The contract with the insurance company has to stipulate what type of risks and responsibilities are transferred to the insurance company. The terms of this contract are extremely important for accounting purposes as they determine whether insured benefits will be considered a defined contribution type or a defined benefit type.

Para. 39 states in this respect: An enterprise may pay insurance premiums to fund a post-employment benefit plan. The enterprise should treat such a plan as a defined contribution plan unless the enterprise will have (either directly, or indirectly through the plan) a legal or constructive obligation to either:

- pay the employee benefits directly when they fall due
- or pay further contributions if the insurer does not pay all future employee benefits relating to employee service in the current and prior periods.

If the enterprise retains such a legal or constructive obligation, the enterprise should treat the plan as a defined benefit plan.

Whether an insured plan qualifies as a defined contribution plan or a defined benefit plan is an extremely important matter, since the way these plans have to be accounted for is totally different. Companies will have a tendency to try to qualify their insured plans as much as possible as defined contribution plans.

Although employers can choose between different types of pension benefit and different ways to organize and finance them, country-specific influences are often encountered. First of all the importance of the pension benefits granted by the employer versus state pensions differs among countries. In countries like the UK, the USA and the Netherlands the benefits of company pension plans are a major source of income for retired people. In countries in the south of Europe and also in Belgium and Scandinavian countries state pensions make up an important part of the income of people after retirement.

Further companies may choose between internal funding or external funding. Very often the national environment, however, determines the choice. For example in the Netherlands and the UK companies usually fund their pension promises externally. German companies use often internal funding. This practice is responsible for large provisions on the balance sheets of German companies (see for example Chapter 27). Very often national legal requirements are the drivers for the observed differences. For example there might be laws which prohibit internal funding. The possibility of withdrawing funds from on external pension fund in times where surpluses are present will also be dependent an the existing laws of a particular country. In fact, IAS 19 has to take into account all these different possibilities existing worldwide.

Another element which relates to organizational issues is whether an employer joins a multi-employer plan for the organizational and financial aspects in relation to pension benefits or whether he decides to set up the organization and financing as a single-employer plan. In some countries such as the Netherlands employers often join multi-employer plans.

In relation to multi-employer plans IAS 19 stipulates that multi-employer plans are defined contribution plans (other than state plans) or defined benefit plans (other than state plans) that:

- pool the assets contributed by various enterprises that are not under common control
- use those assets to provide benefits to employees of more than one enterprise, on the basis that contribution and benefit levels are determined without regard to the identity of the enterprise that employs the employees concerned.

Whether these multi-employer plans are of a defined benefit or a defined contribution type will depend on the terms of the plan.

Impact of company pension plans on the sponsoring company

Activity 20.5

How do you think these different types of pension plan affect the financial situation of the sponsoring company, namely the employer?

Activity feedback

- Pensions represent a cash outflow for the company. The timing of the cash flow will be different according to the funding system which is used by the company: pay as you go system, internal or external funding system and the finance pattern determined by the actuarial funding methods.
- The amount of pension benefits represents a cost for the company. This cost can be reduced through advanced funding if positive investment returns are obtained.
- When an employee renders service, his pension rights accrue. Depending on the terms of the pension plan or the existing company practice the employer has a legal or constructive obligation. At the time of retirement the employer owes the employee a certain amount of money. This amount of money is determined in advance in the case of a defined benefit plan or will be dependent on the realized

investment return on the amounts contributed to a plan under a defined contribution plan.

In this respect the concept of vested benefits is important as vested employee benefits are those benefits that are not conditional on future employment. The terms of a pension plan stipulate when pension benefits become vested. Usually an employee has to be in service for a minimum period (e.g. five years) before his pension rights become vested. If the benefits are vested, this means that the employee has earned his/her pension rights independent of whether the employee will stay further with the firm.

From the feedback of Activity 20.4, we have learned that pension benefits do have an impact on the result, the cash flow and the financial position of a company. As a result these elements have to be accounted for in the financial statements of the employer. The way these benefits are accounted for will depend largely on the type of pension promise which has been made to the employee, namely a defined contribution into a plan or a promise for a defined benefit at the moment of retirement. Defined contribution plans are much simpler to account for. With regard to the recognition and valuation of pension benefits granted under a defined benefit plan, many technical issues have to be agreed on first.

Accounting for defined contribution plans

Under a defined contribution plan, the finance pattern and the responsibility of the employer can be determined in a very straightforward way. The amounts to be contributed, according to the terms of the pension plan, should be treated as pension costs for that particular period. If the employer has transferred all the contributions stipulated in the pension plan to a pension scheme, then the employer has fulfilled his pension commitments and no provision has to be shown on the balance sheet.

Paras 44 to 46 of IAS 19 stipulate reporting and disclosure requirements in relation to a defined contribution plan as follows: When an employee has rendered service to an enterprise during a period, the enterprise should recognize the contribution payable to a defined contribution plan in exchange for that service as a liability (accrued expense), after deducting any contribution already paid. If the contribution already paid exceeds the contribution due for service before the balance sheet date, an enterprise should recognize that excess as an asset (prepaid expense) to the extent that the prepayment will lead to, for example, a reduction in future payments or a cash refund. The contribution payable to a defined contribution plan should also be recorded as an expense, unless another International Accounting Standard requires or permits the inclusion of the contribution in the cost of an asset (see, for example, IAS 2, *Inventories*, and IAS 16, *Property, Plant and Equipment*).

A company should always disclose in the notes the amount recognized as an expense in relation to the defined contribution plans of the company.

Accounting for defined benefit plans

As mentioned earlier, the pension benefit under this type of plan is determined by the pension plan formula and as such is defined in advance. The formula can be a function of the salary of the beneficiary or another variable.

Under a defined benefit scheme the exact total amount of the benefit is known only at the moment of retirement (in case of a lump sum payment) or when the pensioner dies (in case of annual payments). Only at that moment are all uncertainties gone. The main problem, however, is how to charge this total cost over the subsequent service years of the employee. In many countries actuarial funding methods are used for this accounting allocation problem and IAS 19 has also opted for this approach by choosing one particular actuarial funding method, namely the projected unit credit method for accounting purposes. Because of the important role of actuarial funding methods in the recognition of pension costs and pension liabilities for accounting purposes we will pay attention in this section to the function and the mechanisms of those actuarial funding methods (often called by actuaries actuarial cost methods).

Mechanisms of actuarial funding methods

We will illustrate the purpose and the mechanisms of actuarial funding methods with a numerical example relating to one person, Mr Dupont. This example is highly simplified for pedagogic reasons.

Activity 20.6

Assume Mr Dupont enters a pension scheme with a pension formula based on his final salary. The pension benefit he is entitled to receive is defined as follows:

$$Br = k(r-y)Sr$$

whereby:

Br = pension benefit to be received at retirement
k = % of salary
r = retirement age
y = age at which the employee is entitled to receive benefits
Sr = last salary before retirement

The pension benefit for Mr Dupont is a lump sum payment at retirement. We will further assume the $k = 10\%$ and that Mr Dupont enters the company in year 1. His pension benefits are vested from the first moment of employment. The salary levels over the five years of his employment are:

Year 1: 100 000
Year 2: 110 000
Year 3: 120 000
Year 4: 140 000
Year 5: 160 000

Calculate the amount of earned pension benefit Mr Dupont is entitled to receive at the end of each year of service rendered.

Activity feedback

The pension benefit Mr Dupont is entitled to increases over the years in the following way.

$$\text{Year 1: } B1 = 0.1 \times 1 \times (100\,000) = 10\,000$$
$$\text{Year 2: } B2 = 0.1 \times 2 \times (110\,000) = 22\,000$$
$$\text{Year 3: } B3 = 0.1 \times 3 \times (120\,000) = 36\,000$$
$$\text{Year 4: } B4 = 0.1 \times 4 \times (140\,000) = 56\,000$$
$$\text{Year 5: } B5 = 0.1 \times 5 \times (160\,000) = 80\,000$$

Several actuarial cost or funding methods exist to determine the financing or funding pattern for the pension benefits. These different methods will all lead to different funding patterns for the same pension benefit to attain in the end, in the case of Mr Dupont at the end of year 5. The group of actuarial cost or actuarial funding methods which are most commonly used can be divided in two subgroups namely accrued valuation methods and projected valuation methods. The first group, the accrued valuation methods, take into account only the service rendered to date and the current salary level for the calculation of the amounts to be funded. The amount to be funded in a particular year under this method is equal to the present value of the benefit accrual in that particular year. Only the accrued or earned pension rights are financed under this method. Under the accrued valuation method expected future salary levels can be taken into account as well in combination with service already rendered. The accrued benefit valuation method whereby future salary levels are taken into account is called the projected unit credit method. This method is chosen by IAS 19 for cost recognition and pension liability valuation purposes.

The second group of actuarial cost methods used by actuaries is called the projected benefit cost methods or projected valuation methods. These actuarial funding methods calculate the total pension benefit an employee will receive on retirement by taking into account the expected service to be rendered over the total service period and the expected salary level at retirement. They allocate that final amount, over the working life of the employee, as a yearly fixed amount or as a fixed percentage of salary.

The main difference in the funding patterns between the two families of actuarial funding methods (accrued valuation methods versus projected valuation methods) is that under the accrued methods the amounts to be funded at the start of a career of a person are lower than if one would finance the promised benefit under a projected valuation method, which takes into account from the start the whole expected service period.

Accrued benefit valuation methods use the pension plan formula in order to determine the accrual of pension rights over the years. The amount of accrued benefits at a particular moment can be defined as follows:

$$AB_x = B_x(_{r-x}P_xT)v_{r-x}\,\ddot{a}_r$$

whereby:

AB_x = actuarial value of accrued benefits at age x
B_x = accrued pension benefits at age x
$_{r-x}P_xT$ = the probability that the employee stays with the firm from age x till retirement with $P_xT = (1 - q_{mx})(1 - q_{wx})(1 - q_{dx})(1 - q_{rx})$
q_m = probability of mortality
q_w = probability of withdrawal from the plan
q_d = probability of disability
q_r = probability of early retirement

v_{r-x} = discount factor from retirement age to age x

$ä_r$ = present value at retirement age of a long life annuity of a single currency unit at the start of each year (needed if the pension benefit will be paid out as an annual payment)

P_xT as such is often called the plan turnover assumption

The function of actuarial assumptions

It is clear from the formula just examined that in order to calculate the accrued benefits and the finance patterns related to it, the actuary must make assumptions about a number of variables, e.g. life expectancy, employee turnover, future salary levels, investment return and so on. These elements are called actuarial assumptions. Some of them are of a demographic nature (e.g. mortality, number of men and women in the plan) others are of an economic nature (e.g. inflation rate, investment return). When these actuarial funding methods are used to determine the finance pattern of the benefits a company is free to choose the value of these assumptions. When the outcome of the actuarial funding method is used for accounting purposes IAS 19 stipulates that (para. 72) the actuarial assumptions used should be unbiased and mutually compatible. By the latter IAS 19 means that (para. 75) actuarial assumptions are mutually compatible if they reflect the economic relationships between factors such as inflation, rates of salary increase, the return on plan assets and discount rates. For example all assumptions which depend on a particular inflation level (such as assumptions about interest rates and salary and benefit increases) in any given future period assume the same inflation level in that period.

Further, IAS states that financial assumptions should be based on market expectations at the balance sheet date, for the period over which the obligations are to be settled. The choice of the actuarial assumptions is not immaterial. Minor changes in the assumptions might have substantial impacts on the amounts reported, the assumption with the most material effect is the discount rate (see also example in Activity 20.11). That is the reason why IAS 19 has paid special attention to the choice of the discount rate (para. 78). The rate used to discount post-employment benefit obligations (both funded and unfunded) should be determined by reference to market yields at the balance sheet date on high-quality corporate bonds. In countries where there is no deep market in such bonds, the market yields (at the balance sheet date) on government bonds should be used. The currency and term of the corporate bonds or government bonds should be consistent with the currency and estimated term of the post-employment benefit obligations.

It is important to state here that the discount rate reflects the time value of money and *not* the actuarial or investment risk.

Activity 20.7

Calculate the actuarial value of accrued benefits for Mr Dupont in each of the five years he is in service, based on the service rendered to that date and the current salary level of that moment. Assume that the plan turnover assumption is equal to zero and the discount rate is 4%. The pension benefit is paid out as a lump sum at the moment of retirement. The actuarial calculations are made at the end of the year.

Activity feedback

$$AB1 = [0.1 \times (1 \times 100\,000)]/(1.04)^4 = 8\,548$$
$$AB2 = [0.1 \times (2 \times 110\,000)]/(1.04)^3 = 19\,558$$
$$AB3 = [0.1 \times (3 \times 120\,000)]/(1.04)^2 = 33\,284$$
$$AB4 = [0.1 \times (4 \times 140\,000)]/(1.04)^1 = 53\,846$$
$$AB5 = [0.1 \times (5 \times 160\,000)]/(1.04)^0 = 80\,000$$

These actuarial calculations can also be made at the start of each year: the interest factor will then be different. The present value of these accrued benefit obligations increases each year due to the year extra service rendered by the employee and the interest accrual.

We will now analyse the impact on the amount of accrued benefits in Activity 20.6 when future salary levels are included in the calculations. IAS 19 requires the use of the projected unit credit method for the determination of the pension liability as well as for the determination of a part of the total pension cost. The projected unit credit method takes into account future salary increases.

Present value of the defined benefit obligation

Activity 20.8

Take into account the expected future salary levels and calculate the projected benefit obligation (PBO) of Mr Dupont at the end of each year that he is in service. Since we take into account expected future salary levels, we can no longer talk about accrued benefits or earned benefits.

Activity feedback

$$PBO1 = [0.1 \times (1 \times 160\,000)]/(1.04)^4 = 13\,677$$
$$PBO2 = [0.1 \times (2 \times 160\,000)]/(1.04)^3 = 28\,448$$
$$PBO3 = [0.1 \times (3 \times 160\,000)]/(1.04)^2 = 44\,379$$
$$PBO4 = [0.1 \times (4 \times 160\,000)]/(1.04)^1 = 61\,538$$
$$PBO5 = [0.1 \times (5 \times 160\,000)]/(1.04)^0 = 80\,000$$

The present value of the defined benefit obligation, as calculated in Activity 20.7 plays an important role in the valuation of a possible pension liability under IAS 19. The PBO is the starting point for the recognition of a defined benefit liability or a pension asset in the financial statements of the employer (para. 54).

Para. 83 of IAS stipulates further that post-employment benefit obligations should be measured on a basis that reflects:

- estimated future salary increases
- the benefits set out in the terms of the plan (or resulting from any constructive obligation that goes beyond those terms) at the balance sheet date
- estimated future changes in the level of any state benefits that affect the benefits payable under a defined benefit plan, if, and only if, either:
  - those changes were enacted before the balance sheet date

– or past history, or other reliable evidence, indicates that those state benefits will change in some predictable manner, for example in line with future changes in general price levels or general salary levels.

As a result of point 3 of para. 83 we notice in practice that when pension plan formulas are renegotiated or new pension plans are set up, the benefits resulting from state pensions are no longer included as a part of the company pension plan benefit formula. Employers clearly want to avoid elements which increase risk and uncertainty.

Determination of the total pension cost

The PBO increases each year due to the service rendered in each year and the interest accrual on the amount of the PBO at the start of the year. The increase due to service rendered is called the current service cost under IAS 19. The total pension cost in a particular year is defined by IAS 19 as follows:

(a) current service cost (see paras 63–91)
(b) interest cost (see para. 82)
(c) the expected return on any plan assets (see paras 105–107)
(d) actuarial gains and losses, to the extent that they are recognized under paras 92 and 93
(e) past service cost, to the extent that para. 96 requires an enterprise to recognize it
(f) the effect of any curtailments or settlements (see paras 109 and 110).

Current service cost

As illustrated in Activity 20.7, the current service cost should be calculated with the use of the projected unit credit method. The projected unit credit method attributes the amount to be funded each year on the basis of the plan's benefit formula. These amounts to be funded each year, which result from the projected unit credit method, represent the current service cost. However, if an employee's service in later years will lead to a materially higher level of benefit than in earlier years, an enterprise should attribute the benefit on a straight line basis from:

- the date when service by the employee first leads to benefits under the plan (whether or not the benefits are conditional on further service)
- until the date when further service by the employee will lead to no material amount of further benefits under the plan, other than from further salary increases.

In those cases the pension plan formula will no longer determine the cost allocation pattern. In fact IAS 19 allows in this case an allocation pattern which is more similar to the funding patterns used by the projected valuation methods (see earlier in this chapter).

Activity 20.9

Calculate the current service cost and the interest accrual for Mr Dupont with the use of the projected unit credit method which takes into account the service rendered to date and the future salary levels. The calculations are made at the end of the year in this example.

Activity feedback

	Current service cost	*Interest accrual*	*Projected benefit obligation (PBO)*
Year 1	13 677	0	13 677
Year 2	14 224	547	28 448
Year 3	14 793	1 138	44 379
Year 4	15 384	1 775	61 538
Year 5	16 000	2 462	80 000

The current service cost is determined each year by the increase in earned pension rights according to the pension benefit formula:

$$CSC\ 1 = [0.1 \times (1 \times 160\,000)]/(1.04)^4 = 13\,677$$
$$CSC\ 2 = [0.1 \times (1 \times 160\,000)]/(1.04)^3 = 14\,224$$
$$CSC\ 3 = [0.1 \times (1 \times 160\,000)]/(1.04)^2 = 14\,791$$
$$CSC\ 4 = [0.1 \times (1 \times 160\,000)]/(1.04)^1 = 15\,384$$
$$CSC\ 5 = [0.1 \times (1 \times 160\,000)]/(1.04)^0 = 16\,000$$

The interest cost component is determined as follows:

$$IC1 = 0.04 \quad (0) = \quad 0$$
$$IC2 = 0.04\ (13\,677) = \quad 547$$
$$IC3 = 0.04\ (28\,448) = 1\,138$$
$$IC4 = 0.04\ (44\,379) = 1\,775$$
$$IC5 = 0.04\ (61\,538) = 2\,462$$

Interest cost

The current service cost calculated with the use of the projected unit credit method and the interest accrual are two components of the total pension cost which should be charged to the profit and loss account. Based on the data we have available so far the total pension cost in the subsequent years would be as shown in Table 20.1.

The interest cost component in Activity 20.8 is determined with the use of the discount rate of 4%. The discount rate reflects the time value of money. Para. 82 stipulates that the interest cost is computed by multiplying the discount rate as determined at the start of the period by the present value of the defined benefit obligation throughout that period, taking account of any material changes in the obligation. Since the amounts calculated in the activity are calculated at the end of the

Table 20.1 Total cost of pensions

	Current service cost	*Interest accrual*	*Total pension cost*
Year 1	13 677	0	13 677
Year 2	14 224	547	14 771
Year 3	14 793	1 138	15 931
Year 4	15 384	1 775	17 159
Year 5	16 000	2 462	18 642

year there is no interest cost in the first year. (As we said earlier this example is simplified for pedagogic reasons.)

Expected return on plan assets

If the amounts to be funded are invested an investment return can be realized. When investments are successful, meaning when the realized investment return is higher than expected return, the total pension cost can be decreased. Concerning this return on plan assets, we have to distinguish between the expected return on assets (again an actuarial assumption) and the realized return on assets. Note that the expected return on plan assets is not the same as the discount factor used in the actuarial calculation.

At the start of a period an assumption must be made about the investment return to be realized in that period. Remember that the interest component reflects the time value of money. We will now add investment data to our example.

Activity 20.10

Assume that in year 3 the expected return on assets will be 5% and in year 4 the expected return on assets is estimated to be 3%. What will be the impact on the pension cost so far? Determine the total pension cost with the elements you know at this stage.

Activity feedback

In year three when the expected return on plan assets is higher than the discount rate used this has so far a decreasing impact on the total pension cost to be reported, the opposite situation arises the year afterwards.

	Year 3	Year 4
Current service cost	14 793	15 384
Interest cost	1 138	1 775
Expected return on plan assets	− 1 422 = 0.05 (28 448)	− 1 331 = 0.03 (44 379)

Actuarial gains and losses

Intuitively, we feel that something is missing at the moment, namely information on the realized investment return. The difference between the expected return on plan assets and the realized return on plan assets is presented as an actuarial gain if the realized return is higher than the expected return, or as an actuarial loss if the realized return is lower than the expected return.

Activity 20.11

Assume that at the end of year 3 the realized return on assets was 1 300 and at the end of year 4 the realized return was 1 500, present the total pension cost based on the information you now possess and under the assumption that the actuarial gains and losses are fully recognized immediately (=charged to the income statement for the total amount).

Activity feedback

	Year 3	Year 4
Current service cost	14 793	15 384
Interest cost	1 138	1 775
Expected return on plan assets	−1 422	−1 331
Actuarial gains or losses	+122	−169

Actuarial gains and losses arise from two sources. If actuarial assumptions are different from reality a difference will occur. This difference can be positive or negative as in Activity 20.10. These differences are called experience adjustments. If this difference between the actuarial assumption and the reality continues to exist then it could be that the actuarial assumptions used in the actuarial calculations have to be changed. This is a second source of actuarial gains and losses. So actuarial gains and losses can also result from changes in the actuarial assumptions themselves. A change in the actuarial assumptions used has as a consequence that the future amounts to be funded will be higher or lower. Further, the PBO calculated with the new actuarial assumptions can also be higher or lower than the PBO calculated with the old actuarial assumptions. In the view of an actuary actuarial gains and losses mean the following. If the PBO (new assumptions) is higher than the PBO (old assumptions) then an actuarial loss arises, since the difference is not yet funded and needs to be. In the opposite situation, where PBO (new assumptions) is smaller than the PBO (old assumptions), an actuarial gain arises, since there is now more funded than the present PBO (new assumptions).

Activity 20.12

Assume that at the start of year 4 the discount rate used in the calculations in relation to the pension benefit of Mr Dupont will be changed from 4% to 5%. What will be the impact on the projected benefit obligation (PBO) at the start of year 4?

Activity feedback

The projected benefit obligation (PBO) at the start of year 4 using a discount rate of 5% is equal to:

$$PBO4 \text{ (new assumptions)} = [0.1 \times (3 \times 160\,000)]/(1.05)^2 = 43\,537$$

Remember that the PBO at the start of year 4 using the discount rate of 4% was PBO4 (old assumptions) 44 374.

In this situation we have an actuarial gain as the projected benefit obligation calculated with the new assumptions (in this case a new discount rate) is lower than the projected benefit obligation calculated with the old assumptions. The actuarial gain is 837 (we talk about a gain because the new PBO (43 537) is lower than the old PBO (44 374)).

A major question subsequently arises. How should we account for this actuarial result?

It is obvious that differences between reality and the actuarial assumptions used will occur frequently (e.g. realized salary increases or higher or lower than estimated salary increases). These differences are almost inherent to this process. Further, minor changes in the actuarial assumptions used might entail an impact on the amounts of the projected benefit obligation calculated. Immediate recognition of these elements has the consequence that the total pension cost will become a highly volatile element on the income statement. This is something that the business world absolutely does not like (for a further discussion of the this aspect see Chapter 26).

In order to reduce this volatility the IASB has chosen a so-called corridor approach. The recognition procedure which is included in IAS 19 concerning these actuarial gains and losses is probably more inspired by concerns from the business world than by elements of the conceptual framework of the IASB. The corridor approach allows that actuarial gains and losses do not always have to be recognized. An element in support of this corridor approach might be that in the long term actuarial gains and losses may be offset against each other. The corridor approach is stipulated in paras 92 and 93 of IAS 19 in the following way.

An enterprise should recognize a portion of its actuarial gains and losses as income or expense if the net cumulative unrecognized actuarial gains and losses at the end of the previous reporting period exceeded the greater of (para. 92):

- 10% of the present value of the defined benefit obligation at that date (before deducting plan assets)
- 10% of the fair value of any plan assets at that date.

These limits should be calculated and applied separately for each defined benefit plan.

Para. 93 further states that the portion of actuarial gains and losses to be recognized for each defined benefit plan is the excess determined under para. 92, divided by the expected average remaining working lives of the employees participating in that plan. However, an enterprise may adopt any systematic method that results in faster recognition of actuarial gains and losses, provided that the same basis is applied to both gains and losses and the basis is applied consistently from period to period. An enterprise may apply such systematic methods to actuarial gains and losses even if they fall within the limits specified in para. 92.

If we apply these paras (92 and 93) to the example of Dupont, we notice that we indeed exceed the corridor of 10% namely $837 > 443$ ($= 0.10(44\,374)$). The amount above 10% is equal to 394 ($= 837 - 443$). If we recognize the amount above 10% or outside the corridor by dividing it by the expected average remaining working life of Mr Dupont, then we will add an amount of 197 ($= 394/2$) to the total pension cost of year 4 and 197 will be taken into account as unrecognized actuarial gain for the determination of the defined benefit liability. In year 5 the remaining 197 will be charged to the income statement under the heading recognized actuarial gain.

IAS 19, however, also allows other systematic allocation methods on condition that they recognize the actuarial results faster. IAS 19 also allows companies to recognize actuarial results which lie within the corridor of 10%. As a result, companies have many options; however, if their aim is to reduce volatility of the pension cost, they will opt to recognize only actuarial results outside the 10% corridor. For external users of the annual accounts this results in less transparency about the current and future impact of the pension plan on a company's situation, especially if the quality of disclosure of the firm is low.

Past service cost

The last major component of the total pension cost are the past service costs. Past service costs arise when an employer grants pension rights for the service rendered prior to the establishment of the pension plan or when an employer grants an increase in pension benefits also for service rendered in past periods. As a result the projected benefit obligation will increase. This increase in the amount of the projected benefit obligation resulting from those past service benefits should, on the one hand, be funded or financed and, on the other, be recognized for accounting purposes. The amounts recognized in relation to those past service benefits in a particular year on the income statement are called past service costs. The amount not yet recognized will be called a past service liability or a past service cost.

Activity 20.13

Assume that from year 4 on Mr Dupont is entitled to a pension benefit of 0.15% of his final salary for each year he has been with the firm instead of 0.10% of his final salary.

The formula of the pension plan of Mr Dupont then becomes:

$$Br = 0.15 \ (r - y)Sr$$

The employer also grants this increase in pension benefits for the first three years of the career of Mr Dupont. We have to remember that the pension rights of Mr. Dupont are vested from the start of his employment. Calculate the new PBO at the start of year 4 which takes into account this increase in pension benefits granted for past periods.

Activity feedback

$$\text{PBO start year } 4 = 0.15 \ [3 \times (160\,000)]/(1.04)^2 = 66\,568$$

Remember that the PBO at the start of year 4 under the old pension benefit formula was 44 379. This is an increase of the projected benefit obligation with $22\,189 = (66\,568 - 44\,379)$.

How should this increase be accounted for?

IAS 19 makes a distinction between vested past service costs and non-vested past service costs. Remember vested pension benefits are pension benefits which are not conditional on further future employment. So the employee is entitled to them, even if he leaves the firm. When past service costs *are* vested, IAS 19 stipulates (para. 96) that these past service cost should be recognized immediately as cost. If past service costs are non-vested they should be recognized as an expense on a straight-line basis over the average period until the benefits become vested.

In the example of Mr Dupont where these past service benefits are vested, the amount of 22 189 should be recognized immediately as part of the total pension cost in year 4. Because the amount of the past service benefits has been fully recognized on the income statement of year 4, it should not be taken into account for the determination of the amount recognized as a defined pension liability.

Activity 20.14

Assume that the pension rights of Mr Dupont would only become vested at the end of year 5. How would you then account for these past service benefits in accordance with IAS 19?

Activity feedback

The amount of 22 189 should then be allocated over years 4 and year 5. Half of it will be reported as part of the pension cost in year 4 and the other half will be taken into account in the determination of the pension liability at the end of year 4. In year 5 the remaining half would then be charged to the income statement.

Curtailments or settlements

A final item of the total pension cost relates to the effects of a curtailment or settlement. A curtailment arises when (para. 111) an enterprise either:

- is demonstrably committed to make a material reduction in the number of employees covered by a plan
- amends the terms of a defined benefit plan such that a material element of future service by current employees will no longer qualify for benefits or will qualify only for reduced benefits.

A curtailment may arise from an isolated event, such as the closing of a plant, discontinuance of an operation or termination or suspension of a plan. An event is material enough to qualify as a curtailment if the recognition of a curtailment gain or loss would have a material effect on the financial statements. Curtailments are often linked with a restructuring. Therefore, an enterprise accounts for a curtailment at the same time as for a related restructuring. We notice that it is up to the management to judge whether the effect is material.

A settlement occurs (para. 112) when an enterprise enters into a transaction that eliminates all further legal or constructive obligation for part or all of the benefits provided under a defined benefit plan, for example, when a lump-sum cash payment is made to, or on behalf of, plan participants in exchange for their rights to receive specified post-employment benefits.

What kind of treatment does IAS 19 prescribe for the results of those settlements and curtailments?

An enterprise should recognize gains or losses on the curtailment or settlement of a defined benefit plan when the curtailment or settlement occurs. The gain or loss on a curtailment or settlement should comprise:

- any resulting change in the present value of the defined benefit obligation
- any resulting change in the fair value of the plan assets
- any related actuarial gains and losses and past service cost that, under paras 92 and 96, had not previously been recognized.

Before determining the effect of a curtailment or settlement, an enterprise should remeasure the obligation (and the related plan assets, if any) using current actuarial assumptions (including current market interest rates and other current market prices) (para. 110).

Defined benefit liability

All the individual components of the total pension cost have now been discussed; we now focus on the possible impact of company pension plans on the balance sheet of the employer. Para. 54 stipulates in this respect that the amount to be recognized as a defined benefit liability should be the net total of the following amounts:

- the present value of the defined benefit obligation at the balance sheet date (see para. 64)
- plus any actuarial gains (less any actuarial losses) not recognized because of the treatment set out in paras 92–93 and
- minus any past service cost not yet recognized (see para. 96)
- minus the fair value at the balance sheet date of plan assets (if any) out of which the obligations are to be settled directly (see paras 102–104).

The first three components have been illustrated when the determination of the total pension cost was discussed.

The present value of the defined benefit obligation calculated with the use of the projected unit credit method was illustrated in Activity 20.7 without a past service cost and Activity 20.12 when a past service cost *was* present. The treatment of the actuarial gains and losses was illustrated in Activity 20.10. The amounts outside the corridor of 10% and not yet recognized should be included in the determination of the amount of the defined benefit liability. However, we know that companies might also use other recognition procedures or recognize also the amount within the corridor. So some flexibility exists with regard to this component. Also the treatment of past service costs was explained in Activity 20.12. Only the fourth component in para. 54 resulting from the plan assets has not yet been discussed.

Plan assets include (according to the definitions of IAS 19) assets held by a long-term employee benefit fund and qualifying insurance policies. Reading the paragraphs on pension plan assets it becomes clear that the market value is regarded as the fair value. It is stipulated in para. 102 that when no market price is available, the fair value of plan assets is estimated; for example, by discounting expected future cash flows using a discount rate that reflects both the risk associated with the plan assets and the maturity or expected disposal date of those assets (or, if they have no maturity, the expected period until the settlement of the related obligation). Further, unpaid contributions due from the reporting enterprise to the fund, as well as any non-transferable financial instrument issued by the enterprise and held by the fund may not be included in the pension plan assets. Plan assets should be reduced further by any liabilities of the fund that do not relate to employee benefits. Where plan assets include qualifying insurance policies that exactly match the amount and the timing of some or all benefits payable under the plan, the fair value of those insurance policies is deemed to be the present value of the related obligations.

There might be occasions where the amount determined under para. 54 may be negative (an asset). For example, if the investment policy of the fund has been highly successful and a surplus exists. An enterprise should then measure the resulting asset at the lower of:

- the amount determined under para. 54
- and the net total of:
  - any unrecognized actuarial losses and past service cost (see paras 92, 93 and 96)
  - the present value of any economic benefits available in the form of refunds from the plan or reductions in future contributions to the plan. The present value of these economic benefits should be determined using the discount rate specified in para. 78.

We will illustrate this with the following activity.

Activity 20.15

The following data are available in relation to a defined benefit plan:

- the present value of the defined benefit obligation   5 000
- unrecognized actuarial losses   200
- unrecognized past service cost   400
- pension plan assets   6 000
- present value of available future refunds   50

Calculate the amount resulting from the determination of the defined benefit liability (para. 54) and compare this amount with the limit put forward in para. 58(b).

Activity feedback

Negative amount according to para. 54:

- the present value of the defined benefit obligation   5 000
- unrecognized actuarial losses   + 200
- unrecognized past service cost   + 400
- pension plan assets   − 6 000
- negative amount   − 400

The limit under para. 58(b):

- unrecognized actuarial losses   200
- unrecognized past service cost   400
- present value of available future refunds   50
- total amount   650

The amount of 400 is less than 650, so the enterprise will recognize an asset of 400 on its balance sheet.

IAS 19 states further that an enterprise should determine the present value of defined benefit obligations and the fair value of any plan assets with sufficient regularity that the amounts recognized in the financial statements do not differ materially from the amounts that would be determined at the balance sheet date.

Disclosure in the notes in relation to pension benefits

On the face of the balance sheet of the employer a liability or an asset will be presented. The underlying elements taken into account to determine this pension liability or asset have to be disclosed in the notes of the financial statements (para. 120). Some extensive disclosures are the result.

An enterprise should disclose the following information about defined benefit plans:

- the enterprise's accounting policy for recognizing actuarial gains and losses
- a general description of the type of plan
- a reconciliation of the assets and liabilities recognized in the balance sheet, showing at least:
  - the present value at the balance sheet date of defined benefit obligations that are wholly unfunded
  - the present value (before deducting the fair value of plan assets) at the balance sheet date of defined benefit obligations that are wholly or partly funded
  - the fair value of any plan assets at the balance sheet date
  - the net actuarial gains or losses not recognized in the balance sheet (see para. 92)
  - the past service cost not yet recognized in the balance sheet (see para. 96)
  - any amount not recognized as an asset, because of the limit in para. 58 (b)
  - the amounts recognized in the balance sheet
- the amounts included in the fair value of plan assets for:
  - each category of the reporting enterprise's own financial instruments
  - any property occupied by, or other assets used by, the reporting enterprise
- a reconciliation showing the movements during the period in the net liability (or asset) recognized in the balance sheet;

The same remark holds for the total pension cost reported. On the profit and loss account of the employer a single amount will be recorded. The external stakeholder to the firm will gain insight in the individual sub-components of the total pension cost by a disclosure of these elements in the notes together with the actuarial assumptions used (para. 120):

- the total expense recognized in the income statement for each of the following and the line item(s) of the income statement in which they are included:
  - current service cost
  - interest cost
  - expected return on plan assets
  - actuarial gains and losses
  - past service cost
  - the effect of any curtailment or settlement
- the actual return on plan assets
- the principal actuarial assumptions used as at the balance sheet date, including, where applicable:
  - the discount rates
  - the expected rates of return on any plan assets for the periods presented in the financial statements

- the expected rates of salary increases (and of changes in an index or other variable specified in the formal or constructive terms of a plan as the basis for future benefit increases)
- medical cost trend rates
- any other material actuarial assumptions used.

An enterprise should disclose each actuarial assumption in absolute terms (for example, as an absolute percentage) and not just as a margin between different percentages or other variables.

Multi-employer plans

Paras 29 and 30 of IAS define how a multi-employer should be accounted for. The terms of the plan will determine whether a multi-employer plan will be classified as a defined benefit plan or a defined contribution plan. Where a multi-employer plan is a defined benefit plan, the company shall account for its proportionate share of the defined benefit obligation, plan assets and costs with the plan in the same way as for any other defined benefit plans. When sufficient information is not available to use defined benefit accounting for a multi-employer plan that is classified as a defined benefit plan, the company might account for the plan as if it were a defined contribution plan. In this situation, the employer has to disclose in the notes to its accounts that the pension plan is, in fact, a defined benefit plan together with the reason why there is insufficient information to account for the plan as a defined benefit plan. If there is a surplus or a deficit in the plan that may affect the amount of future contributions, information about the surplus or the deficit (basis for the calculation and the implications) should be provided as well.

Termination benefits

Finally IAS 19 deals with termination benefits. An enterprise should recognize termination benefits as a liability and an expense when, and only when, the enterprise is demonstrably committed to either:

- terminate the employment of an employee or group of employees before the normal retirement date
- or provide termination benefits as a result of an offer made in order to encourage voluntary redundancy.

An enterprise is demonstrably committed to a termination when, and only when, the enterprise has a detailed formal plan for the termination and is without realistic possibility of withdrawal. The detailed plan should include, as a minimum:

- the location, function, and approximate number of employees whose services are to be terminated
- the termination benefits for each job classification or function

- the time at which the plan will be implemented. Implementation should begin as soon as possible and the period of time to complete implementation should be such that material changes to the plan are not likely.

Where termination benefits fall due more than 12 months after the balance sheet date, they should be discounted using the discount rate specified in para. 78.

In the case of an offer made to encourage voluntary redundancy, the measurement of termination benefits should be based on the number of employees expected to accept the offer (para. 140).

Accounting by the pension fund

When pension benefits are externally funded the entity to which the amounts are transferred has to prepare financial statements as well. When the amounts are transferred to an insurance company, the financial statements of the insurance company will give a picture of the financial position of the insurance company.

Financial reporting by pension funds is regulated by IAS 26 *Accounting and Reporting by Retirement Benefit Plans*. The last revision of IAS 26 dates from 1994, which is important to stress, since IAS 19, which focuses on the financial statements of the employer, has been revised twice since then. The financial situation of a pension fund will not be presented in the 'classical' format of financial statements, namely consisting of a balance sheet and an income statement. IAS 26 defines the contents of a pension fund 'report' which should be prepared. Also in relation to this report the type of pension benefit (defined contribution or defined benefit) promised plays a role.

When amounts resulting from a defined contribution plan are transferred to a pension fund, the report (para. 13) contain a statement of net assets available for benefits and a description of the funding policy.

When amounts resulting from a defined benefit plan are transferred to a pension fund, the report of the fund should contain either (para. 17):

- a statement that shows:
  - the net assets available for benefits
  - the actuarial present value of promised retirement benefits, distinguishing between vested benefits and non-vested benefits
  - the resulting excess or deficit
- or a statement of net assets available for benefits including either:
  - a note disclosing the actuarial present value of promised retirement benefits, distinguishing between vested benefits and non-vested benefits
  - or a reference to this information in an accompanying actuarial report.

  If an actuarial valuation has not been prepared at the date of the report, the most recent valuation should be used as a base and the date of the valuation disclosed.

We notice immediately that the concept of defined benefit obligation is not introduced here, IAS 26 only mentions actuarial present value of promised retirement benefits. In order to improve the information value of the annual reports of pension funds a revision of IAS 26 in line with the vision of IAS 19 would be welcome. It is not certain, however, whether the business world would also welcome a revision in the near future.

Summary

IAS 19 is considered to be one of the more technical standards. This high level of technicality is for the time being only related to the determination of the total pension cost and a possible pension liability or pension asset. It is to be expected that when recognition and measurement rules are developed for equity benefits, these will be of a highly technical level as well, since they involve valuation of options and possible other financial instruments. For the time being only extensive disclosure requirements are included in IAS 19 in relation to equity benefits. With regard to the reporting of pension benefits the IASB has already shifted from extensive disclosure in the notes to recognition and measurement of the costs and possible liabilities resulting from the company pension plans in the income statement and on the balance sheet. The technical level of the accounting process depends on the type of pension promise made.

Accounting for defined contribution plans is less technical than accounting for defined benefit plans. It has been noticed that in recent years defined contribution plans have become more popular. Could the stricter accounting requirements which make the uncertainties and the risks involved in a defined benefit plan more visible have something to do with this?

EXERCISES

(✔ indicates answers are available on pages 731–734)

✔ 1 Company Rebo has five directors, which all participate in the following share-based remuneration plan with cash alternatives. The directors have the right to choose between 600 shares or the value of 500 shares paid in cash at vesting date. If the directors opt for the shares they may not sell them for three years. The only vesting requirement is that the directors should remain three years with the company.

At the grant date the entity's share price is €30. At the end of years 1, 2 and 3 the share prices are €33, €36 and €40. The fair value of the share alternative is €28 per share. Calculate the remuneration expense for the equity-based remuneration system of Rebo. Indicate also which accounts are credited. Consider further both situations, namely the directors choose the cash alternative and the directors choose the equity alternative.

✔ 2 IAS 19 'Employee Benefits' was issued in February 1998. Amongst other things the standard deals with the treatment of post-employment benefits such as pensions and other retirement benefits.

Post-employment benefits are classified as either defined contribution or defined benefit plans.

Required:

(a) Describe the relevant features and required accounting treatment of defined contribution and defined benefit plans under IAS 19.

(b) Klondike operates a defined benefit post-retirement plan for its employees. The plan is reviewed annually. Klondike's actuaries have provided the information in the table on the next page.

The average remaining working lives of Klondike's employees at 31 March 2001 is 10 years.

Required:

Prepare extracts of Klondike's financial statements for the year to 31 March 2002 in compliance with IAS 19 'Employee Benefits' insofar as the information permits.

(ACCA June 02)

✔ 3 Company Crux grants share options to its employees at 1.1.X1. Each employee will receive ten options if he/she stays with the company for the next two years. At grant date

Klondike

	at 31 March 2001 $000	at 31 March 2002 $000
Present value obligation	1 500	1 750
Fair value of plan assets	1 500	1 650
Current service cost – year to 31 March 2002		160
Contributions paid – year to 31 March 2002		85
Benefits paid to employees – year to 31 March 2002		125
Net cumulative unrecognised gains at 1 April 2001	200	
Expected return on plan assets at 1 April 2001 is	12%	
Discount rate for plan liabilities at 1 April 2001	10%	

the turnover percentage of employees is estimated at 20%. The fair value of the option at grant date is €20. The company grants these options to the 100 employees in service at grant date. During the first year four employees leave and the company revises its estimate on employee turnover from 20% to 15% (=15 employees leaving). During year 2 another four employees leave, the entity revises the estimate to 12%. At the end of the third year six employees leave the company. The share options of the remaining employees vest at the end of year 3.

Calculate the remuneration expense for year 1,2 and 3 following from this share option plan. What is the credit-side when this expense is recorded in the books of the company?

✔ 4 At the beginning of year 1, an entity grants to 20 senior executives 1000 share options, each based on two conditions. First, the executive has to remain with the entity until the end of year 3. Second the share options may not be exercised unless the share price has increased from €100 at the beginning of year 1 to above €130 at the end of year 3. If the share price is above €130 at year 3, the share options may be exercised at any time during the next five years.

The entity applies a binomial option-pricing model, which takes into account the possibility that the share price will exceed €130 at the end of year 3 (in this case the share options become exercisable) and the possibility that the share price will not exceed €130 at the end of year 3 (and then the options will be forfeited). It estimates the fair value of the share options with this market condition to be €48 per option.

At the end of year 1, the company estimates the turnover of senior executives at 2%. In the second year one executive leaves the company, but the turnover estimate remains the same. During the third year two executives leave the company. Calculate the remuneration expense for each year in which an expense needs to be recorded. Which account will be credited when the remuneration expense is recorded.

✔ 5 An entity grants 100 share appreciation rights to its 200 employees on the condition that they remain with the firm for two years. At the end of these two years, the benefits vest and the employees may exercise the options in the two consecutive years. The benefits will be paid out in cash and the cash amount will be determined by the intrinsic value at the date of exercise. The fair value of the appreciation rights and the intrinsic value of the rights are presented below.

Year	Fair value	Intrinsic value
1	31	
2	36	30
3		40

At the end of the first year ten employees leave the company and the company estimates that in the next year 15 more employees will leave. In year 2, 16 employees leave and 74 employees exercise their share appreciation rights immediately when their benefits vest and the remaining 100 exercise their rights in year 3.

Calculate the remuneration expenses and the amount of the liability to be recognized as a result of these share-based payment transaction.

6 Discuss the 'corridor' approach for the recognition of actuarial gains and losses. Take into account in the discussion the framework for the preparation and presentation of financial statements. Do you agree with the 'corridor' approach or are you in favour of another recognition approach? Give arguments to support your decision.

7 For the determination and recognition of the current service cost and the defined pension liability one particular actuarial cost method has been chosen, namely the projected unit credit method. This method takes into account expected future salary increases. Comment on this decision. What is your opinion on taking into account these expected salary increases? What arguments could be used in favour of including future salary increases? Are there any arguments against the inclusion of future salary increases?

8 The actuarial assumptions 'discount factor' and 'expected market return' are different elements in the opinion of the IASB and as a result the impact of both assumptions is included separately in the total pension cost. Would the data be less reliable or value relevant if the same value were used for the discount factor and the expected market return? Comment on your opinion.

9 Consider the assumptions 'discount factor' and 'expected market return' again. Take into account the different funding or financing systems (internal and external funding) which companies can use. Does the separate disclosure of the interest cost component and the return on assets increase the information value of the pension data communicated to external users of the financial statements? Discuss.

10 State pension plans are defined in IAS 19 as multi-employer plans. Multi-employer plans can be either of a defined benefit type or of a defined contribution type. Had you been in the position of the standard setter, would you have included the treatment of the state pension plans in the treatment of the multi-employer plans? Present arguments in favour of your answer.

11 The recognition of equity benefits on the balance sheet and income statement is currently under discussion. If you were in the standard setter's position, how would you recognize and measure equity benefits? Take into account the conceptual framework and try to be consistent with it.

12 The following statements relate to accounting for retirement benefits under the provisions of IAS 19 – *Employee benefits*. [The 'net pension asset' is the fair value of plan assets less the present value of plan liabilities.]

(i) Other things being equal, the net pension asset increases when interest rates increase.

(ii) Other things being equal, the net pension asset decreases when share prices fall.

(iii) Where the terms of retirement benefits are altered so as to provide immediate additional benefits to retired members, then the cost of the additional benefits should be recognised in the income statement over a period equal to the average life expectancy of the retired members.

Which of the statements are true?

A (i) and (ii) only.
B (i) and (iii) only.
C (ii) and (iii) only.
D All of them.

(CIMA Nov 03)

13 E pays contributions into a post-employment defined benefit plan on behalf of its employees. The balance sheet of the enterprise at 30 April 2003 showed a net pension liability of $60 million. During the year to 30 April 2004:

- The enterprise closed down a division and the curtailment of retirement benefits for employees made redundant resulted in a gain of $4 million.
- The estimated current service cost was $8 million.
- The expected return on assets was $6 million.
- The unwinding of the discount on the pension liability was $4 million.
- There was no recognition of actuarial gains or losses in the income statement.

The net pension liability at 30 April 2004 was $65 million [before incorporating the actuarial gain or loss for the year].

What is the actuarial gain or loss for the year ended 30 April 2004?

A   A loss of $1 million

B   A gain of $1 million

C   A loss of $3 million

D   A gain of $3 million

(CIMA May 04)

Changing prices and hyperinflationary economies

> After studying this chapter you should be able to:
> ☐ outline regulatory requirements in relation to the issues of accounting for inflation and changing prices discussed in Chapters 4–7
> ☐ describe, apply and appraise the requirements of IAS 29 concerning hyperinflationary economies
> ☐ explain the implications of adjusting, or not adjusting, for changes in general purchasing power in economies with material inflation.

Introduction

We spent considerable time on the alternative theoretical and practical possibilities regarding measurement alternatives in Part One, Chapters 4–7. We also briefly looked at some of the national attitudes and national regulations of earlier years. It is not necessary to repeat this material or to revisit the thinking behind it. This chapter limits itself to coverage of international regulation on the matter.

EU Fourth Directive

The majority of the Directive is couched in historical terms, but it does, in article 33, permit member states to allow and to require a wide variety of alternative methods, provided only that, if such methods are used, information is given in the notes to the accounts sufficient for the reader to work out what the balance sheet figures would have been under the historical cost approach. National reactions to this in subsequent national legislation by European countries were broadly what we would expect from our discussion in Chapter 2, i.e. UK, Ireland and the Netherlands, for example, do allow such variations and most mainland European countries do not.

IAS GAAP

As we pointed out in Part One, inflation and price increases in the 1970s were much higher in the main developed economies than is the case now.

In 1977 the IASC issued IAS 6, *Accounting Responses to Changing Prices*, which required the disclosure of the effect of any procedures applied to reflect the impact of specific or general price changes. Subsequently the IASC replaced IAS 6 with IAS 15, which required the use of restatement on the basis of either the general price level or current costs when the reporting currency was subject to a significant (but unspecified) degree of inflation. In 1989 the IASC followed an approach similar to that of the FASB, by making IAS 15 optional. In the same year the IASC issued IAS 29, which requires general price level restatement when the reporting currency is subject to hyperinflation. It is worth noting, however, that IAS GAAP are applied in a number of countries with less developed economies, where significant inflation (but not necessarily hyperinflation) may be prevalent. Yet IAS 15 appears to have been little used in practice. It has now been completely withdrawn, with effect from 1 January 2005.

IAS 29, *Financial Reporting in Hyperinflationary Economies*, is another matter. IAS 29 requires that if the functional currency used by an entity is the currency of a hyperinflationary economy, then the entity's financial statements should be restated in units of the same purchasing power, using the measuring unit current at the balance sheet dates (units of current purchasing power). According to IAS 29, para. 37, this restatement should be made using 'a general price index that reflects changes in general purchasing power' and it is preferable that the same index be used by all enterprises that report in the currency of the same economy.

The restated financial statements should be presented as the primary financial statements and separate presentation of the unrestated financial statements is discouraged. The corresponding figures for the previous period required by IAS 1, *Presentation of Financial Statements* (see Chapter 8), and any information in respect of earlier periods should also be restated in terms of units of current purchasing power at the balance sheet date (IAS 29, paras 7–8). The gain or loss on net monetary position (see later) should be separately disclosed as part of net income (IAS 29, para. 9).

The determination of the functional currency in any particular case, previously discussed in SIC 19, is now covered in the newly revised IAS 21 (see Chapter 25). It is defined as the currency of the primary economic environment in which the group operates. As a result of these changes, an entity can no longer avoid restatement under IAS 29 by adopting a stable currency, such as the functional currency of its parent, as its functional currency, a dodge not prevented in the original IAS 21 and 29 taken together. The possible implications are well illustrated in the case study on Aeroflot, which follows on page 421.

IAS 29, para. 3, sets out five characteristics of the economic environment as indicators of hyperinflation, of which the fifth is the most frequently cited:

1 The general population prefers to keep its wealth in non-monetary assets or in a relatively stable foreign currency.
2 The general population regards monetary amounts not in terms of the local currency but in terms of a relatively stable foreign currency.
3 Sales and purchases on credit take place at prices that compensate for the expected loss of purchasing power during the credit period even when it is short.
4 Interest rates, wages and prices are linked to a price index.
5 The cumulative inflation rate over three years is approaching or exceeds 100% (i.e. the average annual inflation rate over three years is approaching or exceeds $33\frac{1}{3}\%$).

The general principles of IAS 29, when applicable, are essentially the CPP approach discussed in Chapter 7. Monetary items are not restated because they are already expressed in terms of the monetary units current at the balance sheet date (current purchasing power unit). In the case of monetary items that are linked by agreement to changes in prices, such as index-linked bonds and loans, their carrying amounts adjusted in accordance with the agreement are used in the restated balance sheet. Other balance sheet amounts are restated to amounts in units of current purchasing power by applying a general price index, unless they are already carried at amounts in units of current purchasing power, such as current market value or net realizable value (IAS 29, paras 11–14).

For items carried at cost or cost less depreciation, the restated cost or cost less depreciation is determined by applying to the historical costs and accumulated depreciation (if any) the change in a selected general price index from the date of acquisition to the balance sheet date. For items carried at revalued amounts, the revalued amount and accumulated depreciation (if any) are restated by applying the change in the price index from the date of the latest revaluation to the balance sheet date.

If records of the acquisition of property, plant, and equipment do not permit the ascertainment or estimation of the acquisition dates, it may be necessary, when the standard is first applied, to use an independent professional valuation of the items concerned as a basis for their restatement. If no general price index is available to cover the period between acquisition and the balance sheet date, an estimate of the changes in general purchasing power of the reporting currency over that period may be made by using the changes in the exchange rate between the reporting currency and a relatively stable foreign currency (IAS 29, paras 11–18).

The restated amount of a non-monetary item is reduced (in accordance with the appropriate IAS) when it exceeds the amount recoverable from the item's future use, sale or disposal (IAS 29, para. 19). It is not appropriate both to restate capital expenditure (fixed assets) financed by borrowing and to capitalize that part of the borrowing costs that compensates for inflation.

At the beginning of the first period of application of IAS 29, the components of owners' equity are restated by applying a general price index from the dates on which the components were contributed or otherwise arose, except for retained earnings and any revaluation surplus. Any revaluation surplus from prior periods is eliminated and restated retained earnings is the residual amount (balancing figure) in the restated balance sheet. Subsequently, all components of owners' equity are restated by applying a general price index from the beginning of the period (or the date of contribution, if later). The movements for the period in owners' equity should be disclosed in accordance with IAS 1, *Presentation of Financial Statements* (see Chapter 9) (IAS 29, paras 24–25).

All items in the income statement should be expressed in terms of end of year current purchasing power units. Hence, all income statement amounts need to be restated by applying the change in general price index between the dates at which the amounts were recorded and the balance sheet date. In practice, average index values for sub-periods, such as months, would normally be used, as in the case of average exchange rates used for the translation of foreign currency amounts under IAS 21 (see Chapter 25).

According to IAS 29, para. 27, the gain or loss on the enterprise's net monetary position may be estimated by applying the change in the general price index to the weighted average for the period of the difference between monetary assets and monetary liabilities.

The gain or loss on the net monetary position should be included in net income. Any adjustment to index-linked assets or liabilities (as mentioned earlier) is offset against the gain or loss on net monetary position. It is suggested that the gain or loss in net monetary position should be presented in the income statement together with interest income and expense and foreign exchange differences related to invested or borrowed funds (IAS 29, paras 27–28).

If an investee accounted for under the equity method reports in the currency of a hyperinflationary country, the financial statements of the investee are restated in accordance with IAS 29 in order to calculate the investor's share of its net assets and results of operations (IAS 29, para. 20).

All items in the cash flow statement should be restated in terms of current purchasing power units at the balance sheet date (IAS 29, para. 33). Comparative figures from the previous reporting period and other comparative information that is disclosed in respect of prior periods should be restated in terms of units of current purchasing power at the balance sheet date (IAS 29, para. 34).

These requirements assume an original historical cost set of financial statements. However, IAS 29 also allows for the possibility of 'current cost' financial statements as the basis. Items stated at current cost are already expressed in units of current purchasing power and so are not restated. Other items are restated as described for historical cost balance sheets earlier (IAS 29, para. 29).

The current cost income statement reports items in terms of the purchasing power of the monetary unit at the times when the underlying transactions or events occurred. For example, cost of goods sold and depreciation are recorded at their current costs at the time of consumption. Therefore, all amounts need to be restated into current purchasing power units at the balance sheet date (IAS 29, para. 30). Gain or loss on net monetary position should be calculated and accounted for as already described (IAS 29, para. 31).

A parent that reports in the currency of a hyperinflationary economy may have subsidiaries that also report in currencies of hyperinflationary economies. The financial statements of such subsidiaries should be restated in accordance with IAS 29 as described earlier, before being included in the process of consolidation. In the case of foreign subsidiaries, financial statements (restated as described earlier if they are in the currency of a hyperinflationary economy) should be translated into the reporting currency at closing rates as required by IAS 21.

If financial statements with different reporting dates are consolidated, all items, whether monetary or non-monetary, should be restated into units of current purchasing power at the date of the consolidated financial statements (IAS 29, paras 35–36).

When an enterprise discontinues the preparation and presentation of financial statements in accordance with IAS 29 because the economy of its reporting currency is no longer hyperinflationary, the amounts that are expressed in current purchasing power units as at the end of the previous reporting period should be treated as the basis for the carrying amounts in its subsequent financial statements (IAS 29, para. 38). In other words, these increased numbers are retained as the new 'cost' figure, which in a sense, they are not.

The following disclosures should be made:

1 The fact that the financial statements and the comparative figures have been restated for changes in the general purchasing power of the reporting currency and are stated in terms of the unit of purchasing power current at the balance sheet date.
2 Whether the underlying financial statements are based on historical costs or current costs.
3 The identity and level of the general price index used at the balance sheet date and the movement in this index during the current and previous reporting periods (IAS, para. 39).

Case study

If you have any doubts about technicalities involved in this discussion, you should reread Chapter 7 at this point. There is no doubt that the Russian airline, Aeroflot, was operating in a hyperinflationary economy according to IAS 29 in the year ended 31 December 1999. The Aeroflot financials quote annual inflation rates for the relevant three years as follows.

For year ended 31 December	Annual inflation
1999	36.7%
1998	84.4%
1997	11.0%

However, Aeroflot, among its 'principal accounting policies', reported as follows:

> The statutory (i.e. Russian statutory) amounts of non-monetary assets and liabilities have been adjusted to their historical cost denominated in US dollars, the functional currency of the Group (except for certain older assets independently valued in US dollars) *so as to present the financial statements in accordance with IAS*. The US dollar has been determined as the reporting currency of the Group on the basis that the majority of revenues are denominated in US dollars and settled in US dollars or other foreign currency, the majority of assets and liabilities are denominated in foreign currency, as is a significant portion of operating expenses. Accordingly, these financial statements are presented in US dollars. . . . Since US dollars are not the currency of a hyperinflationary economy, the provisions of IAS 29 have not been applied. [emphasis added].

The consolidated statement of operations of Aeroflot for 1999 is shown in Table 21.1.

A very significant reduction in the scale of operations is indicated. Revenue in 1999 is 17% down on 1998 and operating costs are 18% down. However the exchange rates for the rouble to the dollar are given in the notes as follows.

At 31 December	Exchange rate
1997	$1 = 5.96 r
1998	$1 = 20.65 r
1999	$1 = 27.00 r

Table 21.1 Aeroflot and subsidiaries' consolidated statements of operations, 1999

	Year ended 31 December 1999	Year ended 31 December 1998
	$ million	$ million
Traffic revenue	865.4	1 000.0
Other revenue	300.8	403.1
Revenue	**1 166.2**	**1 403.1**
Operating costs	(908.9)	(1 103.9)
Staff costs	(118.0)	(170.3)
Depreciation and amortization expense	(132.0)	(135.1)
Operating costs	**(1 158.9)**	**(1 409.3)**
Operating income (loss)	**7.3**	**(6.2)**
Interest expense	(52.2)	(32.2)
Interest income	0.9	2.0
Share of income in associated undertakings	4.6	4.4
Foreign exchange and translation loss, net	(6.8)	(18.4)
Non-operating income (expenses), net	40.1	(25.1)
Loss before taxation and minority interest	**(6.1)**	**(75.5)**
Taxation	52.2	(134.2)
Loss after taxation	**(58.3)**	**(209.7)**
Minority interest	(1.3)	(1.2)
Loss	**(59.6)**	**(210.9)**
Loss per share	**($0.05)**	**($0.19)**

Taking a rough and simplistic calculation, the average rate of exchange for 1999 can be taken as the mid-point of the beginning and end rates and similarly for 1998. This simplistic calculation gives an average range for 1999 of 23.82 and for 1998 of 13.31.

Activity 21.1

Recalculate the figure for revenues and operating costs from Table 21.1 into historical roubles using the multiplicands given in the illustration and comment on the results.

Activity feedback

The figures are as shown in Table 21.2.

Without claiming accuracy for the figures used, it is clear that the trend of activity indicated in nominal roubles is the exact opposite of that suggested in the published financials. A significant *increase* in the scale of operations is now indicated. Also, the

Table 21.2 Aeroflot operating results (recalculated in roubles from Table 21.1)

	Year ended 31 December 1999	Year ended 31 December 1998
	000 million roubles	000 million roubles
Traffic revenue	20.614	13.310
Other revenue	7.165	5.365
Revenue	27.779	18.675
Operating costs	21.650	14.693
Staff costs	2.811	2.267
Depreciation and amortization	3.144	1.798
Operating costs	27.605	18.758
Operating income (loss)	0.174	(0.083)

result for 1999 in nominal roubles is a profit under these assumptions (albeit small), not a loss. A further refinement of the figures in Table 21.2 is possible. The 1998 figures are expressed (as calculated) in 1998 roubles. Arguably, these should be re-expressed into 1999 roubles for comparison with the reported 1999 figures, i.e. the entire 1998 column in Table 21.2 could be multiplied by 136.7%. This would suggest that in real terms that 1998 and 1999 revenues and expenses were not significantly different. Who said that accounting is an exact discipline?!

The other question that arises in relation to the Aeroflot example is whether or not the bold claim in the quoted accounting policy that the treatment used, in avoiding IAS 29 adjustments, was in accordance with IAS, is actually correct. The answer is, possibly but, from 1 January 2005, this treatment would definitely not be permitted.

Summary

In this chapter we explored the IAS regulations relating to accounting for inflation, as contained in IAS 29 and related these regulations to the theoretical issues discussed in Part One.

EXERCISES   (✔ indicates answers are available on page 735)

✔ 1 Which phenomena is IAS 29 adjusting for when it is applied in the preparation of financial statements?

2 The idea that a regular annual inflation rate of 35% requires CPP adjustments, but that a regular annual inflation rate of 25% does not, is quite absurd. Discuss.

3 Rework a numerical exercise from Chapter 7.

22

Cash flow statements

After studying this chapter you should be able to:
- ☐ describe the difference between funds flow and cash flow
- ☐ explain why the IASB found it necessary to require cash flow rather than funds flow statements
- ☐ describe the requirements of IAS 7, *Cash Flow Statements* (revised)
- ☐ prepare cash flow statements
- ☐ identify any problems in relation to cash flow statements
- ☐ compare different GAAPs for cash flow statements.

Introduction

lli'kwidəti|

A cash flow statement, as we will see later, provides additional useful information to users, additional, that is, to the income statement and balance sheet of an enterprise. The cash flow statement emphasizes cash and liquidity rather than revenue, expenses and profit. IAS 7, which was first issued in 1977, originally required a funds flow statement not a cash flow statement. IAS 7 was revised in 1992 and now requires a cash flow statement. We will discuss the difference between funds flow and cash flow within this chapter.

Cash flow reporting

The traditional accounting process is an uncertain and complex process. Not only is profit determination complex, it is potentially misleading. In any accounting year there will be a mixture of complete and incomplete transactions. Transactions are complete when they have led to a final cash settlement and these cause no profit measurement difficulties.

Considerable problems arise, however, in dealing with incomplete transactions, where the profit or loss figure can only be estimated by means of the accruals concept, whereby revenue and costs are:

> Matched with one another so far as their relationship can be established or justifiably assumed and dealt with in the profit and loss account of the period to which they relate.

Thus, the profit for the past year is dependent on the validity of many assumptions about the future, e.g. the future life of assets is estimated in order to calculate the depreciation charge for the past year.

The greater the volume of incomplete transactions, the greater the degree of estimation and, accordingly, the greater the risk that investors could turn out to have been misled if actual outcomes deviated from estimates.

To explore the differences between cash flow and profit reporting, consider the following.

Activity 22.1

Two short statements about the same business in the same year follow. Summarize in words what each statement is telling us and suggest reasons for the differences between them.

A		€000s
	Sales	410
	less Cost of sales	329
		81
	less Other expenses	36
		45
	less Depreciation	13
		32
	less Taxation provided	13
		19
	less Dividend provided	8
	Retained	11

B		€000s
	Sales received	387
	less Payments for goods for sale	333
		54
	less Other expenses paid	32
		22
	less Capital expenditure	20
		2
	less Taxation paid	14
		(12)
	less Dividend paid	7
	Increase in borrowing	(19)

Activity feedback

Clearly, statement *A* is an income statement. It shows the revenues and expenses, calculated on the traditional bases, the taxation charges relating to the year and the dividends which it has been decided should be paid out to shareholders in relation to that year. It shows a profit and implies (although we do not know the size of the business) a successful year.

Statement *B* is a statement of cash movement in the year – a summary of the cash book but analysed into the various reasons the cash has moved. The individual differences between the two statements will be due to changes in accruals, prepayments and the like. Overall, statement *B* shows a reduction in the cash resources of the business before the payment of the dividend and obviously shows an even bigger contraction in the cash resources of the business after the dividend payout in the year. Statement *B* surely implies an unsuccessful year.

People often talk about 'cash flows' or claim to be in favour of 'cash flow statements' or 'cash flow reporting' without being too precise about what they mean. In fact, different people are likely to mean significantly different things and it is very important that we are able to separate out the various situations and arguments one from the other.

At one level, it can be suggested that cash flow reporting, actual and budgeted, should completely replace both the income statement (on whatever basis) and balance sheet. The argument for this (ignoring barter situations) is that only cash represents and demonstrates an increase or decrease in the business resources and that this suggests both that only cash should be reported and that only cash need be reported. This argument is surely untenable. Users need information about changes in the command of a business organization over resources, over goods and services or the power to obtain goods and services.

At a second level, it can be suggested that some form of cash flow statement on the lines of statement *B* in Activity 22.1, since it obviously gives information which is potentially useful and which is additional to and different from the information in the income statement should be required as an additional statement in the final reporting package. This is surely logical. Indeed, it is arguably precisely because an income statement for the year is not a good indicator of the cash flow position for the year and because a cash flow statement for the year is not a good indicator of the profit and loss position for the year that the argument for including both is so powerful.

Funds flow or cash flow?

The funds flow statement as traditionally prepared for many years was, conceptually speaking, an extremely odd animal. It tried to adjust away some, but not all, of the accrual adjustments used in the creation of the income statement to start with. Historically, the reason for much of this obscurity was that the funds flow statement, being an additional statement not required by the law, was deliberately designed not to give additional information, merely to rearrange already available information in a different form. Basically the funds flow statement concentrated on changes in net current assets rather than cash.

So what is funds flow? The next activity should illustrate this for you.

Activity 22.2

An extract from the balance sheet of *A* enterprise as at 31 December 20X2:

	€000s	€000s
	31.12.X2	31.12.X1
Inventory	4 300	4 600
Accounts receivable	2 600	1 300

Cash and bank	1 200	2 500
	8 100	8 400
Accounts payable	6 500	7 900
Working capital	1 600	500

Identify the change in funds.

Activity feedback

If we look solely at cash we could state that *A* had experienced a decrease in cash of €1 300 000 over the year. Contrariwise, looking at working capital/net current assets provides a much better position, an increase of €1 100 000 over the year. But which figure should users of accounts have regard to when taking decisions?

Advantages of cash flow over funds flow

These can be summarized as follows:

- Funds flow data based on movements in working capital can obscure movements relevant to the liquidity and viability of an entity. For example, a significant decrease in cash available may be masked by an increase in inventory or accounts receivable. Entities may, therefore, run out of cash while reporting increases in working capital. Similarly, a decrease in working capital does not necessarily indicate a cash shortage and a danger of failure.
- As cash flow monitoring is a normal feature of business life and not a specialized accounting technique, cash flow is a concept which is more widely understood than are changes in working capital.
- Cash flows can be a direct input into a business valuation model and, therefore, historical cash flows may be relevant in a way not possible for funds flow data.
- A funds flow statement is based largely on the difference between two balance sheets. It reorganizes such data, but does not provide new data. The cash flow statement may include data not disclosed in a funds flow statement.

So does a cash flow statement have the relevant characteristics of useful information? Let us see if you can answer the question.

Activity 22.3

State whether you believe, given your knowledge so far, that cash flow is understandable, relevant, reliable and complete.

Activity feedback

1 *Understandable*. Certainly, cash is a concept that most people understand, whereas accrual accounting takes us a few years to learn and even more years to understand the need for!

2 *Relevant.* Cash certainly is relevant as without it a business cannot operate. Enterprises may be able to show a healthy profit but have a very poor cash position as they are relying on borrowed funds.

3 *Reliable.* Cash is the end product of a transaction. It is realized! Whereas funds based on profit require us to estimate a point of realization of revenue prior to receipt of cash and the ultimate realization of cash can be in doubt. Cash is certainly free from bias.

4 *Complete.* Is anything that is historical information providing a complete picture? A cash flow statement shows information about the reporting entity's cash flows in the reporting period, but this provides incomplete information for assessing future cash flows. Some cash flows result from transactions that took place in an earlier period and some cash flows are expected to result in further cash flows in a future period.

Looking back to Activity 22.2 where we noted that a healthy funds flow (working capital) of €1.1m masked a decrease in cash flow of €1.3m we can see that the selection of funds or cash flow can have a major impact on a user's interpretation of an enterprise's financial position. It is also worth noting that cash is the 'life blood' of an enterprise and without it they cannot operate. Cash is also rather a difficult figure to manipulate.

Requirements of IAS 7

Scope

The IASC viewed cash flow reporting as so important that there are no exemptions for any enterprises. No matter what an enterprise's principal revenue-producing activities might be they need cash to conduct their operation, to pay their obligations and to provide returns to their investors, Their users need this information as they are interested in how the enterprise uses and generates cash.

Generation of cash flows and definitions

Cash flows within an enterprise can broadly be generated by three activities:

1 Operating or principal revenue producing activities defined by IAS 7 as those activities that are not investing or financing.

2 Investing activities; the acquisition and disposal of long-term assets and investments not included in cash equivalents.

3 Financing activities; activities that result in changes in the size and composition of the equity capital and borrowings of the enterprise.

Some other definitions from IAS 7 for completeness are:

- *Cash.* Comprises cash on hand and demand deposits.
- *Cash equivalents.* Short-term, highly liquid investments that are readily convertible to known amount of cash and which are subject to an insignificant risk of changes in value.

Activity 22.4

Provide examples of cash flows, both inflow and outflow, from operating, investing and financing activities. To help we provide an example for each category in Table 22.1.

Table 22.1 Examples of cash flows

Operating activities	Investing activities	Financing activities
Cash receipts from sale of goods and rendering of services	Cash payments to acquire fixed assets	Cash proceeds from issue of shares and other equity instruments

Now extend the table.

Activity feedback

You may not have identified all the following but the definitive list as given by IAS 7 is shown in Table 22.2.

Table 22.2 Definitive list of cash flows as given by IAS 7

Operating activities	Investing activities	Financing activities
Cash receipts from sale of goods and rendering of services	Cash payments to acquire fixed assets	Cash proceeds from issue of shares and other equity instruments
Cash receipts from royalties, fees, commissions and other revenue	Cash receipts from sale of fixed assets	Cash payments to owners to acquire or redeem the enterprise's shares
Cash payments to suppliers for goods and services	Cash payments to acquire equity or debt instruments of other enterprises and interests in joint ventures	Cash proceeds from issuing debentures, loans, notes, bonds, mortgages and other short- or long-term borrowings
Cash payments to and on behalf of employees	Cash advances and loans made to other parties	Cash repayments of amounts borrowed
Cash payments or refunds of income taxes unless they can be specifically identified with financing or investing activities	Cash receipts from the repayment of advances and loans made to other parties	Cash payments by a lessee for the reduction of the outstanding liability relating to a finance lease
Cash receipts and payments from contracts held for dealing or trading purposes	Cash payments for futures, forward contracts, options and swaps except when the contracts are held for dealing or trading purposes or the payments are classified as financing activities	Cash receipts and cash payments of an insurance enterprise for premiums and claims, annuities and other policy benefits

The amount of cash flows from operating activities is highly important for users to assess whether enough cash has been generated from this source for the enterprise to repay loans, make investments in assets and pay dividends. Cash flows under the heading of operating activities are primarily derived from the principal revenue producing activities of the enterprise.

Separating out the cash flows from investing activities is also seen as important as this provides users with information on investment made in resources that will potentially generate future income and cash flows. Users require information on cash flows within financing activities so that they can predict claims on future cash flows from providers of capital to the enterprise.

Activity 22.5

Identify in which category the following cash flows would be included:

1 An enterprise purchases a motor vehicle that it intends to sell on to a customer.
2 An enterprise purchases a motor vehicle that it intends to use as part of its delivery fleet.
3 An enterprise purchases a motor vehicle using a finance lease.
4 An enterprise gains the use of a motor vehicle under an operating lease.
5 An enterprise holds securities for dealing/trading purposes.
6 Interest paid and received and dividends received by an enterprise.
7 Dividends paid by an enterprise.

Activity feedback

1 This is purchase of an inventory item and therefore shown under operating activities.
2 This is purchase of a fixed asset for the enterprise and therefore part of investing activities.
3 The enterprise has acquired the use of a fixed asset but the cash flow of principal payments will be shown under financing activities. There will be no cash flow under investing activities.
4 This time the payments under the operating lease will be treated as cash flows under operating activities as they are viewed as a normal expense payment of the enterprise. Note that the motor vehicle, depending on the revenue-producing activities of the enterprise and how the financing of the motor vehicle is arranged, can be regarded as a cash flow of any of the three categories.
5 These are inventory to the dealing house and therefore part of operating activities as they relate to the principal revenue-producing activities.
6 These are usually classified as operating cash flows for a financial institution but may also be regarded as operating for other enterprises as they form part of the net profit calculation – IAS 7, para. 33. This paragraph also allows them to be treated as financing – interest paid, or investing – interest and dividends received. The later alternative seems more sensible to us.
7 Dividends paid are obviously financing as they are a cost of obtaining finance. However, IAS 7 allows an alternative categorization under operating activities. This is to enable users to judge the ability of the enterprise to pay dividends out of

operating cash flows. We find this lack of consistency over the treatment of interest and dividends received and paid confusing and it will certainly impair comparability of cash flows between enterprises where different alternatives have been used.

Cash and cash equivalents

The definitions of these are important as cash flows are defined as inflows and outflows of cash and cash equivalents. It should be apparent to you that an investment, dependent on our view of short-term or highly liquid could be viewed as a cash and cash equivalent cash flow item or an investing activity. Bank borrowings are generally viewed, according to IAS 7, as financing activities but in certain circumstances bank overdrafts can be viewed as part of cash and cash equivalents. These circumstances are where the overdraft forms an integral part of the enterprise's cash management.

Activity 22.6

Determine whether the following items are cash, cash equivalents, investing activities or financing:

1 An account held with a bank where withdrawals require 90 days' notice.
2 An account held with a bank where withdrawals require 95 days' notice.
3 An overdraft with the bank which is seen as short term and part of everyday cash flows of the enterprise.
4 A loan from the bank for 60 days for a specific purpose.
5 An investment with a bank which has 60 days to maturity, but its final value is subject to significant risk as it is based on the index achievable at that time from a highly fluctuating stock market.

Activity feedback

1 If you view 90 days as short term then this is cash equivalent.
2 If you view 95 days as long term then this would be investing.
3 Cash as part of cash management.
4 Financing as a loan for a specific purpose cannot be viewed as everyday cash management.
5 This investment has a significant risk attached to it in terms of its final value and therefore must be regarded as investing activities.

The decision as regards 1 and 2 is clarified by IAS 7 (para. 7) as follows:

> An investment normally qualifies as a cash equivalent only when it has a short maturity of, say, three months or less from date of acquisition. It must be readily convertible to a known amount of cash and be subject to an insignificant risk of changes in value.

The decisions required here are quite subjective and it is feasible for one enterprise to determine an investment as a cash equivalent and another as an investing item.

Format of a cash flow statement

IAS 7 requires enterprises to report cash flows during a period in a statement identifying cash flows classified by operating, investing and financing activities. This implies a simple statement as follows:

> Cash flow statement
> Cash flows from operating activities   A
> Cash flows from investing activities   B
> Cash flows from financing activities   C
> Net change in cash and cash equivalents   X

However, the standard, in order to provide relevant information to users, requires each of these cash flows to be separated into their constituent parts, i.e.:

1 Gross cash receipts and gross cash payments arising from investing and financing activities. Note here that if a single transaction has cash flows involving financing, investing and operating activities then the transaction will need to be split into its constituent parts. An example of such a transaction is a finance lease payment where the principal repayment will be disclosed as a cash flow under financing and the interest payment can be disclosed under operating or financing.
2 Gross cash receipts and payments from operating activities or net profit adjusted for effects of a non-cash nature.
3 Cash flows under any of the three sections can be reported net where the cash flows reflect the activities of the customer rather than the enterprise or where items are large, maturities short and turnover quick.
4 Cash flows relating to extraordinary items should be identified separately under each category.
5 Cash flows relating to taxes, interest and dividends received and paid, acquisitions and disposals of subsidiaries and other business units.

In addition, the components of cash and cash equivalents are required, together with a reconciliation of the amounts in the cash flow statement with the equivalent items reported in the balance sheets.

Item 2 in the list indicates that there are two methods for determining cash flows from operating activities, from cash receipts and payments known as the direct method or from adjusting net profit for non-cash receipts and payments known as the indirect method. The standard prefers the direct method as it 'provides information which may be useful in estimating future cash flows which is not available under the indirect method'. Strangely, the UK ASB requires the indirect method as it does not believe that the benefits to the users of the direct method outweigh the costs of preparing it.

Activity 22.7

1 What information would the direct method provide that the indirect method would not provide to users?
2 Why might the direct method be more costly to prepare than the indirect?
3 How should a non-cash transaction be dealt with in a cash flow statement?

Activity feedback

1 The direct method would identify cash receipts from customers and cash payments to suppliers and employees whereas the indirect method would only show net profit with its adjustments for depreciation, profit on disposal and changes in working capital etc. The actual disclosure of cash receipts and payments enables users to evaluate future cash flows more easily.

2 Enterprises operate an accounting system that is geared towards accrual accounting. The direct method would require a company to use either an accounting system which directly records and analyses the cash flow in relation to each transaction, thus operating two accounting systems or to adjust sales, costs of sales and other items in the income statement for non-cash items, changes in working capital and other items which relate to investing or financing activities – a time-consuming and costly business. If we take the view that information should be provided that is useful to users, the view of the Framework, then we must support the direct method for the disclosure of operating cash flows.

3 Quite obviously it shouldn't be dealt with as it does not involve a cash flow!

Examples of non-cash transactions given in the Standard are:

- acquisition of assets either by assuming directly related liabilities or by means of a finance lease
- acquisition of an enterprise by means of an equity issue
- conversion of debt to equity.

All these involve the exchange of a non-cash asset for a non-cash liability or conversion from one asset or liability to another. These types of transaction will be reported elsewhere in the financial statements.

Direct/indirect method of determining cash flows

Activity 22.8

From the following information relating to Zen enterprise calculate the cash flows from operating activities using both the direct and indirect method.

Consolidated income statement for the period ended 31 December 20X2

	€000s
Sales	30 650
Cost of sales	26 000
Gross profit	4 650
Depreciation	(450)
Administration and selling expenses	(910)
Interest expense	(400)
Investment income	500
Foreign exchange loss	(40)
Net profit before taxation and extraordinary item	3 350
Extraordinary item – insurance proceeds from earthquake disaster	180

Net profit after extraordinary item		3 530
Taxes on income		(300)
Net profit		3 230

Consolidated balance sheet as at 31 December 20X2

	20X2 €000s	€000s	20X1 €000s	€000s
Assets				
Cash and cash equivalents		410		160
Account receivable		1 900		1 200
Inventory		1 000		1 950
Portfolio investments		2 500		2 500
Property, plant and equipment at cost	3 730		1 910	
Accumulated depreciation	1 450	2 280	1 060	850
Total assets		8 090		6 660
Liabilities				
Trade payables		250		1 890
Interest payable		230		100
Income taxes payable		400		1 000
Long-term debt		2 300		1 040
Total liabilities		3 180		4 030
Shareholders equity		1 500		1 250
Retained earnings		3 410		1 380
Total shareholders equity		4 910		2 630
Total liabilities and shareholders equity		8 090		6 660

Other information is available as follows:

(a) All the shares of a subsidiary were acquired for €590 000. The fair values of assets acquired and liabilities assumed were as follows:

	€000s
Inventories	100
Accounts receivable	100
Cash	40
Property, plant and equipment	650
Trade payables	100
Long-term debt	200

(b) €250 000 was raised from the issue of shares and €250 000 from long-term borrowings.

(c) Interest expense was €400 000 of which €170 000 was paid during the period. €100 000 relating to interest expense of the prior period was also paid during the period.

(d) Dividends paid were €1 200 000.

(e) The liability for tax at the beginning and end of the period was €1 000 000 and €400 000 respectively. During the period a further €200 000 tax was provided for. Withholding tax on dividends received during the period of €200 000 amounted to €100 000.

(f) During the period, the group acquired property, plant and equipment with an aggregate cost of €1 250 000 of which €900 000 was acquired by means of finance leases. Cash payments of €350 000 were made to purchase property, plant and equipment.

(g) Plant with original cost of €80 000 and accumulated depreciation of €60 000 was sold for €20 000.

(h) Accounts receivable as at end 31 December 20X2 include €100 000 of interest receivable.

[adapted from example in Appendix A to IAS 7]

Activity feedback

Direct method

Cash flow from operations:	
Cash receipts from customers (working 1)	30 150
Cash paid to suppliers and employees (working 2)	(27 600)
Cash generated from operations	2 550
Interest paid (170 + 100 note c)	(270)
Income taxes paid (1000 + 200 + 100 − 400)	(900)
Cash flow before extraordinary item	1 380
Proceeds from earthquake disaster settlement*	180
	1 560

(*assume disaster gave rise to loss of operating activities)

Working 1		
Sales – income statement	30 650	
add Opening accounts receivable	1 200	
less Closing accounts receivable	(1 800)	(1 900 − 100 note h)
add Subsidiary debtors	100	
	30 150	

Working 2		
Cost of sales – income statement	26 000	
less Opening stock	(1 950)	
add Closing stock	1 000	
Purchases	25 050	
less Closing trade payables	(250)	
add Opening trade payables	1 890	
	26 690	
Admin and selling expenses	910	
	27 600	
Subsidiary trade payables note a	100	
less Subsidiary inventories note a	(100)	
	27 600	

(Note interest and income taxes paid are treated as part of operating activities, dividends paid are not.)

Indirect method

Net profit before tax and dividends	3 350	
add Back interest	(100)	
Foreign exchange loss	40	
Depreciation	450	
	3 740	
Increase in trade and other receivables	(500)	(700 − 100 subsidiary − 100 interest receivable)
Decrease in inventories	1 050	(950 + 100 subsidiary)
Decrease in trade payables	(1 740)	(1 640 + 100 subsidiary)
Cash generated from operations	2 550	
Interest paid	(270)	
Income taxes paid	(900)	
Cash flow before extraordinary item	1 380	
Proceeds from earthquake disaster settlement	180	
Net cash flow from operating activities	1 560	

Activity 22.9

Now calculate the cash flow from investing activities from the data given in Activity 22.8.

Activity feedback

Investing activities cover cash flows in respect of fixed assets, investments in equity or debt, advances and loans to other parties. The balance sheet changes identify any increases/decreases in portfolio investments and property, plant and equipment and we were also informed about an acquisition of a subsidiary.

Therefore:

Cash flow from investing activities		
Acquisition of subsidiary less cash acquired	(550)	(590 − 40)
Purchase of property, plant and equipment	(350)	(note f) or (working 1)
Proceeds from sale of equipment	20	(note g)
Dividends received	200	(note c)
Interest received (investment income − dividends)	200	
Net cash used in investing activities	(480)	

Working 1	
Opening balance sheet of property etc. at cost	1 910
add Subsidiary bought	650
less Sale	(80)
	2 480
Closing balance sheet at cost	3 730
	1 250
Leased assets so no cash flow	(900)
Therefore assets bought for cash	350

Activity 22.10

Now identify the cash flows from financing activities from the data given in Activity 22.8.

Activity feedback

Cash flow from financing activities covers proceeds from the issue of shares, loans etc. and repayments of amounts borrowed.

Cash flow from financing activities		
Proceeds from issuing shares	250	(note b)
Proceeds from long-term borrowings	250	(note b)
Payments of finance lease (working 1)	(90)	
Dividends paid	(1 200)	(note d)
	(790)	

Working 1	
Opening balance sheet long term debt	1 040
add Finance lease principal	900
	1 940
add Subsidiary long term loan	200
	2 140
New loans	250
	2 390
Closing balance sheet long term debt	2 300
Therefore lease principal repaid	90

If you put the answers of Activities 22.8, 9, and 10 together and add on cash and cash equivalent changes you have a full cash flow statement for the data in Activity 22.8 as follows.

DIRECT METHOD CASH FLOW STATEMENT

Cash flow from operating activities		
Cash receipts from customers (working 1)	30 150	
Cash paid to suppliers and employees (working 2)	(27 600)	
Cash generated from operations	2 550	
Interest paid (170 + 100 note c)	(270)	
Income taxes paid (1 000 + 200 + 100 − 400)	(900)	
Cash flow before extraordinary item	1 380	
Proceeds from earthquake disaster settlement*	180	
Net cash flow from operating activities		**1 560**

Cash flow from investing activities		
Acquisition of subsidiary less cash acquired	(550)	(590 − 40)
Purchase of property, plant and equipment	(350)	(note f) or (working 1)
Proceeds from sale of equipment	20	(note g)
Dividends received	200	(note c)
Interest received (investment income − dividends)	200	
Net cash used in investing activities		**(480)**

Cash flow from financing activities
Proceeds from issuing shares   250   (note b)
Proceeds from longterm borrowings   250   (note b)
Payments of finance lease (working 1)   (90)
Dividends paid   (1 200)   (note d)
Net cash used in financing activities   (790)
Net increase in cash and cash equivalents   290

Cash and cash equivalents at beginning of period (160 – 40 f.e.l.)   120
Cash and cash equivalents at end of period   410

Notes to this cash flow are required in respect of:

- the fair value of asset and liabilities of the subsidiary acquired
- the amount of property, plant and equipment acquired by finance lease
- detailed analysis of the cash equivalents
- segmental cash flows.

IAS 7 Appendix A illustrates these notes.

Activity 22.11

The balance sheet of Axbrit enterprise for the year ended 31 March 20X2 is as follows:

Assets	20X2	20X1
Cash and cash equivalents	27	21
Accounts receivable	15	18
Inventory	25	20
Property, plant and equipment at cost	230	160
Accumulated depreciation	(60)	(44)
Total assets	237	175
Liabilities		
Trade payables	47	39
Income taxes payable	16	12
Long term debt	32	30
Total liabilities	95	81
Shareholders equity		
Share capital	33	27
Capital reserves	30	24
Retained earnings	79	43
Total shareholders equity	142	94
Total liabilities and shareholders equity	237	175

Prepare the cash flow statement for the year ended 31 March 20X2 given that no property, plant and equipment was sold during the period and that the increase in long term debt took place on 1 April 20X2 and carried a 10% rate of interest and that dividends paid during the year were €18.

Activity feedback

As we are not given the income statement or any other information to enable us to derive net cash flow from operating activities using the direct method we have to use the indirect method in this example.

Indirect method net cash flow from operating activities

Net profit (change in retained earnings + dividends)	54	
Add interest on long term loans	3.2	
Add taxation charge (assume liability at end is charge for period)	16	
		19.2
Net profit before taxation		73.2
add Depreciation	16	
Increase in inventories	(5)	
Decrease in accounts receivable	3	
Increase in trade payables	8	22
Cash generated from operations		95.2
Interest paid		(3.2)
Income taxes paid		(12)
Net cash flow from operating activities		80
Cash flow from investing activities		
Purchase of property, plant and equipment	70	
Net cash used in investing activities		(70)
Cash flows from financing activities		
Proceeds from issues of shares	12	
Proceeds from long-term borrowings	2	
Dividends paid	(18)	
Net cash used in financing activities		(4)
Net increase in cash and cash equivalents		6
Cash and cash equivalents at beginning of period		21
Cash and cash equivalents at end of period		27

The next activity requires you to prepare a rather more complicated cash flow than Activity 22.11.

Activity 22.12

From the income statement and balance sheets of Thomas Manufacturing enterprise prepare the cash flow statement for the year ended 31 December 20X5.

Thomas manufacturing income statement for the year ended 31.12.X5

	€000s	€000s
Sales		5 000
Change in inventories		500
Own work capitalized		150
Other operating income		50

Raw materials and consumables	(2 000)	
Other external charges	(750)	(2 750)
Employee costs		(1 500)
Depreciation and amortization		(400)
Other operating charges		(100)
		950
Income from investments – dividends		20
Other interest receivable		5
		975
Interest payable		(160)
Income before income taxes		815
Income taxes		(325)
Income after taxes		490
Extraordinary income	70	
Extraordinary charges	(90)	
Extraordinary loss	(20)	
Tax on loss	8	(12)
Income for period		478

Dividends paid for the period were €250 000.

Balance sheet as at 31.12.X5

31.12.X4

Cost €000s	Net €000s		Cost €000s	Deprec. €000s	Net €000s
		Non-current assets			
200	100	Intangible	350	200	150
1 500	800	Property, plant and equip.	2 500	775	1 725
100	100	Investments	200		200
1 800	1 000		3 050	975	2 075
		Current assets			
	1 000	Inventories		1 600	
	1 000	Accounts receivable		1 200	
	50	Investments			
	250	Cash		30	
	2 300				2 830
	3 300				4 905
		Shareholders equity			
	1 000	Ordinary shares			1 500
	200	Capital reserves			800
	177	Retained earnings			405
	1 377				2 705
		Liabilities			
		Long term			
	980	Loans			790
		Short term			

600	Accounts payable	750
	Loans	257
243	Taxation	274
843		1 281
100	Deferred taxes	129
1 923		1 200
3 300		4 905

Further information is available as follows:

- As at 1 January X5, freehold land was revalued from €500 000 to €1 000 000.
- During the year ended 31 December X5 plant and equipment costing €300 000, written down to €50 000 at 31 December X4, was sold for €75 000. These book gains and losses were adjusted into the depreciation charge in the income statement.
- Own work capitalized refers to development work carried forward as an intangible asset.
- Loans with a nominal value of €190 000 were redeemed at par during the year.
- Shares were issued for cash during the year; there were no purchases of the company's own shares.
- The investments shown as current assets at 31 December X4 and not regarded as cash equivalent were sold during the year for €50 000.

Activity feedback

Indirect cash flow statement for Thomas Manufacturing

	€000s	€000s
Cash flow from operating activities		
Net profit before tax and extraordinary items		815
Adjustments for:		
Depreciation (400 + 25 gain adj. on sale into dep.)	425	
Profit on sale of plant and equipment	(25)	
Investment income	(25)	
Interest expense	160	535
Operating profit before working capital changes		1 350
Increase in trade and other receivables	(200)	
Increase in inventories	(600)	
Increase in trade payables	150	(650)
Cash generated from operations		700
Interest paid		(160)
Income taxes paid (see note 1)		(257)
Cash flow before extraordinary items		283
Proceeds from extraordinary items		(20)
Net cash from operating activities		263
Cash flow from investing activities		
Purchase of intangible fixed assets	(150)	
Purchase of property, plant and equipment (note 2)	(800)	
Purchase of investments	(100)	

Proceeds from sale of investments	50	
Proceeds from sale of equipment	75	
Interest received	5	
Dividends received	20	
Net cash used in investing activities		(900)
Cash flow from financing activities		
Proceeds from issues of shares	600	
Proceeds from long term borrowings	257	
Redemption of loans	(190)	
Dividends paid	(250)	
Net cash from financing activities		417
Net decrease in cash and cash equivalents		(220)
Cash and cash equivalents at beginning of period		250
Cash and cash equivalents at end of period		30

Note 1	
Opening balance of taxes $(243 + 100)$	343
Add income statement charge $(325 - 8)$	317
	660
Closing balance of taxes $(274 + 129)$	403
Therefore taxes paid during the year	257

Note 2	
Opening balance of assets at cost	1 500
add Revaluation during the year	500
less Sale at cost	(300)
	1 700
Closing balance at cost	2 500
Therefore purchase of assets	800

Disclosure

As an example of disclosure required in respect of cash flow statements by IAS 7 we present that relating to the Bayer Group for the year ended 31 December 2001.

CASH FLOW STATEMENT

The cash flow statement shows how the liquidity of the Bayer Group was affected by the inflow and outflow of cash and cash equivalents during the year. The effects of acquisitions, divestitures and other changes in the scope of consolidation are eliminated. Cash flows are classified by operating, investing and financing activities in accordance with IAS 7 (*Cash Flow Statements*). An adjustment is shown to reconcile cash and cash equivalents at the end of the year to the liquid assets reflected in the balance sheet. The amounts reported by foreign consolidated companies are translated at average exchange rates for the year, with the exception of cash and cash equivalents, which are translated at closing rates as in the balance sheet. The effect of changes in exchange rates on cash and cash equivalents is shown separately.

BAYER GROUP CONSOLIDATED STATEMENTS OF CASH FLOW

	Note	2001	2000
		€ million	€ million
Operating result		**1 611**	**3 827**
Income taxes currently payable		(637)	(873)
Depreciation and amortization		2 516	2 139
Change in long term provisions		(193)	(316)
Gains on retirements of non current assets		(374)	(73)
Gross cash provided by operating activities		**2 923**	**4 164**
(Increase) Decrease in inventories		146	(750)
(Increase) Decrease in trade accounts receivable		638	(548)
Increase in trade accounts payable		73	351
Changes in other working capital		79	(126)
Net cash provided by operating activities	39	**3 859**	**3 091**
Of which discontinuing operations	42	159	302
Cash outflows for additions to property, plant and equipment		(2 617)	(2 647)
Cash inflows from sales of property, plant and equipment		521	322
Cash inflows related to investments		109	(45)
Cash outflows for acquisitions		(502)	(4 125)
Interest and dividends received		138	191
Cash inflows from marketable securities		219	115
Net cash used in investing activities	40	**(2 132)**	**(6 189)**
Of which discontinuing operations	42	295	(298)
Capital contributions		0	2
Bayer AG dividend and dividend payments to minority stockholders		(1 028)	(953)
Issuances of debt		2 514	3 952
Retirements of debt		(2 551)	(1 893)
Interest paid after taxes		(484)	(336)
Net cash provided by (used in) financing activities	41	**(1 549)**	**772**
Of which discontinuing operations	42	36	11
Change in cash and cash equivalents due to business activities	42	**178**	**(2 326)**
Cash and cash equivalents at beginning of year		**491**	**2 812**
Change in cash due to changes in scope of consolidation		42	(3)
Change in cash and cash equivalents due to exchange rate movements		8	8
Cash and cash equivalents at end year	43	**719**	**491**
Marketable securities and other instruments		52	213
Liquid assets as per balance sheets		**771**	**704**

NOTES TO THE STATEMENTS OF CASH FLOWS

[39] Net cash provided by operating activities

The cash flow statement starts from the operating result. The gross cash flow for 2001 of €2.9 billion (2000: €4.2 billion) is the cash surplus from operating activities before any changes in working capital. Breakdowns of the gross cash flow by segment and region are given on the table on pages 66–67. The net cash flow of €3.9 billion (2000: €3.1 billion) takes into account changes in working capital.

[40] Net cash used in investing activities

Additions to property, plant and equipment and intangible assets in 2002 resulted in a cash outflow of €2.6 billion (2000: €2.6 billion). Cash outflows for acquisitions amounted to €0.5 billion (2000: €4.1 billion). Sales of property, plant and equipment led to a cash inflow of €0.5 billion (2000: €0.3 billion), while that from interest and dividend receipts and from marketable securities amounted to 0.4 billion (2000: €0.5 billion).

[41] Net cash provided by (used in) financing activities

The net cash outflow of €1.5 billion in 2001 mainly comprises the €1.0 billion dividend payment for 2000 (2000: € billion dividend payment for 1999) and €0.5 billion (2000: €0.3 billion) in interest payments.

[42] Discontinuing operations

Discontinuing operations affected the Group cash flow statements as follows:

€ million	Erdolchemie		Fibers		H & R		DyStar	Total	
	2001	2000	2001	2000	2001	2000	2000	2001	2000
Net cash provided by Operating activities	13	38	28	114	118	84	66	159	302
Net cash provided by (used in) investing activities	474	(87)	(16)	(30)	(163)	(116)	(65)	295	(298)
Net cash provided by (used in) financing activities	0	0	(41)	–	77	(7)	18	36	11
Change in cash and cash equivalents	487	(49)	(29)	84	32	(39)	19	490	15

Table 22.3 FRS 1 and IAS 7 compared

FRS 1	IAS 7
Operating	Operating
Dividends from joint ventures and associates	Operating or investing
Returns on investments and servicing of finance	Operating or financing for interest paid, investing for interest and dividends received
Taxation	Operating
Capital expenditure and financial investment	Investing
Acquisition and disposals	Investing
Equity dividends paid	Financing or operating
Management of liquid resources	Investing or cash equivalent
Financing	Financing

(43) Cash and cash equivalents

Cash and cash equivalents as of 31 December 2001 amounted to €0.7 billion (2000: €0.5 billion). The liquid assets of €0.8 billion (2000: €0.7 billion) shown in the balance sheet also include marketable securities and other instruments.

GAAP comparisons

UK v IAS

The UK standard FRS 1 (revised 1996), *Cash Flow Statements*, defines cash flow as increases or decreases in cash. Thus those items that would be regarded as cash equivalents under IAS 7 are presented in accordance with FRS 1 under a heading of 'management of liquid resources'. FRS 1 also has many more headings than the IAS as can be seen in Table 22.3.

A note of the reconciliation of the movement in net debt is required by FRS 1 but not by IAS 7. There is also a difference in the treatment of cash flows from a foreign subsidiary. IAS 7 requires translation using exchange rates prevailing on dates of cash flows whereas FRS 1 requires the same rate as that used in the income statement, which will be the average or closing rate.

US v IAS

US cash flow statements (SFAS 95 as amended by 102, 104 and 117) use the three headings of IAS 7 but there are some minor differences arising from permitted alternatives within the IAS.

Summary

Within this chapter we have attempted to show you how to draw up a cash flow statement using both the direct and indirect method and we have highlighted some of the problems associated with it. These problems are:

- the arbitrary three month cut off for cash equivalents
- the choice of category for interest and dividends

- the difficulty of producing direct cash flows
- the lack of user information in indirect cash flows.

On the whole, however, the cash flow statement under IAS 7 is certainly an improvement on the previous funds flow statement and the production of cash flow information provides important information to users.

1 Comment on the usefulness of both funds flow statements and cash flow statements to users.

2 *Cash is a very difficult figure to fiddle* (David Tweedie). Discuss.

3 Compare and contrast the direct and indirect method of preparing a cash flow statement and identify and comment on the reasons why the IASB prefers the direct method. (Note: This preference is not universal by accounting standards' boards.)

4 Using the cash flow statement provided in respect of the Bayer Group analyse, as far as the information permits, the performance of the group.

✔ **5** Discuss the proposition that a cash flow statement is more useful to users than an income statement.

6 Differentiate, using illustrative examples where necessary, between cash and cash equivalents.

7 Cash flows should be defined as increases or decreases in cash. Discuss.

✔ **8** Rytetrend is a retailer of electrical goods. Extracts from the company's financial statements are set out below:

Income statement for the year ended 31 March:	2003		2002	
	$000	$000	$000	$000
Sales revenue		31 800		23 500
Cost of sales		(22 500)		(16 000)
Gross profit		9 300		7 500
Other operating expenses		(5 440)		(4 600)
Operating profit		3 860		2 900
Interest payable – loan notes	(260)		(500)	
– overdraft	(200)	(460)	nil	(500)
Profit before taxation		3 400		2 400
Taxation		(1 000)		(800)
Profit after taxation		2 400		1 600
Dividends		(600)		(400)
Net profit for the period		1 800		1 200
Accumulated profit – brought forward		5 880		4 680
Accumulated profit – carried forward		7 680		5 880

Balance Sheets as at 31 March	2003		2002	
	$000	$000	$000	$000
Non-current assets (note (i))		24 500		17 300
Current assets				
Inventory	2 650		3 270	
Receivables	1 100		1 950	
Bank	nil	3 750	400	5 620
Total assets		28 250		22 920

Equity and liabilities

Ordinary capital ($1 shares)		11 500		10 000
Share premium		1 500		nil
Accumulated profits		7 680		5 880
		20 680		15 880
Non-current liabilities				
10% loan notes		nil		4 000
6% loan notes		2 000		nil
Current liabilities				
Bank overdraft	1 050		nil	
Trade payables	2 850		1 980	
Proposed dividends (declared before the year end)	450		280	
Taxation	720		630	
Warranty provision (note (ii))	500	5 570	150	3 040
Total equity and liabilities		28 250		22 920

Notes

(i) The details of the non-current assets are:

	Cost $000	Accumulated depreciation $000	Net book value $000
At 31 March 2002	27 500	10 200	17 300
At 31 March 2003	37 250	12 750	24 500

During the year there was a major refurbishment of display equipment. Old equipment that had cost $6 million in September 1998 was replaced with new equipment at a gross cost of $8 million. The equipment manufacturer had allowed Rytetrend a trade in allowance of $500 000 on the old display equipment. In addition to this Rytetrend used its own staff to install the new equipment. The value of staff time spent on the installation has been costed at $300 000, but this has not been included in the cost of the asset. All staff costs have been included in operating expenses. All display equipment held at the end of the financial year is depreciated at 20% on its cost. No equipment is more than five years old.

(ii) Operating expenses contain a charge of $580 000 for the cost of warranties on the goods sold by Rytetrend. The company makes a warranty provision when it sells its products and cash payments for warranty claims are deducted from the provision as they are settled.

Required:

(a) Prepare a cash flow statement for Rytetrend for the year ended 31 March 2003.

(b) Write a report briefly analysing the operating performance and financial position of Rytetrend for the years ended 31 March 2002 and 2003.

Your report should be supported by appropriate ratios.   (ACCA June 03)

9 The following information relates to Planter, a small private company. It consists of an opening balance sheet as at 1 April 2003 and a listing of the company's ledger accounts at 31 March 2004 after the draft operating profit before interest and taxation (of $17 900) had been calculated.

Planter – Balance sheet as at	1 April 2003	
	$	$
Non-current assets		
Land and buildings (at valuation $49 200 less accumulated depreciation of $5 000)		44 200
Plant (at cost of $70 000 less accumulated depreciation of $22 500)		47 500
Investments at costs		16 900
		108 600
Current assets		
Inventory	57 400	
Trade receivables	28 600	
Bank	1 200	87 200
Total assets		195 800
Equity and liabilities		
Capital and Reserves:		
Ordinary shares of $1 each		25 000
Reserves:		
Share premium	5 000	
Revaluation reserve	12 000	
Accumulated profits	70 300	87 300
		112 300
Non-current liabilities		
8% Loan notes		43 200
Current liabilities		
Trade payables	31 400	
Taxation	8 900	40 300
		195 800

Ledger account listings at 31 March 2004	Dr	Cr
	$	$
Ordinary shares of $1 each		50 000
Share premium		8 000
Accumulated profits – 1 April 2003		70 300
Profit before interest and tax – year to 31 March 2004		17 900
Revaluation reserve		18 000
8% Loan notes		39 800
Trade payables		26 700
Accrued loan interest		300
Taxation	1 100	
Land and buildings at valuation	62 300	
Plant at cost	84 600	
Buildings – accumulated depreciation 31 March 2004		6 800
Plant – accumulated depreciation 31 March 2004		37 600
Investments at cost	8 200	
Trade receivables	50 400	
Inventory – 31 March 2004	43 300	

Bank		1 900
Investment income		400
Loan interest	1 700	
Ordinary dividend	26 100	
	277 700	277 700

Notes

(i)   There were no disposals of land and buildings during the year. The increase in the revaluation reserve was entirely due to the revaluation of the company's land.

(ii) Plant with a net book value of $12 000 (cost $23 500) was sold during the year for $7 800. The loss on sale has been included in the profit before interest and tax.

(iii) Investments with a cost of $8 700 were sold during the year for $11 000. The profit has been included in the profit before interest and tax. There were no further purchases of investments.

(iv) On 10 October 2003 a bonus issue of 1 for 10 ordinary shares was made utilising the share premium account. The remainder of the increase in ordinary shares was due to an issue for cash on 30 October 2003.

(v) The balance on the taxation account is after settlement of the provision made for the year to 31 March 2003. A provision for the current year has not yet been made.

Required:

From the above information, prepare a cash flow statement using the indirect method for Planter in accordance with IAS 7 'Cash Flow Statements' for the year to 31 March 2004.   (ACCA June 04)

Presentation issues

After studying this chapter, you should be able to:
- ☐ explain the purpose of segmental reporting
- ☐ describe what is meant by a business segment and what is meant by a geographical segment
- ☐ explain the criteria for the determination of a reportable segment
- ☐ describe the difference between a primary reporting format and a secondary reporting format
- ☐ explain what is meant by non-current assets held for sale
- ☐ describe how non-current assets held for sale should be recognized and measured
- ☐ explain the purpose of issuing information on discontinuing operations
- ☐ explain how information on discontinued operations should be disclosed
- ☐ describe what is meant by a post-balance sheet event
- ☐ explain the difference between an adjusting event and a non-adjusting event
- ☐ explain the selection process of an accounting policy
- ☐ explain the treatment when an accounting policy is changed
- ☐ explain the treatment of a change in an accounting estimate
- ☐ explain the treatment of an error in the financial statements
- ☐ define basic earnings per share
- ☐ define diluted earnings per share
- ☐ describe the contents and appraise the statement IAS 33 on earnings per share
- ☐ describe the main issues of interim financial reporting under IAS 34.

Introduction

Most of the standards that we are going to discuss in this chapter have in common, that they regulate supplemental information disclosure on top of the data reported in the balance sheet and income statement. The aim of the standards discussed in this chapter is the improvement of the information disclosed in the financial statements for decision usefulness. Stakeholders will make economic decisions based on the reported information. The issues to be discussed are segmental reporting (IAS 14), communication of information on post-balance sheet events (IAS 10), the determination of the earnings per share (IAS 33) and interim financial reporting (IAS 34). Also IAS 8 is discussed in this chapter as it focuses on the comparability and consistency of information disclosed through the financial statements. So IAS 8 does not deal with supplementary information to the balance sheet and profit and loss account, but the standard focuses on the selection process of accounting policies and the change in those policies and accounting estimates. Also the treatment of prior-period errors receives attention.

The basic objective of IFRS 5 is also the improvement of the comparability of financial information. In this respect IFRS 5 provides the rules for how information on non-current assets held for sale and on discontinued operations should be disclosed.

Segmental reporting

The first Standard that we will discuss is IAS 14 on segmental reporting. The latest version of IAS 14 was approved in 1997. With regard to this version there had been substantial cooperation between the FASB and the IASC (at that time). Prior Standards on segmental disclosure had been criticized as the criteria embedded in those Standards were judged not strict enough by parties interested in the financial statements of companies.

Why was segmental reporting a topic of debate?

Purpose of segmental reporting

In order to answer that question we will first define what segmental reporting means and its purpose. On the balance sheet and profit and loss account of a company aggregated data on sales, expenses, assets and liabilities of a company as a whole are communicated to external parties. For companies active in a single industry, e.g. Pizza Hut, the risk and the volatility of the results disclosed by the company in the profit and loss account are tied to the characteristics of risk and volatility of that specific industry. In this case external stakeholders are able to make predictions about the future performance of the company based on an assessment of its prior year and current performance and on an assessment of the future evolution of the industry in which the company is active.

Very often, however, companies sell multiple products and are competing in different industries and on different regional markets, e.g. companies such as Nike and Adidas are active in the sport equipment industry and clothing industry, but they are selling their products worldwide in markets with different levels of purchasing power. A company like the Scandinavian SAS group is active in the airline industry as well as in the hotel business. The corporate risk of these companies or groups is influenced, first, by the individual risks of the different product groups and, second, by the individual risks of the different markets in which they are competing. The risks and volatility of the results of these individual products – or services groups or different markets – can be positively or negatively correlated to each other. If there is a positive correlation between the risks and returns of the individual segments then the risk of the company as a whole is increased and the corporate result will then be highly volatile. If the correlation is negative the corporate risk is reduced. So in order to make predictions about the future performance of multi-business and multinational companies, information on the performance of the individual groups of products or services and the different regional markets is essential.

Providing that financial information about these different product groups and separate markets is called segmental reporting.

Think of some multinationals or other companies you are familiar with and try to determine whether they are single business or multi-business enterprises and if they are competing in different markets. What kind of information would you like about them?

Segmental reporting is dealt with in IAS 14. As mentioned in the introductory paragraph the key objective of this Standard is to assist the user of financial statements in making judgements about the opportunities and risks facing an enterprise by the disclosure of more disaggregated information than that provided in the primary financial statements (meaning the balance sheet and profit and loss account of the group).

Information on the result obtained in each segment should be disclosed together with the capital employed in each segment. As the segmental information to be disclosed is more disaggregated it enables the reader of the financial statements to analyse the financial performance of the enterprise in the various market areas in which it operates. In this respect segmental information increases the value relevance of the accounting information disclosed in the financial statements. Market areas may be understood in the sense of product markets (business segments) and geographic markets (geographic segments).

Companies, however, are not very eager to disclose segmental information as these segmental data are of strategic importance. The profitabilility of individual markets or business lines are revealed by it. Segmental data not only increase the value relevance of the accounts for investors, but also competitors will make use of those segmental data in their own decision process. As disclosing segmental data are experienced by companies as communicating proprietary information, firms have often tried in the past to provide segmental information of little value relevance. Analysts have consistently criticized the quality and inadequacy of the segment disclosures. Firms often argued that the benefits of informing the capital markets about firm value are smaller than the costs of aiding competitors with the information. The degree of flexibility permitted in segment disclosures was an issue for regulators in the 1980s and the 1990s (Fields, Lys and Vincent, 2001). In the mid-1990s the American FASB issued a new Standard on segment reporting requiring disclosures on segment reporting that are consistent with the firm's internal reporting organization. The IASB took a similar approach.

The important step forward in those new Standards was the stricter definition of the segments for which individual data had to be reported.

Before we start with the discussion of the contents of IAS 14, it is important to stress that IAS 14 should be applied by those enterprises whose equity or debt securities are publicly traded and by enterprises that are in the process of issuing equity or debt securities in public securities markets (IAS 14; para. 3). Companies that issue voluntarily segmental information in their IAS accounts should also fully comply with IAS 14 (para. 5).

Definition of segments

IAS 14 requires information to be disclosed for both business segments and geographical segments, with one of these being designated as the primary basis and the other as the secondary basis (less information is required to be disclosed in relation to the secondary basis), depending on which is regarded as providing the more meaningful analysis of the predominant source and nature of risks and returns. The principle underlying the approach in IAS 14 is that an entity's organizational and management structure develops along lines related to the predominant sources of its risks and returns. Accordingly, the process of identifying segments for external reporting purposes begins with the information used by the board of directors and the chief executive officer to evaluate past performance and to make decisions about future allocations of resources. A business segment is defined by IAS as follows (para. 9):

> A *business segment* is a distinguishable component of an enterprise that is engaged in providing an individual product or service or a group of related products or services and that is subject to risks and returns that are different from those of other business segments. Elements which could help in determining whether products and services are related include (IAS 14, para. 9):
>
> (a) the nature of the products or services;
> (b) the nature of the production processes;
> (c) the type or class of customer for the products or services;
> (d) the methods used to distribute the products or provide the services; and
> (e) if applicable, the nature of the regulatory environment, for example, banking, insurance, or public utilities.

We notice in this definition that the difference in the risk profile of the segments is essential in the definition. A single business segment will not include products and services with significantly different risks and returns (IAS 14, para. 11). The products and services included in a single business segment are expected to be similar with respect to the majority of the factors. Consider this information when you solve Activity 27.9 which relates to segmental disclosure and the definition of a business segment in Chapter 27. This activity is also useful in the context of this chapter, but it can only be solved in Chapter 27 as the necessary information is provided there.

A geographical segment is defined in para. 9 of IAS 14:

> A *geographical segment* is a distinguishable component of an enterprise that is engaged in providing products or services within a particular economic environment and that is subject to risks and returns that are different from those of components operating in other economic environments. Factors that should be considered in identifying geographical segments include:
>
> (a) similarity of economic and political conditions;
> (b) relationships between operations in different geographical areas;
> (c) proximity of operations;
> (d) special risks associated with operations in a particular area;
> (e) exchange control regulations; and
> (f) the underlying currency risks.

> Similarly, a geographical segment does not include operations in economic environments with significantly differing risks and returns. A geographical segment may be a single country, a group of two or more countries or a region within a country.
>
> (IAS 14, para. 12).

Further, a geographical segment can be determined by the location of its markets (where its products are sold or services rendered) or by the location of its operations (where its products are produced or where its service delivery activities are based). Companies are free to choose the basis for geographical segmentation. An entity's organizational and internal reporting structure will normally provide evidence of whether its dominant source of geographical risks results from the location of its assets (the origin of its sales) or the location of its customers (the destination of its sales). As a result we observe that companies within the same industry might determine the geographical segments for which segmental information will be disclosed in a different way. If we focus on the segmental disclosure practices in the airline industry we notice that British Airways presents (with regard to their geographical analysis of turnover (annual report, 2003/2004, p. 33)) two different types of geographical segmentations, namely by the area of original sale and by the area of destination. We learn from those data that most tickets are sold in the UK and that the revenue earned on intercontinental flights to North and South America is almost equal to the revenue earned on flights within Europe. Lufthansa which prepares its financial statements in compliance with IAS, uses the following geographical segmentation basis for its revenues (annual report, 2003, note 40):

> The allocation of traffic revenue to regions is based on the original place of sale, the allocation of other operating revenue is based on the geographical location of the customer, and the allocation of other segment income is based on the place of service.

Activity 23.1

As investor but also as competitor which type of geographical segmentation would you appreciate in the airline industry?

Activity feedback

Segmental information which reveals the profitability of the different routes is obviously more interesting than knowing how many tickets are sold in a country. The country of sale of the ticket might even be unrelated to the actual destination flown, e.g. a ticket sold in Brussels for a flight from Paris to Barcelona.

One could wonder whether these elements play a role in the disclosure decisions of the airlines given that most airlines choose the location in which the ticket is sold as the geographical segmentation basis.

Segment data

After the definition of a business segment and a geographical segment, the question arises in general which data should be reported for each individual segment. For each individual segment, segment revenues, segment expenses, segment results, segment liabilities and segment assets should be disclosed. These elements are defined in para. 16 of this Standard. IAS 14 stipulates further that the segment accounting policies should be prepared in conformity with the accounting policies adopted for preparing and presenting the financial statements of the consolidated group or enterprise.

Segment revenue

Segment revenue is defined as revenue reported in the enterprise's income statement that is directly attributable to a segment and the relevant portion of enterprise revenue that can be allocated on a reasonable basis to a segment, whether from sales to external customers or from transactions with other segments of the same enterprise. Segment revenue does not include:

- interest or dividend income, including interest earned on advances or loans to other segments, unless the segment's operations are primarily of a financial nature
- or gains on sales of investments or gains on extinguishment of debt unless the segment's operations are primarily of a financial nature.

Segment revenue includes further an entity's share of profits or losses of associates, joint ventures or other investments accounted for under the equity method only if those items are included in consolidated or total enterprise revenue.

Segment revenue includes also a joint venturer's share of the revenue of a jointly controlled entity that is accounted for by proportionate consolidation in accordance with IAS 31, *Financial Reporting of Interests in Joint Ventures*.

Segment expenses

Segment expense is defined as expense resulting from the operating activities of a segment that is directly attributable to the segment and the relevant portion of an expense that can be allocated on a reasonable basis to the segment, including expenses relating to sales to external customers and expenses relating to transactions with other segments of the same entity. Segment expense does not include:

- interest, including interest incurred on advances or loans from other segments, unless the segment's operations are primarily of a financial nature
- losses on sales of investments or losses on extinguishment of debt unless the segment's operations are primarily of a financial nature
- an entity's share of losses of associates, joint ventures, or other investments accounted for under the equity method
- income tax expense
- or general administrative expenses, head office expenses and other expenses that arise at the entity level and relate to the enterprise as a whole. However, costs are sometimes incurred at the entity level on behalf of a segment. Such costs are segment expenses if they relate to the segment's operating activities and they can be directly attributed or allocated to the segment on a reasonable basis.

Segment expense includes a joint venturer's share of the expenses of a jointly controlled entity that is accounted for by proportionate consolidation in accordance with IAS 31.

For a segment's operations that are primarily of a financial nature, interest income and interest expense may be reported as a single net amount for segment reporting purposes only if those items are netted in the consolidated or enterprise financial statements.

The allocation mechanism for revenues and expenses and also for assets and liabilities, as we will see later, is 'direct attribution' or 'allocation on a reasonable basis'. It is interesting to stress that an element of judgement is introduced here. Although the proposed allocation mechanism of IAS 14 sounds acceptable, companies might use it to decrease the value relevance of their disclosed segmental data. A substantial portion of costs, revenues, assets or liabilities might not be allocated because the management of a company can claim that the allocation cannot be done on a reasonable basis. However, guidance in other standards might be useful in determining what is a 'reasonable basis' for allocating costs to segments such as IAS 2, *Inventories*, and IAS 11, *Construction Contracts*.

Segment assets

Segment assets are those operating assets that are employed by a segment in its operating activities and that either are directly attributable to the segment or can be allocated to the segment on a reasonable basis. If a segment's segment result includes interest or dividend income, its segment assets include the related receivables, loans, investments, or other income-producing assets. Segment assets do not include income tax assets. Segment assets include investments accounted for under the equity method only if the profit or loss from such investments is included in segment revenue. Segment assets include a joint venturer's share of the operating assets of a jointly controlled entity that is accounted for by proportionate consolidation in accordance with IAS 31. Segment assets are determined after deducting related allowances that are reported as direct offsets in the enterprise's balance sheet.

Para. 16 stipulates further that: 'Assets that are jointly used by two or more segments should be allocated to segments if, and only if, their related revenues and expenses also are allocated to those segments.' This is an interesting element. Segment assets do not include assets used for the general entity or head office purposes.

Activity 23.2

Assume an airline transports passengers and cargo on the same planes and on the same flights. The airline does not own separate planes for cargo only. In relation to segmental reporting, the airline decides to consider passenger transport and cargo transport as two individual separate business segments because the risk involved is different. The influence of the economic climate is different on cargo transport than on passenger transport; the business itself is different and the competitors are different to some extent. What does this imply for the disclosure of segmental assets?

Activity feedback

The revenue of passenger transport and cargo transport is directly attributable to both individual segments. The assets used to generate these revenues are the planes. This choice of individual business segments implies that the costs of the airplane (= pilots, fuel, landing rights, maintenance, repair and depreciation) should be allocated over the two business segments unless the management of the airline thinks there is no reasonable allocation method to do so.

Segment liabilities

Segment liabilities are those operating liabilities that result from the operating activities of a segment and that either are directly attributable to the segment or can be allocated to the segment on a reasonable basis. If a segment's segment result includes interest expense, its segment liabilities include the related interest-bearing liabilities. Segment liabilities include a joint venturer's share of the liabilities of a jointly controlled entity that is accounted for by proportionate consolidation in accordance with IAS 31. Segment liabilities do not include income tax liabilities.

Reportable segments

A reportable segment is a business segment or geographical segment for which segment information is required to be disclosed by the standard. We will now focus on the process for determining which segments are reportable in the notes to the balance sheet and the profit and loss account. The identification of reportable segment is accomplished in two steps. The first step is concerned with identifying the primary and the secondary reporting segments. The primary and the secondary reporting format are not given equal weight. The difference between the two relates to the amount of detailed information which has to be disclosed for each individual segment. So if preparers indicate their business segments as primary reporting segments, this implies that much more detailed information will be disclosed in the notes to the financial statements on the business segments than on geographical segments. However, companies are not free to choose which reporting segment is their primary segment. Paras 26–33 of IAS 14 help with deciding to which category of segment (business or geographic) the primary and to which category of segment the secondary reporting format will be applied, if it is reportable. The second step is concerned with the application of size criteria in order to identify those segments for which disclosure of individual segment information (whether primary or secondary) is required.

Choice of the primary and the secondary reporting format
According to paras 26–27 of IAS 14 the internal organization of the company determines the external reporting, as the IASB is convinced that companies structure their business according to different risk patterns. As indicated earlier, IAS 14 requires a 'management approach' to identifying externally reportable segments. This demands a direct link between the segment disclosures in the financial statements and the entity's organizational structure and internal financial reporting system, primarily in respect of information reported to the board of directors and the chief executive officer (para. 33). However, this does not mean that the standard requires the reporting format in the financial statements to be a simple copy of the information given to the board. Internally reported operating segments may be separately disclosed, combined with others or left unallocated, depending on their significance. Para. 26 states that the dominant source and nature of an enterprise's risks and returns should govern whether its primary segment reporting format will be business segments or geographical segments. If the enterprise's risks and rates of return are affected predominantly by differences in the products and services it produces, its primary format for reporting segment information should be business segments, with secondary information reported geographically. Similarly, if the enterprise's risks and rates of return are affected predominantly by the fact that it operates in different countries or other geographical areas, its primary format for reporting segment information should be geographical segments, with secondary information reported for groups of related products and services.

So the choice of the primary reporting segment lies with the company as it decides on its internal management information system. Again, this is an important element which lies within the discretion of the reporting company. The choice of the primary and secondary has to be disclosed in the notes.

For example, the multinational beerbrewer Interbrew, which changed into Imbev after the merger with the Brazilian brewer Ambev, one of the world's leading breweries has chosen as its primary segment its geographical markets. The reason for the choice in favour of the geographical segmentation as primary segment is explained in the notes (annual report, Interbrew, 2003, p. 58) as follows:

> The company is a single product business, products or services provided other than malt-based beverages representing less than 10% of the company's turnover, which is why its chosen segment reporting format is geographical segments. Making a segmentation between the different beers produced is not part of the internally reported financial information and is not feasible especially while the same installations are used to produce the different types of beer and while brand differential between 'premium', 'specialities' and 'standard lager' is different from one geographical market to another for the same brand.

Imbev sells brands such as Becks, Labatt Ice and Stella Artois. Nestlé (annual report, 2000) another company with strong brands has also chosen geographical markets as its primary reporting format.

If the internal organization structure and reporting system of a company follows a 'matrix approach', in which both a product service market (business) focus and a geographic market focus are reflected on the enterprise's organization and systems, then IAS 14 prioritizes business segments over geographic segments as the choice for application of the primary reporting format. The standard permits an enterprise with a 'matrix' organization structure and reporting system to apply the primary reporting format to both business and geographic segments but not to the latter only.

In a situation in which the enterprise's internal organization structure and reporting systems have neither a product-service nor a geographic market focus (for example, the focus might be on legal entities within a group), IAS 14 requires the directors and management of the enterprise to make a choice between business and geographic segments for the application of the primary reporting format on the basis of their identification of the predominant sources and nature of the enterprise's risks and returns (IAS 14, paras 26–30). The internal reporting system may have segments, some of which satisfy the requirements of IAS 14 for identification as either business or geographic segments (see earlier) and some of which do not. In this case, the latter (unsuitable) segments should be analysed into their next lower level of subsegment along either business or geographic lines and the subsegments will then be identified as potentially reportable segments. This should be done 'rather than construct(ing) segments solely for external reporting purposes' (IAS 14, para. 33). However, the resultant potentially reportable segments may be combined with other 'substantially similar' ones in light of the size criteria discussed next. Similarity means according to IAS 14 that, first of all, the segments should exhibit a similar long-term financial performance and, second, that they are similar in all of the factors in the appropriate definition in para. 9.

Application of the size criteria

The second step of defining the reportable segments consists in the application of size criteria to the internal business segments. In other words, the second step will consist in identifying the different segments reported internally and judge on the basis of criteria, set forward in IAS 14 (paras 34–43), which of those segments will classify as externally reportable segments. Some of the internally reported segments will be combined for external reporting purposes or others will be included in an unallocated reconciling item. First of all, the size criteria to identify the individual reportable segments will be presented and this will be followed by an activity.

The size criteria are included in paras 34–43 of IAS 14. Para. 35 states that a business segment or geographical segment should be identified as a reportable segment if a majority of its revenue is earned from sales to external customers and:

- its revenue from sales to external customers and from transactions with other segments is 10% or more of the total revenue, external and internal, of all segments
- its segment result, whether profit or loss, is 10% or more of the combined result of all segments in profit or the combined result of all segments in loss, whichever is the greater in absolute amount
- or its assets are 10% or more of the total assets of all segments.

What is the treatment for an internally reported segment that falls below all the above thresholds mentioned in IAS 14, para. 35? In fact IAS 14, para. 36 foresees three possibilities:

(a) that segment may be designated as a reportable segment despite its size
(b) that segment may be combined into a separately reportable segment with one or more other similar internally reported segment(s) that are also below all the thresholds of significance in para. 35 (two or more business segments or geographical segments are similar if they share a majority of the factors in the appropriate definition in para. 9)
(c) that segment is not separately reported or combined, it should be included as an unallocated reconciling item.

In the end IAS states that if total external revenue attributable to reportable segments constitutes less than 75% of the total consolidated or enterprise revenue, additional segments should be identified as reportable segments, even if they do not meet the 10% thresholds in para. 35, until at least 75% of total consolidated or enterprise revenue is included in reportable segments.

Activity 23.3

The management of a major multinational has identified the following reportable segments:

	Total segment revenues	Inter-segment revenues	Segment result	Identifiable segment assets
Segment A	750		300	800
Segment B	400	40	50	450
Europe	1 150	40	250	1 250

Segment C	950		250	600
Segment D	500	50	200	900
Asia	1 450	50	450	1 500
Segment E	350	35	50	500
Segment F	500		150	700
Africa	850	35	200	1 200
Segment G	550		100	750
Segment H	650		100	400
North America	1 200	0	0	1 150
Total segments	**4 650**	**125**	**900**	**5 100**
Inter-company eliminations	**125**		**50**	**150**
Consolidated total	**4 075**		**850**	**4 950**

1 Assume segments A–H are business segments. Determine which of these business segments would classify as reportable segments.
2 Based on your answer on question 1, determine whether sufficient operations are represented by the reportable segments (75% threshold test).
3 Assume segments A–B are in Europe, segments C–D in Asia, segments E–F in Africa and segments G–H in North America. Determine which geographical segments would classify as reportable segments.
4 Based on your answers on question 3, determine whether enough reportable geographical segments have been identified (75% threshold test).

Activity feedback

1 Reportable business segments

	Segment revenue[1] >465 10% of 4 650	Segment result >105 10% of 1 050[2]	Identifiable segment assets >510 10% of 5 100	Reportable segment
Segment A	Yes	Yes	Yes	Yes
Segment B	*No*	*No*	*No*	*No*
Segment C	Yes	Yes	Yes	Yes
Segment D	Yes	Yes	Yes	Yes
Segment E	*No*	*No*	*No*	*No*
Segment F	Yes	Yes	Yes	Yes
Segment G	Yes	*No*	Yes	Yes
Segment H	Yes	*No*	*No*	Yes

[1] The majority of the segment revenue is from external sales in all segments.
[2] Combined result of segments in profit 1 050
   Combined result of segments in loss 150
   Chose the greater in absolute amounts, i.e., 1 050

2 Number of reportable business segments

Total external segment revenue for reportable segments		**Total consolidated revenue**	
Total segment revenue	4 650	Total segment revenue	4 650
Revenue non-reportable Segment B	400	Inter-segment revenue Segment B	80
Revenue non-reportable Segment E	350	Inter-segment revenue Segment D	50
Inter-segment revenue Segment D	50	Inter-segment revenue Segment E	35
	3 850		**4 525**

Test: 3 850/4 525 = 85% which is greater than the threshold 75%. Enough reportable segments have been identified.

3 Reportable geographical segments

	Segment revenue[1]	Segment result	Identifiable segment assets	Reportable segment
	>465	>105	>510	
	10% of 4 650	10% of 1 050	10% of 5 100	
Europe	Yes	Yes	Yes	Yes
Asia	Yes	Yes	Yes	Yes
Africa	Yes	Yes	Yes	Yes
North America	Yes	No	Yes	Yes

[1] The majority of the segment revenue is from external sales in all segments.
[2] Combined result of segments in profit 1 050
  Combined result of segments in loss 150
  Chose the greater in absolute amounts, i.e., 1 050

4 Number of reportable geographical segments

All identified segments qualify as reportable segments.

Total external segment revenue for reportable segments		**Total consolidated revenue**	
Total segment revenue	4 650	Total segment revenue	4 650
Inter-segment revenue Europe	40	Inter-segment revenue Europe	40
Inter-segment revenue Asia	50	Inter-segment revenue Asia	50
Inter-segment revenue Africa	35	Inter-segment revenue Africa	35
	4 525		**4 525**

Test: 9 050/9 050 = 100%

In Appendix A to IAS 14, a segment definition tree is presented in order to illustrate the decision process by which internally reported segments will be designated to become individual externally reported segments or combined segments or by unallocated information. We reproduce this decision tree in Figure 23.1.

Information disclosure for a primary reporting format
If a reportable segment classifies as the enterprise's primary reporting format, the elements to be disclosed are listed within paras 50–67.

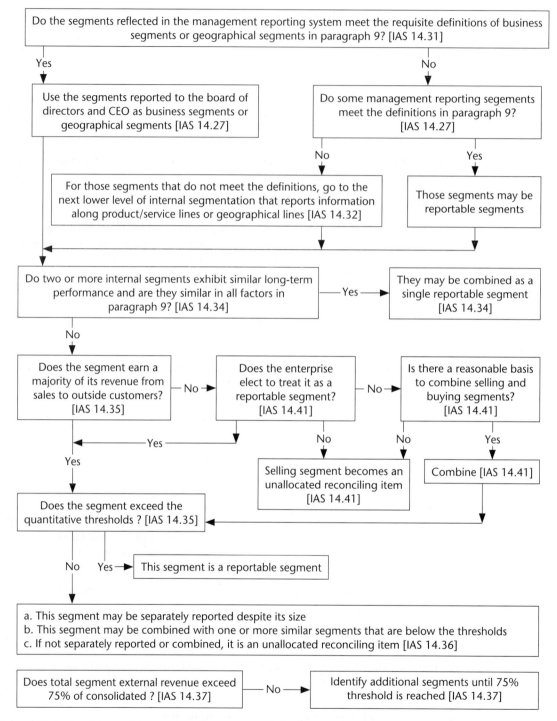

Figure 23.1 Decision to determine allocation of internally reported segments

An entity should disclose segment revenue for each reportable segment. Segment revenue from sales to external customers and segment revenue from transactions with other segments should be separately reported. Further, the segment results together with the total carrying amount of segment assets and segment liabilities should be disclosed for each reportable segment.

An entity should disclose the total cost incurred during the period to acquire segment assets that are expected to be used during more than one period (property, plant, equipment and intangible assets) for each reportable segment. While this is sometimes referred to as capital additions or capital expenditure, the measurement required by this principle should be on an accrual basis, not a cash basis (para. 57).

An entity should disclose the total amount of expense included in segment result for depreciation and amortization of segment assets for the period for each reportable segment (para. 58).

An entity should disclose, for each reportable segment, the total amount of significant non-cash expenses, other than depreciation and amortization for which separate disclosure is required by para. 58, that were included in segment expense and, therefore, deducted in measuring segment result (para. 61).

An entity should disclose, for each reportable segment, the aggregate of the entity's share of the net profit or loss of associates, joint ventures, or other investments accounted for under the equity method if substantially all those associates' operations are within that single segment (para. 64).

If an entity's aggregate share of the net profit or loss of associates, joint ventures, or other investments accounted for under the equity method is disclosed by reportable segment, the aggregate investments in those associates and joint ventures should also be disclosed by reportable segment (para. 66).

An entity should present a reconciliation between the information disclosed for reportable segments and the aggregated information in the consolidated or entity financial statements. In presenting the reconciliation, segment revenue should be reconciled to entity revenue from external customers (including disclosure of the amount of entity revenue from external customers not included in any segment's revenue); segment result should be reconciled to a comparable measure of entity operating profit or loss as well as to entity net profit or loss; segment assets should be reconciled to entity assets; and segment liabilities should be reconciled to entity liabilities (para. 67).

Information disclosure for a secondary reporting format

With regard to those disclosures for the secondary format the requirements are different according to the type of primary format chosen, namely business segments or geographical segments. The information to be disclosed is much less than for the primary segment, for which the information disclosure is quite substantial if IAS 14 is applied properly.

To illustrate the primary reporting format as well as the secondary reporting format, the segmental information of Lufthansa is now given in Table 23.1. We notice that in the notes to the segment reporting the information on the pricing policies for inter-segment sales are given. Concerning the primary format prior year comparative figures have been included in the annual report of Lufthansa (2000) as well. They have not been included here as the illustration is now already quite extensive.

Table 23.1 Primary reporting format – business segment information for financial year 2003 in €m

	Passenger Business Lufthansa Passenger Business group[1]	Logistics Lufthansa Logistics group	MRO[1] Lufthansa Technik group	Catering LSG Sky Chefs group[1]	Leisure Travel Thomas Cook group	IT Services Lufthansa Systems group	Service and Financial Companies[2]	Segment total
External revenue	9 774	2 147	1 587	2 200	–	219	30	15 957
– of which traffic revenue	9 549	2 113	–	–	–	–	–	11 662
Inter-segment revenue	434	14	1 265	467	–	392	0*	2 572
Total revenue	10 208	2 161	2 852	2 667	–	611	30	18 529
Other segment income	1 121	174	171	211	–131	39	335	1 920
– of which from investments accounted for using the equity method	–79	4	6	7	–131	–	17	–176
Cost of materials	5 398	1 391	1 418	1 201	–	54	10	9 472
Staff costs	2 101	315	840	1 109	–	205	45	4 615
Amortisation and depreciation	698	120	152	933	–	32	46	1 981
– of which impairments	19	6	52	705	–	–	36	818
Other operating expenses	2 975	475	455	461	–	304	136	4 806
Segment results	**157**	**34**	**158**	**–826**	**–131**	**55**	**128**	**–425**
– of which from investments accounted for using the equity method	–79	4	6	7	–131	–	17	–176
Segment assets	7 184	1 368	1 908	1 586	283	186	1 746	14 261
– of which from investments accounted for using the equity method	129	8	78	70	283	–	152	720
Segment liabilities	6 622	585	1 330	816	–	222	724	10 299
– of which from investments accounted for using the equity method	–	–	–	–	–	–	–	–
Capital expenditure	678	31	80	148	–	48	99	1 084
– of which from investments accounted for using the equity method	–	–	–	–	–	–	4	4
Other significant non-cash items	183	5	–8	22	–	–1	–	201
Average number of employees	34 935	5 127	17 861	32 967	–	3 121	787	94 798

* below €1 m
[1] Due to changes in the group of consolidated companies the comparability of prior year figures is limited.
[2] Due to changes in the group of consolidated companies (Lufthansa AirPlus Servicekarten GmbH), money market funds allocation, and the deconsolidation of START AMADEUS as from 28 February 2003, comparability with the preceding year is limited.

Reconciliation of segment information with consolidated figures in €m:

	Segment total		Reconciliation		Group	
	2003	2002	2003	2002	2003	2002
External revenue	15957	16971	–	–	15957	16971
– of which traffic revenue	11662	12032	–	–	11662	12032
Inter-segment revenue	2572	2437	–2572	–2437	–	–
Total revenue	18529	19408	–2572	–2437	15957	16971
Other revenue	1920	2516	–163	–398	1757	2118
– of which from investments accounted for using the equity method	–176	–91	176	91	–	–
Cost of materials	9472	9345	–2267	–2149	7205	7196
Staff costs	4615	4684	–3	–24	4612	4660
Amortisation and depreciation	1981	1275	–51	–32	1930	1243
– of which impairments	818	66	–35	–33	783	33
Other operating expenses	4806	5154	–692	–756	4114	4398
Results	–425	1466	278	126	–147	1592
– of which from investments accounted for using the equity method	–176	–91	176	91	–	–
Assets	14261	14704	2471	4433	16732	19137
– of which from investments accounted for using the equity method	720	914	–	–	720	914
Liabilities	10299	10576	3737	4389	14036	14965
– of which from investments accounted for using the equity method	–	–	–	–	–	–
Average number of employees	94798	94135	–	–	94798	94135

The reconciliation column includes both the effects resulting from consolidation procedures and the amounts resulting from the different interpretation of segment item contents in comparison with the corresponding Group items.

The eliminated revenue of the business segments generated with other consolidated business segments may be gathered from the reconciliation column. As regards the other segment revenue, income originating from relationships with the other business segments has been eliminated as well ('other revenue' reconciliation column). In financial year 2003, this concerned especially exchange gains from intra-group loans in foreign currency in the amount of €105m (prior year: €274m) as well as income from intra-group services of €48m (prior year: €48m). In so far as the eliminated revenue and other income is compared with segment expenses with regard to the companies which took up the services, such expenses have been eliminated, too ('expenses' reconciliation column). Certain components of the Group's financial result have also been allocated to the business segment's income, in particular results from the equity accounting of investments of the business segment. Since, in the Group's view, such results are not allocated to the operating result but the financial result, they have to be eliminated upon reconciliation with regard to the Group's operating result.

The amounts included in the 'results' reconciliation column originate mainly from the reallocation of the negative results from accounting at equity, which results are part of the segment results of the business segments, however not of the Group's operating result.

The reconciliation column for segment assets and segment liabilities contains eliminated receivables and payables among the business segments, the difference between market values and carrying amounts of financial instruments as well as, on the assets side, the carrying amounts of equity investments eliminated within the scope of capital consolidation.

Secondary reporting format – geographical segment information for financial year 2003 in €m:

	Europe incl. Germany	North America	Central & South America	Asia/ Pacific	Middle East	Africa	Other	Segment total
Traffic revenue[1]	8 145	1 349	223	1 545	154	246	–	11 662
Other operating revenue	1 812	1 516	112	544	207	104	0*	4 295
Other segment income[2]	1 562	71	8	42	16	8	50	1 757
Income from investments accounted for using the equity method	−193	4	2	11	–	–	–	−176
Segment assets	12 300	1 315	105	431	65	45	–	14 261
– of which from investments accounted for using the equity method	594	47	13	66	–	–	–	720
Capital expenditure	938	62	4	77	0*	3	–	1 084
– of which from investments accounted for using the equity method	4	–	–	–	–	–	–	4

Secondary reporting format – geographical segment information for financial year 2002 in €m:

	Europe incl. Germany	North America	Central & South America	Asia/ Pacific	Middle East	Africa	Other	Segment total
Traffic revenue[1]	8 195	1 470	296	1 681	147	243	–	12 032
Other reporting revenue	1 831	2 021	143	598	253	93	0*	4 939
Other segment income[2]	1 979	35	12	40	22	10	20	2 118
Income from investments accounted for using the equity method	−117	15	−1	12	–	–	–	− 91
Segment assets	11 615	2 442	98	443	44	62	–	14 704
– of which from investments accounted for using the equity method	770	53	14	77	–	–	–	914
Capital expenditure	987	79	3	14	1	0*	–	1 084
– of which from investments accounted for using the equity method	101	1	–	–	–	–	–	102

* below €1m
[1] Traffic revenue is allocated by original places of sale.
[2] Other segment income corresponds to the operating income of the Group (including income from financial assets).

in the group) should be measured in accordance with applicable IFRSs. In other words, an entity should apply its usual accounting policies up until the criteria for classification as held for sale are met.

Thereafter a non-current asset (or disposal group) classified as held for sale should be measured at the lower of its carrying amount and fair value less costs to sell. According to IFRS 5 the fair value is defined as 'the amount for which an asset could be exchanged, or a liability settled, between knowledgeable, willing parties in an arm's length transaction'. Costs to sell are defined as 'the incremental costs directly attributable to the disposal of an asset (or disposal group), excluding finance costs and income tax expense'. When the sale is expected to occur beyond one year, the costs to sell should be measured at their present value. Any increase in the present value of the costs to sell that arises from the passage of time should be presented in profit or loss as a financing cost. There is no similar requirement to present that element of an increase in fair value that also relates to just the passage of time as finance income.

For the disposal groups, the standard adopts a portfolio approach. It requires that if a non-current asset within the scope of its measurement requirements is part of a disposal group, the measurement requirements should apply to the group as a whole, so that the group is measured at the lower of its carrying amount and fair value less costs to sell. It will still be necessary to apportion any write down to the underlying assets of the disposal group, but no element is apportioned to items outside the scope of the standard's measurement provisions.

If a newly acquired asset (or disposal group) meets the criteria to be classified as held for sale (which are subtly different for assets acquired exclusively with a view to subsequent disposal), applying the above requirements will result in the asset (or disposal group) being measured on initial recognition at the lower of its carrying amount had it not been so classified (for example, cost) and fair value less costs to sell. This means that, if the asset (or disposal group) is acquired as part of a business combination, it will be measured at fair value less costs to sell.

While a non-current asset is classified as held for sale or while it is part of a disposal group classified as held for sale it should not be depreciated or amortized. Interest and other expenses attributable to the liabilities of a disposal group classified as held for sale should continue to be recognized.

On subsequent remeasurement of a disposal group, the standard requires that the carrying amounts of any assets and liabilities that are not within the scope of its measurement requirements, be remeasured in accordance with applicable IFRSs before the fair value less costs to sell of the disposal group is remeasured.

Recognition of impairments losses and reversals

The requirement to measure a non-current asset or disposal group held for sale at the lower of carrying amount less costs to sell may give rise to a write down in value (impairment loss) and possibly its subsequent reversal. As noted earlier, the first step is to account for any items without the scope of the standard in the normal way. After that, any excess of carrying value over fair value less costs to sell should be recognized as an impairment.

Any subsequent increase in fair value less costs to sell of an asset up to the cumulative impairment loss previously recognized either in accordance with IFRS 5 or in accordance with IAS 36, *Impairment of Assets*, should be recognized as a gain. In the case of a disposal group, any subsequent increase in fair value less costs to sell should be recognized:

- to the extent that it has not been recognized under another standard in relation to those assets outside the scope of IFRS 5's measurement requirements
- but not in excess of the cumulative amount of losses previously recognized under IFRS 5 or before that under IAS 36 in respect of the non-current assets in the group that are within the scope of the measurement rule of IFRS 5.

Any impairment loss (or any subsequent gain) recognized for a disposal group should be allocated to the non-current assets in the group that are within the scope of the measurement requirements of IFRS 5. The order allocation should be:

- first, to reduce the carrying amount of any goodwill in the group
- then, to the other assets of the group pro rata on the basis of the carrying amount of each asset in the group.

When assets meet the criteria to be classified as held for sale they have to be presented separately on the balance sheet. In the notes disclosures have to be made in relation to the facts and circumstances of the sale and the gains or losses recognized after the classification of the non-current assets as 'held for sale'. If assets are no longer used in the operational activities of the firm, they will no longer generate revenues, expenditures and cash. Information on the impact of the disappearance of these items should be presented as information on discontinued operations.

Discontinued operations

IFRS 5 deals also with the presentation of information on discontinued operations. This type of information disclosure had been regulated already namely under the superseded IAS 35 requires the presentation of a single amount on the face of the income statement relating to discontinued operations, with further analysis either on the face of the income statement or in the notes.

Activity 23.4

Why do you think financial information about these discontinuing operations should be provided to the external user of the financial statements?

Activity feedback

A discontinuing operation is a relatively large component of an enterprise that is either being disposed of completely or substantially or is being terminated through abandonment or piecemeal sale. The effects of such discontinuation are likely to be significant both in their own right and in changing the future results of the remaining component of the enterprise.

Distinguishing between the financial impact of the discontinuing and the continuing operations on the financial situation of an enterprise will improve the ability of investors, creditors and other users of financial statements to make projections of the enterprise's cash flows, earnings generating capacity and financial position.

In order to be useful for decision purposes, the results of an enterprise need to be presented in a manner that will satisfy the two following objectives. First, the activities and results of the year under review must be reported fully and clearly. Second, readers of the financial statements should be able to understand the implications of the current period results for future periods. This relates to the relevance of accounting information. So the objective of IFRS 5 is to establish a basis for segregating information about a major operation that an enterprise is discontinuing from information about its continuing operations and to specify minimum disclosures about a discontinuing operation.

Definition of a discontinued operation

IFRS 5 defines a discontinued operation as 'a component of an entity that either has been disposed of, or is classified as held for sale, and:

(a) represents a separate major line of business or geographical area of operations;

(b) is part of a single co-ordinated plan to dispose of a separate major line of business or geographical area of operations; or

(c) is a subsidiary acquired exclusively with a view to resale.

For the purposes of this definition, a 'component of an entity' is also defined by the standard as comprising 'operations and cash flows that can be clearly distinguished, operationally and for financial reporting purposes, from the rest of the entity. In other words, a component of an entity will have been a cash-generating unit or a group of cash-generating units while being held for use'.

Business enterprises frequently close facilities, abandon products or even product lines and change the size of their workforce in response to market forces. Those kinds of termination do not qualify as discontinuing operations but they can occur in connection with a discontinuing operation. A list of such activities which do not qualify as discontinuing operations is presented below:

■ gradual or evolutionary phasing out of a product line or class of service
■ discontinuing, even if relatively abruptly, several products within an ongoing line of business
■ shifting of some production or marketing activities for a particular line of business from one location to another
■ closing of a facility to achieve productivity improvements or other cost savings
■ selling a subsidiary whose activities are similar to those of the parent or other subsidiaries.

These examples could bring along the recording of impairments or restructuring provisions.

With regard to the presentation of information on those discontinued operations IFRS 5 stipulates that an entity shall disclose:

(a) a single amount on the face of the income statement comprising the total of:
   (i) the post-tax profit or loss of discontinued operations and
   (ii) the post-tax gain or loss recognised on the measurement to fair value less costs to sell or on the disposal of the assets or disposal group(s) constituting the discontinued operation.

    (b) an analysis of the single amount of (a) into:

        (i) the revenue, expense and pre-tax profit or loss of discontinued operations and related income tax expense;

        (ii) the gain or loss recognised on the measurement to fair value less costs to sell or on the disposal of the assets or disposal group(s) consituting the discontinued operation and related income tax expense.

The analysis may be presented in the notes or on the face of the income statement. If it is presented on the face of the income statement it shall be presented in a section identified as relating to discontinued operations, i.e. separately from continuing operations. The analysis is not required for disposal groups that are newly acquired subsidiaries that meet the criteria to be classified as held for sale on acquisition.

    (c) the net cash flow attributable to the operating, investing and financing activities of discontinued operations.

The standard also makes clear that any gain or loss on the remeasurement of a non-current asset (or disposal group) classified as held for sale that does not meet the definition of a discontinued operation should not be included within these amounts for discontinued operations, but be included in profit or loss from continuing operations.

Further, IFRS 5 requires that these disclosures be re-presented for prior periods presented in the financial statements so that the disclosures relate to all operations that have been discontinued by the balance sheet date for the latest period presented. Accordingly, adjustments to the comparative information as originally reported will be necessary for those disposal groups categorized as discontinued operations.

Activity 23.5

Alpha has three segments: pharmaceuticals, chemicals and soft drinks. In 20X3 after an assessment of the corporate strategy for the future, the company decides to concentrate on chemicals and pharmaceuticals.

On 30 September 20X3 the board of directors voted in favour of a disposal plan which would either try to sell off the *soft drinks* segment as a whole or, if not successful by the end of 20X3, dispose of the assets of the segment in a piecemeal fashion. An announcement of the plan was made the same day. A month later the company enters into a legally binding sales agreement with one of the major producers of soft drinks in the world. The parties expect the sale to be completed in February 20X4.

The following information for the soft drink segment is available for the financial year 20X3 (figures and transactions are simplified):

	Book value at 30 September	Recoverable amount at 30 September	Book value/result at 31 December
Assets	450	400	400
Liabilities	200	200	200
Revenue	–	–	300
Operating expenses	–	–	125

An amount of 25 is representing non-cash expenses.

As you are aware, information relating to a discontinuing operation should be presented separately from continuing operations. You should now prepare the information that needs to be disclosed in the financial statements on 31 December 2003. Assume a corporate income tax rate of 30% on the accounting profit for the segment.

Also comment on what other information must be given regarding the discontinuing operation.

Activity feedback

- As a single amount on the income statement, para. 33 (a): profit for the period from discontinued operations

(i) the post-tax result on discontinued operations	122.5
(ii) the post-tax gain or loss on the measurement of the assets held for sale	35
Total	157.5

- An analysis of the single amount para. 33(b)

revenue from discontinued operations	300
expenses from discontinued operations	125
(i) pre-tax result	175
(ii) related income tax expense	52.5
(iii) the loss on non-current assets held for sale	50
(iv) related income tax result	15

- On the asset side of the balance sheet we should present as a single line item: non-current assets classified as held for sale   400
- Among the liabilities we should disclose as a single line item: liabilities directly associated with non-current assets held for sale   200
- Net cash flow attributable to discontinued operations: 200

Note that comparative figures for 20X2 should be restated as well (para. 34). Disclosure requirements (refer to IFRS 5, para. 11):

- a description of the segment soft drinks (also comment on the reason for the disposal)
- segments in which the discontinuing operation is reported (is a segment in this case)
- the date on which the company announced the plan to discontinue the soft drink segment (also comment on the date when it entered into the binding sales agreement)
- the date when the discontinuance is expected to be completed

Events after balance sheet date

Financial statements are used for mainly two purposes. First of all, external stakeholders will use financial statement information as input in their own decision-making process and, second, financial statements can serve as basis for control on stewardship. The latter means that management and directors could be held accountable for their policy decisions and actions on the basis of the financial statements.

With regard to the first aim of financial reporting, namely providing useful and reliable information it is important that external stakeholders get a clear idea about which transactions and their related financial impact are included in the annual accounts and which transactions or events and their related financial impact have not been taken into account in the financial statements. Between the balance sheet date and the publication of the financial statements to the public time passes. Accounts, no matter how sophisticated the information technology, are never prepared, audited and approved by directors in a few days. Generally there is a time lag of a number of months between the balance sheet date and the 'signing off' of the accounts by directors. During this period numerous events can occur that may or may not have an influence on the information which is provided, by the final accounts, for users.

Activity 23.6

Can you think of activities after balance sheet date which might alter the financial picture presented by the financial statements closed at the balance sheet date?

Activity feedback

- The bankruptcy of an important customer.
- The levy of import tariffs in an important export market of the company.
- The acquisition of a large part of the shares of a company.
- A settlement of a court case in which the company is involved.

The events listed will have an impact on the financial situation of the company and it might well be that external stakeholders will change their decisions in relation to the company if they take into account the financial impact of the information becoming available after balance sheet date. IAS 10 deals with the communication of the impact of those post balance sheet events on the financial situation of the company.

Definition of events after balance sheet date

Para. 3 of IAS 10 defines events occurring after the balance sheet date as those events, both favourable and unfavourable, that occur between the balance sheet date and the date when the financial statements are authorized for issue. Two types of event, can be identified:

- those that provide evidence of conditions that existed at the balance sheet date (adjusting events after the balance sheet date)
- those that are indicative of conditions that arose subsequent to the balance sheet date (non-adjusting events after the balance sheet date).

Date of authorization for issue

In order to judge the relevance of the information provided through the financial statements it is of extreme importance for the external stakeholders to know when the financial statements have been authorized for issue, as the financial statements do not reflect events after this date. Therefore para. 17 of IAS 10 states explicitly that an enterprise should disclose the date on which the financial statements were authorized for issue and who gave that authorization. If the enterprise's owner or others have the power to amend the financial statements after issuance, the enterprise should disclose that fact.

Activity 23.7

Check the financial statements on several websites of listed companies. Is information disclosure clear on this issue (= date of authorization for issue and who gave the authorization)?

Activity feedback

As user of the annual report and the financial statements you will have found out that it is not easily retrievable and it is not obvious where to find that information, especially with regard to the item 'who gave the authorization'.

An example of such disclosure is found in the financial statements of Anglo Gold United (annual report, 2000, p. 42) (see Table 23.2).

The process involved in authorizing the financial statements for issue will vary depending on the management structure, statutory requirements and procedures followed in preparing and finalizing the financial statements (para. 4). In some cases, an enterprise is required to submit its financial statements to its shareholders for approval after the financial statements have already been issued. In such cases, the financial statements are authorized for issue on the date of original issuance, not on the date when shareholders approve the financial statements (para. 5). In other cases, the management of an entity is required to issue its financial statements to a supervisory board (made up solely of non-executives) for approval. In such cases, the financial statements are authorized for issue when the management authorizes them for issue to the supervisory board. Care may need to be taken in determining the date 'authorization' for this purpose. The Standard has to allow for a variety of different national systems of corporate governance and of management structure.

IAS 10 makes a distinction between adjusting events after balance sheet date and non-adjusting events after balance sheet date. For both type of events the financial impact of the events has to be disclosed to the readers of the financial statements, however, the way of disclosure differs.

Table 23.2 Annual accounts of Anglo Gold United

Directors' approval

The annual financial statements and group annual financial statements for the year ended 31 December 2000 were approved by the board of directors on 20 February 2001 and are signed on its behalf by:

Directors:			
R M Godsell	**R P Edey**	**J G Best**	**C B Brayshaw**
Chairman and chief executive officer	Deputy chairman	Finance director	Chairman, Audit Committee

Managing secretary: **Ms Y Z Simelane**

Adjusting events

With regard to adjusting events an enterprise should adjust the amounts recognized in its financial statements to reflect adjusting events after the balance sheet date (para. 8). IAS 10 does not give an explicit definition as guidance for what might be an adjusting event. A list of examples of what the IASB considers to be adjusting events is presented. The following examples should serve as a point of reference for preparers of financial statements (para. 9):

- The settlement after the balance sheet date of a court case that confirms that an entity had a present obligation at the balance sheet date. The entity adjusts any provision previously recognized related to this court case in accordance with IAS 37, *Provisions, Contingent Liabilities and Contingent Assets* or recognizes a new provision instead of merely disclosing a contingent liability because the settlement provides additional evidence that would be considered in accordance with para. 16 of IAS 37.
- The receipt of information after the balance sheet date indicating that an asset was impaired at the balance sheet date or that the amount of a previously recognized impairment loss for that asset needs to be adjusted. For example:
  - the bankruptcy of a customer which occurs after the balance sheet date usually confirms that a loss already existed at the balance sheet date on a trade receivable account and that the enterprise needs to adjust the carrying amount of the trade receivable account
  - the sale of inventories after the balance sheet date may give evidence about their net realizable value at the balance sheet date.
- The determination after the balance sheet date of the cost of assets purchased or the proceeds from assets sold before the balance sheet date.
- The determination after the balance sheet date of the amount of profit-sharing or bonus payments, if the entity had a present legal or constructive obligation at the balance sheet date to make such payments as a result of events before that date (see IAS 19).
- The discovery of fraud or errors that show that the financial statements were incorrect.

Non-adjusting events

The name already reveals that the amounts related to this type of post-balance sheet events should not be recognized in the financial statements themselves, but disclosed in the notes to the accounts. If non-adjusting events after the balance sheet date are material, non-disclosure could influence the economic decisions of users taken on the basis of the financial statements (para. 21). Accordingly, an entity shall disclose the following for each material category of non-adjusting event after the balance sheet date in the notes to the accounts:

- the nature of the event
- an estimate of its financial effect, or a statement that such an estimate cannot be made.

Again, examples of non-adjusting events are presented as guidance in IAS 10 (para. 22).

The following are examples of non-adjusting events after the balance sheet date that would generally result in disclosure:

- a major business combination after the balance sheet date (IFRS 3, *Business Combinations*, requires specific disclosures in such cases) or disposing of a major subsidiary;
- announcing a plan to discontinue an operation
- major purchases of assets, classification of assets as held for sale in accordance with IFRS 5, *Non-current Assets Held for Sale and Discontinued Operations,* other disposals of assets or expropriation of major assets by government
- destruction of a major production plant by a fire after the balance sheet date
- announcing or commencing the implementation of a major restructuring (see IAS 37, *Provisions, Contingent Liabilities and Contingent Assets*)
- major ordinary share transactions and potential ordinary share transactions after the balance sheet date (IAS 33, *Earnings Per Share*, requires an entity to disclose a description of such transactions, other than when such transactions involve capitalization or bonus issues, share splits or reverse share splits all of which required to be adjusted under IAS 33)
- abnormally large changes after the balance sheet date in asset prices or foreign exchange rates
- changes in tax rates or tax laws enacted or announced after the balance sheet date that have a significant effect on current and deferred tax assets and liabilities (see IAS 12, *Income Taxes*)
- entering into significant commitments or contingent liabilities, for example, by issuing significant guarantees
- commencing major litigation arising solely out of events that occurred after the balance sheet date.

Since information on adjusting but also on non-adjusting events is extremely important for external parties, the disclosure rules on non-adjusting events became stricter over the past years. If an enterprise receives information after the balance sheet date about conditions that existed at the balance sheet date, they are now obliged to adjust disclosures that relate to these conditions, in the light of the new information.

If we study the list of examples of non-adjusting events described in para. 22 of IAS 10, we notice that some events lie within the decision power of the management (e.g. acquisitions, discontinuing operations) and other events are beyond the influence of the management (e.g. fire, change in tax laws). It is interesting to observe that many acquisitions or major investments seem to take place between the balance sheet date and the 'signing off' of the accounts. By signing the contract after balance sheet date, the acquisition becomes a non-adjusting event. If, through the acquisition, control was obtained over another entity, full consolidation of the entity in the group accounts could be avoided and the influence of the liabilities of that entity and goodwill paid on acquisition could be postponed for one year on the group's financial statements.

For more information on these items see also Part Three on group accounts of this book. Further, the subjectivity inherent in the item of possible disclosure of non-adjusting events is not removed by the inclusion in IAS 10 of a list of examples. Words such as 'major' or 'significant' appear in nearly all the examples given, so the expert subjective judgement of the accountants responsible for the preparation of the financial statement package remains crucial.

Dividends

In the latest revision of IAS 10 the treatment of dividends was dealt with more explicitly. Para. 12 states that if dividends to holders of equity instruments (as defined in IAS 32, *Financial Instruments: Disclosure and Presentation*) are declared after the balance sheet date, an entity shall not recognize those dividends as a liability at the balance sheet date. In many countries dividends under these circumstances are disclosed as a liability in the national GAAP accounts, the IAS treatment is different.

The issue of going concern

There is, however, one item which applies to the definition of a non-adjusting event, but which entails an adjustment of the financial statements. We refer to para. 14 of IAS which stipulates that if management determines after the balance sheet date either that it intends to liquidate the enterprise or to cease trading or that it has no realistic alternative but to do so, the financial statements should no longer be prepared on a going concern basis.

This implies that the accounts have to be completely redrawn on a non-going concern basis. The latter has a tremendous impact on the data which will subsequently be presented in the financial statements.

Accounting policies, changes in accounting estimates and errors

By now we have mentioned several times that financial statements serve as a means for communicating the economic health of a company to external parties. For a proper assessment of the performance and the financial status of a company external stakeholders need a benchmark with which to compare the financial accounting information. This will be discussed and illustrated extensively in Chapter 27. Data taken from the financial statements of other companies are often used for benchmarking purposes. In this respect comparability of financial accounting information is extremely important. Comparability refers not only to inter-firm comparability but also to the comparability over time of company data of the same enterprise. Techniques for inter-firm comparisons and within firm comparisons over time are presented in Chapter 27.

The objective of IAS 8 is to enhance comparability of financial statement data over time within the same firm and between firms. In order to improve comparability IAS 8 focuses on the criteria for selecting accounting policies, the accounting treatment and disclosure of changes in accounting policies, changes in accounting estimates and errors. The purpose of the standard is to ensure that entities prepare and present their financial statements on a consistent basis. IAS 8 shall be applied in selecting and applying accounting policies and accounting for changes in accounting policies, changes in accounting estimates and corrections of prior period errors. The tax effects of corrections of prior period errors and retrospective adjustments made to apply changes in accounting policies are accounted for and disclosed in accordance with IAS 12, *Income Taxes*.

The first part of IAS 8, which deals with accounting policies, determines first how to select and apply accounting policies (see paras 7–13). Accounting policies are defined as specific principles, bases, conventions, rules and practices adopted by an entity in preparing and presenting financial statements (para. 5). The selection process for an accounting policy starts with determining if there is a specific standard that deals with the transaction or event that has to be reported.

IAS 8 states that when a Standard or an interpretation specifically applies to a transaction, other event or condition, the accounting policy or policies applied to that item shall be determined by applying the Standard or Interpretation and considering any relevant Implementation Guidance issued by the IASB for the Standard or Interpretation (paras 7–9). It is interesting to note that the IASB stipulates that the Implementation Guidance for Standards does not form part of those Standards, and therefore does not contain requirements for financial statements (para. 9).

In the absence of a particular Standard or an interpretation of a Standard that specifically applies to an item in the financial statements, management shall use its judgement in developing and applying an accounting policy that results in information that is (para. 10):

- relevant to the decision-making needs of users; and
- reliable in that the financial statements:
  - represent faithfully the results and financial position of the entity
  - reflect the economic substance of transactions and other events, and not merely the legal form
  - are neutral, i.e. free from bias
  - are prudent
  - are complete in all material respects.

In making the judgement described in para. 10, management shall consider the following sources in descending order (para. 6):

- the requirements and guidance in Standards and interpretations of Standards, dealing with similar and related issues
- the definitions, recognition criteria and measurement concepts for assets, liabilities, income and expenses set out in the Framework for the Preparation and Presentation of Financial Statements
- the most recent pronouncements of other standard-setting bodies that use a similar conceptual framework to develop accounting standards, other accounting literature and accepted industry practices, to the extent, but only to the extent, that these are consistent with the first two points of this paragraph.

IAS 8 states explicitly that accounting policies should be applied consistently for similar transactions, other events and conditions, unless a Standard or an Interpretation specifically requires or permits categorization of items for which different policies may be appropriate. If a Standard or an Interpretation requires or permits such categorization, an appropriate accounting policy shall be selected and applied consistently to each category (para. 13).

Accounting policy changes

Once an accounting policy is chosen it needs to be applied on a consistent basis over the years. Although consistency is the rule, changes in accounting policies are permitted if the change:

(a) is required by a Standard or an Interpretation
(b) or results in the financial statements providing reliable and more relevant information about the effects of transactions, other events or conditions on the entity's financial position, financial performance or cash flows (para. 14).

IAS 8 addresses changes of accounting policy arising from three sources:

1 initial application (including early application) of a Standard or Interpretation containing specific transitional provisions;
2 initial application of a Standard or Interpretation which does not contain specific transitional provisions
3 voluntary changes in accounting policy.

Activity 23.8

Can you think of events or elements which might induce a voluntary change in accounting policies?

Activity feedback

- Company *A* becomes a subsidiary of company *B*, subsequently the accounting policies within company *A* should be harmonized with the accounting policies of company *B*.
- All changes between benchmark treatments and allowable treatments prescribed in the IAS/IFRS, e.g. a switch from capitalizing borrowing costs to expensing them, due to changes in the finance policy of a company.

Policy changes under 1 should be accounted for in accordance with the specific transitional provisions of that Standard or Interpretation.

A change of accounting policy under 2 or 3 should be applied retrospectively, that is applied to transactions, other events and conditions as if it had always been applied (paras 5–19). The standard goes on to explain that retrospective application requires adjustment of the opening balance of each affected component of equity for the earliest prior period presented and the other comparative amounts disclosed for each prior period presented as if the new accounting policy had always been applied (para. 22). The Standard observes that the amount of the resulting adjustment relating to periods before those presented in the financial statements (which is made to the opening balance of each affected component of equity of the earliest prior period presented) will usually be made to retained earnings. However, it goes on to note that the adjustment may be made to another component of equity (for example, to comply with a Standard or an Interpretation). IAS 8 also makes clear that any other information about prior periods, such as historical summaries of financial data, should be also adjusted (para. 26).

It will frequently be straightforward to apply a change in accounting policy retrospectively. However, the Standard accepts that sometimes it may be impractical to do so. Accordingly, retrospective application of a change in accounting policy is not required to the extent that it is impracticable to determine either the period-specific effects or the cumulative effect of the change (para. 23). The concept 'impracticable' occurs also in relation to the accounting treatment of prior period errors. As noted above, in the absence of a specifically applicable Standard or an Interpretation an entity may apply an accounting policy from the most recent pronouncements of another standard-setting body that uses a similar conceptual framework. The standard makes clear that a change in accounting policy reflecting a change in such a pronouncement is a voluntary change in accounting policy which should be accounted for and disclosed as such (para. 21).

We have noticed that the IASB introduced the concept of impracticability in relation to the retrospective application of accounting policy changes. Since this concept can be used to circumvent the retrospective application of an accounting policy change, the Standard devotes a considerable amount of guidance to discussing what 'impracticable' means for these purposes.

The Standard states that applying a requirement is impracticable when an entity cannot apply it after making every reasonable effort to do so. It goes on to note that, for a particular prior period, it is impracticable to apply a change in an accounting policy retrospectively or to make a retrospective restatement to correct an error if:

1   the effects of the retrospective application or retrospective restatement are not determinable
2   the retrospective application or retrospective restatement requires assumptions about what management's intent would have been in that period
3   or the retrospective application or retrospective restatement requires significant estimates of amounts and it is impossible to distinguish objectively information about those estimates that:
    (i)   provides evidence of circumstances that existed on the date(s) as at which those amounts are to be recognized, measured or disclosed
    (ii) would have been available when the financial statements for that prior period were authorized for issue, from other information.

IAS 8 observes that it is frequently necessary to make estimates in applying an accounting policy and that estimation is inherently subjective and that estimates may be developed after the balance sheet date. But developing estimates is potentially more difficult when retrospectively applying an accounting policy or making a retrospective restatement to correct a prior period error, because of the longer period of time that might have passed since the affected transaction, other event or condition occurred.

However, the objective of estimates related to prior periods remains the same as for estimates made in the current period, namely, for the estimate to reflect the circumstances that existed when the transaction, other event or condition occurred. Hindsight should not be used when applying a new accounting policy to, or correcting amounts for, a prior period, either in making assumptions about what management's intentions would have been in a prior period or estimating the amounts recognized, measured or disclosed in a prior period. For example, if an entity corrects a prior period error in measuring financial assets previously classified as held-to-maturity investments in accordance with IAS 39, it should not change their basis of measurement for that period if management decided later not to hold them to maturity.

Therefore, retrospectively applying a new accounting policy or correcting a prior period error requires distinguishing information that:

(a) provides evidence of circumstances that existed on the date(s) as at which the transaction, other event or condition occurred

(b) and would have been available when the financial statements for that prior period were authorized for issue from other information.

The Standard states that for some types of estimate (e.g. an estimate of fair value not based on an observable price or observable inputs), it is impracticable to distinguish these types of information. When retrospective application or retrospective restatement would require making a significant estimate for which it is impossible to distinguish these two types of information, it is impracticable to apply the new accounting policy or correct the prior period error retrospectively.

The concept of impracticability introduces limitations to the retrospective application of accounting policy changes. The future will tell us if this concept of impracticability will be used to avoid the retrospective application of accounting policy changes.

Although IAS 8 and similar standards of other GAAP systems require all these types of disclosure, we do observe in practice a difference in the quality of disclosure relating to changes in accounting policy or accounting methods. Less quality implies that external parties are hindered in comparing financial data from subsequent years or between firms. If accounting changes are used for example for earnings management purposes, then there is an incentive to drop the quality level of these disclosures. As disclosure requirements concerning these accounting method changes have become stricter over the years, accounting method changes are now less used for annual accounts' management purposes. The stricter disclosure requirements allow external parties to 'undo' the effect of the change and to detect the 'real' underlying economic performance.

The issue of accounting quality will be discussed further in Chapter 26.

First-time Adoption of IFRS

When a company changes from its domestic GAAP to IAS/IFRS Standards, this change does not belong to the scope of IAS 8. IFRS 1, *First-time Adoption of IFRS*, provides guidance for all companies, which change either compulsorily, or voluntarily to IAS/IFRS Standards.

An entity's first IFRS financial statements are the first annual financial statements in which the entity adopts IFRSs, by an explicit and unreserved statement in those financial statements of compliance with IFRSs. Financial statements under IFRSs are an entity's first financial statements if, for example, the entity:

(a) presented its most recent previous financial statements:
   (i) under national requirements that are not consistent with IFRSs in all respects;
   (ii) in conformity with IFRSs in all respects, except that the financial statements did not contain an explicit and unreserved statement that they complied with IFRSs;
   (iii) containing an explicit statement of compliance with some, but not all, IFRSs;

    (iv) under national requirements inconsistent with IFRSs, using some individual IFRSs to account for items which national requirements did not exist; or

    (v) under national requirements, with a reconciliation of some amounts to the amounts determined under IFRSs;

(b) prepared financial statements under IFRSs for internal use only, without making them available to the entity's owners or any other external users;

(c) prepared a reporting package under IFRSs for consolidation purposes without preparing a complete set of financial statements as defined in IAS 1, *Presentation of Financial Statements*; or

(d) did not present financial statements for previous periods.

If a company presents its financial figures for a particular financial year, these figures are usually accompanied by prior-year figures. For the sake of comparability these figures should be prepared using the same GAAP. This implies that the prior-year figures in an entity's first IFRS financial statements should also be prepared with the use of IAS/IFRS. If we apply this principle to the compulsory change to IAS/IFRS for listed companies in the EU we obtain the following situation.

    The reporting date for entity A's first IFRS financial statements is 31 December 2005. If entity A decides to present comparative information in those financial statements for one year only, the date of transition to IFRSs is the beginning of business on 1 January 2004 (or, equivalently, close of business on 31 December 2003). Entity A will have presented financial statements under its previous GAAP annually to 31 December each year up to and including 31 December 2004. In this case entity A is required to apply the IFRSs effective for periods ending on 31 December 2005 in:

- preparing its opening IFRS balance sheet at 1 January 2004
- and preparing and presenting its balance sheet for 31 December 2005 (including comparative amounts for 2004), income statement, statement of changes in equity and cash flow statement for the year to 31 December 2005 (including comparative amounts for 2004) and disclosures (including comparative information for 2004).

If a new IFRS is not yet mandatory but permits early application, entity A is permitted, but not required, to apply that IFRS in its first IFRS financial statements. For many preparers which present their first IFRS financial statements the main question is: 'Which accounting policies need to be applied for the recognition and measurement of the items of the financial statements?' The main rule is that an entity shall use the same accounting policies in its opening IFRS balance sheet and throughout all periods presented in its first IFRS financial statements. Those accounting policies shall comply with each IFRS effective at the reporting date for its first IFRS financial statements. This general rule implies that an entity shall not apply different versions of IFRSs that were effective at earlier dates.

    In its opening IFRS balance sheet an entity shall (para. 10):

(a) recognize all assets and liabilities whose recognition is required by IFRSs;

(b) not recognize items as assets or liabilities if IFRSs do not permit such recognition;

(c) reclassify items that it recognized under previous GAAP as one type of asset, liability or component of equity, but are a different type of asset, liability or component of equity under IFRSs; and

(d) apply IFRSs in measuring all recognized assets and liabilities

The accounting policies that an entity uses in its opening IFRS balance sheet may differ from those that it used for the same date using its previous GAAP. The resulting adjustments arise from events and transactions before the date of transition to IFRSs. Therefore, an entity shall recognize those adjustments directly in retained earnings (or, if appropriate, another category of equity) at the date of transition to IFRSs (para. 11).

In essence, companies have to use all IFRSs that are effective at reporting date for all the information included in the annual accounts. However, there are two categories of exception. First, IFRS 1 specifies a number of optional exemptions from retrospective application (paras 13–25). First-time adopters can elect to apply all, some or none of the six optional exemptions. These optional exemptions relate to items with regard to business combinations, fair value, employee benefits, cumulative translation differences, compound financial instruments and assets and liabilities of subsidiaries, associates and joint ventures. Second, IFRS 1 foresees mandatory exceptions from retrospective application. These mandatory exceptions relate to derecognition of financial assets and financial liabilities, hedge accounting, estimates and assets classified as held for sale and discontinued operations.

The switch from a previous GAAP system to IFRS will have an impact on the published figures of a company. IFRS 1 requires that in the notes to the accounts the impact of the transition from the previous GAAP to IAS/IFRS on the financial position, the financial performance and the cash flow should be explained.

Changes in accounting estimates

IAS 8 defines a change in accounting estimates as an adjustment of the carrying amount of an asset or a liability, or the amount of the periodic consumption of an asset, that results from the assessment of the present status of and expected future benefits and obligations associated with assets and liabilities. Changes in accounting estimates result from new information or new developments and, accordingly, are not corrections for errors.

Valuing balance sheet and profit and loss account items often involves making estimates.

Activity 23.9

Think of some balance sheet or profit and loss account elements in which estimates are needed for valuation purposes.

Activity feedback

Estimates are required for example in the valuation of:

- allowances for bad debts
- inventory obsolescence

- determination of the fair value of assets
- determination of the useful life of an asset.

Indeed it is difficult to think of elements that do not include estimations.

The use of reasonable estimates is an essential part of the preparation of financial statements. However, estimates may need to be revised over the years in light of new or changing information. The revision of an estimate does not affect the original classification of the transaction. As changes of accounting estimates imply in most circumstances elements of judgement, the IASB states explicitly in IAS 8 that the change of the estimate should not undermine the reliability of the financial statements.

IAS 8 requires that changes in estimate be accounted for prospectively; defined as recognizing the effect of the change in the accounting estimate in the current and future periods affected by the change (IAS 8, paras 36–38). The Standard goes on to explain that this will mean (as appropriate):

- adjusting the carrying amount of an asset, liability or item of equity in the balance sheet in the period of change
- recognizing the change by including it in profit and loss in:
  - the period of change, if it affects that period only (for example, a change in estimate of bad debts)
  - or the period of change and future periods, if it affects both (for example, a change in estimated useful life of a depreciable asset or the expected pattern of consumption of the economic benefits embodied in it).

Further, the Standard states explicitly that a change in an accounting estimate does not result from a change in the measurement basis or method applied, which is a change in an accounting policy. When it is difficult to distinguish between a change in an accounting policy and a change in an accounting estimate, the change is treated as a change in an accounting estimate, with appropriate disclosure.

Prospective recognition of the effect of a change in an accounting estimate means that the change is applied to transactions, other events and circumstances from the date of the change to estimate. A change in an accounting estimate may affect the current period only or both the current period and future periods.

So a change in an accounting estimate involves less administrative work and is somehow less visible than a change in accounting policy or method. The latter is applied retrospectively and therefore prior year comparative data need to be restated as well. All these changes will probably catch the eye of the user of the annual accounts sooner or later. Empirical evidence exists (this will be discussed in Chapter 26) that changes in accounting estimates are now more popular for earnings management purposes than accounting policy changes as they are less costly and less visible.

Activity 23.10

Think of an example of a change in an accounting estimate which affects only the current period. Then think of an example which might affect the current period as well as subsequent periods.

Activity feedback

For example, a change in the estimate of the amount of bad debts affects only the current period and is therefore recognized in the current period. However, a change in the estimated useful life of or the expected pattern of consumption of the future economic benefits embodied in a depreciable asset affects depreciation expense for the remainder of the current period and for each future period during the asset's remaining useful life. In both cases, the effect of the change relating to the current period is recognized as income or expense in the current period. The effect, if any, on future periods is recognized in future periods.

An entity shall disclose the nature and amount of a change in an accounting estimate that has an effect in the current period or is expected to have an effect in future periods, except for the disclosure of the effect on future periods when it is impracticable to estimate that effect (para. 39).

If the amount of the effect in future periods is not disclosed because estimating it is impracticable, an entity shall disclose that fact (para. 40).

Errors

IAS 8 also deals with the treatment of prior period errors. Prior period errors are omissions from, and mis-statements in, the entity's financial statements for one or more prior periods arising from a failure to use, or misuse of, reliable information that:

- was available when financial statements for those periods were authorized for issue
- could reasonably be expected to have been obtained and taken into account in the preparation and presentation of those financial statements.

Such errors include the effects of mathematical mistakes, mistakes in applying accounting policies, oversights or misinterpretations of facts and fraud.

Para. 4 stipulates that the correction of the error has to be accounted for in a retrospective way, in the first set of financial statements authorized for issue after their discovery by:

- restating the comparative amounts for the prior period(s) in which the error occurred
- or, if the error occurred before the earliest prior period presented, restating the opening balances of assets, liabilities and equity for the earliest prior period presented.

In this way the financial statements are presented as if the error had never occurred.

Also in the case of prior period errors, comparative information presented for a particular prior period need not be restated if restating the information would be impracticable (paras 43–45).

Special disclosure requirements apply in relation to such prior period errors (para. 49):

(a) the nature of the prior period error;
(b) for each prior period presented, to the extent practicable, the amount of the correction:
  (i) for each financial statement line item affected; and
  (ii) if IAS 33 applies to the entity, for basic and diluted earnings per share;

(c) the amount of the correction at the beginning of the earliest prior period presented; and

(d) if retrospective restatement is impracticable for a particular period, the circumstances that led to the existence of that condition and a description of how and from when the error has been corrected.

Financial statements of subsequent periods need not repeat these disclosures.

Activity 23.11

During 20X2, company A discovered that certain products that had been sold during 20X1 were incorrectly included in inventory at 31 December, 20X1 at €3 250.

Company A's accounting records for 20X2 show sales of €52 000, cost of goods sold of €43 250 (including €3250 for error in opening inventory) and income taxes of €2 625.

In 20X1, company A reported:

Sales	36 750
Cost of goods sold	26 750
Profit from ordinary activities before	
Income taxes	10 000
Income taxes	(3 000)
Net profit	7 000

20X1 opening retained earnings were 10 000 and closing retained earnings were 17 000.

Company A's income tax rate was 30% for 20X2 and 20X1.

Show the necessary disclosures in the financial statements for the year 20X2.

Activity feedback

Company A – an extract from the income statement

	20X2	20X1 (restated)
Sales	52 000	36 750
Cost of goods sold	40 000	30 000
Profit form ordinary activities before Income taxes	12 000	6 750
Income taxes	3 600	2 025
Net profit	8 400	4 725

Company A
Statement of retained earnings

	20X2	20X1 (restated)
Opening retained earnings as previously reported	17 000	10 000
Correction of fundamental error (Net of income taxes of 975) (Note 1)	2 275	–
Opening retained earnings as restated	14 725	10 000
Net profit	8 400	4 725
Closing retained earnings	23 152	14 725

Extracts from notes to the financial statements

1 Certain products that had been sold in 20X1 were incorrectly included in inventory at 31 December, 20X1 at 6500. The financial statement of 20X1 has been restated to correct this error.

Once again, we notice that the restatement is made on the judgement of the management whether or not the restatement is impracticable.

Earnings per share

Most people or companies buy shares of other companies for investment purposes. Probably only fans of listed football clubs such as Manchester United, Barcelona or Ajax buy shares for purely emotional reasons. An indicator frequently used in the context of evaluating the investment performance of a company is earnings per share. Earnings per share (EPS) is found by dividing profit attributable to the ordinary shareholders by the number of ordinary shares in issue. As an absolute, however, it has no meaning or relevance. Earnings per share becomes relevant in the context of the price/earnings ratio or when the growth rate of the EPS of a company is considered. This will be explained with the following example. If we are told that company A has an EPS of 6c whereas company B has an EPS of 25c, we are unable to compare the performance of the two because we know nothing about their relative size or, more specifically, about the number or value of shares in issue. For the same reasons, the quoted share price of the two companies provides no basis for comparison of the stockmarket's perceptions of either.

Thus analysts and investors require a basis of comparison and an indicator of confidence in particular companies. Such an indicator is the price/earnings (PE) ratio, which is simply calculated by dividing the share price by the EPS, thereby relating company performance to external perception.

The calculation and use of the PE ratio is illustrated in the following activity, where the PE ratio for company X is calculated to be 7.5 and for company Y, 12.

Activity 23.12

In which company would you invest?

Company	X	Y
Price per share (a)	150c	96c
Earnings per share (b)	20c	8c
PE ratio (a/b)	7.5	12

Activity feedback

Company X has a higher share price and greater EPS, but company Y is expected to perform better in the future. Why? The normal action of supply and demand has bid up the share price of Y relative to current earnings and the market is therefore saying something about its confidence in Y relative to X. Obviously, a very high PE would indicate such extravagant expectations that there may be some element of risk, but generally a high PE is a good indicator of market support. People are willing to pay more for something they think more highly of.

If the PE ratio is used in this way, being quoted in the financial press and elsewhere, it matters greatly that its derivation is consistent and comparable. There are no problems with the price of the share, but what about the earnings per share?

In this section we will discuss the calculation of the EPS and in Chapter 27 we further illustrate the use of EPS in the context of the price/earnings ratio. In order to calculate earnings per share, first of all, the earnings number has to be defined and, second, the determination of the number of shares to be used in the denominator has to be specified as well. To enhance the comparability of the EPS measure between companies the IASB has issued standard IAS 33 which deals with the determination of EPS. The IASB is well aware of the fact that IAS 33 mainly improves the consistency in the determination of the denominator of the EPS ratio. Companies can still influence their results by using different accounting valuation methods and accounting estimates, as we discuss in Chapter 26.

IAS 33 shall be applied by entities whose ordinary shares or potential ordinary shares are publicly traded and by entities that are in the process of issuing ordinary shares or potential ordinary shares in public securities markets (IAS 33, para. 2). An entity that discloses earnings per share shall calculate and disclose earnings per share in accordance with IAS 33, if they state that their annual accounts comply with IAS/IFRS, even those companies that disclose voluntarily EPS data in their IAS financial statements.

Two types of EPS ratio can be calculated: basic earnings per share (BEPS) and diluted earnings per share (DEPS). The main difference between the two EPS figures is the number of shares they take into account in the denominator. In the calculation of basic earnings per share (BEPS) the outstanding equity share capital during the financial year is taken under consideration. The diluted earnings per share (DEPS) takes into account, besides the outstanding shares, the existence of securities with no current claim on equity earnings, but which will give rise to such a claim in the future.

As the main objective of IAS 33 is achieving consistency in the determination of the denominator of the EPS ratio, the elements to be included in the denominator should be defined first. Paras 5 and 6 of IAS 33 provide the following definitions:

An ordinary share is an equity instrument that is subordinate to all other classes of equity instruments. Ordinary shares participate in net profit for the period only after other types of shares such as preference shares.

A potential ordinary share is a financial instrument or other contract that may entitle its holder to ordinary shares.

Warrants, options and their equivalents are financial instruments that give the holder the right to purchase ordinary shares.

Contingently issuable ordinary shares are ordinary shares issuable for little or no cash or other consideration upon the satisfaction of certain conditions pursuant to a contingent share agreement, whereby a contingent share agreement is an agreement to issue shares that is dependent on the satisfaction of specified conditions.

Put options on ordinary shares are contracts that give the holder the right to sell ordinary shares at a specified price for a given period.

Dilution is a reduction in earnings per share or an increase in loss per share resulting from the assumption that convertible securities were converted, that options or warrants were exercised or that ordinary shares were issued upon the satisfaction of certain conditions.

Anti-dilution is an increase in earnings per share or a reduction in loss per share resulting from the assumption that convertible instruments are converted, that options and warrants are exercised, or that ordinary shares are issued upon the satisfaction of specified conditions.

Listed companies have to disclose the basic earnings per share and diluted earnings per share. We concentrate, first of all, on the basic earnings per share figure and all the issues which might arise in the calculation of the BEPS. Later on we discuss the diluted earnings per share.

Basic earnings per share

The basic earnings per share (BEPS) figure represents the amount attributable to the ordinary shareholders by dividing the earnings figure by the weighted average number of ordinary shares outstanding (the denominator) during the period. The calculation of the earnings figure is determined in para. 12. The earnings are equal to the profit and loss attributable to the parent entity. If there are discontinuing operations (see pp. 470–8 for a discussion on 'discontinuing operations') in a company then the BEPS should also be calculated on the basis of the profit or loss for the period from the continuing operations attributable to the parent entity. If there are no discontinuing operations there is just one basic earnings per share figure. Again, this is to improve the relevance of the information communicated.

The calculation of the earnings included in the numerator shall be the profit or loss adjusted for the after-tax amounts of preference dividends, differences arising on the settlement of preference shares and other similar effects of preference shares classified as equity. The reason is that ordinary shares are not entitled to those elements. The weighted average number of ordinary shares outstanding during the period will figure in the denominator.

Activity 23.13

The summarized income statement for EPS SA for the year ended 20X6 is as follows:

	€	€
Profit before taxation		1 000 000
Taxation (including deferred adjustment)		400 000
		600 000
Preference dividend	50 000	
Ordinary dividend	100 000	
		150 000
		450 000

The number of ordinary shares in issue is 200 000.
Calculate the basic EPS.

Activity feedback

From the definition of earnings per share:

$$\text{Basic EPS} = \frac{\text{Profit after tax} - \text{preference dividend}}{\text{Number of ordinary shares}}$$

$$= \frac{600\,000 - 50\,000}{200\,000}$$

$$= €2.75 \text{ per share}$$

Changes in equity share capital during the year

In Activity 23.13 the number of shares in issue is given and remains constant over the financial period. However, in reality, there can be changes in the equity share capital during the financial year under consideration. For the purpose of calculating basic earnings per share, the number of ordinary shares should be the weighted average number of ordinary shares outstanding during the period. This is the number of ordinary shares outstanding at the beginning of the period, adjusted by the number of ordinary shares bought back or issued during the period multiplied by a time-weighting factor. The time-weighting factor is the number of days that the shares are outstanding as a proportion of the total number of days in the period; a reasonable approximation of the weighted average is adequate in many circumstances.

Activity 23.14

Fullmar plc had issued share capital on 31 December X5 as follows:

500 000 preference shares (value €1 each) a preference dividend of 7% is attached
4 000 000 ordinary shares (value €0.25 each)

Profit after tax for the year ended 31 December X5 was €435 000. On 1 October X5 Fullmar had issued 1 million ordinary shares at full market price (= €0.25 each).
Calculate the EPS for Fullmar plc for the year ended 31 December X5.

Activity feedback

The number of ordinary shares in issue on 1 January X5 was 3 million and 1 million were issued on 1 October X5. Thus the time weighted average number of ordinary shares in issue for the year was

$$(3\,000\,000 \times 9/12) + (4\,000\,000 \times 3/12) = 3\,250\,000$$
$$\text{or}$$
$$(3\,000\,000 \times 12/12) + (1\,000\,000 \times 3/12) = 3\,250\,000$$

The earnings for the year attributable to the ordinary shareholders is €435 000 − €35 000 preference dividend = €400 000. Therefore:

$$\text{EPS} = \frac{400\,000}{3\,250\,000} \text{ per share}$$

$$= €0.1230 \text{ per share}$$

In reality, shares can be issued at a price different from the market price or shares can be issued without a corresponding change in resources. Related to this, para. 26 of IAS 33 states that the weighted number of ordinary shares outstanding during the period and for all periods presented shall be adjusted for events, other than the conversion of potential ordinary shares, that have changed the number of ordinary shares outstanding without a corresponding change in resources. Ordinary shares may be issued or the number of ordinary shares outstanding may be reduced, without a corresponding change in resources. Examples include:

- a capitalization or bonus issue (sometimes referred to as a stock dividend)
- a bonus element in any other issue, for example a bonus element in a rights issue to existing shareholders
- a share split
- a reverse share split (consolidation of shares).

A bonus issue

In a capitalization or bonus issue or a share split, ordinary shares are issued to existing shareholders for no additional consideration. Therefore, the number of ordinary shares outstanding is increased without an increase in resources. The number of ordinary shares outstanding before the event is adjusted for the proportionate change in the number of ordinary shares outstanding as if the event had occurred at the beginning of the earliest period presented. For example, on a two-for-one bonus issue, the number of ordinary shares that are outstanding before the issue is multiplied by three to obtain the new total number of ordinary shares or by two to obtain the number of additional ordinary shares.

In all these examples more shares have been issued at no 'cost'. The earnings of the business during the year can only be regarded as relating to the shares at the end of the year, i.e. to all the shares including the new ones. No distortion arises, as no resources were passed into the business when the new shares were created.

Activity 23.15

Using the same data as in Activity 23.14 but assuming that the shares issued on October X5 were a capitalization issue, calculate the EPS for the year. This means that we have a bonus issue for no additional consideration, whereby for each three existing shares a new share is issued.

Activity feedback

We now have a capitalization issue, not a full market price issue of shares, and therefore we assume 4 million shares in issue for the whole of the year. (Note this assumption would be the same no matter at what point during the year the capitalization was made.)

The number of shares in issue can also be calculated from the following:

$$3\,000\,000 \times \frac{9}{12} \times \frac{4}{3} + 4\,000\,000 \times \frac{3}{12}$$
$$\text{(bonus factor)}$$
$$= 3\,000\,000 + 1\,000\,000 = 4\,000\,000$$

Remember this for more complicated examples:

$$\text{EPS} = \frac{400\,000}{4\,000\,000} = \text{€}0.10 \text{ per share}$$

We need to think about the implications of such changes for meaningful comparison with prior year's figures. Adjusted earnings per share could be calculated. This ratio then consists of the earnings of the year before divided by the new amount of outstanding shares of the current year.

A consolidation of ordinary shares generally reduces the number of ordinary shares outstanding without a corresponding reduction in resources. However, where a share consolidation is combined with a special dividend and the overall effect is a share repurchase at fair value, the reduction in the number of ordinary shares outstanding is the result of a corresponding reduction in resources. The weighted average number of ordinary shares outstanding for the period in which the combined transaction takes place is adjusted for the reduction in the number of ordinary shares from the date the special dividend is recognized.

Rights issue at less than full market price

In a rights issue, the exercise price is often less than the fair value of the shares. Therefore, such a rights issue includes a bonus element as indicated earlier. The number of ordinary shares to be used in calculating basic earnings per share for all periods before the rights issue is the number of ordinary shares outstanding before the issue, multiplied by the following factor:

$$\frac{\text{Fair value per share immediately before the exercise of rights}}{\text{Theoretical ex-rights fair value per share}}$$

The theoretical ex-rights fair value per share is calculated by adding the aggregate fair value of the shares immediately before the exercise of the rights to the proceeds from the exercise of the rights and dividing by the number of shares outstanding after the exercise of the rights. Where the rights themselves are to be publicly traded separately from the shares before the exercise date, fair value for the purposes of this calculation is established at the close of the last day on which the shares are traded together with the rights.

This is complicated! A rights issue combines the characteristics of a capitalization issue and a full market price issue. New resources are passing into the business so a higher earnings figure, related to these new resources, should be expected. But at the same time there is a bonus element in the new shares, which should be treated like a capitalization issue. To the extent that the rights issue provides new resources, i.e. equates to an issue at full market price, we need to calculate the average number of shares weighted on a time basis. To the extent that the rights issue includes a discount or bonus element we need to increase the number of shares deemed to have been in issue for the whole period. The theoretical ex-rights price can be calculated as follows:

1 Calculate the total market value of the equity before the rights issue (actual cumulative rights price × number of shares).

2 Calculate the total proceeds expected from the right issue (issue price × number of shares).

3 Add these two amounts and divide by the total number of shares involved altogether (i.e. by the total number after the rights issue).

Activity 23.16

Trig plc as at 30 June X5 has €600 000 ordinary shares in issue with a current market value of €2 per share. On 1 July X5 Trig plc makes a four for six rights issue at €1.75 and all rights are taken up. Earnings for the year after tax and preference dividends are €81 579 and the previous year's EPS was declared as 9c. Calculate the EPS figure that should be shown in the financial statements for the year ended 31 December X5.

Activity feedback

We first need to calculate the theoretical ex-rights price of the shares:

$$\begin{array}{lll}
\text{Market value of equity before rights} & = \quad 600\,000 \times €2 & = 1\,200\,000 \\
\text{Proceeds from rights issue} & = \dfrac{400\,000 \times €1.75}{1\,000\,000} = & \dfrac{700\,000}{1\,900\,000}
\end{array}$$

$$\text{Theoretical ex-rights price} = \frac{1\,900\,000}{1\,000\,000} = €1.90$$

Second, we calculate the weighted average number of shares:

$$\underset{\text{(time weighting)}}{600\,000 \times \frac{1}{2} \times \frac{2}{1.9}} + \underset{\text{(time weighting)}}{1\,000\,000 \times \frac{1}{2}} = 815\,789$$

Therefore EPS for year ending 31 December X1 $= \dfrac{8\,157\,900}{815\,789} = 10c$ per share

Third, we need to recalculate the previous year's EPS:

$$9 \times 1.9/2 = 8.55c \text{ per share}$$

A reduction has occurred in the previous year's EPS as we have inserted the bonus element of the rights.

Diluted earnings per share

Besides the basic earnings per share, a company must also disclose its diluted earnings per share. Where there are securities existing at the year end that will have a claim on equity earnings from some time in the future, then it is clear that at this future time the claim of each currently existing share will, other things being equal, be reduced (or diluted). It is likely to be useful information to current shareholders and others to give them a picture of what the EPS would be if this dilution takes place. This is done by recalculating the current year's EPS as if the dilution had already occurred.

For the calculation of the numerator of the diluted EPS, the starting amount will be the earnings amount of the BEPS adjusted for the after-tax effect of:

1 any dividends or other items related to dilutive potential ordinary shares deducted in arriving at profit or loss attributable to ordinary equity holders of the parent entity as calculated in accordance with the calculation done for the BEPS
2 any interest recognized in the period related to dilutive potential ordinary shares
3 any other changes in income or expense that would result from the conversion of the dilutive potential ordinary shares.

In the denominator of the DEPS the number of ordinary shares shall be the weighted average number of ordinary shares calculated in accordance with paras 19 and 26 (which relate to the denominator of the BEPS), plus the weighted average number of ordinary shares that would be issued on the conversion of all the dilutive potential ordinary shares into ordinary shares. Dilutive potential ordinary shares shall be deemed to have been converted into ordinary shares at the beginning of the period or, if later, the date of issue of the potential ordinary shares.

Further potential ordinary shares shall be treated as dilutive when, and only when, their conversion to ordinary shares would decrease earnings per share or increase loss per share from continuing operations (para. 41). Potential ordinary shares are anti-dilutive when their conversion to ordinary shares would increase earnings per share or decrease loss per share from continuing operations. The calculation of diluted earnings per share does not assume conversion, exercise, or other issue of potential ordinary shares that would have an antidilutive effect on earnings per share (para. 43). In determining whether potential ordinary shares are dilutive or antidilutive, each issue or series of potential ordinary shares is considered separately rather than in aggregate. The sequence in which potential ordinary shares are considered may affect whether they are dilutive. Therefore to maximize the dilution of basic earnings per share, each issue or series of potential ordinary shares is considered in sequence from the most dilutive to the least dilutive, i.e. dilutive potential ordinary shares with the lowest 'earnings per incremental share' are included in the diluted earnings per share calculation before those with a higher earnings per incremental share. Options and warrants are generally included first because they do not affect the numerator of the calculation.

IAS 33 considers a number of financial instruments as potential dilutive and describes their effect on the DEPS figure in the following order:

- options, warrants and equivalent instruments (paras 45–48)
- convertible instruments (paras 42–51)
- contingently issuable shares (paras 52–61)
- purchase options (para. 62)
- written put options (para. 63).

The latest version of IAS 33 also pays attention to retrospective adjustments. IAS 33 (para. 64) states in this respect that if the number of ordinary or potential ordinary shares outstanding increases as a result of capitalization, bonus issue or share split, or decreases as a result of a reverse share split, the calculation of basic and diluted earnings per share for all periods presented shall be adjusted retrospectively. If these changes occur after the balance sheet date but before the financial statements are authorized for issue, the per share calculations for those and any prior period financial statements presented shall be based on the new number of shares. The fact that per share calculations reflect such changes in the number of shares shall be disclosed. In addition, basic and diluted earnings per share of all periods presented shall be adjusted for the effects of errors and adjustments resulting from changes in accounting policies accounted for retrospectively.

Activity 23.17

The summarized income statement for EPS plc for the year ended 20X1 is as follows:

	€	€
Profit before taxation		1 000 000
Taxation (including deferred adjustment)		400 000
		600 000
Preference dividend	50 000	
Ordinary dividend	100 000	
		150 000
		450 000

The number of ordinary shares in issue is 2 million.

In addition to the 2 million ordinary shares already in issue, however, there exists convertible loan stock of €500 000 bearing interest at 10%. This may be converted into ordinary shares between 20X3 and 20X6 at a rate of one ordinary share for every €2 of loan stock. Corporation tax is taken for convenience as 50%. Calculate the fully diluted EPS.

Activity feedback

The fully diluted EPS is found as follows. If the conversion is fully completed then there will be two effects:

1 The share capital will increase by 250 000 shares (1 share for every €2 of the €500 000 loan).
2 The profit after tax will increase by the interest on the loan no longer payable less the extra tax on this increase. The interest at 10% on €500 000 is €50 000, but the extra tax on this profit increase would be 50% of €50 000, i.e. €25 000.

So profit after tax, and therefore 'earnings', will increase by $50 000 - 25 000 = €25 000$. Fully diluted EPS will therefore be:

$$\frac{600 000 + 25 000 - 50 000}{2 000 000 + 250 000}$$

$$= \frac{575 000}{2 250 000c}$$

$$= 25.6c \text{ per share}$$

Remember that the fully diluted EPS is a hypothetical calculation. It assumes total conversion into equity participation. The extent to which this assumption is likely in any particular circumstance is irrelevant.

The IASB attaches importance to the EPS figure as it requires in IAS 33 that the basic EPS as well as the diluted EPS should be disclosed on the face of the income statement for the current year as well as for all other years for which information is presented. EPS should be presented for each class of ordinary shares that has a different right to share in net profit for the period. We know that if there are discontinuing operations, two EPS figures have to be disclosed. An entity that reports a discontinuing operation shall disclose the basic and diluted amounts per share for this line item either on the face of the income statement or in the notes to the financial statements. Even if the EPS figure is negative the amounts should be presented.

On the face of the income statement EPS is presented as a single figure. In the notes to the accounts the user of the financial statements can obtain information on the composition of the numerator and the denominator of the basic EPS and the diluted EPS.

It is perhaps useful at this point to look at an example of a calculation of EPS involving more than one type of share issue. The following example appears complicated but only requires a clear thought process and a knowledge of IAS requirements.

Activity 23.18

Part of a listed company's consolidated profit and loss account is as follows:

Chasewater Public Limited Company
Consolidated P&L account (extract) for the year ended 30 June 20X5

	€	€
Group net profit before taxation		500 000
Taxation		270 000
Group net profit after taxation		230 000
Minority interests in subsidiaries		20 000
Attributable to shareholders in Chasewater Plc		210 000
Extraordinary items (after taxation)		11 000
Net profit for year		221 000
Dividends (net)		
Preference	25 000	
Ordinary	100 000	
		125 000
Retained earnings for year		96 000

Notes
1 Issued share capital (fully paid), 1 July 20X4: 250 000 10% cumulative preference shares of €1 each and 4 million ordinary shares of 25c each.
2 Loan capital, 1 July 20X4: €500 000 7% convertible debentures (convertible into 200 ordinary shares per €100 debenture, with proportionate increases for subsequent bonus issues and for the bonus element in subsequent rights issues).
3 Changes during the year ended 30 June 20X5:
   1 October 20X4 Rights issues of ordinary shares (ranking for dividend 20X4–5): 1 for 4 at €0.90 per share: market price before issue, €1.00
   1 January 20X5 Conversion of €100 000 of 7% convertible debentures
   1 March 20X5 Bonus issue of ordinary shares, 1 for 3

4 Basic earnings per share for the year ended 30 June 20X4 was 4c.
5 Corporation tax, 52%; income tax basic rate, 30%.
   Required:
   (a) compute the company's basic earnings per share for the current year and *its comparative BEPS for the previous year;* and
   (b) to compute the company's fully diluted earnings per share for the current year only.

Activity feedback

On reading the question you should have noted the following:

1 a rights issue on 1 October 20X4 of 1 million shares
2 a conversion of debentures on 1 January 20X5 to 200 000 shares plus the bonus element of the rights issue 3 a bonus issue on 1 March 20X5.

A quantity of convertible debentures still remain in issue.
First, we calculate the earnings for the EPS calculation. This is straightforward:

Profit after tax after extraordinary items	221 000
Preference dividend	25 000
Earnings for basic EPS calculation	196 000

Second, as a rights issue has taken place we need to calculate the adjusting factor, i.e.:

$$\frac{\text{Actual cumulative rights}}{\text{Theoretical } ex\text{-rights}}$$

Market value of equity *before rights* $= 4\,000\,000 \times €1 = 4\,000\,000$

Proceeds of rights issue $=$	$1\,000\,000 \times 90c$	$= 900\,000$
	$5\,000\,000$	$4\,900\,000$
Theoretical ex-rights price $=$	$4\,900\,000$	$= 98c$
	$5\,000\,000$	

Adjusting factor $= 100/98$ (this represents the bonus element of the rights issue).

Third, we need to calculate the time weighted *average number* of shares and remember to include the bonus issue for the whole of the year and multiply the proportion of capital in issue before rights by a factor of 100/98. Note the conversion of debentures on 1 January 20X5 will be to $200\,000 \times 100/98$ shares $= 204\,082$ shares 98 and that the bonus issue will be calculated as follows:

Number of shares in issue *before bonus* $=$

$$4\,000\,000 + 1\,000\,000 \text{ rights} + 204\,082 \text{ conversion} = 5\,204\,082$$

$$\text{Bonus issue at 1 for 3} = \frac{5\,204\,082}{7} = 743\,440$$

Number of shares in issue after bonus $= 6\,938\,776$

Time weighted number of shares $=$

$$\left[4\,000 \times \frac{3}{12} \times \frac{100}{98} + 5\,000\,000 \times \frac{3}{12} \times 5\,204\,082 \times \frac{2}{12} \right]$$

$$\frac{4}{3}(\text{bonus factor}) + 6\,938\,776 \times \frac{4}{12}$$

$$= (1\,020\,408.1 + 1\,250\,000 + 867\,347)\,\frac{4}{3} + 2\,312\,925.3$$

$$= 3\,137\,755.1 \times \frac{4}{3} + 2\,312\,925.3 = 6\,496\,598.6$$

The fourth, fifth and sixth steps are as follows:

$$\text{Basic EPS 20X5} = \frac{19\,600\,000}{6\,496\,598.6} = 3.02\text{c}$$

$$\text{Revised EPS 20X4} = 4\text{c} \times \frac{3}{4}\,(\text{bonus factor}) \times \frac{98}{100}\,(\text{rights factor}) = 2.94\text{c}$$

Fully diluted EPS also needs to be calculated to see if there is a 5% dilution:

	£
Basic earnings	196 000
Add back debenture interest assuming full conversion took place at 1 July 20X4	
$\frac{6}{12} \times 7\% \times 500\,000 + 6\,\frac{6}{12} \times 7\% \times 4\,000\,000 =$	31 500
Corporate tax adjustment for non-payment of debenture interests	(16 380)
Diluted earnings	211 120

The weighted number of shares will need recalculating assuming all convertible debentures converted on 1 July 20X4, i.e. 1 million shares issued. Note the bonus issue will now be 2 083 333 shares on 1 March 20X5, and the rights issue 1 250 000 shares on 1 October 20X4.

Time weighted number of shares.

$$\left[5\,000\,000 \times \frac{3}{12} \times \frac{100}{98} + 6\,250\,000 \times \frac{5}{12}\right]\frac{4}{3} + 8\,333\,333 \times \frac{4}{12} = 7\,950\,680$$

$$\text{Diluted EPS} = \frac{21\,112\,000\text{c}}{7\,950\,680} = 2.66\text{c}$$

Interim financial reporting

All the standards discussed in this chapter relate to the disclosure of information with the purpose of enhancing the decision usefulness of the data communicated through the financial statements. Investors, creditors, suppliers, the government and the workforce all make use of data taken from the financial statements. The financial statements are prepared on a yearly basis only. The investors' community, however, appreciates the provision of financial information on a more frequent basis.

Many stock exchanges require half-year interim reports. The US SEC even asks for quarterly interim reports. In Europe, the normal frequency of reporting is biannual. Relatively few European companies follow the North American practice of reporting every quarter. The European Union's Council of Economics and Finance Ministers

(ECOFIN) is expected to approve and issue the *Proposal for a Directive of the European Parliament and of the Council on the harmonization of transparency requirements with regard to information about issuers whose securities are admitted to trading on a regulated market and amending Directive 2001/34/EC* (draft Transparency Directive) in its final form in the autumn of 2004. Article 5.3 of that Directive will require in respect of half-yearly financial reports that 'where the issuer is required to prepare consolidated accounts, the condensed set of financial statements shall be prepared in accordance with the international accounting standard applicable to the interim financial reporting as adopted pursuant to the procedure provided for under Article 6 of Regulation (EC) No. 1606/2002.' This means that half-yearly reports are expected to comply with IAS 34 once the draft Transparency Directive has been approved. However, quarterly reports will be exempt from this requirement. A company can publish interim financial reports as a result of a requirement by a stock exchange or another regulatory body. The practice of publishing an interim report can also result from a voluntary disclosure decision.

Activity 23.19

Look at websites of listed companies and find out how they present their interim financial reports. Do they present other types of financial short-term information?

Activity feedback

Interim financial reports usually consist of a consolidated statement in a kind of abbreviated format and explanatory notes accompanied by a management report. Besides interim financial statements companies also often disclose on their website operating data on a half-year, quarterly or even monthly basis. If you look at the websites of some major airlines you will even find traffic statistics updated on a monthly basis.

Before we present the contents of IAS 34, we want to underline that IAS does not require companies to publish interim financial reports. Only if an enterprise reporting under IAS does choose (or is required by other authorities) to issue such interim reports, then IAS prescribes the minimum content of an interim financial report and the principles for recognition and measurement in complete or condensed financial statements for an interim period.

Format of interim reports

Concerning the format of the interim report, IAS 34 leaves two options from which management has to choose. As an interim financial report a company can publish either a complete set of financial statements or a set of condensed financial statements for an interim period. The interim period is defined as a financial reporting period shorter than a full financial year. If an enterprise publishes a complete set of financial statements in its interim financial report, the form and content of those statements should conform to the requirements of IAS 1 for a complete set of financial statements.

If, however, the company chooses for a set of condensed financial statements then the minimum components of the interim financial report are presented in para. 8 of IAS 34, as follows:

- condensed balance sheet
- condensed income statement
- condensed statement showing either (i) all changes in equity or (ii) changes in equity other than those arising from capital transactions with owners and distributions to owners
- condensed cash flow statement
- selected explanatory notes.

What is meant by 'condensed' is explained further in the Standard. 'Those condensed statements should include, at a minimum, each of the headings and subtotals that were included in its most recent annual financial statements.' Additional line items or notes should be included if their omission would make the condensed interim financial statements misleading. Further basic and diluted earnings per share should be presented on the face of an income statement, complete or condensed, for an interim period.

It is important to stress that IAS 34 starts from the assumption that anyone who reads an enterprise's interim report will also have access to its most recent annual report. As a result, virtually none of the notes to the annual financial statements is repeated or updated in the interim report. Instead, the interim notes include primarily an explanation of the events and changes that are significant to an understanding of the changes in financial position and performance of the enterprise since the last annual reporting date. IAS 34 pays explicit attention to the notes accompanying the interim report.

Notes to the interim reports

Concerning these selected explanatory notes, which are typical for interim reports, para. 16 states which information as a minimum should be included if material and if not disclosed elsewhere in the interim financial report. The information should normally be reported on a financial year-to-date basis. However, the enterprise should also disclose any events or transactions that are material to an understanding of the current interim period:

- a statement that the same accounting policies and methods of computation are followed in the interim financial statements as compared with the most recent annual financial statements or, if those policies or methods have been changed, a description of the nature and effect of the change
- explanatory comments about the seasonality or cyclicality of interim operations
- the nature and amount of items affecting assets, liabilities, equity, net income or cash flows that are unusual because of their nature, size or incidence
- the nature and amount of changes in estimates of amounts reported in prior interim periods of the current financial year or changes in estimates of amounts reported in prior financial years, if those changes have a material effect in the current interim period

- issuances, repurchases and repayments of debt and equity securities
- dividends paid (aggregate or per share) separately for ordinary shares and other shares
- segment revenue and segment result for business segments or geographical segments, whichever is the entity's primary basis of segment reporting (disclosure of segment data is required in an entity's interim financial report only if IAS 14, *Segment Reporting*, requires that entity to disclose segment data in its annual financial statements)
- material events subsequent to the end of the interim period that have not been reflected in the financial statements for the interim period
- the effect of changes in the composition of the entity during the interim period, including business combinations, acquisition or disposal of subsidiaries and long-term investments, restructurings and discontinued operations. In the case of business combinations, the entity shall disclose the information required to be disclosed under paras 66–73 of IFRS 3, *Business Combinations*
- changes in contingent liabilities or contingent assets since the last annual balance sheet date.

IAS 34 gives the following examples of disclosures required in interim financial reports (para. 17):

- the write-down of inventories to net realizable value and the reversal of such a write-down;
- recognition of a loss from the impairment of property, plant and equipment, intangible assets, or other assets, and the reversal of such an impairment loss;
- the reversal of any provisions for the costs of restructuring;
- acquisitions and disposals of items of property, plant and equipment;
- commitments for the purchase of property, plant and equipment;
- litigation settlements;
- corrections of prior period errors;
- any loan default or breach of a loan agreement that has not been remedied on or before the balance sheet date; and
- related party transactions.

Furthermore, individual standards and interpretations also provide guidance regarding disclosures for many of these items.

Valuation rules for interim reports

IAS 34 stipulates that an enterprise should apply the same accounting policies in its interim financial report as are applied in its annual financial statements, except for accounting policy changes made after the date of the most recent annual financial statements that are to be reflected in the next annual financial statements.

In many firms revenues and costs have a seasonal pattern. Think, for example, of firms in the tourism industry or in the ice cream industry. But in industries where one would not think about seasonal patterns, they may indeed exist, e.g. sale of cars.

With regard to revenue and expense recognition explicit guidance is given on revenues and costs which occur unevenly during the year. Revenues that are received seasonally, cyclically or occasionally within a financial year should not be anticipated or deferred as of an interim date if anticipation or deferral would not be appropriate at the end of the enterprise's financial year. Costs that are incurred unevenly during an enterprise's financial year should be anticipated or deferred for interim reporting purposes if, and only if, it is also appropriate to anticipate or defer that type of cost at the end of the financial year.

But, what shall we do with costs and revenues resulting from discretionary decisions by the management? The costs can be allocated evenly over the quarters or they can be changed to a specific quarter only according if they have occurred in that specific quarter. Consider again the valuation rules of IAS 34 mentioned earlier. They don't give *that* much guidance. To overcome this issue the IASB has presented in Appendix B to IAS 34 a list of examples of how to apply the general recognition and measurement principles in relation to interim reports. The examples relate to maintenance, provisions, pensions, intangible assets, year-end bonuses, tax credits and inventories, among other things.

Explicit attention is paid in IAS 34 to the use of accounting estimates. Para. 41 stipulates that the measurement procedures to be followed in an interim financial report should be designed to ensure that the resulting information is reliable and that all material financial information that is relevant to an understanding of the financial position or performance of the enterprise is appropriately disclosed. While measurements in both annual and interim financial reports are often based on reasonable estimates, the preparation of interim financial reports generally will require a greater use of estimation methods than annual financial reports. Again an appendix is used to give more guidance. Appendix C presents *Examples of the use of estimates* (for example, contingencies, pensions, income taxes, provisions, inventories etc.).

The frequency of an enterprise's reporting – annual, half-yearly, or quarterly – should not affect the measurement of its annual results. To achieve that objective, measurements for interim reporting purposes are made on a year-to-date basis.

What does this mean?

The requirement to present information on a financial year-to-date basis and to ensure an understanding of the current interim period should be noted carefully. It logically has no effect in the context of half-yearly interim statements, but if interim statements are issued quarterly, then its implications could be significant. The financial report must satisfy the requirements of providing an understanding of the latest quarter (and its comparatives) and also an understanding of the year-to-date (and its comparatives). For example, a first-quarter report (e.g. 1.1.20X2–31.3.20X2) has to show the data for the three months and comparable figures for the first three months of the previous year (1.1.20X1–31.3.20X1). For example a third-quarter report has to show the data for the first nine months of the current year (e.g. 1.1.20X2–30.9.20X2) and comparative data for the first nine months of the previous year (1.1.20X1–30.9.20X1) and data of the last three months as well (1.7.20X2–30.9.20X2) and the same period in the previous year (1.7.20X1–30.9.20X1).

In order to help the preparers of interim financial reports an extensive appendix can be found accompanying IAS 34 in which a large number of examples is given in relation to applying the recognition and measurement principles of IAS to interim financial reports.

With regard to interim reporting the IASB takes a framework-based approach in the standard IAS 34 itself. As such, it seems that the IASB merely sees interim reporting as a frequent version of annual reporting, whereas the business community often uses the interim reports as a signalling device towards the total result of the financial period of at the end of the year.

Summary

In this chapter a set of individual Standards has been discussed and illustrated. They all had in common that their purpose is to increase the usefulness of the reported information so that external users of the annual accounts can make better decisions. We remember, however, that although the Standards have become stricter over the years, room for judgement is still left and this might threaten the value relevance of the accounting information. For example, the choice of the primary or secondary reporting format related to segmental reporting, the disclosure on non-adjusting events, the judgement about the impracticability of a restatement in relation to a change in an accounting policy or discovery of an error. However, we must admit that judgement is almost inherent to the process of financial reporting.

EXERCISES	(✔ indicates answers are available on pages 737–740)

✔ 1 Calculate from the following information:
   (a) the basic eps
   (b) the fully diluted eps.
   The capital of the company is as follows:
   ■ £500 000 in 7% preference shares of £1 each
   ■ £1 000 000 in ordinary shares of 25p each
   ■ £1 250 000 in 8% convertible unsecured loan stock carrying conversion rights into ordinary shares as follows: on 31 December 120 shares for each £100 nominal of loan stock.
   The P&L account for the year ended 31 December showed:
   (a) profit after all expenses, but before extraordinary items, loan interest and corporation tax – £1 200 000. Extraordinary items £100 000 (expense)
   (b) corporation tax is to be taken as 35% of the profits shown in the accounts after all expenses and after loan interest.

✔ 2 Extracts from the consolidated financial statements of Worldwide for the year ended 31 March 2004

INCOME STATMENT – YEAR ENDED 31 March 2004

	$'000
Revenue	665 000
Cost of sales	(312 000)
Gross profit	353 000
Distribution costs	(99 000)
Administrative expenses	(118 000)
Profit from operations	136 000
Income from investments	6 000
Finance cost	(25 000)
Profit before tax	117 000

	$'000	
Income tax expense	(28 000)	
Profit after tax	89 000	
Minority interests	(8 000)	
Net profit for the period	81 000	

BALANCE SHEET AS AT 31 March 2004

	$'000	$'000
ASSETS		
Non-current assets:		
Property, plant and equipment	340 000	
Financial assets	50 000	
		390 000
Current assets:		
Inventories	75 000	
Trade receivables	104 000	
Bank balances	24 000	
		203 000
		593 000
EQUITY AND LIABILITIES		
Capital and Reserves:		
Issued capital	150 000	
Accumulated profits	180 000	
		330 000
Non-current liabilities:		
Interest bearing borrowings	140 000	
Deferred tax	36 000	
		176 000
Current liabilities:		
Trade and other payables	70 000	
Short term borrowings	17 000	
		87 000
		593 000

Requirement:
Prepare a segment report for Worldwide for the year ended 31 March 2004 that complies with IAS14. You need not address disclosures required by IAS14 that cannot be given from the information available. (ACCA June 04)

3 As the recently qualified accountant of Aveler plc, a food retailer with balance sheet date 31 December 20X1, you notice the following items occurring before the accounts are approved by the directors:

   (a) the sale, during the period from 31 December 20X1 to the date the accounts are approved by the directors, of 1000 tins of baked beans
   (b) the purchase, during the period from 31 December 20X1 to the date the accounts are approved by the directors, of 750 tins of baked beans
   (c) the incurrence of other expenses, during the period from 31 December 20X1 to the date the accounts are approved by the directors, amounting to €125
   (d) notification that a customer who owes the company €10 000 as at 31 December 20X1 has gone into liquidation on 17 January 20X2
   (e) a fire on 4 January 20X2 destroys all the stock in one warehouse
   (f) the receipt of a letter from the company's insurers stating that it is unclear whether Aveler was actually insured for loss of stock by fire.

Which of these items are relevant to the accounts for the period ending 31 December 20X1?

4 Outline the circumstances in which post-balance sheet events affect the contents of financial statements. In what different ways are those contents affected? Give examples to illustrate your points.

5 Consider Table 23.1 again in which the segmental data from Lufthansa are included. Write up a short summary of what you learn from the segmental data on the corporate structure of Lufthansa.

6 Outline the main difficulties with the disclosure for segmental information and outline possible arguments against the disclosure of segmental information.

7 From the annual report of Interbrew we learn that their primary reporting segment is geographical. Look for annual reports of other large breweries on their websites and find out whether the segmental data they disclose are somehow comparable with the data of Interbrew and what you learn from them.

8 In preparing the financial statements for the year ended 31 December 20X5 Alpha plc discovers the following, all of which are material in the context of the company's results:

■ development expenditure that met the required criteria of IAS 38 was previously capitalized and amortized. Alpha now believes that writing off all expenditure on development work would give a fairer presentation of the results

■ a debt that was previously considered to be collectable as at 31 December 20X4 now requires writing off

■ the estimate of costs payable in respect of litigation was €250 000 as at 31 December 20X4. This has now materialized at €280 000

■ the directors of Alpha are of the view that depreciating vehicles by the reducing balance method rather than the straight line method as previously used will present a fairer view of the financial performance of the company.

How would you threat the information above in preparing the financial statements at the end of 31 December 20X5? The treatment should be in line with IAS/IFRS.

9 Discuss the advantages and disadvantages of earnings per share as a measure of corporate performance.

10 Consider the information given in Table 23.3 and explain to the holders of equity in Interbrew the usefulness of information like basic earnings per share and diluted earnings per share.

Table 23.3 Interbrew shareholder information: **Information to our Shareholders**

Earnings, dividends, share and share price	2001 IAS	2000 IAS	2000	1999	1998	1997
Adjusted net profit per share {1} {2} (euro)	1.44	1.04	1.21	0.92	0.69	0.51
Dividend per share {1} (euro)	0.29	0.21	0.21	0.18	0.15	0.12
Average number of shares (in millions)	429	335	333	323	322	322
Fully dilated number of shares (in millions)	434	343	436	332	336	338
Share price high (euro)	37.5	38.1	38.1	N/A	N/A	N/A
Share price low (euro)	25.5	34.0	34.0	N/A	N/A	N/A
Year-end share price (euro)	30.75	37.12	37.12	N/A	N/A	N/A

{1} Adjusted for stack splits
{2} Net profit (share of the group) (before extraordinary xxxx goodwill impairment) plus amortization of goodwill, divided by the number of shares outstanding

Source: Annual report, 2001, p. 118

11 Consolidated financial statements effectively aggregate the results of members of the group. Whilst this achieves the objective of showing the results of the group as if it were a single entity, it does have the disadvantage of hiding the relative performance of the different components of the entity. The international Accounting Standards Board's solution to this problem is to require disclosures relating to the different segments of the entity.

Required:

(a) (i) Discuss the objectives and usefulness of reporting segment information.

   (ii) Define a reportable segment under IAS 14 'Segment Reporting'.

   (iii) Identify the main problems of providing segment information.

(b) Portico has identified the following distinguishable business segments, together with their relative sizes:

Engineering	23%
Textiles	22%
Chemicals	20%
Travel agency	8%
House building	7%
Four others of 5% each	20%

None of the smaller segments are similar enough to be combined with other segments. The sizes above can be taken to relate to segment revenues, profits and assets.

The following additional information has been obtained:

(i) For cost control purposes, Portico's holding company is invoiced centrally and pays the utility costs (electricity and water) of each of its three reportable segments.

(ii) In its management accounts, central head office expenditure on research and development expenditure is allocated to reportable segments in relation to the relative turnover of each segment.

(iii) Certain assets, liabilities and expenses for the segments have been identified:

	Engineering $000	Textiles $000	Chemicals $000
Leased assets at cost	12 000	25 000	18 000
Annual depreciation based on life of lease	1 200	1 250	1 500
Outstanding lease liability (at year end)	7 000	15 000	8 000
Lease interest for current year	800	1 300	600

Required:

Identify the reportable segments for Portico and state how you would recommend the items in (i) to (iii) above should be treated in Portico's segment report. (ACCA June 02)

12 The IASB issued IAS 33, *Earnings per Share* in 1997 with the objective of determining the principles for the calculation and presentation of earnings per share in order to improve performance comparison. Its main focus is on the denominator of the calculation.

Required:

(a) Explain the usefulness of disclosing:

   (i) A company's basic earnings per share;

   (ii) A company's diluted earnings per share.

(b) Below are extracts from the financial statements of Bovine for the year to 31 March 2003: Income statement:

	Continuing operations $000	Discontinuing operations $000	Total $000
Profit (loss) before tax	1,580	(200)	1,380
Tax (charge) relief	(280)	50	(230)
Profit from the ordinary activities	1,300	(150)	1,150
Extraordinary item as part of continuing operations (net of tax relief of $60)			(120)
			1,030
Balance sheet:			
Ordinary shares of 25 cents each			1,800
6% Non-redeemable preference shares			500
10% Convertible preference shares $1 each			1,000
Non-current liabilities			
8% Convertible loan stock			1,500

Notes: all shares and loan stocks were in issue prior to the beginning of the current accounting year. The 10% convertible preference shares are convertible to ordinary shares on the basis of three ordinary shares for every five preference shares on 31 March 2005 at the option of the preference shareholders. The 8% convertible loan stock is redeemable on 31 March 2005 or can be converted to ordinary shares on the basis of 120 ordinary shares for each $100 of loan stock at the holder's option.

There are also in issue directors' share options for four million ordinary shares. These were issued on 31 March 2002 and are exercisable on 31 March 2005 at a price of $1.40 per share. The market price of Bovine's shares can be taken as $2.00 each.

Preference dividends are paid out of taxed profits. Interest on loan stock is an allowable tax reduction. The rate of income tax is 25%.

Required:

Calculate Bovine's basic and diluted earnings per share for the year ended 31 March 2003.

(ACCA June 03)

13 Earnit plc is a listed company. The issued share capital of the company at 1 April 1999 was as follows:
- 500 million equity shares of 50p each.
- 100 million £1 non-equity shares, redeemable at a premium on 31 March 2004. The effective finance cost of these shares for Earnit plc is 10% per annum. The carrying value of the non-equity shares in the financial statements at 31 March 1999 was £110 million.

Extracts from the consolidated profit and loss account of Earnit plc for the year ended 31 March 2000 showed:

	£ million
Turnover	250
Cost of sales	(130)
Gross profit	120
Other operating expenses	(40)
Operating profit	80
Exceptional gain	10
Interest payable	(25)
Profit before taxation	65

Taxation	(20)
Profit after taxation	45
Appropriations of profit	(26)
(see note)	
Retained profit	19

Note appropriations of profit:
■ to non-equity shareholders	11
■ to equity shareholder	15
	26

The company has a share option scheme in operation. The terms of the option are that optionholders are permitted to purchase 1 equity share for every option held at a price of £1.50 per share. At 1 April 1999, 100 million share options were in issue. On 1 October 1999, the holders of 50 million options exercised their option to purchase, and 70 million new options were issued on the same terms as the existing options. During the year ended 31 March 2000, the average market price of an equity share in Earnit plc was £2.00.

There were no changes to the number of shares or share options outstanding during the year ended 31 March 2000 other than as noted in the previous paragraph.

Requirements:

(a) Compute the basic and diluted earnings per share of Earnit plc for the year ended 31 March 2000. Comparative figures are not required.

(b) Explain to a holder of equity shares in Earnit plc the usefulness of both of the figures you have calculated in part (a). (CIMA May 00)

14 IAS 10 (revised) was issued in May 1999. It deals with the accounting treatment of events occurring after the balance sheet date.

Required:

(i) In assessing the results of a company for the current year, explain why events occurring after the balance sheet date may be of importance; and describe the circumstances where the financial statements should and should not be adjusted.

(ii) During a review of Penchant's draft financial statements (for the year ended 30 September 2003) in October 2003, the following matters came to light:

- The company's internal auditors discovered a fraud on one of the company's contracts. A senior employee had accepted an inducement of $200 000 for awarding the construction of roadways on one of the company's contracts to a particular sub-contractor. Investigations showed that the price of the sub-contracting was $1 million higher than another comparable tender offer. At 30 September 2003 the contract was approximately 50% complete.

- An earthquake occurred on 10 October 2003. It caused damage to an in progress contract that it is estimated will cost $500 000 to rectify.

- At 30 September 2003 the company's head office premises were included in the draft financial statements at a value of $12 million. A building surveyor's report showed that they had fallen in value by $2 million. This was due partly to the discovery of ground subsidence and partly to a general fall of 10% in property prices caused by a sharp unexpected rise in interest rates announced in October 2003.

- In October 2003 there was a sharp fall in the value of a foreign currency. Penchant was owed a substantial amount for the final instalment of a completed contract whose price was fixed in that currency. The estimated loss due to the fall in the exchange rate has been translated at $250,000.

Note: you may assume the above figures are material.

Required:

For each of the items above, explain how Penchant should treat them under International Financial Reporting Standards. (ACCA Dec 03)

✔ 15 Classify the events below as adjusting events or non-adjusting events according to IAS 10

  (a) shortly after the balance sheet date a survey of an item of property, plant and equipment revealed significant structural problems with the asset

  (b) a lawsuit alleging damages suffered from an accident that occurred after balance sheet date

  (c) a bankruptcy of a customer that occurs after the balance sheet date

  (d) at year end, management has the intention to decide upon the implementation of a restructuring plan. After balance sheet date but prior to the issuance date of the company's financial statements, management approves and anounces the plan.

16 Hamlet, a publicly listed company, is preparing its financial statements to 30 September 2003. In previous years it has chosen to write off all of its development expenditure even where management have been confident that the related projects would be profitable. The company is aware that development expenditure meeting the definition of an intangible asset in IAS 38 'intangible Assets' should be capitalised. In the near future Hamlet intends to prepare its financial statements under International Financial Reporting Standards and as a step towards this, the management of Hamlet are to change their accounting policy for development expenditure for the current year to comply with IAS 38. Reproduced below are details of Hamlet's development expenditure for the relevant years. For the purpose of implementing the new policy management consider four years to be an appropriate amortisation period for all development expenditure. Amortisation should commence in the year following initial capitalisation.

		$million
Amounts written off in year to 30 September:	1999	500
	2000	400
	2001	900
	2002	640
	2003	720

No development expenditure occurred in any year prior to 30 September 1999. The accumulated profit of Hamlet at 1 October 2001 was $2,500 million. You may assume that the above development expenditure meets the definition of a recognisable intangible asset in IAS 38.

Required:

(i) Describe the circumstances in which companies are permitted to change their accounting policies under International Financial Reporting Standards and discuss what constitutes a change of accounting policy

(ii) Prepare extracts of Hamlet's income statement and balance sheet for the year to 30 September 2003 together with comparative figures to reflect the change in accounting policy in respect of development expenditure; and calculate the restated accumulated profits at 1 October 2001.

Hamlet uses the benchmark treatment in IAS 8 'Net Profit or Loss for the Period, Fundamental Errors and Changes in Accounting Policies'. Ignore deferred tax.

(ACCA Dec 03)

Part Three

Consolidated Accounts and the Multinational

In this part we look in some detail at the preparation of financial statements for several enterprises which could be regarded as a group. Such statements are known as consolidated accounts and the techniques for preparing them are complicated and require detailed regulations. In addition, many of these groups consist of enterprises which operate in different countries and, therefore, different currencies, so we need rules and regulations for conversion from one currency to another. We also need to consider the accounting for the relatively simple operation of receiving or making payments in a foreign currency. The accounting for this may not be as easy as it first appears.

At the end of this part we invite you to form your own opinion as to whether the information provided by consolidated accounts and in respect of foreign enterprises and different currency transactions is helpful to users.

Consolidated financial statements

> After studying this chapter you should be able to:
> ☐ explain a business combination and the requirements of IFRS 3
> ☐ explain the entity and proprietary concept
> ☐ outline the need for consolidated financial statements
> ☐ consider the mechanics of preparing consolidated financial statements
> ☐ state the requirements of European directives in relation to consolidated financial statements
> ☐ describe the requirements of IAS 27, *Consolidated and Separate Financial Statements*
> ☐ define an associated undertaking
> ☐ describe the requirements of European directives and IAS 28, *Investments in Associates*, and IAS 31, *Interests in Joint Ventures*
> ☐ practise the preparation of consolidated financial statements involving inter-company trading, unrealized profits, pre-acquisition profits and inter-company balances
> ☐ describe the issues surrounding IAS 24, *Related Party Disclosures*.

Introduction

Most people are vaguely familiar from their daily newspapers with such words as 'takeover', 'merger', etc. but few have need to understand how such business combinations are actually structured. There are two basic possibilities:

1 A new company may be formed in order to absorb one or more existing companies. The essential feature here is that the new company would physically take over the assets and liabilities of the companies absorbed and the latter would then cease to exist.

2 A company may be taken over by another company, but in this case the company being taken over would continue to exist (and would still, of course, keep its own assets and liabilities).

It is important here to recognize that in case 2 the acquiring company obtains control over the action of the company taken over, as opposed to simply acquiring the assets of that company (case 1). In effect, with case 2 the purchasing company is acquiring an investment rather than a collection of sundry assets and the cost of this investment would itself appear in the purchasing company's balance sheet as an asset (in much the same way as individuals purchase investments (shares) in companies).

The twin elements in this transaction are an acquiring (or holding) company and a company (or companies) being acquired (subsidiaries) and these form the basis for an examination of the structure of groups of companies.

Activity 24.1

Company A, an engineering firm, owns buildings and plant and machinery with NBV of $500 000. Company B buys these assets on 1 January 200X from A at a cost of $650 000 and leases them back to A on an operating lease.

Company C, on the 1 January 200X purchases 55% of the ordinary voting shares of Company A on the open market.

Which company, B or C, has control of A?

Activity feedback

What do we mean by control? In relation to enterprises we are seeking to identify who controls, commands, regulates the use of that enterprise's resources. We are seeking to identify who controls the decision making in the enterprise.

B owns the assets A is using but in no way does B control the decisions of A's directors. Presumably, A could gain the use of assets from another company if necessary. C owns A's shares and therefore has controlling voting power over who is appointed to the board of directors and thus controls A.

Need for group accounts

If we examine the separate accounts of two enterprises, H and S, where H holds 55% of the ordinary voting shares of S then we will find the following information available to us. We will refer to H as the 'holding' enterprise, S as the 'subsidiary' and when considering both enterprises together we will regard them as a 'group'.

In H's balance sheet the shareholding (interest) in S will simply appear as an investment recorded at its cost of acquisition, historical cost. However, as with other assets in a balance sheet, the use of historical cost as the basis of valuation would not normally give the shareholders of H any indication of the value of the subsidiary or the underlying assets.

In relation to the holding enterprise's income statement the only reference to the subsidiary would be 'dividends received from S' (assuming there were any) and, of course, this would give no indication of the subsidiary's profitability.

As far as the group is concerned the holding enterprise's accounts give no meaningful information about the group's activities, hence it would be useful to find a way to prepare information about the related activities of H and S in a consolidated (combined) format.

This is where the need for group accounts arises; to provide useful information to shareholders and other users of the holding enterprise's financial statements about the group as a whole.

At this point, note that in our example of H and S, H only owned 55% of S's shares and therefore the other 45% will be held by other shareholders. We will refer to these other shareholders as the minority interest shareholders.

Seventh Council Directive of the European Communities

This Directive issued in 1983 also identified the need to prepare consolidated accounts. It requires a member state to require any undertaking governed by its national law to draw up consolidated accounts and a consolidated annual report if that undertaking has control of another by its share ownership, voting rights or ability to exercise dominant influence. The directive further requires that the consolidated accounts drawn up provide a true and fair view of the assets, liabilities, financial position and profit or loss of the undertakings included.

Several accounting alternatives have been developed to accommodate this need to report fully on the activities of group enterprises.

The parent company approach/proprietary concept

With this method of accounting the assumption is made that the group accounts are being prepared to be primarily of use by the shareholders of the controlling parent enterprise and the minority interests are credited with their share of the net tangible assets of the subsidiary. This minority shareholding can then be reflected either as a quasi-liability or by omitting it entirely from the consolidated financial statements (see proportional consolidation method, p. 520).

A simple example is given here to demonstrate the proprietary concept (parent company approach).

Big Company acquired the whole of the outstanding common shares of Little Company at a price of €1.5 per share for cash as at 30 June, at which their respective balance sheets were as follows:

	Big €	Little €
Investment in Little	75 000	
Land and buildings	100 000	25 000
Plant	40 000	20 000
Sundry other assets	20 000	15 000
	235 000	60 000
Share capital	150 000	50 000
Reserves	85 000	10 000
	235 000	60 000

As at this date, the estimated fair values of Little's assets were:

Land and buildings	30 000
Plant	22 000
Sundry other assets	15 000
Total	67 000

In Big's balance sheet, the investment in Little is shown at €1.50 × 50 000 shares, i.e. €75 000. In the group's balance sheet the subsidiary's assets would be best brought in at fair value amounting to €67 000, as this can be regarded as more useful than historic cost. We would need to account for the difference between this figure and the cost of the investment in Little of €75 000 and we refer to this difference as goodwill on consolidation (€8000). The consolidated balance sheet would look like this:

Land and buildings	130 000
Plant	62 000
Goodwill on consolidation	8 000
Sundry other assets	35 000
	235 000
Share capital	150 000
Reserves	85 000
	235 000

It should be noted in passing that goodwill might perhaps be thought of as an intangible fixed asset, but should certainly not be regarded as a current asset.

Proprietary concept consolidation with minority interest

Let's suppose Big only acquires 75% of the shares of Little at a price of €1.6 per share for cash. The fair value of Little's assets is:

Land and buildings	30 000
Plant	22 000
Sundry other assets	15 000
	67 000

and the balance sheets of the respective enterprises are:

	Big €	Little €
Investment in Little	60 000	
Land and buildings	100 000	25 000
Plant	40 000	20 000
Sundry other assets	20 000	15 000
	220 000	60 000
Share capital	150 000	50 000
Reserves	70 000	10 000
	220 000	60 000

The goodwill calculation is:	
Paid for investment	60 000
Acquired 75% of fair value	
Of net assets (67 000)	50 250
	9 750

On consolidation we need to remember to bring in 75% of the assets of Little at fair value, i.e. the group share, but to only incorporate the minority interest share, 25%, at net book value. This is because the proprietary concept is only concerned with the fair value in relation to the holding (parent) enterprise share not that of the minority interest.

The consolidated balance sheet is then:

	Calculation	€
Goodwill	See previous calculations	9 750
Land and buildings	$100\,000 + 25\% \times 25\,000 + 75\% \times 30\,000$	128 750

Plant	$40\,000 + 255 \times 20\,000 + 75\% \times 22\,000$	61 500
Sundry assets	$20\,000 + 15\,000$ (NBV = FV)	35 000
		235 000
Share capital	Big only	150 000
Reserves	Big only	70 000
Minority interest	$25\% \times 60\,000$	15 000
		235 000

Goodwill (premium) on acquisition

From previous chapters you should by now be aware of the inadequacies of historic cost as a measure of asset value. It will be realized that the net book value (NBV) of an asset (or collection of assets) in the balance sheet of a company will not necessarily bear any relationship to the market value of these assets or of that company.

Obviously, when one company acquires shares in another company, then the price it is willing to pay for these shares will be computed by reference to the underlying value of the assets of the company to be acquired and not of their book value as shown in the balance sheet. One would normally expect the assets of the company being acquired to be revalued on the basis of the fair value of those assets for consolidation purposes. Further, since one company is acquiring control of another company (i.e. as opposed to simply buying a small (minority) shareholding), then the price to be paid for that controlling interest is very often a price in excess of the total of the fair value of the net assets of the subsidiary. Fair value is the price at which an asset would be purchased in an arm's length transaction.

For accounting purposes this excess is termed goodwill or premium on acquisition. Obviously this 'difference' referred to earlier needs to be accounted for (if only to ensure that double entry is maintained) and it is usual for the total of such premium (goodwill) on acquisition of all group subsidiaries to be shown as an asset in the group balance sheet.

IAS GAAP, under IFRS 3, *Business Combinations*, requires that after initial recognition this business combination goodwill should be measured at cost less any accumulated impairment losses. Thus this goodwill *is not* amortized but tested for impairment. This impairment test is carried out in accordance with IAS 36, *Impairment of Assets*. Previously IAS GAAP did permit amortization of business combination goodwill. Whether this change will result in a more robust view of goodwill on the balance sheet will depend on the robustness of the impairment reviews. The IASB states that goodwill arising from an acquisition represents a payment made by the acquirer in anticipation of future economic benefits which may result from synergy between the identifiable assets acquired or from assets which, individually, do not qualify, for recognition in the financial statements but for which the acquirer is prepared to make a payment in the acquisition.

The rationale for carrying goodwill on the balance sheet of the combined business at its impaired cost as opposed to amortizing that goodwill through the profit or loss account is outlined in the IASB's *Basis for Conclusions* to IFRS3. The Board initially considered three possible treatments for goodwill arising on a business combination:

(a) straight line amortization but with an impairment test whenever there was an indication that the goodwill might be impaired

(b) non-amortization but with an impairment test annually or more frequently if events or changes in circumstances indicated that the goodwill was impaired

(c) permitting entities a choice between (a) and (b).

Point (c) was soon discounted in the deliberations as permitting such choices impairs the usefulness to users, as both comparability and reliability are diminished. However, many respondents to ED3 supported method (a) as the acquired goodwill can be considered to be consumed over time and replaced with internal goodwill. The respondents felt that straight line amortization over an arbitrary period, given that the pattern of use and useful life of goodwill is difficult to predict, with impairment tests was a reasonable balance between conceptual soundness and operationality. In other words, (a) was the pragmatic solution. However, the Board was not impressed with pragmatism, being doubtful of the benefits of amortizing acquired goodwill but not recognizing internal goodwill. They felt that the amortization was unhelpful as unlike a tangible fixed asset, goodwill does not have a finite physical utility life. Thus the Board decided that (b) was the way forward; as long as a rigorous and operational impairment test could be devised (see IAS 36, Chapter 13) then more useful information would be provided to users by the use of (b). The proof of this decision will be tested in the future. Whatever method we use to account for acquired or inherent goodwill in the financial statements has a very large impact on the net assets and profit or loss recorded for the year. If users are not aware of this fact the decisions they make from using the information given could be flawed.

Discount on acquisition can also occur. This relates to the possibility of one company acquiring control of another at a discounted price (i.e. as opposed to at a premium).

In practice, this is not so far fetched as it might at first sight appear, in that an acquiring company may for various reasons (e.g. empire building) be quite willing to purchase a company with a recent history of trading losses, together with a forecast future of losses. This discount on the purchase price (i.e. the surplus of the fair value of tangible assets acquired over purchase consideration) at the date of acquisition may be thus thought of as compensation for anticipated future losses to the acquiring group. (One might also reasonably assume that in the medium term future the group would hope to turn this subsidiary into profitability.) Alternatively, this discount may arise because the asset values agreed on acquisition may not be deemed to be fair values by the acquiring company and may be revalued downwards on consolidation.

It must be emphasized at this stage that the calculation of the goodwill or discount on acquisition should be made after a fair valuation has been made of the net assets acquired. In practice, in many cases no revaluation occurs and it is then assumed that the book value reflects the fair value, as is the case with some of the illustrations used later in this chapter. Note also that for purposes of computation of goodwill or discount on acquisition we usually take the fair value of net assets as being equal to the proportion of the subsidiary's share capital plus reserves as at date of acquisition. The discount on acquisition is generally referred to as negative goodwill.

If negative goodwill is identified then IFRS 3 requires the acquirer to reassess the calculation and to then recognize the negative goodwill that still exists in profit or loss.

(See Chapter 13 for goodwill in more detail.)

The entity concept

This concept views the group as a unit and makes no distinction between shareholders. The difference between the proprietary and entity concept only occurs where there is less than 100% purchase of the shares of an enterprise.

Illustration

A buys 80% of B for cash $2200 when net assets have a fair value of $2000 and net book value was $1500. A's balance sheet as at the date of acquisition was:

	$	
Net assets	5 000	(including the investment in B)
Share capital	4 000	
Reserves	1 000	
	5 000	

Calculation of goodwill

	Proprietary	Entity
Purchase consideration	2 200	2 200
80% of fair value of net assets	1 600	1 600
Goodwill	600	600
(attributable on majority shareholding)		
Implicit total goodwill in B (600 represents 80% of goodwill of B)		750

Consolidated financial statements

	Proprietary	Entity
Net assets	4 700 ^{w1}	4 800 ^{w2}
Goodwill	600	750
	5 300	5 550
Share capital	4 000	4 000
Reserves	1 000	1 000
Minority interest	300	550 ^{w3}
	5 300	5 550

Working 1

Net assets are A [5000 − 2200 investment in B]	2 800
Plus 80% of fair value (FV) of B's assets	1 600
Plus minority share of net book value (NBV) of B's assets	300
	4 700

Working 2

The net assets under the entity concept reflect the full revaluation of B, i.e. 80% of B is valued at $2200 thus the full valuation is $2750 − of this $750 is goodwill.

Working 3

If the full valuation of B is $2750 then the minority interest of 20% is $550.

Activity 24.2

Comment on the asset figure of $4700 shown under the proprietary method.

Activity feedback

This figure consists of a mix of fair values (1600) for 80% of B's assets and net book values (300) for 20% of B's assets. The net assets of A (2800) could be at fair value at date of acquisition or net book value depending on the accounting policies adopted by A.

The proprietary method, because of this anomaly, has been adapted into a further two methods.

Proprietary concept – parent company extension

This method adopts a fair value method to value the full net assets excluding goodwill of the group but does not include the full valuation of goodwill, only the group share.

Activity 24.3

Show the consolidated financial statement for A group using the parent company extension method to the proprietary concept.

Activity feedback

Net assets [2800 + 2000]	4 800
Goodwill [80% of the full value of goodwill]	600
	5 400
Share capital	4 000
Reserves	1 000
Minority interest	400
(20% of net assets FV 2000)	5 400

Proprietary concept – proportional consolidation

This method completely excludes the minority interest from the consolidated financial statement which is in accord with the proprietary concept of providing information primarily for the majority shareholders.

Activity 24.4

Show the consolidated financial statements for A group using proportional consolidation.

Activity feedback

Net assets [2800 A + 80% of B's at FV]	4 400
Goodwill	600
	5 000

Share capital	4 000
Reserves	1 000
	5 000

Proportional consolidation also has another disadvantage. When one company acquires control of another company (even though as in this case it does not acquire the whole of *B*'s equity share capital), then *A* can determine the future action of *B* and can dictate the way in which *B* should utilize all (i.e. 100%) of its assets. This is the reality of the relationship between *A* and *B* (i.e. control) and it is quite different from the impression given in our balance sheet above, which implies that the group controls only 80% of *B*'s various assets. Neither, of course, does this method give any indication of the existence of an external (minority) interest in *B*.

Comparison of all four methods of consolidation

Activity 24.5

Compare and contrast the information provided in the balance sheet using all four methods of consolidation.

Activity feedback

This can best be seen by drawing up Table 24.1, containing information from the previous Activities 24.2–24.4.

This shows that the consistent figures throughout the four methods are only those of share capital and reserves of the holding company. The net assets change depending on how much of the fair value of the net assets each method considers attributable to the group. The proportional method excludes all reference to the portion of assets owned by the minority asset whereas the entity and extension method assume that the group might not own all of the subsidiary's assets but it certainly controls them. The proprietary method only incorporates the net book value of the portion of assets owned by the minority, it disregards the fair value of this portion. The goodwill only changes under the entity method where we include what could be regarded as the minority goodwill. The minority interest is shown at either 25% of NBV of net assets excluding goodwill (proprietary) or 25% of all net assets at fair value including goodwill (entity) or

Table 24.1 Information on balance sheets gleaned from Activities 24.2–24.4

	Proprietary	Entity	Proprietary extension	Proportional
Net assets	4 700	4 800	4 800	4 400
Goodwill	600	750	600	600
	5 300	5 550	5 400	5 000
Share capital	4 000	4 000	4 000	4 000
Reserves	1 000	1 000	1 000	1 000
Minority interest	300	550	400	N/A
	5 300	5 550	5 400	5 000

25% of fair value of net assets excluding goodwill (extension). The proportional method of course makes no reference to a minority interest.

This plethora of methods requires us to decide which method we should use to reflect the consolidation of subsidiaries.

IFRS 3 regulation for consolidation of subsidiaries and concept used

IFRS 3 does not permit the use of the entity concept or proportional consolidation for the consolidating subsidiary enterprise but does allow the proprietary concept method.

The acquiree's identifiable assets and liabilities recognized should be measured at their fair values as at the date of acquisition. Any goodwill or negative goodwill should be accounted for in accordance with IFRS 3 paras 51–57. Any minority interest should be stated at the minority's proportion of the fair values of the identifiable acquiree's assets and liabilities recognized.

> Under this approach, the net identifiable assets over which the acquirer has obtained control are stated at their fair value, regardless of whether the acquirer has acquired all or only some of the capital of the enterprise or has acquired the assets directly.
>
> Consequently, any minority interest is stated at the minority's proportion of the fair values of the net identifiable assets of the subsidiary.

Equity accounting

This particular method is only appropriate when there is no 'control'. One type of 'control', majority voting power, we looked at in Activity 24.1. We will look at other types of control later in this chapter. Equity accounting is not a method to be used where we have a subsidiary company situation, but could be used where one enterprise has a significant interest in another, and in this connection the words 'associated company' rather than 'subsidiary company' are appropriate. A fuller discussion of the equity accounting method and its use for dealing with associated companies is given later in this chapter, together with a consideration of IAS 28 and 31.

Parent company approach – extension method revisited

The parent company approach used in the UK became known as acquisition accounting and the following activity allows you to practise this method again as it is the method identified in IFRS 3. It is generally referred to as the purchase method.

Activity 24.6

Large Company acquired 75% of the share capital of Small Company at a price of €3.50 per share for cash as at 30 September, at which date their respective balance sheets were:

	Large Co	Small Co
	€	€
Land and buildings	210 000	43 000
Investment in Small	115 500	–
Plant and equipment	75 000	22 000
Net current assets	63 500	18 000
	464 000	83 000
€2 shares	246 000	66 000
Reserves	218 000	17 000
	464 000	83 000

The estimated fair values at 30 September of Small assets were:

Land and buildings	49 000
Plant and equipment	19 000
Net current assets	18 000
	86 000

Prepare the consolidated balance sheet of Large as at 30 September using the parent company extension method of IFRS 3.

Activity feedback

Goodwill calculation

	€
Purchase consolidation	115 000
Purchased 75% of fair value	64 500
	51 000

Consolidation balance sheet for Large Group

	€
Land and buildings [210 000 + 49 000]	259 000
Plant and equipment [75 000 + 19 000]	94 000
Goodwill	51 000
Net current assets [63 500 + 18 000]	81 500
	485 500
Share capital	246 000
Reserves	218 000
	464 000
Minority interest [25% × 86 000]	21 500
	485 500

Note again that under this treatment all the assets except goodwill are consolidated at 100% of fair value; goodwill included is only that in relation to the majority shareholding; the minority interest is only valued at its share of fair value of net assets excluding goodwill.

From our discussion so far we can highlight several issues that need dealing with/defining/clarifying in relation to consolidated financial statements:

- definition of control
- investments that do not lead to control but perhaps should be reflected in consolidated financial statements
- the need to define fair value
- the need to define detailed regulation in relation to the preparation of consolidated financial statements.

Control and subsidiaries

IFRS 3 defines a 'business combination as the bringing together of separate entities or businesses into one reporting entity. The result of nearly all business combinations is that one entity, the acquirer, obtains control of one or more other businesses, the acquiree [para. 4].

Control is the power to govern the financial and operating policies of an entity or business so as to obtain benefits from its activities. A parent is an entity that has one or more subsidiaries. A subsidiary is an entity controlled by another entity.

Note in these definitions that the word 'entity' is used, not 'company', so a subsidiary could be a partnership or unincorporated body as well as a company as long as the enterprise is controlled by another. 'Control is presumed to be obtained when one of the combining enterprises acquires more than one half of the voting rights of the other combining enterprise unless it can be demonstrated that such ownership does not constitute control'. Even when ownership is not 50% or more of the voting shares control could still be exercised by the holding (parent) enterprise.

Activity 24.7

Identify in each of the following circumstances whether B is a subsidiary of A, i.e. A exercises control over B.

1 A owns 40% of the voting rights of B and has an agreement with a shareholder who holds a further 15% of the voting rights that enables him to vote for these shares as well.
2 A owns 42% of the voting rights of B but also has an agreement to govern the financial and operating policies of B.
3 A owns 48% of voting rights of B.
4 A owns 35% of the voting rights of B and also has the power to appoint or remove five of the nine members of the board of directors.
5 A owns 33% of the voting rights of B and 100% of the voting rights of C which in turn holds 20% of the voting rights of C.

Activity feedback

The examples are derived from IFRS 3, para. 19, which states control is:

- power over more than half of the voting rights of the other enterprise by virtue of an agreement with other investors;
- power to govern the financial and operating policies of the other enterprise under a statute or an agreement
- power to appoint or remove the majority of the members of the board of directors or equivalent governing body of the other enterprise; or
- power to cast the majority of votes at meetings of the board of directors or equivalent governing body of the other enterprise.

In cases **1**, **2** and **4** *A* clearly controls the decisions of *B* and therefore *B* is a subsidiary of *A*. These are all examples of the IAS use of de facto control.

Case **3** is not an example of a parent–subsidiary relationship.

Case **5** is an example of a subsidiary relationship and Figure 24.1 should show this more clearly.

A controls *C* and therefore also 20% of *B* which together with its own 33% holding gives it control over 53% of *B*. This is an example of a mixed group.

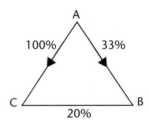

Figure 24.1 A subsidiary relationship

Further mixed groups

Activity 24.8

In the examples given identify the parent subsidiary relationships:

1 *H* owns 75% of the voting shares of *S* which in turn owns 40% of the voting shares of *S1*. *H* also owns directly 15% of the voting shares of *S1*.
2 *H* owns 100% of the voting shares of *S*, which in turn owns 30% of *S1*. *H* also owns 75% of *S2* which in turn owns 25% of *S1*.
3 *H* owns 60% of the voting shares of *S* which in turn owns 20% of the voting shares of *S1*. *H* also owns directly 20% of the voting shares of *S1*.

Activity feedback

1

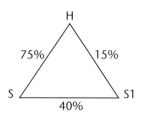

- *S* is a subsidiary of *H* (75% ownership), *S1* is not a subsidiary of *S* (assuming no information in respect of dominant influence).
- *H* directly owns $75\% \times 40\%$ of $S1 + 15\%$ of $S1$:

  $= 30\% + 15\%$
  $= 45\%$ which would imply no subsidiary relationship.

- However, *H* controls *S* thus controls 40% of *S1* plus 15%.
- Therefore, *S1* is a subsidiary of *H* and will be consolidated with a minority interest of 55%.

2

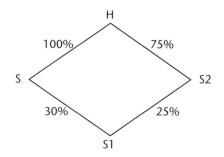

- *S* and *S2* are subsidiaries of *H*.
- *H* directly owns $100\% \times 30\% + 75\% \times 25\%$ of $S1$:

  $= 30\% + 18.75\%$
  $= 48.75\%$ only.

- However, *H* controls $30\% + 25\% = 55\%$.
- Thus, *S1* is a subsidiary of *H* and will be consolidated with a minority interest of 51.25%.

3

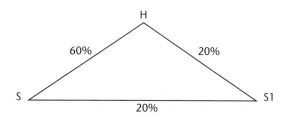

- *S* is a subsidiary of *H*.
- *H* owns 60% × 20% + 20% of *S1* = 32% of *S1*.
- *H* controls 20% + 20% of *S1* = 40%.
- Thus, *S1* is not a subsidiary of *H* (assuming no indication of dominant influence) and will not be consolidated.

Accounting for business combinations

IFRS 3, as we have seen, requires business combinations to be accounted for using the purchase method. This method necessarily requires us to identify the acquirer and the acquiree in any business combination. The acquirer is, in short, the one that obtains control as defined at p. 524. This acquirer is not always easy to identify but the standard tells us that we have to identify one and that usually there are indications available to us. For example:

- If the fair value of one of the combining entities is significantly greater than that of the other combining entity, the entity with the greater fair value is likely to be the acquirer.
- If the business combination is effected through an exchange of voting ordinary equity instruments for cash or other assets, the entity giving up the cash or other assets is likely to be the acquirer.
- If the business combination results in the management of one of the combining entities being able to dominate the selection of the management team of the resulting combined entity, the entity whose management is able so to dominate is likely to be the acquirer.

Note the use of the word likely in the examples.

This requirement to always identify an acquirer and acquiree and subsequently to prepare financial statements using the purchase method has now banned the use of merger/pooling of interests method. The merger method was previously used under IAS 22 (which was withdrawn on the issue of IFRS3), to account for business combinations known as 'uniting of interests'.

The purchase method requires the acquirer, from the date of acquisition to incorporate into the income statement the results of operations of the acquiree and to recognize in the balance sheet the identifiable assets and liabilities of the acquiree and any goodwill or negative goodwill arising on the acquisition.

The date of acquisition is defined as the date on which the acquirer obtains control of the acquiree.

Applying the purchase method involves three steps:

1 identifying an acquirer (see page 525)
2 measuring the cost of the business combination
3 allocating, at the acquisition date, the cost of the business combination to the assets acquired and liabilities and contingent liabilities assumed.

Measuring the cost

IFRS 3 states that the acquirer should measure the cost of a business combination as the aggregate of:

(a) the fair values, at the date of exchange, of assets given, liabilities incurred or assumed, and equity instruments issued by the acquirer, in exchange for control of the acquiree

(b) plus any costs directly attributable to the business combination.

The items listed under (a) have to be measured at fair value and therefore if any settlement for the combination is deferred, the fair value of the deferred component is discounted to the present value at the date of exchange. As regards the liabilities in item (b) future losses or other costs incurred as a result of the combination must not be regarded as liabilities and therefore are not included in the cost of the combination. However, in contrast, any costs directly attributable to the combination such as professional fees, legal advisors, valuers and other consultants to effect the combination are regarded as part of the cost of the combination. In addition to these costs business combinations are sometimes agreed that include an adjustment to the costs dependent on future events. For example, an adjustment to the cost might be dependent on a given level of profits being achieved in future years. If this adjustment can be measured reliably and is probable then the cost of the combination should be adjusted at the outset.

Allocating the cost to the assets, liabilities and contingent liabilities

IFRS 3 requires us to allocate the cost of the combination by recognizing the assets, liabilities and contingent liabilities at their fair values. The difference between the cost and the fair value is recognized as goodwill, which is subsequently, measured at cost less any accumulated impairment losses. By recognizing the assets, liabilities and contingent liabilities of the acquiree at total fair value then the minority interest in the acquiree is of necessity stated at their proportion of the net fair value of those items. It is also important to note that the acquirer can only recognize intangible assets of the acquiree if these meet the definitions in IAS 38 at the acquisition date.

The following illustrates the consolidation process where a minority interest is involved in accordance with IFRS 3.

Illustration

Alpha plc bought 75% of the shares of Beta Ltd for cash at the price of €4.00 per share when the balance sheets of the two companies were as follows:

	€ Alpha	€ Beta
Net current assets	75 000	12 000
Fixed assets (before investment in Beta)	400 000	75 000
	475 000	87 000
Share capital	350 000	60 000

Reserves	125 000	27 000
	475 000	87 000

The nominal value of Alpha and Beta shares is respectively €2 and €2.50 and the fair value of Beta's fixed assets at acquisition is €83 000 and the net current assets €12 000.

The first point to note in this example is that Alpha has not yet recorded the purchase of 75% of Beta in its books. This must be done prior to consolidation and thus Alpha's balance sheet will become:

	€ Alpha
Net current assets	3 000
Fixed assets (before investment in Beta)	400 000
Investments in Beta (18 000 shares at €4 per share)	72 000
	475 000
Share capital	350 000
Reserves	125 000
	475 000

We can now calculate goodwill on acquisition (or cost of control):

Cost of Alpha's control of Beta is		72 000
For which Alpha bought		
75% of share capital of Beta	45 000	
75% of reserves of €27 000	20 250	
75% of revaluation to FV	6 000	71 250
Goodwill on acquisition		750

At this point it is worth calculating the minority interest holding at date of acquisition. The minority interest is obviously 25% of the shares and reserves of Beta but also includes 25% of the revaluation created in recording Beta's assets at fair value. Thus minority interest is:

25% share of capital of Beta	15 000
25% of reserves at acquisition	6 750
25% of fair value reserve	2 000
Minority interest at date of acquisition	23 750

The consolidated balance sheet can now be prepared as follows:

Goodwill on acquisition	750
Fixed assets	483 000
Net current assets	15 000
	498 750
€2 share capital	350 000
Reserves	125 000
	475 000
Minority interest	23 750
	498 750

Note that the minority interest is recorded as a one line entry on the consolidated balance sheet.

Acquisition accounting later than date of acquisition

Activity 24.10

1 *H* Ltd purchased 80% of the equity share capital of *S* Ltd for cash at 31 December year 1 at a price of €1.50 per share, when the balance on *S* Ltd's reserves stood at €2000.

2 The consolidation is required to be made at 31 December year 2, at which point the individual balance sheets of the two companies are as follows:

	€ H Ltd	€ S Ltd
Sundry current assets	35 000	6 000
Investment in *S* Ltd	9 600	–
Plant and machinery	60 000	5 000
	104 600	11 000
Represented by		
Shares of €1	40 000	8 000
Reserves	64 600	3 000
	104 600	11 000

Activity feedback

The consolidated balance sheet as at 31 December year 2 would then be as follows:

	€
Sundry current assets	41 000
Plant and machinery	65 000
Goodwill on acquisition (note 1)	1 600
	107 600
Represented by	
Shares of €1	40 000
Group reserves (note 2)	65 400
	105 400
Minority interests (note 3)	2 200
	107 600

Notes

	€	€
1 Cost of investment in *S* Ltd		9 600
Acquired ordinary shares at 31 December year 1		
(80% × 8000)	6 400	
Acquired reserves at 31 December	1 600	
(being 80% of balance of £2000 on reserves of *S* Ltd at		
31 December)		8 000
Goodwill on acquisition		1 600

2 Reserves of *H* Ltd at 31 December year 2 .... 64 600
   Reserves of *S* Ltd accruing to groups since date of acquisition
     to 31 December year 2 (3000 − 2000) × 80% 800
                         65 400

3 Share capital as 31 December year 2 of *S* Ltd accruing to
   minorities (20% × 8000) 1 600
   Reserves at 31 December year 2 of *S* Ltd accruing to
   minorities (20% × 3000) 600
                         2 200

Inter-company trading and the elimination of unrealized profits

When one member of a group, *S*, buys from an external supplier at a price (say) of €100, and sells those goods to a fellow group company, *S1*, at a price of €140, then *S* can legitimately show a profit of €40 in its own income statement. However, on consolidation of the accounts of *S* and *S1* it should be recognized that this sale from *S* to *S1* cannot give rise to a profit as far as the group income statement is concerned as the sale is in effect an internal group transfer. In order for the group to realize a profit on sale, the sale must be made to a customer outside the group. This is shown diagrammatically in Figure 24.2 (the arrows represent sales either within or outside the group as indicated. R = realized group sales; UR = unrealized group sales).

Note, again, that although internal group sales reflect unrealized profit as far as the group is concerned, there is nonetheless a realized profit to be had from such transactions as far as the income statement of individual companies within the group is concerned.

Referring to the previous example if the individual accounts of *S* and *S1* are combined for consolidation purposes without further adjustment, then the group

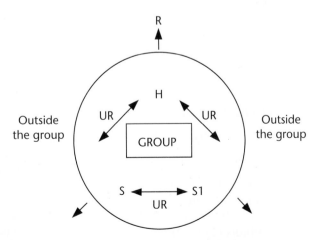

Figure 24.2 Inter-company trading and elimination of unrealized profits

profit will show €40 and group stock will stand at €140. In other words, group profit will be overstated by €40 and also the stock of the group will be stated at €40 in excess of cost to the group (as opposed to S).

IAS 27, para. 24 on the subject of inter-group transaction has this to say:

> Intra-group balances, transactions, income and expenses should be eliminated in full.

Activity 24.11

A enterprise owns 75% of the shares in B enterprise bought when the reserves of B were €200 000. The individual balance sheets of A and B as at 30 June 200X are given below. During the year B has sold goods to A at a profit margin of 25% on cost. €50 000 of these goods lie in A's closing stock as at 30 June 200X. Also B owes C an outside supplier €2000 and C owes A €5000 as at 30 June 200X.

	A €000s	B €000s
Assets		
Land and plant	1 000	200
Stock	600	400
Debtors	200	40
Investment in B	275	–
	2 075	640
Liabilities		
Creditors	30	16
	2 045	624
Represented by		
Shares of €1	1 000	100
Reserves	1 045	524
	2 045	624

Prepare the consolidated balance sheet as at 30 June 200X.

Activity feedback

Consolidated balance sheet as at 30 June 200X:

	€000s
Assets	
Goodwill (note 1)	50
Land and plant	1 200
Stock (1000 – 10)	990
Debtors (240 – 2)	238
	2 478

Liabilities

Creditors (46 − 2)		44
		2 434

Represented by:

Shares of euro		1 000
Reserves		1 280.5
		2 280.5
Minority interest (note 3)		153.5
		2 434

Note 1

Cost of investment in B		275
Less ordinary shares acquired	75	
Reserves acquired 75% × 200	150	225
		50

Note 2

Reserves A	1 045
Reserves post-acquired B	
75% (524 − 10 − 200)	235.5
	1 280.5

Note 3

Minority interest	25
25% ordinary shares	128.5
25% reserves = 25% × 514	153.5

Reconciliation of inter-company balances

It is commonplace for companies within a group to shuffle liquidity and stocks between themselves as and when required and indeed this is one of the advantages of a group structure. Obviously with reference to such transactions, the indebtedness to/from member companies will need to be recorded in the individual companies' books of account as appropriate. Hence, each company will carry balances within the group. In relation to the group's position as regards the outside world, these balances are internal balances and will, therefore, not require to be shown in the group balance sheet. They are, in fact, cancelled on consolidation across the individual balance sheets of group members. Occasionally, however, it is not possible to cancel out such inter-company balances, and this may often be due to transfer of goods or cash between group companies straddling the financial year end. A consolidation adjustment is required at the year end to adjust for goods or cash in transit between two companies before we can carry out the consolidation of accounts. The adjustment assumes that we account for the transit item as though it had reached its destination. It is important to note that these adjustments we are making here only affect the consolidated accounts; we make no adjustment for these inter-company balances to the individual accounts of each enterprise.

Activity 24.12

The financial year end of two companies A and B within the same group is 31 December. On 29 December A despatched goods to B to invoice value of €40 000 and charges B's ledger account accordingly. *B* does not receive either goods or invoice until 4 January. Prepare the consolidation adjustment on *B*'s books and note any other adjustment that may be required on consolidation.

Activity feedback

The adjustment will bring the goods into *B*'s books as at 31 December.

B ledger books	Dr	Cr
Goods in transit	€40 000	
A current account		€40 000

On consolidation the respective inter-company balances in the current accounts which are now in agreement will cancel out.

However, we must remember that this stock of €40 000 in transit will contain an element of unrealized profit and this will need eliminating on consolidation.

Consistency of reporting dates and accounting policies within the group

Generally, the financial statement of a parent and its subsidiaries will be drawn up to the same date to enable easy preparation of consolidated financial statements. However, sometimes it is impracticable to do this and consolidation can take place using the accounts prepared to different dates provided the difference is no greater than three months. IAS 27 paras 26 and 27 explain the process.

On the issue of consistency of accounting policies IAS 27, para. 28 states the following:

> Consolidated financial statements should be prepared using uniform accounting policies for the transactions and other events in similar circumstances.

Acquisition by stages

Sometimes one enterprise will acquire shareholdings in another in stages. For example, *A* may acquire 25% of the voting shares of *B* at 1.4. X1, a further 20% six months later and a further 30% 12 months later. In this example, it is only at the third stage that a subsidiary/parent relationship exists. The difficulty with staged acquisitions is in determining the date when a subsidiary relationship exists, what the cost was and what the fair value of the assets and liabilities acquired was.

The date of an acquisition by stages is fairly straightforward. This remains at the date when control is transferred. In our example, this is the third stage and therefore consolidation would take place as from that date. Prior to this date the investment would be recorded as a trade investment, associate (see p. 548 and IAS 28) or joint venture (see p. 553 and IAS 31).

> When an acquisition involves more than one exchange transaction the costs of the acquisition is the aggregate cost of the individual transactions. When an acquisition is achieved in stages, the distinction between the date of

acquisition and the date of the exchange transaction is important. While accounting for the acquisition commences as from the date of acquisition, it uses cost and fair value information determined as at the date of each exchange transaction.

When an acquisition is achieved by successive purchases, the fair values of the identifiable assets and liabilities may vary at the date of each exchange transaction. If all the identifiable assets and liabilities relating to an acquisition are restated to fair values at the time of successive purchases, any adjustment relating to the previously held interest of the acquirer is a revaluation and is accounted for as such.

The following activity should help to clarify this.

Activity 24.13

H acquired an interest in *S* as follows:

- 10% of the voting shares for $150 000 on 1.4.01
- 30% of the shares for $450 000 on 1.4.02
- 40% of the voting shares for $800 000 on 1.4.03
- the remaining 20% for $350 000 on 31.3.05.

The fair values of the recognized assets and liabilities of *S* at these dates were $1m, $1.5m, $1.75m and $2m respectively. Accounts are drawn up as at 31 March. Identify at what date *S* becomes a subsidiary of *H* and the goodwill to be shown in the consolidated financial statements after the final acquisition.

Activity feedback

S becomes a subsidiary of *H* at the third purchase, 1.4.03, when 80% is then controlled.

Goodwill will be recognized at the third stage but calculated by reference to each exchange transaction.

	$
FV at first stage	1 000 000
Acquired 10%	100 000
Cost	150 000
Goodwill Stage 1	50 000
FV at second stage	1 500 000
Acquired 30%	450 000
Cost	460 000
Goodwill stage 2	10 000
FV at third stage	1 750 000
Acquired 40%	700 000
Cost	800 000
Goodwill stage 3	100 000
Total goodwill after third purchase	160 000

FV at fourth stage	2 000 000
Acquired 20%	400 000
Cost	250 000
Negative goodwill stage 4	50 000

The goodwill on acquisition to be shown in the consolidated financial statements as at 31 March 2005 will be 160 000. The negative goodwill of 50 000 will be taken to profit and loss account in accordance with the IFRS 3 treatment of negative goodwill. The fair value of the assets acquired in Activity 24.13 would be as follows:

Stage	FV
1	100 000
2	450 000
3	700 000
4	400 000
	1 650 000

Now the problem is that H is adding $1.65m of net assets to its own on consolidation but the fair value of these assets is actually $2m. This is resolved by revaluing the assets separately to the consolidation exercise to the stepped up fair value (para. 59 of IFRS 3).

Thus, the consolidated accounts would incorporate the net assets at $2m and show a revaluation reserve of $350 000. The goodwill on consolidation would only be adjusted in this revaluation exercise if there was an indication of impairment.

Reverse acquisitions

Normally in an acquisition the acquirer, who issues shares to the acquiree shareholders to gain control, still retains control of the combined enterprises.

Illustration

Enterprise *A* with a share capital of €100 shares issues a further 50 shares to acquire the complete shareholding of enterprise *B* consisting of 200 €1 shares, a one *A* share for four *B* shares exchange. In this case *A* now owns all *B* shares, 200, and *A's* shareholders hold 100 *A* shares. *B* shareholders hold 50 *A* shares. Thus *A* shareholders retain control of *A*. If, however, *A* had issued 200 *A* shares to acquire the 200 *B* shares then *B* shareholders would now hold two-thirds of the shareholding of *A* and in 'substance' the acquiree, *B*, becomes the acquirer.

When an enterprise obtains ownership of the shares of another enterprise but as part of the exchange transaction issues enough voting shares as consideration such that control of the combined enterprises passes to the owners of the enterprise whose shares have been acquired. This situation is described as a reverse acquisition. Although legally the enterprise issuing the shares may be regarded as the parent or continuing enterprise, the enterprise whose shareholders now *control* the combined enterprise is the acquirer. The enterprise issuing the shares is deemed to have been acquired by the other enterprise; the latter enterprise is deemed to be the acquirer and applies the purchase method to the assets and liabilities of the enterprise issuing the shares.

Adjustments to purchase consideration

IFRS 3, paras 32–35 cover this issue. Acquisition agreements often provide for adjustment to the cost of an acquisition dependent on future events. These future events can be:

- the results of acquiree's operations exceeding or falling short of an agreed level
- the market price of securities issued as part of the purchase consideration being made.

IFRS 3 requires that a reasonable estimate of the purchase consideration in the circumstances just described is made at the point of acquisition based on the adjustment being probable and measurement of the adjustment being reliable.

If the cost of the acquisition is subsequently resolved at a different amount than envisaged then this is accounted for by an adjustment to goodwill. This is the case except in the following circumstances:

> In some circumstance, the acquirer may be required to make subsequent payment to the seller as compensation for a reduction in the value of the purchase consideration. This is the case when the acquirer has guaranteed the market price of securities or debt issued as consideration and has to make a further issue of securities or debt for the purpose of restoring the originally determined cost of acquisition. In such cases, there is no increase in the cost of acquisition and, consequently, no adjustment to goodwill or negative goodwill. Instead, the increase in securities or debt issued represents a reduction in the premium or an increase in the discount on the initial issue (para. 35).

Activity 24.14

Company A acquires all the issued share capital of company B when the fair value of B's net assets was €1m. The cost of the acquisition was €1.5 but included a proviso that unless earnings of B remained at 10% above the previous year the consideration would be reduced by €0.1m for each percentage point below that required. In addition, A guaranteed the market price of the securities issued to B's shareholders on the acquisition for six months. The acquisition date was 1 October 2001 and consolidated financial statements were drawn up as at 31 December 2001.

In the year ended 31 December 2002 it was noted that B's earnings were 8% in excess of the previous year and that the market price of the securities had fallen by €0.2m.

Identify the goodwill on acquisition and adjustments necessary in the consolidated financial statements 31 December 2002. Assume goodwill has not been impaired.

Activity feedback

	€m
Purchase consideration	1.5
Fair value of net assets	1.0
Goodwill	0.5

Subsequent events change the purchase consideration to €1.3m and thus goodwill to €0.3m.

Cost of acquisition will be shown in *A*'s individual books as €1.3m and the goodwill in the consolidated financial statements at 31.12.02 as €0.3m

The fall in the market price of the securities will be dealt with by a further issue of securities by *A* to *B*. The increase in securities will reduce the premium or increase the discount on the initial issue; it will not affect the purchase consideration.

Adjustments to identifiable assets or liabilities

These can occur because:

- the acquirer was unaware of certain assets or liabilities of the acquiree
- the assets or liabilities did not satisfy recognition criteria
- or further information comes to light which enables more accurate estimation of fair values.

How these adjustments are dealt with depends on whether they occur before or after the first complete annual accounting period subsequent to acquisition:

- Before and the adjustment is reflected in goodwill providing the amount will be recovered from expected future economic benefits, otherwise it would be recognized as an expense.
- After and the adjustment is reflected in income or expense *not* goodwill.

Disposal of part-interest

When a group disposes of part of an interest in a subsidiary undertaking a profit or loss on disposal will obviously arise but how do we calculate this? According to IAS 39 it should record any profit or loss arising calculated as the difference between the carrying amount of the net assets of that subsidiary undertaking attributable to the group's interest before the reduction and the carrying amount attributable to the groups interest after the reduction together with any proceeds received.

Activity 24.15

The value of a subsidiary's net assets at 31 March 200X is €400,000. At this date the parent, which held a 100% share in the subsidiary, disposes of 40% for €200 000. On the original acquisition of the subsidiary, goodwill of €80 000 arose. This goodwill has not subsequently been impaired and is in addition to the net assets of €400 000. Calculate the profit or loss on disposal.

Activity feedback

	€
Group share of net assets before disposal including goodwill	
(100% × (400 000 + 80 000))	480 000
Group share of net assets after disposal including goodwill	
(60% × (400 000 + 80 000))	288 000
Disposal proceeds	200 000
	488 000
Profit on disposal	8 000

If, for example the goodwill had been impaired to €60 000, then the impairment loss would have been recognized in previous profit and loss accounts. The profit on disposal, assuming no change in the proceeds, would then have been calculated as follows:

Group share of net assets before disposal including value of	
goodwill remaining (100% × 460 000)	460 000
Group share of net assets after disposal including goodwill	
(60% × 460 000)	276 000
Disposal proceeds	200 000
	476 000
Profit on disposal	16 000

The profit increases in this case by the €8 000 (40% of €20 000) which has previously been debited to profit and loss account.

We can usefully refresh our memory of group accounts and work through a full example at this point.

Activity 24.16

The balance sheets of Alexander and Britton on 30 June 20X1 were as follows:

	Alexander		Britton	
	€000s	€000s	€000s	€000s
Fixed assets				
Land and buildings	108		64	
less Depreciation	20	88	32	32
Plant and machinery	65		43	
less Depreciation	25	40	29	14
		128		46
Investments				
Shares in Britton		35		
Current assets				
Stock	25		27	
Debtors	48		21	
Bank	22		6	
	95		54	

Creditors <1 year				
Creditors	112	(17)	34	20
		146		66
Represented by				
Ordinary €1 share		100		50
Capital reserves		10		
Revenue reserves		36		16
		146		66

1 Alexander acquired 37 500 shares in Britton several years ago when there had been a debit balance on the revenue reserve of €3000.
2 During the year ended 30 June 20X1 Alexander purchased a machine from Britton for €5000 which had yielded a profit on selling price of 30% to that company. Depreciation on the machine had been charged in the accounts at 20% on cost.
3 Britton purchases goods from Alexander providing Alexander with a gross profit on invoice price of $33\frac{1}{3}$%. On 30 June 20X1 the stock of Britton included an amount of €8000 being goods purchased from Alexander for €9000.

Required:
Prepare the consolidated balance sheet of Alexander and its subsidiary as at 30 June 20X1.

Activity feedback

	€000	€000
Cost of control		35
Shares of net assets 75% (50 − 3)		35.25
Negative goodwill		0.25
Inter-group transfer of machine – unrealized profit		1 500
Excess depreciation charged 20% × 1 500		300
Britton's accounts unrealized profit		1 200
Inter-group stock transfer – unrealized profit		
$33\frac{1}{3}$% × €9 000		3 000
		1 000
Reduction in value		2 000

Consolidated balance sheet as at 30 June 20X1

Fixed assets		
Land and buildings		120
Plant and machinery		52.8
		172.8
Current assets		
Stock	50	
Debtors	69	
Bank	28	
	147	
Creditors <1 year		
Creditors	146	1
		173.8

Represented by	
Ordinary €1 shares	100
Capital reserves	10
Revenue reserves	47.6
	157.6
Minority interest (25% (66 − 1.2))	16.2
	173.8

Note 1		
Reserves of Alexander	36	
Unrealized profit on stock	(2)	
Post-acquisition profits of Britton:		
75% (16 (30.6.X1) + 3 (debit balance at acq. date) −		
1.2 (unrealized profit on sale of machine))	13.35	
Negative goodwill	0.25	
	47.6	

Consolidated income statement

It is worthwhile at this point considering the preparation of a consolidated income statement for a group. The principles of preparation are the same as those for the balance sheet. Thus the aspect of control over profits is highly important. A simple example demonstrates the preparation of a consolidated income statement.

Illustration

The individual income statements of High and Low as at 31 December 200X are as follows:

	High	Low
	€	€
Turnover	100 000	50 000
Cost of sales	75 000	30 000
Gross profit	25 000	20 000
Distribution expenses	4 000	3 000
Administration expenses	7 000	8 000
	14 000	9 000
Investment income:		
Dividends received	2 250	
	16 250	
Taxation	7 000	3 000
Earnings	9 250	6 000
Retained earnings	22 000	4 000
	31 250	10 000

The share capital of Low consists of 100 000 €1 shares of which High bought 75 000 on 1 January 200X for €90 000. The fair value of Low's assets at date of acquisition equated to net book values and the only reserves existing when High bought in were retained profits. During the year High sold goods to Low for €12 000 which included a profit of €2000. As at 31.12.0X half of these goods still remain in Low's stocks. The dividends paid and proposed by Low are all paid out of current profits.

First, we need to identify the goodwill on acquisition:

	€	€
Cost of High's control of Low		90 000
Bought 75% of Low's shares	75 000	
Bought 75% of Low's retained profits	3 000	78 000
Goodwill		12 000

Next, we need to sort inter-company trading:

		€
Reduce High's sales by		12 000
Reduce High's profits by		1 000
Reduce Low's stock by		1 000

Consolidated income statement for the year ended 31.12.0X

		€
Turnover (150 000 − 12 000)		138 000
Cost of sales (105 000 − 12 000 + 1 000)		94 000
		44 000
Distribution expenses	7 000	
Administration expenses	15 000	22 000
		22 000
Taxation		10 000
Consolidated earnings on ordinary activities after tax		12 000
less Minority interest (25% × 6 000 − Low's profit after tax)		1 500
Consolidated earnings for the financial year		10 500
Retained earnings		22 000
		32 500

Note that all allocation of profit to minority interest for the year takes place after calculating consolidated earnings after tax and that the inter-company transactions in relation to Low's dividends paid to High is eliminated.

Acquisition part-way through a year

When the acquisition of a subsidiary occurs part–way through the year then a proportion of that year's profits of the subsidiary will be regarded as pre-acquisition. When preparing the consolidated profit and loss account for the year of acquisition it is appropriate to bring in only the post-acquisition amount at each line of consolidation (i.e. turnover, cost of sales etc.) on a time basis.

Preparation of consolidated accounts involving more than one subsidiary

These are relatively straightforward if you remember the rules already explained. We include an activity here of a consolidation involving several companies to test your understanding and application of the techniques of consolidation.

Activity 24.17

A plc acquired 5m €1 shares of B Ltd five years ago when the reserves of B stood at £6m. B Ltd acquired 2.25m €1 shares in C Ltd four years ago when the accumulated reserves of C were €½m. A plc also acquired 3m €1 share of D Ltd 2 years ago when D's reserves were €0.3m. At the date of acquisition the net book value of all assets equated to fair value. There has been no issue of shares in any of these companies throughout the five-year period. The balance sheets relate to the group companies as at 31.12.200X.

	A €m	B €m	C €m	D €m
Fixed assets	45	5	1.5	2
Investment in B	16	–	–	–
Investment in C	–	4.5	–	–
Investment in D	4	–	–	–
Net current assets	32	18	2.5	1
	97	27.5	4	3
Share capital	18	7.5	3	4
Reserves	79	20	1	(1)
	97	27.5	4	3

Prepare the consolidated balance sheet of A group as at 31.12.200X.

Activity feedback

B and D are subsidiaries of A with controlling interests of 66.6% and 75% respectively. C is a subsidiary of B at an ownership of 75% but as B is a subsidiary of A then C is also a subsidiary of A at a controlling interest of 50%. Figure 24.3 aids understanding here.

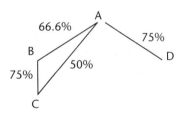

Figure 24.3 Subsidiaries and controlling interest

The goodwill calculations at acquisition are:

	B €m	C €m	D €m	Total €m
Cost of control	16	4.5	4	
Shares bought	5	2.25	3	
Reserves bought	4	0.375	0.225	
	9	2.625	3.225	
Goodwill	7	1.875	0.775	
Group share	7	1.25	0.775	9.025
Minority calculations:				
Total net assets	23	4	3	
MI% share	33.3	50	25	
MI	7.67	2	0.75	10.42

Consolidated balance sheet as at 31 December 200X

	€m
Goodwill	9.025
Fixed assets	53.5
Net current assets	53.5
	116.025
Share capital	18
Reserves	
$[79 + (20 - 6)2/3 + (1 - 0.5)1/2 + (-1 - 0.3)3/4]$	87.605
Minority interest	10.42
	116.025

Uniting of interests

Prior to the issue of IFRS 3, which requires that in any business combination an acquirer is identified, IAS 22 identified a 'uniting of interests' business combination. IAS 22 defined this as follows:

> A uniting of interests is a business combination in which the shareholders of the combining enterprises combine control over the whole, or effectively the whole, of their assets and operations to achieve a continuing mutual sharing in the risks and benefits attaching to the combined entity such that neither party can be identified as an acquirer.

Many respondents to the Board on this issue believe such uniting of interests still occur, even if only rarely, and that it will be impossible in such cases to identify an acquirer as required by IFRS 3. It was also previously the case that such uniting of interests was accounted for using the pooling of interests/merger method of accounting. IFRS 3 has now eliminated the use of merger accounting because:

- it has virtually eliminated the idea of uniting of interests
- in no circumstances, according to the Board, does the pooling of interests method provide superior information to that provided by the purchase method.

The *Basis for Conclusions* to IFRS 3 does conclude that if true mergers exist, which it doubts, then a better accounting method to use for them could be the 'fresh start method'. This method requires *both* companies in the business combination to value all assets at fair value.

Another reason why the Board eliminated merger accounting was harmonization as US GAAP prohibits it and UK GAAP is likely to follow the IASB treatment.

Differences between acquisition accounting and merger accounting

The main differences between the two methods can be examined under the headings of:

1 goodwill
2 share premium (paid-in surplus)
3 pre-acquisition profits.

Goodwill

With a merger, there is no change in ownership and we merely have a pooling of resources, a consolidated balance sheet produced for a merger situation will simply combine the existing balance sheets and the assets will therefore remain at the book values at which they appear in the original balance sheets of the separate enterprises, that is to say no goodwill is recognized in the new balance sheet (since none is in fact acquired).

However, with acquisition accounting the net assets of the enterprise acquired will usually be revalued as at the date of acquisition and, of course, the difference between the purchase consideration and this asset revaluation will give rise to goodwill (premium) on acquisition.

Share premium

With an acquisition where an enterprise issues shares to acquire another enterprise the cost of the investment is recorded in the acquirer's balance sheet and, of course, any shares issued in consideration are recorded at market value, i.e. nominal value plus share premium created. However, with a merger situation, shares issued in the share-for-share exchange involved are recorded at nominal value, i.e. no share premium is created.

Pre-acquisition profits

For acquisition accounting purposes and in accordance with the concept of capital maintenance, the distributable profits of any acquired enterprise are frozen, i.e. are not legally regarded as available for distribution by the group.

By the same token, with merger accounting and in keeping with the spirit of a pooling of resources, the reserves of each participant company are merely pooled, i.e. those that were distributable before the merger remain distributable after the merger.

It is obvious when one considers these differences why merger accounting was popular. Following from this, it can be seen that with merger accounting the balance sheet of the new enterprise does not carry a goodwill figure that might have to be reduced against income. Neither is there a non-distributable share premium account arising in the merged balance sheet and also the distributable reserves of the group are enlarged as opposed to the situation which would have prevailed under the acquisition accounting method.

It is appropriate here to consider an example of the application of merger accounting and also to contrast it with acquisition accounting.

Activity 24.18

Two companies, *A* and *M* have the following respective balance sheets as at 30 June 200X:

	A	M
	$	$
Common shares ($1)	9 000	6 000
Earned surplus	2 000	3 000
	11 000	9 000

Represented by		
Net current assets	5 000	2 000
Plant and machinery	6 000	7 000
	11 000	9 000

A acquired the whole of the share capital of M on the basis of a one-for-one share exchange as at the given date, at which point the market values of their respective shares were:

A	$4
M	$4

The fair values of *M*'s tangible assets as at 30 June 200X were:

	$
Plant and machinery	8 000
Net current assets	2 500

Prepare the consolidated balance sheet for *A* using both purchase and pooling methods.

Activity feedback

Consolidated balance sheet as at 30 June 200X

	Purchase		Pooling
Common shares ($1)	15 000	(note 1)	15 000
Share premium (paid-in surplus)	18 000	(note 2)	–
Earned surplus	2 000	(note 3)	5 000
	35 000		20 000
Represented by:			
Net current assets	7 500	(note 4)	7 000
Plant and machinery	14 000	(note 4)	13 000
Goodwill on acquisition	13 500	(note 4)	–
	35 000		20 000

Notes

1 Based on a one-for-one exchange, *A* will need to issue a further 6000 $1 shares (i.e. 9000 + 6000 = 15 000).
2 Issued at a price of $4 per share the share premium on the issue of *A* shares for acquisition accounting purposes will be $3 per share (i.e. 6000 × €3 = €18 000).
3 For acquisition accounting purposes (but not for merger accounting) the reserves of M of €3000 as at the date of acquisition will be frozen.
4 Cost of investment (i.e. 6000 shares at $4 each) 24 000
   less Fair value of net assets acquired (i.e. $8000 + 2500) (10 500)
   13 500

Despite the simplicity of this example the differences are amply illustrated:

1 Under acquisition accounting a non-distributable share premium account arises.

2 Under merger accounting the reserves of M at the date of acquisition are regarded as distributable by the group.

3 For acquisition accounting the assets of M are recorded at fair values, whereas for merger accounting purposes book values prevail.

Disclosure requirements

IFRS 3 requires such disclosure that 'enable users of financial statements to evaluate the nature and financial effect of business combinations' (para. 66). Disclosure is required as follows:

- names and descriptions of combining entities
- acquisition date
- percentage of voting equity instruments acquired
- cost of the combination and the components of the cost
- details of operations disposed of due to the combination
- details of fair values and carrying values of assets, liabilities and contingent liabilities acquired
- amount of any negative goodwill
- amount of acquiree's profit or loss since the acquisition date included in the acquirer's profit or loss.

Information is also required on any adjustments in the current period of the business combination and any changes to the carrying amount of goodwill.

An example of such disclosure is taken from the accounts for the year ended 31 December 2000 of Charles Vögele Group (p. 51)

Composition of goodwill	Depreciation period	Cost	Depreciation 2000	Accumulated depreciation	Book values
Acquisition of store locations in Switzerland 1995	5 years	9 500	(1 900)	(9 000)	500
Initial consolidation in connection with LBO 1997	20 years	76 632	(3 832)	(11 495)	65 137
Purchase of the minority interest in Charles Vögele (Austria) AG in 1998	20 years	33 012	(1 650)	(3 301)	29 711
Acquisition of store locations in the Netherlands 1999	20 years	4 663	(239)	(425)	4 238
Acquisition MacFash Group 2000	20 years	24 575	(5 029)	(4 915)	19 660
Balance 31.12.2000		148 382	(12 650)	(29 136)	119 246

Comments on acquisition of the MacFash Beteiligungsgesellschaft mbH as at 1 January 2000:

Purchase price	27 763
Cash	(3 045)
Other receivables	(15 409)
Inventories	(477)
Deferred tax assets	(1 915)

Bank overdraft	1 729
Trade payables	5 574
Accruals	1 395
Current tax liabilities	17
Provisions	9 512
Goodwill at the time of acquisition	25 144
Effect of exchange rates	(569)
Goodwill as at December 2000	24 575

The value of the goodwill represents the takeover of a profitable location already introduced in the market. In 2000, these 40 acquired stores contributed net sales of CHF 83.5 million. The goodwill was determined in local currency (DEM) at the time of acquisition and reported at 31 December 2000 in CHF using the year end exchange rate. The purchase price was deposited in a fiduciary account in 1999 until the final conclusion of the transaction. Through the acquisition, the group at 1 Janaury 2000 received cash and cash equivalents amounting to net CHF 1.3 million.

Special purpose enterprises

These are entities that have been created to accomplish a narrow and well-defined objective. For example, such a special purpose enterprise (SPE) could be set up to carry out a specific research project. The SPEs are generally set up under tight legal arrangements and the sponsor may transfer assets and liabilities to it. Within such arrangements we need to determine whether the sponsor has control over the SPE, as if he has, then it must be consolidated in accordance with IAS 27. SIC 12, *Consolidation – Special Purpose Enterprises*, requires that: 'An SPE should be consolidated when the substance of the relationship between an enterprise and SPE indicates that the SPE is controlled by that enterprise.' The SIC identified the following as indicating control:

- the activities of the SPE are being conducted on behalf of the enterprise according to its specific business needs so that the enterprise obtains benefits from the SPE's operation
- the enterprise has the decision-making powers to obtain the majority of the benefits of the activities of the SPE or, by setting up an 'autopilot' mechanism, the enterprise has delegated these decision-making powers
- the enterprise has rights to obtain the majority of the benefits of the SPE and therefore may be exposed to risks incident to the activities of the SPE
- or the enterprise retains the majority of the residual or ownership risks related to the SPE or its assets in order to obtain benefits from its activities.

Equity accounting and associates

Introduction

We identified equity accounting as a method available to report on the activities of groups of enterprises at p. 522.

Illustration

On 31 December 200X *A* enterprise acquired 1200 common shares in *B* enterprise (4000 common shares) at a cost of €3 per share. *B*'s net assets at 31.12.20X1 had a book value of €5600 and no *B* shares have been issued for several years.

The balance sheets of *A* and *B* as at 31.12.20X2 are as follows:

	A	B
	€	€
Net current assets	2 000	3 600
Property, plant and equipment	30 000	6 400
Investment in B	3 600	–
	35 600	10 000
Common shares €1	16 000	4 000
Reserves	19 600	6 000
	35 600	10 000

A is required to issue consolidated financial statements and decides to apply equity accounting to its investment in *B*.

First, we need to identify the goodwill, if any, in the investment as we did for acquisition accounting.

	€
Cost of investment	3 600
Purchased 30% of B's net assets	1 680 (or 30% of shares 4 000 = 1 200
Goodwill	1 920 + 30% of reserves 1 600 = 480
	note reserves are €6000 so earnings
	since purchase are €4400

Consolidated balance sheet of *A* enterprise 31.12.02 using equity accounting for *B*

	€
Net current assets	2 000
Property, plant and equipment	30 000
Investment in B	
3600 + 30% × earnings since purchase 4400	4 920
	36 920
Common shares €1	16 000
Reserves (19 600 + 1 320 share of B since	
purchase)	20 920
	36 920

Activity 24.19

Using the illustration define equity method of accounting.

Activity feedback

Equity method of accounting records the investment at its initial cost adjusted for post acquisition change in investor's net assets of the investee (IAS 28, para. 2).

In Activity 24.19 we assumed book value equated to fair value. Unrealized profits on inter-enterprise transactions would be eliminated as they are in acquisition accounting.

Goodwill in equity accounting

In Activity 24.19 we identified goodwill but then appeared to do nothing with it. In accordance with IAS 28 this goodwill, if positive, is included in the carrying amount of the investment. (Under the previous version of IAS 28 the goodwill was amortized but, remember, amortization of goodwill is no longer permitted under IASs.) The goodwill, unlike that in the case of a subsidiary, is not identified separately or subject to a separate impairment test. The investment in its entirety is tested for impairment. To do this test, in accordance with IAS 36, the recoverable amount of the investment, which is the higher of value in use and fair value less costs to sell, is compared with its carrying amount whenever there is an indication of impairment as prescribed by IAS 39. If the goodwill on the purchase of the associate is negative then this is excluded from the carrying amount of the investment and is included as income in the determination of the investor's share of the associate's profit or loss in the period in which the investment is acquired.

Illustration

If the cost of the investment in Activity 24.19 is €1500 and the reserves of the parent €17 500 then the identified goodwill would be as follows:

	€
Cost of investment	1 500
Purchased 30% of net assets	1 680
Negative goodwill	(180)

The balance sheet would be as follows:

	€	€
Net current assets		2 000
Property, plant and equipment		30 000
Investment in B – cost	1 500	
– share of earnings since purchase	1 320	
– exclusion of goodwill	180	3 000
		35 000
Capital shares		16 000
Reserves	17 500	
Reserves since purchase	1 320	
Negative goodwill	180	19 000
		35 000

Use of equity method

The equity method in consolidated financial statements provides the user of the statements with much more information than recording the investment at cost and accounting for any distributions from the investee. The user is able to see his share of the results of the investment and calculate more useful ratios. The issue in respect of equity accounting is what type of investment it should be applied to. General consensus around the world is that it should be applied to those investments in which the investor has significant influence defined as: 'The power to participate in the financial and operating policy decisions of the investee but not control over those policies' (IAS 28, para. 2).

This type of investee is known as an *associate*, defined by IAS 28 as: 'An enterprise in which the investor has significant influence and which is neither a subsidiary nor a joint venture of the investor.'

Significant influence is amplified in IAS 28 as a situation where the investor holds, directly or indirectly through subsidiaries, 20% or more of the voting power of the investee and that if such a situation exists significant influence will be presumed unless it can be clearly evidenced otherwise and vice versa. Significant influence is usually evidenced by:

- representation on the board of directors or equivalent governing body of the investee
- participation in policy making processes
- material transactions between the investor and the investee
- interchange of managerial personnel
- provision of essential technical information.

Exemptions from the use of equity method

'An investment in an associate shall be accounted for using the equity method except when:

(a) the investment is classified as held for sale in accordance with IFRS 5 *Non-current Assets held for Sale and Discontinued Operations*;

(b) the exception in paragraph 10 of IAS 27, allowing a parent that also has an investment in an associate not to present consolidated financial statements, applies; or

(c) all of the following apply:

(i) the investor is a wholly-owned subsidiary, or is a partially-owned subsidiary of another entity and its other owners, including those not otherwise entitled to vote, have been informed about, and do not object to, the investor not applying the equity method;

(ii) the investor's debt or equity instruments are not traded in a public market (a domestic or foreign stock exchange or an over-the-counter market, including local and regional markets);

(iii) the investor did not file, nor is it in the process of filing, its financial statements with a securities commission or other regulatory organisation, for the purpose of issuing any class of instruments in a public market; and

(iv) the ultimate or an intermediate parent of the investor produces consolidated financial statements available for public use that comply with International Financial Reporting Standards.'

(IAS 28, para. 13)

Associate enterprises and losses

In the illustration on p. 541 if the reserves of B at 31.12.20X2 had stood at €14 000 debit then careful consideration would need to be given to how the loss was shown in the consolidated financial statements. If equity accounting was strictly applied the consolidated balance sheet would be:

	€
Net current assets	2 000
Property, plant and equipment	30 000
Investment in B	
3600 + 30% (15 600)	(1 080)
	30 920
Common shares €1	16 000
Reserves (19 600 − 4 680)	14 920
	30 920

This would imply that A has an obligation to transfer economic benefits of €1272 to the associate but this may not be the case.

IAS 28, para. 29 states:

If an investor's share of losses of an associate equals or exceeds its interest in the associate, the investor discontinues recognizing its share of further losses. The interest in an associate is the carrying amount of the investment in the associate under the equity method together with any long-term interests that, in substance, form part of the investor's net investment in the associate. For example, an item for which settlement is neither planned nor likely to occur in the foreseeable future is, in substance, an extension of the equity's investment in that associate. Such items may include preference shares and long-term receivables or loans but do not include trade receivables, trade payables or any long-term receivables for which adequate collateral exists, such as secured loans. Losses recognized under the equity method in excess of the investor's investment in ordinary shares are applied to the other components of the investor's interest in an associate in the reverse order of their seniority (i.e. prior to liquidation).

Thus, the consolidated balance sheet of A should be shown as follows if there is no obligation:

	€
Net current assets	2 000
Property, plant and equipment	30 000
Investments in B	−
	32 000
Common shares €1	16 000
Reserves [19 600 − 3 600]	16 000
	32 000

Alternatively, if there is an indication that the value of an investment may be impaired then IAS 36, *Impairment of Assets*, must be applied. The issue of impairment is dealth with in paras 33 and 34 of IAS 28. The associate must then be recorded at its value in use determined by estimating the enterprise's share of the present value of the estimated future cash flows expected to be generated by the investee as a whole, including the cash flows from the operations of the investee and the proceeds on the ultimate disposal of investment or the present value of the estimated future cash flows expected to arise from dividends to be received from the investment and from its ultimate disposal.

Both methods generally give the same result.

Disclosure requirements for associates

These are identified in paras 37 to 40 of IAS 28.

Joint ventures

So far we have defined investment in another enterprise as either a subsidiary relationship, a uniting of interests, an associate relationship, or a simple trade investment.

There is one other type of investment we need to consider and that is a joint venture: 'A joint venture is a contractual arrangement whereby two or more parties undertake an economic activity which is subject to joint control' (IAS 31, para. 3). 'Joint control is the contractual agreed sharing of control over an economic activity' and exists only when the strategic financial and operating decisions relating to the activity require the unanimous consent of the parties sharing control (the venturers) (IAS 31, para. 3).

IAS 31 was issued in 1990, reformatted in 1994 and revised to be comparable with IAS 36, *Impairment of Assets* in July 1998. The area of joint ventures is one where we find major differences between IAS, UK and US GAAPs.

A joint venture is dependent on a contractual arrangement, usually in writing. This contract will cover several issues such as duration of the activity, reporting obligations, appointment of the governing body of the venture, capital contributions by each party (venturer) and the sharing of income, expenses or results. The contract will establish joint control by all ventures involved and will ensure that no one venture can control the activity. Quite often though one venturer may be appointed as the operator or manager of the venture but he will still have to act within the financial and operating policies agreed by all the venturers. If this is not the case and one venturer can act unilaterally then the venture is not a 'joint venture' but probably a subsidiary of one venturer (IAS 31, paras 10, 11 and 12).

Activity 24.20

Serp Company, a building firm, is involved in the following arrangements with other building entities:

- An interest in a project Castle Residential with Locking Company and Crawford Company. The project involves the renovation of the castle building to provide resident accommodation. The participants have equal shares in the project and are to share profits equally. Invoices are sent to Cork Company, which has contracted with the venturers for the work by each of the participants for their work done.

- A 30% interest in Alpha company to the board of which Serp appoints two directors.
- A 70% interest in Beta company.
- An equal interest with *X* company in Gamma. The consent of Serp and *X* is required to all decisions on financial and operating policies of Gamma essential to activities, economic performance and financial position.
- A 15% interest in Wimp plc.
- A 22% interest in Alpine plc which is seen as a short-term investment.
- An interest in Delta Company. Serp, Delta and Condo are to share equally in the income, expenses and results of Delta and they have each contributed the same capital. Condo has the power to vary the financial and operating policies of Delta as it sees fit.

Identify what type, in accordance with IAS GAAP, each of these arrangements is, as far as SERP is concerned.

Activity feedback

Castle Residential is a joint venture as the venturers have joint control.
Alpha is an associate as we can presume significant influence from two directors.
Beta is a subsidiary if we assume 70% interest implies 70% voting rights.
Gamma is a joint venture as it is jointly controlled by Serp and *X*.
Delta is actually a subsidiary of Condo, not of Serp, and thus Serp will only account for the results of Condo as a trade investment.
Wimp and Alpine are trade investments as the former investment does not demonstrate any significant influence and the latter is for a short term.

GAAP comparisons

US GAAP does not specifically define joint ventures. UK GAAP is similar to IAS but requires that the joint venture is a separate entity. In Activity 24.19 the Castle Residential project would not be regarded as a joint venture as it is not a separate entity. UK GAAP would define this venture as a joint arrangement.

Forms of joint venture

A joint venture can take many different forms both legally and in substance but IAS 31 categorizes them into three areas:

- jointly controlled operations
- jointly controlled assets
- jointly controlled entities.

Jointly controlled operations are ventures where the assets and resources of the individual ventures are used. If a joint venture was established by three venturers to construct a spacecraft with one manufacturing the shell and furbishing the interior, the second the engines and the third the computer hardware and software, and each carried out the work alongside its normal activities using its own employees and incurring its own expenses and liabilities then this would be regarded as a jointly controlled operation. This presumes, of course, that the venture met the requirements to be defined a joint venture.

Joint controlled assets occur when venturers jointly own and control specific assets for the purpose of a joint venture. For example, if two venturers acquired a refurbished castle and rented out rooms in the castle, each venturer receiving rents and bearing expenses, then this would be regarded as a joint venture with jointly controlled assets. Many examples of this type of joint venture occur in oil, gas and mineral extraction industries. For example, three venturers could purchase a mine where each extracts a distinct mineral, each bearing their own costs of extraction and receiving sale revenues for their particular mineral.

Jointly controlled entities are examples of joint ventures where a distinct entity is formed in which each venturer has an interest. IAS 31 gives the following example:

> (*Para. 26*) A common example of a jointly controlled entity is when two enterprises combine their activities in a particular line of business by transferring the relevant assets and liabilities into a jointly controlled entity. Another example arises when an enterprise commences a business in a foreign country in conjunction with the government or other agency in that country, by establishing a separate entity which is jointly controlled by the enterprise and the government or agency.

> (*Para. 27*) Many jointly controlled entities are similar in substance to those joint ventures referred to as jointly controlled operations or jointly controlled assets. For example, the venturers may transfer a jointly controlled asset, such as an oil pipeline, into a jointly controlled entity, for tax or other reasons. Similarly, the venturers may contribute into jointly controlled entity assets, which will be operated jointly. Some jointly controlled operations also involve the establishment of a jointly controlled entity to deal with particular aspects of the activity, for example, the design, the marketing, distribution or after-sales service of the product.

Activity 24.21

Identify what form of joint venture Castle Residential and Gamma is (Activity 24.20) in accordance with IAS 31.

Activity feedback

Castle Residential is a jointly controlled operation.
Gamma is a jointly controlled entity.

GAAP comparison

UK GAAP – a jointly controlled operation and jointly controlled assets would not be a joint venture. As we will see later, though, the accounting for these ventures will be the same under IAS and UK GAAP. A jointly controlled entity would be regarded as a joint venture under UK GAAP but the accounting is different under UK and IAS GAAP.

US GAAP only refers to jointly controlled entities and again the accounting is different for the two GAAPs.

Accounting for joint ventures

Jointly controlled operations will be accounted for in the venturer's own financial statements already as in this operation the venturer is using its own assets and liabilities and incurring its own income and expenses. There may need to be some adjustments to the venturer's statements for inter-venture transactions.

Separate financial statements for the joint venture are not required by law (as it is not a legal entity) but generally they are prepared for management purposes.

Jointly controlled assets are again already recorded in the venturer's financial statements so no further entries are required in the consolidated financial statements except to eliminate inter-venture transactions.

The accounting for a jointly controlled entity is by necessity different to the other two forms of joint venture as legally the entity must maintain its own accounting records and prepare financial statements. The venturer will have made contributions to the joint venture in terms of cash or other assets and these will be recorded in the venturer's individual statements as their investment in the jointly controlled entity.

However, this record of investment does not show the substance and economic reality of the joint venture to the user of the consolidated financial statements. In essence, without some different accounting method being used, the consolidated financial statements will not reflect the venturer's share of future economic benefits.

IAS 31 requires either proportional consolidation (the benchmark treatment/ preferred method) or the equity method (allowed alternative treatment) to be used for jointly controlled entities. Both of these methods have been discussed already.

Under the proportional consolidation method it is permitted either to combine the venturer's share of assets, liabilities, income and expenses in the joint venture with its own or to show the share of joint venture items as individual items at each line on the balance sheet and income statement. The latter method is preferred by some, as it does not sum whole and part items.

The equity method is as used for associates and is supported by those whose belief that joint control is similar to significant influence. The IAS does not support this view but does, however, permit the alternative treatment. Equity method is not recommended by the Board because it believes 'proportionate consolidation better reflects the substance and economic reality of a venturer's interest in a jointly controlled entity, that is to say, control over the venturer's share of the future economic benefits' (para. 40). Note that if an enterprise had two investments, one in an associate and the other in a joint venture defined as a jointly controlled entity then in the consolidated financial statements of the venturer there would be no difference in the accounting for either investment if the alternative treatment was used for the joint entity.

GAAP comparison

UK GAAP does not permit the use of proportional consolidation but agrees with the IAS that equity accounting is not appropriate for joint ventures. UK GAAP uses gross equity accounting for joint ventures. US GAAP uses equity accounting, as it does not permit proportional consolidation.

Activity 24.22

X company acquired 600 €1 common shares in Y company at a price of €1.50 per share on 31 December 20X1 at which point the income statement of Y had a credit balance of €800. The respective balance sheets of X and Y as at 31 December 20X2 are summarized here:

	X	Y
	€	€
Net current assets	1 000	1 800
Property plant and equipment	15 000	3 200
Investment in Y	900	–
	16 900	5 000
Common shares €1	8 000	2 000
Reserves	8 900	3 000
	16 900	5 000

X is required to prepare consolidated financial statements as it has several subsidiaries for the year ended 31 December 20X2. You are required to draft the initial consolidated balance sheet of the group as at December 20X2 before the inclusion of the subsidiaries but after the inclusion of Y assuming, first, that the investment in Y is an associate and, second, a jointly controlled entity. Amortize goodwill over a life of ten years.

Activity feedback

Y as an associate or as a jointly controlled entity using the alternative accounting treatment as permitted by IAS 31

	€	€
Net current assets	1 000	
Property, plant and equipment	15 000	
Investment in Y (see note 1)	1 560	
	17 560	
Common shares € 1	8 000	
Reserves (see note 2)	9 560	
	17 560	

Note 1: Goodwill calculation

Cost of investment	900
Assets acquired 30% × 2800	840
Goodwill	60

Note 2: Reserve calculation

X reserves	8 900
30% of Y post-acquisition (2200)	660
	9 560

Share of net assets 30% × 5000 + goodwill 60 = 1 560

Y as a joint controlled entity using proportional consolidation as preferred by IAS 31 (summed method).

Net current assets [1000 + 30% × 1800]	1 540
Property plant and equipment [15 000 + 30% × 3200]	15 960
Goodwill in joint venture [60]	60
	17 560
Common shares €1	8 000
Reserves (see note 2)	9 560
	17 560

Y as a jointly controlled entity using proportional consolidation as preferred by IAS 31 (individual line method).

Net current assets	1 000	
Net current assets joint venture	540	
		1 540
Property, plant and equipment	15 000	
Joint venture	960	15 960
Goodwill of consolidation of JV		60
		17 560

Transactions between a venturer and a joint venture

IAS 31, para. 48

When a venturer contributes or sells assets to a joint venture, recognition of any proportion of a gain or loss from the transaction should reflect the substance of the transaction. While the assets are retained by the joint venture and provided the venturer has transferred the significant risks and rewards of ownership, the venturer should recognize only that portion of the gain or loss which is attributable to the interests of the other venturers. The venturer should recognize the full amount of any loss when the contribution or sale provides evidence of a reduction in the net realizable value of current assets or impairment loss.

IAS 31, para. 49

When a venturer purchases assets from a joint venture, the venturer should not recognize its share of the profits of the joint venture from the transaction until it resells the assets to an independent party. A venturer should recognize its share of the losses resulting from these transactions in the same way as profits except that losses should be recognized immediately when they represent a reduction in the net realizable value of current assets or impairment loss.

Activity 24.23

A joint venture, Gamma company, is set up between A, B, and C companies. All venturers share equally in the joint venture. After establishment of the joint venture A sells to Gamma for cash some items of equipment, carrying value in A's books €1m, for €1.6 m.

Show the adjustments to be made in A's consolidated financial statements in respect of the above transaction.

Activity feedback

In *A's* individual statements the transaction will have been recorded as a sale of equipment thus:

Dr Cash	1.6m
Cr Equipment gain	1m
Cr Income statements – gain on sale	0.6m

The gain on sale of 0.6m, in accordance with IAS 31, should only be recognized in the consolidated financial statements as that part which is attributable to the other venturers. Thus only $2/3 \times 0.6m = €0.4$ m should be recognized.

In the consolidated financial statements using proportional consolidation the following adjustments to *As* individual accounts will be required.

Cr Cash	0.533
Dr Equipment	0.333
Dr Income statement gain on sale	0.2

Thus the consolidated statements will still show one-third of the equipment and the gain on sale will have been reduced to €0.4m. It will be as though only two-thirds of the equipment has been sold.

Under the equity method the following adjustments will be required.

Cr Investments in JV	0.2
Dr Income statement	0.2

SIC 13, *Jointly Controlled Entities – Non-monetary Contribution by Venturers*, provides further guidance on accounting for situations where a venturer transfers assets in exchange for an interest in the entity.

Disclosure in respect of joint ventures

These are as expected:

- listing and description of interest in significant joint ventures
- proportion of ownership interest held
- aggregate amounts of each of current assets, long-term assets, current liabilities, long-term liabilities, income and expenses related to interest in joint ventures
- aggregate amount of certain contingencies incurred in relation to joint venture
- share of capital commitments of joint venture
- method it uses to recognize its interest in jointly controlled entities.

Summary of accounting methods for business combinations

The following might be a useful summary at this stage.

Business combination	*Method of accounting in CFS*
Subsidiary relationship	Purchase (acquisition)
Associate relationship	Equity accounting

Joint venture:

Jointly controlled operations}	Already accounted for, make adjustments
Jointly controlled assets}	for transactions between venturers only
Jointly controlled entity	Proportional consolidation or equity accounting

The following activity brings together several of these accounting methods for practice purposes.

Activity 24.24

The following information is available in respect of Serp company and the other entities for the year ended 31 March 20X8 (see Activity 24.20)

Income statement for the year ended 31.3.X8

	Serp	Gamma	Alpha	Beta
	€000	€000	€000	€000
Turnover	9 000	6 000	15 000	10 000
Cost of sales	3 900	2 200	8 000	5 000
Gross profit	5 100	3 800	7 000	5 000
Administration and distribution	900	1 200	2 100	1 100
Operating profit	4 200	2 600	4 900	3 900
Dividends received	50			
Interest payable	150	170		1 100
Profit before tax	4 100	2 430		2 800
Taxation	1 750	1 100	4 900	1 100
Profit after tax	2 350	1 330	2 100	1 700

1 Serp has not received any dividends from any of its investments except for those from Wimp and Alpine.
2 Net assets of Alpha at acquisition, 1 April 20X3 were €18 000 000 and of Beta purchased 1 April 20X4 €15 000 000.
3 Serp bought its share in Gamma at 1 April 20X7.
4 Information in respect of Castle Residential project is as follows:

Memorandum income statement as at 31.3.X8

	Serp	Locking	Crawford
	€000	€000	€000
Turnover	2 000	700	500
Cost of sales	950	400	600
Gross profit	1 050	300	900
Administration and distribution	300	20	100
Operating profit	750	280	800
Interest payable	50		100
Profit before tax	700	280	700
Taxation	170		100
Profit after tax	530	280	600

These figures in respect of Serp are included in Serp's profit and loss account but no adjustment has been made in respect of the turnover and costs reported by Locking and Crawford on the Project.

Balance sheet as at 31.3.X8 for Serp and other entities

	Serp €000	Gamma €000	Alpha €000	Beta €000
Non-current assets	16 500	10 130	30 000	27 500
Investments in:				
Beta	12 000			
Gamma	2 500			
Alpha	5 700			
Wimp, Alpine	5 000			
Current assets	3 200	1 000	4 000	2 500
Current liabilities	(2 900)	(800)	(2 700)	(900)
	42 000	10 330	31 300	29 100
Long-term liabilities	(2 200)	(4 000)	(7 500)	(9 000)
	39 800	6 330	23 800	2 010
Share capital	10 000	5 000	4 000	8 000
Reserves	29 800	1 330	19 800	1 210
	39 800	6 330	23 800	2 010

The accounting policy of Serp is to write goodwill off over a period of 15 years.

Required:
Prepare the consolidated accounts for the Serp group for the year ended 31.3.X8.

Activity feedback

1 The jointly controlled operation, Castle Residential, has to be accounted for in Serps accounts in accordance with the terms of that arrangement, i.e. equal shares:

	Project €000	Equalization €000	Equal shares €000
Turnover	4 200	(600)	1 400
Cost of sales	1 950	(300)	650
Gross profit	2 250	(300)	750
Administration and distribution	420	(160)	140
Operating profit	1 830	(140)	610
Interest payable	150	0	50
Profit before tax	1 680	(140)	560
Taxation	270	(80)	90
Profit after tax	1 410	(60)	470

2 Goodwill calculations:

		€000
Joint venture Gamma	Purchase price	2 500
	50% × 5000	2 500
	Goodwill	0

Subsidiary Beta	Purchase price	12 000
	70% × 15m	10 500
	Goodwill	1 500
Associate Alpha	Purchase price	5 700
	30% × 18m	5 400
	Goodwill	300

3 Consolidated income statement for Serp group for the year ended 31.3.X8

	€000	€000
Group turnover (9000 − 600 equal + 10 000 subsid)		18 400
Cost of sales (3900 − 300 equal + 5000 sub)		8 600
Gross profit		9 800
Administration and distribution costs (900 − 160 + 1100)		1 840
Group operating profit		7 960
Share of operating profit in:		
Joint venture	1 300	
Associate	1 470	
		2 770
		10 730
Dividends received trade investments		50
		10 780
Interests payable		
Group (150 + 1100)	1 250	
Associate		
Joint venture	85	1 335
Profit on ordinary activities before tax		9 445
Tax:		
Group (1750 + 1100 − 80)	2 770	
Joint venture (50% × 1100)	550	
Associate (30% × 2100)	630	3 950
Profit on ordinary activities after tax		5 495
Minority interest (30% × 1700)		510
Retained profit for group and its share of associate and joint ventures		4 985

Consolidated balance sheet for Serp group as at 31.3.X8

Non-current assets		
Goodwill (1500)		1 500
Property, plant and equipment (16 500 + 27 500)		44 000
Investments		
Investments joint ventures		3 165
Investments in associates:		
Share of net assets (30% × 23 800)	7 140	
Goodwill	300	7 440
Trade investments		5 000
		61 105

Current assets (3200 + 2500)		5 700
Current liabilities	3 860	1 840
		62 945
Long term liabilities (2200 + 9000)		11 200
		51 745
Equity minority interest (30% × 20 100)		6 030
		45 715
Share capital		10 000
Reserves		35 715
		45 715

Reserves		
Serp	29 800	
less Equalization	60	29 740
Alpha (5800 × 30%)		1 740
Gamma		665
Beta (5 100 × 70%)		3 570
		35 715

An example of a disclosure note in respect of consolidation methods is shown from Bayer financial report 2002.

Consolidation methods:

Capital consolidation is performed according to IAS 22 (*Business Combinations*) by offsetting investment in subsidiaries against the underlying equities at the dates of acquisition. The identifiable assets of subsidiaries and joint ventures are included at their fair values in proportion to Bayer's interest. Remaining differences are recognized as goodwill.

Where the statements of individual consolidated companies reflect write-downs or write-backs of investments in other consolidated companies, these are reversed for the Group statements.

Intragroup sales, profits, losses, income, expenses, receivables and payables are eliminated.

Deferred taxes are recognized for temporary differences related to consolidation entries.

Joint ventures are included by proportionate consolidation according to the same principles.

Intercompany profits and losses on transactions with companies included at equity were immaterial in 2002.

Activity 24.25

Determine from Bayer's disclosure whether accounting methods used are in accordance with current IASs.

Activity feedback

Bayer has obviously used the benchmark treatment under the previous version of IAS 22, as fair values have only been included in proportion to Bayer's interest. Thus, the value of assets and liabilities displayed in the group accounts will include the subsidiaries' assets partly at fair value (that part owned by Bayer), and partly (the minority interest), at some other value which equates to balance sheet carrying value of the subsidiary before taking account of fair value on consolidation. Thus the assets and liabilities displayed by Bayer in the consolidation are a mix of values. The allowed alternative treatment would have avoided this mix of values being incorporated from subsidiaries, as 100% of these would have to be incorporated at fair value (including the minority interest share).

Would Bayer's accounts have been more understandable and/or 'truer and fairer' if the alternative treatment had been used? Note, as stated earlier, that the alternative treatment is set to become the only method permitted by the IASB.

Related party transactions

So far in this chapter we have dealt with accounting for business combinations, subsidiaries, associates and joint ventures. However, what we have not considered is that the parties in these business combinations often enter into transactions with each other that unrelated parties would not undertake. For example:

- Assets and liabilities may be transferred between parties at values above or below market value.
- One party may make a loan to another at a beneficial interest rate or without taking into account the full risk involved.
- Services carried out by one party for another may be charged for at a reduced rate.

When working through the accounting techniques for business combinations we learnt that such transactions required eliminating in the group consolidated accounts.

However, one of our basic assumptions within accounting is that transactions are carried out at arm's length between independent parties. If they are not, then users of financial statements will be misled if they are not provided with information in respect of these related party transactions. However, if we wish to give such information to users we need to have uniformity of information provided by enterprises and to clearly define when parties are related. This issue is dealt with by IASB in IAS 24 first issued in July 1984 and updated as part of the Board's improvement project.

Related party issue

IAS 24 in its consideration of the related party issue maintains that related party relationships could have an effect on the financial position and operating results of the reporting enterprise and that this effect can occur even if no transactions have taken place.

Activity 24.26

Identify a related party situation where:

- A transaction occurs that affects the financial position and operating results of the reporting enterprise.

■ A situation where no transaction occurs but an effect is still felt on the financial position and operating results of the reporting enterprise.

Activity feedback

■ There are several situations you could have identified here and three of them we identified for you above. Others are agency arrangements, leasing arrangements, licence agreements, guarantees and collaterals, management contracts and transfer of research and development.

■ Such a situation could be where a subsidiary may terminate relations with a trading partner on acquisition by the parent of a fellow subsidiary engaged in the same trade as the former partner. Another such situation would be where a subsidiary, once acquired, is instructed by its parent not to engage in certain activities, e.g. research and development.

IAS 24 definitions

Related part – A party is related to an entity if:

(a) Directly, or indirectly through one or more intermediaries, the party:
   (i) controls, is controlled by, or is under common control with, the entity (this includes parents, subsidiaries and fellow subsidiaries)
   (ii) has an interest in the entity that gives it significant influence over the entity
   (iii) or has joint control over the entity.
(b) The party is an associate (as defined in IAS 28, *Investments in Associates*) of the entity.
(c) The party is a joint venture in which the entity is a venturer (see IAS 31, *Interest in Joint Ventures*).
(d) The party is a member of the key management personnel of the entity or its parent.
(e) The parent is a close member of the family of any individual referred to in **(a)** or **(d)**.
(f) The party is an entity that is controlled, jointly controlled or significantly influenced by or for which significant voting power in such entity resides with, directly or indirectly, any individual referred to in **(d)** or **(c)**.
(g) The party is a post-employment benefit plan for the benefit of employees of the entity, or of an entity that is a related party of the entity.

Close members of the family of an individual are defined as those family members who may be expected to influence, or be influenced by, that individual in their dealings with the entity. They may include:

■ the individual's domestic partner and children
■ children of the individual's domestic partner
■ dependants of the individual or the individual's domestic partner.

Compensation includes all employee benefits (as defined in IAS 19, *Employee Benefits*) including employee benefits to which IFRS2, *Share-based Payment*, applies. Employee benefits are all forms of consideration paid, in exchange for services rendered to the entity. It also includes such consideration paid on behalf of a parent of the entity in respect of the entity. Compensation includes:

(a) short-term employee benefits, such as wages, salaries, and social security contributions, paid annual leave and paid sick leave, profit sharing and bonuses (if payable within twelve months of the end of the period) and non-monetary benefits (such as medical care, housing, cars and free or subsidised goods or services) for current employees;

(b) post-employment benefits such as pensions, other retirement benefits, post-employment life insurance and post-employment medical care;

(c) other long-term employee benefits, including long-service leave or sabbatical leave, jubilee or other long-service benefits, long-term disability benefits and, if they are not payable wholly within twelve months after the end of the period, profit-sharing, bonuses and deferred compensation;

(d) termination benefits; and

(e) share-based payments.

(IAS 24, Para. 9)

Related party transaction – a transfer of resources, services or obligations between related parties, regardless of whether a price is charged.

Control – the power to govern the financial and operating policies of an entity so as to obtain benefits from its activities.

Significant influence (for the purpose of this standard) – participation in the financial and operating policy decisions of an enterprise, but not control of these policies. Significant influence may be gained by share ownership, statute or agreement (IAS 28, para. 9).

Disclosure requirements of IAS 24

This breaks down into two areas:

1 Where no transactions have occurred between the parties but control exists. In this case the relationship must be disclosed so that the user can form a view about the effect of the relationship on the reporting enterprise.

2 Where transactions have occurred between related parties. In this case the nature of the relationship, the types of transactions and elements of the transactions necessary for an understanding of the financial statements must be disclosed.

Activity 24.27

Identify those elements of a related party transaction that you believe should be disclosed so as to provide an understanding of the financial statements.

Activity feedback

You probably identified:

■ name of related party
■ volumes and amounts involved in the transactions
■ amounts and volumes outstanding at the balance sheet date

- amounts written off in respect of debts due from the related party
- pricing policies
- transfer of a major asset at a reduced price
- those where a free service was given.

IAS 24 requires disclosure of four elements:

1. amount of the transactions
2. amount of outstanding balances
3. provision for doubtful debts
4. expense recognized during the period in respect of bad or doubtful debts

together with the name of the entity's parent and key management personnel compensation in total and for each of:

1. short-term employee benefits
2. post-employment benefits
3. other long-term benefits
4. termination benefits
5. share-based payment.

Summary

Within this chapter we have looked at methods of accounting for an enterprise's investment in another enterprise: as a trade investment, as an associate, as a joint venture; as an acquisition; or as a merger. We have formulated consolidated statements using all these methods and considered their implications. We have looked in detail at the accounting requirements for the consolidation of a subsidiary undertaking using acquisition accounting in accordance with IAS GAAP. We have also identified the issues surrounding related party transactions.

The whole area of accounting for business combinations is highly complex and we have not been able to deal with all aspects here. However, we hope we have provided you with a great deal of food for thought, and you may like to consider whether you believe the current regulation actually does provide a true and fair view to stakeholders. This might be particularly pertinent in the light of the Enron bankruptcy in the USA and other such failures.

It is worth noting that in the preparation of consolidated financial statements, we are using:

- acquisition accounting for subsidiaries
- equity accounting for associated companies
- proportional consolidation or equity accounting for joint ventures.

There is also still a debate outstanding on the fresh-start method, a review of which is promised under Phase II of the business combinations project. Phase II will also deal in more detail with the application of acquisition accounting to step-by-step purchases, minority interests, the fair value of the consideration and complex combination issues such as mutual entities, dual-listed entities and entities under common control.

Is this a suitable point to question whether the characteristic of understandability can be applied to consolidated accounts?

At this stage we provide a further activity for you to practise your consolidation skills. The provision of an activity at the summary stage in a chapter is most unusual in this text but it is essential that you learn to apply the techniques of consolidation.

Activity 24.28

On 1 April 20X5 Hardy enterprise acquired 4 million of Sibling enterprise's common shares. paying €4.50 each. At the same time it also purchased at nominal value €500 000 of its 10% redeemable preference shares. At the date of acquisition the retained profit reserves of Sibling enterprise were €8 400 000. The draft balance sheets of the two enterprises at 31 March 20X8 were as follows:

	Hardy €000	Hardy €000	Sibling €000	Sibling €000
Non-current assets				
Land and buildings		22 000		12 000
Plant and equipment		20 450		10 220
Investment in Sibling: common shares		18 000		
Preference shares		500		
		60 950		22 220
Current assets				
Inventory	9 850		6 590	
Accounts receivable	11 420		3 830	
Cash	490		0	
	21 760		10 420	
Current liabilities				
Accounts payable	6 400		4 510	
Bank overdraft	0		570	
Provision for taxation	2 470		1 980	
	(8 870)		(7 060)	
Net current assets		12 890		3 360
Long-term liabilities				
10% loans		(12 000)		(4 000)
Net assets		61 840		21 580
Common shares of €1		10 000		5 000
10% preference shares				2 000
Retained profit reserves		51 840		14 580
		61 840		21 580

Extracts from the income statement of Sibling enterprise before intra-group adjustments, for the year to 31 March 20X8 are:

	€000
Profit before tax	5 400
Taxation	(1 600)
	3 800

The following information is relevant:

1 Included in the land and buildings of Sibling is a large area of developed land at its cost of €5 million. Its fair value at the date Sibling was acquired was €7 million and by 31 March 20X8 this had risen to €8.5 million. The group valuation policy for development land is that it should be carried at fair value and not depreciated.

2 Also at the date of Sibling's acquisition the plant and equipment included plant that had a fair value of €4 million in excess of its carrying value. This plant had a remaining life of five years. The group calculates depreciation on a straight line basis. The fair value of Sibling's other net assets approximated to their carrying values.

3 During the year Sibling sold goods to Hardy for €1.8 million. Sibling adds a 20% mark-up on cost to all its sales. Goods with a transfer price of €450 000 were included in Hardy's stock at 31 March 20X8. The balance on the current accounts of the parent and subsidiary was €240 000 on 31 March 20X8.

Prepare the consolidated balance sheet of Hardy as at 31 March 20X8.

Activity feedback

Consolidated balance sheet of Hardy as at 31 March 20X8

	€000	€000
Non-current assets		
Land and buildings (working 1)		37 500
Plant and equipment (working 2)		32 270
Goodwill		2 480
		72 250
Current assets		
Inventory (working 4)	16 365	
Accounts receivable (11 420 + 3830 − 240 current accs)	15 010	
Cash	490	
	31 865	
Current liabilities		
Accounts payable (6400 + 4510 − 240)	10 670	
Bank overdraft	570	
Provision for taxation	4 450	
	15 690	16 175
Long-term liabilities		
Loans		(16 000)
Net assets		72 425
Common shares		10 000
Revaluation reserve		1 200
Retained profits (working 6)		54 804
Minority interests (working 5)		6 421
		72 425

	Land and buildings	Plant
Working 1 and 2		
Balance from question Hardy	22 000	20 450
Sibling	12 000	10 220

Revaluation	3 500	4 000
Additional depreciation		(2 400)
	37 500	32 270

Working 3 Goodwill		
Paid common shares	18 000	
preference shares	500	18 500
Bought		
80% common shares	4 000	
Preference shares	500	
80% pre-acquisition reserves	6 720	
80% revaluations at date of acquisition	4 800	16 020
		2 480

Working 4		
Balance as per question 9850 + 6590	16 440	
less Unrealized profit on transfer still in inventory	(75)	
	16 365	

Working 5 Minority interest		
Net assets Sibling less preference shares 19 589 × 20%	3 916	
add Minority preference shares	1 500	
add Revaluations of 7500 × 20%	1 500	
less adjustments for:		
Additional depreciation 2400 × 20%	(480)	
Unrealized profit on inventory 75 × 20%	(15)	
	6 421	

Working 6		
Retained profits Hardy		51 840
Post-acquisition profits Sibling	6 180	
less Additional depreciation	(2 400)	
less Unrealized profit on inventory	(75)	
	3 705 × 80% =	2 964
		54 804

EXERCISES

(✔ indicates answers are available on pages 740–746)

1 Construct (using appropriate assumptions) a mixed group structure bringing together a holding enterprise, a subsidiary and a sub-subsidiary.

2 Define a subsidiary, associate and related party enterprise.

3 Identify how a subsidiary, associate and related party will be dealt with in the financial statements of a group.

4 Appraise the effects on a group's financial statements of the use of merger accounting as opposed to acquisition accounting in order to account for business combinations.

✔ 5 Explain why the fair value of an enterprise's assets is used in the preparation of consolidated financial statements.

6 The preparation of consolidated financial statements provides useful information to users. Discuss.

7 Disclosure of related party transactions in financial statements provides no useful information to users. Discuss.

8 Explain what a special purpose enterprise is and identify how the IASB requires these to be accounted for.

9 Using any information you can find in respect of 'Enron' discuss the following statement: *If Enron had prepared its financial statements using IAS GAAP instead of US GAAP it would have had to account for special purpose enterprises differently.*

10 What is 'control' as used in relation to consolidated financial statements?

11 Appraise the need for group accounts.

✔ **12** Identify the essence of proportional consolidation and equity accounting and explain when each can be used in the preparation of consolidated financial statements in accordance with IAS GAAP.

✔ **13** The following draft balance sheets relate to Largo, a public limited company, Fusion, a public limited company and Spine, a public limited company, as at 30 November 20X3.

	Largo $m	Fusion $m	Spine $m
Non-current assets			
Tangible non-current assets	329	185	64
Investment in Fusion	150		
Investment in Spine	30	50	
Investment in Micro	11		
	520	235	64
Current assets	120	58	40
	640	293	104
Capital and reserves			
Called up ordinary share capital of $1	460	110	50
Share premium account	30	20	10
Accumulated reserves	120	138	35
	610	268	95
Non-current liabilities – deferred tax	20	20	5
Current liabilities	10	5	4
	640	293	104

The following information is relevant to the preparation of the group financial statements:

(i) Largo acquired ninety per cent of the ordinary share capital of Fusion and twenty-six per cent of the ordinary share capital of Spine on 1 December 20X2 in a share for share exchange when the accumulated reserves were Fusion $136 million and Spine $30 million. The fair value of the net assets at 1 December 20X2 was Largo $650 million, Fusion $330 million and Spine $128 million. Any increase in the consolidated fair value of the net assets over the carrying value is deemed to be attributable to property held by the companies. There had been no new issue of shares since 1 December 20X2.

(ii) In arriving at the fair value of net assets acquired at 1 December 20X2, Largo has not accounted for the deferred tax arising on the increase in the value of the property of both Fusion and Spine. The deferred tax arising on the fair valuation of the property was Fusion $15 million and Spine $9 million.

(iii) Fusion had acquired a sixty per cent holding in Spine on 1 December 19W9 for a consideration of $50 million when the accumulated reserve of Spine was

$10 million. The fair value of the net assets at that date was $80 million with the increase in fair value attributable to property held by the companies. Property is depreciated within the group at five per cent per annum.

(iv) The directors of Largo wish to account for the business combination as a uniting of interests. On 1 December 20X2, before the share exchange, the market capitalisation of the companies was $644 million: Largo; $310 million: Fusion; and $310 million: Spine. The number of employees of Largo was fifty per cent more than the combined total of the employees of both Fusion and Spine. The new Board of Directors will comprise ten directors, seven of whom will be nominated by Largo. As a result of the directors' wish to use the pooling accounting method, the cost of the investment in Fusion and Spine, shown in the financial statements of Largo, is simply the nominal value of the share capital issued. The directors feel that pooling accounting is appropriate as former institutional shareholders of Fusion own a substantial amount of equity in the new business combination with the result that Largo cannot dominate the new business combination because of their influence over the management of the new entity.

(v) Largo purchased a forty per cent interest in Micro, a limited liability investment company on 1 December 20X2. The only asset of the company is a portfolio of investments which is held for trading purposes. The stake in Micro was purchased for cash for $11 million. The carrying value of the net assets of Micro on 1 December 20X2 was $18 million and their fair value was $20 million. On 30 November 20X3, the fair value of the net assets was $24 million. Largo exercises significant influence over Micro. Micro values the portfolio on a 'mark to market' basis.

(vi) Fusion has included a brand name in its tangible non-current assets at the cost of $9 million. The brand earnings can be separately identified and could be sold separately from the rest of the business. The fair value of the brand at 30 November 20X3 was $7 million. The fair value of the brand at the time of Fusion's acquisition by Largo was $9 million.

Required:

Prepare the consolidated balance sheet of the Largo Group at the year ended 30 November 20X3 in accordance with International Financial Reporting Standards, explaining the reasons why pooling of interests accounting would not be used for the business combination.   (ACCA Dec 03)

14 Barking, an unlisted company, operates in the house building and commercial property investment development sector. The sector has seen an upturn in activity during recent years and the directors have been considering future plans with a view to determining their impact on the financial statements for the financial year to 30 November 20X4.

(a) Barking wishes to obtain a stock exchange listing in the year to 30 November 20X4. It is to be acquired by Ash, a significantly smaller listed company in a share for share exchange whereby Barking will receive sufficient voting shares of Ash to control the new group. Due to the relative values of the companies, Barking will become the majority shareholder with 80% of the enlarged capital of Ash. The executive management of the new group will be that of Barking.

As part of the purchase consideration, Ash will issue zero dividend preference shares of $1 to the shareholders of Barking on 30 June 20X4. These will be redeemed on 1 January 2005 at $1.10 per share. Additionally Ash will issue convertible interest free loan notes. The loan notes are unlikely to be repaid on 30 November 20X5 (the redemption date) as the conversion terms are very favourable. The management of Ash have excluded the redemption of the loan notes from their cash flow projections. The loan notes are to be included in long term liabilities in the balance sheet of Ash. As part of the business combination Ash will change its name to Barking inc.

(b) The acquisition will also have other planned effects on the company. Barking operates a defined benefit pension scheme. On acquisition the scheme will be frozen and replaced by a group defined contribution scheme, and as a result no additional benefits in the old scheme will accrue to the employees. Ash's employees are also in a defined benefit scheme which has been classified as a multi-employer plan but it is currently impossible to identify its share of the underlying assets and liabilities in the scheme. After acquisition, Ash's employees will be transferred to the group's defined contribution scheme, with the previous scheme being frozen.

(c) As a result of the acquisition the company will change the way in which it recognises sales of residential properties. It used to treat such properties as sold when the building work was substantially complete, defined as being when the roof and internal walls had been completed. The new policy will be to recognize a sale when a refundable deposit for the sale of the property has been received and the building work is physically complete. Legal costs incurred on the sale of the property are currently capitalised and shown as current assets until the sale of the property has occurred. Further, it has been decided by the directors that as at 30 November 20X4, the financial year end, some properties held as trading properties of both companies would be moved from the trading portfolio to the investment portfolio of the holding company, and carried at fair value.

(d) The directors intend to carry out an impairment review as at 30 November 20X4 in order to ascertain whether the carrying amount of goodwill and other non-current assets can be supported by their value in use. The plan is to produce cash flow projections up to 20X4 with an average discount rate of 15% being used in the calculations. The ten year period is to be used as it reflects fairly the long term nature of the assets being assessed. Any subsequent impairment loss is to be charged against the income statement.

Required:

Draft a report to the directors of Barking, setting out the financial reporting implications of the above plans for the financial statements for the year to 30 November 20X4.

(ACCA Dec 03)

15 The consolidated financial statements of Dietronic, a public limited company, for the year ended 30 November 20X3 are:

Income Statement

	$000
Group operating profit	13 000
Interest income	940
Profit on sale of subsidiary	100
Profit before tax	14 040
Taxation	(5 000)
Minority Interests	(3 000)
Profit after tax	6 040

Balance Sheet

	$000
Tangible non current assets	18 500
Goodwill	1 500
Current Assets	8 000
	28 000
Share capital $1 ordinary shares	5 000
Reserves	10 000
Minority Interest	6 000
	21 000
Current Liabilities	4 000
Long term debt	3 000
	28 000

There have been a number of changes in the composition of the group during the year. The changes in the group and the accounting practices used are set out below:

(i) Dietronic had created on 1 July 20X3 a new management company in which it holds 80% of the ordinary share capital with the remainder being held by an employee share ownership trust. Dietronic had invested $160 000 in the company at the balance sheet date, and had incurred $400 000 in administrative set-up costs. These costs have been treated as goodwill on consolidation as the setting up of the new company constitutes a 'notional' acquisition with the set up costs being included in the cost of acquisition. The shares held by the employee share ownership trust were issued at a price of $2 per share and are included in the consolidated balance sheet of Dietronic at this amount within current assets. The share capital of the management company is 100 000 ordinary shares of $1.

(ii) Dietronic acquired 70% of the ordinary share capital of Dairy, a public limited company, on 31 October 20X2. On acquisition of Dairy, the financial assets of the company were reduced from the book value of $1.2 million to $600 000. This reduction came about as a result of the directors' assessment of the fair value of the investments after taking intoaccount the 'marketability' of the portfolio. On 31 December 20X2, all the investments were sold for $1 million net of costs and the profit on disposal reported in 'interest income' in the consolidated income statement. The financial assets sold were wholly unquoted investments.

(iii) Dietronic had a 100% owned German subsidiary which was set up in 20X0 by Dietronic. The subsidiary was sold on 1 December 20X2 for 600 000 euros ($400 000). The subsidiary is included in the holding company's accounts at a cost of $300 000 at 30 November 20X2 and the net assets at the same date included in the consolidated financial statements were 540 000 euros ($360 000). All exchange differences arising on the translation of the subsidiary's financial statements have been taken to a separate exchange reserve and the cumulative total on this reserve is $40 000 debit as at 1 December 20X2 before the receipt of the dividend. Dietronic has calculated the gain on the sale of the subsidiary as follows:

	$000
Sale proceeds	400
Cost of investment	(300)
Gain on sale	100

The closing rate/net investment method was used to consolidate the financial statements of the subsidiary. During the year to 30 November 20X2, the German subsidiary had declared and accounted for a proposed dividend of 48 000 euros. This had been included in the holding company's financial statements at the exchange rate ruling when the dividend was declared ($1 = 1.6 euros). This dividend was received on 1 December 20X2 by Dietronic and recorded in the cash book and dividends receivable account. The shareholders of the subsidiary approved the dividend on 1 October 20X2 and the exchange rate at 1 December 20X2 was ($1 = 1.5 euros).

(iv) On 1 June 20X3 Dietronic acquired a 25% share in a newly formed company, Diet, a public limited company. Diet has been classified as an associated company in the financial statements but no details have been shown on the face of the balance sheet or income statement as Dietronic feels that the results and net assets of the associate are immaterial. The only amount included in the financial statements as regards the associate is the purchase consideration of $2.1 million which has been added to tangible non-current assets. The fair value of the net assets of Diet at the date of acquisition was $6.8 million. The directors are confident that Diet will be successful in future years with profits in the next financial year and dividends of 10c per share forecast for five years. If the investment in Diet were to be sold at 30 November 20X3, it is anticipated that it would realise $1.8 million.

The directors are seeking advice as to the acceptability of the accounting practices used for the above changes in the composition of the group. A discount rate of 5% should be used in any calculations.

Summarised Balance Sheet at 30 November 20X3

	Diet	
	$000	$000
Tangible non-current assets		5 000
Net Current Assets		2 000
		7 000
Ordinary Share Capital of $1		7 600
Reserves at 30 November 2002	80	
Loss for year to 30 November 2003	(680)	(600)
		7 000

Required:

(a)   Discuss the nature of any amendments required to the consolidated financial statements of Dietronic in order to bring the accounting practices used for the changes in the composition of the group into line with International Financial Reporting Standards.

(b)   Redraft the consolidated financial statements of Dietronic in accordance with these amendments.   (ACCA Dec 03)

16 Base, a public limited company, acquired two subsidiaries, Zero and Black, both public limited companies, on 1 June 20X1. The details of the acquisitions at that date are as follows:

Subsidiary	Ordinary Share Capital of $1	Reserves	Fair value of net assets at acquisition	Cost of Investment	Ordinary Share Capital acquired
	$m	$m	$m	$m	$m
Zero	350	250	770	600	250
Black	200	150	400	270	120

The draft income statements for the year ended 31 May 2003 are:

	Base	Zero	Black
	$m	$m	$m
Revenue	3 000	2 300	600
Cost of Sales	(2 000)	(1 600)	(300)
Gross profit	1 000	700	300
Distribution costs	(240)	(230)	(120)
Administrative expenses	(200)	(220)	(80)
Profit from operations	560	250	100
Finance cost – interest expense	(20)	(10)	(12)
Investment income receivable (including inter company dividends paid May 20X3)	100	–	–

Profit before tax	640	240	88
Income tax expense	(130)	(80)	(36)
Net profit from ordinary activities	510	160	52
Accumulated profit 1 June 20X2	1 400	400	190

The following information is relevant to the preparation of the group financial statements:

(i) On 1 December 20X2, Base sold 50 million $1 ordinary shares in zero for $155 million. The only accounting entry made by Base was to record the receipt of the cash consideration in the cash account and in a suspense account.

(ii) On 1 March 20X3, Black issued 100 million ordinary shares of $1 at a price of $2.65 per share. It was fully subscribed and paid up on that day. Base decided not to subscribe for the shares but the directors of Base had significant influence over the decision to issue the shares. The directors of Black had prepared financial information as at 28 February 20X3 for the purpose of the new issues of shares showing the carrying values of the net assets of Black to be $480 million.

(iii) Black had sold $150 million of goods to Base on 30 April 20X3. There was no opening inventory of inter-company good but the closing inventory of the these goods in Base's financial statements was $90 million. The profit on these goods was 30% on selling price.

(iv) Base has implemented in full IAS19 'Employee Benefits' in its financial statements. The directors have included the following amounts in the figure for cost of sales:

	$m
Current service cost	5
Actuarial deficit on obligation	4
Interest cost	3
Actuarial gain on assets	(2)
Charged to cost of sales	10

They are unsure as to the treatment of these amounts given their stated objective of maximising current year profit. The fair value of the plan assets at 31 May 20X2 was $48 million and the present value of the defined benefit obligation was $54 million at that date. The net cumulative unrecognised actuarial loss at 31 May 2002 was $3 million and the expected remaining working lives of the employees was ten years.

(v) Base invested on 1 June 20X2 in a convertible debt instrument at a cost of $20 million. The debt is repayable in four years at $16 million but the conversion terms are extremely favourable. Base has included the convertible debt in its balance sheet at $20 million.

(vi) Base had carried out work for a group of companies (Drum Group) during the financial year to 31 May 20X2. Base had accepted one million share options of the Drum Group in full settlement of the debt owed to them. At 1 June 2002 these share options were valued at $3 million which was the value of the outstanding debt. The following table gives the prices of these shares and the fair value of the option.

	Share price	Fair value of option
31 May 20X2	$13	$3
31 May 20X3	$10	$1

The options had not been exercised during the year and remained at $3 million in the balance sheet of Base. The options can be exercised at any time after 31 May 20X5 for $8.50 per share.

(vii) Base had paid a dividend of $50 million in the year and Zero had paid a dividend of $70 million in May 20X3.

(viii) The fair value adjustments have been incorporated into the subsidiaries' records.

(ix) Ignore the tax implications of any capital gains made by the Group and assume profits accrue evenly throughout the year.

Required:

Prepare a consolidated income statement for the Base Group for the year ended 31 May 20X3 in accordance with International Accounting Standards/International Financial Reporting Standards. (ACCA June 03)

17 Highmoor, a public listed company, acquired 80% of Slowmoor's ordinary shares on 1 October 20X2. Highmoor paid an immediate $2 per share in cash and agreed to pay a further $1·20 per share if Slowmoor made a profit within two years of its acquisition. Highmoor has not recorded the contingent consideration.

The balance sheets of the two companies at 30 September 20X3 are shown in the table below.

	$ million	**Highmoor** $ million	$ million	**Slowmoor** $ million
Tangible non-current assets		585		172
Investments (note (ii))		225		13
Software (note (iii))		nil		40
		810		225
Current assets				
Inventory	85		42	
Accounts receivable	95		36	
Tax asset	nil		80	
Bank	20	200	nil	158
Total assets		1 010		383
Equity and liabilities				
Capital and reserves:				
Ordinary shares of $1 each		400		100
Accumulated profits – 1 October 20X2	230		150	
profit/loss for year	100	330	(35)	115
		730		215
Non-current liabilities				
12% loan note	nil		35	
8% Inter company loan (note (ii))	nil	nil	45	80
Current liabilities				
Accounts payable	210		71	
Taxation	70		nil	
Overdraft	nil	280	17	88
Total equity and liabilities		1 010		383

The following information is relevant:

(i) At the date of acquisition the fair values of Slowmoor's net assets were approximately equal to their book values.

(ii) Included in Highmoor's investments is a loan of $50 million made to Slowmoor. On 28 September 20X3, Slowmoor paid $9 million to Highmoor. This represented interest of $4 million for the year and the balance was a capital repayment. Highmoor had not received nor accounted for the payment, but it had accrued for the loan interest receivable as part of its accounts receivable figure. There are no other intra group balances.

(iii) The software was developed by Highmoor during 20X2 at a total cost of $30 million. It was sold to Slowmoor for $50 million immediately after its acquisition. The software had an estimated life of five years and is being amortised by Slowmoor on a straight-line basis.

(iv) Due to the losses of Slowmoor since its acquisition, the directors of Highmoor are not confident it will return to profitability in the short term.

(v) For the purposes of realising any negative goodwill, in its acquisition plan, Highmoor had estimated at the date of acquisition that Slowmoor would make losses of $15 million (of which $12 million would be attributable to Highmoor) before returning to profitability. The remaining weighted average useful life at the date of acquisition of the acquired depreciable non-monetary assets can be taken as four years (straight-line basis).

Required:

(a) Prepare the consolidated balance sheet of Highmoor as at 30 September 20X3, explaining your treatment of the contingent consideration.

(b) Describe the circumstances in which negative goodwill may arise. Your answer should refer to the particular issues of the above acquisition. (ACCA Dec 03)

18 In recent years Hillusion has acquired a reputation for buying modestly performing businesses and selling them at a substantial profit within a period of two to three years of their acquisition. On 1 July 20X2 Hillusion acquired 80% of the ordinary share capital of Skeptik at a cost of $10 280 000. On the same date it also acquired 50% of Skeptik's 10% loan notes at par. The summarised draft financial statements of both companies are:

Income statements: Year to 31 March 20X3

	Hillusion $000	Skeptik $000
Sales revenue	60 000	24 000
Cost of sales	(42 000)	(20 000)
Gross profit	18 000	4 000
Operating expenses	(6 000)	(200)
Loan interest received (paid)	75	(200)
Operating profit	12 075	3 600
Taxation	(3 000)	(600)
Profit after tax for the year	9 075	3 000
Accumulated profit brought forward	16 525	5 400
Accumulated profit per balance sheet	25 600	8 400

Balance Sheets: as at 31 March 20X3

	Hillusion	Skeptik
Tangible non-current Assets	19 320	8 000
Investments	11 280	nil
	30 600	8 000
Current Assets	15 000	8 000
Total assets	45 600	16 000

Equity and liabilites		
Ordinary shares of $1 each	10 000	2 000
Accumulated profits	25 600	8 400
	35 600	10 400
Non-current liabilites		
10% Loan notes	nil	2 000
Current liabilities	10 000	3 600
Total equity and liabilities	45 600	16 000

The following information is relevant:

(i) The fair values of Skeptik's assets were equal to their book values with the exception of its plant, which had a fair value of $3.2 million in excess of its book value at the date of acquisition. The remaining life of all of Skeptik's plant at the date of its acquisition was four years and this period has not changed as a result of the acquisition. Depreciation of plant is on a straight-line basis and charged to cost of sales. Skeptik has not adjusted the value of its plant as a result of the fair value exercise.

(ii) In the post acquisition period Hillusion sold goods to Skeptik at a price of $12 million. These goods had cost Hillusion $9 million. During the year Skeptik had sold $10 million (at cost to Skeptik) of these goods for $15 million.

(iii) Hillusion bears almost all of the administration costs incurred on behalf of the group (invoicing, credit control etc.). It does not charge Skeptik for his service as to do so would not have a material effect on the group profit.

(iv) Revenues and profits should be deemed to accrue evenly throughout the year.

(v) The current accounts of the two companies were reconciled at the year-end with Skeptik owing Hillusion $750 000.

(vi) Time apportionment should be used in the year of acquisition.

Required:

(a) Prepare a consolidated income statement and balance sheet for Hillusion for the year to 31 March 20X3

(b) Explain why it is necessary to eliminate unrealised profits when preparing group financial statements; and how reliance on the entity financial statements of Skeptik may mislead a potential purchaser of the company.

Note: your answer should refer to the circumstances described in the question.

(ACCA June 03)

✔ 19 (a) **Hapsburg, a public listed company, acquired the following investments:**

– On 1 April 2003, 24 million shares in Sundial. This was by way of an immediate share exchange of two shares in Hapsburg for every three shares in Sundial plus a cash payment of $1 per Sundial share payable on 1 April 2006. The market price of Hapsburg's shares on 1 April 2003 was $2 each.

– On 1 October 2003, 6 million shares in Aspen paying an immediate $2.50 in cash for each share.

Based on Hapsburg's cost of capital (taken as 10% per annum), $1 receivable in three years' time can be taken to have a present value of $0.75.

Hapsburg has not yet recorded the acquisition of Sundial but it has recorded the investment in Aspen.

The summarised balance sheets at 31 March 2004 are:

	Hapsburg	Sundial	Aspen			
Non-current assets	$000	$000	$000	$000	$000	$000
Property, plant and equipment		41 000		34 800		37 700
Investments		15 000		3 000		nil
		56 000		37 800		37 700

Current Assets							
Inventory	9 900		4 800		7 900		
Trade and other receivables	13 600		8 600		14 400		
Cash	1 200	24 700	3 800	17 200	nil	22 300	
Total assets		80 700		55 000		60 000	
Equity and liabilities							
Capital and reserves							
Ordinary shares $1 each		20 000		30 000		20 000	
Reserves:							
Share premium	8 000		2 000		nil		
Accumulated profits	10 600	18 600	8 500	10 500	8 000	8 000	
		38 600		40 500		28 000	
Non-current liabilities							
10% loan note		16 000		4 200		12 000	
Current liabilities							
Trade and other payables	16 500		6 900		13 600		
Bank overdraft	nil		nil		4 500		
Taxation	9 600	26 100	3 400	10 300	1 900	20 000	
Total equity and liabilities		80 700		55 000		60 000	

The following information is relevant:
(i)   Below is a summary of the results of a fair value exercise for Sundial carried out at the date of acquisition:

Asset	Carrying value at acquisition $000	Fair value at acquisition $000	Notes
Plant	10 000	15 000	remaining life at acquisition four years
Investments	3 000	4 500	no change in value since acquisition

The book values of the net assets of Aspen at the date of acquisition were considered to be a reasonable approximation to their fair values
(ii)   The profits of Sundial and Aspen for the year to 31 March 20X4, as reported in their entity financial statements, were $4.5 million and $6 million respectively. No dividends have been paid by any of the companies during the year. All profits are deemed to accrue evenly throughout the year.
(iii)   In January 20X4 Aspen sold goods to Hapsburg at a selling price of $4 million. These goods had cost Aspen $2.4 million. Hapsburg had $2.5 million (at cost to Hapsburg) of these goods still in inventory at 31 March 20X4.
(iv)   All depreciation is charged on a straight-line basis.
Required:
Prepare the Consolidated Balance Sheet of Hapsburg as at 31 March 20X4 in accordance with current IASs.
(b) Some commentators have criticised the use of equity accounting on the basis that it can be used as a form of off balance sheet financing.
Required:
Explain the reasoning behind the use of equity accounting and discuss the above comment.
                                                                    (ACCA June 04)

20 The balance sheets of George and its subsidiary enterprises Zippy and Bungle at 30 June 20X3 (the accounting date for all three enterprises) are given:

	George $000	$000	Zippy $000	$000	Bungle $000	$000
ASSETS						
Non-current assets:						
Property, plant and equipment (*Note 3*)	45 000		25 000		20 000	
Financial assets (*Notes 1* and *2*)	20 000		Nil		Nil	
		65 000		25 000		20 000
Current assets:						
Inventories (*Notes 3* and *4*)	18 000		12 000		11 000	
Trade and other receivable (*Notes 3* and *4*)	15 000		10 000		9 000	
		33 000		22 000		20 000
Total assets		98 000		47 000		40 000
EQUITY AND LIABILITIES						
Capital and reserves:						
Issued ordinary share capital ($1 shares)	25 000		15 000		10 000	
10% $1 preferred shares	Nil		10 000		Nil	
Share premium account	10 000		Nil		4 000	
Accumulated profits	24 000		8 000		9 300	
		59 000		33 000		23 300
Non-current liabilities						
Interest bearing borrowing (*Note 3*)	20 000		Nil		4 000	
Deferred tax (*Note 3*)	2 000		1 000		1 500	
		22 000		1 000		5 500
Current liabilities						
Trade payables (*Note 4*)	10 000		6 500		6 000	
Tax payable	2 000		1 500		1 000	
Proposed dividend (*Note 5*)	Nil		1 000		Nil	
Bank overdraft	5 000		4 000		3 000	
Provisions (*Note 3*)	Nil		Nil		1 200	
		17 000		13 000		11 200
Total equity and liabilities		98 000		47 000		40 000

Notes to the balance sheets

1 On 1 July 19W0, the date of incorporation of Zippy, George subscribed for all the ordinary shares of Zippy at par. Then, on 1 July 19W5, when its balance of accumulated profits was $3 million, Zippy issued 10 million $1 preferred shares at par. George subscribed for 50% of these shares.

2 On 30 June 20X3, George purchased 8 million $1 shares in Bungle. The terms of the purchase consideration were as follows:

    2.1   On 30 June 20X3, George issued 3 $1 ordinary shares for every 4 shares purchased in Bungle. The market value of the ordinary shares at 30 June 20X3 was $4 per share.

2.2 On 30 June 20X5, George will pay the former shareholders of Bungle $1 in cash for every share in Bungle they have purchased. This payment is contingent on the cumulative profits after tax of Bungle for the two years ending 30 June 20X5 being at least $3 million.

At the date of carrying out the fair value exercise (see *Note* 3 below), the directors of George considered it probable that this cash payment would be made.

2.3 No entries in respect of the purchase of shares in Bungle have been made in the balance sheet of George.

3 Following the acquisition of Bungle, the directors of George carried out a fair value exercise as required by IAS *22 – Business combinations*. The following matters are relevant and all potential fair value adjustments are material:

3.1 Property, plant and equipment comprise land and buildings and plant and machinery. At 30 June 20X3, the land and buildings had a carrying value of $12 million and a market value of $18 million. The plant and machinery had a carrying value of $8 million. All the plant and machinery was purchased on 30 June 20X0 and was being depreciated on a straight-line basis over 8 years. No reliable estimate was available of the current market value of the plant and machinery, but at 30 June 20X3, the plant would have cost $22 million to replace with new plant.

3.2 The inventory at 30 June 20X3 comprised:
- Finished good which could be sold for $14.5 million. A reasonable profit allowance for the selling effort of the group would be $3 million.
- Finished goods that had been damaged and could only be sold for $100 000, representing a significant loss on sale.

3.3 Trade receivables includes an amount of $400 000 that the directors of George consider doubtful.

3.4 The interest-bearing borrowing of Bungle is repayable at par on 30 June 20X6. Interest at 10% per annum is payable annually in arrears and the payment due on 30 June 20X3 has already been made. The relevant discount rate is 7%.

3.5 The other provisions of Bungle comprise:
- $400 000 in respect of the closure of various retail outlets to which the directors of Bungle became committed prior to entering into acquisition negotiations with the directors of George.
- $800 000 in respect of the estimated cost of integrating Bungle into the George group. No detailed integration plans had been formulated by 30 June 20X3.

3.6 The additional deferred tax that needs to be provided on the adjustments that are necessary as a result of the fair value exercise is a liability of $3 million.

4 George supplies a component to Zippy at cost plus a mark up of 20%. At 30 June 20X3, the inventories of Zippy included $1.5 million in respect of this component. At 30 June 20X3, the receivables of George showed an amount receivable from Zippy of $1.2 million, while the grade payables of Zippy showed an amount payable to George of $600 000. On 29 June 20X3, George sent a consignment of components to Zippy at an invoiced price of $600 000. The consignment was received and recorded by Zippy on 2 July 20X3.

5 On 15 July 2003, Zippy paid its preferred share dividend for the year ended 30 June 20X3. George made no entries in its financial statements in respect of this dividend unit it was received in cash.

Required:

(a) Compute the goodwill on consolidation of Bungle that will be shown in the consolidated balance sheet of George at 30 June 20X3. Provide justification for your figures where you consider this is needed.

(b) Prepare the consolidated balance sheet of George at 30 June 2003. (IFRI Nov 03)

Foreign currency translation

After studying this chapter you should be able to:
- [ ] explain the necessity for foreign currency conversion and translation
- [ ] describe the IAS regulations in respect of foreign currency transactions for individual enterprises
- [ ] appraise the position where foreign currency investments and borrowings are matched
- [ ] critically appraise the IAS regulations in respect of translation of the accounts of foreign branches and subsidiaries etc.
- [ ] translate accounts of foreign enterprises
- [ ] describe the disclosure requirements of IAS regulations in respect of foreign currency translation.

Introduction

Business is increasingly international. Whenever a business has any dealings abroad, it will be involved in 'foreign' currencies. Since an enterprise generally keeps its accounting records and prepares its accounting reports in its own 'home' currency, figures expressed in foreign money units need to be re-expressed in 'home' units or whatever the reporting currency is. If foreign currency exchange rates remain absolutely constant, i.e. if the value of one currency in terms of the other does not change, then no difficulties arise. But this is rarely the case and, as we all know, exchange rates can and do fluctuate very considerably over relatively short periods of time.

Currency conversion

Currency conversion is required when a foreign currency transaction is completed within an accounting period. A transaction, foreign or otherwise, can be regarded as comprising two events:

- the purchase or sale of an asset or the incurring of an expense or item of income
- the receipt or payment of monies for these assets, expenses or items of income.

These events need to be recorded in an enterprise's books as they occur.

Activity 25.1

A UK company sells goods to a Swiss company on 1 May 20X2 for SWFr750 000. Payment is received on 1 August 20X2.

Exchange rate 1 May 20X2 is £1 = SWFr3.5544.

1 August 20X2 is £1 = SWFr3.7081.

The year end for the company is 30 September 20X2 and the reporting currency is sterling. Record this transaction in the company's books and name the balance on the accounts receivable account.

Activity feedback

Remembering the transaction comprises two events, we need to record the sale of goods immediately, but we must record the event in £s not SWFrs.

Sales account	Accounts receivable
1.5.X2 acc rec, 211 006	1.5.X2 sales 211 006

750 000/3.5544 (exchange rate 1.5.X2) = 211 006. When payment is received on 1 August X2 it will be in the form of SWFr750 000 which we must convert to sterling at the exchange rate at the time = 750 000/3.7081 = £202 260.

Event will be recorded as:

		£	£
Dr.	Cash	202 260	
Cr.	Accounts receivable		202 260

Thus, there will be a balance on the accounts receivable account of £8746, which is obviously a loss on exchange which will need to be reported in the income statement for ordinary activities.

Similarly, if the exchange rate had decreased from May to August a profit on exchange would have occurred which again would be reported as profit on ordinary activities.

Currency translation

Activity 25.1 involved a transaction that was completed by the year end but we need to consider how to deal with foreign transactions that are not completed by the year end.

Activity 25.2

Let us assume in Activity 25.1 that the company's year end is 30 June 20X2 when the exchange rate is £1 = SWFr3.6573. Record this transaction in the company's books.

Activity feedback

The initial sale will be recorded as before but at the year end 30 June 20X2 the accounts receivable account will show a balance of £211 006. This balance is not correct because if the debt was paid at this date we would receive SWFr750 000 = 205 069 which is the value of the debt at 30 June 20X2. Thus we translate the accounts receivable account at the year end at the exchange rate ruling, which is known as the spot rate, at a given date:

Accounts receivable

1.5.X2 sales	211 006	30.6.X2 Income statement	5 937
		loss on exchange 30.6.X2 balance c/d	205 069
	211 006		211 006
1.7.X2 balance b/d	205 069	1.8.X2 cash	202 260
		30.6.X3 IS loss on exchange	2 809

The balancing figure of £5937 is the loss on exchange identified as at 30 June X2, which will be debited to the income statement. When the debt is finally paid on 1 August 20X2 a further loss of £2809 is identified for the next year. Notice the total loss of £8746 is now split over the two years.

The currency translation follows the idea of prudence as we are taking account of the loss as soon as we are aware of it. However, what would we have done if on 30 June 20X2 the exchange rate were £1 = SWFr3.4973?

This time at the year end the debtor would translate as 750 000/3.4973 = £214 451 giving a profit on exchange of £3445 and on 1 August 20X2 when the debt is finally settled a loss of £12 191. The gain of £3445 is an unrealized gain and prudence might suggest that we should not recognize this gain.

Let us see what IAS 21 says on this issue.

IAS 21 requirements for individual enterprise's foreign currency transactions

The Standard was issued in 1983, revised in 1993 and revised again under the improvement project 2004. IAS 21 states in para. 28:

> Exchange differences arising on the settlement of monetary items or on translating monetary items at rates different from those at which they were translated on initial recognition during the period, or in previous financial statements, should be recognized in profit or loss in the period in which they arise, except as described in para. 32.

Further, para. 29 goes on to state:

> When monetary items arise from a foreign currency transaction and there is a change in the exchange rate between the transaction date and the date of settlement, an exchange difference results. When the transaction is settled within the same accounting period as that in which it occurred, all the exchange difference is recognized in that period. However, when the transaction is settled in a subsequent accounting period, the exchange difference recognized in each period up to the period of settlement is determined by the change in exchange rates during each period.

Thus, the IAS is telling us to recognize an unrealized gain in the accounts (in the activity this was £3445). This treatment can be justified on the grounds that:

- Where exchange gains arise on short-term monetary items their ultimate cash realization can normally be assessed with reasonable certainty and they are therefore realized in accordance with realization conventions.
- It provides symmetry with losses.

Activity 25.3

An enterprise, Axel, purchases an asset for €10 000 from a foreign enterprise on 1.3.X2 when the exchange rate between the two currencies involved was 1FC = €2. The functional currency of Axel is FCs. At the balance sheet date of Axel, 30.6.X2, the exchange rate is 1FC = €1. Show the entries by Axel to record this transaction initially and those required at the balance sheet date.

Activity feedback

Assets in FC				Accounts payable in FCs		
1.3.X2 purchase	5 000	Bal. c/d	5 000	30.6.X2	1.3.X2	
Bal. b/d	5 000	30.6.X2		bal. c/d 10 000	purchase	5 000
30.6.X2					Exchange diff.	5 000
					Bal. b/d	10 000

In Activity 25.3 only the monetary item, accounts payable, has been reported using the closing rate at the balance sheet date. Under the requirements of IAS 21 only foreign currency monetary items should be reported using closing rate; non-monetary items which are carried at historical cost denominated in a foreign currency should be reported using the exchange rate at the date of acquisition or, if the fair value is used, the exchange prevalent when the fair value was determined.

Reporting currency

The improvement project to IAS 21 removed the notion of 'reporting currency' and replaced it with two further definitions of currency.

Functional currency is the currency of the primary economic environment in which the entity operates.

Presentation currency is the currency in which the financial statements are presented.

When determining its functional currency an entity has to consider the following in accordance with IAS 21 paras 9–12:

The primary economic environment in which an entity operates is normally the one in which it primarily generates and expends cash. An entity considers the following factors in determining its functional currency:

(a) the currency:

(i) that mainly influences sales prices for goods and services; and

(ii) of the country whose competitive forces and regulations mainly determine the sales prices of its goods and services;
   (b) the currency that mainly influences labour, material and other costs of providing goods or services.

The following factors may also provide evidence of an entity's functional currency:

- the currency in which funds from financing activities are generated
- the currency in which receipts from operating activities are usually retained.

The following additional factors are considered in determining the functional currency of a foreign operation, and whether its functional currency is the same as that of the reporting entity:

- Whether the activities of the foreign operation are carried out as an extension of the reporting entity, rather than being carried out with a significant degree of autonomy. An example of the former is when the foreign operation only sells goods imported from the reporting entity and remits the proceeds to it. An example of the latter is when the operation accumulates cash and other monetary items, incurs expenses, generates income and arranges borrowings, all substantially in its local currency.
- Whether transactions with the reporting entity are a high or low proportion of the foreign operation's activities.
- Whether cash flows from the activities of the foreign operation directly affect the cash flows of the reporting entity and are readily available for remittance to it.
- Whether cash flows from the activities of the foreign operation are sufficient to service existing and normally expected debt obligations without funds being made available by the reporting entity.

When these indicators are mixed and the functional currency is not obvious, management uses its judgement to determine the functional currency that most faithfully represents the economic effects of the underlying transactions, events and conditions.

Once determined the functional currency is not changed unless the factors just outlined change.

An entity entering into a foreign currency transaction records that transaction initially by applying to the foreign currency amount the spot exchange rate between the functional currency and the foreign currency at the date of the transaction. This is what we did in Activity 25.3.

As far as preparation of financial statements is concerned an entity can present them in any currency. This means that where the functional and presentation currency differ then a further translation of results and financial position into the presentational currency is required. This commonly occurs where individual entities within a group who all have different functional currencies have to present in the group currency.

The translation from functional to presentation currency occurs as follows:

1 assets and liabilities for each balance sheet presented shall be translated at the closing rate at the date of that balance sheet
2 income and expenses for each income statement shall be translated at exchange rates at the date of the transactions
3 all resulting exchange differences shall be recognized as a separate component of equity.

Activity 25.4

The balance sheet of Zhou Ltd at 31.12.X4 is as follows:

	FCs	FCs
Share capital		300
Retained profits		100
		400
Equipment at cost	350	
less Depreciation	50	300
Inventory	80	
Net monetary current assets	60	140
Long-term loans		(40)
		400

The presentation currency for Zhou Ltd. is Crowns (CRs) and as at:

	FCs to CRs
1 January X4	5
Average for the year to 31 December X4	4.5
Average for closing inventory acquisition	4.6
31 December X4	4.2

Income statement for the year ended 31.12.X4 is as follows:

	FCs
Sales	600
less Cost of sales	400
Gross profit	200
less Depreciation	(50)
Less other expenses	(50)
	100

Translate the financial statements of Zhou Ltd. into the presentation currency from the functional currency and show clearly where any exchange difference is recognized.

Activity feedback

Balance sheet as at 31.12.X4:

	Rate	CRs	CRs
Share capital	5	60	
Retained profits		21.4	
Exchange difference		13.8	95.2
Equipment at cost	4.2	83.3	
Depreciation	4.2	11.9	71.4
Inventory	4.2	19	
Net monetary current assets	4.2	14.3	
Long-term loans	4.2	(9.5)	23.8
			95.2

Income statement for the year ended 31.12.X4:

Sales	4.5		133.3
less Cost of sales	4.5		88.9
Gross profit			44.4
Depreciation	4.2	11.9	
Other expenses		11.1	23
			21.4

The exchange difference is the amount required to balance the statements.

Loans

AS 21 defines 'monetary items as units of currency held and assets and liabilities to be received or paid in fixed or determinable number of units of currency' (para. 7). Thus a loan will be translated as any other monetary item at closing rate and the exchange gain or loss credited or charged to income. We might question the rationale for taking the unrealized exchange gain on the loan at the balance sheet date to the income statement here but it at least provides consistent symmetrical treatment with the loss which is equally unrealized.

Hedge accounting or investments matched by borrowings

An enterprise that has made a foreign entity investment is exposed to an exchange risk on that investment. However, it is possible for the investing enterprise to protect itself by raising loans in a foreign country denominated in the foreign currency and using the money from these borrowings to make the investment. From the point of view of the home (investing) enterprise it has:

- an asset, exposed to an exchange risk
- a liability also exposed to an exchange risk.

Since the asset and liability, in principal equal in amount, are in effect part of one overall transaction and since the exchange risks are equal and opposite, the effects of exchange rate movements on these items should simply be cancelled out.

Normally, however, a foreign currency investment, a long-term non-monetary item, would not be translated in the accounts at the year end but the loan, a long-term monetary item, *would* be translated. IAS 21 allows us to classify as equity exchange differences arising on a foreign currency liability where that liability is used as a 'hedge'. Once the investment is disposed of then the exchange difference on the loan will be recognized as income or expense.

Interestingly, IAS 21 does not deal with hedge accounting for foreign currency items in much detail and we have to refer to IAS 39 for further guidance. The criteria in IAS 39 used to identify a hedge are as follows:

- At the inception of the hedge there is a formal document to support classification as a hedge.
- The hedge is expected to be highly effective.
- A forecasted transaction which is the subject of the hedge must be highly probable.
- The effectiveness of the hedge can be reliably measured.

■ The hedge was assessed on an ongoing basis and determined actually to have been highly effective throughout the financial reporting period.

Activity 25.5

An enterprise whose year end is 31 March, and which prepares its accounts in £s sterling, takes out two loans on 1 August, one for 5 000 000 pesetas and one for FF200 000 when the exchange rates were £1 = 180 pesetas = FF10. The French franc loan is used to make an equity investment of $30 000; £1 = $1.60. At the same time another equity investment is the purchase of 100 000 Australian dollars (A$). £1 = A$1.9. How would this be shown in the enterprise's books at the year end when £1 = 186 pesetas = FF9.7 = $1.5 = A$1.95 given the reporting currency is £.

Activity feedback

Initially, when the loans and investments are taken up they will need to be recorded in the books in £s as follows:

Loan pesetas		Loan FF	
	1/8 cash 27 778		1/8 cash 20 000
	(5 000 000/180)		(200 000/10)

Investment $		Investment A$	
1/8 cash 18 750		1/8 cash 52 632	
(30 000/1.6)		(100 000/1.9)	

Long-term monetary items, i.e. pesetas loan and French franc loan will be translated at year end exchange rates, but can the investments be translated at year end? The answer is generally no. In this case, however, it is possible that the dollar investment is hedged with the French franc loan therefore the loss on this loan avoids the income statement and is taken directly to equity.

Loan pesetas		Loan FF	
31/3 gain IS 896	1/8 cash 27 778	31/3bal.c/d 20 619	1/8 cash 20 000
31/3 bal c/d 26 882			31/3 loss equity
			reserves 619

Note that in Activity 25.5 we assume there is no need for the hedged loan and investment to be in the same currency. It is perfectly clear that where investments and loans are in the same currency the loss on one will offset the gain on the other due to the change in currency rate. However, the logic of hedging using different currencies is rather unclear, as you cannot be certain the risk will be covered. It is interesting to note, in Activity 25.5, that if the French franc loan and dollar investment had not been treated as hedged then the income statement would have borne a further loss of £619!

Summary of individual enterprise transactions

1 Settled transactions: gain or loss is obviously realized and reflected in cash flows.

2 Unsettled transactions: short-term monetary items translate at year end exchange rate and gain or loss, although unrealized, is taken to income statement, as it is reasonably certain.

3 Long-term monetary items treated the same as short term.

4 If a liability forms a hedge to a net investment then the exchange difference on the liability is classified as equity.

Translation methods for financial statements of foreign operations

When translating any particular item we can take two basic possible views:

1 We can use the exchange rate ruling when the item was created (historic rate).

2 We can use the exchange rate ruling when the item is being reported (current or closing rate).

Since we can apply this choice to each item in the financial statements one at a time, it is clear that many different combinations are possible. Four that have been suggested are now outlined.

Single rate (closing rate)

This is based on the idea that the holding enterprise has a net investment in the foreign operation and that what is at risk from currency fluctuations is this net financial investment. All assets, liabilities, revenues and expenses will be translated at the closing (balance sheet date) rate. Exchange differences will arise if the closing rate differs from the previous year's closing rate or from the date when the transaction occurred.

Mixed rate (current/non-current)

Here, current assets and liabilities would be translated at the closing rate whereas fixed assets and non-current liabilities would be translated at the rate ruling when the item was established (i.e. current items are translated at current rates and fixed items are translated at fixed rates).

Mixed rate (monetary/non-monetary)

This proposal would translate monetary assets and liabilities at the closing rate and all non-monetary assets and liabilities at the rate ruling when the item was established. There is an analogy here with the arguments for CPP accounting. Monetary items are automatically expressed in current monetary units, so use the current rate for them and non-monetary items are expressed in out-of-date monetary units, so use the out-of-date rate for them.

Mixed rate (temporal)

This is based on the idea that the foreign operations are simply a part of the group that is the reporting entity. Some of the individual assets and liabilities of the group just 'happen' to be abroad. The valuation basis used to value the assets and liabilities determines the appropriate exchange rate. Those assets recorded on a HC basis would be translated at the historic rate – the rate ruling when the item was established. Assets recorded on a current value basis would be translated at the current (closing) rate. Revenues and expenses should theoretically be translated at the rate ruling on the date when the amount shown in the accounts was established, i.e. assuming an even spread of trading at the average rate for the year.

It is important to avoid the assumption that the temporal method means using historic exchange rates. The words temporal and historic are sometimes, quite wrongly, used interchangeably in this context. 'Temporal' means literally 'at the time', i.e. consistent with the underlying valuation basis. So the temporal method does mean using historic exchange rates when applied to HC accounts. But the temporal method means using current exchange rates when applied to current value accounts. This would broadly reduce the temporal method to the single rate method.

There has been controversy over the appropriate method to use. The two favoured possibilities are the closing rate method and the temporal method but both the UK and the US have had changes of heart over the years as to which method should be used when.

IAS 21 rules for translation of financial statements of foreign operations

IAS 21 requires each entity to determine its functional currency and to then translate its foreign currency items into the functional currency using the temporal method. Exchange differences arising are recognized in the profit or loss of the period. Where an entity has to translate from its functional currency to a presentation currency, for example where consolidated financial statements are required for a group containing individual entities using functional currencies different to the presentation currency, then essentially the closing rate method is used.

However, the closing rate method requires that income and expenses are translated at the dates of transactions and this is usually approximated by an average rate for the period and exchange gains and losses are classified as equity until the disposal of the net investment. There is an exception to this and that is when the foreign entity operates in a hyperinflationary economy when IAS 29 applies.

Tables 25.1 and 25.2 provide a useful summary of both methods.

Table 25.1 Financial statements of a foreign operation translated into functional currency

Item	Translation rate
Cost and depreciation of property, plant and equipment and intangible assets	Rate at date of acquisition or fair valuation date
Inventories	Rate when cost incurred
Monetary items	Closing rate
Income and expense items	Rate at date of transaction or average rate for period if rates do not fluctuate significantly
Exchange difference	Income statement

Table 25.2 Financial statements of a foreign operation translated into presentation currency

Item	Translation rate
All assets and liabilities whether monetary or non-monetary	Closing rate
Income and expense items	Rate at date of transaction
Exchange difference	Equity

The following activity will show the differences between the two methods.

Activity 25.6

Home established a 100% ownership of Away on 1 January year 8 by subscribing to €25 000 of shares in cash when the exchange rate was 12 'tickets' to the €. Away raised a long-term loan of 100 000 tickets locally on 1 January year 8 and immediately purchased equipment costing 350 000 tickets, which was expected to last ten years with no residual value. It was to be depreciated under the straight line method. The accounts of Away in the foreign currency for year 8 follow, during which the relevant exchange rates were:

	Tickets to €
1 January	12
Average for year	11
Average for period in which closing inventory acquired	10.5
31 December	10

Income statement for year 8

	Tickets
Sales	450 000
less Cost of sales	(360 000)
Gross profit	90 000
less Depreciation	(35 000)
Other expenses	(15 000)
Net profit	40 000

Balance sheet as at 31 December year 8

Share capital	300 000
Retained profits	40 000
	340 000
Equipment at cost	350 000
less Depreciation	35 000
	315 000
Inventory	105 000
Net monetary current assets	20 000
less long-term loans	(100 000)
	340 000

Translate the accounts for the foreign operation using both the closing rate and temporal method and identify what to do with the exchange differences.

Activity feedback

Income statement for year 8	Rate	Closing	Temporal	Rate
Sales	11	40 909	40 909	11
less Cost of sales	11	32 727	32 727	11
Gross profit		8 182	8 182	
less Depreciation	10	(3 500)	(2 917)	12
Other expenses	11	(1 364)	(1 364)	11
Net profit		3 318	3 901	

Balance sheet as at 31 December year 8	Rate	Closing	Temporal	Rate
Share capital		25 000	25 000	
Retained profits		3 318	3 901	
		28 318	28 901	
Equipment at cost	10	35 000	29 167	12
less Depreciation	10	3 500	2 917	12
		31 500	26 250	
Inventory	10	10 500	10 000	10.5
Net monetary current assets	10	2 000	2 000	10
less Long-term loans	10	(10 000)	(10 000)	10
		34 000	28 250	
Exchange difference		(5 682)	651	
		28 318	28 901	

The share capital figure in the closing rate method is translated at the original rate to highlight the exchange differences.

The exchange difference, a loss, of €651 under the temporal method should be charged to the income statement for the current year. Had it been a gain it would have been credited to the income statement in accordance with IAS 21. You might question whether this is prudent but it is treating the exchange differences of the foreign entity as if they were the exchange differences of the reporting entity.

Under the closing rate method, the issue is more complex. Differences have arisen in respect of each type of balance sheet item because the opening balances (representing the net investment in the overseas subsidiary by the holding company) have been retranslated back into sterling at the closing rate. The total gain of €5682 can be broken down as in Table 25.3.

IAS 21 requires that this gain is taken to equity. You could argue that the gain of €833 on the short-term monetary items be taken to income statement and only the long-term items to equity. The allocation of these exchange differences to either equity

Table 25.3 Retranslation at closing rate

Item	Closing rate	Opening rate	Difference
Opening fixed assets	350 000/10	350 000/12	£5 834 credit
Opening net current assets	50 000/10	50 000/12	£ 833 credit
Opening long-term loans	100 000/10	100 000/12	£1 667 debit
Net profit	40 000/10 = 4 000	40 000/average = 3 318	£ 682 credit

or income certainly has an effect on the information provided to users as can be seen from the example and the final balance sheets.

	Closing rate – foreign entity	Temporal method – integral
Share capital	25 000	25 000
Equity reserves	5 682	
	30 682	
Retained profits	3 318	3 250
Net assets	34 000	28 250

Note the difference in the net assets, once translated, of the foreign enterprise.

Try the following activity to test your understanding of foreign currency translation and the requirements of IAS 21.

Activity 25.7

The final accounts for the year to 31 March year 5 of Otters, an overseas wholly owned subsidiary of Seals of London, follow.

The relevant exchange rates of the two currencies were:

Date	Tails to €s
1 January year 1	16.00 when shares issued
1 April year 1	16.20 when property bought
1 September year 3	18.00 when loans issued
31 March year 4	19.80
Average for January – March year 4	19.70 when opening inventory bought
31 March year 5	20.10
Average for January – March year 5	20.05 when closing inventory bought
Average for year to 31 March year 5	20.00

Retained profits from previous years were €10 240 under temporal and €9950 under closing rate. Paid dividends were 150 000 tails, €7 934 as received in London.

Income statement for year to 31 March year 5

	Tails 000s	Tails 000s
Sales		10 000
less Cost of sales		
Opening inventory	1 800	
Purchases	7 700	
	9 500	
less Closing inventory	2 000	7 500
Gross profit		2 500
less Wages and salaries	600	
Sundry expenses	380	
Property depreciation	100	
Equipment depreciation	100	
Loan interest	120	1 300

Net profit	1 200
Tax	600
	600
Retained profits previous years	200
	800

Balance sheet as at 31 March year 5

Ordinary shares		3 000
Retained profits		650
		3 650
8% loans		1 500
Current liabilities		
Accounts payable	2 000	
Tax	600	2 600
		7 750
Property	2 500	
Depreciation	500	2 000
Plant and equipment	500	
Depreciation	250	250
Current assets		
Inventory	2 000	
Accounts receivable	2 000	
Cash	1 500	5 500
		7 750

Translate the accounts of Otters using both the closing rate and temporal rate. Identify the exchange gain or loss and its accounting treatment according to IAS 21.

Activity feedback

Income statement for year to 31 March year 5:

		Temporal Method			Closing	Rate
		€	€		€	€
Sales	20		500 000	20		500 000
less Cost of sales						
Opening inventory	19.7	91 371		19.7	91 371	
Purchases	20	385 000		20	385 000	
		476 371			476 371	
Closing inventory	20.05	99 751	376 620	20.05	99 751	376 620
Gross profit			123 380			123 380
Wages and salaries	20	30 000		20	30 000	
Sundry expenses	20	19 000		20	19 000	
Property depreciation	16.2	6 173		20	4 975	
Equipment depreciation	18	5 556		20	4 975	
Loan interest	20	6 000	66 729	20	6 000	64 950
Net profit			56 651			58 430
Tax	20		30 000	20		30 000
			26 651			28 430

Profits previous years	Given		10 240	Given		9 950
			36 891			38 380
Dividends	Actual		7 394	Actual		7 394
			29 497			30 986

Balance sheet as at 31 March year 5

Shares	16		187 500	16	187 500	
Exchange difference	Balancing figure				(36 895)	150 605
Retained profits	Above	29 497		Above		30 986
Exchange difference	Balancing figure	(26 033)	3 464			
			190 964			
8% loan	16.5		90 909	20.1		74 627
Current liabilities						
Accounts payable	20.1	99 502		20.1	99 502	
Tax	20.1	29 851	129 353	20.1	29 851	129 353
			411 226			385 571
Property	16.2	154 321		20.1	124 378	
Depreciation	16.2	30 864	123 457	20.1	24 876	99 502
Equipment	18	27 778		20.1	24 876	
Depreciation	18	13 889	13 889	20.1	12 438	12 438
Current assets						
Inventory	20.05	99 751		20.1	99 502	
Accounts receivable	20.1	99 502		20.1	99 502	
Cash	20.1	74 627	273 880	20.1	74 627	273 631
			411 226			385 571

Under the temporal method the loss of €26 033 on exchange is charged to profits for the year and will need to be shown within the income statement as an operating expense, i.e. profits for the year will only be €618.

Under the closing method the exchange loss of €36 895 is taken to equity not profit.

The figures for incorporation with the reporting enterprise are noticeably different under each method.

Some other issues

Disposal of a foreign entity is dealt with in accordance with para. 48 of IAS 21:

> On the disposal of a foreign operation, the cumulative amount of the exchange differences deferred in the separate component of equity relating to that foreign operation should be recognized in profit or loss when the gain or loss on disposal is recognized.

Presumably now we can assume the gain or loss is realized and therefore treated as other realized gains or losses.

IAS 21 does allow a change in an entity's functional currency. However, this can only happen where there is a change in the underlying transaction events and conditions. This could occur when there is a change in the currency that mainly influences the sale prices of goods and services. A good example of this is when European countries adopt the euro. Para. 37 of IAS 21 tells us to account for the change in the functional currency prospectively as follows:

> An entity translates all items into the new functional currency using the exchange rate at the date of the change. The resulting translated amounts for non-monetary items are treated as their historical cost. Exchange differences arising from the translation of a foreign operation previously classified in equity in accordance with paragraphs 32 and 39(c) are not recognized in profit or loss until the disposal of the operation.

Disclosure requirements

We refer you to paras 51–57 of the standard for these, but the following from the Illustrative Corporate Consolidated Financial Statements 2004 [Footsy & Co. Group] published by Pricewaterhouse Coopers illustrates the disclosure required.

2.4 Foreign currency translation

(a) *Functional and presentation currency*
Items included in the financial statements of each of the Group's entities are measured using the currency of the primary economic environment in which the entity operates ('the functional currency'). The consolidated financial statements are presented in euros, which is the Company's functional and presentation currency.

(b) *Transactions and balances*
Foreign currency transactions are translated into the functional currency using the exchange rates prevailing at the dates of the transactions. Foreign exchange gains and losses resulting from the settlement of such transactions and from the translation at year-end exchange rates of monetary assets and liabilities denominated in foreign currencies are recognised in the income statement, except when deferred in equity as qualifying cash flow hedges and qualifying net investment hedges.
   Translation differences on non-monetary items, such as equities held at fair value through profit or loss, are reported as part of the fair value gain or loss. Translation differences on non-monetary items, such as equities classified as available-for-sale financial assets, are included in the fair value reserve in equity.

(c) *Group companies*
The results and financial position of all the group entities (none of which has the currency of a hyperinflationary economy) that have a functional currency

different from the presentation currency are translated into the presentation currency as follows:

(i) assets and liabilities for each balance sheet presented are translated at the closing rate at the date of that balance sheet;

(ii) income and expenses for each income statement are translated at average exchange rates (unless this average is not a reasonable approximation of the cumulative effect of the rates prevailing on the transaction dates, in which case income and expenses are translated at the dates of the transactions); and

(iii) all resulting exchange differences are recognised as a separate component of equity.

On consolidation, exchange differences arising from the translation of the net investment in foreign entities, and of borrowings and other currency instruments designated as hedges of such investments, are taken to shareholders' equity. When a foreign operation is sold, such exchange differences are recognised in the income statement as part of the gain or loss on sale.

Goodwill and fair value adjustments arising on the acquisition of a foreign entity are treated as assets and liabilities of the foreign entity and translated at the closing rate.

27. Net foreign exchange gains/(losses)

The exchange differences (charged)/credited to the income statement are included as follows:

	2004	2003
Sales	333	(150)
Cost of goods sold	(125)	50
Selling and marketing costs	(250)	200
Administration expenses	(235)	100
Finance costs – net (Note 25)	2 594	(1 995)
	2 317	(1 795)

Financial reporting in hyperinflationary economies

At several points throughout this chapter we noted differences to the requirements for IAS 21 for those entities reporting in a currency of a hyperinflationary economy. The financial statements of such a foreign entity have to be dealt with in accordance with IAS 29 before the requirements of IAS 21 are applied. IAS 29 requires (in para. 8) that:

The financial statements of an enterprise whose functional currency is the currency of a hyperinflationary economy, whether they are based on a historical cost approach or a current cost approach, should be stated in terms of the measuring unit current at the balance sheet date. The corresponding figures for the previous period required by IAS 1, *Presentation of Financial Statements*, and any information in respect of earlier periods should also be stated in terms of the measuring unit current at the balance sheet date.

Para. 9 goes on to state: The gain or loss on the net monetary position should be included in profit or loss and separately disclosed.

GAAP comparisons

IAS v UK
Foreign currency is dealt with under SSAP 20 in the UK. This is similar to IAS 21 except:

- When foreign currency loans are used to hedge foreign currency investments both can be retranslated and exchange differences taken to equity and offset.
- There is no requirement in SSAP 20 for exchange differences resulting from severe devaluation of a currency to be included as part of the initial cost of an asset.
- Under the closing rate method used for foreign entities in the UK there is a permitted choice between using the average rate or the closing rate to translate the income statement.
- When disposal of a foreign entity occurs under UK GAAP the exchange differences remain under equity.

IAS v US
Foreign currency is dealt with in SFAS 52, which is generally similar to IAS 21.

Summary

A fascinating topic but not an easy one. It is difficult to get to grips with the logic of applying one set of rules to translation to functional currency and another to presentation currency. Some of the logic used might also be questionable and the information that is eventually provided for users might be less than understandable.

Remember:

- For individual enterprise transactions non-monetary items are translated at originating exchange rate but monetary items at balance sheet rate if not settled. Thus unrealized gains and losses due to foreign currency fluctuations will be taken to the income statement generally as part of ordinary activities.
- Foreign enterprises recording to functional currency use the temporal method.
- Foreign enterprises translating to reporting currency use the closing rate for balance sheet and average rate (generally) for income statement.
- Where exchange differences result from severe devaluations and there is no practical means to hedge these are carried as part of the cost of the asset.
- Foreign operations in hyperinflationary economies have to be stated in the measuring unit current at the balance sheet date before translation.

EXERCISES   (✔ indicates answers are available on page 746–750)

1 Explain the differences in treatment and the effect of translating financial statements using the temporal and closing rate method.
2 Identify the circumstances under which IAS 21 permits the use of the closing rate method and the temporal method for translation of financial statements.

✔ **3** Should exchange differences appear in the income statement of an enterprise or be charged direct to reserves? State the reasons for your answer.

4 What is the difference between foreign currency conversion and foreign currency translation?

✔ **5** Critically appraise the concepts on which the closing rate and temporal methods are based and discuss the factors that will be taken into account by a group choosing between the two methods.

6 What is 'hedge accounting'? Identify the requirements of IAS 21 in accounting for hedges.

✔ **7** Memo, a public limited company, owns 75% of the ordinary share capital of Random, a public limited company which is situated in a foreign country. Memo acquired Random on 1 May 2003 for 120 million crowns (CR) when the retained profits of Random were 80 million crowns. Random has not revalued its assets or issued any share capital since its acquisition by Memo. The following financial statements relate to Memo and Random:

Balance Sheets at 30 April 2004

	Memo $m	Random CRm
Tangible non current assets	297	146
Investment in Random	48	–
Loan to Random	5	–
Current Assets	355	102
	705	248
Capital and Reserves		
Ordinary shares of $1/1CR	60	32
Share premium account	50	20
Accumulated profit	360	95
	470	147
Non current liabilities	30	41
Current liabilities	205	60
	705	248

Income Statements for year ended 30 April 2004

	Memo $m	Random CRm
Revenue	200	142
Cost of sales	(120)	(96)
Gross profit	80	46
Distribution and administrative expenses	(30)	(20)
Operating profit	50	26
Interest receivable	4	–
Interest payable	–	(2)
Profit before taxation	54	24
Income tax expense	(20)	(9)
Profit after taxation	34	15

The following information is relevant to the preparation of the consolidated financial statements of Memo:

(a) The directors wish to treat goodwill in accordance with recent proposals as a foreign currency asset. Goodwill has been subjected to an impairment review as at 30 April 2004 and is deemed to be impaired by $2 million.

(b) During the financial year Random has purchased raw materials from Memo and denominated the purchase in crowns in its financial records. The details of the transaction are set out below:

	Date of transaction	Purchase price $m	Profit percentage on selling price
Raw materials	1 February 2004	6	20%

At the year end, half of the raw materials purchased were still in the inventory of Random. The inter-company transactions have not been eliminated from the financial statements and the goods were recorded by Random at the exchange rate ruling on 1 February 2004. A payment of $6 million was made to Memo when the exchange rate was 2.2 crowns to $1. Any exchange gain or loss arising on the transaction is still held in the current liabilities of Random.

(c) Memo had made an interest free loan to Random of $5 million on 1 May 2003. The loan was repaid on 30 May 2004. Random had included the loan in non-current liabilities and had recorded it at the exchange rate at 1 May 2003.

(d) The fair value of the net assets of Random at the date of acquisition is to be assumed to be the same as the carrying value.

(e) Random operates with a significant degree of autonomy in its business operations.

(f) The following exchange rates are relevant to the financial statements:

Crown to $

30 April/1 May 2003	2.5
1 November 2003	2.6
1 February 2004	2
30 April 2004	2.1
Average rate for year to 30 April 2004	2

(g) Memo has paid a dividend of $8 million during the financial year and this is not included in the income statement.

Required:

Prepare a consolidated income statement for the year ended 30 April 2004 and a consolidated balance sheet at that date in accordance with International Financial Reporting Standards.

(Candidates should round their calculations to the nearest $100 000.) (ACCA June 04)

8 Small was incorporated in 1985 and prior to its acquisition by Big had built up its own customer base and local supplier network. This was not disturbed when Small became a subsidiary of Big as the directors of Big were anxious that the local expertise of the management of Small should be utilised as much as possible. Therefore all the day-to-day operational decisions regarding Small continued to be made by the existing management, with the directors of Big exercising 'arms' length' strategic control.

The balance sheets of Big and Small at 31 March 2003 are given below. The balance sheet of Small is prepared in florins, the functional currency for Small.

	Big $000	$000	Small FI'000	FI'000
Non-current assets:				
Property, plant and equipment	60 000		80 000	
Investments	9 500			
		69 500		80 000

Current assets:				
Inventories	30 000		40 000	
Trade receivables	25 000		32 000	
Cash	3 000		4 000	
		58 000		76 000
		127 500		156 000
Issued capital and reserves:				
Called up share capital (50 cents/$\frac{1}{2}$ florin shares)		30 000		40 000
Revaluation reserve		15 000		–
Accumulated profits		34 500		44 000
		79 500		84 000
Non-current liabilities:				
Interest-bearing borrowings	15 000		30 000	
Deferred tax	5 000		9 000	
		20 000		39 000
Current liabilities:				
Trade payables	12 000		15 000	
Tax	16 000		18 000	
		28 000		33 000
		127 500		156 000

NOTES TO THE BALANCE SHEETS
Note 1 – Investment by Big in Small
On 1 April 1997, Big purchased 60 million shares in Small for 57 million florins. The accumulated profits of Small showed a balance of 20 million florins at that date. The accounting policies of Small are the same as those of Big except that Big revalues its land, whereas Small carries its land at historical cost. Small's land had been purchased on 1 April 1994. On 1 April 1997, the fair value of the land of Small was 6 million florins higher than its carrying value in the individual financial statements of that enterprise. By 31 March 2003, the difference between fair value and carrying value had risen to 11 million florins. Apart from this accounting policy difference, no other fair value adjustments were necessary when initially consolidating Small as a subsidiary.

Note 2 – Intra-group trading
On 6 March 2003, Big sold goods to Small at an invoiced price of $6 000 000, making a profit of 25% on cost. Small recorded these goods in inventory and payables using an exchange rate of 5 florins to $1 (there were minimal fluctuations between the two currencies in the month of March 2003). The goods remained in the inventory of Small at 31 March 2003 but on 29 March 2003 Small sent Big a cheque for 30 million florins to clear its payable. Big received and recorded this cash on 3 April 2003.

Note 3 – Exchange rates

Date	Exchange rate (florins to $1)
1 April 1994	7
1 April 1997	6
31 March 2002	5.5
31 March 2003	5
Weighted average for the year to 31 March 2003	5.2

Weighted average
for the dates of
acquisition of closing
inventory   5.1

Required:

Translate the balance sheet of Small at 31 March 2003 into $s and prepare the consolidated balance sheet of the Big group at 31 March 2003.   (CIMA May 03)

Part Four

Financial Analysis

In Part One we focused on what financial reporting is all about – what it is trying to achieve and how the accountant sets about achieving it. Parts Two and Three presented the rules that accountants have created for themselves to govern financial reporting. In those three parts, a preparer's approach to financial reporting is taken as we describe the mechanisms and rules through which financial information is provided to users. In Part Four, a user's approach is followed. In this part we analyse how different stakeholders of a company can use the information provided in the annual accounts to gain some insight as to the reporting entity's stability, performance, future prospects and/or whatever else may interest them.

Interpretation of financial statements

After studying this chapter you should be able to:
- ☐ explain how industry analysis can be useful in the context of financial analysis
- ☐ explain why knowledge of the corporate strategy is important for financial analysis
- ☐ describe the different incentives for annual accounts' management
- ☐ identify the practices which are used for annual accounts' management purposes
- ☐ explain the purpose of entity analysis
- ☐ describe what is meant by quality of disclosure.

Introduction

Financial statements provide valuable information for different stakeholders. In Chapter 1 we identified the users of accounting information and their differing needs. The following activity provides a useful piece of revision.

Activity 26.1

Identify the users of accounting information and their needs/objectives.

Activity feedback

- Investors/owners – is the money invested in the business making a suitable return for them or could it earn more if invested elsewhere? Is the business a safe investment, that is, is it likely to become insolvent/bankrupt? Should the investors invest more money in the business?
- Suppliers – is the business able to pay for the goods bought on credit? Will the business continue to be a recipient of the goods the supplier produces?
- Customers – is the business able to supply the goods the customer requires and when it requires them? Will the business continue in operation so that guarantees on goods purchased will be met?
- Lenders – is there adequate security for the loan made? Does the business make a sufficient profit and have enough cash available to make the necessary payments to the lender of interest and capital?

- Employee – does the business make sufficient profit and have enough cash available to make the necessary payments to the employees? Will the business continue in operation at its current level so that the employee has secure employment?
- Government – for example to calculate taxation due or to aid decision-making in respect of the economy as a whole of a country.
- Public – the majority of their needs is in respect of employment, pollution and health and safety which is not particularly, as yet, provided by financial statements.

From the feedback to this activity it is possible to identify three general areas of interest in which users' needs and objectives may lie:

- Financial status – can the business pay its way, is it in fact *liquid*?
- Performance – how successful is the business, is it making a reasonable profit, is it utilizing its assets to the fullest, is it in fact profitable and efficient?
- Investment – is the business a suitable investment for shareholders or would returns be greater if they invested elsewhere, is it a good investment?

Since the financial statements serve as a means of communication with the external stakeholders of a firm, these annual accounts may sometimes be 'managed' to convey a certain message to the outside world. Therefore, it is extremely important that users of financial accounting information are well aware of the incentives a company may have to influence the annual accounts and the means they have available for this purpose.

The knowledge about 'annual accounts management incentives and practices' is as important as a sound knowledge about the techniques of financial analysis in order to understand and judge properly the information provided through the annual accounts. In Part Four we discuss both elements in depth. The 'annual accounts management incentives and practices' will be discussed in this chapter. The techniques of financial analysis (trend analysis, common size financial statements, ratio analysis and cash flow analysis) are presented and illustrated in Chapter 27.

Financial statements are a source of information about a company since they present a picture of the economic performance of a firm. This economic performance, however, is influenced to a large extent by the adopted business strategy of a firm and by the economic and industrial environment in which a firm is operating. As a result the business strategy of a firm and the industry characteristics will have an impact on the accounting data represented in the financial statements. Therefore, it is worthwhile gaining a clear insight into the industry and business characteristics of a company before starting with the analysis of its financial statements. Studying the economic and industrial environment of a company together with its strategy is often called 'industry analysis' in textbooks on financial and corporate reporting and analysis.

Industry analysis

In order to determine whether a business is, in fact, liquid or whether it is making a reasonable profit or is worthwhile to invest in, we need to compare the performance of the company with a benchmark. Besides gaining insight into how a firm's strategy and its business environment have an impact on the data in the annual accounts, industry analysis also provides benchmarking data to financial analysts and other users of accounting information. Through industry analysis we can obtain benchmarks against which the current performance, the financial status and the investment potential of a particular company can be compared. However, we need to take great care in carrying out this benchmarking so that we do not invalidate the results. In setting benchmarks against which we can compare a company, we must remain aware of the limitations of this comparison. This item will be further elaborated in the next chapter.

Activity 26.2

What other benchmarks/indicators could you think of besides benchmarks taken from industry analysis? Consider also their limitations.

Activity feedback

- *Past period achievements*. Uses – to identify whether current activity is better or worse than previous periods. Limitations – external factors may have influenced activity levels, e.g. public awareness of environmental issues may have necessitated a change in manufacturing process leading to increased costs.
- *Budgets*. Uses – has current activity matched planned activity? Limitations – the budget may not be a valid standard of performance, e.g. underlying assumptions may have been unrealistic or set at too high a level.

Activity 26.3

Within the scope of industry analysis data from other businesses in the same industry or industry averages could be used for benchmarking purposes. What could be their limitations?

Activity feedback

- *Other businesses*. Uses – is our business performing as well? Limitations – businesses may not be truly comparable with regard to size and type, e.g. grocery sole trader compared to supermarket; manufacturer compared to retailer. Further external factors may affect one business, e.g. a lengthy strike. Accounting standards and accounting policies on which accounting information is prepared may be different, e.g. stock valuations, depreciation, historic cost or revalued amount, treatment of research and development, treatment of goodwill.
- *Industry averages*. Industry averages have uses and limitations very similar to those of other businesses. Additionally, an average is simply a figure which takes account of the best but also of the worst.

Each of the four benchmarks identified is commonly used in assessing business status, performance and potential, but interpretation of accounts is highly subjective and requires skilled judgement, bearing in mind the limitations of these benchmarks.

In the next two sections a brief overview of the elements to be considered in the context of industry analysis will be presented.

Analysis of the business environment

As different elements of the business and the economic environment of a company have an impact on the revenue and costs levels of the firm, we may state that the environment determines to a certain extent the profit potential of a company. An important element with regard to industry profitability is the level of competition in an industry. This level of competition is influenced by the type of competition, the barriers to entry, the production capacity available in the industry, the existing relationships, agreements and alliances.

The degree of competition in an industry determines to a large extent the price which can be charged for the products or services to the customer. The competion can be perfect competition, monopoly or any form in between. Firms in a monopoly position with no substitutes for their products or services can charge higher prices than firms in a situation of perfect competition with a high number of substitutes and high price elasticity of demand. The danger of substitute products can be avoided if firms are able to differentiate their products or services. This possibility will be determined by the existing switching costs.

The level of price competition in an industry is also a function of the cost structure which is related to the technology used and the existence of economies of scale. If the ratio fixed to variable costs is high, firms have a tendency to engage in price wars in order to fully utilize the production capacity they have invested in. Many economic textbooks mention the airline industry as a typical example of an industry where such a policy is often applied. However, if we analyse more closely the value chain of an airline company then this observation (= high fixed costs) relates only to the transport activities in the value chain of the airline. Other activities in the value chain (such as reservations and sales, catering, handling) have a higher proportion of variable costs in their total cost structure. Therefore, price wars intended to fill up the empty seats in the airplanes will increase costs in the other activity areas of the value chain of an airline, where costs are much more variable. The outcome of such a policy of filling up seats through price reductions is not always beneficial, as we will see later.

Another element which characterizes the competitive environment of a firm is the presence of high or low barriers to entry. In industries with low barriers to entry the pricing of existing firms within that industry is more constrained and so is the potential for abnormal profits. Barriers to entry could be created through the technology used, the access to channels of distribution, the supplier relationships and the existence of excess capacity.

A further important aspect of industry analysis is the study of the relation of the input and output market of a firm. As input market we distinguish the labour market, the capital market and the suppliers' market. The power relations in these different markets and the scarcity of the resources determine to a large extent the price a company has to pay for those inputs. For example in times of economic prosperity the bargaining power of airline pilots with regard to their salaries is much higher than in times of economic downturn, when there is labour-related overcapacity in the airline industry.

The power relations with the buyers in the output market of the firm determine to a large extent the margin which a company can earn. If 80% of the turnover of company X is bought by company Y, then the bargaining position with regard to a price increase on the goods delivered to Y of company X is very weak.

Regulation or the absence of it further characterizes the environment in which a firm operates. Regulation includes among other things government regulations, legal requirements and taxation.

The environment of the firm consists mainly of factors that are beyond the control of the management. The only way to avoid certain environmental characteristics is often to switch to another industry or another country, such changes, however, are not always obvious.

Analysis of the business strategy and corporate strategy

Business strategy

The management of a firm will choose what type of business to be in by taking into account environmental and industry characteristics together with an analysis of strengths and weaknesses of the company. The next step is to decide in which manner the firm is going to compete with other firms within the same industry. This implies choices with regard to the products or services and their characteristics which will be offered, with regard to the type of customers to attract and with regard to how these products or services will be produced. The firm's business strategy is the strategy that managers choose to achieve a competitive advantage. Several typologies to define strategy exists. The most well known is that of Porter. He defines two generic competitive strategies, namely a low-cost strategy and a differentiation strategy (Porter, 1985). Cost leadership can be achieved through economies of scale and scope, economies of learning, efficient production, simpler product design, lower input costs, cost control and leaner organizational processes. A firm following a low-cost strategy in the automobile industry is Hyundai. In the airline business Ryanair, easyJet and Southwest airlines are important low-cost airlines. Until now they have been successful in their strategy through a combination of several elements like lower input costs (lower wage levels), efficient production (higher asset utilization through reduced set-up time, so more flights a day can be operated), different organizational processes (ticket sales only through the Internet) and simpler product design (only transport is offered and passengers need to pay for the extras e.g. food and drinks). In Chapter 27 we investigate whether the ratios and the underlying balance sheet and profit and loss structure of those low-cost airlines such as Ryanair reflect the strategy followed and if the ratios and balance sheet and profit and loss account structures are indeed different from the financial picture we get from the annual accounts of the traditional airlines such as Lufthansa, SAS, British Airways, KLM or Austrian Airlines.

A firm following a differentiation strategy seeks to sell a unique product or service. Uniqueness can be achieved through superior customer service, product design and product features, brand loyalty, distribution network or technology. Mercedes Benz or BMW follow a differentiator strategy in the automobile sector.

Whether a firm can develop or sustain cost leadership or differentiation depends on the organization of the value chain. 'The value chain is defined as the sequence of business functions in which utility [usefulness] is added to the products or services of an organization' (Horngren, Bhimani, Datar and Foster, 2002, p. 8) These functions are research and development, design of products, services or processes, production, marketing, distribution and customer service. The activities in the value chain of a low coster will be organized differently from the activities in the value chain of a differentiator.

We learn, for example, from the annual reports of Ryanair that their turnaround time between two flights has been brought down to 25 minutes. This is much shorter than traditional airlines and results in a higher asset utilization (meaning more flights a day using the same plane).

Firm profitability will not only be influenced by the chosen strategy but also by structural cost drivers such as scale, scope, experience, technology, complexity, executional cost drivers like workforce involvement, total quality management, capacity utilization, plant layout efficiency, product configuration, linkages with suppliers or customers (Shank and Govindarajan, 1992) and operational cost drivers which are cost drivers specific to activities in the value chain. Although these mentioned cost drivers are usually firm-specific, certain drivers can be distinguished for an industry as a whole.

Research into the cost drivers in the airline industry (Banker and Johnston, 1993) revealed the existence of two different types of cost driver – those related to actual outputs and those related to output capacity. Actual outputs are the number of passengers carried or tons of cargo handled. The number of passengers are the cost drivers for handling and catering. Fuel consumption and labour hours for scheduled flight crews and attendants vary more with aircraft size, seating capacity, distance and other characteristics of flights and aircrafts than with the actual number of passengers carried or tons of cargo handled. The cost of aircraft maintenance varies more with the number of flights, hours flown and characteristics of the aircraft such as number of engines than with actual outputs such as number of passengers carried. So, transport costs such as fuel, labour cost, maintenance and depreciation or rentals are driven by the output capacity of the airline. The output capacity is measured by the amount of seats offered by the airline (available seat kilometre or mile) and by the cargo capacity available (available ton kilometre or mile).

Summarizing these results means that an increase in passengers will increase the handling and catering costs of an airline but not the costs related to the output capacity. However, if an airline starts more flights or adds more planes to its fleet the costs related to output capacity will increase not incrementally but stepwise. Executional cost drivers in the airline business are elements such as density of the network and hub concentration.

Corporate strategy

Some firms operate in only one industry but others are competitive in more industries.

Activity 26.4

Think of companies such as Unilever, Walt Disney Corporation, McDonald's and Airbus. In how many businesses are they competitive?

Activity feedback

Single industry	Multiple businesses
McDonald's (fast food)	Unilever (food, cleansing agents, skincare products)
Airbus	Walt Disney Corporation (movies, TV channel, theme parks, real estate)

At corporate level the management can choose to be active only in one business or to operate in multiple businesses. Corporate strategy decisions focus on where corporate resources will be invested. Business strategy decisions are concerned with how to compete in defined product markets.

Some companies prosper by competing in one industry whereas others operate successfully in different industries. Imbev, one of the world largest breweries, started to become a global player after the decision was taken to sell off the soft drinks and to concentrate solely on the beer market. They are now the number three (at the time of writing) worldwide in the brewing industry and produce and distribute brands such as Beck's, Bass, Labatt Ice, Stella Artois, Hoegaarden and MacCaffrey's.

For financial analysis purposes it is important to know whether a company is a multi-business company, in which case, the consolidated annual accounts reflect the performance of the group as a whole. In the consolidated profit and loss account, costs of different businesses will be presented in an aggregated way. Only through the segmental data included in the notes to the financial statements can the user of these statements get a glimpse of the profitability of the individual businesses. The Scandinavian SAS group, for example, is active in the airline business but is also a well-known player in the hotel sector. This implies that, for example, the item leasing costs in the profit and loss account of the group's financial statements of SAS not only relates to lease expenses for airplanes, but also to the lease costs of assets employed in the hotel business of the group. In the case of inter-firm comparison one must be vigilant as regards whether or not companies are in the same business or in the same portfolio of businesses.

The main aim of undertaking industry analysis before one starts with accounting analysis is to get to know the business as the business context gives meaning to the information presented in the annual accounts. According to the industry or strategy chosen the value of certain ratios will be lower or higher or the volatility of earnings will be different.

Accounting analysis

We have already illustrated that the performance of a firm is influenced to a large extent by the adopted business strategy and by the economic and industrial environment in which the firm is operating. As a result, the business strategy of the firm and the industry characteristics will be reflected in the accounting data. An understanding of that process is useful for an analysis of the accounts in a meaningful way. However, there is more to be taken into account before one can start with financial analysis. As annual accounts are used to communicate the underlying business reality to outside investors, managers may use financial reporting strategies to manipulate investors' perceptions or the perception of other stakeholders. Managers may choose accounting and disclosure policies that make it more or less difficult for external users of financial statements to understand the true economic performance of the business.

Besides adopting a business strategy, the management can also adopt what is called an 'accounting strategy'. The purpose of accounting analysis is to gain insight into the 'accounting strategy' of the firm. The 'accounting strategy' of a firm consists of the incentives management has to influence the annual accounts, the adopted reporting strategy and the methods which have been used to manage these accounts according to the reporting strategy. Knowledge about the adopted 'accounting strategy' will enable the external user of the annual accounts to detect more easily the underlying economic performance of the firm and make a more reliable judgement about the performance of that firm.

Accounting strategy: incentives to manage the annual accounts

The management of a company can have different incentives to manage the financial statements. The most important and the most common ones follow. Most of these incentives have been the subject of empirical research, the results of which confirm the existence of these incentives listed.

Incentives driven by capital market considerations

Reducing the perceived risk of a company

Investors and analysts evaluate an investment in a firm as more risky when the reported results are volatile. This volatility of the earnings has an impact on the market price of the shares. A higher risk perception means a lower share price. So, managers might have an incentive to influence the perception of the capital market.

Listed firms reduce the volatility of the reported income in order to reduce the perceived risk of the company. Research findings provide empirical evidence that a firm's relation with capital markets can create incentives to influence earnings (Dechow *et al.*, 1996, Rangan, 1998, Shivakumar, 1998). This incentive leads to reducing the volatility of reported earnings.

Raising additional financing through the stock market

In periods preceding a capital increase by an equity offer the management of the company might be tempted to produce a steady stream of increasing results over the years. In this situation earnings are not only smoothed and reported as less volatile but an upward trend of the results also needs to be present. Some recent studies find that earnings are managed prior to or around initial public offerings (Friedlan, 1994, Neil *et al.*, 1995) or seasoned equity offerings (Shivakumar, 1998, Rangan, 1998).

Debt contracts – accounting-based debt covenants

Very often the terms of a lending agreement involve debt covenants which are specified as accounting ratios and may not be violated. A violation of these debt covenants might entail an increase of the interest rate applied to a loan or an immediate repayment of that loan or an extra collateral. So managers have an incentive to choose those accounting methods and estimates which reduce the violation of the debt covenant (Sweeney, 1994). Sweeney found further that firms approaching default respond with income increasing accounting changes. Using actual debt covenant violations, Defond and Jiambalvo (1994) found support for earnings management by managers of firms with debt covenant violations.

It is not compulsory under most GAAP systems to disclose information about debt covenants. The following example taken from the annual accounts of Barry-Callebaut (the largest manufacturer worldwide of cocoa and chocolate products, with sales around

CHF 3.6 billion in the 2002/2003 fiscal year) is the result of a voluntary disclosure decision made by the firm:

> The term and revolving facilities agreement also contains certain financial covenants, including, amongst others, a maximum senior leverage ratio, a minimum interest cover ratio and a minimum solvency ratio, next to a number of potentially restrictive undertakings limiting or preventing specific business transactions.
>
> (Note 13, financial statements 2002/2003, p. 96)

Management compensation

Top management compensation often consists of three individual components, a base salary, a bonus plan linked to a certain indicator and shares or share options. When the bonus plans of top management are linked to reported profits, there is an incentive to choose those accounting methods and accounting estimates which make the company exceed the profit targets stipulated in their compensation contract. This finding not only holds for top management compensation but also for lower level managers compensated on the basis of accounting numbers. Linking compensation to accounting numbers does not only create incentives for managing those numbers. Jensen and Murphy (1990) claim that paying executives on the basis of accounting profits rather than on changes in shareholder wealth not only generates incentives to manipulate the accounting system but also generates incentives to ignore projects with large net present values in favour of less valuable projects with larger immediate accounting profits.

In his seminal paper in this area Healy (1985) found support for earnings management by managers of firms with bonus plans linked to accounting numbers. Healy shows that ceilings (i.e. the upper earnings found in the bonus scheme) in compensation contracts have a predictable effect on accounting accruals.

Due to this possible negative effect of accounting numbers-based compensation other forms of management compensation emerged. Stock option plans became very popular and 'stock-based performance measures' are often argued to be superior to accounting-based performance measures. However, short-term behaviour of the management might arise when the exercise period of the options is short.

In order to avoid short-termism compensation plans based on stock options should have a long-term perspective. Imbev called its stock option plan 'Long-term incentive programme' and included an extended conversion period:

> In 1999 the company established a long-term incentive program for key management employees. Under this program, subscription rights can be offered for free to key management employees and secondarily to directors. Each subscription right entitles the holder to subscribe for one new ordinary share of Interbrew SA, paying the average price over the 30 trading days before it was offered. Subscription rights have a term of ten years, and can be exercised over a three-year period. The issues of rights are in accordance with the interest of the company and its shareholders, since they aim to motivate the management with a view to the development of the activities of the company in the long run.
>
> (annual report 2003, Interbrew, note 22, employee benefits, p. 73)

Another possibility is to base compensation on performance measured relative to aggregate performance in the industry. An example of such a plan are the 'performance' programmes that Lufthansa offers to its senior executives (annual report 2003, Lufthansa, p. 86):

> Last year, for the first time, senior staff with individual salary contracts were also offered a stock option programme based on outperformance. LH-PerformanceAT runs for three years and enables the participants to receive a bonus payment depending on the outperformance of the Lufthansa share compared with the stock of other companies. The benchmark index is identical to that used in the executive programme. 'LH-Performance 2003'.

Small loss avoidance behaviour

It has been noticed that companies tend to avoid small losses and prefer to report small profits instead. Earnings management research has provided evidence for this practice which the research calls 'small loss avoidance'. De George *et al.* (1999) and Burgstahler and Dichev (1997) present evidence that managers of US firms use accounting discretion to avoid reporting small losses. Small losses are more likely to lie within the bounds of insiders' reporting discretion and, consequently, can be avoided through earnings management. This implies, further, that if a loss cannot be avoided by accounting decisions companies have a tendency to go for a one-time big loss which is called big bath accounting.

'Big bath accounting' to manage future earnings

Setting the objective to maximize the loss is referred to in the literature as big bath accounting. Of course, there are limits to the loss one can present to the stakeholders without influencing their actions. Big bath accounting occurs in two circumstances. First of all, big bath accounting can occur in case of a (one-time) heavy loss that cannot be avoided by income maximizing accounting interventions (see small loss avoidance). Faced with such a situation the firm's management may choose to maximize the loss in the current accounting period. In years of economic downturn, this practice is often observed.

Second, big bath accounting can occur when the annual accounts will be cleaned up before or after an acquisition, a merger or other form of business cooperation. Big bath accounting usually implies the frontloading of costs through large asset write downs and increases in provisions (restructuring provisions are extremely popular for this purpose) in order to enhance the future performance of the firm. In the financial year where 'a bath is taken' a substantial loss is reported, however, in the following years, performance will rise partly due to reduced depreciation charges or a decreases of provisions. This practice has received increasing levels of critique over the last years. The reinforcement of the conditions for creating restructuring provisions under IAS 37 are a result of those practices.

Cookie jar reserves

One of the *accounting 'hot spots' that we are considering this morning* is accounting for restructuring charges and restructuring reserves. A better title would be accounting for general reserves, contingency reserves, rainy day reserves or cookie jar reserves.

Accounting for so-called restructurings has become an art form. Some companies like the idea so much that they establish restructuring reserves every year. Why not? Analysts seem to like the idea of recognizing as a liability today, a budget of expenditures planned for the next year or next several years in down-sizing, right-sizing or improving operations and portraying that amount as a special, below-the-line charge in the current period's income statement. This year's earnings are happily reported in press releases as 'before charges'. CNBC analysts and commentators talk about earnings 'before charges'. The financial press talks about earnings before 'special charges'. (Funny, no one talks about earnings before credits-only charges.) It's as if special charges are not real. Out of sight, out of mind . . .

The occasion of a merger also spawns the wholesale establishment of restructuring or merger reserves. The ingredients of the merger reserves and merger charges look like the makings of a sausage. In the Enforcement Division, I have seen all manner and kind of things that ordinarily would be charged to operating earnings instead being charged 'below the line'. Write-offs of the carrying amounts of bad receivables. Write-offs of cost of obsolete inventory. Write-downs of plant and equipment costs, which, miraculously at the date of the merger, become non-recoverable, whereas those same costs were considered recoverable the day before the merger. Write-offs of previously capitalized costs such as goodwill, which all of a sudden are not recoverable because of a merger. Adjustments to bring warranty liabilities up to snuff. Adjustments to bring claim liabilities in line with management's new view of settling or litigating cases. Adjustments to bring environmental liabilities up to snuff or in line with management's new view of the manner in which the company's obligations to comply with EPA will be satisfied. Recognition of liabilities to pay for future services by investment bankers, accountants and lawyers. Recognition of liabilities for officers' special bonuses. Recognition of liabilities for moving people. For training people. For training people not yet hired. For retraining people. Recognition of liabilities for moving costs and refurbishing costs. Recognition of liabilities for new software that may be acquired or written, for ultimate sale to others. Or some liabilities that go by the title 'other'.

It is no wonder that investors and analysts are complaining about the credibility of the numbers.

Source: Speech by Walter R. Schuetze, Chief Accountant, Enforcement Division, US Securities and Exchange Commission, 22 April 1999 http: *www.sec.gov/news/speeches/spcha76.htm*

Third, the practice of big bath accounting may also be observed when there is a CEO change. We will discuss this later.

Executive changes

Annual accounts management can sometimes be observed when executive changes take place in companies. Executive changes can be forced or voluntary (e.g. retirement). The outgoing CEO or executive team as well as the incoming CEO or executive team can have incentives to influence the accounts. Research on CEO turnover and annual accounts management distinguishes between CEO turnover in troubled firms versus CEO turnover in non-troubled firms. Dechow and Sloan (1991) investigated the hypothesis that CEOs in their final years of office (before retirement) manage discretionary investment expenditures to improve short-term earnings performance (for example, spending less on R&D). LaSalle *et al.* (1993) report evidence that is consistent with the hypothesis that new CEOs exploit their accounting discretion to blame the predecessor for poor performance, establish a lower benchmark for subsequent performance evaluation and relieve future earnings of charges that would otherwise have to be made. Murphy and Zimmerman (1993) also found evidence that incoming CEOs of poorly performing firms took 'baths'.

However, it is important to stress that reduced profits or losses when a new CEO or new management team comes in could also be the result of the 'income borrowing behaviour' of the former CEO. The outgoing CEO could have improved his performance through accounting decisions in the immediate years before the turnover which increases the reported results or through income smoothing behaviour above sustainable levels for several years. So, the outgoing CEO in this case has increased the reported income by using accounting practices which borrow income from the future. In these circumstances, the new CEO will be faced with less profit or even a loss due to the reversal effect of the practices used by his predecessor (this is discussed later).

Other incentives

Political and regulatory elements

Tax authorities use accounting data in order to determine the tax base of a company. Accounting methods might be chosen with a tax effect in mind. Especially in continental Europe (e.g. Germany, Belgium, France) there is a strong link between the reported income in the individual accounts of the company and the tax income.

Regulatory agencies might use accounting data to evaluate regulatory policies (e.g. import tariffs, ant-trust actions). In the literature empirical evidence can be found that earnings management is induced by political or regulatory processes (Key, 1997, Guenther *et al.* 1997).

Articles in company laws with regard to dividend payments, companies in distress and bankruptcy conditions often refer to ratios in the individual or group accounts of a company which may or may not be exceeded or violated. This results in an incentive to manage these ratios if there is a danger of violation.

Competitive pressures

Data from the annual accounts might be useful for the competition. Especially in a situation where one company is obliged to disclose more proprietary information due to national GAAP requirements, companies have a tendency either to avoid this disclosure or to decrease the quality of disclosure. For example, segmental data will be disclosed on a more aggregated level or high recurring profits might be topped off to avoid entry in the industry by new firms.

Union negotiations

Facing forthcoming union negotiations the management might have an incentive to decrease the net result of the company. Strong company profits might incite the unions to ask for a salary increase. These incentives will be more present in companies, industries or countries with strong labour union power.

If we consider the incentives listed we can see that some of them are recurring and others are non-recurring incentives to manage the accounts.

Activity 26.5

Which of the incentives listed could be classified as 'recurring' and which could be classified as 'non-recurring'?

Activity feedback

Recurring incentives could be: reducing earnings volatility for listed companies, efforts to sustain share prices when stock options are granted. Further, regulatory incentives can be recurring if, for example, a company is located in a country where there is a link between tax income and accounting income. Non-recurring incentives could be present in the situation of an individual public offering, a merger or acquisition or an executive change.

In current research related to earnings management the notion of explicit and implicit contracts is introduced. Earnings management can either be induced by explicit contracts (e.g. debt covenants based on accounting numbers, compensation contracts based on accounting numbers) or by implicit contracts. Implicit contracts can be between the firm and its customers, suppliers, short-term creditors, employees, capital providers and other stakeholders. Bowen *et al.* (1995) and Kasanen *et al.* (1996) find evidence that implicit contracts induce earnings management. While explicit contracts seem important incentives for earnings management in companies with widespread ownership, implicit contracts are especially important in creating earnings management incentives in firms with concentrated ownership. Concentrated ownership might create implicit contracts between a firm and its major shareholders which often have a seat on the board of directors. (Kasanen *et al.* (1996) reveals implicit contracts on dividends with institutional shareholders.)

The story of Sabena and the airline industry

Different companies from the airline industry will be used for illustrative purposes throughout Part Four. The published financial statements and annual reports of Austrian Airlines, KLM, British Airways, Lufthansa, Ryanair, easyJet, SAS, the former SAir Group and the late Sabena will be used. In relation to the airline Sabena, data from the last ten years of its existence (1991–2001) will be used throughout both this chapter and for educational purposes. Sabena was the Belgian national flag carrier which was declared bankrupt in 2001. Within the time span covered the analysis will mainly focus on the period 1995–2001 during which Sabena was linked to the SAir Group. The SAir Group was the majority shareholder of the airline Swissair which also ceased to exist in the beginning of 2002. A short overview of the last ten years of the existence of Sabena is now presented.

Activity 26.6

When reading the following information about Sabena, keep in mind the overview of the literature given above. Which elements from the literature could possibly be related to this company?

Sabena, Belgium's national flag carrier, was founded in 1923. Sabena was a state-owned enterprise, characterized by a weak financial performance for as long as it existed. Due to the deregulation of the airline industry which would gradually take place in the European Union from the beginning of the 1990s, airlines were investigating all forms of cooperations and alliances with each other. It was already clear at that time that it would be extremely difficult for Sabena to survive on its own. In order to make Sabena an attractive bride for a partnership a major restructuring had taken place in 1991. Subsequently Sabena entered in 1992 into a cooperation with Air France. The French partner acquired 37% of the shares of Sabena. The partnership with Air France came to an end two years later in 1994. Mid-1995 Swissair acquired a large minority holding of 49.5% in the capital of Sabena. Together with the investment in the share capital of Sabena, a loan of 151 million CHF was granted by Swissair to the Belgian government, which remained the majority shareholder with 50.5% of the shares. The loan to the Belgian government entitled Swissair at that time to raise its equity holding in Sabena from 49.5% to 62.25% later on.

The shareholder agreement signed by the two shareholders (SAir and the Belgian government) included, among other things, the following items. The articles of the shareholders' and masters' agreement stipulated that the managing director (CEO) be appointed at the suggestion of both shareholders (Belgian state and SAir). Further, the articles stipulated that the other members of the management committee of Sabena could be appointed or dismissed by the board of directors on the proposal of the managing director.

In February 1996 one of the top executives of the SAir Group became President and CEO of Sabena. From the management team in place at Sabena at the beginning of 1996 only one person remained on board of the management team at the time of the bankruptcy in 2001. In this short time frame many management positions were occupied by several persons; the position of chief financial officer changed hands three times in those five years.

Sabena was the first airline in which the SAir Group took a substantial minority shareholding. The acquisition of this substantial minority shareholding (49.5%) fitted into the new strategy of Swissair. Their new corporate strategy was presented in their annual report of 1996 (p. 1)

> Swissair has moved from its traditional structure as an airline to become a corporate group that conducts airline-related activities in addition to actual airline operations. The new group structure, named the SAir Group will underscore the diversity of the new corporation.

Together with this new corporate strategy, a new CEO, a former controller from within the company, was appointed in the SAir group. The strategy of the business segment airlines of the SAir Group was to obtain a market share of 20% in Europe (Lüchinger, p. 210). This strategy, called the 'hunter' strategy would be pursued by taking substantial minority shareholdings in EU airlines. Sabena was the first one and later on French (AOM, Air Litoral), German (LTU), Italian (Volare) and Portuguese Airlines (Portugalia, TAP) followed. As Switzerland was not a member of the European Union, acquiring a majority shareholding in the EU airlines would result in these airlines becoming non-EU airlines.

The acquisition of minority holdings by SAir in other airlines was beneficial not only for obtaining a market share of 20% but also for the so-called second pillar of the SAir Group, namely the airline-related business segments (e.g. catering, ground handling, technics, logistics, information systems). Illustrations of this practice can be found in several annual reports of the SAir Group. The following evidence is found on p. 18 of the annual report of the SAir Group, 1996.

> Atraxis' first year as an independent information technology company was very challenging ... Several reservations and handling systems were delivered to third-party customers and made operational, including the complete migration of the Sabena booking and handling system.

Further:

> On December 16, Swisscargo and Sabena signed an agreement whereby Swisscargo's distribution network would market the entire freight capacity of Sabena's fleet of aircraft as of January 1, 1997. Swisscargo thereby enlarged its freight capacity by almost one quarter and is taking full advantage of the chance to create a cargo hub in Brussels.
>
> (p. 20; annual report, SAir Group 1997)

In the notes to the annual accounts of the SAir Group of 1997 we find the following explanation concerning the operating revenues: 'Results for 1997 also include the assumption by Swisscargo of Sabena's cargo business, which increased the relevant operating revenue item by CHF160 million.' It is interesting to note here that the so-called 'assumption' of the cargo business of Sabena by SAir is, in fact, a non-event in the annual report of Sabena. In the annual reports of Sabena the titles in the narrative part switch from cargo to cargo handling and in the five-year overview of summary airline operating statistics the statistics relating to cargo are replaced by the words 'assumed by SAir'. The growth in the airline-related activities came from acquisitions and from providing services to the Qualiflyer Group, which included all the airlines in which SAir hold substantial shareholdings. (SAir Group, annual report 2000, p. 4): 'Group companies active in the airline-related businesses generated added revenue by performing maintenance, catering, IT and cargo services for Qualiflyer Group airlines.'

Whereas Sabena had only two shareholders (the Belgian government 50.5% and the SAir Group 49.5%), the SAir Group was listed with dispersed ownership. Even employees held shares in SAir as we learn from the notes to the annual accounts of the SAir Group (e.g. note 4 of the annual report of the SAir Group of 1998, p. 19): 'The SAir Group also issues shares to its personnel. These shares carry dividend and voting rights, but cannot be sold for three years after their issuance.' As in many large listed groups stock options were also granted to staff members.

At the end of 1996 both SAir and Sabena were headed by new CEOs who had committed themselves to growth and profitability. With regard to Sabena evidence of this commitment to profitability can be found in the consecutive annual reports of 1995, 1996 and 1997. 1995 annual report, Sabena, p. 5:

> Our collaboration with Swissair, the strengthening of our balance sheet achieved in 1995 and the commercial growth witnessed over the last three years are all strong building blocks which enable us to achieve our objective of profitability from 1998.

1996 annual report p. 5:

> A year of transition for Sabena, 1996 was hallmarked by the creation of a new management team headed by a new CEO. The Horizon '98 plan points the way to a return to profitability in 1998.

Annual report Sabena, 1997, p. 5:

> Sabena succeeded in 1997 in reaping the first benefits of the Horizon '98 programme in the drive to balance the books and make the airline profitable again. ... [page 9] The aim of all these measures (Horizon '98 plan) is to return Sabena to profitability in 1998.

In 1998 Sabena 'showed' the promised profit. Figure 26.1 shows the operating result and the net result of Sabena NV over the period 1991–2000 and the 1998 figures are, indeed, in the black.

Sabena NV represents the holding company of the Sabena Group but at the same time it is also the airline. The revenue of Sabena NV makes up 90% of the revenue of the Sabena Group and the total assets of Sabena NV represent 85% of the total assets of the Sabena Group. For this reason it makes sense to look at the behaviour of the individual accounts of

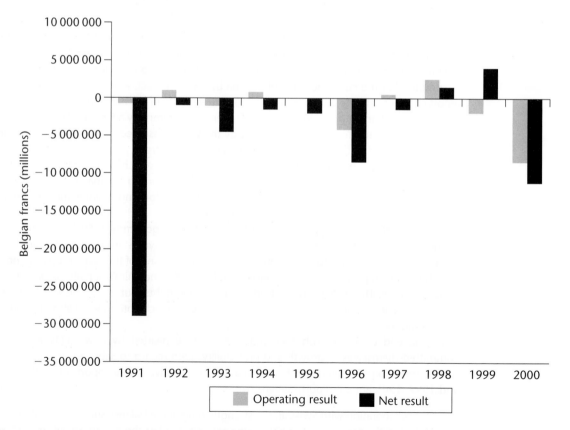

Figure 26.1 Ten-year overview of the operating and net result of Sabena NV
Source: Annual accounts of Sabena NV, 1991–2000

Sabena NV. These individual accounts are prepared according to Belgian GAAP for the whole time frame.

The results of 1998 were commented on by the board of directors in the annual report as follows:

> The main reason why the year has been such a turning point is because we have managed to re-establish our profitability. The efforts made to cut costs, to increase productivity and to occupy more aircraft seats, have clearly borne fruit ... In summary we can state that, this year, Sabena has finalized the groundwork done in 1996 and 1997 within the framework of the 'Horizon '98 Plan'. Its task is now to ensure profitable growth based on continued restraint in matters of expenditure.

The fact that in 1997, and especially 1998, the economic climate was very favourable for the airline industry was not mentioned as a possible explanation for the positive figures. In line with the growth strategy of the SAir Group the board of directors of Sabena took the decision in 1997 to renew and expand the fleet in the coming years. To fill this extra seat capacity offered on the market Sabena engaged heavily in price competition. The number of passengers indeed grew as we will see later, but the mix of passengers was very unfavourable. In the main, it was economy class passengers who were attracted, among them many transfer passengers. These transfer passengers create extra variable costs (handling, etc.) and are therefore not very profitable for an airline. The percentage of business class passengers decreased especially from 2000 on, the year when the sale of the tickets for both airlines (Swissair and Sabena) was for the first time carried out for a period of 12 months through the newly created Airline Management Partnership (AMP) between the two airlines.

The results of the Sabena Group over the same time frame show a rather similar pattern, except for 1992 and 1999 (group accounts are only available from 1992 on) (see Figure 26.2). In those years the results of the individual accounts of Sabena NV were positively influenced by gains on intra-group sale of assets (for example, in 1999, the creation of a new 100% owned subsidiary Sabena Technics NV which would be responsible for maintenance, repair and overhaul of planes). These intra-group results are, of course, eliminated in the process of consolidation (see Chapter 24).

From 1999 on the group accounts of Sabena are prepared with the use of IAS. The group loss of 1999 was told in the message of the board of directors as follows:

> 1999 turned into another year of strong growth for the Sabena Group in spite of an ever more demanding competitive climate. It was a year that saw us exceed the 10-million passenger mark. But the unexpected increase in certain costs, particularly in the price of fuel, lowered operating results. Because of certain extraordinary transactions, amongst which the sale of Equant shares, the net results of the Sabena Group show a slight profit. Nonetheless, the Board has decided to absorb into the 1999 figures part of the restructuring costs linked to the Airline Management Project (AMP).

The message of the board of directors reported further on the start of AMP and what it meant for Swissair and Sabena:

> As initially provided in the 1995 agreements, the two airline companies have decided to combine their commercial activities by the formation of a partnership.

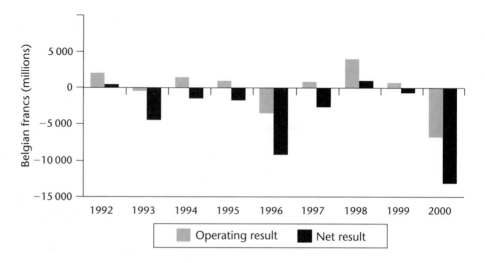

Figure 26.2 Overview of the operating and net result of the Sabena Group
Source: Annual accounts of Sabena Group, 1992–2000

The divisions of the two companies have been restructured and spread over 2 administrative headquarters: Brussels for Marketing, Product and Sales, Zurich for the Management of the network and support functions. Because of the permanency of this new agreement, the Board of Directors asked the 2 main shareholders of Sabena, being the Belgian State and the SAir Group, for an agreement on matters pertaining to the future shareholding structure.

It is obvious from the description in the annual report that the creation of AMP will have an impact on the structure of the Sabena Group and maybe on the SAir Group as well. Employees from the SAir Group and from Sabena were transferred to AMP. Concerning the impact on costs and revenues, the annual report remains vague.

The agreement between the shareholders on the future shareholding structure, talked about in the report of 1999, was reported in the annual report of Sabena of 2000 as follows (annual report, 2000 p. 3):

> Two principal events distinguished the year 2000: the agreement between the shareholders under which the SAir Group would take a majority holding of 85 per cent in Sabena as soon as the bilateral agreements between Switzerland and the 15 Member States of the European Union have been ratified. This ratification is expected to take place by the end of 2001. . . . The establishment of the AMP as a partnership under British law with affiliates in every country in which Sabena and Swissair operate.

The agreement talked about in the Sabena report of 2000, was signed on 25 January 2001.

The economic climate deteriorated in 2000 (economic crises, high fuel prices and an unfavourable exchange rate with the dollar) and Sabena's financial situation became dramatic. At the level of the SAir Group difficulties also started to emerge mid-2000.

The 'old' CEO left Sabena mid-2000 and the company was headed by a new CEO whom the Swiss had recruited a year earlier from a competitor airline. At the beginning of 2001 two CEO changes shortly after each other were witnessed at the top of the SAir Group as well. Both new CEOs got the task to turn the tide and restore profitability. In both annual reports the reader is informed about how each company will proceed in achieving this target. Annual report of Sabena 2000:

> In order to improve the result sharply in the short term, the 'Blue Sky' restructuring programme was launched. . . . The Board of Directors will give every priority in 2001 to redressing the performance of the Group and to signing sustainable partnerships.

Annual report of SAir Group, Message from the new Chairman, p. 5:

> Our main priority is to reorganise the Group's airline sector, the first pillar of the dual strategy, and restore it to a sound financial condition. . . . The SAir logistics, SAir services and SAir relations divisions, forming the second pillar of our dual strategy, have either met or surpassed their performance targets.

The reorganization of the airline segment at the SAir Group meant that the 'hunter' strategy was abandoned in 2001. SAir Group annual report, 2000, p. 4:

> Beginning in 1995 the Group began to follow a strategy of acquiring minority holdings in foreign airlines. . . . The Board realised that the depth of the resources required to implement the chosen strategy, in terms of time, capital and management capacity, was greater than the Group could provide. The lack of ample financial resources to pursue additional acquisitions and to carry out the required refinancing plans in Germany, Belgium and France forced the abandonment of this strategy. Subsequent to a thorough investigation, the Board decided to shift the strategy of the Group's airline sector in January 2001.

Due to the further deterioration of the economic climate, the events of 11 September 2001, social unrest, an extreme unfavourable cost structure due to prior management decisions and, last but not least, the withdrawal of the SAir Group at the end of September 2001 from Sabena, the Belgian airline had to file for bankruptcy. The oldest carrier in Europe at that time was declared bankrupt on 7 November 2001 and ceased to exist, at the age of 78 years old. Thousands of jobs (directly and indirectly) were lost (some estimates suggest a figure of 17 000) and, as a result of the bankruptcy the economic growth rate of Belgium was reduced by 0.2%. In Switzerland, too many people lost their jobs due to the serious financial problems at the SAir Group.

Activity feedback

- Sabena was looking for a partner in the beginning of the 1990s, the annual accounts had to look attractive. Accumulated losses from the years before were cleaned up in a major restructuring.
- There is evidence of implicit contracts on the part of the board of directors of Sabena towards profit. The texts of the board of directors in the annual reports of 1995, 1996 and 1997 contain implicit contracts which make a promise for profitability from 1998 on.

- Two CEO changes are observed: one in 1996 and the other in 2000. However, there is a difference between the first CEO change and the second. The CEO coming on board in 1996 had the goal of pursuing growth and profitability. The CEO of the new millennium was facing a company in distress.
- Regulatory aspects could also play a role.

Taxes: In Belgium, there is a strong link between reported accounting income in the individual accounts and the income which is used to determine taxable profit.

Regulatory aspects: Although there has been deregulation since the beginning of the 1990s, the airline business is still a highly regulated industry.

Accounting analysis: reporting strategy

In the former section we have discussed several existing incentives for annual accounts' management. According to the kind of incentive a different reporting strategy and as a result a different type of annual accounts management will be used. For example, if a firm is involved in union negotiations the aim will be the decrease of the reported profits in the period before the negotiations. In the literature on reporting strategies a distinction is often made between management of the profit and loss account (also called earnings management) and management of the balance sheet structure. Further, when earnings management is used to present the published results in a more favourable way than the underlying economic results, we are able to distinguish two major patterns. First of all, the result of one particular year might be influenced in a particular direction (increase or decrease) and, second, earnings management can also take the form of income smoothing. The purpose of income smoothing is to reduce the variability in reported earnings. Although a wide variety of incentives to manage the financial statements exists, the same reporting strategy can often be used for different incentives.

Activity 26.7

Consider some of the different existing incentives presented earlier to manage the annual accounts. What type of accounting strategy would be appropriate for these different types of incentives?

Activity feedback

- *Capital market considerations.*
  - *Risk perception.* The accounting strategy of the firm would be to engage in earnings management with the purpose of presenting earnings or results which are less volatile than the underlying economic results that the firm has obtained. In this situation income smoothing would be pursued and this practice would be a 'recurring activity'. In periods with 'high' economic income, profits would be topped off and in periods with 'lower' income increasing measures would be used.
  - *Prepare for an initial public offering.* In this case the accounting strategy could consist of showing a good performance over the years before the IPO and an

improvement of the balance sheet structure. Different types of annual accounts management might be combined into the overall reporting strategy: income smoothing in order to influence the perceived risk of the company, balance sheet management to improve the structure of the balance sheet and increasing the result upwards over a time period before the IPO.

- *Tax incentives.* In countries where there is a link between accounting income and taxable income, the accounting strategy is to decrease the reported profit in order to reduce taxable profit. This type of management will be recurring as long as the company exists.
- *Compensation contracts.* In the case of stock options, an increasing share price is desired. The reporting strategy could consist of income smoothing practices, undertaken to reduce the perceived risk of the company, and further income increasing measures might be used as well. Bonus plans with ceilings might entail one time earnings management upwards to the ceiling or one time earnings management below the ceiling.

Discussing the concept of reporting strategy, it is also worthwhile mentioning that, although a distinction is made between earnings management and balance sheet management, the *impact* of the methods used for those purposes are not isolated to the income statement or the balance sheet alone. In reality, earnings management also has an indirect impact on certain balance sheet items. For example, an accounting method change with regard to depreciation (change from declining method to straight line method) will influence not only the depreciation expense on the profit and loss account, but also the reported book value of the assets on the balance sheet. The same indirect effect can be observed when a company decides to manage the balance sheet. If a company wants to improve the debt/equity ratio through switching from owned assets to assets acquired under operational leasing contracts, not only the liability structure of the balance sheet will be altered. As a consequence the character of the costs involved will change as well. A large part of the costs related to the use of the asset will switch from depreciation costs to rental costs. For financial analysis purposes the former are regarded as non-cash costs whereas the latter are considered as cash costs.

To conclude this section on accounting strategy the operating results, the extraordinary results (which relate to gains and losses on sales of assets) and the net result of a company named DAT Airlines NV are presented in Figure 26.3 for the period 1997–2000. DAT was a 100% subsidiary of Sabena NV and these data were taken from the individual accounts of DAT. The data reflect two items which evolve in the opposite way (operating result and extraordinary result) and the sum of the two reflects a more stable pattern (net result). Can you think of a possible explanation?

Accounting analysis: practices of annual accounts management

After the discussion on the incentives for annual accounts management and the applied accounting strategy (earnings management and management of balance sheet elements) we now focus on the methods or practices used to influence these annual accounts. The practices or methods used for annual accounts management are usually divided in most textbooks and articles into three categories, namely accounting method choices, accounting estimate choices and real decisions (operating decisions, financing

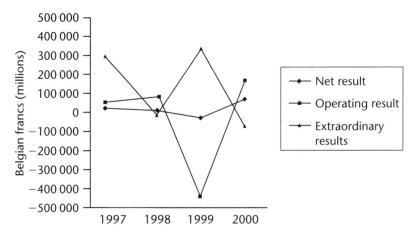

Figure 26.3 Results of DAT Airlines NV, 1997–2000
Source: Annual accounts of DAT Airlines NV, 1997–2000

decisions or investment decisions). Besides these three main instruments of earnings management, other mechanisms can be used as well to manage the impression of the reader of the financial statements towards a more favourable impression about the performance of the company. In this respect J. Francis (2001) lists the following elements: timing of adoption of new standards; choices about display (number of statements, layout of statement); aggregation decisions; and classification decisions. Accounting method choice and accounting estimate choice are accounting decisions with no direct first order effect on cash flows (Jiambalvo, 1996). These practices are called accrual methods in the literature and the use of them is called accruals management. The use of accounting estimates for earnings management purposes is often referred to in the literature as 'discretionary accruals management'. Further, a company can pick a single element to manage the accounts but most often a portfolio of elements is used. A portfolio could mean either several individual methods or practices used to achieve a reporting strategy or a combination of an accrual method linked to a real decision.

As we saw in the earlier parts of this volume, preparing financial statements implies complying with the regulation which governs financial reporting (general accepted accounting principles: e.g. US GAAP, IAS/IFRS, UK GAAP, German GAAP). However, since most GAAP are not a rigid set of principles, the management of a company has a certain flexibility with regard to the choice of valuation methods and accounting estimates to use. The level of flexibility will depend on the GAAP being applied. Insight into the accounting flexibility available to a company might enable the external analyst to separate true information from noise or distortion to a certain extent. An explicit consideration of the flexibility allowed by GAAP applied for the presentation of the annual accounts is a necessity for financial analysis.

Accounting standards that are characterized by more flexibility allow managers more easily to report income in those financial periods when managers have incentives to present better results. Empirical research has provided evidence that the so-called 'low-quality' accounting standards provide more flexibility to management for earnings management purposes (see Chapter 2). These standards are found in countries with a code law system and a creditor orientation in financial reporting. However, we also learned in Chapter 2 that 'high-quality' accounting standards on their own are no guarantee for 'high-quality' financial reporting. The institutional environment (= shareholder protection, degree of enforcement of accounting standards and risk of litigation) play a significant role in the quality of financial reporting in a country.

The aim of the IASB (Foundation Constitution, part A, para. 2) is 'to develop in the public interest, a single set of high-quality, understandable and enforceable global accounting standards that require high-quality, transparent and comparable information in financial statements and other financial reporting to help participants in the world's capital markets and other users make economic decisions'. As a result, we observe over the last years that the flexibility in the IAS/IFRS standards becomes less. In most standards, the allowable treatment has been removed, leaving only the prior benchmark treatment in place (e.g. IAS 8 the prospective application of accounting method or policy changes was deleted from the Standard).

The following is a brief discussion of the practices used for annual accounts management.

Accounting method choice

Accounting method choice is present when there are several possible valuation methods for the same item under the GAAP which has to be applied for the preparation of the annual accounts. Some examples are listed now which could be categorized under the heading accounting method choice:

- choice of depreciation method (e.g. declining method, straight line or accelerated method)
- choice of inventory valuation (LIFO, FIFO or weighted average)
- choice whether or not to capitalize certain expenditures.

With regard to accounting method choice the possibility of influencing the accounts can be limited by the accounting standard setter. A standard setter can always remove options from the available set of accounting principles. This evolution is observable recently in relation to IAS/IFRS. The IASB has been removing a number of alternative treatments from the Standards. This implies that level of accounting flexibility with regard to accounting method choice is declining.

Accounting method choices are not the most popular item to be used for annual accounts' management purposes as the visibility of those choices is perceived as rather high. If one applies an accounting method change the impact on the results of the company and the equity should be disclosed in the notes (for further discussion see the section on quality of disclosure). Chapter 23 presented the accounting treatment of accounting method changes and the necessary information disclosure in relation to such a change. The aim of IAS 8 is to enhance comparability in a situation of an accounting method change.

The use of accounting estimates for annual accounts' management purposes is often preferred by management above accounting method changes because they are less visible and less costly than changes in accounting methods.

Accounting estimates

For the preparation of the financial statements accounting decisions not only relate to the choice of valuation methods to be applied but also to the accounting estimates to be used for valuation purposes. Below a few items of the financial statements in which accounting estimates play a role are now presented.

Bad debt allowances

Research has revealed that this type of accrual is often used for management purposes (e.g. McNichols and Wilson, 1988). A change in the amount of bad debt allowance is often not visible as this amount is netted off from the receivables.

Inventory

Related to inventories there is, first of all, the accounting method choice (FIFO, LIFO, weighted average). In industrial companies, however, overhead should be allocated to the production if full costing is required for valuation purposes. Many standards on inventory valuation require that the allocation of the overhead be based on the company's normal level of activity. Companies in distress are sometimes tempted to allocate part of the unused capacity to the products instead of charging that amount to the P&L account. As a result, these costs related to the unused capacity will be carried forward through the inventory to 'hopefully' more favourable financial years.

Provisions

Provisions are a very popular balance sheet item for managing earnings. Provisions are used for smoothing purposes as well as for one time increases or decreases of the results. External analysts should always investigate the reasons why provisions are created. Sometimes they have the character of amounts set aside for intentional use later on.

This use of provisions for the increase of reported profit when 'economic profit' is lower is also called rainy day accounting. An example of this rainy day accounting can be found in the annual accounts of Sabena in the time frame 1991 to 1995. A substantial amount of provisions was created in the annual accounts of 1991 before the cooperation with Air France. These provisions were then released until 1996 when a new management team headed by a Swiss CEO had taken over. The gradual release of these provisions reduced the negative reported results over that period.

Provisions can also be used to 'frontload' costs, frontloading meaning bringing future costs to the current period. The purpose is to enhance the profitability in future periods. This frontloading of costs by increasing provisions was encountered in the first years of the cooperation between Sabena and the SAir Group. Evidence of this practice is found in the following annual reports:

> (Annual report Sabena, 1995, p. 5) The group result for 1995 remained in the red to the tune of BEF 1.620 Million. This includes an exceptional provision of BEF 1.090 million for the renewal of the fleet ... [p. 22]. Following the decision by the Board of Directors to make exceptional provisions of BEF 1.090 million to effect a rapid standardization of the long haul fleet, consolidated results in 1995 showed a net loss of BEF 1.620 million BEF.

Activity 26.8

Is this provision created in 1995 in accordance with conceptual frameworks governing financial reporting?

Activity feedback

This provision does not really match with definitions and concepts found in the conceptual frameworks.

More provisions follow in the financial year 1996 (annual report, 1996, p. 9):

> The Board of Directors has decided to set off the exceptional charges in 1996 against major reductions in values and provisions designed to ease the fleet harmonisation and modernisation process. The total amount of money involved in the reduction of values and provisions for the fleet (A310-B747) is BEF 1531 million.

The evolution of the provisions over the period 1991–2000 in the annual accounts of Sabena is presented in Figure 26.4.

High-quality standards are characterized by their stringent rules for the creation and the use of provisions. A provision for the renewal of the fleet, would under strict compliance with IAS/IFRS standards not have been possible. So these practices are more easy to apply for managers when they use low-quality accounting standards. However if managers are operating in countries with weak shareholder protection and low risk of litigation it might be tempting to use this type of earnings management even when high-quality accounting standards are used for the preparation of the financial statements.

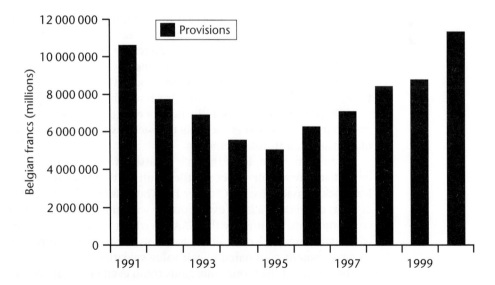

Figure 26.4 Evolution of provisions of Sabena NV
Source: Annual accounts of Sabena NV, 1991–2000

Impairment of assets

Through impairment of assets costs in the current period are increased. The remaining book value is lower and, as a result, future depreciation costs will be lower. Sabena recorded, beside the creation of provisions for fleet renewal, impairment of assets on the aircraft present in their fleet as we saw in the extract of the annual report of 1996 (p. 9), cited earlier. Large impairments of assets also occurred in 1997 (annual report 1997, p. 9):

> The board of directors decided actively to pursue the recovery plan to redress the accounts of Sabena and its subsidiaries in order to provide them with the maximum resources for the future. Within Sabena, the pursuit of this recovery plan was mainly reflected in the value reductions made to aircraft, above all in the case of the 2 Boeing 747s.

These aircraft were later the subject of sale and leaseback transactions. The surplus realized at the moment of the sale of the aircraft was spread over the leasing period of those planes in 1998 and in 1999. As a result the impact of the leasing costs of those planes on the profit and loss account was softened in those years. Here we observe a combination of an accrual accounting decision (recording of impairments) followed by a real transaction (sale and leaseback of a plane).

Under low-quality accounting standards there is usually less guidance on how to determine the amount of the impairment. Very often these standards of lower quality only stipulate that in case of a major reduction in value an impairment should be recorded. In this book we illustrated how under IAS 36 the amount of the impairment should be determined. We recall from Chapter 12 in Part Two that managers have fewer degrees of freedom for the determination of the impairment than under standards of higher quality.

Real transactions

Companies are constantly engaged in operating, financing and investment transactions. These real transactions, however, can also be used for annual account's management purposes. Common examples are the deferral of transactions to future periods, such as purchases and R&D. In some cases, the choice of a particular transaction (e.g. financing through a finance lease or operating lease) is not neutral with regard to the impact on the annual accounts. As a result the choice of operating, investment and financing decisions might be influenced or even determined by accounting valuation or presentation issues. Sometimes, real transactions are only undertaken with the purpose of annual accounts management.

A common example is the sale of assets with a gain on disposal. This has an immediate favourable effect on the result of that year (except for certain sale and leaseback transactions; see Chapter 14). The possibility of creating profit through a sale of assets depends to a large extent on the valuation principles which are applied in the company or are required by the GAAP to which the company complies. In a historical cost environment the possibilities for these one-time big gains are much larger than in an environment dominated by fair value valuation.

The impact of these one-time gains could even be enhanced by combining the real transactions (sale of asset) with a large write down or impairment the year before the sale. This practice was applied by Sabena. The airplanes on which large impairments had been recorded were sold. A number of those planes were leased back for a short time period. The profits realized on those planes were deducted from the rental costs for the years 1998 and 1999; as a result the operating costs for the airline were lower in 1998 and 1999.

Gains or losses realized on the sale of assets always have an influence on the individual accounts of the entity that undertakes the transaction. However, if the sale is realized within a group, these intra-group sales with gains or losses have no influence on the group accounts. In circumstances in which individual accounts are used for regulatory, tax or legal purposes, one must be vigilant for these intra-group profits. The profit reported in 1999 in the individual accounts of Sabena NV was mainly created through the transfer of assets from Sabena NV to a newly created subsidiary Sabena Technics NV. It had no effect on the result in the group accounts.

It is clear that not all changes in accounting estimates, accounting method changes and real transactions are induced by earnings management motives or balance sheet management motives. It is important for an analyst to consider all possible explanations for these changes or transactions when they occur. This will be illustrated with the following example.

In the individual accounts of Sabena NV a change in allowances for bad debts is noticed in the year 2000. A year in which the company is already seriously in distress. The evolution of allowances for bad debts is presented in Table 26.1.

In 2000 there is a decrease in the allowances for bad debt, whereas in prior years there was an increase related to the change in allowances for bad debt.

Activity 26.9

If you relate the change in bad debt allowance to the elements of the annual accounts (balance sheet total, turnover, equity) of Sabena do you think the amount is material (balance sheet total 61 billion BEF, revenue see Table 26.1, equity at 31.12.2000, 220 392 (000) BEF)?

Activity feedback

At first sight the amount does not seem to be material, at least not in relation to the balance sheet total of 61 billion BEF or to the total revenue of 94 billion BEF. However if we relate the amount to the equity of the company we get a different picture. The

Table 26.1 Evolution of turnover and bad debt allowances in the financial statements of Sabena NV and Sabena Technics NV

In (000 BEF)	Turnover		Changes in bad debt allowances	
	Sabena	Sabena + Technics	Sabena	Sabena + Technics
1997	65 384 958	65 384 958	38 266	38 266
1998	80 363 967	80 363 967	90 515	90 515
1999	76 975 634	89 544 618	47 634	138 294
2000	94 747 785	106 598 381	(57 069)	(204 309)

Source: Financial statements of Sabena NV and Sabena Technics NV

equity in 2000 declined to 220 392 (000) BEF. The difference between an increase of bad debt allowances of $+/-40$ million BEF (year 1999) and a decrease 57 million BEF (year 2000) amounts to 90 million BEF. This 90 million BEF compared with 220 million BEF is not that immaterial. However, economic explanations for this change in allowances for bad debts should always be considered. It could be that the separation of Sabena Technics from Sabena NV in 1999 was the explaining factor. Maybe customers of Sabena Technics have another payment profile. In order to investigate for this possibility the data of Technics are added in 1999 and 2000 to the Sabena NV data.

Another explanation could be the creation of the Airline Management Partnership. Does the AMP play a role in the treatment of uncollectable receivables? Note that in the annual report of Sabena AMP is announced as a major restructuring for a number of activities under which come 'marketing, product and sales'. A further explanation could be that Sabena is pursuing a stricter collection policy due to her own liquidity problems. In an effort to improve cash flow, the management of firms in serious distress usually take action to accelerate the collection of receivables. This leads to a lower balance in receivables and a decrease in allowances for bad debt. These are questions which cannot be answered by an external analyst on the basis of published information. Only insiders know the answer.

At the end of the discussion on annual accounts' management practices it is important to highlight that most methods of annual accounts management have what is called a *reversal effect*. Reversal means that income increasing accounting interventions in the current period lead to a decrease in income in future periods and vice versa. In fact, many of the methods applied involve only inter-temporal shifts in accounting income. In the literature accounting method choices are often labelled as having a reversal effect (declining depreciation will have lower profits in the beginning than the straight line method, but after a certain moment in the life span of the asset the situation reverses), whereas a real transaction is often labelled as having a one time effect. However, all three practices (accounting method changes, accounting estimates and real transactions) might entail reversing effects. If one sells, for example, a fuel hedge contract to have an increase in profits in the year the contract is sold, the company will probably suffer from higher fuel prices in the period thereafter. So the sale of the contract is not limited to a one-time effect.

An element that might differ between the different methods for annual accounts management is the timing of the reversal effect.

Activity 26.10

Think of some methods to be used for annual accounts management purposes with a short reversal time and methods with a longer reversal time.

Activity feedback

A change in accounting methods or estimates in the area of the working capital of a firm might have a short reversal period e.g. a switch from one inventory valuation method to another, a change in the estimates of bad debt allowances.

Working capital accruals reverse in the short term as these elements are short-term assets and liabilities. This implies that if the results fall short the year after, additional earnings influence practices must be used if one does not want the result to drop. The reversal period in relation to non-working capital items is longer. For example the gain realized on sale and leaseback transactions is spread out over the life span of the leased asset.

Bowen *et al.* (1995) found that management in general chooses accounting interventions with a long-term positive effect on accounting income. However, if the compensation scheme of the management had short-term perspectives, practices with shorter reversal periods were used.

The story of Sabena

In Figure 26.1 we presented the net results of Sabena NV over the years 1991–2000 and in Figure 26.2 the results of the Sabena Group over the years 1992–2000. In this section we link together all the information we have collected so far on Sabena and re-analyse the evolution of the reported results. The aim of this illustration is to analyse the accounting and reporting strategy and to get an idea of the underlying economic result.

In 1991 big bath accounting was practised in order to enhance the future of Sabena. Figure 26.1 clearly illustrates this. In 1992 the cooperation with Air France started. The figure presents the operating result and the net result of the individual accounts of Sabena NV over the period 1992–2000. Figure 26.2 presents the consolidated results of the Sabena Group over the same period. In Figure 26.5 the important company events are mentioned.

In the first time frame, namely the cooperation with Air France, the results fluctuate almost within a more narrow band-width. The results were kept within that band-width partly due to the release of provisions over those years (see Figure 26.4) In 1992 the individual accounts were positively influenced due to the sale of a subsidiary with profit within the group (Sobelair, the charter company, was sold to Sabena leasing NV). This last item was only beneficial for the individual accounts of Sabena.

At the start of the second time frame, namely the cooperation with the SAir Group, especially in 1996, the financial year where the new CEO comes in, the results drop sharply. The subsequent messages of the board of directors even provide information on the goal they were pursuing and on the methods they were using to obtain the goal. The accounting strategy was making it possible for Sabena to show profit from 1998 on. The subsequent messages of the board of directors could be regarded as implicit contracts for profitability from 1998 on. For example (annual report 1997, p. 30):

> In 1997 the Sabena Group's exceptional result was influenced, as it had been in 1996, by the implementation of the balance sheet recovery plan with the intention that certain factors should no longer have an adverse effect on the profit and loss account in the coming years.

(For further evidence on this message see earlier in this text.)

The two time frames can also be distinguished if we represent the exceptional costs and exceptional revenues in a graphical way (Figure 26.6). During the cooperation with Air France it is a rather stable pattern. From 1996 to 1999 we observe a gradual increase of exceptional revenue. In 2000 a new CEO comes in.

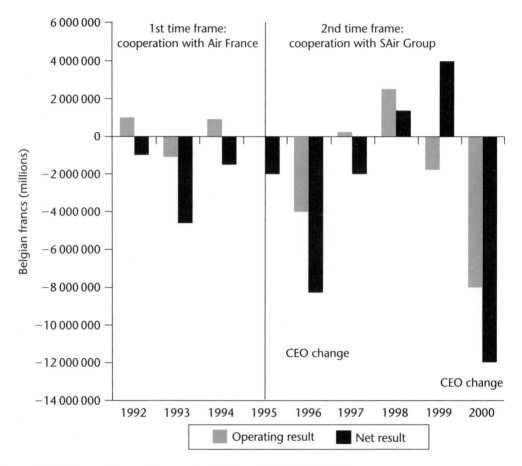

Figure 26.5 Net and operating result of Sabena NV, 1992–2000
Source: Annual accounts of Sabena NV, 1992–2000

If we return to the second time frame in Figure 26.5 we might state that the frontloading of costs, a favourable economic climate and gains on disposal of assets resulted in the 'promised' profit in 1998 in the individual accounts as well as in the consolidated accounts. The gain in the number of planes (mainly Boeings) acquired under a sale and leaseback agreement also favourably influenced the result of 1999, as part of the gain was carried forward. In 1999 the group results were negative again (see Figure 26.2), the individual accounts, however, showed a good profit figure of 4 billion BEF through intra-group sales as explained earlier. The 'reported' results of Sabena looked fair in 1998, although whether the underlying economic performance had also improved could not yet be judged. This would only become clear after a few years, since Sabena had practised to some extent what is called big bath accounting in the literature in the years before 1998. Many stakeholders involved considered this reported profit as a major breakthrough. In many textbooks, however, warnings with

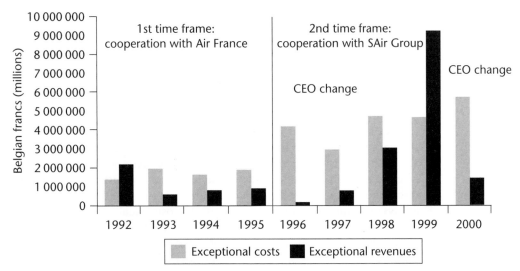

Figure 26.6 Evaluation of exceptional results within Sabena NV, 1992–2000
Source: Annual accounts of Sabena NV, 1992–2000

regard to big bath accounting can be found. For example, Penmann (2001, p. 601):

> This intertemporal shifting of income means that earnings quality is not only doubtful in the year of the manipulation but also in subsequent years when borrowing or saving of income 'comes home to roost'.

It is important to note here that the board of directors of Sabena had made in their messages the necessary disclosures, so that external parties who had taken the time to look at the annual reports of prior years, knew they had to judge the results of 1998 with the necessary caution.

Due to the elements mentioned in the introduction to this chapter on Sabena – unfavourable economic climate, raising costs due to prior management decisions extensive and expensive fleet renewal and to a lesser extent rather expensive outsourcing of activities (evidence of the latter can be found in interviews given by the management of Sabena to the press and by declarations of the members of the management before the parliamentary investigation committee in Belgium), high fuel prices, unfavourable exchange rate with the dollar – but also due to the reversal effect of certain of the accounting methods used, the results of 2000 collapsed.

The purpose of this section on practices of annual accounts' management was to highlight the importance of gaining understanding into the accounting flexibility which is available to the management of a company. For financial analysis purposes it is not only important to understand the accounting flexibility which was available, but it is also necessary to know which valuation rules and estimates are used in the presentation of those annual accounts. In order to get an idea about the valuation methods used and accounting estimates applied the quality and the level of disclosure in the financial statements is an important determinant of the visibility of accounting interventions. Unfortunately, the level of disclosure differs among companies.

Quality of disclosure

When management provides the necessary disclosures in the notes to the balance sheet, profit and loss account and cash flow statement and in the management discussion report, it facilitates the analysis of the business reality of the company by external parties. Financial statements are meant to inform the stakeholders of the firm about the result, the cash flow and the financial position of the firm. In principle, the published figures should represent the underlying economic situation of the firm. However, due to the flexibility that exists in the accounting standards to be applied and the incentives that face top executives towards earnings management a situation might be created in which the published figures in the financial statements do not translate the underlying economic condition of the firm. Although companies must provide a minimum level of disclosure as required by the GAAP they are complying with, the management team can always make more voluntary disclosures. Disclosure quality refers to the compliance of a company to all the disclosures required by the GAAP and to the informativeness of the voluntary disclosures which are presented in the annual report. So disclosure quality and the level of disclosure can also be extended to the narrative part of the annual report. This will be discussed further in Chapter 27. Empirical and analytical accounting research have paid attention to disclosure practices. Most empirical research studies provide evidence that an increase in disclosure leads to lower costs of capital due to the reduction in information asymmetry. The analytical research, however, indicates that there is all optimal level of disclosure for a company.

Disclosure quality is an important benchmark when inter-firm comparisons are made and it relates to several aspects. Some examples of disclosure quality will now be illustrated.

Description of accounting methods and accounting estimates

So far we have learned that the choice of accounting valuation methods and accounting estimates can influence the reported profit and the balance sheet structure. Adequate disclosure in the notes on the methods and the estimates used might enable external analysts to get an idea of the impact of the choice and to reconcile earnings of different firms when executing a comparative financial analysis of companies. Further, a company can also explain why a particular choice has been made. If we compare the different airlines we notice that the level of explanation with regard to, for example, how frequent flyer obligations are accounted for differs. Frequent flyer programmes could create obligations for an airline. However, the obligation is dependent on several terms of the contract between the airline and the customer. On top of that several ways exist to account for these obligations: the incremental cost approach whereby the costs are charged to P&L when passengers make use of the bonus miles or the revenue minus approach whereby part of the revenue of the ticket sale is deferred to the moment the passenger makes use of the bonus miles (a provision is then created).

In the notes containing the description of the accounting policies of Sabena we find the following brief disclosure:

> Annual report, 2000, p. 50, note 5.7: Appropriate provisions are also made for liabilities arising from mileages accrued via the Qualiflyer frequent flyer programme. These provisions are equal to the costs to be incurred as such credits are redeemed.

In the accounts of British Airways, the programmes themselves are described together with the way they are accounted for under UK GAAP as well as under US GAAP:

> Annual report, 2003/2004, note 1, p. 35: The group operates two principal frequent flyer programmes. The Airline scheme, 'Executive Club', allows frequent travellers to accumulate 'BA Miles' mileage credits which entitle them to a choice of various awards, including free travel and are sold to participating partners to use in promotional activities. The AIRMILES scheme, operated by the company's wholly-owned subsidiary Airmiles Travel Promotions Limited allows companies to purchase miles for use in promotional incentives.
>
> Revenue from the sale of BA Miles and AIRMILES to third parties is recognised when miles are issued to participants. The estimated direct incremental cost of providing free redemption services, including British Airways flights, in exchange for redemption of miles earned by members of the group's Executive Club and AIRMILES schemes is accrued as members of these schemes accumulate mileage. Costs accrued include incremental fuel, catering, servicing costs and cost of redemptions on air and non-air partners; these costs are charged to cost of sales… [p. 63] Under US GAAP, following the implementation of SAB 101 'Revenue Recognition in Financial Statements' a proportion of frequent flyer revenue is deferred until the frequent flyer airmiles are redeemed.

Explanation of significant changes in accounting methods and accounting estimates

Accounting method changes hinder external users of the financial statements in comparing the results and the balance sheet structures over the years. Adequate disclosure of the new accounting method applied and the impact on comparability could facilitate the analysis.

When Ryanair changed its accounting policies for the provision for maintenance of aircraft and for depreciation of aircraft (annual report 1999, p. 29, note 1 prior year adjustment) extensive explanation was provided regarding the impact of this change on the profit and loss account, the tangible assets, the provisions and the equity of the company.

For airlines complying with IAS the issuance of SIC 23 (*Property, Plant and Equipment – Major Inspection or Overhaul Costs*) implied changes with regard to the treatment of major inspection or overhaul costs. The level of disclosure with regard to this change, however, differed among the airlines.

Level of information disclosure

Another example which relates to quality of disclosure is the level of compliance with disclosures required by GAAP and the extra-voluntary disclosure provided on that item. With regard to related parties a separate disclosure has to be made under several GAAP e.g. IAS/IFRS (see Chapter 24). If we compare the item 'related party disclosures' between the annual accounts of Lufthansa and those of the SAir Group we observe differences, however, both airlines prepare their annual accounts using IAS/IFRS.

SAir limits the explicit note on related parties to note 29 'Transactions with board members and key shareholders'. Board members and key shareholders are indeed third parties, however, we know that the airlines in which SAir holds a substantial minority shareholding qualify as related parties due to the way they are accounted for in the books of SAir, namely by using the equity method. Information on those third parties is distributed over several different items in the notes of the financial statements of the SAir Group (annual report SAir, 2000, p. 33). For example note 12, p. 21 on the accounts receivable includes elements which classify in fact as related party disclosures:

Trade accounts receivable: of which CHF 66 million due from associated undertakings, other accounts receivable: of which CHF 12 million due from associated undertakings, current loans: of which CHF 13 million due from associated undertakings.

Related party information is also found in the notes on lease payments (see Chapter 27).

In the annual accounts of Lufthansa, however (annual report 2003, note 41) the information on related party disclosures is bundled into one note, namely note 40, and is much more extensive. Together with the kind of relationship a list is presented with the amount of services rendered to the related party and the amount of services utilized:

Company	Volume of services rendered		Volume of services utilized	
	2003	2002	2003	2002
	E m	E m	E m	E m
Condor Flugdienst GmbH	179	155	21	2
British Midland	11	79	31	69

Entity analysis

In the earlier section of this part on methods of annual accounts management we saw that results of the individual accounts can be influenced through intra-group sales. If there is a relationship of control these results are eliminated in the group accounts in the consolidation process (see Chapter 24). This means, however, that it is important to look into the different relationships one company might have with other companies. There are different kinds of relationship between an investor company and the company it has invested in. These different kinds of relationship need different accounting treatments. The following treatments are laid down in all GAAP: control (the investee is consolidated), significant influence (equity method) and no influence (valuation at cost).

When there is a control relationship, there is always the possibility of transferring profits from one company to the other by means of transfer prices for goods and services transferred between group members. These intra-group profits are eliminated when all companies over which a holding company has control are fully consolidated.

In case of a significant influence in a company, but without control, the undertaking is accounted for by the equity method. In situations where there is control but the undertaking is accounted for by the equity method, the accounts of both parties involved do not present a true picture of the underlying relationship and position of the group.

The 'real' nature of the relationship should be considered and compared with the accounting treatment applied in the annual accounts. Sometimes it might be that the accounting treatment does not comply with the underlying relationship. As an external analyst it is extremely useful to know why there is this difference and what the impact on the published accounts is. Especially under rules-based GAAP, companies can set up separate entities using legal constructions in such a way that the legal form of the relationship does not comply with the definition of control embedded in the GAAP used by the controlling company. In these circumstances, a change in the accounting standards, might turn an associated company into a subsidiary for reporting purposes. We will elaborate this item further at the end of this section.

Through the following activity we will illustrate the impact on the annual accounts of the investor according to the accounting method applied: full consolidation or equity method. This activity illustrates further the reporting procedures presented in Chapter 24.

Activity 26.11

Company A owns 45% of the shares of company B; company A bought the shares on 1.1.X. Company A sells goods or services to company B. Company B sells the goods or services further to their clients. The beginning balance sheets of the individual accounts of company A and B follow. Assume that company A sells a product to company B, at year end 31.12.X company B has sold all products to third parties. The cost of the products for company A amounts to €40 000. Company A sells the products to company B for €50 000. In the first situation company B is able to realize a turnover of €56 000 with the sale of the products to its customers. In the second situation company B realizes only a turnover of €42 000. This sale of products is the only activity for company A and B in the year X.

	Balance sheet company A 1.1.X	Balance sheet company B 1.1.X
Financial assets	45 000	
Other assets	755 000	400 000
Total assets	800 000	400 000
Equity	300 000	100 000
Liabilities	500 000	300 000
Total equity + liabilities	800 000	400 000

Consider, for both situations, the impact on the profit and loss account for company B. Take further into account the regulation on accounting for associated enterprises and consider the impact on the profit and loss account of company A, the investor, if the shareholding in B is accounted for under the equity method. When solving this activity bear in mind what you learned about the equity method and accounting for associated companies in prior chapters of this book.

Activity feedback

Situation 1: Company *B* is able to sell the products for 56 000

	Individual accounts, company A	Individual accounts, company B	Group accounts, company A
Balance sheet			
Financial assets	45 000		47 700
Other assets	765 000	406 000	765 000
Total assets	810 000	406 000	812 700
Equity	310 000	106 000	312 700
Liabilities	500 000	300 000	500 000
Equity + liabilities	810 000	406 000	812 700
Profit and loss account			
Operating revenue	50 000	56 000	50 000
Operating costs	40 000	50 000	40 000
Operating results	10 000	6 000	10 000
Results from associated undertakings			2 700
Net result	10 000	6 000	12 700

Situation 2: Company *B* sells the products for 42 000

	Individual accounts, company A	Individual accounts, company B	Group accounts, company A
Balance sheet			
Financial assets	45 000		41 400
Other assets	765 000	392 000	765 000
Total assets	810 000	392 000	806 400
Equity	310 000	92 000	306 400
Liabilities	500 000	300 000	500 000
Equity + liabilities	810 000	392 000	806 400
Profit and loss account			
Operating revenue	50 000	42 000	50 000
Operating costs	40 000	50 000	40 000
Operating results	10 000	(8 000)	10 000
Results from associated undertakings			(3 600)
Net result	10 000	(8 000)	6 400

Activity 26.12

Assume that there are underlying contracts between the management of *A* and the shareholders of *B* in which agreements are made that *A* has the power to control the operating and financing activities of B. Remember what you learned about consolidation in Chapter 24. Consider also the definition of control in IFRS 3 and the accounting method prescribed in IAS 27. How should company *A* now account for company *B* and what would be the difference with the situation presented under Activity 26.11.

Activity feedback

Company *A* would now have to consolidate company *B*. The consolidated accounts of the group *AB* would present the following picture.

	B sold the products for 56 000	B sold the products for 42 000
Group balance sheet		
Total assets	1 171 000	1 157 000
Equity (capital + reserves)	300 000	300 000
Results of the year	12 700	6 400
Minority interests	58 300	50 600
Liabilities	800 000	800 000
Total equity and liabilities	1 171 000	1 157 000
Group profit and loss account		
Operating revenue	56 000	42 000
Operating costs	40 000	40 000
Operating result	16 000	2 000
Net result	16 000	2 000
Share of minority interests	(3 300)	4 400
Net result for the group	12 700	6 400

We notice that if the transactions with associated enterprises are accounted for in a correct manner the impact on the net result of the investor company is the same as under full consolidation. The only difference concerning the profit and loss account relates to the lines where the result is eliminated. The operating result under the equity method is always 10 000, in the case of consolidation the loss or profit made by *B* on the sale is reflected in the operating result. Although the net result is the same amount under both the equity method and full consolidation, the amounts representing the operating revenue and the operating result are different. This might have an impact on ratios calculated where sales or operating results are included in the nominator or denominator. (See Chapter 27 for more information on ratio analysis.) The main difference with regard to full consolidation or equity relates mainly to the balance sheet. The amount of debt is much higher in the case of full consideration.

A further element with regard to entity analysis is the question whether all entities with which a company has a link have been included in the consolidated accounts and are properly accounted for (consolidated, equity method or valued at cost according to the relation). In this context the creation of special purpose entities is important.

In the last decades of the 20th century SPEs were created for various reasons, in the beginning especially for lease purposes and later on, for other reasons (e.g. increasing revenue). The entity analysis performed should take into account whether or not all special purpose entities set up by a company are included or left out from the consolidation process. However, there can be differences in the GAAP which is applied. It is said that the SPEs which Enron had created and which they could exclude from consolidation under US GAAP would have been consolidated if Enron would have applied IAS/IFRS.

In the wake of the accounting scandals, the FASB looked into these issues. In January 2003, the FASB issued FASB Interpretation no. 46, *Consolidation of Variable Interest Entities – VIE (FIN 46)* and amended it in October 2003. Variable interest entities are entities that lack sufficient equity to finance their activities without additional financial support from other parties or whose equity holders lack adequate decision making ability based on the criteria set forth in that Interpretation.

Economic criteria such as 'lack of sufficient equity to finance the activities' or 'lack of decision-making ability' now dominate the decision whether or not to consolidate an entity in the group accounts. Due to this change in the standards on variable interest entities, the Walt Disney Company will now have to include its two theme parks, Euro Disney in France and Hong Kong Disneyland, in its group accounts with the use of the full consolidation method. Up until 2003 both theme parks were included in the group accounts of the Walt Disney Company with the use of the equity method. With regard to the investment Euro Disney, the economic situation of Euro Disney and its relationship with the Walt Disney Company are now presented in Activity 26.13.

Activity 26.13

When you read the following information, consider the characteristics of a variable interest entity. Which elements embedded in FIN 46 do you recognize in the relation between the Walt Disney Company and Euro Disney?

The Walt Disney Company holds 39% of the capital of Euro Disney SCA, but Euro Disney SCA is managed by Euro Disney SA, which is an indirect 99% owned subsidiary of the Walt Disney Company. Further in connection with a financial restructuring of Euro Disney in 1994, Euro Disney Associés SNC, a wholly owned affiliate of the Walt Disney Company, entered into a lease arrangement with a financing company with a non-cancellable term of 12 years related to substantially all of the Disneyland Park assets and then entered into a 12-year sub-lease agreement with Euro Disney on substantially the same terms. At the conclusion of the sub-lease term, Euro Disney will have the option of assuming Disney SNC's rights and obligations under the lease for a payment of $90 million over the ensuing 15 months. If Euro Disney does not exercise its option, Disney SNC may purchase the assets, continue to lease the assets or elect to terminate the lease. In the event the lease is terminated, Disney SNC would be obligated to make a termination payment to the lessor equal to 75% of the lessor's then outstanding debt related to the Disneyland Park assets, which payment would be approximately $1.3 billion. Disney SNC would then have the right to sell or lease the assets on behalf of the lessor to satisfy the remaining debt, with any excess proceeds payable to Disney SNC. Euro Disney's financial difficulties, notwithstanding, the company believes it is unlikely that Disney SNC would be required to pay the 75% lease termination payment as the company currently expects that in order for Euro Disney to continue its business it will either exercise its assumption option in 2006 or that the assumption of the lease by Euro Disney will otherwise be provided for in the resolution to Euro Disney's financial situation.

Activity feedback

We distinguish the 'lack of management power'. Euro Disney is, in fact, managed by a subsidiary of the Walt Disney Company. Further we notice that due to the weak financial situation of Euro Disney from the start, a subsidiary of the Walt Disney

Company bears the financial risks in relation to the lease agreements Euro Disney has with the lessor of the assets. Euro Disney SNC is obliged to fulfil the commitments towards the lessor if Euro Disney SCA is not able to pay the lessor.

Although the economic situation and the legal situation of the relationship between the Walt Disney Company and Euro Disney did not change from 2003 to 2004, the accounting method the Walt Disney Company will use to account for its investment in Paris will be different. This change in method is a result of a change in accounting standards. In its annual report the Walt Disney Company informs its readers (see the extract from the annual report, which follows).

The impact of a change in accounting standards is illustrated with the use of the economic situation of the Walt Disney Company and Euro Disney. The financial figures of Euro Disney will also be used in the last section of Chapter 26.

Impact of FIN 46 on Equity Investments

As discussed in Note 2, the implementation of FIN 46 will likely require the Company to consolidate both Euro Disney and Hong Kong Disneyland for financial reporting purposes in the first quarter of fiscal 2004. The following tables present consolidated results of operations and financial position for the Company as of and for the year ended September 30, 2003 as if Euro Disney and Hong Kong Disneyland had been consolidated based on our current analysis and understanding of FIN 46.

	As Reported	Euro Disney	Hong Kong Disneyland	Adjust-ments	As Adjusted
Results of Operations					
Revenues	$ 27 061	$ 1 077	$ 5	$ (10)	$ 28 133
Cost and expenses	(24 330)	(1 032)	(7)	9	(25 360)
Amortization of intangibles assets	(18)	–	–	–	(18)
Gain on sale of business	16	–	–	–	16
Net interest expense	(793)	(101)	–	–	(894)
Equity in the income of investees	334	–	–	24	358
Restructuring and impairment charges	(16)	–	–	–	(16)
Income before income taxes, minority interest and the cumulative effect of accounting change	2 254	(56)	(2)	23	2 219
Income taxes	(789)	–	–	13	(776)
Minority interests	(127)	–	–	22	(105)
Cumulative effect of accounting change	(71)	–	–	–	(71)
Net income/(loss)	$ 1 267	$ (56)	$ (2)	$ 58	$ 1 267

Balance Sheet:

Cash and cash equivalents	$ 1 583	$ 103	$ 76	$ –	$ 1 762
Other current assets	6 731	191	9	(9)	6 922
Total current assets	8 314	294	85	(9)	8 684
Investments	1 849	–	–	(623)	1 226
Fixed assets	12 678	2 951	524	–	16 153
Intangible assets	2 786	–	–	–	2 786
Goodwill	16 966	–	–	–	16 966
Other assets	7 395	128	9	–	7 532
Total assets	$ 49 988	$ 3 373	$ 618	$ (632)	$ 53 347
Current portion of borrowings[1]	$ 2 457	$ 2 528	$ –	$ (388)	4 597
Other current liabilities	6 212	487	61	(85)	6 675
Total current liabilities	8 669	3 015	61	(473)	11 272
Borrowings	10 643	–	237	–	10 880
Deferred income taxes	2 712	–	–	–	2 712
Other long-term liabilities	3 745	289	–	(71)	3 963
Minority interests	428	–	–	301	729
Shareholders' equity	23 791	69	320	(389)	23 791
Total liabilities and shareholders' equity	$ 49 988	$ 3 373	$618	$(632)	$ 53 347

[1]All of Euro Disney's borrowings are classified as current as they are subject to acceleration if a long-term solution to Euro Disney's financing needs is not achieved by March 31, 2004.

Impact of accounting standards used on annual accounts

As already mentioned, we know that accounting analysis involves an evaluation of the accounting flexibility available to the management of a company. This accounting flexibility is, to a large extent, determined by the type of GAAP which is applied. Some GAAP systems allow more valuation choices for one item than others or simply require other valuation or presentation methods. According to the GAAP applied the same transactions or operations can be accounted for in a different way.

A clear illustration of the impact which GAAP can have on the annual accounts, is found in the annual accounts of Euro Disney SCA. The structure of Euro Disney SCA is presented in note 1 of the consolidated financial statements 2003:

> Euro Disney SCA (the 'Company') and its wholly-owned subsidiaries (collectively, the 'Group') commenced operations with the official opening of Disneyland Park on April 12, 1992. The Group operates the Disneyland Resort Paris, which includes two theme parks, Walt Disney Studios Park and the Disneyland Park (the 'Theme Park'), seven themed hotels, two convention centres, the Disney Village entertainment centre and a golf course in

Marne-la-Vallée, France. In addition, the Group manages the real estate development and expansion of the related infrastructure of the property. The company, a publicly held French company, is owned 39% by indirect, wholly-owned subsidiaries of the Walt Disney Company ('TWDC') and managed by Euro Disney SA (the Company's Gérant), an indirect, 99%-owned subsidiary of TWDC. The General Partner is EDL Participations SA, also an indirect, wholly-owned subsidiary of TWDC.

The balance sheet structure and the cost structure of the company differ significantly according to the GAAP applied. Euro Disney SCA presents its financial statements according to French GAAP *and* according to US GAAP. The biggest difference relates to the treatment of the lease agreements in the accounts of Euro Disney SCA (notes 1–2, consolidated financial statements 2001):

> The Group owns Walt Disney Studios Park, the Disneyland Hotel, the Davy Crockett Ranch, the golf course, the underlying land thereof and the land on which the five other hotels and the Disney Village entertainment centre are located and leases substantially all the remaining operating assets.

This implies that all attractions in the theme park, the hotels (New York, Newport Bay Club, Sequoia Lodge, Cheyenne and Santa Fe) and the Disney Village entertainment centre are operated under lease agreements which qualify under French GAAP as operational leases (note 2, consolidated financial statements 2003).

The balance sheet and profit and loss account of Euro Disney SCA under French GAAP have the following outlook.

Profit and loss account of Eurodisney SCA (in € million)	Year ended September 30			
	2003	2002	2001	2000
Revenues	1 053.1	1 076.0	1 005.2	959.2
Cost and expenses	(920.7)	(900.3)	(820.0)	(783.4)
Income before lease and financial charges	132.4	175.7	185.2	175.8
■ lease rental expense	(193.8)	(188.8)	(185.8)	(151.1)
■ financial income	49.0	59.1	89.8	74.8
■ financial expense	(55.5)	(41.1)	(51.5)	(62.0)
Income before exceptional items	(67.9)	4.9	37.7	37.5
■ exceptional income/(loss) net	11.9	(38.0)	(7.2)	1.2
Net income	(56.0)	(33.1)	30.5	38.7

Balance sheet Euro Disney SCA (€ in millions)	Year ended September 30			
	2003	2002	2001	2000
Current assets	210.7	232.4	784.5	645.9
Deferred charges	55.1	86.7	88.1	63.3
Fixed assets	2 317.8	2 389.5	2 233.5	2 084.6
Total assets	2 583.6	2 708.6	3 106.1	2 793.8
Current liabilities	271.2	359.5	425.8	379.6
Deferred revenues	87.6	94.7	77.3	75.3
Provisions	120.1	35.5	31.1	21.8

Borrowings	867.5	821.3	1 141.2	916.8
Shareholders' equity	1 084.4	1 244.8	1 277.9	1 247.5
Quasi-equity	152.8	152.8	152.8	152.8
Total liabilities and equity	2 583.6	2 708.6	3 106.1	2 793.8

In the annual accounts a reconciliation to US GAAP is included. The largest impact stems from a different treatment of the lease contracts:

> The Group leases substantially all of its operating assets under various agreements. Under French GAAP, the Group has not capitalized these leases and is accounting for them as operating leases. Under US GAAP, the underlying assets and liabilities and related depreciation and interest expense are reflected in the Group's financial statements.

Besides the reconciliation of the leasing agreements, there are other elements which also have an impact on the accounts but the amount is minor compared to the lease impact (see annual accounts).

	Year ended September 30			
(€ in millions)	2003	2002	2001	2000
Net result, as reported under French GAAP	(56.0)	(33.1)	30.5	38.7
Lease and interest adjustments	7.2	(35.7)	(78.4)	(106.0)
Other	(5.6)	1.5	(2.7)	1.1
Net loss under US GAAP	(54.4)	(67.3)	(50.6)	(66.2)
Comprehensive income items:				
Interest rate hedges	2.1	0.7	(8.1)	–
Comprehensive loss under US GAAP	(52.3)	(66.6)	(58.7)	(66.2)

This reconciliation to US GAAP brings the result of Euro Disney SCA in the red. After the reconciliation of shareholders' equity to US GAAP a much smaller amount of equity is left.

Reconciliation of shareholders' equity	Year ended September 30			
(€ in millions)	203	2002	2001	2000
Shareholders' equity, as reported under French GAAP	1 084.3	1 244.8	1 277.9	1 247.5
Cumulative lease and interest adjustments	(1 279.8)	(1 278.0)	(1 251.3)	(1 172.9)
Effect of revaluing the ORAs and sale/leaseback transactions	178.1	178.1	178.1	178.1
Other	77.8	(23.3)	(25.0)	(14.6)
Shareholders' equity under US GAAP	60.4	112.6	179.7	238.1

It is not only a change from one set of GAAP to another set of GAAP that could entail enormous differences; new standards within the same set of GAAP could result in major differences with regard to balance sheet and profit and loss accounts.

British Airways experienced this some time ago. British Airways had to make substantial changes to its accounts when several new financial reporting standards (FRS) were introduced by the Accounting Standards Board in the UK at the beginning of the 1990s. FRS 5 especially had a tremendous impact. The following illustration relates to it.

British Airways plc

This company, because of FRS 5, *Reporting the Substance of Transactions* is having to make very significant changes to its published financial statements. For example, as of 1994 twenty-four aircraft previously accounted for under extendable operating lease arrangements, and therefore off the balance sheet, will need to be included as assets on the balance sheet with the corresponding liabilities also included. British Airways also, in order to avoid problems of protection policies by foreign governments, has set up 49%-owned operating companies, i.e. TAT European airlines and Deutsche BA. Under FRS 2 these were classified as associate undertakings and dealt with accordingly in the group accounts. However, under FRS 5 they will need to be classified as quasi-subsidiaries and therefore treated in the accounts as if they were subsidiary undertakings. There are obviously a whole variety of detailed effects on the numbers in the published financial statements resulting from FRS 5. Noteworthy, for example, is an increase in the value of fixed assets and related borrowings by some £1100 million!

Summary

The purpose of financial statements is to give external parties a picture of the performance of a company and its financial position. At the same time, however, financial statements are viewed by the management of a company as a means of communication to the outside world. Sometimes, a tension may arise to publish a result somewhat different from the underlying economic result. In this case, the company will adopt a certain accounting strategy. The aim of this chapter was to describe and analyse the different building blocks of such an accounting strategy (incentives, reporting strategy and practices used). Trying to detect the accounting strategy of a firm and undo the published result from the disturbing elements of the accounting strategy is called accounting analysis. The purpose of accounting analysis is to get an idea of the underlying economic result and only this result is useful or value relevant for decision-making purposes.

EXERCISES   (✔ indicates answers are available on pages 750–751)

✔ **1** Identify as many examples as possible where the choice of accounting policy could significantly affect the analysis and interpretation of published financial statements.

✔ **2** The summarized balance sheets of three businesses in the same industry are shown below for 200X.

	A	B	C
	£000	£000	£000
Intangibles	100	–	10
Tangible fixed assets	886	582	580
Current assets	920	580	950
Current liabilities	(470)	(252)	(486)
	1 436	910	1 054
Long-term liabilities	(100)	(20)	(50)
	1 336	890	1 004
Share capital	200	40	300
Revaluation reserve	80		
Retained profits	1 056	850	704
	1 336	890	1 004

The operating profit and sales for the three companies for the years in question were:

	A	B	C
operating profit	282	194	148
sales	2 100	1 500	1 750

The companies had different treatments for the intangibles. Company A is amortizing this at £10 000 per annum and company C at £2 000 per annum. Company B has written off goodwill of £40 000 to retained profits in the year. Included in the depreciation expense of company A is an extra £4 000 over and above the historical cost depreciation caused by an earlier revaluation of its premises.

Appraise the financial performance and stability of each of these three companies within the limits of the information given.

3 If you consider companies such as Mc Donald's, Kentucky Fried Chicken, Burger King etc., what are the value drivers in their industries? What are the critical factors in their industrial environment? Comment on these. Subsequently, contrast your findings with an analysis of the value drivers of companies like Boeing and Airbus. What do you observe? How will these different industry characteristics and value drivers have an impact on the financial statements of these companies? You might look up their annual reports on their websites for inspiration.

4 Identify as many examples as possible where the choice of accounting methods, accounting estimates or even real transactions could significantly affect the analysis and interpretation of the financial statements. Comment on how these choices affect the financial statements.

5 Consider again the examples you have listed in answering question 3. Relate these findings to the national GAAP of your own country. Does the national GAAP in your country allow accounting flexibility on many of the items listed?

6 Compare the accounting flexibility of the national GAAP in your own country with the flexibility in IAS/IFRS. Which of the two systems allows less flexibility to the preparer of the financial statements?

7 Would the information provided through financial statements improve if you could eliminate accounting flexibility from the standards?

8 You, as an accountant, are asked by your financial director, to choose suitable companies to compare your own company with. Explain, in a report to her, what would influence your choice and how you would adjust for differing accounting policies, if any.

Techniques of financial analysis

After studying this chapter you should be able to:
- ☐ identify potential red flags that obstruct comparability of financial accounting data
- ☐ perform the following types of analysis and appraise the results:
  - – trend analysis
  - – common size analysis
  - – ratio analysis
  - – segmental analysis
  - – cash flow analysis.

Introduction

The purpose of financial analysis is to evaluate the performance of a firm given the strategy of the firm, the economic and industrial environment in which the company is competitive and the accounting strategy applied. Several techniques of financial analysis exist. The most well-known technique is the technique of ratio analysis, in which items of the balance sheet and profit and loss account are related to each other. Each introductory course on financial accounting usually has a chapter on ratio analysis.

Activity 27.1

Using the annual accounts of Euro Disney 2003 which ratios would you calculate?

Activity feedback

Any reader of this text who has some introduction to this topic will come up with ratios such as:

- current assets/current liabilities to judge the ability of a company to repay its debt in the short term
- debt/equity to evaluate the financial risk of a company in the long term
- results/equity to decide whether or not the investments are used in a profitable way.

Activity 27.2

Can you judge the financial situation of Euro Disney SCA properly based only on the ratios of 2003? Why or why not?

Activity feedback

Judging the performance of a firm based on the results of a particular year or even two years is not that meaningful. First of all, one has no external benchmark to compare the performance of the firm with, for example, a competitor in the same industry. Second, information from one or two years is too short a time frame to build an internal benchmark on.

Think of the example of Sabena in Chapter 26. Had you been given only the annual accounts of 1998 or even 1998 and 1999, would you have been able to make a proper judgement on the economic and financial situation of Sabena? The answer is simply, *No!* The profits of 1998 and the figures of 1999 tell a different story if the data from 1995, and more especially 1996 and 1997, are added.

In order to evaluate the performance of a firm in a meaningful way a comparison is needed with firms in the industry, with the past performance of the firm or with an absolute benchmark. In ratio analysis, however, no absolute benchmarks exist, except maybe that profitability should be above the weighted average cost of capital. But even that absolute benchmark in some industries is not always fulfilled.

From the illustrations in the activities thus far it becomes clear that the performance of a firm should be judged in a relevant time frame and against some industry benchmarks. The analysis of the performance of the firm over time is called horizontal analysis or trend analysis. The comparison with the performance of other companies or a whole industry is done by vertical analysis or common size analysis. Before trend analysis and vertical analysis can be undertaken, it is necessary to check if there are no elements present which would disturb the comparison over time and between companies.

Activity 27.3

Which elements can you think of that would disturb the comparison of firm performance over time or between companies?

Activity feedback

- Changes in the structure of the company through a merger, acquisition or creation of new subsidiaries
- differences in valuation rules or accounting methods applied
- differences in presentation rules applied
- different time spans.

In the following section below we illustrate these pitfalls related to comparability.

Elements of non-comparability in financial statements

Activity 27.3 listed some red flags that should be checked before one starts with analysing the performance and the financial position of a company. A number of red flags will now be illustrated with real life examples taken from the airline industry.

Changes with regard to the time span of the financial year

Companies might decide to change the time span of a particular year for several reasons. We can observe this practice if a company suffers from a huge loss (e.g. trading losses on financial contracts), the company may decide to extend the financial year from 12 months to 15 months by changing the reporting date. As a result, this huge loss is then compensated by profits of 15 months instead of 12.

Companies can also create very short financial years in which huge losses or restructurings are accounted for. An example can be found in the annual accounts of the financial year of Sabena 1991. For the purpose of big bath accounting, the financial year 1991 of Sabena was split into two financial years. The first financial year covered three months (1.1.1991–31.3.1991). The second financial year of 1991 covered the other nine months (1.4.1991–31.12.1991). The bath was located in the first annual report of 1991, the second annual report of 1991 showed a profit.

Financial year	1.1.1991–31.3.1991	1.4.1991–31.12.1991
	in 000 BEF	in 000 BEF
Operating profit/(loss)	(2 808 673)	2 161 465
Net profit/(loss)	(30 230 650)	1 132 000

When the ten-year overview of the results of Sabena (1991–2000) were presented (Figure 26.1) the results of the two annual reports of the year 1991 were added up. In this way we obtained a result for a period of 12 months which does not disturb the ten-year comparability over those ten years. In the annual reports of Sabena, however, the data of 1991 were never included in an overview of comparative data over a time frame. The following argument was always put forward: The data of 1991 are not comparative with the other data due to restructuring of Sabena World Airlines in 1991. The comparative figures in the annual accounts of 1992 were those of the second annual report of 1991.

As mentioned earlier for comparative purposes in this text, Sabena's two financial years of 1991 have been combined to gain results for a 12-month period. This is done in the figures presented in this book and also in the data used for trend analysis and common size analysis later on in this chapter.

Different balance sheet dates

Companies use different closing dates for their financial statements. Even within the same industry differences can be observed. For example, in the airline business the following dates are used as balance sheet dates by the different airlines:

31 March: British Airways, KLM, Ryanair
31 September: easyJet
31 December: Austrian Airlines, Lufthansa, Sabena, SAir Group, SAS.

If we compare the annual accounts of the two low-cost carriers for the financial year with closing date in 2001, we have to take into account that easyJet closed its financial statements after the 11 September terrorist attacks on the WTC in New York and Pentagon in Washington by terrorists; and Ryanair had done so before that event.

Changes in company structure

Over the years companies merge, acquire other companies or parts of other companies or restructure activities into different separate legal business entities. If a company is involved in mergers or acquisitions observed growth is often not organic but rather through acquisition. This should be considered in a different way.

Often companies disclose in the notes to the accounts the main drivers of the growth. For example, the SAir Group, to which the airline Swissair belonged, grew mainly through acquisitions in the last years of the 20th century. In note 1 of the annual report of SAir (financial year 2000) information is provided on the causes of the growth in revenue:

> The increase of 24.8% in operating revenue from 1999 to 2000 can be split up in 48% growth through acquisition, 14% positive impact of currency movements and 38% resulting from organic growth.
>
> (Annual accounts, 2000, p. 14, note 1)

These changes in company structures are especially hindering for trend analysis. Some company restructurings can create an impression of decline, although in reality part of the activities has been moved to a separate entity. The accounts of the airline Sabena NV seem to suggest a decline in total operating revenue from 1998 to 1999 (see Table 27.1).

In reality, however, the activities of maintenance and repair were, in 1999, separated into Sabena Technics NV. In order to make a proper comparison over three years we need a constant entity structure. If we add up the data of Sabena Technics NV with those of Sabena NV and correct for intra-group transactions then (data taken from the segmental information in the group accounts) we get a picture which shows growth. In Table 27.2. we present the evolution of the total operating revenue and some operating cost items of Sabena NV, whereby the necessary corrections are made to obtain a constant entity.

Although we have now managed to keep the entity of analysis constant, the influence of the changes in book value of the assets is not eliminated. With the transfer

Table 27.1 Operating revenue and some operating cost items of Sabena NV (%)

	1998	*1999*	*2000*
Operating revenue	100	97.51	110.88
Materials and consumables	100	92.04	139.11
Services and goods delivered	100	111.68	139.02
Personnel cost	100	91.24	88.38
Depreciation fixed assets	100	50.58	46.16

Source: Annual reports of Sabena NV, 1998, 1999 and 2000

Table 27.2 Operating revenue and some operating cost items of Sabena NV totalled with operating revenue and operating cost items of Sabena Technics NV (%)

	1998	1999	2000
Operating revenue	100	105.17	118.77
Materials and consumables	100	112.41	158.11
Services and goods delivered	100	112.61	139.98
Personnel cost	100	109.18	107.42
Depreciation fixed assets	100	74.96	93.44

Source: Annual reports of Sabena NV, 1998, 1999 and 2000 and Sabena Technics NV, 1999 and 2000

of assets from Sabena NV to Sabena Technics NV, the book value of those assets was increased as well. As a result the depreciation costs rise.

As Sabena Technics was a 100% subsidiary of Sabena NV the accounts of the Sabena Group were not influenced by this restructuring. The increase in book value of the assets now remaining with Sabena Technics has no influence on the group accounts, because this increase is eliminated in the consolidation process.

Although group accounts are not affected by this kind of restructuring whereby the new entity is fully consolidated in the group accounts, we must always keep in mind that individual accounts are still used for different purposes, for example, tax. It also happens that group management decides to undertake an IPO in relation to individual legal entities belonging to the group. For example, the Deutsche Post Group offered a part of the shares of its subsidiary the Deutsche Post Bank to the capital market in 2004. The individual accounts are then used as a piece of information in the business valuation process of that particular business unit. If, restructurings take the form of bringing activities into joint ventures or other forms of cooperation which are no longer fully consolidated, then there is also an impact on the consolidated accounts. When operations are discontinued due to a restructuring of activities, shareholders need information on the share of these discontinued activities in the result, the financial position and the cash flow of the group. IFRS 5 stipulates that in case of discontinued activities the impact should be disclosed to the reader of the accounts (see Chapter 23). The main objective is to ensure comparability for the reader of the annual accounts.

Accounting method changes and accounting estimate changes

All GAAP have the consistency principle in their standards: companies are supposed to apply the same accounting policies from one period to the next. The purpose of this consistency principle is enhancing comparability between financial statements over time. However, in practice, changes are observed and the user of the financial statements should take them into account. As these elements have been discussed extensively in Chapter 26 in the context of annual accounts management we will not elaborate on them further here.

A change in GAAP applied

Companies not only change accounting methods or estimates over the years, they sometimes switch from one set of accounting regulation or standards to another set of standards. This is a one-time change that might have a serious impact on the results and on the balance sheet of company. The impact of a different set of GAAP on the financial statements of a company was illustrated at the end of Chapter 26 with the difference between the net result and the equity of Euro Disney SCA presented both according to French and US GAAP.

In the airline industry several major airlines have switched from their national GAAP to IAS/IFRS. The financial year of the change differed between them, the first financial years in which IAS group accounts were published for the different airlines were: Lufthansa in 1997, SAS in 1997, the SAir Group in 1996, Austrian Airlines in 2000 and Sabena in 1999. This hinders not only the comparability of company data over a longer time span, but it also makes inter-firm comparisons less obvious. The switch to IAS/IFRS is usually done for the group accounts only.

Differences in presentation

With regard to differences in presentation we will discuss two items. The first example relates to the contents of the items used in the annual accounts. In the second different companies use different ways of presentation and layout.

Differences in contents of profit and loss account and balance sheet items

Many airlines use headings such as operating profit (British Airways, Ryanair), operating income (KLM, SAS) or result from operating activities (Austrian Airlines, Lufthansa). These items sound similar and one is tempted to calculate an operating margin (operating result/operating revenue) in order to compare the operating profitability of the different airlines.

Activity 27.4

Analyse the profit and loss accounts and the notes on the operating revenue and operating costs on the websites of those airlines and try to find out whether the concept operating result covers the same elements for each airline.

Activity feedback

If we investigate the contents of the profit and loss accounts and the notes on the operating revenues and operating costs of the different airlines, for example, for the financial years 1999 and 2000 we notice certain differences. An element to be reckoned which are the different balance sheet dates (see earlier discussion). Further the differences relate mainly to the treatment of gains and losses on disposal of assets and on whether or not the income from associated companies is included in the operating income.

- Ryanair, British Airways, easyJet and KLM exclude results on the sale of fixed assets and financial assets from the operating revenues, operating costs and operating result. Income from associated enterprises is also not included in the operating result. British Airways has two separate lines in its profit and loss account: operating profit and operating profit including associates.
- SAS includes items as share of income in affiliated enterprises, income from the sale of shares in affiliated companies, income from the sale of aircraft as separate items

contributing to the operating income. For a comparison with BA, KLM, Ryanair and easyJet these elements need to be excluded.

■ Austrian Airlines includes under other operating revenue, income from disposal of non-current assets excluding financial assets. For comparison, these items should be excluded.

■ Lufthansa includes under other operating revenue income from disposal of fixed assets, the operating expenses include losses from the disposal of fixed assets.

In Table 27.3 the operating margin of each airline before and after correction for comparability is presented. For some airlines we notice a not insignificant difference.

The table only illustrates how comparability can be obstructed by including different elements under the same heading. This correction does not imply that the data on operating margins are now straightforwardly comparable. We still have to bear in mind that these airlines are using different GAAP, which on its own is a threat for comparability. Corrections of this type can only be executed if one is analysing a small number of companies, however, in large-scale analyses (e.g. for large industry analyses or for academic research) these corrections are often not made.

Table 27.3 Operating margin of different European airlines before and after some corrections to improve comparability (%)

Operating margin	Before correction		After correction for comparability	
	31.12.1999 or 31.3.2000	31.12.2000 or 31.3.2001	31.12.1999 or 31.3.2000	31.12.2000 or 31.3.2001
UK GAAP				
Ryanair	22.71	23.39	22.71	23.39
easyJet (31.9)	10.87	11.74	10.87	11.74
BA	0.94	4.10	0.94	4.10
Dutch GAAP				
KLM	1.51	3.98	1.51	3.98
IAS/IFRS				
Lufthansa	7.12	8.78	5.32	6.53
SAS	3.99	6.42	1.51	3.22
Austrian Airlines	1.23	4.22	0.59	−0.69

Source: Annual accounts of Ryanair, easyJet, British Airways, KLM, Lufthansa, SAS and Austrian Airlines

Differences in presentation

Standardized formats for balance sheet and profit and loss accounts facilitate comparison. In practice, however, companies use different formats and layouts. Several GAAP require a minimum layout with which companies have to comply.

Activity 27.5

Look at the website of British Airways and Lufthansa. Can you compare operating costs of both airlines with regard to contents of the different cost items relating to operating costs. Which items can easily be compared?

Activity feedback

Besides different valuation rules (British Airways uses UK GAAP and Lufthansa IAS/IFRS) the two companies use a different form of presentation for the profit and loss account. British Airways presents the operational costs by function on the profit and loss account and Lufthansa uses an approach that classifies costs by nature in the first place.

An example of the presentation by function is included in the section trend or horizontal analysis. A cost classification by nature consists of the following items on the profit and loss account of Lufthansa: cost of materials, staff costs, depreciation and amortization expense, other operating expenses, further changes in inventories and work performed by the enterprise and capitalized.

Analysing further the notes on operational costs of British Airways and those on the operational costs of Lufthansa we notice that the only cost components which are directly comparable on the basis of the published information are the fuel costs, the staff and personnel costs, the depreciation and amortization cost and the lease and rental costs. These elements will be considered later.

Trend analysis or horizontal analysis

That benchmarks are necessary to make a sound judgement about the performance of a company has already been illustrated in this chapter. With the use of trend analysis we compare the performance of the firm to its own history. In annual reports we often find change statistics comparing the figures of two subsequent years. However, some caution is needed when using this published information.

Activity 27.6

Table 27.4 gives percentages of change between 1999 and 2000 published in the annual report of Sabena (year 2000, p. 9). Is a reported increase always positive?

Table 27.4 Sabena Group Consolidated: key figures, 2000/1999

	1999 (million EUR)	2000 (million EUR)	% 2000/1999
Turnover	2 228	2 436	9.3
Operating result	15	(163)	− 1 208.7
Net result	(14)	(325)	2 226.1
Operating cash flow	138	(51)	− 137.1
Cash flow net result	124	(108)	− 187.1
Changes in treasury position	(80)	(225)	182.1
Balance sheet total	2 471	2 358	− 4.6
Equity	223	(97)	− 143.3
Ratio long-term debt/equity	5.0	10.9	118.0

Source: Annual report of Sabena, 2000, p. 9

Activity feedback

If negative amounts are involved, care should be taken with the presented statistics. The change in net result and the change in treasury position is not favourable at all.

With trend analysis or horizontal analysis we analyse how financial statement items have changed over time. According to the litterature a five-year time frame is necessary, longer periods, for example, ten years are also possible, although the number of elements which disturb comparison only increases over such a long period. For the purpose of trend analysis a base year is chosen and all the financial statement items are then expressed as an index relative to the base year. Therefore, the choice of the base year is relatively important, as the performance over the years to follow is benchmarked to this base year.

If trend analysis is applied on the items of the profit and loss account the focus lies on the evolution of the revenue or turnover and the costs related to it. Whether or not the relation between the evolution of the sales and the costs should be linear, depends on the industry characteristics. From the section on industry analysis we know that for the airline industry only catering and handling costs are somewhat variable and are a function of the number of passengers transported. The other costs related to the air transport are a function of the output capacity of the airline which is measured as available seat kilometre or available ton kilometre. We illustrate trend analysis on the basis of the evolution of the operating revenue and operating costs of British Airways and Ryanair in Tables 27.5 and 27.6.

If we analyse the data of British Airways we observe a low growth rate of turnover. Until 2001 and afterwards turnover declined due to increased competition, the war on terror and SARS. The results of British Airways were further negatively influenced in 2002 and 2003 by exceptional charges relating to phasing out Concorde from the fleet

Table 27.5 Horizontal analysis British Airways 1998–2004 (%)

	1998	*1999*	*2000*	*2001*	*2002*	*2003*	*2004*
Turnover	100.00	103.16	103.45	107.36	96	88	87
Operating costs	100.00	104.12	108.82	109.34	103	90	87
Fuel and oil	100.00	89.24	101.77	139.49	130	106	116
Staff	100.00	106.70	112.21	107.46	108	95	98
Depreciation + amortization	100.00	112.34	117.60	129.76	139	133	123
Aircraft leasing	100.00	118.11	149.61	174.02	156	148	106
Engineering and other aircraft cost	100.00	104.89	107.65	107.82	109	96	83
Landing fees and route charges	100.00	104.69	97.01	91.75	87	81	78
Handling, catering and other operating costs	100.00	108.40	112.64	110.52	94	81	79
Selling cost	100.00	101.40	97.62	93.26	67	58	45
Accommodation, ground equipment and currency difference	100.00	100.67	117.16	99.06	110	91	92
Exceptional items	100.00	100.00	100.00	100.00	8000	8400	100.00
Operating result	100.00	87.70	16.67	75.40	− 21	58	80
Net profit	100.00	44.78	−4.57	24.78	− 28	18	31

Source: Annual reports of British Airways, 1997/1998–2000/2001, 2002/2003–2003/2004

Table 27.6 Horizontal analysis of Ryanair, 1998–2004 (%)

	1998	1999	2000	2001	2002	2003	2004
Operating revenue	100.00	127.56	159.64	210.21	271	366	466
Operating costs	100.00	129.80	162.93	212.66	264	332	472
Fuel and oil	100.00	135.87	154.90	235.90	377	468	636
Staff	100.00	129.98	158.37	199.78	257	306	406
Depreciation	100.00	144.03	175.23	235.39	236	308	406
Aircraft rentals	100.00	56.89	41.01	142.49	79	–	227
Maintenance, materials and repairs	100.00	165.58	233.76	278.84	367	414	605
Marketing and distribution	100.00	118.37	154.55	103.57	59	70	78
Route charges	100.00	137.64	173.99	236.18	311	456	735
Aircraft charges	100.00	121.05	179.66	276.27	356	453	618
Other	100.00	130.80	157.64	194.31	231	301	396
Operating result	100.00	120.58	149.35	202.57	291	471	449
Net profit	100.00	126.24	159.29	229.51	813	1257	1640

Source: Annual reports of Ryanair, 1997/1998–2000/2001, 2002/2003–2003/2004

and restructurings. Handling, catering and operating costs which are rather variable seem to be more in control again, since they were growing much faster than revenue, especially in the financial year 2000. However, related to this aspect we must bear in mind that the number of passengers decreased from 2000 to 2001 (p. 61, annual report, British Airways, 2001). Selling costs are decreasing which could be explained by the fact that many airlines are now using, besides the traditional travel agent, the system of ticket sales through the Internet.

Although fuel costs are a function of distance flown and the number of take-offs, the steep increase of fuel costs in 2001 does not necessarily mean that more flights were offered. The fuel cost component is also a function of the kerosene price and fluctuations in the dollar currency. From 2000 the kerosene price started to rise again and airlines were facing higher fuel costs for the same flights offered. The impact could be postponed for a period if the airline had been able to hedge against these fuel price increases. The costs related to output capacity (e.g. depreciation, amortization and aircraft leasing) increased substantially, although the output capacity measures (available seat miles) do not show an increase from 2000 to 2001 (p. 61, annual report British Airways, 2001).

The first element which catches the eye looking at the trend data of Ryanair is the growth rate. The operating result and the net result are growing at the same pace as the revenue. What is further remarkable is that marketing and distribution costs remain constant during the growth. Also staff costs and the remaining other costs grow at a slower rate.

As an external user of financial statements one must always keep in mind that competitors also watch evolutions of costs and breakdown of those costs (common size analysis). Anecdotal evidence exists that smoothing around certain levels for certain cost items is practised in several industries. Consumers also keep an eye on the annual accounts. For example, which airline in the world would publish a profit and loss account showing decreasing costs with regard to maintenance if the fleet capacity remains constant or increases?

Common size analysis

The benchmark to compare the performance of a firm with in trend analysis was its own past performance. In common size analysis the benchmarking element is the performance of other firms, usually taken from the same industry. For the purpose of external benchmarking the size effect needs to be eliminated and this is done by expressing the items of the profit and loss account as percentage of sales and the items of the balance sheet in percentages of total assets. Through common size balance sheets we are able to compare, on the one hand, the financing structure of different companies and, on the other, where they have invested these resources. The items of the balance sheets of Lufthansa, British Airways and Ryanair will now be reformulated or regrouped so that the headings include similar items which are comparable. Valuation rules are still different (British Airways and Ryanair use UK GAAP and Lufthansa uses IAS/IFRS).

For the year 2000 (British Airways and Ryanair balance sheet date 31.3.2001) the common size balance sheets reveal the following structure (see Table 27.7).

Studying the way in which those companies are financed we notice that British Airways is mostly financed through external debt (75%). In the case of Lufthansa, provisions make up a large portion of the equity and liability side of the balance sheet. These provisions relate to a large extent to pension benefits which are financed through internal funding. In Chapter 20 we mentioned that there are significant differences in the organization and the funding of these benefits. Internal funding is a common

Table 27.7 Common size analysis of group balance sheet of British Airways, Lufthansa and Ryanair (%)

	Lufthansa 31.03.2003	British Airways 31.03.2004	Ryanair 31.03.2004
Fixed assets	65.05	77.20	55.15
Intangible assets	5.69	1.38	1.51
Aircraft	43.14	58.55	53.16
Other tangible assets	7.76	12.64	0.48
Financial assets	8.46	4.63	0.00
Current assets	34.94	22.79	44.85
Inventories	2.51	0.62	0.89
Liquid assets and securities	16.26	13.76	42.78
Other current assets	16.17	8.41	1.18
Total	100	100	100
Equity	15.85	18.28	49.51
Minority interests	0.25	1.73	0.00
Provisions	48.12	0.70	3.20
Non-current liabilities	19.36	54.59	30.71
Other liabilities	16.42	24.70	16.58

Source: Annual reports of British Airways, 2003/2004, Lufthansa, 2003 and Ryanair, 2003/2004

practice in German companies and this is an illustration of it. At Ryanair equity represents half of the financial resources. This substantial amount of equity is not only a result from the profit generated by the company, but it results also from the appeal the company has made to the capital market in the past year and the years before. On the asset side of the balance sheet we notice that fixed assets make up a large proportion of the assets of the two traditional airlines. Ryanair has a substantial part of current assets. These liquid assets and securities result probably from the share issues and those amounts will be needed for investments in new growth projects. We have to mention that this common size analysis is carried out on the group accounts of those companies. Whether the groups have similar structures will be discussed later in this chapter.

Common size analysis carried out on the profit and loss accounts is only meaningful if the individual items of the profit and loss account can be compared. From a number of airlines in Europe we have taken those cost items which are comparable and used them in a common size profit and loss account with regard to operating revenue, some operating costs and operating result. Since the following illustrations and those further in this chapter benefit from the presence of the data of the SAir group and Sabena, we present the figures for the year 2000. Further the corrections for comparability with regard to the inclusion of gains and losses on disposal of assets have been taken into account (see Table 27.5) We still have to remember that British Airways and Ryanair use UK GAAP, KLM uses Dutch GAAP and all the other use IAS/IFRS (see Table 27.8).

Table 27.8 Common size analysis of operating revenue and operating cost components (%)

	BA	Lufthansa	SAS	AA	KLM	Ryanair	SAir	Sabena
Operating revenue	100	100	100	100	100	100	100	100
Operating costs	95.90	93.47	96.78	100.69	96.02	76.61	96.28	105.75
Fuel	11.88	9.13	8.33	11.38	14.91	13.02	6.35	10.74
Staff	25.61	22.08	31.40	18.76	24.07	12.56	27.77	22.17
Depreciation	7.71	6.23	4.61	12.88	6.16	12.14	6.11	4.75
Lease cost	2.38	0.38	3.99	1.66	4.89	1.49	5.47	13.89
Other	48.32	55.66	8.45	56.01	45.99	37.40	50.59	54.19
Operating result	4.10	6.53	3.22	−0.69	3.98	23.39	3.72	−5.75

Source: Annual reports of Austrian Airlines, 2000, British Airways, 2000/2001, KLM, 2000/2001, Lufthansa, 2000, Ryanair, 2000/2001, Sabena, 2000, SAir, 2000, and SAS, 2000

Activity 27.7

What kinds of difference do you notice? Can you think of an explanation, taking into account all the elements which have been discussed already concerning airlines?

Activity feedback

Ryanair has substantially lower staff costs than the other companies. Further, the lease costs differ among the airlines. However, the lease costs which refer to operating lease contracts should always be considered in combination with depreciation and amortization costs. Airlines which own a large percentage of their fleet or operate their fleet under financial lease agreements have higher depreciation costs than airlines leasing most of their aircraft under operating lease contracts. The quality of disclosure with regard to the item owned aircraft, aircraft under financial lease or aircraft under operating lease differs among the airlines. Some comparative data are presented with regard to this item. Some airlines disclose in the narrative part of the annual accounts the breakdown of their fleet according to the way it is financed. A few examples are listed in Table 27.9.

We learn from this comparative analysis that Lufthansa is the only carrier which still owns a large part of its fleet. Whether or not a plane is accounted for as a financial lease or an operating lease depends not only on the contract, but also on the GAAP applied. To illustrate the impact we present an historic overview of the composition of the fleet and the way it is accounted for in Table 27.10. The data included in Table 27.10 will be used again later in this chapter.

The fuel cost expressed as a percentage of operating revenue differs drastically among these companies. We know already that distance flown, number of take-offs and kerosene price has an influence, but that alone does not explain the differences which appear in Table 27.8.

Table 27.9 Information on fleet capacity of British Airways, KLM, Lufthansa and Sabena

	Aircraft owned	Financial leading	On balance sheet	Operational leasing	Total
Lufthansa	273 (82%)	49 (15%)	322 (97%)	9 (3%)	331 (100%)
KLM	87 (41%)	78 (37%)	165 (77%)	48 (23%)	213 (100%)
Sabena	8 (9%)	32 (37%)	40 (46%)	47 (54%)	87 (100%)
British Airways			226 (67%)	112 (33%)	338 (100%)

Source: Annual reports of British Airways, KLM, 2000/2001, Lufthansa, 2000 and Sabena 2000

Table 27.10 Aircraft operated by the Sabena Group

Year	Aircraft owned		Aircraft under financial leasing		Aircraft under operational leasing		Total
1993	33	49.25%	15	22.39%	19	28.36%	67
1994	27	38.57%	19	27.14%	24	34.29%	70
1995	26	33.77%	19	24.68%	32	41.56%	77
1996	38	48.72%	8	10.26%	32	41.03%	78
1997	35	50.00%	4	5.71%	31	44.29%	70
1998	10	13.51%	3	4.05%	61	82.43%	74
1999	8	9.76%	31	37.80%	43	52.44%	82
2000	8	9.20%	32	36.78%	47	54.02%	87

Source: Annual reports of Sabena, 1993–2000

Activity 27.8

Can you think of another explanation, bearing in mind for this purpose the discussions in the section on industry analysis in Chapter 26?

Activity feedback

When we compare British Airways and Ryanair at 31.3.2001 these companies are almost 100% airlines, with very few other activities at that time. The group accounts of SAS, however, do not only present revenues and costs from the airline business, the costs and the revenues stemming from their hotel business are included as well. Further Lufthansa and SAir have, besides their airlines, other airline-related businesses such as catering, ground handling, IT etc. This explains the lower percentage of fuel costs in relation to operating revenue, whereas British Airways and Ryanair were not active in these airline-related businesses at that time.

Corporate strategic decisions determine the different business lines in which a company is active. The consolidated group accounts represent the overall performance of the different industries or businesses in which a company competes. Segmental information provides an overview of the different businesses and the proportion of each business unit in the total revenue and the results before interest and taxes (EBIT). A discussion on segmental reporting under IAS can be found in Chapter 23. In the next section we illustrate how the use of segmental data could shed extra light on the analysis of the group's profit and loss account and balance sheet included in the group accounts.

Segmental analysis

Segmental reporting informs the user of the group accounts on the breakdown of the total revenue over the different business segments. For an evaluation of the breakdown of the operational costs in the common size analysis (see Tables 27.7 and 27.8) in a more meaningful way, the segmental data included in the accounts need to be considered as well. A comparative analysis between airline activities (passengers and freight and mail) versus airline related activities reveals that SAS, Lufthansa but especially the SAir Group have diversified activities (Table 27.11).

Table 27.11 Breakdown of total group revenue over different business segments (%)

	Passenger traffic	Freight and mail	Other (technics, ground handling, catering etc.)
Ryanair	88		12
British Airways	84	6	10
SAS	70	5	25
Lufthansa	61	14	25
KLM	65	17	18
Austrian Airlines	75	6	19
SAir Group	41	10	49
Sabena	85	Assumed by SAir in 1997	15

Source: Financial statements of 2000, Austrian Airlines, 2000, British Airways and KLM, 2000/2001, Lufthansa, 2000, Ryanair, 2000/2001, Sabena, SAir, and SAS, 2000

Table 27.12 Horizontal analysis of different business segments of the SAir Group (%)

	1997	1998	1999	2000
External revenue	100	107.02	123.17	153.74
SAirlines	100	106.54	116.37	130.40
SAir Services	100	120.37	147.00	243.86
SAir Logistics	100	105.18	110.61	141.77
SAir Relations	100	104.61	131.79	170.58
SAir Group	100	2700	2400	8200

Source: The annual report of the SAir Group, 1997, 1998, 1999, 2000

The data of the SAir Group do not come as a surprise, as their corporate strategy since 1996 is their so-called two pillar strategy. Growth in the so-called second pillar is among acquisitions and organic growth also obtained by integrating the airline-related activities of the airlines in which they acquire a substantial minority shareholding into the SAir Group. If we analyse the annual report of Sabena of 1994, we observe that before the cooperation with SAir (annual report of Sabena, 1994, p. 6) passenger traffic made up 75.1% of total revenue, cargo and other airline related activities amounted to 25% of the total revenue. These proportions have been changing up to 2000. So we learn from the annual report of Sabena (2000, p. 24) that in 2000 the catering activities have been further integrated and outsourced to Gate Gourmet, the catering company from the SAir Group.

The analysis of the segmental disclosure of a company can shed light on the corporate strategy of the group and on the importance of the different business or geographical segments of the group. In Table 27.12 the horizontal analysis of the different business segments of the SAir Group are presented (the analysis is based not on total revenue, which includes inter-segment revenue, but on external revenue).

Focusing on the business segment airlines of the SAir Group we learn from their annual report that for the years 1998, 1999 and 2000 the revenue and earnings before interest and taxes (EBIT) of the leasing activities of their company, Flightlease, are combined with the revenue and EBIT of the airlines Swissair, Crossair and Balair into one business segment airline.

Activity 27.9

The combination of leasing and airline activities into one business segment, airlines, in the financial years 1999 and 2000: what do you think of this approach?

Activity feedback

Earlier in the chapter we mentionned that depreciation and rental and lease costs should always be considered together in order to determine the impact of the airplane capacity costs on the results. According to the financing policy chosen (financial leasing, operational leasing or owned and financed through equity or loans) the depreciation and rental costs will be higher or lower. In 1998 Swissair sold and leased back a large part of its fleet. The leasing company, Flightlease, was involved in these transactions. In order to make EBIT and other data of the SAirlines (Swissair, Crossair and Balair) comparable with other airlines, the leasing activities were added to the business segment airlines. That was the explanation given by financial analysts.

This argument would have been acceptable had Flightlease been responsible only for the leasing activities of Swissair, Crossair and Balair, the airlines in which the SAir Group was the majority shareholder. However, Flightlease also leases planes to associated enterprises such as Sabena and its subsidiary, Sobelair, LTU and several other airlines. Taking that information into account the argument is less acceptable. In the notes to the annual accounts of SAir we find with regard to leased assets the following information (SAIR annual accounts, 2000, note 26, p. 30) 'Future lease income from aircraft lease agreements amounts to CHF 1.6 billion and will stem largely from associated undertakings.'

Illustration

The case of Sabena (1991–2000)

Before we turn to the next technique of financial analysis, ratio analysis, we apply trend analysis and common size analysis on the operating revenue and operating cost data of Sabena NV over the last ten years (1991–2000) of its existence. We use the individual accounts of Sabena NV because they have been prepared according to Belgian GAAP for the whole time frame of the analysis, whereas the group accounts were published in Belgian GAAP up to 1998 and from 1999 according to IAS. As already mentioned Sabena NV represents the airline and accounts for 90% of the revenue of the Sabena Group. In the data presented, comparability is enhanced by adding the cost and revenue data of Sabena Technics (the subsidiary created in 1999) to the data of Sabena NV after correction for inter-segment revenue. Many elements resulting from the accounting strategy of Sabena (see subsequent reports of the board of directors, discussed in Chapter 26) were reported as exceptional costs and exceptional revenue, so the operating revenue and operating costs reported relate to the operating activities. The evolution of some airline operating statistics is also presented.

Activity 27.10

Taking into account the information given about Sabena in Chapter 26, the discussion on trend analysis, common size analysis and segmental analysis, what evolutions do you observe in Table 27.13 and 27.14? What explanations can you give? What extra information would you like to have in addition in order to make a better judgement?

Activity feedback

Most meaningful is to focus the analysis on those operating cost components which are less influenced by accrual accounting decisions. Operating cost items such as changes in values in current assets and provisions will therefore be left out of this analysis.

Table 27.13 Horizontal analysis of the operating result of Sabena NV + Sabena Technics (%)

Sabena + Technics	1991	1992	1993	1994	1995	1996	1997	1998	1999	2000
Operating revenue	100.00	98.24	100.99	108.86	112.82	115.24	132.98	162.43	170.83	192.92
Mat. cons	100.00	90.96	102.68	105.23	94.94	107.78	71.51	71.84	80.75	113.58
Serv. goods	100.00	99.81	112.49	121.94	133.11	145.49	192.05	247.31	278.48	346.18
Personnel cost	100.00	92.81	86.09	86.08	93.75	100.87	99.73	108.32	118.26	116.35
Dep fix assets	100.00	117.11	115.97	118.36	118.02	118.17	111.48	112.54	84.36	105.16
Current assets	100.00	33.33	−8.89	8.92	3.62	10.66	−36.65	15.65	−7.02	−33.40
Provisions	100.00	88.30	6.88	29.63	−27.62	2.60	−33.90	0.66	57.50	68.22
Other	100.00	88.42	81.07	72.06	55.70	110.21	98.41	132.60	138.52	128.85
Operating cost	100.00	95.33	101.71	106.02	111.45	121.44	130.79	156.08	171.21	205.54
Operating result	100.00	−140.97	160.05	−125.10	−0.42	625.45	−47.75	−359.65	202.21	1231.30

Activity data	1991	1992	1993	1994	1995	1996	1997	1998	1999	2000
Actual production										
# passengers	100.00	104.11	120.96	141.20	165.69	171.41	227.69	289.86	332.46	362.19
# hours	100.00	104.74	118.31	126.41	142.99	164.98	170.88	208.46	239.94	258.51
# km	100.00	104.15	117.54	126.69	143.57	162.00	166.11	209.33	243.61	263.82

Source: Annual reports of Sabena, 1991–2000

Table 27.14 Vertical analysis of the operating result of Sabena NV + Sabena Technics NV (%)

Sabena + Technics	1991	1992	1993	1994	1995	1996	1997	1998	1999	2000
Operating rev	100.00	100.00	100.00	100.00	100.00	100.00	100.00	100.00	100.00	100.00
Mat. cons	23.61	21.86	24.01	22.83	19.87	22.08	12.70	10.44	11.16	13.90
Serv. goods	40.44	41.09	45.05	45.30	47.71	51.06	58.40	61.57	65.93	72.57
Personnel cost	32.66	30.85	27.84	25.82	27.13	28.58	24.49	21.78	22.61	19.69
Dep fix assets	4.39	5.23	5.04	4.77	4.59	4.50	3.68	3.04	2.17	2.39
Current assets	1.64	0.56	−0.14	0.13	0.05	0.15	−0.45	0.16	−0.07	−0.28
Provisions	−1.86	−1.67	−0.13	−0.51	0.46	−0.04	0.47	−0.01	−0.63	−0.66
Other	0.35	0.32	0.28	0.23	0.17	0.34	0.26	0.29	0.29	0.24
Operating cost	101.23	98.23	101.95	98.59	100.00	106.68	99.56	97.28	101.46	107.85
Operating result	−1.23	1.77	−1.95	1.41	0.00	−6.68	0.44	2.72	−1.46	−7.85

Source: Annual reports of Sabena and Sabena Technics NV, 1991–2000

Taking into account all the data presented so far on Sabena in Chapters 26 and 27 we know that there have been at least three 'events' which had an impact on the structure of Sabena NV in that period, namely the 'assumption' of cargo by the SAir Group, the creation of Sabena Technics NV and the creation of the Airline Management Partnership. Only with regard to the creation of Sabena Technics can the external user of the annual accounts judge the impact as Sabena Technics is fully consolidated in the group accounts and its individual accounts are published. The impact of the 'assumption of the cargo business' by SAir on the operating revenue and the operating costs of Sabena is not clear for an external user of the annual accounts. We only know from the annual report of SAir that their group operating revenue increased positively as a result from the assumption of Sabena's cargo business. The impact of this assumption on the revenues and costs of Sabena is not disclosed. This hinders further the comparability of the airline statistics over time. So more information on the impact of the 'assumption' of the cargo business by SAir would be welcome.

That the creation of the AMP will have an impact on the operating revenues and operating costs of Sabena is clear. Personnel costs, for example, decrease in 2000 as a number of employees of Sabena are transferred to the Airline Management Partnership. The same happens at the level of the SAir Group, employees from SAir are also transferred to the AMP. Evaluating the impact of the AMP on the situation of Sabena is rendered more difficult for the external analysts as the AMP was organized under the legal form of a partnership located in the UK. One of the characteristics of a partnership under the European Directives is that the financial statements do not have to be made public.

Further we learn from the annual report of SAir (see Chapter 26, extract annual report SAir 1999, financial statements p. 19 and financial statements year 2000, p. 17) that in 1998 and in 1999 shares which could be sold after three years have been given to personnel and share options were also granted to staff members. It would be interesting to know how many of the AMP employees own shares of the SAir Group.

We will now turn to the evolution of the individual operating cost items.

In this ten-year period the two time frames (namely the cooperation with Air France and the cooperation with the SAir Group) clearly step out of the data. Different patterns can be observed from 1991 to 1995 and from 1996 until 2000. In the first time frame, the cooperation with Air France, there is a smooth growth of operating revenue. The different operating cost categories follow more or less at the same pace. The vertical analysis shows that the proportion of each cost component in total revenue remains stable in the first half of the last decade of the 20th century. In the second time frame when the SAir Group took a substantial minority shareholding (49.5%) in Sabena, the growth rate increased. The aim of SAir was to acquire, together with its associated undertakings, a market share of 20% in Europe. Those airline operating statistics, which are comparable over the ten-year time span show an enormous increase in the last years of the 20th century. This was a result of the fleet expansion. From Table 27.10 we learn that there is an enormous increase in the fleet capacity in the year 1999. From Chapter 26 we know that Sabena tried to fill up the increased seat capacity by price reductions. This policy did result in a growing number of passengers carried, however, most of the extra passengers were economy class. These passengers increase the rather variable costs such as handling and catering, which represent activities which had to be bought for a large part from the airline-related segments or the second pillar of the SAir Group in the last years of the existence of Sabena. As a result of this policy, the trend pattern of the cost components and the proportion of each cost component in the total revenue lost their stability in the second half of the 1990s.

The decrease in the component 'materials and consumables' until 1998 can be explained by the policy of outsourcing, but also by the favourable fuel prices and the favourable exchange rate to the dollar. An unfavourable change in these last two years at the end of the 20th century explains the steep rise in component materials and consumables costs.

Due to the outsourcing of activities the component 'services and other goods' rose, but that is not the sole explanation. The steep rise in this component in the last two years is also due to the enormous fleet expansion of Sabena, financed through operating lease contracts. The impact of this fleet expansion on the cost of 1999 was somewhat softened as the realized gains on the sale of planes were offset with the lease costs. In 2000 this effect disappeared to a large extent and the costs of the fleet expansion now hit the profit and loss account with their full impact. (The impact of this fleet expansion on the finance structure of Sabena is illustrated in the section on ratio analysis.) The personnel cost decreases in 2000; this could be due to the creation of the AMP, but we cannot be completely sure of this as the only information received about AMP is that: 'The partnership constituted a complete merger of the commercial departments of Sabena and Swissair . . . From the economic aspect of achieving savings, AMP realised a reduction in expenditure for the two airlines of around EUR 100 million per annum' (annual report, Sabena, financial year 2000, p. 14).

Depreciation costs remain rather stable over the ten-year period. This is due to the fact that capacity cost for the airplanes switch from depreciation to lease costs over the years (Sabena NV used Belgian GAAP). The increase from 1999 to 2000 can be explained by the increase in book values of the fixed assets transferred from Sabena NV to Sabena Technics NV together with the goodwill created in the course of the creation of this subsidiary. This results in higher depreciation costs.

Further care should be taken in evaluating the trend data of the operating result. As the base year had a negative operating result, years with a positive operating result get a negative sign. Years with a negative operating result have a positive sign.

Ratio analysis

Financial statements identify a multitude of figures for us, for example, profit before tax, gross profit, total of fixed assets, net current assets. As already mentioned these figures do not mean very much unless we can compare them to something else. In previous sections of this chapter on techniques of financial analysis we have benchmarked the whole balance sheet and profit and loss account of a company against its own historical data (trend analysis) or against the data of other companies (common size profit and loss account and common size balance sheets) in order to be able to evaluate the overall performance. With the technique of ratio analysis we are able to focus on specific questions concerning the financial stituation of the company. Examples of those questions are:

- Can the business meet its financial commitments? Can the business pay its debt? Is it liquid (financial status)?
- How successful is the business? Is it making a reasonable profit? Is it utilizing its assets to the fullest? Is it, in fact, profitable and efficient?
- Is the business a suitable investment for shareholders or would returns be greater if they invested elsewhere? Is it a good investment?

Balance sheet items or profit and loss account items related to these questions will be combined in a ratio to provide useful information to the user of the accounts for his/her decision making.

For example, looking at a set of financial statements of a high street retailer may tell us that profit before tax is £3 million, but will not tell us if this is a good profit. It will probably be more than the profit of a sole trader in the same industry but does it mean the high street retailer is really performing better?

Activity 27.11

You have €1150 to invest and discover that type 1 investment will provide interest of €68 per annum and type 2 investment will provide a single interest payment of €341 after five years. Which investment would you choose, assuming no compound interest and no change in the value of the pound?

Activity feedback

Investment 1 provides a return of 68/1150 = 5.91% per annum, investment 2 a return of 68.2/1150 = 5.93% per annum. Thus investment 2 provides the higher return. In the activity we compared the return with the amount invested and expressed the figures in the same units – percentage per annum. We were then able to identify which investment provided the better return.

With ratios we relate certain items of the balance sheet and profit and loss account to each other in order to evaluate the financial status, the performance or the investment potential of a business.

Before starting with ratio analysis, one always has to check the pitfalls which may hinder the comparability of financial statement data. We have discussed these pitfalls to a large extent in the first part of this chapter so we will not repeat them here. Besides data from the airline industry, in this section on ratio analysis we will also use data from the annual accounts of Henkel and Nestlé from their financial year 2003. The main objective in including these accounts is to illustrate the different ratios which might be calculated on the basis of these financial statements rather than compare the financial situation of the two multinationals, which have as similarities that they are recognizable worldwide and are active in consumer goods. Nestlé is active in the following business segments: beverages, milk products, nutrition and ice cream, prepared dishes, cooking aids and petcare, chocolate, confectionery and biscuits and pharmaceutical products. Henkel competes in the following business lines: adhesives, cosmetics and toiletries, laundry and homecare, hygiene/surface technology and chemical products (information taken from their segmental data in their annual reports).

In the following tables the data on the balance sheet and profit and loss account of Henkel (Table 27.15) and Nestlé (Table 27.16) are presented.

We will start with a discussion of those ratios which are helpful in assessing the following questions:

■ How successful is the business?
■ Is it making a reasonable profit?
■ Is it utilizing its assets to the fullest?
■ Is it in fact profitable and efficient?

Table 27.15 Henkel Group consolidated balance sheet

Assets

in million euros	Notes	31 Dec 2002	31 Dec 2003
Intangible assets	14	1 786	1 641
Property, plant and equipment	15	1 717	1 683
Shares in associated companies		790	716
Other investments		115	145
Long-term loans		519	538
Financial assets	16	1 424	1 399
Fixed assets		**4 927**	**4 723**
Inventories	17	1 073	1 053
Trade accounts receivable	18	1 545	1 581
Other receivables and miscellaneous assets	19	416	521
Liquid funds/Marketable securities	20	226	1 188
Current assets		**3 260**	**4 343**
Deferred tax assets	21	**326**	**296**
Total assets		**8 513**	**9 362**

Shareholders' Equity and Liabilities

	Notes	31 Dec 2002	31 Dec 2003
Subscribed capital	22	374	374
Capital reserve	23	652	652
Revenue reserves	24	2 510	2 788
Unappropriated profit		156	167
Gains and losses recognized in equity	25	−413	−670
Equity excluding minority interests		**3 279**	**3 311**
Minority interests	26	84	75
Equity including minority interests		**3 363**	**3 386**
Provisions for pensions and other post-employment benefits	27	1 644	1 642
Other provisions	28	1 146	1 056
Provisions for deferred tax liabilities	29	242	181
Provisions		**3 032**	**2 879**
Borrowings	30	859	1 855
Trade accounts payable	31	858	789
Other liabilities	32	401	453
Liabilities		**2 118**	**3 097**
Total equity and liabilities		**8 513**	**9 362**

Table 27.15 (continued)

in million euros

	Notes	2002	2003
Sales	1	**9 656**	**9 436**
Cost of sales	2	−5 103	−4 965
Gross profit		**4 553**	**4 471**
Marketing, selling and distribution costs	3	−2 951	−2 915
Research and development costs	4	−259	−257
Administrative expenses	5	−538	−508
Other operating income	6	164	158
Other operating charges	7	−111	−77
Amortization of goodwill	8	−140	−125
Restructuring costs	9	−52	−37
Exceptional items	10		
Sale of participation in Wella		−	81
Extended restructuring costs		−	−85
Operating profit (EBIT)		**666**	**706**
Net income from associated companies		161	174
Income from Clorox share buy-back		−	30
Net result from other participation		−9	−2
Net interest expense		−154	−140
Financial items	11	**−2**	**62**
Earnings before tax		**664**	**768**
Taxes on income	12	**−233**	**−238**
Net earnings		**431**	**530**
Minority interests	13	4	−11
Earnings after minority interests		**435**	**519**
Allocation to revenue reserves		−279	−352
Unappropriated profit		156	167

Performance of the firm

Ratios which try to give a picture of a firm's profitability combine the result of a firm with the investments made for the generation of that result. The two most common ratios are return on equity (ROE) and return on assets (ROA).

$$\text{Return on equity (ROE)} = \text{Profit/Equity}$$

The profit figure used in this ratio can be before or after tax. In case of group accounts one has to make sure that if the minority interests are not added up to the equity of the

Table 27.16 Nestlé consolidated income statement, 31 December 2003

in millions of CHF	Notes	2003	2002
Sales to customers	1	**87 979**	89 160
Cost of goods sold		**(37 583)**	(38 521)
Distribution expenses		**(7 104)**	(7 112)
Marketing and administration expenses		**(31 081)**	(31 379)
Research and development costs		**(1 205)**	(1 208)
EBITA[(a)]	1	**11 006**	10 940
Net other income (expenses)	2	**(534)**	1 686
Amortization and impairment of goodwill		**(1 571)**	(2 277)
Profit before interest and taxes		**8 901**	10 349
Net financing cost	3	**(594)**	(665)
Profit before taxes	4	**8 307**	9 684
Taxes	5	**(2 307)**	(2 295)
Net profit of consolidated companies		**6 000**	**7 389**
Share of profit attributable to minority interests		**(380)**	(329)
Share of results of associates	6	**593**	504
Net profit		**6 213**	7 564
As percentages of sales			
EBITA(a)		**12.5%**	12.3%
Net profit		**7.1%**	8.5%
Earnings per share			
(in CHF)			
Basic earnings per share	7	**16.05**	19.51
Fully diluted earnings per share	7	**15.92**	19.30

Assets

	Notes		2003		2002
Current assets					
Liquid assets	8				
Cash and cash equivalents		**7 074**		6 338	
Other liquid assets		**8 054**		7 953	
			15 128		14 921
Trade and other receivables	9		**12 851**		12 666
Inventories	10		**6 995**		6 794
Derivative assets	11		**669**		959
Prepayments and accrued income			**590**		632
Total current assets			**36 233**		35 342

Table 27.16 (continued)

In millions of CHF	Notes	2003		2002	
Non-current assets					
Property, plant and equipment	12				
Gross value		**41 778**		40 797	
Accumulated depreciation		**(24 339)**		(23 772)	
			17 439		17 025
Investments in associates	13		**2 707**		2 561
Deferred tax assets	23		**1 398**		1 519
Financial assets	14		**2 394**		2 862
Employee benefit assets	21		**1 070**		1 083
Goodwill	15		**26 745**		25 718
Intangible assets	16		**1 575**		1 242
Total non-current assets			**53 328**		52 010
Total assets			**89 561**		87 352
Liabilities, minority interests and equity					
Current liabilities					
Trade and other payables	17		**9 852**		9 932
Financial liabilities	18		**15 419**		18 702
Tax payable			**549**		825
Derivative liabilities	19		**846**		384
Accruals and deferred income			**3 699**		3 894
Total current liabilities			**30 365**		33 737
Non-current liabilities					
Financial liabilities	20		**14 064**		10 548
Employee benefit liabilities	21		**3 363**		3 147
Deferred tax liabilities	23		**576**		492
Tax payable			**4**		15
Other payables			**305**		400
Provisions	24		**3 061**		3 381
Total non-current liabilities			**21 373**		17 983
Total liabilities			**51 738**		51 720
Minority interests			**943**		813
Equity					
Share capital	25		**404**		404
Share premium and reserves					
Share premium		**5 926**		5 926	
Reserve for treasury shares		**2 458**		2 830	
Translation reserve		**(5 630)**		(4 070)	
Retained earnings		**36 093**	**38 847**	**32 307**	36 993
			39 251		37 397
Less:					
Treasury shares	26		**(2 371)**		(2 578)
Total equity			**36 880**		34 819
Total liabilities minority interest and equity			**89 561**		87 352

group, the share in the profit of the company of the minority interests should be excluded from the profit in the numerator as well. Besides ROE another widely used profitability ratio is ROA.

$$\text{Return on assets (ROA)} = (\text{Profit before tax} + \text{Interest})/\text{Total assets}$$

Instead of using the total assets in the denominator, net total assets can be used. The net assets are equal to the equity of the company and the long term debts. This ratio is also often called return on capital employed (ROCE) or return of net total assets.

$$\text{Return on capital employed (ROCE)} = (\text{Profit before tax}$$
$$+ \text{Long-term interest})/(\text{Equity} + \text{Long-term debt})$$

A remark which applies to the calculation of all performance ratios, ROA, ROE and ROCE or RNA is the question with regard to the choice of the investment base to which one should compare the result: investment base of the beginning of the year or an average equity base. In practice, very often the equity base at the end of the year is taken. If one has data available only for one year, then in that case there is not much of a choice.

In order to determine whether the obtained profitability is sufficient or excellent, one needs a benchmark. As benchmarks for these ratios could serve besides the already known time series data and competitor or industry data, the proceeds of an investment in risk-free loans. The latter could answer the question: would the owners be better off selling the business and placing the proceeds in a bank deposit account?

Activity 27.12

Calculate the ROA and ROE of Henkel and Nestlé. Evaluate what the difference between the outcome of the ratios will be according to the different investment bases used (investment base at the beginning of the year, average investment base, investment base at the end of the year).

Activity feedback

	Henkel	Nestlé
ROA – investment base beginning of the year	$(768 + 140)/8\,513 = 10.66\%$	$(8\,307 + 594)/87\,352 = 10.18\%$
ROA – average investment base	$(768 + 140)/8\,937 = 10.16\%$	$8\,307 + 594/88\,456 = 10.06\%$
ROA – investment base end of the year	$(768 + 140)/9\,362 = 9.69\%$	$8\,307 + 594/89\,561 = 9.93\%$
ROE – investment base beginning of the year	$530/3\,363 = 15.74\%$	$6\,213/34\,819 = 17.84\%$
ROE – average investment base	$530/3\,374 = 15.70\%$	$6\,213/35\,849 = 17.33\%$
ROE – investment base at the end of the year	$530/3\,386 = 15.65\%$	$6\,213/36\,880 = 16.84\%$

When a company is making profit then ROA and ROE are always lower if the investment base at the end of the year is taken.

The return on total assets can be calculated at corporate level, at the business segment level or at the regional level depending on the choice of the primary segment concerning segmental reporting (see Chapter 23). The segmental information included in the notes of the IAS/IFRS financial statements discloses the assets and liabilities which can be allocated to a business segment or geographical segment. If one calculates ROA at the business level or at the geographical level one has to take into account that there will always be assets in a company used by different segments or regions and therefore they will not be attributed to the individual segments or regions. The same argument holds for a number of expenses which are consumed by many segments or regions but which will not be attributed to the different segments or regions.

In the ratios just discussed profitability is evaluated by relating results to the investment bases. The profitability ratio ROA can further be broken down by relating results to sales and sales to the investment base:

$$\text{Return on assets} = \frac{\text{Profit}}{\text{Total sales}} \times \frac{\text{Total sales}}{\text{Assets}}$$

The first ratio (profit/total sales) is called the profit margin ratio which expresses the result in a currency generated by each currency unit of sales. This ratio focuses on profitability. The second ratio (total sales/assets) focuses on efficiency.

Activity 27.13

Which 'profit' is the most meaningful to combined with sales in the ratio (profit/total sales)? Look at the profit and loss account of Henkel and Nestlé.

Activity feedback

There is the choice between the operating result and the net result of the company. The operating result is related directly to the sales, whereas the net result is also influenced by financing activities and extraordinary or exceptional results. So the most obvious choice is the operating result. If the net result is used, then the combination with the asset turnover (total sales/assets) results in the ROA figure again.

Activity 27.14

Calculate both ratios for Nestlé and Henkel.

Activity feedback

	Henkel	Nestlé
Profit margin	908/9436 = 9.62	8 901/87 979 = 10.11
Asset turnover	9436/9362 = 1.00	87 979/89 561 = 0.98

We notice that Nestlé succeeds in obtaining a higher profit margin and a similar turnover on assets. This explains the higher ROA of Nestlé compared to Henkel.

In the section on industry analysis in Chapter 26 we discussed factors influencing the pricing policy of a company and those influencing the cost levels. Sales price levels and cost levels together determine the profit margin. An analysis of the different cost components in relation to the sales figures could reveal interesting differences between companies. If costs are classified in the profit and loss account according to their function, then the following ratios could be calculated:

- cost of sales/sales
- marketing and sales costs/sales
- distribution cost/sales
- administrative cost/sales.

Activity 27.15

Try to calculate these ratios for Henkel and Nestlé. What do you observe when you analyse the profit and loss account?

Activity feedback

The layouts of the profit and loss accounts are different. The ratios which analyse the different cost components can therefore not be calculated separately. For comparative purposes we have to add up marketing, sales, distribution and administrative costs for both companies.

	Henkel	Nestlé
Cost of goods sold/sales	52.61%	42.71%
Marketing, sales, distribution and administrative costs/sales	36.27%	43.4%

The information obtained from these ratios which relate the different cost components to the sales figure can also be obtained from a common size analysis of the profit and loss account. For example, the common size analysis of the operating cost items revealed similar information.

The next group of ratios to be examined concentrates on the effectiveness of certain operations. The performance of a firm is influenced not only by the profit margin obtained on its products or services but also by the effectiveness of its operations. The turnover of assets can be regarded as an efficiency ratio, however, it is one of a very general nature. Long-term as well as short-term assets are included in the overall ratio total sales/total assets. With regard to efficiency, the short-term elements are the centre of attention, although in some industries the efficient use of the long term assets is much more crucial.

The following ratios focus on the turnover of short-term assets.

Turnover of inventory

The turnover of inventory is calculated as the 'cost of goods sold/inventory'. The average inventory level is used as denominator. The turnover of the inventory could also be expressed in days, the ratio then becomes ((average inventory/cost of goods sold) × 365).

Activity 27.16

Calculate the inventory turnover and the number of inventory days of Henkel and Nestlé.

Activity feedback

	Henkel	Nestlé
Inventory turnover	4 965/1063 = 4.6	3 7583/6 894.5 = 5.45
Inventory days	(1 063/4 965) × 365 = 78 days	(6 894/37 583) × 365 = 67 days

Nestlé reaches a higher inventory turnover. The observed differences, however, in these ratios could relate to elements other than differences in effectiveness. Industry-specific elements also have an influence. If a company has perishable goods, then these ratios will be higher.

Using the same ratio structure the turnover of trade receivables and trade payables can be calculated, and the average collection or payment period. The following ratios provide that information:

- sales/trade receivables
- (trade receivables/sales) × 365
- purchases/trade payables
- (trade payables/purchases) × 365.

Activity 27.17

Calculate those ratios for Henkel and Nestlé for which you possess data.

Activity feedback

	Henkel	Nestlé
Trade receivables turnover	9436/1563 = 6.03	87 979/12 758 = 6.89
Collection period	(1 563/9436) × 365 = 60	(12 758/87 979) × 365 = 53

Nestlé obtains a higher turnover, but again the same comments have to be made. Not only efficiency influences the outcome of these ratios. They could be influenced by industry characteristics. Average collection periods are often determined by industry practice.

The ratios concerning the trade payables can only be calculated if information on the purchases is provided in the annual accounts.

Not only the value obtained for the ratios presented will differ between industries, the usefulness of the ratios will also differ according to the industry.

Industry-specific ratios

The ratio cost of goods sold/sales is more meaningful for companies active in consumer and industrial goods than for companies in a service industry such as insurance companies and banks. Some industries have their own specific ratios (like banks, insurance companies, airlines) which characterize the key drivers of performance in that specific industry. For the airline industry such ratios are for example, unit revenue or yield which represent the average amount of traffic revenue per RPK/RPM or RTK/RTM. In this ratio revenue passenger kilometres/miles (RPK/M) is defined as the number of paying passengers multiplied by the distance they are flown in kilometres/miles. Revenue tonne kilometres/miles (RTK/M) is defined as the number of tonnes of paid traffic (passengers, freight and mail) multiplied by the distance this traffic is flown in kilometres or miles.

These operating statistics or industry-specific key ratios are disclosed by companies on a voluntary basis. Industry practice is usually the driving force for this type of disclosure. This implies that the level of disclosure of these industry-specific ratios differs significantly between companies. The issue of quality of disclosure, which was discussed in Chapter 26, is relevant in this context. Further it is essential to keep in mind that these operating statistics or ratios are presented in the non-audited part of the annual report. A proper comparison between companies based on these voluntary disclosed industry ratios is therefore not always possible and should be executed with great caution as it concerns non-audited data.

If we compare the annual report of the Scandinavian SAS Group with the annual report of Sabena in the year 2000, we observe that SAS provides an extensive list on operating statistics to the external stakeholders with regard to their airline business. Sabena discloses only a limited amount of airline operating statistics, we even notice that the five-year overview of the main operating statistics relating to the airline business together with financial indicators disappears from their annual report. Until 1999 each year a five-year comparative table on a limited set of airline statistics was included in the annual report. Empirical evidence exist that the quality and the level of disclosure is very often an indicator for the financial health of a company. This evidence seems to confirm it.

Financial status

In order to judge the financial situation of a firm the external stakeholders want answers to questions such as: Can the business meet its financial commitments? Can the business pay its debt? Is it liquid? External stakeholders need information on the financial status of a company. It is essential for a business to be able to pay its debts as and when they fall due, otherwise its chances of remaining in operation become remote. For that purpose there is a need to analyse the assets available to the company to meet its liabilities. This can be done in the short, medium and long term.

Short-term financial status or the liquidity of a firm

If we analyse the assets available in order to meet the short-term liabilities of the firm, we focus on the structure of the working capital of a company, namely the relation between current assets and current liabilities. The acid test ratio or quick ratio and the current ratio can be used for this purpose.

$$\text{Current ratio} = \text{Current assets/Current liabilities}$$
$$\text{Acid test ratio} = (\text{Current assets} - \text{Inventory})/\text{Current liabilities}$$

Activity 27.18

Calculate both ratios for Nestlé and Henkel.

Activity feedback

	Henkel	Nestlé
Current ratio	4 343/1 242 = 3.49	36 233/30 365 = 1.19
Acid test ratio	3 290/1 242 = 2.64	29 238/30 365 = 0.96

Current assets are supposed to be converted into cash in the current operating cycle of the company. The higher the ratio the more resources a company has available to repay the short-term debts. In the acid test or quick ratio the inventory is excluded from the current assets as it is the least convertible item of the group. It is often observed that companies in distress keep production levels constant although their sales drop. If these companies use a full cost approach for inventory valuation purposes then they are able to capitalize a part of their overhead in a growing inventory amount. The IAS/IFRS standards only allow the full cost approach for inventory valuation purposes (see Chapter 15). This improves the comparability among the data published by firms complying with IAS/IFRS.

Calculating the liquidity ratios for Henkel and Nestlé we have not taken into account the amounts due within 12 months which represent a 'possible' repayment of long-term debt. The amounts of the long-term borrowings which are due within 12 months have not been taken into account, since both companies have included this amount under long-term debt. If Henkel and Nestlé fully comply with IAS/IFRS, their information implies that there is already a refinance agreement for those amounts (see IAS 1) and as such these amounts are not, 'economically speaking', due within 12 months.

Long-term financial status

The financial status of a company also refers to the ability of a company to meet its debt in the long run. A key element in this respect is the capital structure of the firm. Companies have two main sources of funds, namely debt and equity. Each has different well-known characteristics (e.g. fixed versus variable rewards, fixed repayment schedules versus repayment when the company liquidates). The financial risk or financial strength of a company is measured by ratios which relate debt to equity. The most commonly used ratio worldwide in this respect is the debt/equity ratio. A high debt/equity ratio implies higher financial risk, since a higher ratio points at higher interest charges and a wider exposure to possible interest changes. Further debt needs to be repaid often at a fixed date irrespective of whether the company has sufficient funds available or not.

Several alterations can be made to the numerator and the denominator of this ratio in relation to the focus of the analysis: e.g. Debt/(Equity + Debt), Long-term debt/ Equity.

Activity 27.19

Calculate these ratios in relation to the long term financial status for Henkel and Nestlé.

Activity feedback

	Henkel	Nestlé
Debt/Equity	$5\,976/3\,386 = 1.76$	$51\,738/37\,823 = 1.36$
Debt/(Equity + Debt)	$5\,976/9\,362 = 0.63$	$51\,738/89\,561 = 0.57$
(Long-term debt + provisions)/Equity	$9\,468/3\,386 = 1.39$	$21\,373/37\,823 = 0.56$
Long-term debt/Equity	$1\,855/3\,386 = 0.54$	$18\,312/37\,823 = 0.48$

Nestlé has a larger proportion of equity funding than Henkel. This could be the result of a corporate decision with regard to financing or it could be the result of lower pay-out levels with regard to profits in the past.

Further, the debt/equity ratio could be influenced by national or institutional differences (see Chapter 2). In countries with a shareholder orientation the debt/equity ratio will be lower than in countries with a credit orientation. Information on the financial risk of a company can be provided by the ratios but also by a common size analysis of the balance sheet structure (see the section on common size analysis in this chapter) or by trend analysis with ratios as input data.

Ratio analysis and common size analysis are complementary techniques of analysis rather than substitutes. This will be illustrated with those ratios which focus on the long-term financial status of the airlines British Airways, Lufthansa and Ryanair at the end of their financial year 2003 or 2003/2004 (Table 27.17).

At the respective balance sheet dates (2002/2003–2004) Ryanair seems to have the lowest financial risk. This is due to the fact that the company had recently raised extra capital through share issues. The debt/equity ratio gives the impression that Lufthansa and British Airways perform in a rather similar way with regard to debt financing. If we combine the ratio analysis with the data from the common size analysis, we notice that the composition of the debt of the two airlines is totally different. The external debt of Lufthansa is much smaller than the external debt of British Airways; Lufthansa is financed for a substantial part by the internal funding policy for the retirement benefits of the workforce.

Table 27.17 Long-term financial status ratios of British Airways, Lufthansa and Ryanair

	British Airways	Lufthansa	Ryanair
Debt/equity	9 704/2 428 = 3.99	14 036/2 696 = 5.20	1 483/1 455 = 1.01
Debt/(equity + debt)	9 704/12 132 = 0.79	14 036/16 732 = 0.83	1 483/2 938 = 0.50
Long-term debt + provisions)/ equity	6 708/2 428 = 2.76	11 293/2 696 = 4.18	996/1 455 = 0.68
Long-term debt/equity	6 623/2 428 = 2.72	3 240/2 696 = 1.20	902/1 455 = 0.62

Source: Annual reports of British Airways, 2003/2004, Lufthansa, 2003 and Ryanair, 2003/2004

The debt/equity ratio's calculated in Table 27.17 for Ryanair, Lufthansa and British Airways are single point observations of the financial risk of those companies. Evaluating the future financial risk of those companies, based on just one single point observation, is therefore not appropriate. A trend analysis of this ratio would provide more information on that question. Ratios always became more meaningful if they are compared with a benchmark.

Up to now in this section on ratio analysis we have used ratios taken from other companies as benchmarks. Another possibility is to benchmark a ratio against its own historical performance within the same firm. In this type of analysis, trend analysis is combined with ratio analysis. The red flags of comparability should also be taken into account when interpreting the data. As an illustration of a trend analysis performed on ratios we will analyse the evolution of the debt/equity ratio of the Sabena Group over the years 1992–2000. The trend analysis of the debt/equity ratio clearly reveals an increasing financial risk over the years towards the final stage of bankruptcy. Before we start with the analysis of the data the pitfalls of comparability need to be checked. If we check for comparability over time, we notice the following elements. With regard to the Sabena Group as a whole no major structural changes have taken place over the time frame considered except for the year 2000 when the Airline Management Partnership was created. Further, we have noticed some structural changes within the group (e.g. 1992 the sale of the charter company Sobelair from Sabena NV to Sabena Leasing, 1999 the creation of a new subsidiary Sabena Technics NV). These within-group structural changes have no influence on the overall group structure. A second element which needs to be taken into account in the period of analysis (1992–2000) is the change of the applied GAAP. Up to 1998 the annual group accounts complied with Belgian GAAP. From 1999 on the group accounts were published using IAS/IFRS. The group accounts of 1999 include comparative data on 1998 which were also prepared with the use of IAS/IFRS.

In Table 27.18 the evolution of the debt/equity ratio of the Sabena group is presented. For the year 1998 the debt/equity ratio is calculated twice, once with data originating from the Belgian GAAP group accounts (D/E = 6.31) published in 1998 and then with the comparative data included in the IAS group accounts data (D/E = 8.49) of 1999.

We notice that when in 1998 Belgian GAAP data are used the debt/equity ratio is lower. The higher ratios under IAS are due to the fact that a number of lease contracts which could be accounted for as operating lease contracts under Belgian GAAP qualified under IAS/IFRS as finance lease contracts. Since from 1995 on we could find in the notes to the annual accounts information on future operating lease payments,

Table 27.18 Evolution of the debt situation of the Sabena Group, 1992–2000

	1992	1993	1994	1995	1996	1997	1998	1999	2000
Debt/equity IAS switch in 1999	5.87	7.28	6.10	3.14	5.42	6.23	6.31	9.68	−26.92
Debt/equity IAS switch in 1998							8.49	9.68	−26.92
'Extended' debt/Equity (*)				3.99	6.7	9.28	9.17	13.21	−42.73

(*) balance sheet debt + off balance sheet debt relating to operating lease contracts
Source: Group accounts of Sabena, 1992–2000

we have added up these future operating lease payments with the debt included on the face of the balance sheet. Using this amount (balance sheet debt + off balance sheet debt relating to operating lease contracts) in the numerator, we have calculated a ratio which we have labelled the 'extended' debt/equity ratio.

The 'Belgian' debt/equity ratio fluctuates around six until 1998. The improvement of the ratio in 1995 was due to a capital increase, the positive effect of which did not last very long. Due to the accounting strategy followed by the board of directors, which was communicated in the annual report of 1996, equity decreased substantially.

The debt/equity ratio shows an increase in financial risk only from 1999 (or 1998 with IAS accounts) on. The 'extended' debt/equity ratio revealed the deterioration of the financial situation of the Sabena Group much sooner.

The evolution of the 'extended' debt/equity ratio shows clearly that from the start of the cooperation with the SAir Group in 1995 the financial risk deteriorated each year. In 1997 the situation has become critical; in 2000 both ratios (debt/equity and 'extended' debt/equity) point to a dramatic situation. The extreme deterioration of the debt/equity ratio in 2000 is caused by two elements. First of all the huge losses of 2000 turns the equity into the red. The second cause of the steeply rising ratios is the increasing lease commitments due to the fleet expansion.

The debt/equity ratio is often used in debt covenants. In Chapter 26 we discussed how a threat of a possible violation of the debt covenants could lead to annual accounts management. A ratio which tries to circumvent the effect of these practices of annual accounts management is the interest cover ratio. This ratio indicates the safety margin between profit and interest charges.

Interest cover ratio = Profit before tax/Net interest costs

Activity 27.20

Calculate this ratio for Henkel and Nestlé.

Activity feedback

	Henkel	Nestlé
Interest cover ratio	768/140 = 5.48	8 307/594 = 13.98

The interest cover ratio is much higher for Nestlé. This is no surprise since Nestlé makes greater use of equity financing of its activities than Henkel (see debt/equity ratio).

The financial risk of a company is directly linked to the capital structure of a company. A company with a high proportion of debt financing is highly *leveraged*. High financial leverage implies high risk. To get an idea about the leverage of the firm the debt/equity ratio is often used. Financial leverage influences the financial risk of a company and further it has an impact on the relation between ROE and ROA.

Activity 27.21

In the case of Henkel and Nestlé ROE is always higher than ROA. What factors do you think influence this relation or is it coincidence?

	Henkel	Nestlé
ROA	10.16%	10.06%
ROE	15.70%	17.33%

Activity feedback

Whether or not ROE is bigger than ROA depends on two elements. First of all the leverage of the company and second the difference between ROA and the interest cost of the firm. The latter is often called the *spread*. If the obtained ROA is higher than the interest cost, a company can increase the level of ROE compared to ROA by switching from equity financing to debt financing. If, however, ROA is lower than the interest cost of the firm, the relation works in the opposite way. ROE will be lower than ROA and the difference will increase with higher leverage.

The companies Henkel and Nestlé obtain a return on assets which is higher than their interest cost. The spread is higher in the case of Nestlé; this implies that Nestlé could increase its ROE more than Henkel just by higher debt financing. The financial risk ratios however, tell us that Henkel is making more use of debt than Nestlé.

Investment perspective

Potential investors in a company use different sets of information in order to decide whether or not to buy shares of a certain company. The question on their mind is whether the company is a worthwhile investment. When investors possess shares in a company they continously assess their investment. The decision to be taken is a 'hold' or 'sell' decision.

Although for these 'buy' or 'sell' decisions the ratios on the profitability, efficiency and financial status of a company provide useful information, specific ratios are developed with regard to this investment decision. These ratios focus on those elements which are specifically relevant for shareholders, namely the return obtained on their investment. This return can take the form of dividends and/or capital appreciation.

Activity 27.22

Obtain a recent copy of a financial newspaper in your country (e.g the *Financial Times*, *Het Financieel Dagblad*, *De Financieel Economische Tijd*, the *Wall Street Journal*). Look up the share information in these newspapers and make a note of the data provided for each company. Also read the 'company news' either in a financial newspaper or any other quality newspaper and note down any ratios or indicators used to evaluate the companies. You could also check the section investors' relations on the websites of listed companies and make a note of the information they provide in that section.

Activity feedback

Your list possibly included the following: book value per share compared with market value per share, net dividend, dividend cover, earnings per share, gross dividend yield, price earnings ratio. Some of these ratios which relate financial statement data to market data could change almost daily. For example, the very popular and widely used price/earnings ratio can change daily. Other ratios like EPS (earnings per share), and ratios related to dividend performance remain constant over the year. We will look at each of these ratios in turn.

Book value per share/market value per share
The book value per share is the ordinary shareholders funds or equity divided by the number of shares. This book value is the value each share would have if the company's assets and liabilities were sold at their balance sheet (book) value. The market value is the price a potential shareholder is willing to pay to acquire a share in the company. Comparing these two values identifies whether the market values the company at more or less than its book value. One could call the book value per share the intrinsic value of the shares. For listed companies ratios based on book values are not that useful since there is a market appreciation for the company. Several ratios will include this market appreciation by using the market price of the share.

Net dividend
This is the amount of dividend declared in any one year per share which equals paid and proposed dividends divided by the number of shares. People invest in shares for one of two reasons: either to earn dividends or capital growth in the value of the share; or both. The level of dividend and its comparison with previous years is generally regarded as an important indicator of future expectations. However, one danger with this comparison is that dividends are not necessarily just paid out of the current year's earnings but can be paid out of retained earnings. It is, therefore, important to look at dividend cover in any one year.

Dividend cover
The dividend cover ratio gives an idea to external parties about the amount with which the results might drop leaving the amount of dividends to be paid from the result of the year unchanged. The dividend cover ratio is calculated as follows:

$$\frac{\text{Net profit available to ordinary shareholders}}{\text{Total ordinary dividend}}$$

$$\text{or} \quad \frac{\text{Profit} - \text{Preference dividends}}{\text{Ordinary dividends}}$$

A ratio higher than one indicates that the ordinary dividends can be paid out of the available result of the year.

Activity 27.23

The following information is available in respect of Kit plc:

	20X2	20X3
	€	€
Ordinary shares issued €1	1 875 000	1 875 000
8% preference shares €1	660 000	660 000
Dividend ordinary shares	225 000	187 500
Net profit after tax	257 500	231 900

Calculate dividend per share in cents for both preference and ordinary shares and dividend cover.

Activity feedback

Dividend per share in cents preference	8c	8c
Dividend per share ordinary	12c	10c
Dividend cover	204 700/225 000	179 100/187 500
	0.90	0.95

Thus the ordinary dividend per share has reduced from 20X2 to 20X3, but the dividend cover has improved. However, this dividend cover is less than one which indicates that the company is not earning enough in either year to pay the dividend and is therefore using past earnings retained to fund the dividend payment. This may be a danger sign for potential investors.

The dividend cover ratio is opposite from the pay-out ratio. The pay-out ratio is defined as follows:

$$(1/\text{dividend cover}) \times 100$$

For Kit the pay-out ratio is:

20X2	20X3
$(1/0.90) \times 100 = 111$	$(1/0.95) \times 100 = 105$

The pay-out ratio is higher than 100, implying that retained earnings are used to pay out dividends.

Earnings per share

In Chapter 23 we discussed how the earnings per share ratio has to be calculated (basic earnings per share and diluted earnings per share). Listed companies are required to publish both EPS ratios in their financial statements. They represent the amount of profit the company has earned during the year for each ordinary share or for each outstanding ordinary share together with potential ordinary shares. The earnings per share ratio is not distorted by the dividend policy of the company (see Table 27.19).

Table 27.19 Earnings per share data of Lufthansa and Ryanair

EPS in Euro	2002	2003
Lufthansa		
Basic	1.88	2.58
Diluted	1.75	–
Ryanair		
Basic	31.71	27.28
Diluted	31.24	27.00

Source: Annual reports of Lufthansa, 2003 and Ryanair, 2003/2004

As already discussed in Chapter 23, the EPS figure is not useful just as a number. The EPS ratio cannot be used to compare performance between companies. Two companies with exactly the same earnings and exactly the same equity amount can have different EPS values. Why?

If the number of shares differs among the two companies then the EPS will differ as well, although there are no performance differences. Also, when the rate of growth of EPS is used as a measure of performance over time within the same company, a careful interpretation is needed. For example, a bonus issue can take place which will increase the number of shares outstanding without a capital increase as a result. The EPS will change although the economic performance has remained unchanged.

Dividend yield

The dividend yield can be calculated as gross dividend yield or as net dividend yield. In the latter case the yield is calculated on the net amount received without taking into account the tax credit.

This is calculated from the formula:

$$\frac{\text{Dividend}}{\text{Market price of ordinary share}}$$

The gross dividend yield is calculated by grossing up the dividend declared in the accounts for basic rate taxation as dividends are always declared and paid net of basic income tax. For example, in the case of Kit plc, if the basic rate of tax is 20% then the gross dividend is:

	20X2	20X3
	225 000/80%	187 500/80%
	281 250	234 375
or per share	15c	12.5c

If the market value per share for Kit was €1.75 in 20X2 and €1.82 in 20X3, then the gross dividend yield is:

15/175	12.5/182
8.6%	6.9%

Shareholders may be willing to accept a low gross dividend yield if there is a greater than average capital growth in share value expected or if the company is a safe investment.

Price earnings ratio

A popular widely used ratio by analysts and the investment community is the P/E ratio. This ratio is also published daily in financial newspapers and often referred to in business programmes on television. The ratio is calculated by dividing the market price of a share by the earnings per share.

The formula for this is:

$$\frac{\text{Market price per share}}{\text{Earnings per share}}$$

For Kit this is:	20X2	20X3
	175/10.9	182/9.6
	16.1	19

Like the dividend yield the PE ratio will change as the market price per share changes. It represents the market's view of the growth potential of the company, its dividend policy and the degree of risk involved in the investment. The ratio reflects the multiple of earnings the market is willing to pay and as a result the P/E ratio reflects the investors' appreciation about the future of the company. This appreciation or confidence level is based on several elements, namely the evolution of the market in which the firm is active together with how the market expects the firm to cope with opportunities in the market, the economic climate for the coming years and the current performance of the firm.

In general a high PE indicates the market has a high/good opinion of these factors, a low PE a low opinion of these factors. Another way of looking at the PE is that it represents the number of years' earnings it is necessary to have at the current rate to recover the price paid for the share. For Kit, this was 19 years at the 20X3 rate of earnings.

However, a high P/E ratio could not only point at investors' confidence, it could also mean an anticipation of a takeover bid or the fact that current earnings are temporarily low. P/E is also regarded as an indicator for risk, a low P/E might indicate that future earnings are less certain or riskier.

Shareholder value and total shareholder return

These ratios could be labelled as the more 'traditional' ones to use for assessing the attractiveness of an investment in certain shares. In the 1980s the concept of shareholder value emerged. Total shareholder return represents the change in capital value of a company over a one-year period, plus dividends, expressed as a plus or minus percentage of the opening value.

The Scandinavian airline group SAS presents total shareholder return obtained each year over a period of ten years:

> The last distinct recession for the airline industry reached its lowest point in 1990–1991. A calculation of the performance of SAS shares over the ten years 1991–2000 shows an average annual total return of 16.3%. This exceeds SAS's target for a total return of 14% over a business cycle by 2.3 percentage points.
> (Annual report, SAS, financial year 2000, p. 14)

The founding father of the concept of shareholder value was Rappaport (1998) and the idea behind the concept was that the future stream of forecast earnings would be a much better starting point to evaluate the future economic potential of a firm. Future cash flows are often used as a proxy for future earnings. Various metrics were developed in the wake of this shareholder value approach. Within the set of 'new' ratios two groups can be distinguished, namely one group of metrics which is developed around the economic value added concept and, second, a group of ratios which focuses on the future cash flows of a firm.

Some of these new metrics have really been developed recently, while others have already been around for years under another name. Those that have been around for years have been relabelled after minor modifications to the existing metric. The most well known is the EVA® concept which builds on the residual income concept and has been trademarked by Stern Stewart & Co:

> The foundations for these new performance measures are residual income and internal rate of return concepts developed in the 1950s and 1960s. Stern Stewart & Co's trademarked 'economic value added' however this is the firm's proprietary adaptation of residual income.
>
> (Ittner and Larcker, 2001)

In essence, economic value added is created when the net operating profit after tax is higher than the company's cost of capital (including debt and equity). Stern and Stewart suggest several corrections to the different items of the concept in order to undo accounting distortions resulting from accrual accounting.

As EVA® is a single-period measure, in order to be useful for financial analysis it should be judged against prior year data. Further, EVA® is a monetary measure which is less useful for inter-firm comparison. These shortcomings for external analysis are not surprising since EVA® was developed in the first place as a management tool for driving the value creation within the firm. A firm can increase its economic value added through the following actions:

- increasing the net operating profit after tax by operational measures which could increase revenues, decrease costs or both of them
- reducing the cost of capital by changing the financing structure of the company
- improving the utilization of the capital employed.

The second group of 'new' ratios represents multi-period metrics which are built on cash flow information. The most well-known metric is the cash flow return on investment (CFROI). This concept is developed by the Boston Consulting Group and represents an economic measure of a company's performance that reflects the average underlying IRR on all existing investment projects. The CFROI can be defined as annual gross cash flow relative to the invested capital of the business unit.

Based on a simplified CFROI rate the Boston Consulting Group developed a residual income measure, which is called cash value added (CVA). CVA is the spread between CFROI and the real cost of capital, multiplied with the investment in fixed assets plus working capital.

These new metrics not only serve as a communication tool to the outside world, but they are also used internally for management and strategic purposes. We learn from the annual report of Lufthansa, financial year 2003 (p. 99) that CFROI and CVA are used for communication purposes and for management purposes:

Cost of capital
For the Group and the individual business segments in per cent

WACC	2003
Group	8.6
Passenger Business	8.6
Logistics	8.9
MRO	8.3
Catering	7.7
IT Services	8.9

Since the beginning of 2000 the entire Lufthansa Group has been controlled in accordance with the principles of value-added management. The basis is the cash value added (CVA) concept. Lufthansa has put in place a closed system of value-added management which in the meantime is firmly entrenched in all planning, steering and control processes. Within this system the CVA is planned, reported and monitored at Group, segmental and divisional level. In addition, the CVA is included as an assessment variable in the remuneration system of top management.

Owing to the overall economic environment and the crisis in the air traffic industry in particular, we fell well short of maintaining the existing level of value with a CVA of −€745 m in 2003. The development of the CVA over time shows that in our industry, with its strongly cyclical pattern of economic activity, it is difficult to achieve a positive CVA every year. The key requirement is to generate a positive contribution to the company value over a complete cycle.

Value creation
Of the Lufthansa Group and the individual business segments in €m

CVA	2003	2002	2001	2000
Group	−745	404	−628	588
Passenger Business	−217	77	−217	114
Logistics	−43	510	−90	151
MRO	37	114	34	15
Catering	−363	−229	−423	7
IT Services	30	37	34	8
Service and Financial Companies	25	29	30	371

From the annual report of SAS we learn that their target CFROI is at least 20% over a business cycle.

SAS is increasing its focus on value growth in its different operating areas. In order to achieve highly accurate control and measurement, the cash flow measure CVA is currently being evaluated as a return measure in the various business units. SAS presents the evolution of the 'realized' CFROI and 'realized' ROCE in a graphical way compared to the target in their annual report.

Limitations of ratio analysis

These limitations of ratio analysis also apply to analysis of financial statements in general. We have already discussed items such as changes in environment, absence of comparable data, different accounting policies, which may limit the usefulness of the information resulting from ratio analysis, horizontal analysis or common size analysis. In this section we point out a few more limitations.

Non-monetary factors

Non-monetary factors are not reflected in financial statements. Thus, such factors as the quality of the product or service are not reflected, neither is whether labour relations are good or bad. In the section on disclosure of non-financial data we will see how companies are trying to overcome this lack of information. More and more non-financial indicators of performance are introduced in the annual reports.

Historic cost accounting

The historical nature of accounts must always be borne in mind as our interpretation of the business is based on this historical information, but this may not be the best guide as to the future performance, financial status and investment potential. However, with recent evolutions in IAS/IFRS and US GAAP the impact of historical cost accounting might diminish in the coming years.

Short-term fluctuations

Ratio analysis does not identify short-term fluctuations within one year in assets and liabilities as our appraisal is based on a balance sheet which provides values of assets and liabilities as at a point in time. By using these year end figures we may, for example, present a better view of liquidity than has been the case throughout the year.

Changes in the value of money

We all know how inflation can affect the value of the euro, pound, dollar, yen in our pocket and this is no different for a business. In fact, inflation and price changes could render the whole of our ratio analysis invalid. Short-term fluctuations are better reflected in interim reports.

Multivariate analysis

The ratio analysis we have considered so far is of a univariate type. This is where one ratio is considered at a time and then all ratios, once calculated, are assessed together and the analyst makes a considered judgement on the state of the entity. By way of contrast, multivariate analysis combines some of the ratios together in a specified manner by applying weightings to each of the ratios. The result is an index number that is compared to previous years, other companies and industrial averages. Multivariate analysis has been widely used in predicting corporate failure. In 1968 Professor Altman combined five ratios to produce what he named a Z score:

$$Z = 0.012X1 + 0.014X2 + 0.033X3 + 0.006X4 + 0.999X5$$

X1 = Working capital/Total assets
X2 = Retained earnings/Total assets

X3 = Earnings before interest and tax/Total assets

X4 = Market capitalization/Book value of debt

X5 = Sales/Total assets.

In his seminal article companies with Z scores above 2.99 had not failed whereas those companies with a Z score below 1.81 had. His research was undertaken in the manufacturing sector of the United States. In the context of this type of multivariate analysis it is important to remember that results of such multivariate analyses in relation to the economic health of a company must be used with extreme caution. The results of these multivariate analyses are only valid for companies located in the same region, active in the same industry and existing more or less in the same time period. The reason for this limited application is that national environments influence reporting practices (see Chapter 2), that the economic climate constantly changes and that the value of the ratios is influenced by industry characteristics.

Another internationally well-known model is that of Taffler, who carried out similar work in the UK, but have not published the details of this as it is used as a working model and they need to retain the commercial interest. What we do know about the model are the ratios included:

$$Z = c_0 + c_1 X1 + c_2 X2 + c_3 X3 + c_4 X4$$

X1 = Profit before tax/Current assets

X2 = Current assets/Current liabilities

X3 = Current liabilities/Total assets

X4 = Length of time which the company can continue to finance its operations using its own assets with no revenue inflow.

The usefulness of these models is, unfortunately, still often limited to the region from which the company data were taken for the estimation procedure. Our view is that the use of several ratios with additional information (such as trend, common size, industry and accounting analysis) and a good deal of common sense should enable you to make a reasonable assessment of a company's financial status, performance, potential and position in the market. The multivariate models used the individual ratios as input without making a proper assessment on the quality of the data and typical characteristics of the data.

Disclosure of non-financial data

The current company performance as well as the long-term company performance is influenced by several factors which are called in the literature drivers of performance or drivers of value creation. These drivers relate to elements such as customer satisfaction, internal organization of the business processes, the quality and service of the products, the innovation capability of the firm. In the last two decades of the 20th century these drivers of performance played a much more prominent role in the management control systems of companies. Internal performance evaluation systems within companies are now built around financial as well as non-financial performance indicators. Many of these indicators are chosen because they are the drivers of future value creation. The most well-known scorecard in which financial indicators are combined with non-financial indicators is the balanced scorecard, a normative concept developed by Kaplan and Norton (1992).

Since elements such as customer satisfaction, innovative capabilities, organizational efficiency etc. are key drivers of performance in the long run, information on these value drivers or performance drivers is also interesting for external users of annual accounts. These indicators might help external users to forecast future performance.

Over recent years we observe that companies which have this information on non-financial indicators available in their internal management information systems also include them in their annual reports. This information on non-financial key drivers for success is always included in the narrative or descriptive part of the annual report and is therefore non-audited.

Since these non-financial data became integrated in a number of annual reports, the academic community started to research the information content of this non-financial information. The focus of the research relates to the information contents of non-financial data and to the predictive value of the data or what is called the value relevance of the data (e.g. Amir and Lev, 1996; Ittner and Larcker, 2001). Research results so far show that non-financial data are complementary to financial data and the value relevance of financial accounting data continues. Further (using customer satisfaction data) Ittner and Larcker obtained evidence that non-financial data have predictive value, however the relation is non-linear.

The practice of disclosure of non-financial data in the annual reports of companies is widely introduced in Scandinavian companies.

Activity 27.24

Look at the annual report of SAS on the website of that company and find out which non-financial key drivers with an impact on long-term company performance are included in the key company statistics. Do you have any problems in assessing these non-financial indicators?

Activity feedback

The key figures of the SAS Group include, besides financial ratios with regard to profitability and investment performance, non-financial data relating to customer satisfaction, human resources and environmental performance. Although for each of these indicators a historic evolution and a target is presented, one has at the moment no external benchmarks to compare the performance with. These data are valuable but not suitable as such for inter-firm comparison (see Table 27.20).

Table 27.20 Non-financial indicators in the annual report of SAS

	Target 2003	Actual 2003	Actual 2002	Actual 2001	Actual 2000	Actual 1999	Actual 1998	Actual 1997	Actual 1996
SAS customer satisfaction	71	67	69	70	72	74	70	70	65
SAS environmental index	79	78	78	80	82	88	96	97	100

Source: Annual report of SAS

We learn further from the narrative part of the annual report that the most significant factors for customer satisfaction are:

- personal attention
- punctuality and regularity
- product offering
- timetable/route network.

Cash flow statement

The cash flow statement, its preparation and its contents have been discussed in Chapter 22. Cash flow information helps the external user to get an idea whether or not a company is able to generate net positive cash flows. To be able to sort out the different origins of cash, the cash flows are divided in three groups in the cash flow statement, namely cash flow from operating activities, cash flow from investment activities and cash flow from financing activities.

Studying cash flow data users of this statement want to know, in the first place, if a company can generate cash from its operations. In second place, the analyst will try to find out whether this internally generated cash is sufficient to finance the investments of the company or whether the firm needs to rely on external borrowing or an equity increase. The relations between the three components of the cash flow will differ according to the financial situation of the company. The cash flow patterns in a fast growing company will differ from those of a company in distress. For example, if we analyse the cash flow statement of the fast growing low-cost airline Ryanair we notice that the growth is financed through a combination of internally generated operating cash flow, external borrowing and an increase in equity. The stock market is an important provider of capital for Ryanair.

Companies in distress often show different patterns, their cash flow generated from operating activities is often negative. This negative cash flow can be compensated through a disposal of assets and borrowing extra funds from creditors or a capital increase. However, cash flow patterns are not always that predictable. If we analyse the cash flow statement of Sabena the year before bankruptcy we still find a positive operating cash flow; however, the remainder of the picture is not that positive (see Table 27.21).

Looking into the details of the operating cash flow of 2000 of Sabena we notice that the loss of 2000 is almost offset by non-cash expenses which were recorded in the profit and loss account. The operating cash flow turns positive in the end through a rather substantial decrease in working capital, especially if we compare the movement in working capital with the previous year (1999). Further, the company keeps investing, however external funds from creditors are not used to finance these investments. The cash flow from financing activities has turned negative and represents substantial cash outflows. Finally, looking at the bottom line of the cash flow, we notice that the company suffers from a substantial decrease in liquid assets in the year 2000.

Although one might have the impression that the comparability issue is less important with cash flow data, one still has to be alert for differences. For example, dividends, taxation and interests can be presented differently among companies. Further, one has to be sure that the bottom line represents an increase or decrease in

Table 27.21 Consolidated cash flow statement of the Sabena Group, 1999 and 2000

	1999 in million euros	2000 in million euros
Net result for the year	(10)	(323)
Minority interests	(3)	(2)
Depreciation of intangible, tangible fixed and financial assets	127	128
Profits/losses realized sustained on assets sales	(30)	(14)
Taxation	1	2
Other corrections and value adjustments	115	204
Cash flow operations before changes in working capital	**200**	**(5)**
Changes in working capital excluding disposable funds	123	330
Interest paid	(56)	(34)
Taxes paid	(1)	(11)
Interest received	14	19
Dividends received		
Decrease in liabilities	(82)	(129)
Total	(124)	(155)
Net cash inflow operating activities (A)	**199**	**170**
Investments in tangible fixed and financial assets	(315)	(143)
Proceeds from sales of tangible fixed assets	169	40
Net cash inflow from investment activities (B)	**(146)**	**(102)**
Net cash inflow from financing activities	**(99)**	**(202)**
Net decrease/increase in disposable funds (A + B + C)	**(46)**	**(134)**
Cash and cash equivalents at beginning of year	324	278
Decrease/increase in disposable funds	(46)	(134)
Adjustments for foreign currency translations on opening		(1)
Cash and cash equivalents at year-end	**278**	**143**

Source: Group account Sabena, year 2000

cash and cash equivalents available in the company. Sometimes the bottom line is working capital movements.

From Chapter 26 we know that information provided through the balance sheet and profit and loss account might be biased or distorted through annual accounts management (accounting method choices, changes in accounting estimates or real transactions). It is believed that in situations where large accruals are recorded cash flow information gives a more reliable picture of the performance of the firm than the result reported in the profit and loss account. However, the usefulness of cash flow information in general and in relation to undo the effect of accrual accounting varies from firm to firm (empirical evidence can be found in Dechow, 1994).

So in order to make a proper assessment about the economic situation and performance of a company data from the balance sheet, profit and loss account, the notes and the cash flow statement should always be combined. This is often called the cash flow check.

If we analyse the profit and loss account of the SAir Goup of the year 2000 in combination with the cash flow statement of the same group we notice indeed that cash flows are less influenced by accruals.

Table 27.22 Cash flow and result information of SAir, 1999–2000

CHF million	1999	2000
Net result	273	(2 885)
Cash flow from operations	1 423	1 191

According to the report of the new incoming CEO, the financial difficulties at the SAir group necessitated the following measures:

> The realignment of our Group's overall business thrust requires corrective action in balance sheet terms, with the charging of extensive depreciation and provisions to the 2000 results. This will enable the Swissair Group to focus on its new corporate objectives free of the financial burdens of the past.
>
> (Annual report, SAir Group, 2000, p. 5)

The financial year 2000 ended for the SAir Group with a loss of 2885 million CHF whereas the year 1999 ended with a profit of 273 million CHF. Looking at the cash flow statements of 1999 and 2000 we notice in both years positive cash flows from operating activities and an increase in cash and cash equivalents at the bottom line of the cash flow statement (see Table 27.22).

With the discussion of the analysis of the cash flow statement the most important techniques of financial analysis have been discussed.

Summary

External parties use financial statement data to obtain information on several aspects of a company, e.g. is the company liquid, can the company repay its debt, is the company performing well? Several techniques exist to extract information from the financial statements in order to answer those questions. One purpose of this chapter was to explain and illustrate these techniques (trend analysis, common size analysis, ratio analysis, segmental analysis and cash flow analysis). A common characteristic of all these techniques is that benchmarks (internal and external) with which to compare the company data are needed in order to have information value for decision purposes. A necessary condition for benchmarking is the comparability of data. As a result, the second purpose of this chapter was to point out and illustrate several pitfalls which might hinder the comparability of financial accounting data. If accounting analysis is combined with several techniques of financial analysis, external parties should be able to judge the performance and the financial position of a company in a proper perspective.

EXERCISES (✔ indicates answers are available on pages 752–753)

✔ 1 You are the management accountant of Expand, a company incorporated in Dollarland. The company is seeking to grow by acquisition and has identified two potential investment opportunities. One of these, Hone, is also a company incorporated in Dollarland. The other, Over, is a company incorporated in Francland.

You have been presented with financial information relating to both companies. The financial information is extracted from their published financial statements. In both cases, the financial statements conform to domestic Accounting Standards. The financial statements of Hone were drawn up in $s while those of Over were drawn up in Francs. The information relating to Over has been expressed in $s by taking the figures in Francs and dividing by 1.55 – the $/Franc exchange rate at 31 December 2000. The financial information is given below.

Income statements

	Hone		Over	
Year ended	31 March 2001 $ million	31 March 2000 $ million	31 December 2000 $ million	31 December 1999 $ million
Revenue	600	550	620	560
Cost of sales	(300)	(250)	(320)	(260)
Gross profit	300	300	300	300
Other operating expenses	(120)	(105)	(90)	(85)
Profit from operations	180	195	210	215
Finance cost	(20)	(18)	(22)	(20)
Profit before tax	160	177	188	195
Income tax expense	(50)	(55)	(78)	(90)
Net profit for the period	110	122	110	105

Statements of changes in equity

	Hone		Over	
Year ended	31 March 2001 $ million	31 March 2000 $ million	31 December 2000 $ million	31 December 1999 $ million
Balance brought forward	470	418	265	240
Net profit for the period	110	122	110	105
Dividends	(70)	(70)	(80)	(80)
Balance carried forward	510	470	295	265

Balance sheets

	Hone		Over	
	31 March 2001 $ million	31 March 2000 $ million	31 December 2000 $ million	31 December 1999 $ million
Non-current assets	600	570	455	440
Inventories	60	50	55	50
Trade receivables	80	75	90	80
Cash	10	20	15	15
	750	715	615	585
Issued share capital	150	150	110	110
Reserves	360	320	185	155
	510	470	295	265
Interest-bearing borrowings	150	150	240	240
Current liabilities	90	95	80	80
	750	715	615	585

Expand is more concerned with the profitability of potential investment opportunities than with liquidity. You have been asked to review the financial statements of Hone and Over with this concern in mind.

Required:
(a) Prepare a short report to the directors of Expand that, based on the financial information provided, assesses the relative profitability of Hone and Over.
(b) Discuss the validity of using this financial information as a basis to compare the profitability of the two companies.   (CIMA May 01)

✔ 2 It has been suggested that cash is king and that readers of a company s accounts should pay more attention to information concerning its cash flows and balances than to its profits and other assets. It is argued that cash is more difficult to manipulate than profit and that cashflows are more important.

Required:
(a) Explain whether you agree with the suggestion that cash flows and balances are more difficult to manipulate than profit and non-cash assets.
(b) Explain why it might be dangerous to concentrate on cash to the exclusion of profit when analysing a set of financial statements.

(CIMA – adapted)

3 Look up the financial statements of two companies competing in the same industry in your country. Calculate their return on equity (ROE). First, try to explain the difference observed with the use of ratio analysis. Subsequently, add trend analysis, common size analysis, segmental analysis and cash flow analysis to it. What extra information do these supplemental analyses give you? If you were to carry out an industry analysis, would this give you extra information on top of it?

4 Look up the P/E ratios of several airlines; what do you observe? How does the market value the prospects of each of these companies? Do the underlying financial statements confirm the market appreciation? Or do you observe conflicts?

5 Question 4 can be repeated for listed companies in several industries. Do you observe industry differences?

6 In which industries would you expect inventory turnover to be lower, in which industries would you expect this ratio to be higher? Comment on this (discuss this in relation to asset turnover also).

7 In which industries would you expect profit margins to be lower, in which industries would you expect this ratio to be higher?

8 Heavy Goods plc carries on business as a manufacturer of tractors. In 2004 the company was looking for acquisitions and carrying out investigations into a number of possible targets. One of these was a competitor, Modern Tractors plc. The company's acquisition strategy was to acquire companies that were vulnerable to a takeover and in which there was an opportunity to improve asset management and profitability.

The chief accountant of Heavy Goods plc has instructed his assistant to calculate ratios from the financial statements of Modern Tractors plc for the past three years and to prepare a report based on these ratios and the industry average ratios that have been provided by the trade association. The ratios prepared by the assistant accountant and the industry averages for 2004 are set out as follows.

Required:
You are required to write a full appraisal and report.

		2002	2003	Industry average 2004	2004
Sales growth	%	30.00	40.00	9.52	8.25
Sales/total assets		1.83	2.05	1.60	2.43
Sales/net fixed assets		2.94	3.59	2.74	16.85
Sales/working capital		−21.43	−140.00	38.33	10.81
Sales/debtors		37.50	70.00	92.00	16.00
Gross profit/sales	%	18.67	22.62	19.57	23.92
Profit before tax/sales	%	8.00	17.62	11.74	4.06
Profit before interest/interest		6.45	26.57	14.50	4.95
Profit after tax/total assets	%	9.76	27.80	13.24	8.97
Profit after tax/equity	%	57.14	75.00	39.58	28.90
Net fixed assets/total assets	%	62.20	57.07	58.54	19.12
Net fixed assets/equity		3.64	1.54	1.75	0.58
Equity/total assets	%	18.29	37.07	33.45	32.96
Total liabilities/total assets	%	81.71	62.93	66.55	69.00
Total liabilities/equity		4.47	1.70	1.99	2.40
Long-term debt/total assets	%	36.59	18.54	29.27	19.00
Current liabilities/total assets	%	45.12	44.39	37.28	50.00
Current assets/current liabilities		0.84	0.97	1.11	1.63
(Current assets − stock)/current liabilities		0.43	0.54	0.72	0.58
Stock/total assets	%	17.07	18.54	14.63	41.90
Cost of sales/stock		8.71	8.55	8.81	4.29
Cost of sales/creditors		6.10	6.25	6.17	12.87
Debtors/total assets	%	4.88	2.93	1.70	18.40
Cash/total assets	%	15.85	21.46	25.08	9.60

Note
Total assets = (fixed assets at net book value + current assets) and net fixed assets = fixed assets at net book value. (ACCA – adapted)

9 Seville plc is a rapidly expanding trading and manufacturing company. It is currently seeking to extend its product range in new markets. To achieve this growth it needs to raise €800 000. The directors are considering two sources of funds:
(i) A rights issue at €2.00 per share. The shares are trading at €2.50 (2000 €2.20) per share.
(ii) A bank loan at an interest rate of 15% and repayable by instalments after two years. The bank would want to secure the loan with a charge over the company's property. The following are extracts from the draft financial statements.

Seville plc
Draft P&L account extract year ended 31.12.01

	2000 €000	2001 €000
Turnover	1 967	1 991
Operating profit	636	698

Interest payable	(45)	(55)
Profit before taxation	591	643
Taxation	(150)	(140)
Profit after taxation	441	503
Extraordinary item	(90)	–
Profit for the year	361	453
Fixed assets		
tangible	1 132	1 504
intangible	247	298
	1 379	1 802
Current assets		
stocks	684	679
debtors	471	511
cash in hand and at bank	80	117
Creditors: due within one year		
trade	(336)	(308)
taxation	(140)	(190)
dividends	(80)	(80)
Creditors: due after more than one year		
10% debentures, repayable 2004	(450)	(450)
finance lease	–	(100)
	1 608	1 981
Capital and reserves		
ordinary share capital €1 shares	800	800
revaluation reserve	144	144
profit and loss	664	1 037
	1 608	1 981

Operating profit

Operating profit has been arrived at after charging or crediting the following:

	2000	2001
	€000	€000
Depreciation	110	150
Gain on disposal of property (as part of a sale and leaseback transaction)	–	95

Extraordinary item

The extraordinary loss consists of reorganization costs in a branch where a reduction in activity involved various measures including redundancies. Attributable tax credit is €38 000.

Deferred taxation

Deferred taxation has not been provided because it is not considered probable that a liability will crystallize. If deferred taxation had been provided in full then a liability for the year of €7000 would have arisen (2000 €8000).

Contingent liability

There is a contingent liability of €85 000 (2000 €80 000) in respect of bills of exchange discounted with bankers.

Further investigation has revealed that stock includes items subject to reservation of title of €40 000 and obsolete or slow moving items of €28 000 (2000 €28 000).

An age analysis of debtors has revealed that debts overdue by more than one year amount to €40 000 (2000) €40 000.

The auditors are yet to report and there is some discussion as to the classification of the gain on disposal and the reorganization costs.

The directors forecast that the new funds will generate an operating profit of €300 000, and that the 2001 operating profit will be repeated. If new shares are issued the dividend will increase to €150 000.

Required:

Prepare a full report on progress, strengths and weaknesses, supported by ratio analysis.

(ACCA – adapted)

10 Recycle plc is a listed company which recycles toxic chemical waste products. The waste products are sent to Recycle plc from all around the world. You are an accountant (not employed by Recycle plc) who is accustomed to providing advice concerning the performance of companies, based on the data which are available from their published financial statements. Extracts from the financial statements of Recycle plc for the two years ended 30 September 2007 are as follows:

Profit and loss accounts – year ended 30 September:

	2007	2006
Turnover	3 000	2 800
Cost of sales	(1 600)	(1 300)
Gross profit	1 400	1 500
Other operating expenses	(800)	(600)
Operating profit	600	900
Interest payable	(200)	(100)
Profit before taxation	400	800
Taxation	(150)	(250)
Profit after taxation	250	550
Proposed dividend	(200)	(200)
Retained profit	50	350
Retained profit b/fwd	900	550
Retained profit c/fwd	950	900

Balance sheets at 30 September

	2007		2006	
	€m	€m	€m	€m
Tangible fixed assets		4 100		3 800
Current assets:				
Stocks	500		350	
Debtors	1 000		800	
Cash in hand	50		50	
	1 550		1 200	

Current liabilities:			
Trade creditors	600		600
Taxation payable	150		250
Proposed dividend	200		200
Bank overdraft	750		50
	1 700		1 100
Net current (liabilities)/assets		(150)	100
Long-term loans (repayable 2009)		(1 000)	(1 000)
		2 950	2 900
Capital and reserves:			
Called-up share capital (€1 shares)		2 000	2 000
Profit and loss account		950	900
		2 950	2 900

You ascertain that depreciation of tangible fixed assets for the year ended 30 September 2007 was €1 200 million. Disposals of fixed assets during the year ended 30 September 2007 were negligible. You are approached by two individuals.

A is a private investigator who is considering purchasing shares in Recycle plc. *A* considers that Recycle plc has performed well in 2007 compared with 2006 because turnover has risen and the dividend to shareholders has been maintained.

B is resident in the area immediately surrounding the premises of Recycle plc and is interested in the contribution made by Recycle plc to the general well-being of the community. *B* is also concerned about the potential environmental effect of the recycling of chemical waste. *B* is uncertain how the published financial statements of Recycle plc might be of assistance in addressing social and environmental matters.

Required:

Write a full report addressed to *A*, supported by appropriate ratios. (CIMA – adapted)

11 H plc manufactures vehicle parts. The company sells its products to a number of independent distributors who resell the goods to garages and other retail outlets in their areas. H plc has a policy of having only one distributor in any given geographical area. Distributors are selected mainly on the basis of financial viability. H plc is keen to avoid the disruption of sales and loss of credibility associated with the collapse of a distributor.

The company is currently trying to choose between two companies which have applied to be its sole distributor in Geetown, a new sales area.

The applicants have supplied the following information:

	Applicant X			Applicant Y		
	1993	1994	1995	1993	1994	1995
Sales (£000)	1280	1600	2000	1805	1900	2000
Gross profit %	22	20	18	23	22	24
Return on capital employed %	8	12	16	14	15	16
Current ratio	1.7:1	1.9:1	2.1:1	1.7:1	1.65:1	1.7:1
Quick ratio	1.4:1	1.1:1	0.9:1	0.9:1	0.9:1	0.9:1
Gearing %	15	21	28	29	30	27

Requirements:
(a) Explain why trends in accounting ratios could provide a more useful insight than the latest figures taken on their own.
(b) Using the information provided above, explain which of the companies appears to be the safer choice for the role of distributor.

(CIMA – adapted)

12 Arizona plc has carried on business for a number of years as a retailer of a wide variety of 'do it yourself' goods. The company operates from a number of stores around the United Kingdom.

In recent years, the company has found it necessary to provide credit facilities to its customers in order to achieve growth in turnover. As a result of this decision, the liability to the company's bankers has increased substantially.

The statutory accounts of the company for the year-ended 31 March 1998 have recently been published, and extracts are provided below, together with comparative figures for the previous two years.

Profit and loss accounts for the years ended 31 March

	1996	1997	1998
	£m	£m	£m
Turnover	1850	2200	2500
Cost of sales	(1250)	(1500)	(1750)
Gross profit	600	700	750
Other operating costs	(550)	(640)	(700)
Operating profit	50	60	50
Interest from credit sales	45	60	90
Interest payable	(25)	(60)	(110)
Profit before taxation	70	60	30
Taxation	(23)	(20)	(10)
Profit after taxation	47	40	20
Dividends	(30)	(30)	(20)
Retained profit	17	10	–

Balance sheets at 31 March

	1996	1997	1998
	£m	£m	£m
Tangible fixed assets	278	290	322
Stocks	400	540	620
Debtors	492	550	633
Cash	12	12	15
Trade creditors	(270)	(270)	(280)
Taxation	(20)	(20)	(8)
Proposed dividends	(30)	(30)	(20)
Bank overdraft	(320)	(520)	(610)
Debentures	(200)	(200)	(320)
	342	352	352
Share capital	90	90	90
Reserves	252	262	262
	342	352	352

Other information:

■ Depreciation charged for the three years was as follows:

year-ended 31 March	1996	1997	1998
	£m	£m	£m
	55	60	70

■ The debentures are secured by a floating charge over the assets of Arizona plc. Their repayment is due on 31 March 2008.
■ The bank overdraft is unsecured. The bank has set a limit of £630 million on the overdraft.
■ Over the past three years, the level of credit sales has been:

year-ended 31 March	1996	1997	1998
	£m	£m	£m
	213	263	375

Given the steady increase in the bank overdraft which has taken place in recent years, the company has recently written to its bankers to request an increase in the limit. The request was received by the bank on 15 May 1998, two weeks after the 1998 statutory accounts were published.

You are an accountant employed by the bankers of Arizona plc. The bank is concerned at the steep escalation in the level of the company's overdraft and your regional manager has asked for a report on the financial performance of Arizona plc for the last three years.

Required:

Write a report to your regional manager which analyses the financial performance of Arizona plc for the period covered by the financial statements.

Your report may take any form you wish, but should specifically address the particular concern of the bank regarding the rapidly increasing overdraft. Therefore, your report should identify aspects of poor performance which could have contributed to the increase in the overdraft.

(CIMA)

13 You are an investment analyst. A client of yours, Mr A, owns 3.5% of the share capital of Price. Price is a listed company and prepares financial statements in accordance with International Accounting Standards. The company supplies machinery to agricultural businesses. The year end of Price is 31 July and the financial statements for the year ended 31 July 2001 were approved by the directors on 30 September 2001. Following approval, copies of the financial statements were sent to all shareholders in readiness for the annual general meeting which is due to be held on 30 November 2001. Extracts from these financial statements are given below:

Income statements – year ended 31 July	2001	2000
	$000	$000
Revenue	54 000	51 000
Cost of sales	(42 000)	(40 000)
Gross profit	12 000	11 000
Other operating expenses	(6 300)	(6 000)
Profit from operations	5 700	5 000
Finance cost	(1 600)	(1 000)
Profit before tax	4 100	4 000

	2001		2000	
Income tax expense	(1 200)	(1 200)		
Net profit for the period	2 900	2 800		

Balance sheets – at 31 July	_2001_		_2000_	
	_$000_	_$000_	_$000_	_$000_
Non-current assets:				
Property plant and equipment		44 200		32 000
current assets:				
Inventories	8 700		7 500	
Receivables	13 000		12 000	
Cash and cash equivalents	200		1 500	
		21 900		21 000
		66 100		53 000
Capital and reserves:				
Issued share capital		20 000		20 000
Reserves		20 300		14 000
		40 300		34 000
Non-current liabilities		15 400		10 000
Current liabilities:				
Trade payables	8 000		7 800	
Tax	1 200		1 200	
Bank overdraft	1 200		Nil	
		10 400		9 000
		66 100		53 000

Statement of changes in equity	
	_$000_
Balance at 31 July 2000	34 000
Surplus on revaluation of properties	5 000
Net profit for the period	2 900
Dividends	(1 600)
Balance at 31 July 2001	40 300

Extracts from notes to the financial statements		
Finance cost – year ended 31 July	2001	2000
	$000	$000
On 10% interest-bearing borrowings	1 000	1 000
On zero-rate bonds	400	Nil
On bank overdraft	200	Nil
	1 600	1 000

Non-current liabilities at 31 July	_2001_	_2000_
	_$000_	_$000_
10% borrowings repayable 31 July 2006	10 000	10 000
Zero-rate bonds	5 400	Nil
	15 400	10 000

The zero-rate bonds were issued for proceeds of $5 million on 1 August 2000. The lenders are not entitled to interest during their period of issue. The bonds are repayable on 31 July 2004 for a total of $6 802 450. The bonds are quoted on a recognised stock exchange. However, the company intends to hold the bonds until they mature and then repay them.

Revaluation of properties:
This is the first time the company has revalued any of its properties.

Depreciation of non-current assets:
Depreciation of non-current assets for the year totalled $4 million (2000 – $3 million).
   Your client always attends the annual general meeting of the company and likes to put questions to the directors regarding the financial statements. However, he is not a financial specialist and does not wish to look foolish by asking inappropriate questions. Mr A intends to ask the following three questions and seeks your advice based on the information provided. The points he wishes to make are as follows:

Point 1:
Why, when the company has made almost the same profit as last year and has borrowed more money through a bond issue, has the company got a bank overdraft of $1.2 million at the end of the year when there was a positive balance of $1.5 million in the bank at the end of the previous year? This looks wrong to me.

Point 2:
The company has a revaluation surplus of $5 million included in the statement of changes in equity. I have never understood this statement. Surely surpluses are shown in the income statement. Perhaps our accountants are unaware of the correct accounting treatment?

Point 3:
I don't understand the treatment of the zero-rate bonds. The notes tell me that these were issued for $5 million and no interest was paid to the investors. The accounts show a finance cost of $400 000 and a balance owing of $5.4 million. Is this an error? On the other hand, perhaps the $5.4 million is the fair value of the bonds? I feel sure an International Accounting Standard has been issued that requires companies to value their borrowings at fair value.
Required:
Prepare a reply to Mr A that evaluates the issues he has raised in the three points and provides appropriate advice. You should support your advice with references to International Accounting Standards.

(CIMA Nov 01)

14 You are the Management Accountant of Drax. The enterprise prepares financial statements to 31 March each year. Earnings per share is regarded as a key performance indicator and the executive directors receive a bonus if the earnings per share exceeds a given target figure. Good corporate governance is ensured by the appointment of a number of non-executive directors, who rigorously scrutinise the financial statements each year to ensure that the earnings per share figure has been correctly computed.
   Drax has recently appointed a new non-executive director who seeks your advice regarding the financial statements for the year ended 31 March 2003. Extracts from these financial statements (excluding the comparative figures) are given below. The financial statements comply with relevant Accounting Standards in all material respects.

STATEMENTS OF FINANCIAL PERFORMANCE:

Income statement – year ended 31 March 2003

	Continuing operations $ million	Discontinuing operations $ million	Total $ million
Revenue	1 000	100	1 100
Cost of Sales	(520)	(70)	(590)
Gross profit	480	30	510
Other operating expenses	(200)	(40)	(240)
Profit from operations	280	(10)	270
Loss on disposal of discontinuing Operations (*Note 1*)	–	(30)	(30)
Profit before finance costs	280	(40)	240
Finance costs			(55)
Profit before tax			185
Income tax expense			(55)
Profit after tax			130
Minority interests			(45)
Group profit for the period			85

Earnings per equity share 59.13 cents

Statement of changes in equity – year ended 31 March 2003

	$million	$million
Balance at 1 April 2002		270
Profit for the financial year		85
Unrealised surplus on the revaluation of properties		22
Currency translation differences on foreign currency net investments	12	
Less exchange losses on related foreign currency loans	(9)	
		3
Dividends (all equity)		(50)
Issue of share capital (*Note 2*)		60
Balance at 31 March 2003		390

NOTES TO THE FINANCIAL STATEMENTS:
Note 1
During the year Drax disposed of a subsidiary. The loss on disposal shown in the income statement consists of two elements:

Disposal proceeds less related net assets less related goodwill	$45 million **loss**
Gain on curtailment of retirement benefits relating to disposal	$15 million **profit.**

Note 2
At the start of the period, Drax had 120 million $1 equity shares in issue. Drax had no non-equity shares. On 1 July 2002, Drax made a rights issue to existing shareholders of one share for every four held at $2 per share. The market value of each share immediately before the rights issue was $2.50.

Note 3 – Defined benefit pension plan

	At 31 March 2003 $ million	At 31 March 2002 $ million
Present value of funded obligations	5 000	4 500
Fair value of plan assets	(2 600)	(2 700)
Unrecognised actuarial losses	(380)	(350)
Net liability in balance sheet	2 020	1 450

The new non-executive director has sent you a list of questions to which he requires answers:

(a) Please show how the earnings per share figure has been computed.

(b) I am a non-executive director for another enterprise operating in the same industry as Drax with roughly the same revenue and with very similar unit costs of raw materials. The nominal value of the shares of this other enterprise is $1 yet its earnings per share is quite different from that of Drax. How can this be?

(c) I am very suspicious about some of the figures in the statement of changes in equity and in the pension plan liability. It would seem to me that exchange losses on loans and actuarial losses relating to the pension plan should be in the income statement. Are the executive directors trying to maximise the earnings per share for their own ends?

(d) I don't understand how the 'gain on curtailment of retirement benefits' is a gain that goes to the income statement. Shouldn't it be treated in the same way as the actuarial losses that seem to be included in the balance sheet figure for the pension plan liability?

Required:

Prepare a reply to the questions the non-executive director has raised. You should refer to the provisions of relevant Accounting Standards where appropriate. Assume that the non-executive director has a reasonable general knowledge of business but that he is not familiar with the detail of Accounting Standards. (CIMA May 03)

15 You are the accountant of Acquirer. Your enterprise has the strategy of growth by acquisition and your directors have identified an enterprise, Target, which they wish to investigate with a view to launching takeover bid. Your directors consider that the directors of Target will contest any bid and will not be very co-operative in providing background information on the enterprise. Therefore, relevant financial information is likely to be restricted to the publicly available financial statements.

Your directors have asked you to compute key financial ratios from the latest financial statements of Target [for the year ended 30 November 2002] and compare the ratios with those for other enterprises in a similar sector. Accordingly, you have selected ten broadly similar enterprises and have presented the directors with the following calculations:

Ratio	Basis of calculation	Ratio for Target	Spread of ratios for comparative enterprises		
			Highest	Average	Lowest
Gross profit margin	$\frac{\text{Gross profit}}{\text{Revenue}}$	42%	44%	38%	33%
Operating profit margin	$\frac{\text{Profit from operations}}{\text{Revenue}}$	29%	37%	30%	26%

Return on total capital	$\dfrac{\text{Profit from operations}}{\text{Total capital}}$	73%	92.5%	69%	52%
Interest cover	$\dfrac{\text{Profit from operations}}{\text{Finance cost}}$	1.8 times	3.2 times	2.5 times	1.6 times
Gearing	$\dfrac{\text{Debt capital}}{\text{Total capital}}$	52%	56%	40%	28%
Dividend cover	$\dfrac{\text{Profit after tax}}{\text{Dividend}}$	5.2 times	5 times	4 times	3 times
Turnover of inventory	$\dfrac{\text{Cost of sales}}{\text{Closing inventory}}$	4.4 times	4.5 times	4 times	3.2 times
Receivables days	$\dfrac{\text{Trade receivables}}{\text{1 day's sales revenue}}$	51 days	81 days	62 days	49 days

Required:

(a) Using the ratios provided, write a report that compares the financial performance and position of Target to the other enterprises in the survey. Where an issue arises that reflects particularly favourably or unfavourably on Target, you should assess its relevance to a potential acquirer.

(b) Identify any reservations you have regarding the extent to which the ratios provided can contribute to an acquisition decision by the directors of Acquirer. You should highlight the extent to which the financial statements themselves might help you to overcome the reservations you have identified.   (CIMA Nov 03)

References

Chapter 2

Alexander, D. and Nobes, C. (2004) *Financial accounting: an international introduction*, 2nd edn, Pearson Education, Harlow.

Ali, A. and Hwang, L-S. (2000) 'Country-specific factors related to financial reporting and the value relevance of accounting data', *Journal of Accounting Research*, 38 (1), Spring.

American Accounting Association (1977) *The Accounting Review*, Supplement to volume 52.

Ball, R. and Shivakumar, L. (2002) 'Earning quality in UK private firms', Working paper, London Business School, 53.

Ball, R., Kothari, S.P. and Robin, A. (2000) 'The effect of international institutional factors on properties of accounting earnings', *Journal of Accounting and Economics*, 29, 1–51.

Basu, S. (1997) 'The conservatism principle and the asymmetric timeliness of earnings', *Journal of Accounting and Economics*, 24, 3–37.

Choi, F. and Mueller, G. (1992) *International Accounting*, Prentice Hall, Englewood Cliffs.

da Costa, R.C., Bourgeois, J.C., and Lawson, W.M. (1978) 'A classification of international financial accounting practices', *The International Journal of Accounting (education and research)*, Spring, 73–85.

Frank, W.G. (1979) An empirical analysis of international accounting principles, *Journal of Accounting Research*, Autumn, 593–605.

Gonzalo, J.A. and Gallizo, J.L. (1992) *Spain*, Routledge, London.

Gray, S. (1988) 'Towards a theory of cultural influence on the development of accounting systems internationally', *Abacus*, March.

Guenther, D. and Young, D. (2000) 'The association between financial accounting measures and real economic activity: A multinational study', *Journal of Accounting and Economics*, 29, 53–72.

Hatfield, H.R. (1966) 'Some variations in accounting practices in England, France, Germany and the US', *Journal of Accounting Research*, Autumn.

Hofstede, G. (1984) *Culture's consequences: international differences in work-related values*. Sage, Beverly Hills, CA.

La Porta, R., Lopez-de-Silanes, F., Schleifer, A. and Vishny, R. (1997) 'Legal determinants of external finance', *Journal of Finance*, 52, 1131–50.

La Porta, R., Lopez-de-Silanes, F., Schleifer, A. and Vishny, R. (1998) 'Law and finance', *Journal of Political Economy*, 106, 1113–55.

Leuz, C. and Verrechia, R.E. (2000) 'The economic consequences of increased disclosure', *Journal of Accounting Research*, 38, supplement, 91–124.

Leuz, C., Nanda, D. and Wysocki, P. (2003) 'Earnings management and investor protection: An international comparison', *Journal of Financial Economics*, 69(3), 505–28.

Maijoor, S. and Vanstraelen, A. (2002) 'Earnings management: The effects of national audit environment, audit quality and international capital markets', unpublished working paper, January 2002.

Mey, A. (1996) 'Theodore Limperg and his theory of values and costs', *Abacus*, 2 (1), September 3–23.

Mueller, G.G. (1967) *International Accounting*, Macmillan, New York.

Nair, R.D. and Frank, W.G. (1980) 'The impact of disclosure and measurement on international accounting classificating', *The Accounting Review*, July, 426–50.

Nobes, C.W. (1980) 'International classification of accounting systems', unpublished paper.

Nobes, C.W. and Parker, R. (2003) *Comparative International Accounting*, 7th edn, Prentice Hall, London.

Ordelheide, D. and KPMG (eds) (2001) *Transnational Accounting*, 2nd edn, Palgrave, London.

Penman, S.H. and Zhang, X-J. (2002) 'Accounting conservatism, the quality of earnings, and stock returns', *The Accounting Review*, 77 (2), April, 237–64.

Pope, P. and Walker, M. (1999) 'International differences in the timeliness, conservatism and classification of earnings', *Journal of Accounting Research*, 37, supplement, 53–87.

Schipper, K. (2000) 'Accounting research and the potential use of international accounting', *British Accounting Review*, 32, 243–56.

Schmalenbach, E. (1927) 'Der Kontenrahmen', *Zeitschrift für betriebswirtschaftliche Forschung*, 21, 385–402.

Seidler, L.J. (1967) 'International accounting – the ultimate theory course', *The Accounting Review*, October, 775–81.

Chapter 4

Edwards, E.O. and Bell, P.W. (1961) *The Theory and Measurement of Business Income*, University of California Press, Berkeley, CA.

Fisher, I. (1930) *The Theory of Interest*. Macmillan, New York. (Reprinted as 'Income and capital', in Parker and Harcourt, 1969.)

Hicks, J. (1946) *Value and Capital*, Clarendon Press, Oxford. (Reprinted as 'Income' in Parker and Harcourt, 1969.)

Parker, R.H. and Harcourt, G.C. (1969) *Readings in the Concept and Measurement of Income*, Cambridge University Press, Cambridge.

Chapter 7

Bonbright, J.C. (1937) *The Valuation of Property*, McGraw-Hill, New York.
Mey, A. (1966) 'Theodore Limperg and his theory of values and costs', *Abacus*, 2 (1), September, 3–23.
Sandilands Report (1975) *Inflation Accounting Committee*, MND 6225, HMSO, London.
Schmalenbach, E. (1959) *Dynamic Accounting*, Gee & Co., London.
Sweeney, H.W. (1936) *Stabilized Accounting*, Harper & Bros, New York.

Chapter 8

Belkaoui, A. (2000) *Accounting Theory*, 4th edn, Thomson Learning, London.
Devine, C.T. (1960) 'Research methodology and accounting theory formation', *The Accounting Review*, July.
Edwards, E.O. and Bell, P.W. (1961) *The Theory and Measurement of Business Income*, University of California Press, Berkeley, CA.
Hendriksen, E.S. (1977) *Accounting Theory*, 3rd edn, Irwin, Homewood, IL.
Jensen, M.C. (1976) *Reflections on the state of accounting research and the regulation of accounting*, Stanford lectures in Accounting, Stanford University.
Lehman, G. (2001) *Accounting Forum* Editorial 25, March.
Littleton, A.C. (1953) *Structure of Accounting Theory*. Monograph no. 5. American Accounting Association.
McDonald, D.L. (1972) *Comparative Accounting Theory*, Addison-Wesley, Reading, MA.
Paton, W.A. (1922) *Accounting Theory*, The Ronald Press, New York.
Scott, D.R. (1941) 'The basis for accounting principles', *Accounting Review*, December.
Sorter, G.H. (1969) 'An events approach to basic accounting theory', *The Accounting Review*, January.
Yu, S.C. (1976) *The Structure of Accounting Theory*, The University Press of Florida, Gainesville.

Chapter 10

Adams, R. (1997) *Linking environmental and financial performance: a survey of best practice techniques*, International standards of accounting and reporting.
Adams, R. (1994) 'Ready for a greening' *Accountancy Age*, 5 May.
Bayer Ag annual report 2001.
Beiersdorf annual report 2000.
Corporate report 1975, UK Accounting Standards Committee.
Gray, R.H., Owen, D. and Adams, C. (1996) *Accounting and accountability: changes and challenges in corporate social and environmental reporting*, Prentice Hall, London.
Hicks, J.R. (1946) *Value and capital*, 2nd edn, Oxford University Press, Oxford.
Kaplan, R.S. and Norton, D. (1996) *The balances scorecard: translating strategy into action*, Boston, Harvard Business School Press.
Moore, D. (1997) *Position paper on accounting for environmental costs and liabilities*, Canadian Institute of Chartered Accountants.

Chapter 20

Black, F. and Scholes, M. (1973) 'The pricing of options and corporate liabilities', *Journal of Political Economy*, 81, 637–59.

Chapter 23

Fields, T., Lys, T. and Vincent L. (2001) 'Empirical research on accounting choice', *Journal of Accounting and Economics*, 31, 255–307.

Chapter 26

Banker, R. and Johnston, H. (1993) 'An empirical study of cost drivers in the U.S. airline industry', *The Accounting* Review, 68 (3), July, 576–601.

Bowen, R., DuCharme, L. and Chores, D. (1995) 'Stakeholders implicit claims and accounting method choice', *Journal of Accounting and Economics*, 255–96.

Burgstahler, D. and Dichev, I. (1997) 'Earning management to avoid earnings decreases and losses', *Journal of Accounting and Economics*, 99–126.

Dechow, P.M. and Sloan, R.G. (1991) 'Executive incentives and the horizon problem: An empirical investigation', *Journal of Accounting and Economics*, 51–89.

Dechow, P.M., Sloan, R.G. and Sweeney, A.P. (1996) 'Causes and consequences of earnings manipulation: an analysis of firms subject to enforcement actions by the SEC', *Contemporary Accounting Research*, 13, 1–36.

DeFond, M.L. and Jiambalvo, J. (1994) 'Debt covenant violation and manipulation of accruals', *Journal of Accounting and Economics*, 17, 145–76.

DeGeorge, F., Patel, J. and Zeckhauser, R. (1999) 'Earnings management to exceed thresholds', *Journal of Business*, 72, 1–33.

Francis, J. (2001) 'Discussion of empirical research on accounting choice', *Journal of Accounting and Economics*, 31, 309–19.

Friedlan, J.M. (1994) 'Accounting choices of issuers of initial public offerings', *Contemporary Accounting Research* 11, 1–31.

Guenther, D., Maydew, E., Nutter, S. (1997) 'Financial reporting, tax costs and book-tax conformity', *Journal of Accounting and Economics*, 23, 225–48.

Healy, P.M. (1985) 'The effect of bonus schemes on accounting decisions', *Journal of Accounting and Economics*, 7, 85–107.

Horngren, C., Bhimani, A., Datar, S. and Foster, G. (2002) *Management and Cost Accounting*, 2nd edn, Financial Times – Prentice Hall, London.

Jensen, M. and Murphy, K. (1990) 'Performance pay and top management', *Journal of Political Economy*, 98, 2, 225–64.

Jiambalvo, J. (1996) 'Causes and consequences of earnings manipulation: an analysis of firms subject to enforcement actions by the SEC', *Contemporary Accounting Research*, 13, 37–47.

Kasanen, E., Kinnunen, J. and Niskanen, J. (1996) 'Dividend based earnings management: empirical evidence from Finland', *Journal of Accounting and Economics*, 283–312.

Key, K.G. (1997) 'Political cost incentives for earning management in the cable television industry', *Journal of Accounting and Economics*, 309–37.

LaSalle, R.E., Jones, S.K. and Jain, R. (1993) 'The association between executive succession and discretionary accounting changes: earning management or different perspectives?' *Journal of Business Finance and Accounting*, 653–71.

Leuz, C., Nanda, D. and Wysocki, P. (2002) 'Investor protection and earnings management: an international comparison', unpublished working paper, The Wharton School for the University of Pennsylvania.

Lüchinger, R. (2001) *Swissair, l'histoire secrète de la debacle,* Editions Bilan, Lausanne.

McNichols, M. and Wilson, G.P. (1988) 'Evidence of earnings management from the provision for bad debts', *Journal of Accounting Research*, 1–31.

Murphy, K.J. and Zimmerman, J.L. (1993) 'Financial performance surrounding CEO turnover', *Journal of Accounting and Economics*, 273–316.

Neil, J.D., Pourciau, S.G. and Schaefer, T.F. (1995) 'Accounting method choice and IPO valuation', *Accounting Horizons*, 9, 68–80.

Palepu, K., Healy, P. and Bernard, V. (2000) *Business Analysis and Valuation: Using Financial Statements*, 2nd edn, South-Western College Publishing, Cincinatti, OH.

Penman, S. (2001) *Financial Statement Analysis and Security Valuation*, McGraw-Hill/Irwin, Boston, MA.

Porter, M. (1985) *Competitive Advantage: Creating and Sustaining Superior Performance*, The Free Press, New York.

Rangan, S. (1998) 'Earnings management and the performance of seasoned equity offerings', *Journal of Financial Economics*, 50, 101–22.

Shank, J. and Govindarajan, V. (1992) 'Strategic cost management and the value chain', *Journal of Cost Management*, winter, 5–21.

Shivakumar, L. (1998) 'Market reaction to seasoned equity offering announcements and earnings management', working paper, London Business School.

Sweeney, A.P. (1994) 'Debt-covenant violations and managers' accounting responses', *Journal of Accounting and Economics*, 17, 281–308.

Chapter 27

Altman, E. (1968) 'Financial ratios, discriminant analysis and the prediction of corporate bankruptcy', *Journal of Finance*, 23 (4), 589–609.

Amir, E. and Lev, B. (1996) 'Value-relevance of non-financial information: the wireless communications industry', *Journal of Accounting and Economics*, 22, 3–30.

Dechow, P. (1994) 'Accounting earnings and cash flows as measures of firm performance: The role of accounting accruals', *Journal of Accounting and Economics*, 138–56.

Decraene, S., Denruyter, P. and Sciot, G. (2002) *De crash van SABENA*. Uitgeverij Van Halewyck, Leuven.

De Zitter, A. (2002) *Het avontuur van SABENA: groei en val van een* luchtvaartmaatschappij, Lannoo, Tielt.

Ittner, C. and Larcker, D.F. (2001) 'Assessing empirical based research in managerial accounting: a value based management perspective', *Journal of Accounting and Economics*, 349–411.

Kaplan, R. and Norton, D. (1992) 'The balanced scorecard – measures that drive performance', *Harvard Business Review*, Jan–Feb, 71–79.

Lüchinger, R. (2001) *Swissair: l'histoire secrète de la debacle*, Editions Bilan, Lausanne.

Moser, S. (2002) *Bruchlandung: wie die Swissair zugrunde gerichtet wurde*, Orell Füssli Verlag AG, Zürich.

Rappaport, A. (1998) *Creating Shareholder Value*, The Free Press, New York.

Stewart, S. (1999) *The Quest for Value*, Harper Business, Boston, MA.

Taffler, R. (1982) 'Forecasting company failure in the UK using discriminant analysis and financial ratio data', *Journal of the Royal Statistical Society*, Series A, 145 (3), 342–58.

Solutions to the Exercises

Chapter 1

2 Accounting information is usually mainly past information, but user decisions are by definition future directed. Consider:
- relevance vs reliability
- objectivity vs usefulness
- producer convenience vs user needs.

3 Perhaps it all depends on what 'reasonably' means. The needs of different users are certainly different (illustration required), but greater relevance from multiple reports would need to be set against:
- costs of preparation
- danger of confusion and the difficulties of user education.

7 It is really much less objective than people often claim. Examples of 'unobjectivity' include:
- problem of determining purchase cost
- overhead allocation
- depreciation calculation
- provisions and their estimation
- prudence (a subjective bias by definition).

Chapter 2

1 You will notice that the answer to this question will be influenced to a large extent by the national background of the student. In the Anglo-Saxon world students will more easily argue that accounting is, in essence, economics based. In those countries, accounting standards are rather broad and derived from general principles. These principles are often derived from economic valuation concepts. Students living under a codified law system and in countries with a creditor orientation will argue more often that accounting is law based. If we consider IAS we might argue that IAS is economics based (e.g. substance over form).

2 The answer to this question is strongly influenced by the items put forward in the section 'national differences will they still play a role in the future?' in Chapter 2. As large companies become more global and seek multi-listings, they will be strongly in favour of harmonization and even uniformity. For small local firms the national environment will remain an important factor shaping their financial reporting practices.

Chapter 3

1 As so often, this is partly a matter of perception. In theory, the proposition is not correct, for two reasons. The first is that accounting regulation, and accounting practice, in Europe is bound by the contents of European Directives, especially the 4th, for individual companies, and the 7th, for groups. The second is the creation of the endorsement mechanism for emerging IFRSs, described in the text.

Chapter 4

2 The two businesses will have different depreciation charges (if they depreciate the buildings at all) and significantly different capital employed totals. They will therefore certainly have different efficiency and return ratios, but are they, economically speaking, different situations? In one sense, yes: more money was put into one than the other; but in another sense, no: opportunity costs and future potential are logically identical. Discuss generally.

3 A tricky one. In one sense, a capital maintenance concept must be defined before income can be determined, suggesting separation is not possible. But since one, in a sense, leads to the other, it could be suggested that perhaps we can define one of them and then automatically deduce the other (which therefore does not need separate definition). Discussion of interrelationships is the key issue.

Chapter 5

2 An interesting question. Replacement cost accounting, given rising cost levels, leads to a lower operating profit figure, which is more prudent. It also leads to higher asset figures in the balance sheet, which is *less* prudent. These two effects considered together will lead to much lower profitability and return on resources ratios, which perhaps sounds more prudent!

6 **I.M Confused, computer dealer**
   (a) Historical cost accounting
   Profit and loss accounts for the years:

	20X1	20X2
	€	€
Sales	3 000	3 600
Cost of sales	(2 000)	(2 000)
Gross profit	1 000	1 600
Expenses – rent	(600)	(700)
Net profit	400	900
Tax@50%	(200)	(450)
Retained profit	200	450

Balance sheets at year ends:

	20X1		20X2	
		€		€
Inventory				
@€1000	(4)	4 000	(2)	2 000
@€1200	(2)	2 400	(2)	2 400
@€1400	(0)	0	(2)	2 800
		6 400		7 200

Cash		3 800	3 450
		10 200	10 650

	€	€
Capital	10 000	10 000
Retained profits	200	650
	10 200	10 650

(b) Replacement cost accounting

Profit and loss accounts for the years:

		20X1		20X2
		€		€
Sales		3 000		3 600
Cost of sales		(2 200)		(2 600)
Gross profit		800		1 000
Expenses – rent		(600)		(700)
Operating profit		200		300
Tax paid		(200)		(450)
Profit/(loss)		0		(150)
Realized holding gain	(2 × 100)	200	(2 × 300)	600
Historical cost profit		200		450

Balance sheets at year ends:

		20X2		20X2
Inventory		€		€
@€1300	(6)	7 800	(0)	0
@€1400	(0)	0	(6)	8 400
Cash		3 800		3 450
		11 600		11 850

	€	€
Capital	10 000	10 000
Realized holding gain	200	800
	10 200	10 800
Distributable profits	0	(150)
Unrealized holding gains	1 400	1 200
	11 600	11 850

(c) The figures show that, given an intention to continue the operations of the business at the current level, the historical cost profit figure is entirely mythical – indeed in the second year the business has an operating loss on this basis.

Chapter 6

3 Arguably, the suggestion would give an income statement with a useful long-run operating perspective (note that this would perhaps be even more relevant if based on *future* RC rather than on *current* RC figures!) at the same time as a balance sheet of current cash equivalents, i.e. meaningful current market values. Discuss advantages of both of these. Against this, there would be a loss of internal consistency in the reporting package, which seems significant. Discuss this too.

6 Steward plc

Trading and profit and loss account for the year ended 31 December:

		1		2
		€		€
Sales		12 000		10 000
Less: cost of sales		8 000		5 900
Gross profit		4 000		4 100
Expenses	1 000		1 200	
Depreciation (note (c))	1 000		1 000	
		2 000		2 200
		2 000		1 900
Holding gain (note (d))		1 000		2 500
		3 000		4 400

Balance sheet as at 31 December:

		1		2
		€		€
Fixed assets				
Machine at NRV (note (a))		9 000		8 000
Current assets				
Inventory at NRV (note (b))	3 000		10 000	
Bank	21 000		19 400	
		24 000		29 400
		33 000		37 400
Share capital		30 000		30 000
Profit		3 000		7 400
		33 000		37 400

Notes

(a) *Fixed assets.* At the end of each year the machine is brought into the balance sheet at its net realizable value.

(b) *Inventory.* The inventory is also brought into the balance sheet at the end of each year at its net realizable value.

$$31.12.1\ 200 \text{ units} \times €15 = £3\,000$$
$$31.12.5\ 500 \text{ units} \times €20 = £10\,000$$

(c) *Depreciation.* The depreciation is the difference between the NRV of the asset at the end of each year, less the NRV of the asset at the beginning of the year.

$$\text{Year 1}\ €9\,000 - €10\,000$$
$$\text{Year 2}\ €8\,000 - €9\,000$$

(d) Holding gain. In Year 1 the holding gain is the unrealized holding gain on the closing inventory:

$$200 \text{ units} \times €5 \text{ (i.e. } €15 - €10) = €1\,000$$

In Year 2 the holding gain of Year 1 has now been realized (and therefore included in the trading account for Year 2) whilst there is an unrealized holding gain on the closing inventory of:

$$500 \text{ units} \times €7 \text{ (i.e. } €20 - €13) = €3\,500$$

Therefore, in Year 2 the holding gain is:

	€
Unrealized holding gain in Year 2	3 500
Less unrealized holding gain from Year 1 now realized in Year 2	1 000
	2 500

If in Year 2 we were to include the €1000 holding gain from Year 1, we would be double counting the holding gain.

Chapter 7

1 In essence, CPP adjustments attempt to update financial measurements for changes in the value of the measuring unit, without altering or affecting the underlying basis of valuation – usually, but not necessarily, historical cost. They do it by using general averaged index adjustments – usually, but again not necessarily, by means of a retail price index. Perhaps give or invite illustration.

7 **Calgary plc current cost profit and loss accounts for the year ended 30 June Year 4**

	€000	€000
Sales		7 000
Profit before interest and taxation on the historical cost basis		1 560
Cost of sales (note (5))	57	
Monetary working capital (note (6))	11	
Depreciation (note (2))	32	
		100
Current cost operating profit		1 460
Gearing adjustment (note (7))	(10)	
Interest	140	
		130
Current cost profit before taxation		1 330
Taxation		300
Current cost profit attributable to shareholders		1 030
Dividends		300
Retained current cost profit for the year		730
Balance brought forward		1 420
Balance carried forward		2 150

Current cost balance sheet as at 30 June

	Year 3 €000	Year 4 €000
Fixed assets		
Land (note (1))	1 697	2 035
Plant and machinery (note (2))	1 277	1 359

Less depreciation		(255)		(544)
		2 719		2 850
Current assets				
Inventory (note (3))	662		912	
Debtors	830		1 300	
Bank	10		620	
	1 502		2 832	
Less:				
Current liabilities				
Creditors	790		1 060	
		712		1 772
		3 431		4 622
Share capital		1 040		1 040
Current cost reserve (note (4))		271	(note (8))	732
Profit and loss		1 420		2 150
		2 731		3 922
Loan capital		700		700
		3 431		4 622

Workings

1 Land

Year 3: Current cost at 30 June Year 3

$$1\,500 \times \frac{241}{213} = 1\,697 \quad \text{€000}$$

Year 4: Current cost at 30 June Year 4

$$1\,500 \times \frac{289}{213} = 2\,035$$

2 Plant and machinery

Year 3: Current cost at 30 June Year 3

$$1\,200 \times \frac{649}{610} = 1\,277 \quad \text{€000}$$

Depreciation for year $\quad 1\,277 \times 20\% = 255$

Year 4: Current cost at 30 June Year 4

$$1\,200 \times \frac{691}{610} = 1\,359$$

Depreciation for year $\quad 1\,359 \times 20\% = 272$

Current cost depreciation at 20% straight line	272
Historical cost depreciation	240
Depreciation adjustment	32
Accumulated depreciation $1\,359 \times 20\% \times 2$ years	= 544

3 Inventory

Year 3: Current cost at 30 June Year 3

$$650 \times \frac{431}{423} = 662 \quad \text{€000}$$

Year 4: Current cost at 30 June Year 4

$$900 \times \frac{462}{456} \qquad = \underline{\underline{912}}$$

4 Current cost reserve 30 June Year 3

	€000
Net increase arising during Year 3 on the restatement of assets to current cost:	
Land	197
Plant and machinery	62
Inventory	12
	271

5 COSA

	€000
Historical cost closing stock	900
Less: historical cost opening stock	650
	250

$$\text{Less} \quad 900 \times \frac{442}{456} - 650 \times \frac{442}{423} \qquad = \underline{193}$$

COSA $\qquad \underline{\underline{57}}$

6 MWCA

	€000
Monetary working capital 30 June Year 3 (debtors less creditors)	240
Monetary work capital 1 July Year 4 (debtors less creditors)	40
	200

$$\text{Less:} \quad 240 \times \frac{442}{462} - 40 \times \frac{442}{431} \qquad = \underline{189}$$

MWCA $\qquad \underline{\underline{11}}$

7 Gearing adjustment

R = gearing ration
L = average net borrowings
S = average of net borrowings and the shareholders' interest (based on CCA)

$$R = \frac{L}{L+S}$$

Average net borrowings

	30 June Year 3 €000	30 June Year 4 €000
Loan	700	700
Less: bank	10	620
Net borrowings	690	80
Average		385

Average of net borrowings and shareholders' interest

	30 June Year 3 €000	30 June Year 4 €000
Total of net assets (excluding bank) in CC accounts	3 439	4 007
Less: net borrowings	690	80
	2 749	3 927
Average		3 338

$$\text{Gearing ratio} = \frac{385}{3723} = 10.3\%$$

Gearing adjustment

Current cost operating adjustments

	€000
Cost of sales	57
Monetary working capital	11
Depreciation	32
	100 × 10.3% = 10

8 Current cost reserve 30 June Year 4

		€000
Balance at 1 July Year 3		271
Net increase arising during Year 4 on the restatement of assets to current cost:		
Land	338	
Plant and machinery	33	
Inventory	–	
Cost of sales adjustment	57	
Monetary working capital adjustment	11	
Depreciation adjustment	32	
Gearing adjustment	(10)	
		461
Balance as at 30 June Year 4		732

Chapter 8

1 There are those who regard it as essentially a practical activity. Certainly, like any service industry, financial reports have to have a practical usefulness. It is also fair to say that financial reporting cannot be theorized about in the sense that pure science can be. However, in our view, theorizing about financial reporting is essential, for two main reasons. First, it will help to produce more consistent and therefore, hopefully, more useful treatments of accounting difficulties. Second, it will make clear to us all what uncertainties and subjectivities still remain. Knowledge of one's weaknesses is always useful!

2 To paraphrase the question, the proposition is that we need to know what tends actually to happen, so that we can discuss what should happen instead in an informed, sensible and knowledgeable way, but automatic acceptance of what does

actually happen is not acceptable. Discussion needed; we would agree with the proposition.

Chapter 9

2 It is often argued that realized results must be distinguished from the results of valuation changes or capital-related movements and that the best way to do this is to produce two separate statements. The trouble with this in practice is that the existence of two statements may enable managers to put good favourable elements in the more high-profile statement (i.e. the income statement) and less favourable items in the other statement. Discussion generally.

Chapter 10

6 This can be answered by determining the advantages and disadvantages of providing additional information.

Advantages:
- promotion of harmony between users and management
- better educated users
- possibly easier change management
- possible influence on users
- users having more relevant information on which to base their decisions.

Disadvantages:
- risk of providing information to competitors
- possibly misleading as they are management opinion of the future in many cases
- not audited
- may not be produced at the appropriate level, e.g. plant level, department level
- increases costs.

7 The answer here is similar to the disadvantages listed in question 6. Overcoming these disadvantages is something enterprises are currently working on evidenced by moves towards environmental and social report auditing.

Chapter 12

7 It certainly seems useful, and consistent, to *require* the revaluation of land, which, after all, does not depreciate. Such information increases relevance, but arguably at some sacrifice of reliability. Discussion needed.

8 This is more difficult. There are two arguments in favour of requiring the revaluation of buildings. First, it makes balance sheet numbers more relevant and, second, through the resulting increase in depreciation changed to up-to-date cost levels, it makes the reported profit a better estimate of long-run future performance. Note that the resulting reported operating profit, being usually lower, is *more* prudent when upward revaluation takes place. But, again, there are reliability considerations.

Chapter 13

1 Intuitively, it seems to us that goodwill is an asset. The only difficulty with this, given IASB definitions, is whether or not an enterprise can control goodwill. It certainly can be expected to give benefit.

6 The answer is **D.**

Workings

The overall impairment loss is $2 million [$27 million – $25 million]. This loss is first allocated to the asset that has suffered obvious impairment, leaving the balance of $1 million to be allocated to goodwill.

Chapter 14

1 Students should be able both to quote the IAS 17 definitions and to explain them in their own words. The essential point is that with a finance base, the lessee is, in substance, in the same business position (but not legal position) as if it had actually bought the item.

7 (i) The accounting treatment of leases is an example of the application of substance over legal form. If this principle is not followed it can lead to off balance sheet financing. The treatment of a lease is determined by the extent to which party receives the risks and rewards incidental to ownership. If a lease transfers substantially these risks and rewards to the lessee it is classed as a finance lease; if not it is an operating lease.

The accounting treatment for the lessee of an operating lease is that the income statement is simply charged with the periodic rentals and there is no effect on the balance sheet other than possibly an accrual or prepayment of the rentals. By contrast a finance lease is treated as a financing arrangement whereby the lessee is treated as having taken out a loan to purchase an asset. This means that both the obligations under the lease and the related asset are shown on the lessee's balance sheet. The impact on the income statement of treating a finance lease as an operating lease is minimal. Over the life of the lease substantially the same amount would be charged to income, however the inter-period timing of the charges would differ. It is the effect on the balance sheet that is important. Treatment as an operating lease means that neither the asset nor the liability is included on the lessee's balance sheet and this would hide the company's true level of gearing and improve its return on capital employed – these are two important ratios.

The Standard gives examples of situations that would normally lead to a lease being classified as a finance lease:

- the lease transfers the ownership of the asset to the lessee at the end of the lease (in some countries these are described as hire purchase agreements)
- the lessee has the option to purchase the asset (normally at the end of the lease) at a favourable price, such that the option is almost certain to be exercised
- the term of the lease (including any secondary period at a nominal rent) is for the major part of the economic life of the asset
- the present value of the minimum lease payments amounts to substantially the fair value of the asset
- the asset is of such a specialized nature that only the lessee could use it without major modification

– the lease is non-cancellable or only cancellable with a penalty to the lessee
– fluctuations in residual gains or losses fall to the lessee.

(ii)

	$
Gemini – Income statement extracts year to 31 March 2003	
Depreciation of leased asset (w (i))	48 750
Lease interest expense (w (ii))	12 480
Balance sheet extracts as at 31 March 2003	
Leased asset at cost	260 000
Accumulated depreciation (w (i))	113 750
Net book value	146 250
Current liabilities	
Accrued lease interest (w (ii))	12 480
Obligations under finance leases (w (ii))	47 250
Non-current liabilities	
Obligations under finance leases (w (ii))	108 480

Workings

(i) Depreciation for the year ended 31 March 2002 would be $65 000 ($260 000 × 25%)

Depreciation for the year ended 31 March 2003 would be $48 750 (($260 000 – $65 000) × 25%)

(ii) The lease obligations are calculated as follows:

Cash price/fair value at 1 April 2001	260 000
Rental 1 April 2001	(60 000)
	200 000
Interest to 31 March 2002 at 8%	16 000
	216 000
Rental 1 April 2002	(60 000)
Capital outstanding 1 April 2002	156 000
Interest to 31 March 2003 at 8%	12 480

Interest expense accrued at 31 March 2003 is $12 480. The total capital amount outstanding at 31 March 2003 is $156 000 (the same as at 1 April 2002 as no further payments have been made). This must be split between current and non-current liabilities. Next year's payment will be $60 000 of which $12 480 is interest. Therefore capital to be repaid in the next year will be $47 520 (60 000 – 12 480). This leaves capital of $108 480 (156 000 – 47 250) as a non-current liability.

Chapter 15

1 (a) **Upright pianos.** Since the stock is reduced to nil by 30 September then profits under all assumptions will be the same as differences in calculated profit arise only

because of different assumptions about usage.

	€
Sales	2 700
Cost of sales	1 750
Gross profit	950
Value of closing stock	250

However, under replacement cost:

	€
Operating profit	1 050
Holding loss realized	100
	950

Grand pianos
(i)   FIFO

	€	
Sales	3 200	
Opening stock	1 200	
Purchases	2 400	
	3 600	
Closing stock		
(1 @ 800)		
(1 @ 900)	1 700	1 900
Gross profit		1 300

(ii) LIFO

	€	
Sales	3 200	
Opening stock	1 200	
Purchases	2 400	
	3 600	
Closing stock		
(1 @600)		
(1 @900)	1 500	2 100
Gross profit		1 100

(iii) Weighted average

Stock

		€		
2 at €600	=	1 200	Sales	3 200
1 at €700	=	700	Cost of sales	
			1 @ 633	
3		1 900	2 @ 689	2 011
			Gross profit	1 189

30 June weighted average = €633

		€
2 at €633	=	1 266
1 at €800	=	800
3		2 066

30 September weighted average = €689

		€	
1 at €689	=	689	
1 at €900	=	900	
2		1 589	Closing stock

(iv) Replacement cost

			€
As at 30 June			
Replacement cost of stock 3 × €700	=		2 100
Profit on sale	=		300
Holding gains	=		200
As at 30 September			
Replacement cost of stock 3 × €800	=		2 400
Profit on sale	=		600
Holding gains	=		200
As at 30 November			
Replacement cost of stock = 2 × €900	=		1 800
Holding gain	=		100
Operating profit	=		900
Holding gains	=		500

(b) FIFO – older, smaller expense figure.
LIFO – older, smaller asset figure.
Weighted average – a bit of both!
RC – both expense and asset current.

6 IAS 11 assumes that management can always make a judgement on contract costs, estimated costs to completion and the stage of completion, whereas USGAAP assumes there may be circumstances in which this judgement is questionable. We leave the debate to you. It is also worth noting that enterprises do receive stage payments for contracts and that IAS 11 treats these as income rather than a liability.

Chapter 16

1 FIs have a significant impact on an enterprise's financial performance, position and cash flow. If these FIs are carried off balance sheet then the user cannot assess the impact. Such instruments are highly risky and a movement in the instrument in favour of or against the enterprise can significantly change its risk profile.

8 Discussion should revolve around the issues of realization and the provision of useful information to users. Whether a gain or loss has to be realized before it is recognized in financial statements is at the heart of this discussion. Note that emphasis is now placed on recognition and measurement with reasonable certainty rather than realization.

Chapter 17

1 Revenue is regarded by many as simply the cash that you are paid for selling things and this simple idea also implies exchange – cash for things. We have carried this idea of exchange through to the balance sheet. Consider the simple exchange of selling an item of inventory for cash: the accounting entries would be to derecognize the item of inventory in the balance sheet and recognize the asset of cash. The asset of cash would qualify as revenue and against this we would match relevant expenses to determine profit. Traditionally, we have not regarded the item of inventory as revenue until it is sold or at least until we have exchanged it for another asset, perhaps a debtor. This approach seems to equate revenue with economic activity involving exchange with a customer and ignores other items such as gains on assets that are revalued or carried at current value.

   IAS 18 defines revenue as: 'The gross inflow of economic benefits during the period arising in the course of the ordinary activities of an enterprise when those inflows result in increases in equity, other than increases relating to contributions from equity participants. (para. 7)'

3 Activities 17.8 and 17.9 can be used to demonstrate the use of substance over form in the Standard.

8 Given that the recognition of revenue requires management to make a number of subjective decisions, it would be difficult to describe it as objective.

Chapter 18

6 A provision and a contingent liability have been distinguished throughout the text, so refer to the definitions. In order to provide relevant information to users, it is generally accepted that the provision should be accounted for in the financial statements, whereas the contingent liability should only be disclosed by way of note. This is so that the accounts do not take an overly prudent view of the state of affairs at the balance sheet date.

9 Many people would argue that IAS 37 lacks prudence in that it does not require the recognition of and accounting for all future expenses. We would not argue this, as we view prudence as a state of being free from bias, not being overly pessimistic.

Chapter 19

4 These are fully explained in the text. You are expected to demonstrate your understanding by the use of examples similar to but not identical to those used in the text.

7 You should set your answer out in a clear style covering the following areas:
   - definition of deferred tax – what is it?
   - approach to providing for deferred tax – flow through, full deferral, partial deferral?
   - provision for deferred tax – deferral vs liability?

Liability method
Calculates deferred tax on current rate of tax thus showing the best estimate of a future liability. Emphasis on balance sheet.

Deferral method

Calculates deferred tax at the tax rate at date difference arose. The balance on deferred tax account is not affected by change in tax rate. Emphasis on income statement.

The approach adopted by the IASB which clearly opts for a balance sheet view full provisioning where the tax is seen as a liability – not an income statement view which advocates flow-through or at best partial provision.

A conclusion to the memo can be formed from questions 1 and 2 and it would be useful to make mention of discounting which reduces the effect of full provisioning.

Chapter 20

1 In this assignment the terms of the arrangement provide the counterparty with a choice of settlement. In this situation a compound financial instrument has been granted, i.e. a financial instrument with debt and equity components (see discussion of IAS 39); IFRS 2 requires the entity to estimate the fair value of the compound instrument at grant date, by first measuring the fair value of the debt component, and then measuring the fair value of the equity component, taking into account that the employee must forfeit the right to receive cash in order to receive the equity instruments.

If we apply this to this assignment, we will start by measuring the fair value of the cash alternative = $3000 \times €30 = €90\,000$. The fair value of the equity alternative is $2\,500 \times €28 = €70\,000$. The fair value of the equity component of the compound instrument is $€20\,000$ ($€90\,000 - €70\,000$). This share-based payment transaction will be recorded as follows. Each year an expense will be recognized. The expense will consist of the change in the liability due the remeasurement of the liability. The fair value of the equity component is allocated over the vesting period.

The following amounts will be recognized:

Year	Calculation	Expense	Equity	Liability
1	Liability component $(3\,000 \times €33)/3 = 33\,000$ Equity component $(20 \times 1/3) = 6\,666$	39\,666	6\,666	33\,000
2	Liability component $(3\,000 \times €36)2/3 - 33\,000 = 39\,000$ Equity component $(20.000 \times 1/3) = 6\,666$	45\,666	13\,332	72\,000
3	Liability component $(3\,000 \times 40) - 72\,000 = 48\,000$ Equity component $(20\,000 \times 1/3) = 6\,667$	54\,667	20\,000	120\,000

Suppose that at the end of year 3 the directors choose the cash alternative. In that situation €120 000 will be paid to the directors and the value of the liability will be nil afterwards. The equity component remains unchanged.

When the directors choose a payment in shares then 25 000 shares will be issued. The liability amount will be transferred to the equity account.

2 (a) Defined contribution plans:

These are relatively straightforward plans that do not present any real problems. Normally under such plans employers and employees contribute specified amounts (often based on a percentage of salaries) to a fund. The fund is often managed by a third party. The amount of benefits an employee will eventually receive will depend upon the investment performance of the fund's assets. Thus in such plans the actuarial and investment risks rest with the employee. The accounting treatment of such plans is also straightforward. The cost of the plan to the employer is charged to the income statement on an annual basis and (normally) there is no further on-going liability. This treatment applies the matching concept in that the cost of the post-retirement benefits is charged to the period in which the employer received the benefits from its employee. Post-retirement benefits are effectively a form of deferred remuneration.

Defined benefit plans:

These are sometimes referred to as final salary schemes because the benefits that an employee will receive from such plans are related to his/her salary at the date they retire. For example, employees may receive a pension of 1/60th of their final year's salary for each year they have worked for the company. The majority of defined benefit plans are funded, i.e. the employer makes cash contributions to a separate fund. The principles of defined benefits plans are simple, the employer has an obligation to pay contracted retirement benefits when an employee eventually retires. This represents a liability. In order to meet this liability the employer makes contributions to a fund to build up assets that will be sufficient to meet the contracted liability. The problems lie in the uncertainty of the future, no one knows what the eventually liability will be, nor how well the fund's investments will perform. To help with these estimates employers make use of actuaries who advise the employers on the cash contribution required to the fund. Ideally the intention is that the fund and the value of the retirement liability should be matched, however, the estimates required are complex and based on many variable estimates, e.g. the future level of salaries and investment gains and losses of the fund. Because of these problems regular actuarial estimates are required and these may reveal fund deficits (where the value of the assets is less than the post-retirement liability) or surpluses. Experience surpluses or deficits will give rise to a revision of the planned future funding. This may be in the form or requiring additional contributions or a reduction or suspension (contribution holiday) of contributions. Under such plans the actuarial risk (that benefits will cost more than expected) and the investment risk (that the assets invested will be insufficient to meet the expected benefits) fall on the company. Also the liability may be negative, in effect an asset.

Accounting treatment:

The objective of the new standard is that the financial statements should reflect and adequately disclose the fair value of the assets and liabilities arising from a company's post-retirement plan and that the cost of providing retirement benefits is charged to the accounting periods in which the benefits are earned by the employees.

In the balance sheet:

An amount should be recognized as a defined benefit liability where the present value of the defined benefit obligations is in excess of the fair value of the plan's assets (in an unfunded scheme there would be no plan assets). This liability will be increased by any unrecognized net actuarial gains (see below).

Where an actuarial gain or loss arises (caused by actual events differing from forecast events), IAS 19 requires a '10% corridor test' to be made. If the gain or loss is within 10% of the greater of the plan's gross assets or gross liabilities then the gain or loss may be recognized (in the income statement) but it is not required to be. Where the gain or loss exceeds the 10% corridor then the excess has to be recognized in the income statement over the average expected remaining service lives of the employees. The intention of this requirement is to prevent large fluctuations in reported profits due to volatile movements in the actuarial assumptions.

The following items should be recognized in the income statement:

- current service cost (the increase in the plan's liability due to the current year's service from employees)
- interest cost (this is an imputed cost caused by the 'unwinding' of the discounting process; i.e. the liabilities are one year closer to settlement)
- the expected return on plan assets (the increase in the market value of the plan's assets)
- actuarial gains and losses recognized under the 10% corridor rule
- costs of settlements or curtailments.

(b) Income statement

	$000
Current service cost	160
Interest cost (10% × 1 500)	150
Expected return on plan's assets (12% × 1 500)	(180)
Recognized actuarial gain in year	(5)
Post-retirement cost in income statement	125

Balance sheet

	$000
Present value of obligation	1 750
Fair value of plan's assets	(1 650)
	100
Unrecognized actuarial gains (see below)	140
Liability recognized in balanced sheet	240
Movement in unrecognized actuarial gain	
Unrecognized actuarial gain at 1 April 2001	200
Actuarial gain on plan assets (w (i))	10
Actuarial loss on plan liability (w (i))	(65)
Loss recognized (w (ii))	(5)
Unrecognized actuarial gain 31 March 2002	140

Workings:

(i)

	Plan assets	Plan liabilities
	$000	$000
Balance 1 April 2001	1 500	1 500
Current service cost		160
Interest		150
Expected return	180	
Contributions paid	85	
Benefits paid to employees	(125)	(125)
Actuarial gain (balance)	10	
Actuarial loss (balance)		65
Balance 31 March 2002	1 650	1 750

(ii) Net cumulative unrecognized actuarial gains at 1 April 2001	200
10% corridor (10% × 1 500)	150
Excess	50 /10 years = $5 000

actuarial gain to be recognized.

3

Year	Calculation	Expense	Equity and cumulative expense
1	(1000 × 0.85 × 20)/3	5 666	5 666
2	(1000 × 0.88 × 20)2/3 − 5 666	6 067	11 733
3	(10 × 86 × 20) − 11 733	5 467	17 200

4 Since IFRS requires the entity to recognize the services received from a counter-party who satisfies all other vesting conditions (e.g. services received from an employee who remains in service for the specified period), irrespective of whether that market condition is satisfied, it makes no difference whether the share price target is achieved. The possibility that the share price target might not be achieved has already been taken into account when estimating the fair value of the share options at grant date.

Year	Calculation	Expense	Liability
1	(20 000 × 0.98 × 48)/3	313 600	313 600
2	((20 000 × 0.98 × 48)2/3) − 313 600	313 600	627 200
3	(1 000 × 17 × 48) − 627 200	188 800	816 000

5

Year	Calculation	Expense	Liability
1	(100 × (200 − 25) × 31)/2 = 271 250	271 250	271 250
2	(100 × (200 − 26 − 74) × 36) − 271 250 = 88 750		
	+ 74 × 100 × 30 = 222 000	310 750	360 000
3	− 360 000 + 100 × 100 × 40 = 400 000	40 000	0

Chapter 21

1 IAS 29 is adjusting for general inflation, i.e. for the fall in the value of money. It applies a *general* inflation adjustment to the original, i.e. normally, historical cost figures. It is in no sense, therefore, concerned with valuation of financial statement items.

Chapter 22

5 Cash flow statement must be looked at together with balance sheet and income statement. It cannot be used in isolation.

The cash flow provides additional information as follows:

- cash flow generated from operations
- cash flow effect of taxation charge
- amounts expended on capital and financial investment are nearly as great as that generated from operations
- capital expenditure and investments have been financed from operations, issued share capital and long-term debt
- minority interest payments and cash from associates can be clearly seen
- whether acquisition of subsidiary has had a positive effect on cash flow.

8 (a) Rytetrend – Cash Flow Statement for the year to 31 March 2003:

	$000	$000
Cash flows from operating activities		
(Note: figures in brackets are in $000)		
Operating profit per question		3 860
Capitalization of installation costs		
less depreciation (300 − 60) (w (i))		240
Adjustments for:		
depreciation of non-current assets (w (i))	7 410	
loss on disposal of plant (w (i))	700	8 110
increase in warranty provision (500 − 150)		350
decrease in inventory (3 270 − 2 650)		620
decrease in receivables (1 950 − 1 100)		850
increase in payables (2 850 − 1 980)		870
Cash generated from operations		14 900
Interest paid		(460)
Income taxes paid (w (ii))		(910)
Net cash from operating activities		13 530
Cash flows from investing activities (w (i))		(15 550)
		(2 020)
Cash flows from financing activity:		
Issue of ordinary shares (1 500 + 1 500)	3 000	
Issue of 6% loan note	2 000	
Repayment of 10% loan notes	(4 000)	
Ordinary dividends paid (280 + (600 − 450) interim)	(430)	570
Net decrease in cash and cash equivalents		(1 450)
Cash and cash equivalents at beginning of period		400
Cash and cash equivalents at end of period		(1 050)

	$000
(i) Non-current assets – cost	
Balance b/f	27 500
Disposal	(6 000)
Balance c/f (37 250 + 300 re-installation)	(37 550)
Cost of assets acquired	(16 050)
Trade in allowance	500
Cash flow for acquisitions	(15 550)
Depreciation	
Balance b/f	(10 200)
Disposal (6 000 × 20% × 4 years)	4 800
Balance c/f (12 750 + (300 × 20%))	12 810
Difference – charge for year	7 410
Disposal	
Cost	6 000
Depreciation	(4 800)
Net book value	1 200
Trade in allowance	(500)
Loss on sale	700
(ii) Income tax paid:	
Provision b/f	(630)
Income statement tax charge	(1 000)
Provision c/f	720
Difference cash paid	(910)

(b) Report on the financial performance of Rytetrend for the year ended 31 March 2003

To:

From:

Date:

Operating performance

(i)   revenue up $8.3 million representing an increase of 35% on 2002 figures.

(ii)   costs of sales up by $6.5 million (40% increase on 2002)

Overall the increase in activity has led to an increase in gross profit of $1.8 million, however the gross profit margin has eased slightly from 31.9% in 2002 to 29.2% in 2003. Perhaps the slight reduction in margins gave a boost to sales.

(iii) operating expenses have increased by $600 000 (($5 440 000 – $240 000) – $4 600 000), an increase of 13% on 2002 figures.

(iv) interest costs reduced by $40 000. It is worth noting that the composition of them has changed. It appears that Rytetrend has taken advantage of a cyclic reduction in borrowing cost and redeemed its 10% loan notes and (partly) replaced these with lower cost 6% loan notes. From the interest cost figure, this appears to have taken place half way through the year. Although borrowing costs on long-term finance have decreased, other factors have led to a substantial overdraft which has led to further interest of $200 000.

(v) The accumulated effect is an increase in profit before tax of $1.24 million (up 51.7% on 2002) which is reflected by an increase in dividends of $200 000.

(vi) The company has invested heavily in acquiring new non-current assets (over $15 million – see cash flow statement). The refurbishment of the equipment may be responsible for the increase in the company's sales and operating performance.

Analysis of financial position

(vii) Inventory and receivables have both decreased markedly. Inventory is now at 43 days from 75 days, this may be due to new arrangements with suppliers or that the different range of equipment that Rytetrend now sells may offer less choice requiring lower inventory. Receivables are only 13 days (from 30 days). This low figure is probably a reflection of a retailing business and the fall from the 2002 figure may mark a reduction in sales made by credit cards.

(viii) Although trade payables have increased significantly, they still represent only 46 days (based on cost of sales) which is almost the same as in 2002.

(ix) A very worrying factor is that the company has gone from net current assets of $2 580 000 to net current liabilities of $1 820 000. This is mainly due to a combination of the above mentioned items: decreased inventory and receivables and increased trade payables leading to a fall in cash balances of $1 450 000. That said, traditionally acceptable norms for liquidity ratios are not really appropriate to a mainly retailing business.

(x) Long-term borrowing has fallen by $2 million; this has lowered gearing from 20% (4 000 000/19 880 000) to only 9% (2 000 000/22 680 00). This is a very modest level of gearing.

The cash flow statement

This indicates very healthy cash flows generated from operations of $14 900 000, more than sufficient to pay interest costs, taxation and dividends. The main reason why the overall cash balance has fallen is that new non-current assets (costing over $15 million) have largely been financed from operating cash flows (only $1 million net of new capital has been raised). If Rytetrend continues to generate operating cash flows in the order of the current year, its liquidity will soon get back to healthy levels.

Note: The above analysis takes into account the net effect of capitalising the staff costs.

Chapter 23

1 (a) **Basic eps**   €

   Profit   1 100 000

   Loan interest   100 000

   _____

                                                                 1 000 000

   Tax at 35%   350 000

   _____

                                                                   650 000

   Preference dividends   35 000

   _____

                                                                   615 000

   _____

   $$\text{eps} = \frac{61\,500\,000}{4\,000\,000} = 15.4\text{c}$$

(b) **Fully diluted eps**   €

Profit   1 100 000

Loan interest

                                                             1 100 000

Tax at 35%   385 000

                                                              715 000

Preference dividends   35 000

                                                              680 000

Number of shares $= 4\,000\,000 + 12\,500 \times 120$ (conversion)

                                  $= 5\,500\,000$

Fully diluted eps $= \dfrac{68\,000\,000}{5\,500\,000} = 12.36\text{c}$

2 (a) The objective of segment reporting is to provide information about the different types of products and services of an enterprise and the different geographical areas in which it operates. This information assists users of financial statements to:
 – Understand the enterprise's past performance.
 – Assess the enterprise's risks and returns.
 – Make more informed judgements about the enterprise as a whole.

Many enterprises provide groups of products or services or operate in geographical areas that are subject to different rates of profitability, opportunities for growth, future prospects and risks. Information about an enterprise's different types of products or services and its operations in different geographical areas is relevant to assessing the risks and returns of a diversified or multinational enterprise, but may not be discernible from the aggregated data. Therefore segment information is widely regarded as necessary to meeting the needs of users of financial statements.

A key problem with segment reporting is the manner in which the reportable segments are identified. IAS14 does provide some guidance in this area, requiring an enterprise to identify segments on the basis of internal reporting systems wherever practicable. The materiality threshold for a segment is basically set at one which contributes at least 10% of total revenue, profits, or total assets. Even with this guidance however, segment identification is a somewhat subjective exercise and comparisons of segment information provided by different enterprises needs to be performed with caution.

A further problem is the method of allocation of costs and assets relating to more than one segment. IAS14 requires that common costs and assets that can reasonably be allocated to individual segments should be included in arriving at results and assets on a segment by segment basis. However, the standard does allow for common items to be left unallocated and this inevitably introduces an element of subjectivity into the segment report.

(b) **Segment report for Worldwide**

	Europe	North America	Asia	Total
	$'000	$'000	$'000	$'000
REVENUE				
External sales (40:35:25)	2 66 000	2 32 750	1 66 250	6 65 000

Inter-segment sales	20 000	16 000	13 000	49 000
Total revenue	286 000	248 750	179 250	714 000

RESULT

Segment result (W1)	60 400	47 100	38 500	146 000
Unallocated corporate expenses				(10 000)
Profit from operations				136 000
Investment income				6 000
Finance cost				(25 000)
Income taxes				(28 000)
Minority interests				(8 000)
Net profit				81 000

OTHER INFORMATION

Segment assets (W2)	204 060	193 320	139 620	537 000
Unallocated corporate assets				
(50 000 + 6 000)				56 000
Consolidated total assets				593 000
Segment liabilities (W3)	26 600	25 200	18 200	70 000
Unallocated corporate liabilities				
(176 000 + 17 000)				193 000
Consolidated total liabilities				263 000

Working 1 – segment result

	Europe $'000	North America $'000	Asia $'000
Segment revenue	286 000	248 750	179 250
Segment costs:			
External*	(207 600)	(181 650)	(129 750)
Intra-group (Note 3 to question)	(18 000)	(20 000)	(11 000)
	60 400	47 100	38 500

– *Total operating costs (excluding intra-group items) are 529 000 (312 000 + 99 000 + 118 000).
– Head office costs are 10 000.
– So costs to be allocated are 519 000. The given ratio is 40:35:25.

Working 2 – segment assets – all allocated 38:36:26

	Europe $'000	North America $'000	Asia $'000
Property, plant and equipment			
(340 000) 38:36:26	129 200	122 400	88 400
Inventories (75 000)	28 500	27 000	19 500
Trade receivables (104 000)	39 520	37 440	27 040
Bank balances (18 000)	6 840	6 480	4 680
	204 060	193 320	139 620

Working 3 – segment liabilities – all allocated 38:26:26

	Europe $'000	North America $'000	Asia $'000
Trade payables (38:36:26)	26 600	25 200	18 200

15 (a) this would be an adjusting event – since these structural problems were pro-bably already present at year end

(b) would be a non-adjusting event

(c) there is strong indication that the customer was already unable to pay before the balance sheet date. Therefore, the provision for bad debts should be recognized at balance sheet date

(d) although this might look like an adjusting event, it is not because at year end, the recognition and measurement criteria of IAS 37 were not met.

Chapter 24

5 Fair value of the assets is used as the acquisition can be regarded in substance as a purchase of the underlying assets at a point in time. Thus the book value of the assets cannot be used, as this in no way reflects the fair value of the assets at date of acquisition. This fair value of assets is then matched with the fair value of the purchase consideration.

12 Proportional consolidation is explained in the text at page 520 and amply demon-strated in Activity 24.4. Equity accounting is explained at page 548. Equity account-ing is used for the consolidation of an investment in an associated enterprise. Proportional consolidation is the benchmark treatment for the consolidation of jointly controlled entities although an alternative is permitted, equity method.

13 Consolidated Balance Sheet as at 30 November 20X3

	Largo $m	$m
Non-current assets		
Tangible non-current assets	665.9	
Intangible non-current assets – brand	7	
Intangible non-current assets – goodwill	80.3	
Investment in associate	12.6	765.8
Current assets		218
Total assets		983.8
Capital and reserves		
Called up share capital		460
Share premium account		264
Accumulated Reserves		121.2
Minority interest		50.6
		895.8
Non-current liabilities		69
Current liabilities		19
		983.8

(i) The business combination should not be accounted for as a uniting of interests because of the following reasons:

    (a) the fair value of the net assets of Fusion and Spine ($315 million + $119 million) is significantly smaller than those of Largo ($650 million). The employees of Largo number fifty per cent more than the combined total of Fusion and Spine and the market capitalization of Largo is significantly larger than that of the two companies ($644 million, Largo, as against $310 million, Fusion, +$130 million Spine, i.e. $440 million).

    (b) the new board of directors comprises mainly directors from Largo. (Seven directors out of ten directors sitting on the Board.)

The arguments concerning the equity holdings are not strong enough to override the overwhelming size and control dominance set out above. The business combination should be treated as an acquisition.

(ii) Largo acquired Fusion and Spine on 1 December 20X2 and, therefore, control was gained for the purpose of the group accounts on that day. For the purpose of the Largo Group, the date of acquisition of Spine by Fusion is not relevant.

Shareholdings	Fusion	Spine	
Largo	90%	26%	)
		90% of 60%	) 80%
Minority Interest	10%	20%	

(iii) Equity of Fusion

	Total	Pre-acquisition	Post-acquisition	Minority Interest
Ordinary share capital	110	99		11
Share premium account	20	18		2
Accumulated reserves	138	122.4	1.8	13.8
Fair value adjustment (w(vii))	49	44.1		4.9
Adjustment for depreciation (w(vii))	(3.2)		(2.9)	(0.3)
Impairment of brands (w(vi))	(2)		(1.8)	(0.2)
	311.8	283.5	(2.9)	31.2
Cost of investment (w(v))		345		
Goodwill		61.5		

Equity of Spine

	Total	Pre-acquisition	Post-acquisition	Minority Interest
Ordinary share capital	50	40		10
Share premium account	10	8		2
Accumulated reserves	35	24	4	7
Fair value adjustment (w(iv))	29	23.2		5.8
Adjustment for depreciation (w(vii))	(1.9)		(1.5)	(0.4)
	122.1	95.2	2.5	24.4
Cost of investment – direct (w(v))		69		
Cost of investment – indirect (90:10)		45		(5)
Goodwill		18.8		19.5

Minority interest is $31.2 m + $19.4 m, i.e. $50.6 million.
Goodwill arising on acquisition of (61.5 + 18.8) i.e. $80.3 million.

(iv) Deferred tax and fair values

Deferred tax should be taken into account in calculation of the fair values of the net assets acquired.

The increase in the value of the net assets to bring them to fair value is attributable to the property. This increase is used to calculate deferred tax which should be deducted from the fair value of the net assets.

The fair value of the net assets should be decreased by the deferred tax on the property.

Fusion

Fair value $330 million (tax $15 million).

Spine

Fair value $128 million ($9 million).

Total increase in deferred tax provision $24 m

(v) Cost of investment:

The group accounts are utilizing acquisition accounting which requires that the consideration should be measured at fair value. Therefore, the cost of the investments in Fusion and Spine should be measured at the market price. The market price on the day of acquisition was $644 million ÷ (460 – 150 – 30) i.e. $2.30 per share. Therefore, the fair value of the consideration is:

	$m
Fusion 150 m × $2.30	345
Spine 30 m × $2.30	69

The share premium account of Largo will then become:	
Balance at 31 May 2004	30
Arising on issue of shares – Fusion	195
– Spine	39
	264

(vi) Brand name

IAS22 'Business Combinations' and IAS38 'Intangible assets' require that intangible assets acquired as part of an acquisition should be recognized separately as long as a reliable value can be placed on such assets. There is no option not to show the intangible asset separately under IAS38. In this case the brand can be separately identified and sold. Therefore, it should be shown separately. Also the brand should be reviewed for impairment as its fair value has fallen to $7 million. The brand should, therefore, be reduced to this value and $2 million charged against the income statement.

(vii) Tangible non-current assets

	$m
Largo	329
Fusion	185
Spine	64
Brand	(9)

Fair value adjustment
  – Fusion (330 – 110 – 20 – 136)   64
  – Spine (128 – 50 – 10 – 30)   38
  Additional depreciation – Fusion   (3.2) (increase in fair
                                           value \$64 m × 5%)
                  – Spine   (1.9) (increase in fair
                                           value \$38 m × 5%)
                               665.9

(viii) Group reserves   **\$m**
    Largo   120
    Fusion   (2.9)
    Spine   2.5
                          119.6
    Income from associate   1.6
                          121.2

(ix) Micro

When an associate is first acquired, the share of the underlying net assets should be fair valued and goodwill accounted for. This has not been carried out in the case of Micro.

                                                      \$m
Fair value of shares at acquisition (40% × \$20 m)   8
Goodwill   3
Carrying value of investment   11

The investments are to be marked to market by Micro and, therefore, a profit will have arisen during the period of \$24 million – \$20 million, i.e. \$4 million. The investment in Micro will, therefore, be stated at (11 + (40% × 4)) million, i.e. \$12.6 million.

19 (a) Consolidated Balance Sheet of Hapsburg as at 31 March 2004:

	\$000	\$000
Non current assets		
Goodwill (16 000 (w (i)))		16 000
Property, plant and equipment (41 000 + 34 800 + 3 750 (w (i)))		79 550
Investments:		
– in associate (w (iv))	15 900	
– ordinary (3 000 + 1 500 (fair value increase)	4 500	20 400
		115 950
Current Assets		
Inventory (9 900 + 4 800 – 300 (w (v)))	14 400	
Trade receivables (13 600 + 8 600)	22 200	
Cash (1 200 + 3 800)	5 000	41 600
Total assets		57 550

Equity and liabilities

Ordinary share capital (20 000 + 16 000 (w (i)))		36 000
Reserves:		
Share premium (8 000 + 16 000 (w (i)))	24 000	
Accumulated profits (w (ii))	12 000	36 000
		72 000
Minority interests (w (iii))		9 150
Non-current liabilities		
10% Loan note (16 000 + 4 200)	20 200	
Deferred consideration (18 000 + 1 800 (w (vi)))	19 800	
		40 000
Current liabilities:		
Trade payables (16 500 + 6 900)	23 400	
Taxation (9 600 + 3 400)	13 000	36 400
Total equity and liabilities		157 550

Note: all working figures in $000.

The 80% (24 m/30 m shares) holding in Sundial is likely to give Hapsburg control and means it is a subsidiary and should be consolidated. The 30% (6 m/20 m shares) holding in Aspen is likely to give Hapsburg influence rather than control and thus it should be equity accounted.

(i)

Cost of control

Investments at cost (see below)	50 000	Ordinary shares (30 000 × 80%)	24 000
		Share premium (2 000 × 80%)	1 600
		Pre acq profit (w (ii))	3 200
		Fair value adjustments (see below)	5 200
		Goodwill	16 000
	50 000		50 000

The purchase consideration for Sundial is $50 million. This is made up of an issue of 16 million shares (24/3 × 2) at $2 each totalling $32 million and deferred consideration of $24 million ($1 per share) which should be discounted to $18 million (24 million × $0.75). The share issue should be recorded as $16 million share capital and $16 million share premium.

Fair value adjustments:

IAS 22 requires the full fair value adjustment to be recorded with the minority being allocated their share.

Fair value adjustment:	Total	group share (80%)	minority (20%)
Property, plant and equipment	5 000	4 000	1 000
Investments	1 500	1 200	300
	6 500	5 200	1 300

The fair value adjustment of $5 million to plant will be realized evenly over the next four years in the form of additional depreciation at $1.25 million per annum. In the year to 31 March 2004 the effect of this is $1.25 million charged to Sundial's profits (as additional depreciation); and a net of $3.75 million added to the carrying value of the plant.

Goodwill on acquisition of Aspen:

Purchase consideration (6 million × $2.50)		15 000
Share capital	20 000	
Profits up to acquisition (8 000 − (6 000 × 6/12))	5 000	
Net assets at date of acquisition	25 000 × 30%	(7 500)
Difference – goodwill		7 500

(ii)

Accumulated profits

	Hapsburg	Sundial	Hapsburg		Sundial
Additional depreciation (w (i))		1 250	Per question	10 600	8 500
URP in inventory (w (v))	300		Post acq profit	2 600	
Unwinding of interest (w (vi))	1 800		Share of Aspen's profit		
Minority interest ((8 500 − 1 250) × 20%)		1 450	(6 000 × 6/12 × 30%)	900	
Pre-acq profit ((8 500 − 4 500) × 80%)		3 200			
Post acq profit ((4 500 − 1 250) × 80%)		2 600			
Balance c/f	12 000				
	14 100	8 500		14 100	8 500

(iii)

Minority interest

		Ordinary shares (30 000 × 20%)	6 000
		Share premium (2 000 × 20%)	400
		Accumulated profits (w (ii))	1 450
Balance c/f	9 150	Fair value adjustments (w (i))	1 300
	9 150		9 150

(iv) Unrealized profit in inventory

As the transaction is with an associate, only the group share of unrealized profits must be eliminated: $1.6 million × 2.5 million/4 million × 30% = $300 000

(b) In recent years many companies have increasingly conducted large parts of their business by acquiring substantial minority interests in other companies. There are broadly three levels of investment. Below 20% of the equity shares of an investee would normally be classed as an ordinary investment and shown at cost (it is permissible to revalue them to market value) with only the dividends paid by the investee being included in the income of the investor. A holding of above 50% normally gives control and would create subsidiary company status and consolidation is required. Between these two, in the range of over 20% up to 50%, the investment would normally be deemed to be an associate (note, the level of shareholding is not the only determining criterion). The relevance of this level of shareholding is that it is presumed to give significant influence over the operating and financial policies of the investee (but this presumption can be rebutted). If such an investment were treated as an ordinary investment, the investing company would have the opportunity to manipulate its profit. The most obvious example of this would be by exercising influence over the size of the dividend the associated company paid. This would directly affect the reported profit of the investing company. Also, as companies tend not to distribute all of their earnings as dividends, over time the cost of the investment in the balance sheet may give very little indication of its underlying value. Equity accounting for associated companies is an attempt to remedy these problems. In the income statement any dividends received from an associate are replaced by the investor's share of the associate's results. In the balance sheet the investment is initially recorded at cost and subsequently increased by the investor's share of the retained profits of the associate (any other gains such as the revaluation of the associate's assets would also be included in this process). This treatment means that the investor would show the same profit irrespective of the size of the dividend paid by the associate and the balance sheet more closely reflects the worth of the investment.

The problem of off balance sheet finance relates to the fact that it is the net assets that are shown in the investor's balance sheet. Any share of the associate's liabilities is effectively hidden because they have been offset against the associate's assets. As a simple example, say a holding company owned 100% of another company that had assets of $100 million and debt of $80 million, both the assets and the debt would appear on the consolidated balance sheet. Whereas if this single investment was replaced by owning 50% each of two companies that had the same balance sheets (i.e. $100 million assets and $80 million debt), then under equity accounting only $20 million $((100 - 80) \times 50\% \times 2)$ of net assets would appear on the balance sheet thus hiding the $80 million of debt. Because of this problem, it has been suggested that proportionate consolidation is a better method of accounting for associated companies, as both assets and debts would be included in the investor's balance sheet. IAS 28 'Accounting for Investments in Associates' does not permit the use of proportionate consolidation of associates, however IAS 31 'Financial Reporting of Interests in Joint Ventures' sets as its benchmark proportionate consolidation for jointly controlled entities (equity accounting is the allowed alternative).

Chapter 25

3 With the temporal method exchange gains and losses are put through the income statement; unrealized gains are the problem. With the closing rate method exchange gains and losses are put through reserves as exchange rate changes will have no effect on cash flow to the holding company. This avoids distortion of income statement due to factors unrelated to trading performance. Losses are the problem with this method.

5 Critical appraisal is required of the concept behind closing rate as compared with temporal method.

The closing rate is based on the idea that the holding company has a net investment in the foreign operation and that what is at a risk from currency fluctuations is the net financial investment. The temporal method is based on the idea that the foreign operations are simply a part of the group, that is, the reporting entity. Thus the closing rate method assumes that business is carried on overseas by semi-independent units that are dependent on the local currencies, whereas the temporal method assumes overseas units are extensions of the home business. The mode of business operation requires assessment to determine which method of translation should be used and the factors involved in this assessment are detailed in the regulations of IAS 21, which are covered in the text.

7 **Memo Group**
Consolidated Balance Sheet for the year ended 30 April 2004

	$m
Tangible non-current assets	367
Goodwill	8
Current Assets	403
	778
Ordinary shares of $1	60
Share premium account	50
Accumulated profits	372
	482
Minority Interest	18
Non-current liabilities	44
Current liabilities	234
	778

Consolidated Income Statement for the year ended 30 April 2004

	$m
Revenue	265
Cost of Sales	(163)
Gross Profit	102
Distribution and Administrative expenses	(40)
Goodwill impairment	(2)
Interest payable	(1)
Interest receivable	4
Exchange gains	1
Profit before taxation	64
Tax	(24)
Profit after taxation	40
Minority Interest	(2)
Profit for year	38

1. **Consolidated Balance Sheet – workings**

	Crowns (m)	Adj	Rate	$m	Notes
Tangible Non-current Assets	146		2.1	69.5	
Current Assets	102		2.1	48.6	
Current Liabilities	(60)	(1.2)	2.1	(29.1)	Exchange loss on inter company debt
Non-current Liabilities	(41)	2	2.1	(18.6)	Exchange gain on inter company loan
	147			70.4	
Ordinary Share Capital	32		2.5	12.8	
Share Premium Account	20		2.5	8.0	

Accumulated profits:

Pre-acquisition	80	2.5	32	
	132		52.8	Net assets at acquisition
Post Acquisition	15	0.8	17.6	Balance
	147	–	70.4	

2. Goodwill

	$m	Crowns
Cost of acquisition (120 ÷ 2.5)	48	120
Less net assets acquired: 75% of $52.8 million (above)	(39.6)	(99)
Goodwill	8.4	21

Goodwill is treated as a foreign currency asset which is translated at the closing rate. Essentially under this method, goodwill is being included in the retranslation of the opening net investment with any gain or loss going to reserves. Therefore, goodwill is 21 million crowns ÷ 2.1 = $10 million.

Therefore a gain of $1.6 million will be recorded in the balance sheet: $2 million will be written off as impairment, giving a balance of $8 m for goodwill.

3. Minority Interest

	$m
Net assets of Random at 30 April 2004	70.4
Minority interest 25% thereof	17.6

4. Post acquisition reserves are 75% of $17.6 million (working 1)   13.2

5. Consolidated Balance Sheet at 30 April 2004

	Memo $m	Random $m	Adjustment $m	Total $m
Tangible Non-current Assets	297	69.5		366.5
Loan to Random	5		(5)	
Current assets	355	48.6	(0.6)	403
Goodwill				8
				777.5
Ordinary Share Capital	60			60
Share Premium Account	50			50
Accumulated profits	360	13.2	(0.6)	
			(0.4)	
				372.2
				482.2
Minority Interest				17.6
Non-current Liabilities	30	18.6	(5)	43.6
Current Liabilities	205	29.1		234.1
				777.5

Adjustments are:

Elimination of inter company loan ($5 m), inter company profit in inventory ($0.6 m) and goodwill gain on retranslation of $1.6 million less impairment of $2 million, i.e. ($0.4 million)

6. Consolidated Income Statement Workings

	Memo $m	Random $m	Inter Company and adjustment $m	Goodwill $m	Total $m
Revenue	200	71	(6)		265
Cost of sales	(120)	(48)	6		(162.6)
Inventory inter company profit (W8)			(0.6)		
Distribution and Administrative Expenses	(30)	(10)			(40)
Goodwill				(2)	(2)
Interest receivable	4				4
Interest payable		(1)			(1)
Exchange gain – loan (W7)		1		1	
Exchange loss – purchases (W8)		(0.6)			(0.6)
Taxation	(20)	(4.5)			(24.5)
	34	7.9	(0.6)	(2)	39.3
Minority Interest		(2)			(2)
Dividends (to statement of changes in equity)	(8)				(8)
	26	5.9	(0.6)	(2)	29.3

The income statement of Random has been translated at 2 crowns = $1, i.e. at the average rate. The closing rate is not allowed under IAS21.

Minority interest is 25% of $7.9 million, i.e. $2 million

7. Loan to Random

There is no exchange difference in the financial statements of Memo as the loan is denominated in dollars. However, there is an exchange gain arising in the financial statements of Random.

	CRm
Loan at 1 May 2003 $5 million at 2.5	12.5
Loan at 30 April 2004 $5 million at 2.1	10.5
Exchange gain	2.0

This will be translated into dollars at 30 April 2004 and will appear in the consolidated income statement (2 million crowns ÷ 2, i.e. $1 million). The reason being that the loan was carried in the currency of the holding company and the subsidiary was exposed to the foreign currency risk.

8. Purchase of raw materials

	$m
Profit made by Memo $6 million × 20%	1.2
Profit remaining in inventory at year end (1/2)	0.6

	CRm
Purchase from Memo ($6 million × 2)	12
less payment made ($6 million × 2.2)	(13.2)
Exchange loss to profit/loss	(1.2)

The exchange loss will be translated at the average rate (2 CR to $1) into dollars, i.e. $0.6 million. Again the fact that the group cash flows have been affected by foreign currency fluctuations could mean that this loss will be reported in the group income statement.

9. Movement on consolidated reserves

	$m
Balance at 1 May 2003	334
Consolidated profit for the period	29.3
Exchange gain on translation	7.3
Exchange gain on goodwill	1.6
Balance at 30 April 2004	372.2

Analysis of exchange gain

	$m
Gain on retranslation of opening equity interest (132 ÷ 2.5 − 132 ÷ 2.1)	10.1
Loss on translation of income statement 7.9 − (7.9 × 2/2.1)	(0.4)
Exchange gain	9.7

75% of exchange gain $9.7 m is $7.3 million

Chapter 26

1 ■ Policy on asset valuation particularly regarding land and buildings – historical cost may or may not be departed from. This will impact on profits via depreciation charges and on balance sheet structure.

■ Depreciation policy will obviously impact on profits and asset values.

■ Stock valuations again will impact on profits and asset values and on liquidity ratios through the cost flow assumptions made (LIFO, FIFO) and also the treatment of overhead costs.

■ Long-term contract assumptions, e.g. the policy on inclusion of activity in annual turnover, and on treatment of possible future losses, and so on.

■ Goodwill valuation and method of elimination from the financial statements.

■ Leases allocation between operating and finance lease, method of allocating finance charges relating to both lessee and lessor.

■ Research and development policy in respect of possible capitalization of development costs and policy on any resulting amortization.

■ Pensions – problems associated with the type of scheme, the valuation of surplus or deficit and the allocation of these and other costs over accounting periods.

■ Use of temporal or closing rate method for translation of foreign trading operations.

■ Consolidation policies – definitions relating to the distinctions between subsidiary and associate, use of acquisition or merger accounting, quantification of fair values will all affect the numbers in the financial statements.

- On a more general level, the subjective judgements relating to conflicting accounting conventions and concepts, e.g. matching and prudence, will all affect the numbers. There may also be changes arising from the issue of new or revised accounting standards, which can cause major differences over time within the financial statements of any particular company or group.

2 Based on the information presented above we try to improve the comparability between the data of company A, B and C, by trying to account for the accounting flexibility and the differences in accounting methods and accounting estimates.

We will make adjustments for the differing accounting policies and the 'reconciliated or recalculated' balance sheets of company A, B and C are presented below.

	Company A in 000	Company B in 000	Company C in 000
Operating profit	282	194	148
Adjustment depreciation	4	–	–
Goodwill	10	–	2
Adjusted profit	296	194	150
Equity	1 336	890	1 004
Less revaluation reserve	(80)	–	–
Less goodwill	(110)	–	(12)
Adjusted equity	1 146	890	992

If we compare the 'original' data with the 'adjusted' data we notice that the performance of company A improves in comparison to the companies B and C. Further the equity of company A decreases. If one compares the obtained result with the equity of the company, company A is now clearly the better peforming company. The financial performance of C improves as well. Not only the relation between profit and invested capital improves for company A after the 'adjustment', but also the operational data taken from the profit account show a nicer performance since the profit of A improves in relation to a non-changed turnover.

After reading Chapter 27 you will be familiar with ratio analysis. At that moment you can compare the ratios of the three companies before and after adjustments for different accounting policies.

Ratios	Company A (%)	Company B (%)	Company C (%)
Before adjustment			
Return on equity	21.1	21.8	14.7
Operating profit/sales	13.4	12.9	8.5
After adjustment			
Return on equity	25.8	21.8	15.1
Operating profit/sales	14.1	12.9	8.6

If one does not take into account the accounting flexibility in comparing companies, Company A and Company B would be regarded as rather similar in relation to financial performance. However, if we do take into account the accounting flexibility, we observe that the performance of company A is better than the performance of Company B.

Chapter 27

1 (a) Report on the relative profitability of Hone and Over.
To evaluate the financial performance and the financial position of Hone and Over several techniques are available like horizontal and vertical analysis, ratio analysis and industry analysis.

Since we only have information available for a time-frame of two years, the results of the horizontal analysis must be interpreted with caution. It seems that both companies face a decline in profitability although the revenue increases. The results of the horizontal analysis show that Over managed to keep its other operating expenses more under control, this resulted in less decline of profit from operations. The increase in the net profit for Over, whereas the net profit for Hone declines must have other causes.

Horizontal analysis based on the two years available, whereby the first year has a value of 100%	Hone	Over
Evolution in revenue	109%	107%
Evolution in cost of goods sold	120%	123%
Evolution in other operating expenses	114%	105%
Evolution in profit from operations	93%	98%
Evolution in net profit	91%	104%

Since the management of Expand is not interested in liquidity data, we will not calculate the current ratio, the acid test ratio, the inventory turnover, the collection period for the revenues and the credit days granted by suppliers.

Using vertical analysis and ratio analysis we obtain the following data:

	Hone 2001	Hone 2000	Over 2000	Over 1999
Gross profit margin	50%	54%	48%	53%
Net profit margin	30%	35%	33%	38%
Total profit margin	18%	22%	17%	18%
Total asset turnover	0,8	0,7	1,00	0,95
Cost of sales/sales	50%	45%	51%	46%
Other expenses/sales	20%	19%	14%	15%
ROA	24%	27%	34%	36%
ROE	21%	25%	37%	39%
Equity/Equity+debt	68%	65%	47%	45%
Debt/Equity+debt	32%	34%	52%	54%
Interest cover	8	10	9,5	10
Dividend cover	1,57	1,7	1,3	1,3

The data above show us that although on the operational side the differences between Over and Hone are not that large, Over is more profitable since it is using debt to a larger extent than Hone and at a much cheaper interest rate than Hone. This might be due to local circumstances (remember the firms are from different jurisdictions).

(b) Comments on the validity of this financial information as a basis to compare the profitability of the two companies.

We have no information to which industry these two companies belong, so we assume for the analysis that both companies belong to the same industry. Only in this way are the data on the operational performance of both firms comparable. Figures like cost structures, asset and inventory turnover, sales margins, profit margins, collection period of receivables and credit granted by suppliers become really comparable if companies belong to the same industries. In order to judge whether Hone and Over are 'best in class' or the worst performers of the industry, industry data must be available in order to benchmark the performance of Hone and Over against industry averages and the best in class in the industry.

Further we observe that both companies belong to different countries. This should be explicitly taken into account. The annual accounts are prepared in the local GAAP of these countries. Are both local GAAP's of high quality? Of low quality? Or of different quality levels? Are the institutional characteristics of both companies the same? What about enforcement of accounting standards, risk of litigation, the audit quality and the rules of the local stock exchange (if Hone and Over are listed companies)?

Since both annual accounts are prepared using different domestic GAAP systems, the accounting flexibility of both systems should be analysed and the accounting method and estimate choices taken by the management should be investigated before the data can be compared.

We observe that the year-ends are different. What about the economic situation of the industry? Was it the same in each of these three years or is it improving or deteriorating?

Given that the companies are located in different countries, local operating and financial characteristics might influence the figures. For example differences in labour cost, financial costs, etc.

Another comment relates to the exchange rate which is used to translate the financial statements of Over into $. Using an exchange rate which differs for monetary and non-monetary assets might create another picture.

2 (a) Cash is exact, profits are calculated via concepts which permit various interpretations/judgements. Profit is a moving traget.

Cash balances can be boosted at year end quite easily by withdrawing payments, taking out loans, encouraging by incentives early debtor settlement etc.

(b) Company needs cash flow and profit to survive. Concentration on increasing cash balances is bad policy as the money will not be earning unless it is invested somehow.

Index